Web Technologies for Commerce and Services Online

Mehdi Khosrow-Pour
Information Resources Management Association, USA

 **INFORMATION SCIENCE REFERENCE**

Hershey · New York

Acquisitions Editor:	Kristin Klinger
Development Editor:	Kristin Roth
Senior Managing Editor:	Jennifer Neidig
Managing Editor:	Sara Reed
Copy Editor:	April Schmidt
Typesetter:	Jamie Snavely
Cover Design:	Lisa Tosheff
Printed at:	Yurchak Printing Inc.

Published in the United States of America by
  Information Science Reference (an imprint of IGI Global)
  701 E. Chocolate Avenue, Suite 200
  Hershey PA 17033
  Tel: 717-533-8845
  Fax: 717-533-8661
  E-mail: cust@igi-global.com
  Web site: http://www.igi-global.com

and in the United Kingdom by
  Information Science Reference (an imprint of IGI Global)
  3 Henrietta Street
  Covent Garden
  London WC2E 8LU
  Tel: 44 20 7240 0856
  Fax: 44 20 7379 0609
  Web site: http://www.eurospanonline.com

Library of Congress Cataloging-in-Publication Data

Web technologies for commerce and services online / Mehdi Khosrow-Pour, editor.

  p. cm.

 Summary: "This book delivers a global perspective on the influence of electronic commerce on organizational behavior, development, and management in organizations, discussing issues such as information security; strategic management of electronic commerce; organizational learning; business process management; mediated enterprises; and electronic marketplaces. It will prove an essential addition to library collections worldwide"--Provided by publisher.

 ISBN-13: 978-1-59904-822-2 (hardcover)

 ISBN-13: 978-1-59904-824-6 (e-book)

 1. Electronic commerce. 2. Web services. 3. Electronic commerce--Security measures. I. Khosrowpour, Mehdi, 1951-

 HF5548.32.W423 2008

 658.8'72--dc22

        2007043378

British Cataloguing in Publication Data
A Cataloguing in Publication record for this book is available from the British Library.

Web Technologies for Commerce and Services Online is part of the IGI Global series named *Advances in Electronic Commerce Series (AEC)* (ISSN: 1935-2921).

All work contributed to this book set is original material. The views expressed in this book are those of the authors, but not necessarily of the publisher.

Advances in Electronic Commerce (AEC)

ISSN: 1935-2921

Editor-in-Chief: Mehdi Khosrow-Pour, DBA

Web Technologies for Commerce and Services Online
Information Science Reference • copyright 2008 • 390 pp • H/C (ISBN: 978-1-59904-822-2)
US $180.00 • Pre-Pub Price: $165.00

Through the last decade, Internet technologies such as electronic commerce have experienced exponential growth, and emerging issues surrounding this phenomenon have necessitated the amassment of research on the cognitive impact of electronic commerce technologies around the world.

Web Technologies for Commerce and Services Online delivers a global perspective on the influence of electronic commerce on organizational behavior, development, and management in organizations, discussing issues such as information security; strategic management of electronic commerce; organizational learning; business process management; mediated enterprises; and electronic marketplaces. With the new insights it delivers on this rapidly evolving technological and commercial domain, this incisive reference will prove an essential addition to library collections worldwide.

Additional titles in the AIRM series:

Advanced Topics in Electronic Commerce
Vol. 1 • H/C ISBN: 1-59140-819-9 • copyright 2005

Utilizing and Managing Commerce and Services Online
H/C ISBN: 1-59140-932-2 • copyright 2006

The Advances in Electronic Commerce (AEC) Book Series is designed to provide comprehensive coverage and understanding of the social, cultural, organizational, and cognitive impacts of e-commerce technologies around the world. These accounts can be viewed from the impacts of electronic commerce on consumer behavior, as well as the influence of e-commerce on organizational behavior, development, and management in organizations. The secondary objective of this book series is to expand the overall body of knowledge regarding the human aspects of electronic commerce technologies and utilization in modern business organizations, assisting researchers and practitioners to devise more effective systems for managing the human side of e-commerce.

Hershey • New York
Order online at www.igi-global.com or call 717-533-8845 x10 –
Mon-Fri 8:30 am - 5:00 pm (est) or fax 24 hours a day 717-533-8661

Table of Contents

Detailed Table of Contents

Chapter I

Business-to-business (B2B) electronic commerce is an important opportunity for small and medium-sized enterprises (SMEs), providing increased competition on a global scale and allowing them to access wider markets. SMEs' B2B electronic commerce success is tied to the ability to foster inter-organizational relationships and customer loyalty. However, this is not always true because many SMEs have difficulty achieving B2B benefits as suggested by media and early research. This study is an empirical examination of the effect of Web tools on the inter-organizational relationships (IOR) between SMEs and their loyal customers. Data collected from 386 SMEs in North America (United States and Canada) and processed with partial least square (PLS) show that the use of Web tools (which include the level of Web content and the level of security on the Internet) has a positive effect on the relationship between cooperation and interdependence, and customer loyalty. However, the effect of Web tools on the relationship between trust and customer loyalty is different because the use of nonsecure Web tools reduces the effect of trust on customer loyalty, and surprisingly, the use of secure Web tools does not increase or decrease the effect of trust on customer loyalty. This research also suggests that one of the factors of the failure or the success of SMEs' B2B e-commerce is the technical skills of the managers in the use of secure Web tools—high skill levels increase the positive effect of trust on customer loyalty. The implications of the results for the study are discussed.

Chapter II

This chapter presents the results of an empirical study recently performed in e-commerce organizations. The purpose of this empirical study was to figure out the usage of electronic product catalogs and especially their systems used for product classification, such as UNSPSC or eCl@ss. The study was performed with the help of a survey, which was sent out to a selection of those product suppliers and manufacturers, where product catalogs are crucial for business. This chapter first presents the necessary fundamentals needed for understanding the results of the survey. Afterwards, it presents the results and identifies problematic areas that should be improved. It will furthermore give some advice for e-commerce organizations, standardization committees, and further research activities to foster the usage of modern classification systems in electronic product catalogs.

Chapter III

Product Complexity as a Determinant of Transaction Governance Structure:
An Empirical Comparison of Web-Only and Traditional Banks/

A transaction governance structure (TGS) is a structure that mediates exchanges of goods or services between different agents or production stages (Williamson, 1979, 1981). According to transaction cost economics (TCE), a selection of TGS for the trade of a particular product depends on the characteristics of the transaction, such as asset specificity, uncertainty, and frequency. This chapter argues that TCE alone is not sufficient to explain the selection of a TGS. Product complexity also plays an important role in explaining why a particular TGS is selected for a particular product. The construct of product complexity originated in the field of industrial marketing and is an important factor in the study of purchasing behaviors of buyers, decision-making processes of suppliers, and dynamic relations between buyers and suppliers. This study integrates industrial marketing with TCE and examines the impact of product complexity on TGS in the context of banking.

Chapter IV

Factors Affecting Online E-Payment Adoption: A Company Perspective /

Online e-payment is playing an important role in the further development of e-commerce and e-business. Research so far has been conducted to analyze the acceptance of online e-payment from consumers' point of view. No research has been carried out to examine the relationship between managers' attitudes towards online e-payment and their influence on the company's e-payment adoption. This research studies the adoption of online e-payment by business enterprises using Rogers' relational model of perceived innovation attributes and the rate of adoption. An online questionnaire survey is developed to collect the data from a sample of Chinese companies. Confirmatory factor analysis is used to validate and refine the instrument. Logistic regression model is employed to test the hypotheses and gain insights into how managers' perceived innovation attributes could affect company's e-payment adoption. The findings suggest that only perceived compatibility has significant influence on online e-payment adoption of Chinese companies. It is suggested that technology-organization-environment (TOE) model could be used in the future study to gain a more comprehensive understanding of nonperceptive factors that may affect company's adoption of online e-payment.

Chapter V

Internet Privacy Policies of the Largest International Companies in 2004 and 2006:

This chapter is a review of Internet privacy policies of the world's largest companies. The report begins with a background on the right to privacy and privacy issues arising out of Internet usage. Attempts to regulate Internet privacy and self-regulatory effectiveness are also reviewed. The methodology for this study is to update and extend Internet privacy analysis by analyzing Web sites of the largest international companies (the Forbes International 100) for inclusion of fair information practices. In addition, a collection of consumer centered practices is defined and studied. The study was initially done in 2004 but the same companies were revisited and reviewed in 2006. Though there was some improvement in results over the approximately two year period, the general finding remains that within the Forbes International 100, fair information practices and consumer centered privacy policies are not being closely followed. It is also found that large U.S. firms are more likely to publish a privacy policy on their Web sites than non-U.S. firms. Finally, if a large international firm does publish a privacy policy on its Web site, the level of compliance with fair information practices and consumer centered policies is not significantly different between U.S. and non-U.S. firms. Implications of the study for researchers and practitioners are reviewed.

Privacy policy statements are one of the more commonly used techniques to alleviate consumers' concerns about information privacy which is generally considered to be one of the primary obstacles to the success of e-commerce. This exploratory study examined the willingness of individuals to provide various types of personal information given varying degrees of protection offered by privacy policy statements. The results demonstrated that the willingness to provide information to Web merchants increased as the level of privacy guaranteed by the statements increased. More interestingly, increasing levels of privacy promised by the statements had the greatest influence on individuals with prior familiarity with policy statements. The results also demonstrated that while most individuals were aware of privacy policy statements, less than half of the respondents had ever read a privacy statement.

Signaling theory provides the framework to address why third-party assurance (TPA) seals may not have the desired positive effect on consumer trust in online merchants. Based on identified antecedents of effective signaling, three research propositions are presented to explore (1) how reliably consumers are able to recall TPA seals on viewed retail Web sites, (2) how familiar consumers are with major TPA seals, and (3) how accurately consumers comprehend the assurances legitimately represented by the TPA seals. Results of this study of three major TPA seals (TRUSTe, BBBOnLine Reliability, and VeriSign) reveal that subjects have relatively poor notice and recall of TPA seals viewed on a Web site, have limited familiarity with TPA programs, and have incomplete and largely inaccurate understanding of the assurances represented by the TPA seals. These results suggest that TPA seals may not fulfill their potential to influence consumer trust in online merchants because the signals are not effectively noticed or accurately interpreted by consumers.

The scope of this work is to explore the transaction profitability of frequent and sporadic buyers in the e-commerce arena. Evidence in relationship marketing literature stressing the impact of purchase frequency on customer profitability, as well as recent academic research challenging this approach and pointing out the importance of sporadic clients, is analyzed and presented. A single case study research methodology was chosen for this chapter due to the exploratory facets associated with the subject and the industry under investigation. In order to gather relevant input to carry out this research, one of the largest retailing groups in Brazil was investigated. Conclusions are drawn showing that greater frequency of purchases does not necessarily translate into increased customer transaction profitability. Implications are presented, enabling practitioners and academics to grasp fully the real value of customers—both frequent and sporadic buyers—in order to develop coherent approaches for dealing with them adequately.

The critical determinant of consumers' commitment to online shopping sites is the information features on a given Web site because online shopping consumers cannot touch or smell the products as they usually do in traditional retail outlets. Customers have to base their judgments on the product information presented on the Web sites. To investigate the relationship between information features and consumers' loyalty to a Web site, the authors have developed two constructs affecting consumer's commitment to online shopping sites. The first construct indicates the consumer's overall evaluation of the online site and the second is the relational benefit of psychological perception about an online site. Results of the online survey with 1,278 Korean customers of online bookstores and ticketing services indicate that information quality, user interface quality, and security perceptions affect information satisfaction and relational benefit. These, in turn, are significantly related to each consumer's commitment to a site. Information satisfaction and relational benefit have a mediating role between online shopping sites' information service quality and site commitment. The effect of information satisfaction and relational benefit appear differently with online bookstores and ticketing services.

Multichannel retailing can offer a wide range of synergies for retailers when their distribution channels accommodate consumer's preferences and their buying behavior. Among the large number of retail types, mail-order companies are well suited to benefit from electronic commerce. Not only can they use their infrastructure and experience with direct selling, but many mail-order companies also seek to use the

Internet to attract new target groups to increase their typically small and narrow customer bases. Currently, they do not know enough about the antecedents of channel choices, especially in the mail-order sector. This chapter addresses this issue and draws special attention to exogenous (i.e., independent of the retailer) factors influencing online shopping behavior. These variables include perceived convenience and perceived security of online shopping in general and consumers' attitudes toward the catalog as the existing distribution channel. One endogenous factor, that is, attitude toward the online shop, is assumed to influence buying behavior at the online shop. To examine relationships between the catalog and the online shop, 2,363 consumers who are familiar with both distribution channels of a mail-order company were surveyed online. The structural equation model developed reveals that attitudes toward the printed catalog most strongly influence attitudes toward the online shop. Further, the analysis has shown that antecedents of buying behavior at the online shop are moderated by gender. Shopping behavior of men is influenced by their attitudes toward the catalog, while that of women is determined by their attitudes toward the online shop.

Chapter XI

Companies are involved in different types of business relationships for various reasons. These include, but are not limited to, efficiency gains, innovation, and influencing other organizations. In the age of digitization, managers have witnessed new ways to manage business relationships, as the number of digital and electronic commerce tools have mushroomed. Business relationships digitization is an under-researched area and therefore the purpose of this chapter is to illustrate how relationships are digitized and what managers as well as academics should know about this emerging phenomenon. With the help of an extensive literature review, this chapter presents an overview of basic features and types of digitized business relationships. The author outlines a model that tackles critical factors while digitizing business relationships. In addition, a case example depicting the digitization process of a business relationship is presented. The chapter concludes with a description of the contribution of the study and presents suggestions for further research.

Chapter XII

Recently, wireless local area network (WLAN) has gained increasing popularity. WLAN equipment manufacturers and practitioners claimed that WLAN had brought dramatic improvements in the forms of productivity gains and attainment of convenience, flexibility, mobility, and time saving to organizations and their employees. However, very little academic research has been conducted to verify these claims and further our understanding of this new phenomenon. By surveying end users and managers, this study investigates the impact of WLAN on users and their work. User satisfaction with WLAN is also assessed. This chapter presents the findings from the study along with a discussion on recent development and future trends of WLAN. Finally, recommendations to researchers, managers, WLAN technology providers, and equipment manufacturers are also provided.

This research deals with two aspects of mobile commerce (m-commerce), namely "killer applications" and critical success factors. After compiling significant information from the related literature, a Delphi panel was assembled by selecting a group of experts who have significant knowledge about m-commerce and wireless communications. The panel was requested to comment on a number of m-commerce issues and scenarios gleaned from the literature review and members of the panel were also asked to indicate which issues were more important and which of the presented scenarios were more likely. Three separate rounds of the Delphi survey were carried out and the final results indicated that the short message service (SMS) and a "killer" portfolio were the two most likely "killer applications" of m-commerce. Additionally, four factors: convenience, ease of use, trust, and ubiquity were identified as the most important to m-commerce success. According to the Delphi results and the experts' comments, the highlighted features of the "killer applications" were found to match the most significant critical success factors as voted by the panel.

This chapter examines the relationship between electronic commerce and the U.S. state sales and use tax system. A framework is used in this study of a high-quality tax system and it is applied to taxing electronic commerce sales. The first part of this chapter analyzes nine principles of an effective tax system and divides these principles into the categories of adequacy of revenue, fairness of revenue, and management of revenue. In the second part of this chapter, these principles are tested to determine what impact electronic commerce taxation has on an effective revenue system. The results of these initial tests suggest that taxation of electronic commerce was associated with fairness in the tax system. In particular, the results suggested that states that had fairer tax systems were more likely to rely less on a sales tax and more on taxing Internet access. Management and adequacy of the revenue systems of states were not found to have a significant bearing on taxing electronic commerce. These results reinforce the existing public finance and legal theories which argue that the sales tax is not a fair revenue stream, and it should be re-evaluated especially in light of the contentious issue of taxing electronic commerce.

Previous research has shown that gender plays a role in the use of information technology by small businesses and that differences exist between the ways in which male and female small business owners/managers perceive information technology, including e-commerce. However, our understanding of whether gender is important in relation to e-commerce adoption barriers is limited. This chapter examines whether differences exist in how male and female owners/managers of small businesses in regional areas in Sweden and Australia perceive e-commerce adoption barriers. The results of a survey of more than

450 small businesses are presented and indicate that, although both male and female owners/managers agree on the key reasons for not adopting e-commerce, they assign different priorities these reasons. In Stheyden, male owners/managers are more concerned about the technical complexities of implementing e-commerce, while females assign a higher importance to the unsuitability of e-commerce. In Australia, the situation is reverse. The results have implications for e-commerce adoption programs and initiatives.

Focus group methodology is introduced in this paper as one appropriate methodology to study the impact of technological innovation factors on e-commerce (EC) adoption in small businesses (SMEs) in New Zealand. The research results suggested two emerging issues pertaining to EC adoption in SMEs in this research. Firstly, SMEs would not invest their scant resources on perceived risky advanced EC initiatives. In adopting simple EC technologies such as Web page and email, factors like cost and compatibility were found not hindering the adoption decision. On the other hand, the proposed drivers to adopt these simple technologies were not highly significant as such. Secondly, the SMEs retained a particular view about advancing their simple EC initiatives. They envisaged that advancing their EC initiatives such as adopting "fully-blown" and interactive Web sites will give more theyight to the impact of the different factors in this research on their adoption decisions of EC. The gulf between the current adoption and usage levels and the envisaged advanced EC initiatives seemed to be increasing further suggesting the weakness of the EC phenomenon in SMEs in this research. The research portrays a path were such gaps could be addressed and hence, this path should guide the SMEs in advancing their EC initiatives. Implications arising from this research with respect to theory and to practice are discussed in this research.

Chapter XVII

Organizational adoption of innovations does not always follow easily comprehendible patterns. This is often the case with interorganizational information systems (IOS), where adoption is dependent on attributes related both to the organization and its environment. The present study operationalizes the Tornatzky and Fleischer (1990) model for organizational adoption in order to investigate reasons for adoption and non-adoption among businesses in the Danish steel and machinery industry. This particular industry segment had been subject to massive information campaigns focusing on the benefits of IOS in the form of EDI from business associations. The study suggests that environmental and organizational attributes rather than technological attributes are the main determining forces for adoption of EDI.

Preface

With the advancement of the Internet, World Wide Web based transactions have opened up immense possibilities for businesses and consumers thereby expanding the popularity of electronic commerce technologies. It is crucial that academicians, researchers, practitioners, and professionals alike have a strong resource to provide ideas and information on the utilization of these new technologies and what possibilities e-commerce offers.

Web Technologies for Commerce and Services Online presents a wide range of the most innovative research in the adoption of e-commerce, e-business, and e-government. This publication provides a comprehensive coverage of social, cultural, organizational, human, and cognitive impacts of the electronic commerce technologies and advances in organizations around the world. Extensive research studies are incorporated covering topics ranging from mobile commerce to virtual enterprises, business-to-business applications, Web services, and enterprise methodologies.

Chapter I, entitled "SME B2B E-Commerce and Customer Loyalty Revisited," by Assion Lawson-Body and Timothy P. O'Keefe, University of North Dakota (USA) examines the effect of Web tools on the inter-organizational relationships (IOR) between small and medium-sized enterprises (SMEs) and their loyal customers. Data collected from 386 SMEs in North America (United States and Canada) and processed with partial least square (PLS) show that the use of Web tools (which include the level of Web content and the level of security on the Internet) has a positive effect on the relationship between cooperation and interdependence, and customer loyalty. However, the effect of Web tools on the relationship between trust and customer loyalty is different because the use of nonsecure Web tools reduces the effect of trust on customer loyalty, and surprisingly, the use of secure Web tools does not increase or decrease the effect of trust on customer loyalty. Additionally, this study suggests that one of the factors of the failure of the success of SMEs' B2B e-commerce is the technical skills of the managers in the use of secure Web tools—high skill levels increase the positive effect of trust on customer loyalty.

Chapter II, entitled "Product Classifications Systems in E-Commerce Organizations," by Sven Abels, Abelssoft Consulting & Services (Germany) and Axel Hahn, University of Oldenburg (Germany), introduces the results of an empirical study recently performed in e-commerce organizations. The study was conducted in order to figure out the usage of electronic product catalogs and especially their systems used for product classification, such as UNSPSC or eCl@ss. A survey was sent out to a selection of those product suppliers and manufacturers, where product catalogs are crucial for business. Presented within this study are the necessary fundamentals necessary for understanding the results of the survey. At the conclusion, the study presents the results and identifies problematic areas that should be improved. Furthermore, advice is given for e-commerce organizations, standardization committees as well as further research activities to foster the usage of modern classification systems in electronic product catalogs.

Chapter III, entitled "Product Complexity as a Determinant of Transaction Governance Structure: An Empirical Comparison of Web-Only and Traditional Banks," by Aimao Zhang and Han Reichgelt,

Georgia Southern University (USA) contends that TCE alone is not sufficient to explain the selection of a transaction governance structure (TGS). Product complexity also plays an important role in explaining why a particular TGS is selected for a particular product. The construct of product complexity originated in the field of industrial marketing and is an important factor in the study of purchase behaviors of buyers, decision-making processes of suppliers, and dynamic relations between buyers and suppliers. The authors integrate industrial marketing with TCE and examine the impact of product complexity on TGS in the context of banking.

Chapter IV, entitled "Factors Affecting Online E-Payment Adoption: A Company Perspective," by Qile He, Middlesex University Business School (UK), Yangqing Duan, University Bedfordshire Business School (UK), Zetian Fu, China Agriculture University (P.R. China), and Daoliang Li, China Agriculture University (P.R. China), examines the online e-payment option which is playing an important role in the further development of e-commerce and e-business. Thus far, research has been conducted to analyze the acceptance of online e-payment from consumers' point of view. However, no research has been carried out to examine the relationship between managers' attitudes towards online e-payment and their influence on the company's e-payment option. This study examines the adoption of online e-payment by business enterprises using Rogers' relational model of perceived innovation attributes and the rate of adoption. The authors developed an online questionnaire survey in order to collect the data from a sample of Chinese companies. The overall findings of this study suggest that only perceived compatibility has significant influence on online e-payment adoption of Chinese companies.

Chapter V, entitled "Internet Privacy Policies of the Largest International Companies in 2004 and 2006: A Review of U.S. and Non-U.S. Companies," by Alan R. Peslak and Norbert Jurkiewicz, Penn State University (USA), reviews Internet privacy policies of the world's largest companies. The primary goal of this study is to update and extend Internet privacy analysis by examining Web sites of the largest international companies (the Forbes International 100) for inclusion of fair information practices. Additionally, a collection of consumer centered practices is defined and studied. The initial study was completed back in 2004. In 2006, the companies were revisited for a second evaluation. Although there was some improvement in results over the two years, the general finding remains that within the Forbes International 100, fair information practices and consumer centered privacy policies are not being closely followed. Other findings, conclude that large U.S. firms are more likely to publish a privacy policy on their Web site than non-U.S. firms. Additionally, if a large international firm does publish a privacy policy on its Web site, the level of compliance with fair information practices and consumer centered policies is not significantly different between U.S. and non-U.S. firms.

Chapter VI, entitled "Strength of Privacy Policy Statements and Consumer Trust," by Dane K. Peterson and David B. Meinert, Missouri State University (USA), John R. Criswell II, Columbia College (USA), and Martin D. Crossland, Oral Roberts University (USA), examines the willingness of individuals to provide various types of personal information given varying degrees of protection offered by privacy policy statements. The results of this study indicated that the willingness to provide information to Web merchants increased as the level of privacy guaranteed by the statement increased. The increasing levels of privacy promised by the statements ahs the greatest influence on those with prior familiarity with policy statements. Also demonstrated through the results was the issue that while most individuals are aware of privacy policy statements, less than half of the respondents have ever read a privacy statement.

Chapter VII, entitled "Seals on Retail Web Sites: A Signaling Theory Perspective on Third-Party Assurances," by Kathryn M. Kimery, Saint Mary's University (Canada) and Mary McCord, University of Central Missouri (USA), explores three research propositions: first, how reliable consumers are able to recall TPA (third-party assurances) seals on viewed retail Web sites; second, how familiar consumers are with major TPA seals; and third, how accurately consumers comprehend the assurances legitimately represented by the TPA seals. This study examines three major TPA seals (TRUSTe, BBBOnLine Reliability, and VeriSign).

Chapter VIII, entitled "The King is Naked: Discovering that Frequent Customers May Not Be Your Best Friend," by Luiz Antonio Joia, Rio de Janeiro State University (Brazil) and Paulo Sergio Sanz, Brazilian School of Public and Business Administration (Brazil), explores the transaction profitability of frequent and sporadic buyers in the e-commerce arena. The authors analyze and present evidence in relationship marketing literature stressing the impact of purchase frequency on customer profitability as well as recent academic research challenging this approach and pointing out the importance of sporadic clients. For this chapter, a single case study research methodology was chosen due to the exploratory facets associated with the subject and the industry under investigation. In order to gather relevant input to carry out this research, one of the largest retailing groups in Brazil was investigated. The findings conclude that greater frequency of purchase does not necessarily translate into increased customer transaction profitability. This study will allow for practitioners and academics to take in the real value of customers, both frequent and sporadic buyers, in order to develop coherent approaches for dealing with them effectively.

Chapter IX, entitled "The Effect of Information Satisfaction and Relational Benefit on Consumer's Online Shopping Site Commitment," by Chung-Hoon Park, Samsung SDS (Korea) and Young-Gul Kim, Graduate School of Management, KAIST (Korea), investigate the relationship between information features and consumers' loyalty to a Web site through two constructs affecting consumer's commitment to online shopping sites. The first construct indicates the consumer's overall evaluation of online site and the second is the relational benefit of psychological perception about an online site. Results of the online survey with 1,278 Korean customers of online bookstores and ticketing services indicate that information quality, user interface quality, and security perceptions affect information satisfaction and relational benefit. These, in turn, are significantly related to each consumer's commitment to a site.

Chapter X, entitled "Online Shopping and Catalog Shopping: Exogenous and Endogenous Antecedents of Consumers' Channel Choice," by Maria Madlberger, Vienna University of Economics and Business Administration (Austria), examines the current issue of many mail-order companies seeking to use the Internet to attract new target groups to increase their typically small and narrow customer bases. Unfortunately, at this time they do not know enough about the antecedents of channel choices, especially in the mail-order sector. In this study, the authors address this issue and draw special attention to exogenous (i.e., independent of the retailer) factors influencing online shopping behavior. These variables include perceived convenience and perceived security of online shopping in general and consumers' attitudes toward the catalog as the existing distribution channel.

Chapter XI, entitled "Digitizing Business Relationship: Some Practical and Theoretical Considerations," by Jari Salo, University of Oulu (Finland), illustrates how relationships are digitized and what managers as well as academics should know about this emerging phenomenon. An extensive literature review is incorporated that provides an overview of basic features and types of digitized business relationships. The author outlines a model that tackles critical factors while digitizing business relationships.

Chapter XII, entitled "Understanding the Impact of Wireless Local Area Networks on Users and Assessing User Satisfaction with Wireless Local Area Networks," by Leida Chen, Ravi Nath, and Jonathan Cowin, Creighton University (USA), investigates the impact of wireless area networks (WLAN) on users and their work. User satisfaction is assessed and recommendations are made to researchers, managers, WLAN technology providers, and equipment manufacturers.

Chapter XIII, entitled "An Exploratory Study of 'Killer Applications' and Critical Success Factors in M-Commerce," by Gordon Xu and Jairo A. Gutiérrez, University of Auckland (New Zealand), examines "killer applications" and critical success factors, two aspects of mobile commerce (m-commerce). After compiling significant information from the related literature, a Delphi panel was assembled by selecting a group of experts who have significant knowledge about m-commerce and wireless communications. The panel was requested to comment on a number of m-commerce issues and scenarios gleaned from the literature review and members of the panel were also asked to indicate which issues were more important and which of the presented scenarios were more likely. The final results of the survey indicated that the short message service (SMS) and a "killer" portfolio were the two most likely "killer applications" of m-commerce. Additionally, four factors: convenience, ease of use, trust, and ubiquity were identified as the most important to m-commerce success. According to the Delphi result and the experts' comments, the highlight features of the "killer applications" were found to match the most significant critical success factors as voted by the panel.

Chapter XIV, entitled "E-Commerce and Sales Taxes in the United States: Adequacy, Fairness, and Management," by Christopher G. Reddick, The University of San Antonio (USA), examines the relationship between electronic commerce and the U.S. state sales and use tax system. The author uses a framework of a high-quality tax system, and it is applied to taxing electronic commerce sales. Nine principles of an effective tax system are analyzed and each of these principles are divided into the categories adequacy of revenue, fairness of revenue, and management of revenue. These principles were then tested to determine what impact electronic commerce taxation has on an effective revenue system. The findings from these initial tests suggest that taxation of electronic commerce was associated with fairness in the tax system. In particular, the results suggested that states that had fairer tax systems were more likely to rely on a sales tax and more on taxing Internet access.

Chapter XV, entitled "Gender and E-Commerce Adoption Barriers: A Comparison of Small Businesses in Sweden and Australia," by Robert MacGregor, University of Wollongong (Australia) and Lejla Vrazalic, University of Wollongong in Dubai (UAE), examines whether differences exist in how male and female owners/managers of small business in regional areas in Sweden and Australia perceived e-commerce adoption barriers. The authors present results of a survey of more than 450 small businesses and there are indications that although both male and female owners/managers agree on the key reasons for not adopting e-commerce, they assign different priorities these reasons.

Chapter XVI, entitled "Personas of E-Commerce Adoption in Small Businesses in New Zealand," by Nabeel Al-Qirim, United Arab Emirates University (UAE) introduces focus group methodology as one appropriate methodology to study the impact of technological innovation factors on e-commerce (EC) adoption in small businesses (SMEs) in New Zealand. The findings suggest two emerging issues pertaining to EC adoption in SMEs. First, SMEs would not invest their scant resources on perceived risky advanced EC initiatives. Second, the SMEs retained a particular view about advancing their simple EC initiatives. In this research, implications arising with respect to theory and to practice are discussed.

Chapter XVII, entitled "Motivators for IOS Adoption in Denmark," by Helle Zinner Henriksen, Copenhagen Business School (Denmark) operationalizes the Tornatzky and Fleischer (1990) model for organizational adoption in order to investigate reasons for adoption and non-adoption among businesses in the Danish steel and machinery industry. This particular industry segment had been subject to massive information campaigns focusing on the benefits of IOS in the form of EDI from business associations. This study suggests that environmental and organizational attributes rather than technological attributes are the main determining forces for adoption of EDI.

This manuscript provides a collection of the latest research related to the effective implementation of e-technologies into the daily lives of professors, researchers, scholars, professionals, and all individuals in general. This innovative volume is a must-read for anyone interested in gaining a more thorough understanding of how to successfully execute e-commerce strategies and how to best adopt the various elements into their own classrooms, workplaces, and organizations.

Chapter I
SME B2B E–Commerce and Customer Loyalty Revisited

Assion Lawson-Body
University of North Dakota, USA

Timothy P. O'Keefe
University of North Dakota, USA

ABSTRACT

Busness-to-business (B2B) electronic commerce is an important opportunity for small and medium-sized enterprises (SMEs), providing increased competition on a global scale and allowing them to access wider markets. SMEs' B2B electronic commerce success is tied to the ability to foster inter-organizational relationships and customer loyalty. However, this is not always true because many SMEs have difficulty achieving B2B benefits as suggested by media and early research. This study is an empirical examination of the effect of Web tools on the inter-organizational relationships (IOR) between SMEs and their loyal customers. Data collected from 386 SMEs in North America (United States and Canada) and processed with partial least square (PLS) show that the use of Web tools (which include the level of Web content and the level of security on the Internet) has a positive effect on the relationship between cooperation and interdependence and customer loyalty. However, the effect of Web tools on the relationship between trust and customer loyalty is different because the use of nonsecure Web tools reduces the effect of trust on customer loyalty, and surprisingly, the use of secure Web tools does not increase or decrease the effect of trust on customer loyalty. This research also suggests that one of the factors of the failure or success of SMEs' B2B e-commerce is the technical skills of the managers in the use of secure Web tools—high skill levels increase the positive effect of trust on customer loyalty. The implications of the results for the study are discussed.

INTRODUCTION

The Internet serves as an intermediary between buyers and sellers for business-to-business (B2B) transactions (Otim & Grover, 2006). One of the most recent applications of Internet technology involves small and medium-sized enterprises (SMEs). SMEs account for the majority of businesses in the USA, employing more than 52% of the private workforce, contributing 51% of gross domestic product and providing two-thirds of all new jobs annually (Levenburg & Klein, 2006). It is no surprise that B2B electronic commerce has received so much attention from entrepreneurs, executives, investors, authors, scholars, and business observers (Porter, 2001). However, while anecdotal evidence and empirical results give the impression that B2B electronic commerce is expanding fast, the fact remains that many SMEs are still sitting on the sidelines (Daniel & McInerney, 2005; Teo, Wei, & Benbasat, 2003).

Since the late 1980s, a growing number of studies on inter-organizational networks have been conducted. One of the primary benefits of such networks is their potential to transform inter-organizational relationships (IOR) (Li & Williams, 1999). Web tools represent one type of inter-organizational network. In this chapter, IOR refers to relationships between SMEs and their customers which are also organizations, quite probably SMEs. Reichheld and Schefter (2000) stress that loyalty via relationship development and improvement is necessary or even the best-designed electronic commerce model will collapse.

Another determinant of customer loyalty is the degree of trust that customers have in the vendor (Reichheld & Schefter, 2000)—trust is important in managing IOR (Komiak, Wang, & Benbasat, 2005). The use of Web tools may have an effect on the relationship between trust and customer loyalty because trust is a precursor to customer loyalty. Trust is a willingness to rely on an exchange partner in whom one has confidence (Berry, 1995). Becoming a trusted partner is key to maintaining IOR. Trust can be achieved by providing the customer with valuable information using a high quality Web site.

Anecdotal evidence shows that the Internet can enable an SME that is involved in an IOR with a customer to globalize and to achieve a multimillion dollar turnover in a couple of years (Poon,

2000). However, such success stories are not widespread. Many SMEs have difficulty achieving the benefits suggested by media and early research (Poon, 2000). In fact, many SMEs have failed to follow the robust technical standards needed to make electronic IOR practice economical (Dai & Kauffman, 2001; Daniel & McInerney, 2005). In addition, there is little existing research that has empirically tested the effect of Web tools on IOR which leads to business partnership/customer loyalty. The primary objective of this study is to examine the effects of Web tools on the IOR between SMEs and their loyal customers/business partners.

This chapter is organized as follows: In the second section, we present the literature review. In the third section, we present the theoretical research model and hypotheses. In the fourth section, we introduce the methodology. In the fifth section, we present analysis and results. In the sixth section, we outline the discussion. In the seventh section, we identify the limitations. In the last section, we draw conclusions and recommendations.

LITERATURE REVIEW

B2B electronic commerce has progressed from the early days when it was used for aggregating buyers and sellers, and it now offers multiple functionalities (Wang & Archer, 2004). B2B exchanges have been significantly affected by the evolution of the Internet (Park & Yun, 2004). Several perspectives have been identified in the literature in assessing the importance of B2B electronic commerce transactions. A relational perspective views transactions as a mechanism to foster inter-organizational relationships (IOR) (Gengatharen & Standing, 2005). B2B electronic commerce creates a virtual marketplace that lowers buyers' cost to acquire information about services and products and reinforces IOR through service delivery (Otim & Grover, 2006).

Empirical research into B2B electronic commerce issues involving SMEs is still in its embryonic development (Elia, Lefebvre, & Lefebvre, 2007). In fact, the Internet and electronic commerce are viewed as a means for SMEs to compete with their larger counterparts—by overcoming distance and size to access global markets and build long-term relationships (Daniel & McInerney, 2005; Gengatharen & Standing, 2005). For SMEs, IORs are particularly critical as they are a primary determinant of customer loyalty (Levenburg & Klein, 2006). It is the way SMEs tend to differentiate themselves from their larger competitors (Levenburg & Klein, 2006).

The relative importance of SMEs in many economies has been long recognized as different from large businesses, and many governments have taken steps to ensure that this sector is not marginalized in the move to the digital age (Gengatharen & Standing, 2005). In any case, there have been many SME e-business successes as well as failures (Korgaonkar & O'Leary, 2006). Most studies indicate that despite growing levels of awareness and enthusiasm for e-business, only a small proportion of SMEs are realizing substantial benefits from the Internet (Gengatharen & Standing, 2005). Korgaonkar and O'Leary (2006) identified 862 SME e-business failures from the year 2000 to the end of the second quarter 2002. Most of those failures occurred in 2000 and continued into 2002.

The reasons for online SMEs success or failure were related to different factors such as managerial, market, and financial issues (Korgaonkar & O'Leary, 2006). The majority of SMEs use the Internet mainly for communication and research, and e-business is not integrated with their business processes (Gengatharen & Standing, 2005). Some of the major challenges facing SMEs are a lack of technological expertise and difficulty identifying the benefits offered by the Internet (Gengatharen & Standing, 2005). Several other studies have addressed the issue of SME B2B e-commerce failures using the quality of the Web

site and the technical skills of the managers as factors. Contrary to expectations, the evidence suggests that e-business has had limited effects on SMEs. One of the key reasons appears to be a lack of understanding of these firm's motivations for engaging in e-business (Levenburg & Magal, 2005). The primary obstacle to the use of e-commerce between SMEs and their customers seems to be the culture and resistance to change that characterize small entrepreneurs (Tagliavini, Ravarini, & Antonelli, 2001). SMEs are often characterized by a lack of specialized staff and a lack of strategic management of the Internet; as a result, SMEs often choose to outsource these activities to reduce costs and improve business performance (Tagliavini et al., 2001).

One empirical study of SME managerial e-business motivations showed that business owners hoped to gain a competitive advantage by improving customer relationships; however, they did not examine the factors that lead to failure (Korgaonkar & O'Leary, 2006). Elia et al. (2007) investigated SME electronic commerce initiatives and their related benefits. Their findings suggest that SMEs have leveraged their electronic commerce initiatives with both their customers and their suppliers. Results also suggest the existence of a close alignment between electronic commerce focus and related benefits (Elia et al., 2007). Gengatharen and Standing (2005) found that the most significant factors affecting SMEs' B2B e-business success or failure are owner innovativeness and management of existing business relationships.

In order to grow, SMEs must evolve their organization and their B2B relationships without impairing competitive advantage (Street & Meister, 2004). Failure to evolve will likely result in harm to the business through loss of customers and may ultimately result in business closure. Although the Internet, particularly the Web, is often relied on to assist growth, SMEs often find technology difficult to implement—in particular due to resource constraints (Street & Meister, 2004).

THE THEORETICAL RESEARCH MODEL AND HYPOTHESES

The key constructs of the research model, identified through the literature, are as follows: the dependent variable will be drawn from the customer loyalty construct, the independent variables will be drawn from the IOR construct, and the moderating variables will be drawn from the Web tools construct. Each is discussed next.

Customer Loyalty

The concept of customer loyalty often used in the literature incorporates behavioral and attitudinal measures (Otim & Grover, 2006). In this chapter, loyalty is defined as building and sustaining a trusted relationship with customers that leads to the customers' repeated purchases of products or services over a given period of time (Lam, Shankar, Erramilli, & Murthy, 2004).

Customer loyalty, in general, increases profit and growth to the extent that increasing the percentage of loyal customers by as little as 5% can increase profitability by as much as 30% to 85%, depending upon the industry involved (Gefen, 2002). Loyal customers are typically willing to pay a higher price and are more understanding when something goes wrong. They are easier to satisfy because the vendor knows the customers' expectations better (Gefen, 2002). It has been found that loyal customers are less price sensitive and lower costs are incurred by providers as the expense of pursuing new customers is reduced (Rowley & Dawes, 2000). The presence of a loyal customer base provides the firm with valuable time to respond to competitive actions (Rowley & Dawes, 2000). Customers demonstrate their loyalty in several ways. They may choose to stay with a provider, whether this continuance is defined as a relationship or not, or they may increase the number of, or the frequency of, their purchases (Rowley & Dawes, 2000).

IOR from SME Perspectives

In this study, an IOR is defined as the process whereby an SME builds long-term relationships with current customers so that both seller and buyer work toward a common set of specified goals (Evans & Laskin, 1994). Trust is a critical factor in any IOR. Trust is required where the trustor does not have direct control over the actions of a trustee, and there are possible negative consequences of one party not fulfilling its obligations (Jarvenpaa & Tractinski, 1999). IOR are built around interactions and can be characterized by a tension between autonomy and interdependence, between team loyalty and individuality, and between competition and cooperation (Nouwens & Bouwman, 1995). The primary goal of an IOR is to achieve a competitive advantage via mutual loyalty in relationship to companies outside the relationship. Therefore an IOR is heavily dependent upon relationships based on cooperation, interdependence, and trust. Each of them is discussed below.

Cooperation

Cooperation is defined in this study as coordinated actions taken by parties to achieve mutual outcomes (Lewin & Johnston, 1997). It has been suggested from the relational perspective that interfirm cooperation is both frequent and desirable (Rindfleisch & Moorman, 2003). Cooperation is proactive because it suggests actively agreeing, for example, to advertise a partner's products (Morgan & Hunt, 1994; Wuyts & Geyskens, 2005). A relationship-committed customer will cooperate with a vendor because of a desire to make the relationship work (Morgan & Hunt, 1994). Advocates of interfirm cooperation argue that alliances, joint ventures, and other forms of collaboration are largely procompetitive because they help firms reduce risk and lower costs (Rindfleisch & Moorman, 2003). Detractors of interfirm cooperation argue that these collaborative activities may be anticompetitive because of the risk that cooperation may lead to outcomes harmful to customer welfare (Rindfleisch & Moorman, 2003). Cooperative behavior allows the relationship to work by ensuring that both parties receive benefits. An enduring desire to maintain a valued cooperative relationship should, in turn, effect loyalty. Thus, we propose the hypothesis below:

H1: *Cooperation will have a positive effect on customer loyalty.*

Interdependence

Interdependence is defined as the level of value that one firm can garner from another firm, compared with the value it can garner from alternative firms, in achieving its goals (Payan & McFarland, 2005). Drawing on theoretical research on electronic communications and IOR, Clark and Lee (2000) developed and tested a model for the link between performance, interdependence, and coordination of firms involved in IOR within the U.S. grocery channel. They found that channel performance, interdependence, and coordination are closely related for IOR-involved firms. Parties involved in an IOR become interdependent when there are significant switching costs associated with replacing the incumbent suppliers (Lewin & Johnston, 1997).

A loyal customer will remain with a vendor, at least in part, because the cost of switching to another vendor is such that it is not worth their while to switch (Reichheld & Schefter, 2000). There is consensus that as customers perceive higher costs in switching service providers than in switching goods suppliers, loyalty is more likely to occur in service-based relationships than in goods-based relationships (Rowley & Dawes, 2000). Some authors propose that a buyer's dependence on a seller is directly related to the buyer's need to maintain the relationship in order to achieve desired goals

(Lewin & Johnston, 1997). Therefore, we offer the following hypothesis:

H2: *Interdependence will have a positive effect on customer loyalty.*

Trust

According to Ganesan (1994), trust is the extent to which the customer believes that the vendor has intentions and motives that are beneficial to the customer (Lewin & Johnston, 1997). Trust is the belief that another can be relied upon with confidence to perform role responsibilities in a fiduciary manner—and is manifest in a willingness to voluntarily increase one's vulnerability to another (Smith, 1997).

Existing research defines organizational trust (trust between organizations) as a critical characteristic of IOR (Bunduchi, 2005). Trust was found to be a critical concept in influencing the development of IOR in many organizational studies (Bunduchi, 2005). Existing research converges on the belief that Internet use affects significantly the level of trust between SMEs and their buyers (Bunduchi, 2005). Based on extensive analysis of existing studies regarding the relationship between IT use and trust in IOR, Gallivan and Depledge (2003) conclude that the use of such technologies can enhance trust between SMEs and their loyal customers, but that outcome depends on the level of IT functionalities used (Bunduchi, 2005). Soliman and Janz (2004) also find that trust is a significant variable influencing the use of inter-organizational systems (Bunduchi, 2005). However, none of these studies have analyzed the effect of trust on the relationships between SMEs and their loyal customers. Accordingly, it is hypothesized that:

H3: *Trust will have a positive effect on customer loyalty.*

Web Tools

There is an existing need to investigate the tools that make a Web site effective for B2B electronic commerce. According to Dholakia and Rego (1998), there are several ways the Web affects electronic commerce, including: (1) the Web is an easy and inexpensive way to advertise, lowering the barriers to entry for SMEs; (2) the Web overturns the traditional hierarchical system of distribution channels; that is, former channel partners become competitors in the global marketplace; (3) unlike traditional means of communication, such as newspapers or television, the Web gives the customer control of choosing and processing information about the firm; (4) the breadth of the medium allows wider availability, accessibility, and selection of hard-to-find products/services (Dholakia & Rego, 1998). Web tools range from simple associatively linked collections of static hypertext documents to interactive, integrated, customizable solutions and agent-based negotiation support; and since Web tools were initially developed to address the development of B2C transactions, they can also be effectively applied in B2B settings as well (Gebauer & Scharl, 1999).

The Web tool components developed in this study are an adaptation of some of the Web site tools presented by Gebauer and Scharl (1999). There are essentially two variables that embody the construct of Web tools: the level of Web content and the level of Web security.

Web Content

Web content is defined as the new Internet-based channels through which SMEs can display information about themselves and the products and services they offer, or better yet, as a dynamic interactive portal (Joseph, Cook, & Javalgi, 2001). This definition encompasses SMEs' interactivity and presence on the Web.

This interactivity concept is complex and multidimensional (Lombard & Ditton, 1997).

According to Rafaeli and Sudweeks (1997), like face-to-face exchange, computer-mediated exchange has the capacity to enable high interactivity. Rafaeli and Sudweeks (1997) identified three levels of exchange involving high degrees of interactivity: two-way non-interactive exchange, quasi-interactive exchange, and totally interactive exchange. One of the major ways in which the Internet differs from other exchange media is that it allows for two-way interaction and multimedia capabilities.

Lombard and Ditton (1997) explained that the concept of presence is central to the use of electronic commerce, and therefore to the usefulness and profitability of such new technologies as the Web. Lombard and Ditton's (1997) conceptualization of presence based on the degree to which a medium can produce seemingly accurate representations of objects, events, and people corresponds, in part, to the definition of the level of Web content used in this article.

H4: *Web content will have a positive effect on the relationship between IOR and customer loyalty.*

Specific institutional mechanisms such as cooperation norms were found to support IOR in B2B electronic commerce (Bunduchi, 2005). The Web allows a cooperative partner to join an exchange alliance—the number of partners who can qualify and participate in online exchanges is greatly increased (Bandyopadhyay, Barron, & Chaturvedi, 2005).

SMEs need to make their Web sites extremely easy to use, since convenience and saving time (and consequently money) are the major thrusts for online cooperation. It is essential for SMEs to offer attractive promotions online backed with high quality products and services to convert potential customers to actual cooperators. Once potential customers are converted to cooperative customers, they are more likely to become loyal customers. SMEs can keep their Web sites fresh, interactive, and relevant to customers' interests by using cookies. Some SMEs use cookies on their Web sites to improve and simplify online cooperation with their loyal customers. Hence, we offer the hypothesis below:

H4a: *Web content will have a positive effect on the relationship between cooperation and customer loyalty.*

A business can use Web content to reach customers all around the world (Jarvenpaa & Tractinski, 1999) in an attempt to initiate and maintain interdependent relationships with them. Web content lets customers who are physically far away from the world's centers of traditional commerce gain access to products and information possibly unavailable via any other delivery mechanism, which may yield customer loyalty and eventually an interdependent relationship. Some researchers argue that Web-based interactivity promotes what some are calling "sticky" transactions that keep buyers locked-in (Steinfield, Chan, & Kraut, 2000). Some researchers propose that a buyer's dependence on a seller is directly related to the buyer's need to maintain the relationship in order to achieve desired goals (Lewin & Johnston, 1997). On this basis, we formulated the hypothesis below:

H4b: *Web content will have a positive effect on the relationship between interdependence and customer loyalty.*

Indeed, companies should use Web content to try to promote their business partners' trust by publishing success stories and partner testimonials on their Web sites or by carrying seals of approval by third parties, and so on. Since the attainment of customer loyalty has customer trust as a prerequisite (Reichheld & Schefter, 2000), electronic relationships supported by trust will lead to customer loyalty. Chow and Holden (1997) verified that trust has a causal effect on loyalty.

When customers trust an online vendor, they will share and communicate strategic information; that electronic communication enables the SME to form a more intimate relationship with customers, offering products and services tailored to their preferences, which in turn increases trust and strengthens loyalty (Reichheld & Schefter, 2000). Hence, we offer the hypothesis below:

H4c: *Web content will have a positive effect on the relationship between trust and customer loyalty.*

Web Security

The IS community has given significant attention to the issue of sharing security information among firms as a tool to minimize security breaches (Gal-Or & Ghose, 2005). The level of security on the Web is defined as the risks associated with Web technology assets such as loss, disruption, and unauthorized access of information, data, and Internet resources (Cavusoglu, Raghunathan, & Mishra, 2002). One of the greatest concerns about doing business via the Internet is the level of security in transactions (Swaminathan, Lepkowska-White, & Rao, 1999). The perception of unsatisfactory security is one of the primary IOR hindrances. Despite advances in security, such as cryptography, authentication, confidentiality, integrity, nonrepudiation, and so forth, companies are still concerned about using an impersonal medium like the Internet for secure transactions (Swaminathan et al., 1999). Although organizational acceptance of the risk of conducting transactions over the Internet is growing, it is still wavering.

Both parties involved in an IOR must develop effective security means together and share information about risk in order to motivate customer participation in online transactions. Both parties also need to secure their Web sites during their inter-organizational exchange which leads to increased customer loyalty.

H5: *Web security will have a positive effect on the relationship between IOR and customer loyalty.*

A lot of research shows that the majority of SMEs are not making use of Web tools due to information security problems (Tagliavini et al., 2001). SMEs engaging in online cooperation employ multiple security technologies such as firewalls and intrusion detection systems (IDS) to internally secure their information (Cavusoglu et al., 2002). Firewalls are network access control devices that attempt to prevent intrusions from external hackers (Cavusoglu et al., 2002). An IDS attempts to detect intrusions by analyzing audit trails that store event histories and network packets (Cavusoglu et al., 2002). For cooperative SMEs, an assessment of the value of these technologies is crucial (Cavusoglu et al., 2002) in order to foster customer loyalty. If high levels of Web security characterize an effective relationship between SMEs and their loyal customers, then we expect:

H5a: *Web security will have a positive effect on the relationship between cooperation and customer loyalty.*

IT security is now widely recognized as an important aspect of an SME's operations realized through the Web site technologies for all types of organizations (Cavusoglu et al., 2002). A secure Web site is necessary because SMEs involved in online interactions need to avoid situations that cause loss of data and resources in the form of destruction, disclosure, denial of service, and fraud. Cavusoglu et al. (2002) identified three internal mechanisms essential in creating a high Web security level: preventive, detective, and responsive. Preventive mechanisms like firewalls allow only authorized traffic between internal and external systems (Cavusoglu et al., 2002). Detective mechanisms try to detect the intrusions when they occur by analyzing log files to detect

suspicious system use (Cavusoglu et al., 2002). Responsive mechanisms are more detailed, directed investigations (typically manual) of system security issues. They typically utilize pattern analysis to detect and confirm, as well as to stop, illegal use of a system (Cavusoglu et al., 2002). An SME's internal mechanisms work in conjunction with customers' external mechanisms. Therefore, using secure Web technology such as digital signatures can help an SME to establish and maintain interdependence leading to customer loyalty. Thus, it is hypothesized:

H5b: *Web security will have a positive effect on the relationship between interdependence and customer loyalty.*

Trust can be achieved by providing the customer with valuable information using a secure Web site. Quelch and Klein (1996) speculate that in the early stages of Internet development, trust is a critical factor in stimulating purchases over the Internet (Jarvenpaa & Tractinski, 1999) primarily due to security issues. SMEs using secure Web site technologies to guarantee identities and other characteristics can maintain credibility, establish customer trust, and increase loyalty. To maintain loyalty, a company must develop IOR, offering products and services through secure, trusted technologies. The customer will then consider its supplier as a trusted company—possibly becoming a loyal customer.

H5c: *Web security will have a positive effect on the relationship between trust and customer loyalty.*

THE RESEARCH MODEL

Since IOR was first developed as a new theory, many researchers have been advancing and augmenting it. Lewin and Johnston (1997) studied six constructs associated with current IOR theory such as interdependence, trust, commitment, communication, cooperation, and equity. These variables are used as descriptors to develop profiles of a successful partnering relationship and a typical relationship between a wood products distributor and two manufacturing principals. They found that the partnering relationship is characterized by a high level of trust, a long-term relationship orientation, intensive information exchange, and a high level of mutual cooperation. Many other authors have studied the transformations that Internet use has brought to the nature of IOR (Bunduchi, 2005; Wang & Archer, 2004). Those studies led to contradictory results regarding the outcome of IT use. Some found that Internet use favors collaborative relationships, whereas others suggested that Internet use creates incentives for organizations to internalize their activities (Bunduchi, 2005; Wang & Archer, 2004).

A reason for such divergent results is that different types of IT can be used to support different kinds of IOR. In general, IS researchers cite transactional relationships and collaborative relationships (Bunduchi, 2005; Wang & Archer, 2004). The former are mainly characterized by low interdependence and low trust. In contrast, the latter are mainly characterized by strong interdependence, high trust, and cooperation. This study addresses IOR between SMEs and their customers because IOR involve a relationship that involves both economic exchange as well as social exchange. Following Christiaanse et al. (2004) cited in Bunduchi (2005), this article focuses on IOR as networks where SMEs' customers or business partners and SMEs meet to engage in relationships such as interdependence, trust, and cooperation.

In the research model, Web tools, such as the level of Web content and the level of Web security, can support the formation and maintenance of IOR because they facilitate the way SMEs cooperate with, depend upon, and trust each other, ultimately affecting customer loyalty.

Figure 1. Research model

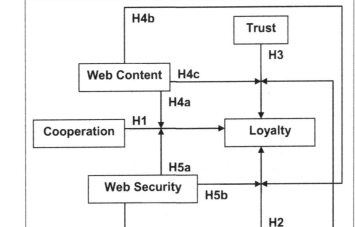

METHODOLOGY

The Study Sample

A total of 1,700 SMEs in the USA and Canada, each having a Web site and an e-mail address, were asked to complete an online survey. Company size is measured by number of employees (Chow & Holden, 1997). In this study, an SME is defined as having fewer than 500 employees. These SMEs were chosen randomly from the Web site of "Industry Canada" (http://strategis. ic.gc.ca), Small Business Administration (SBA) database, and North Dakota Small Business Development Center (SBDC) database. The senior sales representative, company executive, or president of each of the above companies was sent a cover letter by e-mail along with the URL of the Web site containing the research instrument (questionnaire). As an incentive, respondents were told that a summary of the results would be sent at their request. A total of 386 SMEs responded, producing a 22.7% response rate. The response rate achieved is acceptable, given the length of the research instrument, the technical and confidential nature of the information requested, and the nature of the respondents.

Measures

All measures were selected from the survey instrument used by Lawson-Body (2003). After slight modification, the questions measuring all variables, except interdependence, used a 5-point Likert-type scale—interdependence was measured using a 6-point Likert-type scale.

The questions measuring Interdependence used a scale of 1 (disagree very strongly) to 6 (agree very strongly). The scale used to measure Loyalty was 1 (decreasing sharply) to 5 (increasing sharply). All other scales ranged from 1 (never) to 5 (always). Since the instruments have been slightly revised from the original ones, reliability coefficients were calculated.

Table 1 presents the reliability coefficients Rho. Its first column presents the independent and dependent variables of the research model. The second column of Table 1 presents the indicator of the reliability of a measure which is the Rho coefficient. Aubert, Rivard, and Patry (1994) report that the guidelines established by Nunnally (1978) for the interpretation of Cronbach's alpha also apply to the Rho coefficient. These guidelines estimate that acceptable reliability coefficients must be higher than 0.70. All Rho coefficients are between 0.735 and 0.869. This is considered very satisfactory.

To measure the Web tools variables, an evaluation grid was used, mounted according to the guidelines offered by Kassarjian (1977) and found in the study of Lawson-Body (2003). The evaluation grid used in this study contains 42 criteria. Web tools such as the level of Web content and the level of Web security were evaluated by two judges: one of the researchers and a graduate student. The independent judge was an MBA student who was chosen randomly. He did not know the researcher personally and performed the ratings as a professional. Therefore, each judge made 42 judgments per SME Web site (386 SME Web sites in total), which resulted in a total of 16,212 (42*386) decisions. The judges were

Table 1. Reliability coefficient Rho

Variables	Coefficients Rho
Interdependence	0.869
Cooperation	0.754
Trust	0.726
Loyalty	0.735

in agreement on 13,132 of the 16,212 judgments, which yields an average of 34 (13132/386) judgments per SME. Both judges disagreed on 3,080 of 16,212 judgments, which yields an average of 8 (3080/386) decisions per SME Web site. The interjudge reliability coefficient is 81%. Berelson (1952), cited in Kassarjian (1977), specified an acceptable reliability coefficient range between 66% and 95%. The ratio of 81% is satisfactory.

ANALYSIS AND RESULTS

Characteristics of Participating SMEs

The respondents were spread across 10 different industry sectors. As shown in Table 2, 78% of the respondents were primarily involved in Manufacturing, Information Technologies Hardware/Software, and other sectors. In terms of annual sales

volume, 40% of the sample had annual sales of less than $1 million, while 42% had annual sales between $1 and $10 million and 18% chose not to share that information. About 40% of the SMEs had less than 10 employees, while roughly 42% had less than 50 employees. Approximately 14% of the SMEs employed between 50 and 500 people. Only 4% had more than 500 employees.

Most of the participating SMEs (about 64%) have been in business for more than 10 years, while 32% have been in business between 1 and 9 years. A total of 75% of the respondents indicated their company Web site had been in existence for 1 to 6 years, while 18% of SMEs indicated they had been online for less than 1 year. A total of 81% of the SMEs had 10% of their budget invested in Web site development and/or maintenance, while 7% of SMEs invested between 11 and 30% of their budget in online resources. Only 2% of SMEs invested more than 50% of their annual budget in Web site development and/or maintenance.

Table 2. Characteristics of the SMEs sampled

Industry sector	Percentage
Automobile and Transportation	2%
Chemicals	2%
IT (non-Internet) Hardware and Software	9%
Internet Access and Service Providers	2%
Manufacturing	29%
Farmers	2%
Health Industry	4%
Finance	2%
Banks	4%
Consulting Firms	4%
Other Sectors	40%
The number of years SMEs have been in business	**Percentage**
Less than one year	4%
1-3 years	12%
4-6 years	10%
7-9 years	10%
10 years or more	64%

Table 2. Characteristics of the SMEs sampled

The size of SMEs (persons)	Percentage
Less than 10 employees	40%
11-50 employees	42%
51-100 employees	6%
101-500 employees	8%
501 employees or more	4%
The revenue (turnover) of SMEs	**Percentage**
Less than $0.75 million	32%
$0.76-$1 million	8%
$2-5 million	22%
$6-10 million	10%
$11 million or more	10%
Do not want to share	18%
The duration of SMEs Web site's existence	**Percentage**
Less than one year	18%
1-3 years	33%
4-6 years	42%
7-9 years	7%
9 years or more	0%
The percentage of SMEs per region	**Percentage**
Western North Dakota	82%
Eastern North Dakota	18%
Southern North Dakota	9%
Northern North Dakota	43%
Other region	12%
The percentage of SMEs' budget invested in Web site development and/or maintenance	**Percentage**
Less than 10%	81%
11-30%	17%
31-50%	0%
51-70%	2%
71-100%	0%

In terms of location, 82% of SMEs that responded to the survey are from North Dakota. The 12% of respondents are spread across the other sampled regions.

Means and Standard Deviations of the Variables

The means and standard deviations of the variables are reported in Table 3. Results show the variable cooperation has the highest standard deviation and the variable trust has the highest mean.

Table 3. Means and standard deviations

Variables	Sample	Means	Standard Deviations
Interdependence	386	11.6571	2.0613
Cooperation	380	14.4265	4.0672
Trust	384	16.5182	2.7122
Loyalty	379	13.2579	2.8910

Procedures for Testing the Hypothesis

Partial least squares (PLS), a second generation multivariate method, was used to process and analyze the data. The PLS method simultaneously evaluates both the measurement model and the theoretical model. It adjusts the relationships among the variables accordingly (Aubert et al., 1994; Chin, Marcolin, & Newsted, 2003). PLS was selected in this research because it presupposes no distributional form for the data.

Hypothesis Testing (H1, H2, and H3)

The test of Hypothesis H1, H2, and H3 on the sample of the 386 respondents was carried out with a statistical tool named PLS-GRAPH. Table 4 shows that Student's T (t value) of effects of interdependence (2.2856), cooperation (2.0041), and trust (1.7780) on customer loyalty are higher than 1.65 (P<=0.05). This first hypothesis test shows that these three IOR variables have a positive and direct effect on customer loyalty. In other words, customer loyalty is increased ($R^2 = .78$)

by interdependence, by cooperation, and by trust, supporting H1, H2, and H3 respectively.

The coefficient of T-statistic and the weights presented in Table 5 show that only some items contribute to the formation or creation of the variable customer loyalty and the three variables (interdependence, cooperation, and trust) which affect customer loyalty. For example, for loyalty, the frequency of sales to regular customer (2.8707) is viewed as the causal variable that provides the condition under which loyalty developed. This indicator is followed by the firm's customers' repeat purchases of products and/or services (2.5801), the percentage of sales to regular customers out of the firm's total sales (2.3671), the total dollar value sales to the firm's regular customer (1.8856), and the average number of years during which the firm maintains business relationships with its customers (1.7615). The percentage of sales from regular customers instead of one time sales (1.5039), the number of the firm's regular customers (1.5203), and the average yearly revenue per regular customer (1.2700) do not contribute to the formation of the variable loyalty. The remaining asterisked (*) indicators in Table 5 contribute

Table 4. Path coefficient and student's T (t values)

Loyalty ($R^2 = .78$)	Path coefficient	T-Statistic
Interdependence	0.3458	2.2856*
Cooperation	0.2273	2.0041*
Trust	0.193	1.7780*

*T-Student significant at 1.64 (P<= 0.05)

to the creation of the variable to which they are connected. According to their T-statistics, some indicators contribute more than others to the formation of their dependent variables. The indicators presented in Table 5 which are not asterisked do not have a significant role in the formation of their corresponding dependent variables.

Hypothesis Testing (H4, H5, and H6)

To test interaction effects, analysis was performed with the three variables (interdependence, cooperation, and trust) that have a positive and direct effect on customer loyalty. The two variables of Web tools play a moderating role. Therefore,

Table 5. The coefficients of T-statistic, weights, and loadings

Items and variables	Weight	Loading	T-Statistic
Loyalty			
LOYAVE**	0.1888	0.3712	1.7615*
LOYREGS	0.4517	0.5702	2.2299*
LOYPERP	0.7817	0.5455	2.3671*
LOYPERT	-0.0041	0.4002	1.5039
LOYPERF	0.3652	0.5189	2.8707*
LOYPERH	0.5170	0.4520	1.8856*
LOYEXP	0.0014	0.1737	1.2700
LOYNBF	0.0147	0.2415	1.5203
LOYGEN	0.3280	0.5521	2.5801*
Interdependence			
INDCOST	0.6698	0.2244	2.4208*
INDTERM	0.3585	0.5718	1.7997*
INDDIFF	-0.4661	0.1251	0.4473
INDBENEF	1.2068	0.4113	2.8384*
Cooperation			
COOPHELP	0.2262	0.4271	2.4766*
COOPDECI	0.5961	0.8303	1.8230*
COOPOLIC	-0.2407	0.0030	0.6745
COOPRECO	0.5889	0.5543	2.0624*
Trust			
TRUSTPRO	0.0968	0.2306	1.0420
TRUSTHON	0.8102	0.6166	1.9185*
TRUSTIME	0.7682	0.6064	2.4812*
TRUSTCOU	0.7490	0.5259	1.9207*
TRUSTINT	0.3333	0.1423	1.7671*
TRUSTEXP	0.4895	0.3952	2.3651*

*T-Student significant at 1.64 (P<= 0.05)

** See Appendix A for a full definition of the items.

the interaction tests of Hypotheses H4, H5, and H6 were carried out with PLS-GRAPH. Table 6 presents the results of the tests of the magnitude of the interaction effect, including the values of the Student T-statistic.

The results indicate that Web tools (which include the level of Web content and the level of security on the Internet) have a positive effect on the cooperation→loyalty and interdependence→loyalty relationships. However, that effect is mixed for trust. The interaction coefficient is not significant for the effect of Web content on the trust→loyalty relationship. However, the interaction effect of Web security on the trust→loyalty relationship is significant. The interaction betas for the effect of Web security and Web content on the trust→loyalty relationships are 0.3108 and 0.2149 respectively. Consequently,

Table 6. Path coefficient and student's T (t values) for the interaction effect

Dependent Variable – Loyalty R² = 0.78	Path coefficient (β standardized)	T-Statistic
Interdependence	0.2364	2.7410*
Cooperation	0.3331	2.7010*
Trust	0.3104	3.1170*
Interaction Effects		
Web security X Interdependence	0.2895	1.8902*
Web content X Interdependence	0.2960	1.7523*
Web security X Cooperation	0.3419	2.4560*
Web content X Cooperation	0.3459	3.1107*
Web security X Trust	0.3108	3.1114*
Web content X Trust	0.2419	1.5641

*T-Student significant at 1.64 (P<= 0.05)

Figure 2. Results of PLS analysis

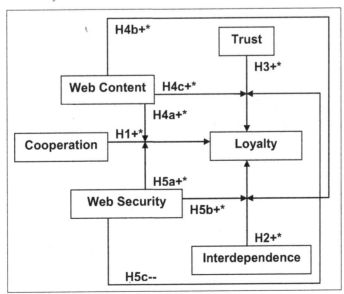

as Web security increases, so does the effect of trust on customer loyalty, but the Web content itself does not increase or decrease the effect of trust on customer loyalty.

The interaction betas for the effect of Web tools on the interdependence→loyalty relationship are 0.2895 (security) and 0.2960 (content). The interaction betas for the effect of Web tools on the cooperation→loyalty relationship are 0.3419 (security) and 0.3459 (content). Web tools have a significant positive effect on the cooperation→loyalty relationship and the interdependence→loyalty relationship.

Discussion and Implications

Eight of nine hypotheses are supported. The use of Web sites increases cooperation and interdependence between SMEs and their loyal customers. The effect of Web site content on the trust→loyalty relationship is neutral, but Web security positively affects that relationship. That means, if SMEs use nonsecure Web sites to maintain relationships with customers, trust in SMEs will be negatively affected, therefore customers will be less loyal to SMEs. There are many explanations for this, which are discussed below.

THE EFFECT OF IOR ON CUSTOMER LOYALTY

The findings of this study appear to be consistent with a number of previous studies. The positive effect of cooperation on customer loyalty appears to support the Kumar's (1996) contention, cited in Son, Narasimhan, and Riggins (2000), that in today's business environment SMEs that are pursuing loyalty as an objective are developing more cooperative and long-lasting customer relationships. Essentially, if an SME's business partner realizes that the information provided about products or services corresponds favorably to the delivered products or services, they will be satisfied with their IOR and will further commit, which leads to repeat purchases.

The study also found that interdependence has a positive effect on customer loyalty. Inter-organizational interdependence refers to mutual dependence between SMEs and their customers; that is, both firms in a mutually dependent relationship can benefit from increased loyalty to each other. Long-term relationships, where both parties over time learn how to best interact with each other, lead to decreasing relationship costs for the customer as well as for the supplier, raise the cost of switching to another supplier, and further stabilize the IOR (Grönroos, 1994). A mutually loyal relationship makes it possible for customers to avoid significant transaction costs involved in shifting the supplier or SME and for SMEs to avoid suffering unnecessary quality costs (Grönroos, 1994). Based on this finding, the notion that interdependence might serve as an important catalyst for an SME in achieving higher customer or business partner loyalty is entirely defendable. In other words, fostering interdependence between SMEs and their business organization might be crucial for the attainment of customer loyalty.

The positive effect of trust on customer loyalty found in this study was previously observed in a study conducted by Chow and Holden (1997). Consistent with conventional wisdom, Chow and Holden (1997) confirmed that the trust held by a buyer toward a seller is an important antecedent of loyalty. Chow and Holden (1997) added that while this may be an expected conclusion in a business environment where the switching costs are high, their findings were drawn from an environment where there were a number of available suppliers and switching costs were considered low. This result suggests that trust evolves as the buyer-seller relationship develops from mere awareness to conducting transactions—not surprisingly, inter-organizational trust ultimately depends on the encounter experience between SMEs and their business partners.

THE EFFECT OF WEB TOOLS ON THE RELATIONSHIP BETWEEN COOPERATION AND CUSTOMER LOYALTY

Web content was found to have a positive effect on the relationship between cooperation and customer loyalty. This finding supports the contention made by many industry leaders that the nature of the cooperative relationship will change as SMEs enter the world of B2B electronic commerce in large numbers (Salam, Lakshmi, & Srikantan, 2001). As SMEs move online, information will become available immediately, thereby forcing cooperative relationships between SMEs and their customers to evolve based on loyalty rather than solely on past relationships. This result indicates that a high level of Web content allows SMEs and their business partners to agree online on how any resource, such as a product, a production plan, a purchase order, and so forth, is described electronically. While cooperation is a well-established strategy, the use of the Web content has made it much more widespread, available, and less costly. Online cooperation that results in mutually derived resource allocation and optimization will yield loyalty. SMEs share ideas, influence views, and establish cooperation potential through news groups, forums, and e-mail, with their business customers and in doing so foster the development of customer loyalty.

The level of Web security positively influences the cooperation loyalty relationship. This result corroborates much of the findings in the literature. SMEs engaging in online cooperation utilize firewalls and intrusion detection systems (IDS) to internally secure their Web sites (Cavusoglu et al., 2002). An assessment of the value of these technologies is crucial (Cavusoglu et al., 2002) for SMEs and their cooperative customers to become loyal to each other. SMEs engaging in online cooperation need to feel that their transactions are secure from prying eyes and safe from alteration. For example, a B2B extranet Web site is a secured business network of several partners that become loyal to each other. Because of the security issue, SMEs that are willing to do online business have to make concerted efforts to allay fears by offering clear security guidelines to their partners and vice versa.

THE EFFECT OF WEB TOOLS ON THE INTERDEPENDENCE: CUSTOMER LOYALTY RELATIONSHIP

The hypothesis that the level of Web content favorably influences the relationship between interdependence and customer loyalty is supported. This confirms the findings in the literature that the formation of an interdependent relationship mediated through the use of Web tools will increase switching costs, therefore create customer loyalty. Web content costs create barriers to exit and raise buyers' costs of switching to new suppliers once an IOR is established. Firms not pursuing cost-based competitive advantages through the Internet will be left behind (Venkatraman, 2000). Therefore, if profits are to be made by online SMEs, loyal customers must be developed. Web tools may be used to foster electronic marketplaces which can result in an increasing number of ephemeral transactions between buyers and sellers. Additionally, Web content strengthens existing commercial relationships and locks in an SME's business partners by increasing the costs of switching to other SMEs.

The hypothesis that the Web security positively influences the interdependence→loyalty relationship is supported. This confirms that Web sites protected by a secured firewall can be used to enhance interdependence between SMEs and their customers. The success of some secured Web sites has been in part due to their ability to increase switching costs (Reichheld & Schefter, 2000). The high cost of switching SMEs renders many IORs unprofitable during early transactions.

Using a secure Web site is necessary because SMEs involved in online interdependence need to avoid situations which cause loss of data and resources in the form of destruction, disclosure, denial of service, and fraud.

The Effect of Web Tools on the Trust→Loyalty Relationship

The results of this study reveal that the trustworthiness of an SME is perceived to be low when Web tools are not secure. Therefore, a nonsecure Web site yields a lack of trust and diminishes the potential for a loyalty advantage. Different levels of experience with an SME's Web tools are expected to give different amounts of evidence for trust. SME business partners may trust based only on indirect or partial experience, such as browsing Web sites, while loyal customers or business partners may rely on additional evidence such as transaction experience. Consequently, even well managed but poorly secured Web tools could lead to the dissolution of pre-existing trust in an IOR and negatively effect customer loyalty.

Quelch and Klein (1996) speculate that trust is an important factor in stimulating purchases over the Internet (Jarvenpaa & Tractinski, 1999) mainly because of security issues. For example, because some SMEs and their customers worry about confidentiality and the use of information from Web content, they attempt to keep pricing and ordering details from competitors. They require that their customers sign legally binding agreements not to misuse information acquired via the IOR. Paradoxically, and in contrast to the speculations of many authors, for the SMEs in this study's sample, Web security was not always considered relevant to level of trust. In other words, and not surprisingly, trust in secure Web sites does not seem to act as a substitute for trust in SMEs.

Based on the literature, the findings of this research can be interpreted as supportive of the position that one factor of SME B2B e-commerce

failure or success is the technical skills of the managers using secure Web tools. The higher the managers' skill level, the higher the affect on the trust→loyalty relationship. Despite increasing use of the Internet for electronic commerce, online security remains an important issue for SMEs and their customers. Several studies, as well as this research, found that security is the primary concern inhibiting SMEs and their customers from engaging in electronic commerce. Security is vital in e-commerce because of the risk involved in information theft, such as e-mail addresses or credit card information which are required for most electronic commerce transactions. Security concerns also include SMEs' potential use of customers' information for electronic surveillance, e-mail solicitation, or data transfer.

One of the findings of this research shows that the use of Web tools (in particular, the nature of the Web content) does not affect the trust→loyalty relationship. This finding corroborates the conclusion of many studies—one of the major challenges for SMEs is uncertainty regarding the benefits offered by electronic commerce. Probably, the main obstacle to the use of electronic commerce among SMEs seems to be a lack of certainty regarding the real advantages these technologies offer. Essentially, this research suggests that Web security is a necessary factor in fostering the effect of trust on loyalty, but that the nature of Web content, at least for the SMEs in this sample, does not affect loyalty beyond that.

Limitations

There were five notable limitations with the study. First, SMEs are in general not good at keeping precise business statistics. Consequently, it is often fruitless to ask for such statistics from SMEs. Even if a small percentage of SMEs maintain such information, it is unlikely that this information would be readily available to researchers due to suspicions regarding the intended use. Whether an SME is successful or not in electronic commerce, there is little incentive to share that information. If an SME is successful, the knowledge of how the success was achieved is valuable and may not be revealed. If an SME has not been successful, then it is very likely that they will have little to tell, and may not wish to share that information either.

Second, there are limitations associated with the survey methodology, in particular, regarding the profile of respondents. From certain statements, we became aware that some respondents were Webmasters who did not necessarily have an extensive background in their SMEs.

The third limitation of this study is the response rate. In all, 386 usable electronic questionnaires were received, a net response rate of 22.7%. Although the number of usable electronic questionnaires was large for a study of this type and permitted the use of appropriate statistical tests, this response rate can be regarded as rather low.

The fourth limitation of this research, given the rather low survey response rate, is nonresponse bias. It is possible that responders are characteristically different from nonresponders in some manner which may bias study results. No attempt was made to assess or identify nonresponse bias.

Another limitation is associated with the geographic distribution of the sample. The majority of respondents are located in a single upper-midwestern state. The extent to which SMEs in that region differ from SMEs in other locations in characteristics salient to this research is a potential source of bias which limits the degree to which this study's results may be generalized.

Finally, while the findings from this study provide some meaningful interpretations and practical recommendations, their generalization should be undertaken with caution. The use of a single researcher and a single MBA student to evaluate the SME Web sites introduces the possibility of a common method bias. A larger number of evaluators independent from the publishing researchers would potentially produce more defendable as unbiased.

CONCLUSION

Recommendations

The main contribution of this study has been to provide empirical evidence on the effect of Web tools on the relationship between cooperation, interdependence, trust, and customer loyalty. In fact, business is based on trust between two parties, whether the business is conducted in person, by phone, or over a Web site. The customer can acquire a sense of the company and the individual from face-to-face discussions or from the appearance and location of the physical site; but the element of trust is difficult to develop in electronic transactions because customer access to trust-building stimuli is limited to what can be observed on the Web site. Therefore, creating trust via the Web depends on fostering IOR through electronic means of well-established Web tools. When SMEs treat the Web as more than just a communication tool, the probability of trust between companies increases, an IOR may develop, and customer loyalty may result.

The findings of this research should help SMEs identify the IOR factors which they should emphasize when Web tools are used to foster customer loyalty.

FUTURE RESEARCH DIRECTIONS

Future research should try to extend the findings of this research and the literature. In particular, the following is suggested:

- SME samples representative of other regions in the world may identify relationship characteristics different from those found in this study and others.
- Certainly the loyalty construct is more complex than is represented in the model presented in this study. The effects of other

moderating variables, such as commitment, for example, on loyalty require study.

- The complex nature of the Web tools construct requires examination in much more detail. The finding that Web content does not significantly affect the trust loyalty relationship is not surprising given the broad definition of content applied in this research. At a minimum, content should probably be subdivided such that the effects of information content is examined separately from the effects of interactivity supportive content.

- Finally, although this was touched upon earlier in this chapter, it warrants further mention. The relationship between loyalty and various independent variables may vary greatly between and among industries and/or business type. For example, the nature of trust and ultimately loyalty may differ between product-oriented IORs and service-oriented IORs.

Researchers are encouraged to build upon the findings of this research, to extend this model, and to identify specific means by which these and other findings may be operationalized in a practical business setting.

REFERENCES

Aubert, B., Rivard, S., & Patry, M. (1994, December 14-17). Development of measures to assess dimensions of IS operation transactions. In *Proceedings of the International Conference on Information Systems,* Vancouver, Canada (Vol. 15, pp. 13-26).

Bandyopadhyay, S., Barron, J. M., & Chaturvedi, A. R. (2005). Competition among sellers in on-line exchanges. *Information Systems Research, 16*, 47-60.

Berry, L. L. (1995). Relationships marketing of services: Growing interest, emerging perspectives. *Journal of Academy of Marketing Science, 23*, 236-245.

Blili, S., & Raymond, L. (1993). IT: Threats and opportunities for small and medium-sized enterprises. *International Journal of Information Management, 13*, 439-448

Bunduchi, R. (2005). Business relationships in Internet-based electronic markets: The role of goodwill trust and transaction costs. *Information Systems Journal, 15*, 321-341.

Cavusoglu, H., Raghunathan, S., & Mishra, B. (2002). Optimal design of information technology security architecture. *International Conference on Information Systems, 23*, 749-756.

Chin, W. W., Marcolin, B. L., & Newsted, P. R. (2003). A partial least squares latent variable modeling approch for measuring interaction effects: Results from a Monte Carlo simulation study and voice mail emotion/adoption study. *Information Systems Research, 14*, 189-217.

Chow, S., & Holden, R. (1997). Toward an understanding of loyalty: The moderating role of trust. *Journal of Managerial Issues, 9*, 275-298.

Clark, T. H., & Lee, H. G. (2000). Performance, interdependence and coordination in business-to-business electronic commerce and supply chain management. *Information Technology and Management, 1*(1-2), 85-105.

Dai, Q., & Kauffman, R. J. (2001, January). Business models for Internet-based e-procurement systems and B2B electronic markets: An exploratory assessment. In *Proceedings of the 34th Hawaii International Conference on Systems Sciences*, Maui.

Daniel, T. A., & McInerney, M. L. (2005). E-commerce and the "reluctant" small business owner:

How technology is changing the business model for small and medium-sized enterprises (SMEs). *The International Journal of Applied Management and Technology, 3*, 183-206.

Dholakia, U. M., & Rego, L. (1998). What makes commercial Web pages popular? An empirical investigation of Web page effectiveness. *European Journal of Marketing, 32*, 724-736.

Elia, E., Lefebvre, L., & Lefebvre, E. (2007). Focus of B2B electronic commerce initiatives and related benefits in manufacturing SMEs. *Journal of Information Systems and E-Business Management, 5*, 1-23.

Evans, J. R., & Laskin, R. L. (1994). The relationship marketing process: A conceptualization and application. *Industrial Marketing Management, 23*, 439-452.

Gal-Or, E., & Ghose, A. (2005). The economic incentives for sharing security information. *Information Systems Research, 16*, 186-208.

Gebauer, J., & Scharl, A. (1999). Between flexibility and automation: An evaluation of Web technology from a business process perspective. *Journal of Computer-Mediated Communication, 5*(2). Retrieved September 1, 2007, from http://jcmc.indiana.edu/

Gefen, D. (2002). Customer loyalty in e-commerce. *Journal of the Association for Information Systems, 3*, 27-51.

Gengatharen, D., & Standing, C. (2005). A framework to assess the factors affecting success or failure of the implementation of government-supported regional e-marketplaces for SMEs. *European Journal of Information Systems, 14*, 417-433.

Grandon, E., & Pearson, J. M. (2004). E-commerce adoption: Perceptions of managers/owners of small and medium sized firms in Chile. *Communications of the Association for Information Systems, 13*, 81-102.

Grönroos, C. (1994). From marketing mix to relationship marketing: Towards a paradigm shift in marketing. *Management Decision, 32*, 4-20.

Jarvenpaa, S. L., & Tractinski, N. (1999). Consumer trust in an Internet store: A cross-cultural validation. *Journal of Computer-Mediated Communication, 5*(2). Retrieved September 1, 2007, from http://jcmc.indiana.edu/

Joseph, V. B., Cook, R. W., & Javalgi, R. G. (2001). Marketing on the Web: How executives feel, what businesses do. *Business Horizons, 44*, 32-40.

Kassarjian, H. H. (1977). Content analysis in consumer research. *Journal of Consumer Research, 4*, 8-18.

Komiak, S., Wang, W., & Benbasat, I. (2005). Trust building in virtual salespersons versus in human salespersons: Similarities and differences. *e-Service Journal, 4*.

Korgaonkar, P., & O'Leary, B. (2006). Management, market, and financial factors separating winners and losers in e-business. *Journal of Computer-Mediated Communication, 11*(4). Retrieved September 1, 2007, from http://jcmc.indiana.edu/vol11/issue4/korgaonkar.html

Lam, Y. S., Shankar, V., Erramilli, M. K., & Murthy, B. (2004). Customer value, satisfaction, loyalty, and switching costs: An illustration from a B-to-B service context. *Journal of the Academy of Marketing Science, 32*, 293-311.

Lawson-Body, A. (2003, August 4-6). An instrument for measuring the effect of trusted electronic inter-organizational relationships on customer loyalty. In *Proceedings of the 2003 Americas Conference on Information Systems (AMCIS 2003)*, Tampa, Florida.

Levenburg, N., & Klein, H. (2006). Delivering customer services online: Identifying best practices of medium-sized enterprises. *Information Systems Journal, 16*, 135-147.

Levenburg, N., & Magal, S. (2005). Applying importance-performance analysis to evaluate e-business strategies among small firms. *eService Journal, 3*.

Lewin, J. E., & Johnston, W. J. (1997). Relationship marketing theory in practice: A case study. *Journal of Business Research, 39*, 23-31.

Li, F., & Williams, H. (1999). Interfirm collaboration through interfirm networks. *Information Systems Journal, 9*, 103-115.

Lituchy, T. R., & Rail, A. (2000). Bed and breakfasts, small inns, and the Internet: The effect of technology on the globalization of small businesses. *Journal of International Marketing, 8*, 86-97.

Lombard, M., & Ditton, T. (1997). At the heart of it all: The concept of presence. *Journal of Computer-Mediated Communication, 3*(2). Retrieved September 1, 2007, from http://jcmc.indiana.edu/

Morgan, R. M., & Hunt, S. D. (1994). The commitment-trust theory of relationship marketing. *Journal of Marketing, 58*, 20-38.

Nouwens, J., & Bouwman, H. (1995). Apart together in electronic commerce: The use of information and communication technology to create network organizations. *Journal of Computer-Mediated Communication, 1*(3). Retrieved September 1, 2007, from http://jcmc.indiana.edu/

Otim, S., & Grover, V. (2006). An empirical study on Web-based services and customer loyalty. *European Journal of Information Systems, 15*, 527-541.

Park, S.-Y., & Yun, G. W. (2004). The effect of Internet-based communication systems on supply chain management: An application of transaction cost analysis. *Journal of Computer-Mediated Communication, 10*(1). Retrieved September 1, 2007, from http://jcmc.indiana.edu/

Payan, J. M., & McFarland, R. G. (2005). Decomposition influence strategies: Argument structure and dependence as determinants of the effectiveness of influence strategies in gaining channel member compliance. *Journal of Marketing, 69*, 66-79.

Poon, S. (2000). Business environment and Internet commerce benefit: A small business perspective. *European Journal of Information Systems, 9*, 72-81.

Porter, M. E. (2001). Strategy and the Internet. *Harvard Business Review, 79*, 63-78.

Rafaeli, S., & Sudweeks, F. (1997). Networked interactivity. *Journal of Computer-Mediated Communication, 2*(4). Retrieved September 1, 2007, from http://jcmc.indiana.edu/

Reichheld, F. F., & Schefter, P. (2000). Your secret weapon on the Web. *Harvard Business Review, 78*, 105-113.

Rindfleisch, A., & Moorman, C. (2003). Interfirm cooperation and customer orientation. *Journal of Marketing Research, 67*, 421-436.

Rowley, J., & Dawes, J. (2000). Disloyalty: A closer look at non-loyals. *Journal of Consumer Marketing, 17*, 538-549.

Salam, A. F., Lakshmi, I., & Srikantan, R. (2001). Relationship marketing and B2B e-commerce. *ICIS*.

Smith, J. B. (1997). Selling alliances: Issues and insights. *Industrial Marketing Management, 26*, 149-161.

Son, J.-Y., Narasimhan, S., & Riggins, J. F. (2000). Factors affecting the extent of electronic cooperation between firms: Economic and sociological perspectives. *ICIS*.

Steinfield, C., Chan, A., & Kraut, R. E. (2000). Computer mediated markets: An introduction and preliminary test of market structure effects. *Journal of Computer-Mediated Communication,*

3. Retrieved September 1, 2007, from http://www. ascusc.org/jcmc/vol5/issue3/steinfield.html

Street, C. T., & Meister, D. B. (2004). Small business growth and internal transparency: The role of information systems. *MIS Quarterly, 28*, 473-506.

Swaminathan, V., Lepkowska-White, E., & Rao, B. P. (1999). Browsers or buyers in cyberspace? An investigation of factors influencing electronic exchange. *Journal of Computer-Mediated Communication, 5*(2). Retrieved September 1, 2007, from http://jcmc.indiana.edu/

Tagliavini, M., Ravarini, A., Antonelli, A. (2001). An evaluation model for electronic commerce activities within SMEs. *Information Technology and Management, 2*, 211-230.

Teo, H. H., Wei, K. K., & Benbasat, I. (2003). Predicting intention to adopt interorganizational linkages: An institutional perspective. *MIS Quarterly, 27*, 19-49.

U.S. SBA, Office of Advocacy. (2000). *Small business expansions in electronic commerce.* Retrieved September 1, 2007, from http://www. SBA.GOV/ADVO/STATS/

Venkatraman, N. (2000). Five steps to a dot-com strategy: How to find your footing on the Web. *Sloan Management Review, 41*, 15-28.

Wang, S., & Archer, N. (2004). Strategic choice of electronic marketplace functionalities: A buyer-supplier relationship perspective. *Journal of Computer Mediated Communication, 10*, 1-30. Retrieved September 1, 2007, from http://jcmc. indiana.edu/

Wuyts, S., & Geyskens, I. (2005). The formation of buyer-supplier relationships: Detailed contract drafting and close partner selection. *Journal of Marketing, 69*, 103-117.

APPENDIX A: FULL DEFINITION OF THE ITEMS USED TO MEASURE THE DEPENDENT AND INDEPENDENT VARIABLES

Loyalty	
Items	**Questions**
LOYAVE	The average number of years during which your firm maintains business relationships with its customers/business partners
LOYREGS	Your firm maintains business relationships with its customers/business partners
LOYPERP	The percentage of sales to regular customers/business partners (customers with whom your firm maintains business relationships) out of your firm's total sales
LOYPERT	The percentage of sales from regular customers/business partners instead of one time sales
LOYPERF	The frequency of sales from your firm's regular customer/business partners
LOYPERH	The total dollar value sales from your firm's regular customer/business partners
LOYEXP	The average yearly revenue per regular customer/business partners
LOYNBF	The number of your firm's regular customers/business partners
LOYGEN	In general, your firm's customers/business partners repeat purchases of products and/or services
Interdependence	
Items	**Questions**
INDCOST	In your judgment, the total costs to your firm in switching to a competitor's product line would be
INDTERM	The average length of time your firm relationship lasts with your customers/business partners
INDDIFF	Differences of opinion between your firm and its customers/business partners will probably be viewed as just a part of doing business
INDBENEF	Differences of opinion between your firm and its customers/business partners will likely results in benefits to both of them
Cooperation	
Items	**Questions**
COOPHELP	Your firm helps out its customers/business partners in whatever ways they ask
COOPDECI	Customers/business partners have considerable latitude in deciding how much technical support they get from your firm for their products
COOPOLIC	Your firm complies with the policies that customers/business partners establish for the marketing of their products
COOPRECO	Customers/business partners follow whatever recommendations your firm makes regarding the marketing and selling of its product line
Trust	
Items	**Questions**
TRUSTPRO	I have found that my firm's customers/business partners can rely on it to keep the promises that it makes
TRUSTHON	My firm is basically honest toward its customers/business partners
TRUSTIME	In my firm's relationship with its customers, it cannot be trusted at times
TRUSTCOU	In my firm's relationship with its customers, it can be counted on to do what is right
TRUSTINT	In my firm's relationship with its customers, it has high integrity
TRUSTEXP	My firm enjoys a high level of trust with its customers

APPENDIX B: FULL DEFINITION OF THE CRITERIA OF THE EVALUATION GRID

Web content	
The home page is presented in text and graphic version	The Web site presents the list of prices of products or services
The Web site presents the firm's realizations	The Web site presents a documentation on products or services
There is a heading like "What's new, What's cool, News" on the Web site	The Web site presents the technical features or characteristics of products or services
Specify the different languages in which the Web site is presented	The Web site presents images and photos about the products
The Web site provides information on customized products or services	The Web site lists the different types of products and services
The Web site provides information on innovative products or services	The Web site presents the firm's partners
The Web site provides information on digital products or services	The links are grouped according to a logical order (for example: by products, by division, etc.)
The Web site provides information on physical products or	The Web site provides convenient internal search engines for finding products or services or other information
The Web site presents press releases	The customer can consult data and information about its portfolio via the Web site
The Web site presents information on the upcoming seminars, conference and expositions in the expertise area of the firm	The Web site provides an order form
The Web site provides up-to-date information	The Web site presents an ordered list of specific e-mail link to each contact employee of the firm
The Web site provides accurate information	The external links refer to the Web site of customers and partners.
In general the Web site presents an informational content on the firm	The Web site is user friendly
The time to load pages and graphics is: (less than 5 seconds, between 6 and 10 seconds, between 11 and 15 seconds, between 16 and 20 seconds, and 21 seconds and more)	Existence of the Web site's map
In general the Web site contains pages and graphics	The Web site promotes business partners' trust by publishing success stories.
Web security	
The Web site provides the personalized customer support to each partner	The Web site provides for the security of your transaction data and privacy
The Web site contains section accessible with a password only to partners	In general the Web site is secure
Partners feel safe in their transaction with the Web site	In general the Web site contributes to the firm's presence on the Internet
The Web site provides a secured fund transfer order	The Web site promotes partner testimonials by carrying seals of approval by third parties, and so on
The Web site presents an option to easy the transactions with the firm	The Web site displays information allowing only authorized traffic between the internal and the external systems
The Web site uses mechanisms in order to detect the intrusions when they occur.	The Web site displays information detecting and confirming, as well as stopping, illegal use of the system

Chapter II
Product Classifications Systems in E-Commerce Organizations

Sven Abels
FlexaDot Information Systems, Germany

Axel Hahn
University of Oldenburg, Germany

ABSTRACT

This chapter presents the results of an empirical study recently performed in e-commerce organizations. The purpose of this empirical study was to figure out the usage of electronic product catalogs and especially their systems used for product classification, such as UNSPSC or eCl@ss. The study was performed with the help of a survey, which was sent out to a selection of those product suppliers and manufacturers where product catalogs are crucial for business. This chapter first presents the necessary fundamentals needed for understanding the results of the survey. Afterwards, it presents the results and identifies problematic areas that should be improved. It will furthermore give some advice for e-commerce organizations, standardization committees, and further research activities to foster the usage of modern classification systems in electronic product catalogs.

MOTIVATION

In recent years, the meaning of e-commerce increased not only for IT companies but also for traditional organizations, not originating from IT environments. Because of the increasing stress of competition, coupled with the need to reduce costs continually, it is most important for companies to develop new business areas and to cooperate with potential business partners. Electronic product catalogs can be a flexible way of cooperating with new business partners in business-to-business (B2B) and business-to-consumer (B2C) environments. One of their advantages compared to traditional product catalogs is that it is possible to automate the integration of product data into existing systems (Handschuh, Schmid, & Stanoevska-Slabeva, 1997; Jeusfeld, 2004). Within the important area of B2B, it is crucial for all participating organizations to minimize their costs for the integration of new business partners and to integrate new product data seamlessly into the product range. Classification systems can be used to classify different products within a homogenous product catalog. They can order products and describe the domain of a product, therefore be used to group a product with other similar products. Standardized classification information can be stored in different formats. Examples for these formats are the classification systems eCl@ss or UNSPSC (eCl@ss, 2001; UN-SPSC, 2001). This information can also be used for creating a semantic order even if products are described with different natural languages, for example, English, German, French, or Spanish. In combination with electronic product catalogs, such as BMEcat (Renner et al., 2001), they offer a high potential for supporting modern e-commerce. Hence, a high number of catalog formats are able to embed classification information of various classification formats in their product descriptions. They enable a usage of this information without changing or enhancing the existing format specification.

Despite the technical maturity and the availability of current standards, a high inconsistency exists in this domain. In the inquiry presented in this chapter, over 96% of all enterprises indicated that they expect an increasing relevance of e-commerce but the survey has also shown that the high potential of e-commerce is often not (yet) used or only used fragmentarily.

To analyze the current situation in organizations and to get an overview about the practical state of the art, a survey was performed during August and September 2004 as an empirical study. This survey aimed at examining electronic product catalogs and especially the usage of classification systems, such as UNSPSC or eCl@ss used in this domain. The survey was sent to companies where electronic or traditional paper-based product catalogs have a high significance for business.

Structure of This Chapter

The following section gives an overview about fundamental definitions needed for the empirical research. It explains concepts and notations and correlates them with a main focus to electronic catalogs and product classification systems. The relevance of those technologies for the e-commerce domain is emphasized. The next section describes the purpose, focus, and execution of the survey itself. The profile of participating companies is described as well as the questions, chosen for the query, which is important to define the validity of the survey as well as the negotiability. The interpretation and the presentation of the results of these surveys are performed in the following section and describe the current situation of the participating organizations. Afterwards, the last section looks at problematic areas identified by these surveys. Moreover, it derivates a call for actions for research and standardizing organizations, needed to foster the usage of modern classification systems in e-commerce environments.

PRODUCT CATALOGS AND CLASSIFICATION SYSTEMS

For storing different products in a common electronic catalog, several different standards and formats were developed in the area of e-commerce. Those formats are not only used for storing different products but also to store the structure of several products by defining product groups. Furthermore, different information such as the product description, the properties of a product, or the manufacturer can be stored (cf. Abecker,

Tellmann, & Grimm, 2001). Electronic product catalogs provide many advantages compared to traditional paper based catalogs. For example, they enable a digital progressing of product data and the integration into existing systems without a need for adding further manual work.

Electronic Product Catalogs

Electronic product catalogs are used to store various product data in a homogenous catalog, which is often divided into different category groups. Baron, Shaw, and Bailey (2000) define an electronic product catalog as "electronic representations of information about the products and/or services of an organization." Muldoon (2000) divides those catalogs into catalogs targeting the end consumer, called the B2C catalog, and catalogs targeting other business partners (B2B). He emphasizes that both are important for modern e-business.

Since several years ago, various different formats are available for storing product catalogs. Most of them are based on XML and provide a high flexibility for different product types differing requirements. Examples for common product catalogs are BMEcat, cXML, OAGIS, or XCBL. A comparison of those formats and their functionality and purposes is, for example, described in Quantz and Wichmann (2003). The choice of a catalog format depends on the application area as well as on the functionalities needed. Moreover, it depends on requirements of business partners and existing software solutions. It is important to consider the version number of a standard used. For example, the catalog formats BMEcat and OAGIS provide many important enhancements in their current version that were not contained in earlier versions. Though both formats are downwards compatible, which in this case means that they allow the usage of files based on a new version in systems that expect files based on the old version and vice versa, the full potential can

only be revealed if both partners are using the same version of a standard.

For this purpose, it is necessary that both the supplier of product data and its consumer, for example, an operator of a Web shop or the user of an e-procurement application, agree on using a common format to exchange product data. The usage of a standard format enables an exchange of different product data with multiple business partners. This makes it easy to integrate the data of new business partners. Dorloff, Schmitz, and Leukel (2002) describe advantages that standardization in this area can have, and they reference Olson (2000) who described differences of catalog exchanges in B2B domains compared to B2C environments: (1) the interaction between information systems is essential; (2) the business content is diverse and complex; and (3) the control mechanism ranges from one-sided to peer-to-peer relationships. Dorloff, Schmitz, and Leukel therefore suggest fostering the usage of standard formats in this area.

By using standard formats, the exchange of data between systems is simplified and therefore an integration of product data in terms of an enterprise application integration (EAI) is enabled. This makes it easier to integrate new products into existing software solutions such as e-procurement systems as mentioned by Böttcher and Groppe (2003). Current catalog solutions offer the possibility to express an update of product catalogs with the usage of special methods. This makes it easy to send only those products that were changed since the last contact with a system or to remove certain products.

Whenever different e-commerce partners are using different catalog formats, a transformation from one format into another one is needed. Marron, Lausen, and Weber (2003) demonstrate this by using XPath (see Clark & DeRose, 1999). Other transformation approaches can be found in Omelayenko and Fensel (2001b) or in Poulovassilis and Brien (1998).

Classification Systems in E-Commerce Environments

Most classification standards available today provide the possibility to arrange products into product groups. Those product groups can then again be ordered into a hierarchy. Whenever a manufacturer of a product stores his product data for an internal usage in a product catalog, the abilities provided by the catalog format are enough to store and manage his products in many ways. He can use the provided functionality to group products, to order them, and to find the products stored in his catalog. However, whenever product data is given to a third person, this method is not sufficient. The reason for this is the loss of semantic information in catalog formats. This can, for example, be easily clarified when looking at a simple example of two different suppliers of product data. Supplier A is using the following hierarchy in her catalog to group toys and to insert a "toy airplane" into her catalog: "Transportation >> Airplanes >> Models (Toys)." Supplier B uses the following structure for the same purpose: "Recreation & Free time >> Toys >> Vehicles." When merging both catalogs, the resulting catalog contains both categories, which is not desirable. Similar problems occur if both catalogs should be integrated into a new common structure, which may be needed whenever an e-commerce partner wants to integrate the product data into her own catalog structure, for example, to arrange the product data into her own product groups available in her Web shop. To solve those problems, adding classification information into the product catalog can be used. This information is normally represented by a string of characters. This string can be used to clearly arrange the information into a product domain. The mentioned information is based on so called classification systems, which define categories for many different product groups that are all identified by a unique string. Because of this, all product groups are unchangeably defined by the classification system (cf. Grabowski, Lossack, & Weißkopf, 2002). Hence, it is enough to add a small string to each product description to classify a product. For example, the string *49-23-15-13* in product descriptions based on the UNSPSC-System,[1] defines this product as a *Toy train*. Furthermore, many modern classification systems allow the adding of additional properties such as the color of a product. Almost all classification systems currently used to classify products are based on a hierarchy to classify products. Favorite classification systems are, for example, UNSPSC or eCl@ss.[2] Furthermore, the Technical Dictionary of RosettaNet (RNTD),[3] which is a subsidiary of the Uniform Code Council (UCC), is often referred to in this domain (see RosettaNet, 2004). However, other order structures are often called classification systems as well in the literature, such as the order structure of Ebay.[4] A comparison between those three classification systems can for example be found in Beneventano et al. (2004).

The classification systems used, and the information according to the product descriptions, are independent from the catalog format used. Classification information can easily be integrated in many modern catalog formats, such as BMEcat, without any problems (cf. Hentrich, 2001). As described in Omelayenko and Fensel (2001a), classification systems can be divided into two different groups: The first group consists of horizontal classification systems, those that try to cover all areas of a certain domain. Well known examples are the ECl@ss-system and UNSPSC. UNSPSC is a hierarchical system based on five hierarchical levels. It consists of more than 12,000 different product groups, which are located on the fourth level (for details, see Ramakrishnan, 2000). UNSPSC is the best-known international classification system for products. A direct competitor is ECl@ss, which is based on five hierarchical levels as well, but in ECl@ss all products are located on the fifth level. Furthermore, ECl@ss defines attributes for all of the 12,700 categories.

Although the number of categories is very high, horizontal classification systems are not detailed enough for all applications. For example, the number of categories for classifying toys might not be high enough for a company that is specialized in producing toys. In this case, the manufacturer will not need any other classification area than those dealing with toys. For this purpose, a vertical classification system is often used. Vertical classification systems concentrate on a certain part of a domain, but they tend to define this part in a very detailed way. An example of a vertical classification system is ETIM, which was defined for classifying electrotechnical products. The RosettaNet Technical Dictionary is another appropriate example in this area. Figure 1 shows the mentioned concepts graphically.

Simple Use Case Scenario

In order to clarify the practical relevance of classification systems in electronic product catalogs, a simple use case scenario is given here. Consider a company called "MegaSell" that wants to offer a broad Web shop containing thousands of office related articles for customers all over the world. This company will now want to offer products from more than one supplier, so obviously an exchange of product data is needed. Since time is limited, MegaSell needs a cheap and error-proof way to exchange the data without creating new

solutions for every supplier. MegaSell therefore uses the BMEcat catalog format to integrate products into the product database. Since BMEcat is a widely accepted standard, most suppliers are able to offer their choice of goods in a BMEcat catalog. The main advantage is that MegaSell will save a significant amount of time and therefore costs because they only have to implement a way of accessing one standard format to communicate with all e-commerce partners. On the other hand, the suppliers do not have to offer their product in a new (yet unknown) format to MegaSell.

There is, however, one thing left to discuss: MegaSell created a number of categories in which the products should be arranged. For example, they offer a paper category with a subcategory "recycled paper," "extra white paper," and so forth. Arranging all products manually will cost a lot, especially if ordering several thousand low-price products such as pencils. In order to avoid this, MegaSell uses the classification information stored in the BMEcat catalog of the suppliers. This information represents the category for each product. Since all suppliers are using the UNSPSC classification system, the UNSPSC initiative has over 4,000 members representing more than 80 countries and offers about 20,000 different categories for products, which are hierarchically ordered. Since the specification can be downloaded from the UNSPSC Web site, it was easy for MegaSell to implement an algorithm to

Figure 1. Horizontal and vertical classification systems

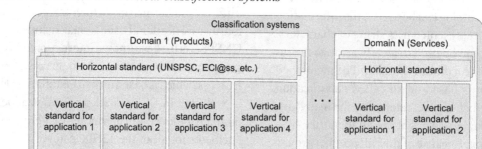

interpret the code and to arrange products into their existing product categories. Moreover, the hierarchical system of this classification system enabled MegaSell to, for example, present all paper products or only "recycled paper" products to their customers by simply interpreting the classification information.

Because of this combination of catalog and classification standards, the whole process of integrating new products from several suppliers can be automated so MegaSell needs no manual work, even if more suppliers are added. Furthermore, updates and product changes can be implemented the same way.

This scenario shows the potential of electronic product catalogs and classification systems. However, reality has shown that there are problems whenever more than one common standard is used. The study has shown that in real-world scenarios, it is most likely that the business partners are either using different standards or different versions of the same standard. The next section will present the results of the empirical study and therefore give an overview about the current situation of e-commerce organizations.

CURRENT SITUATION IN E-COMMERCE ORGANIZATIONS

In the last sections, several formats, standards, and technologies were introduced. Most of them are meanwhile technically matured and can be used for free in commercial applications. Although many of those developments are technically matured and provide a high quality, they are used seldom in practice. There are several reasons for this. For example, there might be another solution, which is technically worse but which was available earlier and therefore became a standard format.

Purpose, Focus, and Execution of the Survey

To find out the current situation and the usage of catalog and classification standards in organizations, an empirical study has been produced in the form of a survey with companies where product catalogs play an important role and where electronic commerce is part of their business strategy. This review of the current situation was performed by the Department of Business Information Systems in Oldenburg, Germany. Sending out a questionnaire to a selection of organizations with a response of 48 questionnaires, which is about two-thirds of the companies that received the questionnaire, did this. Whenever possible, the questionnaire was sent directly to the person responsible for creating product catalogs. If this information was not available, the questionnaire was sent to the e-commerce management team.

Additionally, several one-to-one interviews were conducted in order to react to special circumstances. The location of the companies chosen for this was the European area with a focus on German speaking countries, but almost all selected were acting internationally in more than one country.

The survey's purpose was to get an adequate sample of the current situation. For example, the importance of electronic product catalogs should have been analyzed. Furthermore, it was an aim to find out how the electronic product catalogs were offered. For example, they were offered online for everybody or produced "on demand." The focus of this study was classification systems and their usage in electronic catalogs. An important aim was to find out the degree of automation in this area. Automation can lead to a strong cost reduction and can therefore accentuate the advantages of e-commerce. In many cases, the adoption of a new technology is only cost-effective if the usage is not bound to a high degree of manual work.

Another aim of this study was to find out the distribution of standards in the area of classification systems in order to find out how often standard formats are used in companies compared to proprietary formats, defined by the companies themselves. Another important result of the study was the identification of possible problematic areas and restraints for the usage of modern e-commerce technologies. This information is important to find out the reason potentials are often underachieved.

Of course, not all questions were answered by all companies. For example, if no classification system was used by a company, then the query for the version number was not answered. For the interpretation and presentation of the results in the next section, the numbers of overall answers per query were used to calculate a percentage value for each query. The questionnaire consisted of 23 different questions and subquestions from which all meaningful results will be presented in the following section. In case of interest, the authors can be contacted to receive a copy of the questionnaire.

Survey Result and Interpretation

The following section presents the most important results of the survey in graphical and textual form. First, the section goes into some general questions

regarding to product catalogs. Afterwards, it focuses on the analysis of classification systems, which are used in catalogs.

Electronic Product Catalogs

In companies, the choice of an electronic catalog format is an important decision when offering the product catalog to other business partners. Standard formats allow the usage of data from different partners and they help to avoid a re-definition of product data and formats for every single e-commerce partner. Conversations with participating companies have shown that product data are often stored in an internal format or a database and then exported into standard formats, which are offered to their business partners for processing. Figure 2 shows the formats that are used by the participating organizations. The three most popular formats are cXML, BMEcat, and Excel. While BMEcat and cXML are based on a well-defined structure to store product data, the Excel format, based on the Microsoft Office suite, is a table-based format and not explicitly defined for storing product data. Hence, there are different possibilities to store a product catalog in this format which makes it harder to perform an automatic redistribution and which leads to necessary adoptions of the systems of the product data consumer.

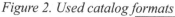

Figure 2. Used catalog formats

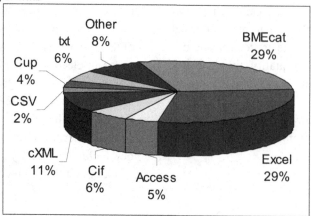

Figure 3. Way of catalog distribution

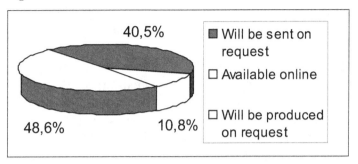

The way of catalog distribution is performed in 48% of the organizations by providing the catalog on demand. This means the catalog is produced on request of business partners. Only 11% of the companies provide their catalog information for public download via the Internet (see Figure 3). It has shown that many organizations produce their catalog in a standard format by using export-filters or self-written conversation programs to transform their internal format into a standardized one.

Usage of Classification Systems

To find out the distribution of classification systems in practical use cases, different questions were sent to the participating companies. It turned out that there are many different situations in companies today when looking at the usage of classification systems.

Arrangement of Product Data into Product Groups

A broad usage of classification systems can be found in the area of automated arrangements of products into product groups. In this area, companies do often use classification information to group products like to arrange product data into product groups, which are then presented in an online shop. As seen in Figure 4, about 77% of the

Figure 4. Arranging product data into product groups

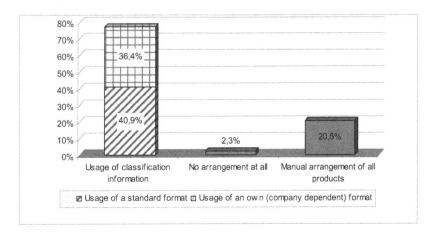

organizations are using classification information to order their products this way. Nevertheless, only 41% are based on standard classification systems such as UNSPSC or eCl@ss, while the rest uses their own classification systems. It turned out that this information for product groups is often extracted directly from the ERP-system of a company or from a database, which was created for the special needs of the company. This is not necessarily a disadvantage, but it makes it harder to exchange the data with other organizations that do not know these "house-made" structures and that therefore have to perform a conversion.

About 20% of all companies preferred a manual arrangement of all products, which is very cumbersome when arranging thousands of products and often needed in e-commerce domains. It is time consuming to integrate those product data into an online shop or other solutions when using a manual integration. On average, the number of products offered by the participating companies was about 34,000 different products, which makes manual processes a time consuming activity, especially with multiple catalog structures.

Classification Systems and Versions

In companies that offer their product catalogs in B2B commerce solutions to other partners, it was declared by 83% of the participating organizations that they already included classification information into their catalog data. They affirmed that this classification information was based on standardized classification systems. For this purpose, the eCl@ss and UNSPSC systems were the most favorite horizontal systems, while the classification system ETIM was mentioned as a well-known and frequently used vertical classification system by the participating companies. An interesting result of this study is the divergence of versions used in classification systems. Within the companies that are using the standardized systems eCl@ss or UNSPSC, different versions of a classification system are circulating as seen in Figure 5. This divergence can lead to problems in the integration of product data from different e-commerce partners because a new version of a system does often contain new categories or it changes existing ones. For example, in version 5

Figure 5. Currently used versions of UNSPSC in organizations

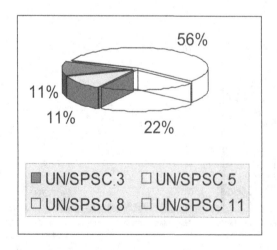

of UNSPSC, a stuffed animal was classified in the category "Stuffed animals or puppets" with the string 49-23-15-06. In Version 7, the same category was represented by the string 60-14-10-04 (see UNSPSC, 2001).

Manual and Automatic Classification

67% of the companies declared that they add the classification information manually to products in their product description. About two-thirds of them perform this manual work when collecting the product data. The other one-third of the organizations perform this work when creating the catalog in the format needed by the business partner. These numbers show an enormous need to foster an automation of this work because a manual classification of several thousand products does not only need time, and therefore high costs, but it is also error-prone, as shown by Wolin (2002). Organizations that use manual methods to classify products declared costs of about 1.5 € per product.

In about half of the companies, an integration of product data into a system that needed classification, information based on a standard system was needed but not supported by their own systems. This means that a conversion was needed. In this situation, it was only possible in 6% of the cases to perform a completely automatic integration. About 44% used a semi-automatic migration and

the other 50% of all organizations performed a manual conversion of all data. In some cases, the integration of classification information based on a completely unknown format did not seem feasible at all. The reasons for this can be seen in Figure 6 and are in most cases connected to high costs, a high number of products, about 34,000 products on average, and requires an immense amount of time and money.

Avoiding a manual classification can save both time and money. Furthermore, an automatic or semi-automatic enrichment of product catalogs with classification information can enable the usage of new classification systems, since it offers an easy and fast classification of products. It is therefore a good decision to consider software applications that help to add classification information automatically or semi-automatically to existing product catalogs. About 32% of all companies testified that they know at least one application that can be used for this purpose. Among them, software products such as Storeserver,[5] e-pro CAT,[6] and Stibo[7] were mentioned.

GLOBAL SIGNIFICANCE OF THE STUDY

As mentioned in an earlier section, the location of the companies chosen got a focus on German speaking countries but it was noted that almost

Figure 6. Reasons for unrealizable integration of an unknown classification system

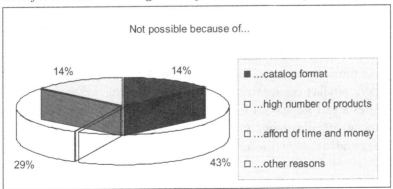

all selected were acting internationally in more than one country. It is supposed that a global analysis or an analysis in another country would deliver similar results in many of the relevant areas. The authors assume that the catalog formats and classification systems used globally will be more focused on international standards such as UNSPSC and probably a mentionable amount will use the RosettaNet Technical Dictionary (RNTD). We therefore assume that the percentage of BMEcat and eCl@ss companies would decrease. Beside those location-depending results, we assume similar results in important areas such as the overall usage of classification systems or the percentage of companies using automatic or semi-automatic classification approaches. For example, the problem of having multiple (incompatible) versions of a classification system (see Figure 5) will probably arise with other standards besides UNSPSC as well. We therefore believe that the problematic areas identified in the next section can be applied to other countries as well.

PROBLEMATIC AREAS AND CALL FOR ACTIONS

This survey has shown in many different areas that a large number of companies are accrediting a high relevance to classification systems. About 70% of the companies expect a high part of their business volumes from the e-commerce domain and most of them believe that the relevance of e-commerce keeps increasing. A positive remark of this survey is the strong distribution of many standards and new formats. However, the last section has also shown some problematic areas. When optimizing these problematic areas, the high potential of modern product catalogs can be exploited. This causes a call for actions for companies, standardizing organizations, and research institutes. They lead to further research and developments in this area:

1. **Call for actions in companies:** In many cases, the full potential of electronic product catalogs and classification systems within the e-commerce domain was not fully used. Many companies already use classification information, but a high amount of them use their own (proprietary) classification systems. Choosing a standardized system not only provides advantages when exchanging with business partners and leads to a high potential of saving costs, but it can also be an argument when finding new business partners, especially in the area of automation which should be considered with much more importance, because in many cases automation enables to significantly save both costs and money. A manual classification of each single product, as performed by about 67% of all cases, can lead to a high number of unnecessary costs. In these cases, a cooperation with research results for accessing latest developments and a usage of software applications should be considered.

2. **Call for actions in standardizing organizations:** From a standardization organizations point of view, that define classification systems such as eCl@ss or UNSPSC and that standardize them, the stability of those formats is important, for example, in the form of providing a downward compatibility. Furthermore, fast reactions to new areas are important. Moreover, it is crucial that the usage of classification systems is simplified by lowering the hurdles that exist in this area. For example, many standards are defined in different specification formats; for example, PDF, CVS, and so forth, that make a comparison for the users unnecessarily hard.

   Additionally, services for using classification systems could help when offered from standardization organizations such as classification services in the form of a Web service that analyzes product data and returns their potential category, as suggested by Beneventano et al. (2004).

The authors of this article argue that there is a need for standardizing organizations to cooperate with competing standards in order to avoid the existence of multiple competing standards, such as eCl@ss and UNSPSC. The parallel development of many different standard formats avoids an easier adoption of classification information in product catalogs and it leads to interoperability problems. In order to perform true global e-business, a common standard of horizontal classification systems would be appreciated.

3.   **Call for actions in research:** Especially in the area of integration costs, it is important to many companies not to adapt to new technology in many cases. It is therefore important to create new approaches and methods to lower costs and allow an easier integration of classification systems into existing environments. There are already approaches existing to analyze product data and to extract their semantics. Approaches for schema analysis, such as the project COMA described in Doan (2003) or approaches for analyzing and merging (product) ontologies such as the SMART-Algorithm (see Noy & Musen, 2000) or the PROMPT-Algorithm (cf. Noy & Musen, 1999) could be transfused to the domain of electronic product data for integrating classification systems. Furthermore, there is a need for research in the area of automatic classification of product data. Existing approaches can be found in Böttcher and Groppe (2003), Wolin (2002), or Beneventano and Magnani (2004). These approaches are often not developed for new formats and catalog standards and will therefore need adoptions.

In the concrete use case of electronic product catalogs in e-commerce, often both the data and the metamodel of the product data are provided. A combined approach of analyzing both could lead to synergy effects and therefore be used to create new approaches. It is important to make results from research available for practical usage and to obey the current situation of organizations and their heterogeneity in systems, data formats, and versioning numbers.

REFERENCES

Abecker, A., Tellmann, R., & Grimm, S. (2001). *Analysis of B2B standards and systems* (Project: SSWS—Semantic Web Enabled Web Services, IST-2001-37134).

Baron, P., Shaw, M.J., & Bailey, A.D. (2000). Web-based e-catalog systems in B2B procurement. *Communications of the ACM, 43*(5), 93-100.

Beneventano, et al. (2004). A Web service based framework for the semantic mapping amongst product classification schemas. *Journal of Electronic Commerce Research, 5*(2).

Beneventano, D., & Magnani, S. (2004). A framework for the classification and the reclassification of electronic catalogs. *ACM Symposium on Applied Computing.*

Böttcher, S., & Groppe, S. (2003). *Automated data mapping for cross enterprise data integration.*

Clark, J., & DeRose, S. (1999). XML path language (XPath) version 1.0. Retrieved September 1, 2007, from http://www.w3c.org/TR/xpath

Doan, A. (2003). *Ontology matching: A machine learning approach.*

Dorloff, F.-D., Schmitz, V., & Leukel, J. (2002). Coordination and exchange of XML catalog data.

In *Proceedings of the 5th International Conference on E-Commerce Research (ICER-5)*.

eCl@ss (2004). eCl@ss White Paper, V0.6. Retrieved September 1, 2007, from http://www.eclass.de

Grabowski, H., Lossack, R., & Weißkopf, J. (2002). *Datenmanagement in der produktentwicklung* [Data management in product developmet]. Hanser.

Handschuh, Schmid, & Stanoevska-Slabeva (1997). The concept of a mediating electronic product catalog. *Electronic Markets Journal, 7*(3).

Hentrich, J. (2001). *B2B-Katalog-Management*. Galileo Business.

Jeusfeld, M. (2004, February 12-14). Integrating product catalogs via multi-language ontologies. In W. Hasselbring (Ed.), *Enterprise Application Integration 2004, Proceedings of the GI-/GMDS Workshop on Enterprise Application Integration (EAI-04)*, Oldenburg, Germany.

Marron, P.J., Lausen, G., & Weber, M. (2003). Catalog integration made easy. In *Proceedings of the ICDE2003*, Bangalore.

Muldoon, K. (2000). *How to profit through catalog marketing*. NTC Business Books.

Noy, N.F., & Musen, M.A. (1999). SMART: Automated support for ontology merging and alignment. In *Proceedings of the 12th Banff Workshop on Knowledge Acquisition, Modeling, and Management*, Banff, Alberta, Canada.

Noy, N.F., & Musen, M.A. (2000). PROMPT: Algorithm and tool for automated ontology merging and alignment. In *Proceedings of the 17th National Conference on Artificial Intelligence (AAAI-2000)*, Austin, TX.

Olson, G. (2000, May). An overview of B2B integration. *Enterprise Application Integration Journal, 4*.

Omelayenko, B., & Fensel, D. (2001a, August 5). Á layered integration approach for product descriptions in B2B e-commerce. In *Proceedings of the Workshop on E-Business & the Intelligent Web at the 17th International Joint Conference on Artificial Intelligence (IJCAI-2001)*, Seattle, WA.

Omelayenko, B., & Fensel, D. (2001b, July 7-10). An analysis of B2B catalogue integration problems. In *Proceedings of the International Conference on Enterprise Information Systems (ICEIS-2001)*, Setúbal, Portugal.

Poulovassilis & Brien (1998). A general formal framework for schema transformation. *Data & Knowledge Engineering, 28*, 47-71.

Quantz, J., & Wichmann, T. (2003). *E-business-standards in Germany*. Research project commissioned by the German Federal Ministry of Economics final report (short version).

Ramakrishnan, A. (2000). *Leveraging the power of UNSPSC for business intelligence* (White Paper).

Renner, et al. (2001). *Specification BMEcat, Version 1.2*. Retrieved September 1, 2007, from http://www.bmecat.org/Download/BMEcatV12e.pdf

RosettaNet. (2004). *RosettaNet technical dictionary: RNTD Specification v4.0*. Retrieved September 1, 2007, from http://www.rosettanet.org

UNSPSC. (2001). *Why coding and classifying products is critical to success in electronic commerce, using the UNSPSC* (White Paper). Granada Research

Wolin, B. (2002). *Automatic classification in product catalogs*. ACM.

ENDNOTES

[1]   http://www.unspsc.org

[2]   http://www.eclass.de

[3]   http://www.rosettanet.org/technicaldiction-ary

[4]   http://www.ebay.com

[5]   http://www.storeserver.net

[6]   http://www.e-pro.de

[7]   http://www.stibocatalog.com

Chapter III
Product Complexity as a Determinant of Transaction Governance Structure:
An Empirical Comparision of Web–Only and Traditional Banks

Aimao Zhang
Georgia Southern University, USA

Han Reichgelt
Georgia Southern University, USA

ABSTRACT

A transaction governance structures (TGS) is a structure that mediates exchanges of goods or services between different agents or production stages (Williamson, 1979, 1981). According to transaction cost economics (TCE), a selection of TGS for the trade of a particular product depends on the characteristics of the transaction, such as asset specificity, uncertainty, and frequency. This article argues that TCE alone is not sufficient to explain the selection of a TGS. Product complexity also plays an important role in explaining why a particular TGS is selected for a particular product. The construct of product complexity originated in the field of industrial marketing and is an important factor in the study of purchasing behaviors of buyers, decision-making processes of suppliers, and dynamic relations between buyers and suppliers. This study integrates industrial marketing with TCE and examines the impact of product complexity on TGS in the context of banking.

INTRODUCTION

E-commerce has given rise to a variety of transaction governance structures (TGSs) such as online electronic transactions, forward and backward auctions, distributor consortia, supply chain networks, and mass catalog compilers (Brack, 2000). The new landscape of TGS raises questions. Is an online TGS more likely to be market or hierarchy oriented? What factors influence the design and selection of an online TGS? Does one have to manage online and off-line differently, and, if so, how? The answers to these questions are important at both the macro and the micro level. At the macro level, they can help policymakers to develop economic and governmental policies regarding e-commerce and the Internet. At the micro level, they can help managers make decisions concerning what to buy (tangible product, searchable product, or digital product), where to buy (from traditional markets or from e-markets), or how to buy (spot purchase or long-term contract).

This study integrates transaction cost economics (TCE) (Williamson, 1979, 1981, 1991) and industrial marketing (Fisher, 1976; Hill, 1973) to examine the impact of product complexity on TGS. The next section of this article reviews the literature that provides the theoretical foundation. The subsequent section proposes the hypotheses and a research model. The following section explains the measurements and tests. The final section discusses the implications and limitations of our study.

LITERATURE REVIEW

Transaction Governance Structure: The Construct

A TGS is defined as a structure that mediates exchanges of goods or services between technologically separable agents or between production stages (Williamson, 1979, 1981). Ring and Van de Ven (2000, p. 173) further defined TGS as "the legal forms of governance that apply to different kinds of transactions (ranging from markets to hierarchies), and the structural and procedural safeguards that parties negotiate into a transaction." There are numerous ways to operationalize

the construct. The two dominant ones are Van de Ven (1976) and Williamson (1991).

In earlier studies (John, 1984; John & Reve, 1982; Klein, 1989; McCabe, 1987), the conceptualization and operationalization of TGS were influenced heavily by sociology. The logic was that an interorganizational relationship is a social system. Since a TGS is a kind of interorganizational structure, the dimensions commonly used to examine social structures, therefore, could be used to define and measure TGS (Van de Ven, 1976). Consequently, the dimensions used for measuring social structures, such as formalization and centralization, were seen commonly in early TGS studies (John, 1984; John & Reve, 1982; Klein, 1989).

The second influential framework of TGS was Williamson's (1991) model. The framework defined TGS with five dimensions: incentive intensity, administrative controls, contract law, adaptation (A), and adaptation (C) (see Table 1).

An incentive mechanism provides a payoff structure to guide actions in a certain direction (Cohendet, Llerena, & Marengo 2000). Incentive intensity is measured by how tightly actions are linked to their consequences. Incentive intensity is high in a pure market-based TGS in which actions of reducing cost and increasing quality are rewarded immediately by profits or demand increases. In a hierarchical TGS, the relationship among supply, demand, and rewards is manipulated by administrative controls. Administrative controls provide a payoff structure to guide agents' behaviors toward an administrative goal.

Types of law distinguish TGSs that govern different types of transactions. Bargaining transactions are governed by classical contract law where transactions are "sharp in by clear agreement; sharp out by clear performance" (MacNeil, 1974, p. 738). Managerial transactions typically take place within an organization and are governed by forbearance law. Under the law of forbearance, "a hierarchy is its own court of ultimate

Table 1. Five dimensions of TGS

	Market	Hybrid	Hierarchy
Incentive Intensity	++	+	0
Administrative controls	0	+	++
Adaptation (A)	++	+	0
Adaptation (C)	0	+	++
Contract law	++	+	0

++ strong; + semi-strong; 0 weak.

appeal" (Williamson, 1991, p. 274), and the parties must resolve their differences internally. Finally, neoclassical contract law applies to rationing transactions in which continuity of a transaction relationship is important. Neoclassical contracts commonly use arbitration to settle disputes and use long-term agreements to maintain continuity. The dimension of contract law reflects the level of court involvement. The role of court is very important for classic contract law to safeguard bargaining transactions. In a neoclassic contract, the court's role is replaced partially by arbitration and mechanisms to deal with unforeseen circumstances. In hierarchical TGSs, the court's involvement is diminished, and disputes must be resolved within administrative hierarchies.

Adaptation (A), where (A) denotes autonomy, is the ability to adapt to a new demand curve or to reach new equilibrium when changes occur. For instance, Japanese automakers had a high level of Adaptation (A). They responded to the oil crisis of the 1970s with small, fuel-efficient vehicles; however, it was not until the 1980s that Detroit finally started to produce small cars (*Sawyers, 1996). Adaptation (C),* where (C) denotes cooperation, is the ability to coordinate among interdependent parties in order to align with a collective goal. In contrast to Adaptation (A), which applies to legally independent agents, Adaptation (C) applies to legally interdependent parties under an implicit or explicit contract.

Table 1 demonstrates how five dimensions vary differently over the market-hierarchy continuum. Incentive intensity diminishes when moving from the market end of the scale to the hierarchy end. Administrative control does the opposite. If we use this multidimensional scale to measure on-line TGS and off-line TGS, then the scores are expected to be different. One group is clustered more closely to market end, and the other group is closer to hierarchy end. In the analysis section, we will use logistic regression to process the scores and to separate the online and off-line into two groups with a significant F value.

Transaction Cost Economics: The Theory

The traditional view of TGS is dichotomous of market vs. hierarchy. In a purely market-based TGS, price is the invisible hand that mediates supply and demand (Smith, 1776). In a purely hierarchical TGS, an administrative hierarchy controls and allocates resources (Chandler, 1977). Transaction cost economics (TCE) attempts to understand how variations in characteristics of transactions lead to the selection of a TGS. Three characteristics of a transaction were identified: asset specificity, uncertainty, and frequency. Asset specificity is the degree to which an asset can be redeployed to alternative uses without losing its productive value. Generally speaking, when asset specificity, frequency, and uncertainty of a transaction are low, a market TGS is more economical. When asset specificity, frequency, and uncertainty of a transaction are high, a hierarchical TGS has the advantage of lower governance costs.

A substantial amount of research has produced results consistent with transaction cost theory (Heide & John, 1992; Walker & Weber, 1987). TCE has been applied broadly in analyzing TGS in human resources management (John & Weitz, 1989), transportation (Maltz, 1993), airline travel (*Christiaanse & Venkatraman, 2002*), international trade (Burgel & Murray, 2000), strategic alliance (Vanhaverbeke, Duysters, & Noorderhaven, 2002), accounting and tax services (Dunbar & Phillips, 2001), R&D (Oerlemans & Meeus, 2001), and supply chain management (Heide & Miner, 1992). This study makes the following two contributions related to research on TGS and TCE:

1. To accelerate the shift from the polar classification toward a multidimensional measurement, this study attempts to build the first multidimensional instrument for measuring TGS. A review of 81 TCE studies from 1982 to 2004 (Zhang, 2005) reported that 36% of studies used the polar classification of market vs. hierarchy. Another 28.5% adopted multichotomous scales to classify TGSs into discrete categories (e.g., market, joint venture, partner relationships, hierarchy). Although researchers readily accepted the notion that TGS was a multidimensional phenomenon, only 11 out of the 81 studies adopted multidimension scales. However, these 11 scales were influenced heavily by the framework of Van de Ven (1976) and used dimensions of social structure to measure TGS. This study is a step toward a multidimensional framework designed for the transactional context.

2. The study brings the concept of TGS into e-commerce and provides an empirical comparison between online TGS and off-line TGS. E-commerce has provided a variety of TGSs, such as online exchanges, distributor consortia, supply chain networks, and mass catalog compilers (Brack, 2000). More than one-third of the Web sites of Fortune 500 are transactional (Young & Benamati, 2000). It is agreed broadly that e-commerce is different from traditional commerce, but little empirical evidence has demonstrated that click-and-order is truly different from brick-and-mortar in terms of TGS. This study provides evidence to show that online and off-line are different along the five dimensions discussed earlier.

Industrial Marketing: Construct of Product Complexity

The concept of product complexity was first introduced by Lawyer (1967) and then incorporated into a model by Fisher (1976). The model speculated that any purchasing decision was determined largely by both product complexity and commercial uncertainty. Originally, Fisher (1976) defined product complexity along three dimensions. Hill (1972, 1973) elaborated Fisher's (1976) definition into seven dimensions (see Table 2). The majority of industrial marketing studies followed Hill's definition (Laios & Moschuris, 1999; McCabe, 1987). Homse (1981) further complicated product complexity by adding another dimension—political complexity. This dimension reflects that a purchase decision is influenced by one's political or social position (e.g., the "buy made in the USA" campaign). Homse's (1981) approach formed the basis for additional studies on product complexity, such as Campbell (1985) and Hollensen and Grünbaum (2003).

The current study makes two contributions in relation to industrial marketing:

1. This study integrates industrial marketing with TCE. The concept of product com-

Table 2. Dimension of product complexity of Hill (1972, 1973)

	Low ← — Product complexity — → High	
7 factors of product complexity	Standardized product Technically simple Established product Previously purchased Existing application Easy to install No after sales service	Differentiated product Technically complex New product Initial purchase New application Specialized installation Technical after sales service

plexity is introduced into TCE studies and, similarly, the construct of TGS into industrial marketing research. This approach potentially may increase the analytical power and generate synergy from both research fields.

2. Another opportunity is to bring a convergence to the diversified e-commerce studies. The categorization schemes used by current e-commerce studies are summarized in Table 3. Empirical studies have been carried out under various schemes. For instance, the intention to shop online was higher for search goods (Chiang & Dholakia, 2003) and a purchasing intention was not influenced by the quality of a Web site if products were low-touch (Lynch, Kent, & Srinivasan, 2001). However, the categorization of products was not consistent and lacked a well-defined construct and measuring instruments.

Industrial marketing research has developed a well-defined construct of product complexity as well as instruments for measuring this concept. The various categorization schemes that currently are used by e-commerce studies duplicate some of the dimensions of product complexity. For instance, search goods is similar to the standardization dimension of product complexity. Experience goods is similar to the dimension of previously purchased. There is a rich research history of using product complexity to analyze the purchasing behavior of buyers (Hill, 1972), the decision making process of suppliers (Burgel & Murray, 2000), cooperative relations between buyers and suppliers (Athaide, Stump, & Joshi, 2003), and product cycle and development process (Griffin, 1997). E-commerce studies can benefit from adopting the concept of product complexity. This study takes an initial step in applying product complexity as the categorization criteria in e-commerce research.

Table 3. Product categorization schemes

Type of Scheme	Examples
tangible and intangible	Sveiby, 1997; Baron, Shaw, & Bailey, 2000
high-touch and low-touch	Lynch, Kent, & Srinivasan, 2001
search goods and experience goods	Nelson, 1974; Chiang & Dholakia, 2003
differentiable and non-differentiable goods	Bond, 1990
frequently purchased goods and infrequently purchased goods	Peterson, Balasubramanian, & Bronnenberg, 1997

RESEARCH FRAMEWORK AND HYPOTHESES

Having reviewed the theoretical foundations and conceptual constructs, we propose a framework to examine the impact of product complexity on TGS (see Figure 1). The first step in the construction of this framework is to demonstrate that online TGS is more market-oriented and that off-line TGS is more hierarchy-oriented. The second step is to establish that product complexity influences selections of TGS. In other words, online TGS is suitable for products with low complexity, and off-line TGS is suitable for products with high complexity. This leads to the following two hypotheses:

Hypothesis 1: *Online TGSs are more market-oriented, while off-line TGSs are more hierarchy-oriented.*

Hypothesis 2: *Online TGSs, because of their market-oriented nature, tend to be used more for products with low product complexity; in contrast, off-line TGSs, because of their hierarchy-oriented nature, tend to be used more for products with high product complexity.*

MEASUREMENTS AND TESTS

Hypothesis 1

Instrument

To measure TGS, an instrument of five dimensions with 22 measurement items was built, based on Williamson's definition discussed earlier (see Appendix A). Twenty-two items were condensed from the items generated from a panel of faculty members and from the literature review. Each item was assigned to a dimension, depending on what the item measured. For instance, item 1 ("There is a big price discrepancy among the same type of products offered by different sellers") measures price sensitivity—a characteristic of market TGS. The dimension of incentive intensity measures how tightly price is linked to supply and demand. Thus, the item was assigned to the dimension of incentive intensity. Each item was accompanied with two 5-point Likert scales for online and off-line, respectively. Respondents checked their levels of agreement accordingly. For example:

There is a big price discrepancy among the same type of products offered by different sellers.

Figure 1. Research framework

Figure 1. Research framework

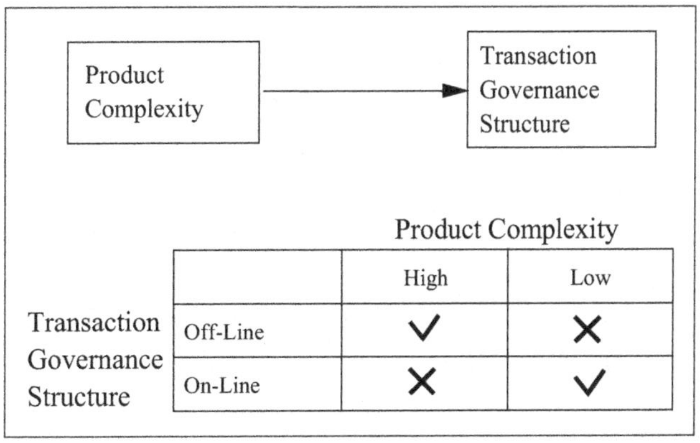

1. *If it is online:* ○ *Strongly disagree* ○ *Disagree* ○ *Neutral* ○ *Agree* ○ *Strongly agree*

2. *If it is off-line:* ○ *Strongly disagree* ○ *Disagree* ○ *Neutral* ○ *Agree* ○ *Strongly agree*

Sample

The sample population was students enrolled in a four-year college located in the southeast United States. The ideal sample should be a random sample from the population of all shoppers. Our sample was a convenience sample that consisted of students from three class sections. One section was from a freshman- and junior-level IT course; the other two sections were from a senior-level IT course. These students majored in business or IT. A total of 124 students participated. All students had online shopping experience. 20% of them had purchased from online stores at least five times; 30% of them had shopped at least 10 times; and 50% had shopped at least 20 or more times. The data collected from 124 subjects were divided arbitrarily into an analysis sample of 102 observations and a holdout sample of 22 observations.

Test

The scores of the items belonging to the same dimension were summated to give a score for that dimension. For instance, the summation of Items 1 and 2 represents the dimension of incentive intensity; the summation of Items 3 through 9 represents the dimension of administrative control.

A logistic regression was performed on the data set based on equation (1) (Hair, Anderson, Tathan, & Black, 1998):

$$p(y = 1 \mid x) = \frac{e^{ax+c}}{1 + e^{ax+c}} \qquad (1)$$

where:

- y is the dependent variable coded 0 for online and 1 for off-line.
- x_1, x_2, x_3, x_4, x_5 are five independent variables representing five dimensions: incentive intensity, administrative control, adaptation (A), adaptation (C), and contract law, respectively. They are summated scales. Each summated scale equaled to the average of measurements of all items of the same dimension.
- $ax = a_1x_1 + a_2x_2 + a_3x_3 + a_4x_4 + a_5x_5$; where a_1, a_2, a_3, a_4, a_5 were obtained from regression. The results are presented in Table 4. Thus, $ax = 0.187x_1 + 2.503x_2 + 1.799x_3 + 0.692x_4 + 1.349x_5 - 19.297$.

In logistic regression, the Hosmer and Lemeshow goodness-of-fit statistic measures the correspondence of the actual and predicted values of

Table 4. Variables in the equation

	B	S.E.	Wald	df	Sig.	Exp(B)
x_1	0.187	.379	0.243	1	.622	1.205
x_2	2.503	.610	16.829	1	.000	12.224
x_3	1.799	.604	8.883	1	.003	6.042
x_4	0.692	.387	3.199	1	.074	1.997
x_5	1.349	.529	6.513	1	.011	3.855
Constant	-19.297	4.308	20.068	1	.000	.000

Table 5. Classification table[a]

		Analysis Sample		% Correct	Holdout Sample		% Correct
		Predicted			Predicted		
		Online	Offline		Online	Offline	
Observed	Online	37	14	73	8	3	73
	Offline	13	38	75	5	6	55
	TOTAL			74			63

[a]*The cutoff value is 0.500*

a dependent variable. A smaller difference in the observed and predicted classification will have a nonsignificant chi-square. In other words, a nonsignificant chi-square indicates that the grouping in reality and grouping predicted by the equation are similar. That was exactly the kind of result obtained from our analysis. The chi-square value was 10.093, which was not significant at $p = 0.259$. Table 5 presents the classification. In the analysis sample, 74% of cases was predicted correctly. In the holdout sample, 63% of cases were predicted correctly.

Since online was coded 0 and off-line was coded 1, the positive values of a_1, a_2, a_3, a_4, a_5 indicated that off-line was measured close to hierarchy end, and online was measured close to market end. It did not imply that online TGS was positioned at the extreme end of the market-hierarchy continuum with pure market characteristics or vice versa for off-line TGS. The result of the logistic analysis indicated that two TGSs were different along five dimensions. The finding supported Hypothesis 1—online TGS is more market-oriented, and off-line TGS is more hierarchy-oriented.

Hypothesis 2

The next step is to establish an association that product complexity influences the selection of TGS. Having established Hypothesis 1, the next task is to prove that online TGS is suitable for products with low complexity, and that off-line TGS is suitable for products with high complexity. To perform ANOVA on product complexity vs. TGS, we need to select two types of TGSs and two types of products. This study selected two TGSs and two products from the banking industry. The reason for focusing on the banking industry is that the banking industry provides a wide range of products from simple checking service to complex commercial lending. The industry has common product specifications and standards. The banking industry is information-intensive and has been leading IT investments. Banks also maintain a relatively synchronized pace in IT implementation. For instance, ATM and Internet Bill Pay were adopted in a relatively short period of time due to competition. Last but not least is the availability of data from online database of Federal Deposit Insurance Corporation (FDIC).

Two Types of Product

The products selected must be as disparate as possible in terms of product complexity. Banks provide various services from simple night deposit boxes to complex commercial lending. For the purposes of this study, the emphasis was on mortgage loans and commercial loans. We need to point out that Web-only banks and traditional banks use the same type of TGS (online) to deliver checking service. Therefore, we cannot compare Web-only TGS with traditional TGS in the context of checking service. However, Web-only banks and traditional banks use different TGSs to process loans. That is why we chose loans to test the hypothesis.

Commercial loans are characterized by many interrelated features, customized terms and conditions, ongoing re-evaluation of borrowers, interactive nonstandard information exchanges, requirement of expertise of lending officers, and high asset specificity of the commercial collateral. The high asset specificity of commercial properties means that commercial assets will lose their productive value when redeployed to alternative uses. A sale of a commercial property requires an industry-specific market, and the resale value of a commercial property is usually lower than the loan value. A $100,000 loan on a piece of industrial equipment usually cannot be recovered fully by liquidating the equipment.

Mortgage loans, by comparison, are simpler products. The terms of mortgage loans are relatively standard. The legal contract written for one mortgage, with minimal and trivial changes, can be used for another mortgage. Typically, a mortgage loan merely involves a property appraisal and a credit rating of the borrower. Required services such as appraisal, credit reporting, title and lien searches, and closing legal services are standardized and, in general, are outsourced. Mortgages also tend to be far less information-intensive than commercial loans. As long as the borrower keeps paying the installments, no reassessments are necessary after a loan is issued. Collateral for a mortgage, such as residential real estate, has low asset specificity due to a general real estate market with a relatively stable demand. The risk of mortgage lending is reduced further by a secondary market that divides the mortgage lending into three major functions: originating, funding, and servicing. Banks can further limit their risks by specializing in one or two functions.

An earlier case study of three types of banking products provided a preliminary assessment of the product complexity (Zhang, Melcher, & Li,

2004). According to the case study, the degree of product complexity becomes progressively higher when ranking products from checking to mortgage lending to commercial lending. In this study, the researchers adopted the argument from the work of Zhang et al. (2004) and assumed that commercial loans have higher product complexity than mortgage loans.

Two Types of TGS

Advances in IT have changed TGSs in the banking industry. The current study considered two types of banking TGS—Web-only banks and traditional commercial banks. Web-only banks depend on the Internet as the primary transaction medium. They did not provide physical lobbies, drive through windows, night deposit boxes, local phone numbers, meeting rooms or offices for face-to-face, or any type of personal interactions with customers. For example, at its Web site, ING DIRECT, one of the 17 Web-only banks, claims "ING DIRECT isn't like other banks. We do business online, over the phone and by mail." On the other hand, traditional commercial banks embraced a wide range of media as transaction structures, including the Internet. They have physical facilities operated and chartered in a particular region in the United States.

Data

Bank financial data as of March 31, 2001, were obtained from the FDIC online database. To maintain an insurance policy from FDIC, banks report to FDIC on a quarterly basis. In March 2001, 22 Web-only banks were registered with the FDIC. These 22 banks were the population of all Web-only banks in the United States at the time of the study. One of 22 Web-only banks, Earth-Star Bank, received FDIC approval in January 2001 and had not posted any financial reports at the time of data collection. Therefore, it was not included in the data set. Four Web-only banks

Table 6. SPSS General linear model report

Source	Type III Sum of Squares	df	Mean Square	F	Sig.
Corrected Model	679.029(a)	3	226.34	8712.39	.000
Intercept	20.809	1	20.81	800.98	.000
Product complexity	10.255	1	10.26	394.74	.000
Type of bank	.020	1	.02	.77	.382
Product complexity * Type of bank	.705	1	.71	27.15	.000
Error	427.153	16442	.03		
Total	3474.965	16446			
Corrected Total	1106.182	16445			

that had neither commercial loans nor mortgage loans were also eliminated. Thus, 17 Web-only banks were included in the study.

Except for those with no commercial loans or mortgage loans, 8,206 commercial banks registered with FDIC were included in the study. The population of commercial banks in the United States at the time of study was 8,206 banks. No sample was drawn from it. The following three sets of data were extracted from balance sheets of the banks: total loans and lease, all real estate loans, and commercial and industrial loans. The percentage of mortgage loans and the percentage of commercial loans were calculated for each bank.

Test

Contrast codes were used on product complexity and type of bank. An ANOVA (Judd & McClelland, 1989) was preformed (see Table 6). The F-statistic of product complexity was 394.74 at a significance level of 0.00. It indicated that both Web-only and traditional banks had significantly more real estate loans than commercial loans. This finding is consistent with a market survey of 1989 that reported a market of $2.43 trillion for commercial property and $8.7 trillion for residential property (*Hartzell, Pittman, & Downs, 1994*).

More importantly for the current study, however, is the F-statistic on "product-complexity *

type of bank." The F is 27.15 at a significance level of 0.00. It clearly confirmed the interaction effect between product complexity and type of bank. The Web-only banks hold significantly higher percentages of mortgage loans than traditional banks, while the traditional banks hold significantly higher percentages of commercial loans.

Having established Hypothesis 1 that online TGSs are more market-oriented and that off-line TGSs are more hierarchy-oriented, we can apply inductive reasoning and assume that Web-only banks are more market-oriented, and that traditional banks are more hierarchy-oriented in the context of loan services. Then we can generalize the ANOVA finding to support Hypothesis 2: a market-oriented TGS is suitable for products with low complexity, while a hierarchical TGS is suitable for products with high complexity. The inductive reasoning may raise a concern of generalization from Web-only banks to online and from traditional banks to off-line.

DISCUSSION AND CONCLUSION

The work of the present study can be summarized into five areas. First, a multidimensional instrument for measuring TGSs was developed, based on Williamson's (1991) framework. This effort may shift TGS studies away from the polar classification and away from dimensions of social structure to a transactional structure. Second, the empirical evidence indicated that click-and-order is truly different from brick-and-mortar along all five dimensions defined by Williamson's (1991) framework. Online is more market-oriented and off-line is more hierarchy-oriented. Third, this study provided evidence that Web-only banks were associated with simple products, while traditional banks were associated with complex products. If we can generalize the finding, one could claim that market-oriented TGS are suitable for products with low product complexity and hierarchy-oriented TGS are suitable for products with high product complexity. Fourth, the integration of industrial marketing with TCE potentially may generate synergy from both research fields. Previous marketing analyses on impact of product complexity on purchasing behaviors and purchasing decision making should be replicated and re-evaluated under the new context of e-commerce. Fifth, the various product categorization schemes currently used in e-commerce studies may converge due to the introduction of product complexity.

Implications

The present study generates some strategic implications for both online and off-line suppliers. A supplier of simple products may want to take advantage of e-commerce and use it as its major marketing channel. For instance, checking service is a simple service with low product complexity. At the microlevel, banks offer free Internet Bill Pay to move checking services online. At the macrolevel, the Federal Reserve has been promoting electronic check processing by lowering automatic clearing house (ACH) processing fees. Since 1996, fees for electronic payment services have declined more than 38%. On the other hand, fees for paper checks increased 3.3% (Dozier,

2000). This regulation reflected the intention of the Federal Reserve System to encourage moving checking services online.

For a supplier of complex products, maintaining or creating an integrated hierarchical market should be its top priority. A supplier should differentiate its products, shorten the product life cycle to maintain newness of the technology, and provide extensive after-sale service. When asked "What do you have to do to beat LendingTree.com or E-loan.com?," a loan officer of a local bank explained that the bank integrated insurance company, appraiser, realtor, attorney, and county assessor to provide integrated services. The officer claimed that she could have her appraiser out to a house the next day. The networking skills enable the officer to provide integrated and timely services. Mergers among banks, security firms, and insurance companies enable nationally chartered banks to extend their ownership and to engage in activities in which they had never engaged before (Pinckney, 2000). Insurance, brokerage, and investment services might be packaged together to provide a total banking service. The cross-functional integration and cross-firm integration potentially may increase product complexity and may maintain an integrated hierarchical market.

This study throws light on the issues raised in the introduction. The construct of product complexity provides a framework to select and design a TGS for a particular good or service. This information is of great importance to managers who make decisions about IT investments and to policymakers who make economic and regulatory policies to regulate the use of e-commerce. The finding of this study suggests that any decision, whether it is at the micro or macrolevel, concerning the use of a particular TGS for trading a particular good or service, has to take product complexity into account.

LIMITATIONS

There are three limitations of the current study. First, the study did not conduct a factor analysis in order to verify if TGS indeed has five distinguished dimensions, as Williamson suggested, or if the instrument items would be loaded the way the researchers designed. Second, this study adopted the argument from the work of Zhang et al. (2004) and assumed that commercial loans have higher product complexity than mortgage loans. The measurement used in Zhang et al. (2004) and other studies was qualitative, and no empirical measurements were made to support the conclusion. Third, we established that online TGS is more market-oriented and off-line TGS is more hierarchy-oriented (Hypothesis 1). However, Hypothesis 2 established that Web-only banks were associated with products with low complexity, while traditional banks were associated with products with high complexity. Can we generalize Web-only banks to online TGS and traditional banks to off-line TGS? If we can, then we can generalize the finding and claim that a market-oriented TGS is suitable for products with low complexity, while a hierarchical TGS is suitable for products with high complexity (Hypothesis 2). This type of inference is inductive from specific to general. It may raise a concern of generalizability.

REFERENCES

Athaide, G.A., Stump, R.L., & Joshi, A.W. (2003). Understanding new product co-development relationships in technology-based, industrial markets. *Journal of Marketing Theory and Practice, 11*(3), 46-58.

Baron, J.P., Shaw, M.J., & Bailey, A.D., Jr. (2000). Web-based e-catalog systems in B2B procurement. *Communications of the ACM, 43*(5), 93-100.

Bond, B. (1990). Sales & marketing—A fundamental difference. *Telephone Engineer & Management, 94*(8), 188-189.

Brack, K. (2000). Your e-options. *Industrial Distribution, 89*(7), 54-58.

Burgel, O., & Murray, G.C. (2000). The international market entry choices of start-up companies in high-technology industries. *Journal of International Marketing, 8*(2), 33-63.

Campbell, N.C.G. (1985). An interaction approach to organizational buying behavior. *Journal of Business Research, 13*(1), 35-49.

Chandler, A.D. (1977). *The visible hand: The managerial revolution in American business.* Cambridge, MA: Belknap Press.

Chiang, K., & Dholakia, R.R. (2003). Factors driving consumer intention to shop online: An empirical investigation. *Journal of Consumer Psychology, 13*(1-2), 177-183.

Christiaanse, E., & Venkatraman, N. (2002). Beyond sabre: An empirical test of expertise exploitation in electronic channels. *MIS Quarterly, 26*(1), 15-39.

Cohendet, P., Llerena, P., & Marengo, L. (2000). Is there a pilot in the evolutionary firm? In N. Foss & V. Mahnke (Eds.), *Competence, governance, and entrepreneurship: Advances in economic strategy research* (pp. 95-115). New York: Oxford University Press.

Dozier, R. (2000, January 18). Federal Reserve changes priced services fee [Editorial]. *Journal Record*, p. 1.

Dunbar, A.E., & Phillips, J.D. (2001). The outsourcing of corporate tax function activities. *The Journal of the American Taxation Association, 23*(2), 35-50.

Fisher, L. (1976). *Industrial marketing*. London: Business Books Limited.

Griffin, A. (1997). The effect of project and process characteristics on product development cycle time. *Journal of Marketing Research, 34*(1), 24-36.

Hair, J.F., Anderson, R.E., Tathan, R.L., & Black, W.C. (1998). *Multivariate data analysis* (5th ed.). Upper Saddle River, NJ: Prentice Hall.

Hartzell, D.J, Pittman, R.H., & Downs, D.H. (1994). An updated look at the size of the U.S. real estate market portfolio. *The Journal of Real Estate Research, 9*(2), 197-212.

Heide, J.B., & John, G. (1992). Do norms matter in marketing relationships? *Journal of Marketing, 56*(2), 32-35.

Heide, J.B., & Miner, A.S. (1992). The shadow of the future: Effects of anticipated interaction and frequency of contact on buyer-seller cooperation. *Academy of Management Journal, 35*(2), 265-292.

Hill, R.W. (1972). The nature of industrial buying decisions. *Industrial Marketing Management, 2*(10), 45-55.

Hill, R.W. (1973). *Marketing technological products to industry*. Oxford: Pergamon Press.

Hollensen, S., & Grünbaum, N.N. (2003). A holistic model for coordinating supplier and customer relationships. In *Proceedings of the 19th Imp-Conference*, Lugano, Switzerland.

Homse, E. (1981). *An interaction approach to marketing and purchasing strategy*. Unpublished doctoral dissertation, University of Manchester, Institute of Science and Technology.

John, G. (1984, August). An empirical investigation of some antecedents of opportunism in a marketing channel. *Journal of Marketing Research, 21, 278-289*.

John, G., & Reve, T. (1982). The reliability and validity of key informant data from dyadic relationships in marketing channels. *Journal of Marketing Research, 19*(4), 517-525.

John, G., & Weitz, B. (1989). Salesforce compensation: An empirical investigation of factors related to use of salary versus incentive compensation. *Journal of Marketing Research, 26,* 1-14.

Judd, C.M., & McClelland, G.H. (1989). *Data analysis: A model-comparison approach*. New York: Harcourt Brace Jovanovich.

Klein, S. (1989). A transaction cost explanation of vertical control in international markets. *Academy of Marketing Science Journal, 17*(3), 253-260.

Laios, L., & Moschuris, S. (1999). An empirical investigation of outsourcing decisions. *Journal of Supply Chain Management, 35*(1), 33-42.

Lawyer, K. (1967, June). *Product characteristics as a function in marketing* [Speech]. London: Polytechnic School of Management Studies.

Lynch, P.D., Kent, R.J., & Srinivasan, S.S. (2001). The global Internet shopper: Evidence from shopping tasks in twelve countries. *Journal of Advertising Research, 41*(3), 15-23.

MacNeil, I.R. (1974). The many futures of contracts. *Southern California Law Review, 47,* 691-816.

Maltz, A. (1993). Private fleet use: A transaction cost model. *Transportation Journal, 32,* 46-53.

McCabe, D.L. (1987). Buying group structure: Constriction at the top. *Journal of Marketing, 51*(4), 89-98.

Nelson, P. (2001). Advertising as information. *Journal of Political Economy, 82*(4), 729-754.

Oerlemans, L.A.G., & Meeus, M.T.H. (2001). R&D cooperation in a transaction cost perspective. *Review of Industrial Organization, 18*(1), 77-90.

Peterson, R.A., Balasubramanian, S., & Bronnenberg, B.J. (1997). Exploring the implications of the Internet for consumer marketing. *Academy of Marketing Science, 25*(4), 329-337.

Pinckney, B. (2000). New law helps banks break barriers. *Capital District Business Review, 27*(3), 20.

Ring, P.S., & Van de Ven, A.H. (2000). Formal and informal dimensions of transactions. In A.H. Van de Ven, H.L. Angle, & M.S. Poole (Eds.), *Research on the management of innovation: The Minnesota studies* (pp. 171-192). Oxford: Oxford University Press.

Sawyers, A. (1996). 1979 oil shock meant recession for U.S., depression for autos. *Automotive News, 70*(5666), 140-144.

Smith, A. (1776). *The wealth of nations*. London: W. Strahau & T. Cadell.

Sveiby, K.E. (1997). *The new organizational wealth: Managing & measuring knowledge-based assets*. San Francisco: Berrett-Koehler Publishers.

Van de Ven, A.H. (1976). On the nature, formation, and maintenance of relations among organizations. *The Academy of Management Review, 1*(4), 24-36.

Vanhaverbeke, W., Duysters, G., & Noorderhaven, N. (2002). External technology sourcing through alliances or acquisitions: An analysis of the application-specific integrated circuits industry. *Organization Science, 13*(6), 714-733.

Walker, G., & Weber, D. (1987). Supplier competition, uncertainty, and make-or-buy decisions. *Academy of Journal Management, 30*(3), 589-596.

Williamson, O. (1979). Transaction cost economics: The governance of contractual relations. *Journal of Law and Economics, 22*(10), 233-261.

Williamson, O. (1981). The economics of organization: The transaction cost approach. *American Journal of Sociology, 87*(3), 549-577.

Williamson, O.E. (1991, June). Comparative economic organization: The analysis of "discrete structural alternatives." *Administrative Science Quarterly, 36*(2), 269-296.

Young, D., & Benamati, J. (2000). Differences in public Web sites: The current state of large U.S. firms. *Journal of Electronic Commerce Research, 1*(3), 94-105.

Zhang, A. (2005). Transaction governance structure: Theories, empirical studies, and instruments. *International Journal of Commerce and Management, 16*(2), 59-85.

Zhang, A., Melcher, A., & Li, L. (2004). Mapping the relationships among product complexity, information technology, and transaction governance structure: A case study. *Journal of Management Systems, 16*(4), 41-54.

APPENDIX A: INSTRUMENT ON TGS

Incentive

- There is a big price discrepancy among the same type of products offered by different sellers.
- I do a lot of price comparison among different sellers when I'm shopping.*

Administrative control

- A seller has influence over a buyer's decision-making.
- A buyer has influence over a seller's decision-making.
- A seller does not know very much about you as a buyer.*
- You as a buyer do not know very much about a seller.*
- A seller can monitor your shopping behaviors.
- A seller can manipulate your shopping behaviors.
- It is easy for a seller to cheat and misrepresent a product.*

Adaptation (A)

- A seller adjusts his price and production quantity according to demand.*
- Fluctuation of market demand has little impact on price.
- There are many suppliers making the same or similar products.*
- The goal of a seller is to maximize his profit regardless of loss of gain of any other players.*
- The goal of a buyer is to minimize his cost regardless of loss of gain of any other players.*
- It is easy to become a seller in terms of initial investment and market entry cost.*

Adaptation (C)

- Negotiations or discussion between a buyer and a seller is required to complete a transaction.
- Explicit communication is required to coordinate activities among sellers and buyers.
- A seller and a buyer usually settle a problem by cooperation and negotiation.
- I would negotiate and cooperate with a seller.

Contract law

- A supplier and a buyer usually go to a court to settle a dispute.*
- A supplier and a buyer usually settle a dispute through discussions, meetings, or arbitration.
- A seller usually has to obey the rules and laws set up by a local community.

* Reversed

Chapter IV
Factors Affecting Online E–Payment Adoption:
A Company Perspective

Qile He
University of Bedfordshire Business School, UK

Yanqing Duan
University of Bedfordshire Business School, UK

Zetian Fu
China Agriculture University, China

Daoliang Li
China Agriculture University, China

ABSTRACT

Online e-payment is playing an important role in the further development of e-commerce and e-business. Research so far has been conducted to analyze the acceptance of online e-payment from consumers' point of view. No research has been carried out to examine the relationship between managers' attitudes towards online e-payment and their influence on the company's e-payment adoption. This research studies the adoption of online e-payment by business enterprises using Rogers's relational model of perceived innovation attributes and the rate of adoption. An online questionnaire survey is developed to collect the data from a sample of Chinese companies. Confirmatory factor analysis is used to validate and refine the instrument. Logistic regression model is employed to test the hypotheses and gain insights into how managers' perceived innovation attributes could affect company's e-payment adoption. The findings suggest that only perceived compatibility has significant influence on online e-payment adoption of Chinese companies. It is suggested that the technology-organization-environment (TOE) model could be used in future study to gain a more comprehensive understanding of nonperceptive factors that may affect company's adoption of online e-payment.

INTRODUCTION

Adoption of information and communication technologies (ICT) innovations is attracting increasing attention from researchers in recent years (Venkatesh, Morris, Davis, & Davis, 2003). Based on various innovation adoption theories, scholars are particularly interested in the factors that affect the adoption of innovations to provide theoretical and practical guidelines to understand behaviors of potential users for the further development of ICT innovations (Chau & Tam, 1997; Harrison, Mykytyn, & Riemenschneider, 1997; Min & Galle, 2003; Teo, Wei, & Benbasat, 2003; Venkatesh & Brown, 2001; Zhu, Kraemer, Xu, & Derick, 2004).

As an emerging technology, online e-payment is playing an important role in the development of e-commerce, in that the lack of online e-payment could hinder the successful implementation of e-commerce (Goldfinger & Perrin, 2001). Research which has been carried out so far is mainly on the acceptance of online e-payment from consumers' point of view. For example, Abrazhevich (2001b, 2001c) conducted a survey to examine consumers' attitudes toward online e-payment to determine the main characteristics that have the most direct effects on user acceptance. Cheng, Sheen, and Lou (2006) investigated the effect of customers' perceptions on their acceptance of channel functions of the Internet, including financial payment. Hung, Chang, and Yu (2006) examined the public acceptance of online tax filing and payment function of e-government from the end user's point of view. Other research focuses on users' requirements in accepting online e-payment instruments without distinguishing commercial users with individual consumers (Buck, 1996; Pilioura, 1998). However, given the importance of companies as e-payment users as well as providers, very little research has been conducted to examine the factors affecting companies' decision on adopting online payment methods. Because companies are organizations, which are different from individual consumers,

the process of adopting new technologies would be more complex than that of consumers. It appears that no empirical research has been carried out so far to systematically analyze business organizations' adoption behavior. Therefore, this research aims to focus on companies' adoption of online e-payment systems and to provide some in-depth understanding of why companies adopt or refuse to use an online e-payment method.

This research attempts to use the innovation diffusion framework of Rogers (1983, 1995) to explore the effect of management's perceptions on the company's adoption of e-payment in order to shed light on understanding the acceptance behavior of the potential e-payment adopters. An online questionnaire survey was conducted with a sample of Chinese companies. The data were used to refine the survey instrument and gain initial understanding of how companies' perceptions of e-payment affect their adoption decision.

The following section discusses the reason why e-payment is viewed as an innovation for companies. This is followed by the demonstration of Rogers' (1983, 1995) relational model, which serves as a theoretical base for the development of research hypotheses. The process of survey development and conduction is described. Confirmatory factor analysis (CFA) is used to validate and refine the survey instrument. The logistic regression model is employed to test the hypotheses to provide initial understanding on the effect of perceived innovation attributes on companies' adoption of online e-payment. Findings from this study call for further research on a company's innovation adoption behavior. The chapter finally discusses other theoretical models that could be used in future research.

ONLINE E-PAYMENT AS AN INNOVATION FOR COMPANIES

Due to the rapid growth of business-to-business (B2B) and business-to-consumer (B2C) e-commerce globally, a significant amount of business transactions have to be conducted over the Internet. Although traditional ways of payments (cash, check, bank draft, etc.) are still playing the dominant role in payment transaction, more and more online e-payment solutions have been introduced to facilitate effective online transactions. Over the last decade, numerous online payment solutions have been developed. However, many of them failed to reach a significant market acceptance or remained at the trial stage. As the electronic payment is the technology in development, its acceptance is still a bottleneck for the growth of the e-commerce industry (Abrazhevich, 2001a, 2001b).

A literature review shows that there is a lack of consistent and clear definition for e-payment, as different researchers may use different working definitions. This research follows the definition given by UNCTAD (2001) that e-payment or online payment refers to "the process of finance or payment mainly using the medium of the Internet" (p. 143). Thus, Internet mediated payment methods are the major concern of this research. Among the various online e-payment instruments, credit/debit card based, electronic check, electronic currency, smart card payment, and centralized account system are found to be typical online payment solutions available in the market (O'Mahony, Peirce, & Tewari, 2001).

According to Rogers (1995), "the innovation is an idea, practice, or object that is perceived as new by an individual or other unit of adoption" (p. 11). Compared to other payment systems, online e-payment is still in the stage of trial and development for many businesses. Although online e-payment is considered one of the key issues in e-commerce, it is frequently regarded as an independent aspect of payment innovation (Mantel, 2001; Mantel & McHugh, 2001, 2002; Wonglimpiyarat, 2002). Ideally, e-commerce should have e-payment as a component, but for some companies engaged in e-commerce, setting up an online payment system is still a technologi-

cal and financial challenge. Due to the security concern and consumers' payment tradition, online e-payment is still a new idea for many businesses, even for those who have already launched e-commerce years ago (UNCTAD, 2002). Online e-payment is believed to be an emerging payment method, which may replace traditional methods. Therefore, it is reasonable to regard e-payment as an innovation to businesses.

LITERATURE REVIEW AND RESEARCH HYPOTHESES

A major focus of previous studies on ICT innovation adoption has been how potential users' perceptions of the innovation influence their adoption or usage (Agarwal & Prasad, 1997; Cheng et al., 2006; Kuan & Chau, 2001; Lewis, Agarwal, & Sambamurthy, 2003; Moore & Benbasat, 1991). Researchers are particularly interested in the impact of subjective perceptions of the potential users on their adoption decisions. The innovation diffusion theory of Rogers (1983; 1995) is frequently cited by those researchers who studied acceptance and diffusion of information systems and information technologies (Adams, Nelson, & Todd, 1992; Agarwal & Prasad, 1997; Chau & Tam, 1997; Davis, 1989; Harrison & Waite, 2006; Premkumar, Ramamurthy, & Nilakanta, 1994; Tung & Rieck, 2005).

Rogers (1983, 1995) proposed a theoretical framework which reveals the relationship between perceived innovation attributes (namely, relative advantage, compatibility, complexity, trialability, and observability) and the rate of adoption. It is regarded as an important theory to understand the adoption behavior of potential adopters and to predict the adoption of technological innovations. Based on this theoretical framework, researchers typically considered perceived innovation characteristics of potential adopters as independent variables, so that the predictive power of those characteristics on the innovation adoption was examined empirically (Adams et al., 1992; Agarwal & Prasad, 1997; Chau & Tam, 1997; Chwelos, Benbasat, & Dexter, 2001; Lee, 2004; Martins, Steil, & Todesco, 2004; Moore & Benbasat, 1991).

Some researchers follow a similar theoretical framework named technology acceptance model (TAM) to study the adoption behaviors. Based on the theory of reasoned action (Fishbein & Ajzen, 1975), the TAM approach advocates that perceived usefulness and perceived ease of use are major influences of an individual's attitude towards using the technology and thus ultimately relating to actual use (Davis, 1989). Although prior research suggests that the TAM model has served well in explaining adoption behavior of users (e.g., Chau, 1996; Henderson & Divett, 2003; Ngai, Poon, & Chan, 2007; Porter & Donthu, 2006), Rogers's relational framework is considered to be a more comprehensive explanation to the perceived characteristics of technological innovations. Therefore, this research will follow Rogers' relational framework to study the companies' adoption of online e-payment.

Rogers' Relational Model

According to Rogers (1983, 1995), relationships among perceived innovation attributes and the rate of adoption, as perceived by the members of a social system, can be described as:

- **Relative advantage and rate of adoption:** The relative advantage of an innovation is positively related to its rate of adoption. This tends to give a reasonable explanation to the adoption of innovations, as the higher the economic or social relative advantages of the innovation, the more likely they will adopt the innovation.
- **Compatibility and rate of adoption:** The compatibility of an innovation is positively related to its rate of adoption; that is, the more an innovation is perceived as consis-

tent with present practices, procedures, and value systems of the potential adopter, the more likely it will be adopted.

- **Complexity and rate of adoption:** The complexity of an innovation is negatively related to its rate of adoption. Since complexity of an innovation can function as an inhibitor to adoption, it is usually negatively related to adoption (Premkumar et al., 1994).
- **Trialability and rate of adoption:** The trialability of an innovation is positively related to its rate of adoption. Rogers and Shoemaker (1971) suggested that innovations will be adopted and implemented more often and more quickly if they can be tried on the installment plan.
- **Observability and rate of adoption:** The observability of an innovation is positively related to its rate of adoption. This means the more visible the results of an innovation, the more likely the innovation will be quickly adopted and implemented (Tornatzky & Klein, 1982).

Rogers' relational model is important in providing practical implications and analytical guidelines for the research on innovation adoption. However, as five attributes measure different perceptions of the potential adopters, the predictive power of perceived innovation attributes was found to be varied with different innovations. According to Rogers (1995), relative advantage is one of the best predictors of an innovation's rate of adoption, while compatibility is of relatively less importance in predicting rate of adoption. Tornatzky and Klein (1982) concluded that relative advantage and compatibility were usually, but not always, consistently related to rate of adoption in a positive direction, and complexity was negatively related to rate of adoption. Surry and Gustafson (1994) found that compatibility, complexity, and relative advantage were important predictors to adoption decisions of computer based learning modules. Martins et al. (2004)

found that observability and trialability are more significant predictors of adoption of Internet in language schools. On the other hand, Lee (2004) indicated that all five perceived characteristics accurately predicted the adoption of nursing workplace innovation.

The significance of those five perceived innovation attributes is found to be different in predicting adoption of innovations, since different studies concentrated on different technological innovations and different user groups in different period. Therefore, it is unreasonable to exclude certain attributes from the theoretical framework simply because they have shown less significance in previous research. The original proposed framework does provide a general theoretical and analytical framework for examining the adoption of innovations. Thus, this research will adapt Rogers' proposed relationship between perceived innovation attributes and adoption of innovation as a theoretical framework (see Figure 1).

In the original framework of Rogers, the rate of adoption of innovation is regarded as the dependent variable. The rate of adoption is the relative speed with which members of a social system adopt an innovation. The relationship between innovation attributes and rate of adoption, therefore, has been examined. Without breaking the consistency of the original framework, many researchers have regarded the adoption or usage of the innovation as the dependent variable instead (Agarwal & Prasad, 1997; Chau & Tam, 1997; Martins et al., 2004; Moore & Benbasat, 1991), so that they studied relationships among perceived attributes and the actual adoption of the innovation successfully. Likewise, this research will also use the adoption status of online e-payment by companies as the dependent variable.

Why Do Perceptions of Adopters Matter?

The relationship model of innovation characteristics and adoption of innovation emphasizes the influence of a potential adopter's perception on the actual adoption behavior. Therefore, it is necessary to clarify the essentiality of perceptions over social behavior. Based on criticism of Downs and Mohr

Figure 1. Theoretical model

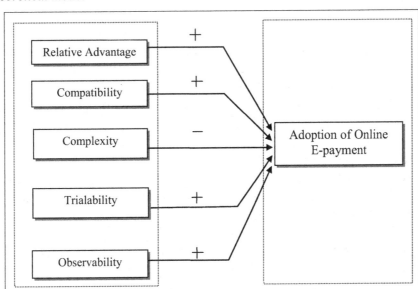

59

(1976) over the inability of innovation research to distinguish primary and secondary characteristics of innovation, Kuan and Chau (2001) point out that secondary or perceived characteristics will serve as more consistent indicators of innovation adoption. The Chicago School of Sociology suggests: "If men perceive situations as real, they are real in their consequences" (Thomas & Znaniecki, 1927). As explained by Rogers (1995), "Perceptions count ... the receivers' perceptions of attributes of an innovation, not the attributes as classified by experts or change agents, affect its rate of adoption." Attitudes of potential adopters, forms the intention to the innovation, so that they will decide to adopt or reject the innovation.

ICT researchers have suggested that intention models or behavioral decision theories from social psychology can provide a foundation for research on IT adoption by firms and IT usage by individuals (Harrison et al., 1997). Moreover, the theory of reasoned action (Fishbein & Ajzen, 1975) reveals that attitudes toward behavior, subjective norm, and perceived behavior control together determine intentions, which in turn determine actions. The predictive power of attitudes to the actual behavior is well supported by the empirical studies (Mathieson, 1991). In this sense, the perception of the decision makers is an effective predictor and explanation to the decision behavior.

Inspired by the consistency between attitudes and social behavior, numerous research is carried out to study the link between the attitudes and the adoption and usage of information technology innovations (Bhattacherjee & Premkumar, 2004). For instance, Davis (1993) applied the attitude theory to study why users accept or reject information systems and how users' acceptance is affected by system design features. Harrison et al. (1997) applied the theory of planned behavior to explain and predict small business executives' decisions to adopt information technology. Karahanna, Straub, and Chervany (1999) combined innovation diffusion and attitude theories in a theoretical framework to examine differences

in pre-adoption and post-adoption beliefs and attitudes over ICT innovation. Kuan and Chau (2001) used the perception-based approach to examine factors affecting the adoption decision of EDI. The results of those studies all confirmed the effectiveness of perceptions and attitudes in predicting and explaining acceptance or adoption behaviors of potential users. Consistently, in this research, it is proposed that managers' perceptions could determine the decision of adopting online e-payment.

Research Hypotheses

In the context of e-payment adoption, some modifications are made to the original framework proposed by Rogers. As shown in Figure 1, the independent variables of the theoretical model are five perceived attributes of online e-payment (relative advantage, compatibility, complexity, trialability, and observability), which are expected to have influences on the online e-payment adoption as the dependent variable. The relationship between perceived innovation attributes and innovation adoption was envisaged to be consistent with Rogers' original model. According to the theoretical framework, the research hypotheses that will be tested are presented as follows:

Hypothesis 1: *The perceived relative advantage of online e-payment positively affects the likelihood of its adoption.*

Hypothesis 2: *The perceived compatibility with online e-payment positively affects the likelihood of adopting online e-payment.*

Hypothesis 3: *The perceived complexity of online e-payment negatively affects the likelihood of its adoption.*

Hypothesis 4: *The perceived trialability of online e-payment positively affects the likelihood of its adoption.*

Hypothesis 5: *The perceived observability of online e-payment positively affects the likelihood of its adoption.*

RESEARCH METHOD

Survey Instrument Development

A survey questionnaire has been developed to collect managers' perceived level of attributes and their adoption status. Survey items were designed based on the validated instrument of Moore and Benbasat (1991), who systematically examined the perceived characteristics of IT innovations and developed an instrument to measure users' perceptions. The instrument is intended to be an effective tool for the study of the initial adoption and eventual diffusion of IT innovations within organizations. Some original items of Moore and Benbasat (1991) have been modified to suit the purpose of this study. For example, constructs

Table 1. Origional constructs and items

Construct	Dimensions	Items
Perceived Relative Advantage	ADV 1: Operational cost	E-payment system is relatively cheaper to use compare to the traditional payment methods
	ADV 2: Relative security	E-payment is more secure than traditional payment methods
	ADV 3: Profitability	E-payment system will strengthen your company's profitability
		E-payment system will strengthen your company's competitive power
	ADV 4: Competitiveness	E-payment system will increase the efficiency of your company
	ADV 5: Efficiency	Utilization of e-payment will enhance your company's prestige
	ADV 6: Prestige	
Perceived Compatibility	COMP 1: Fit needs	E-payment fits your company's needs
	COMP 2: Complement	E-payment is a good complement to the traditional payment methods
		E-payment does not conflict with the traditional payment methods
	COMP 3: Conflict	E-payment fits well with the operation style of your company
		E-payment system is compatible with the overall operation of your
	COMP 4: Fit style	company
	COMP 5: Overall compatibility	
Perceived Complexity	CLEX 1: Setup difficulty	E-payment is difficult to set up compared to traditional payment
	CLEX 2: Maintenance difficulty	methods
		E-payment system is difficult to maintain compared to traditional payment methods
	CLEX 3: Operation difficulty	E-payment system is difficult to operate compared to traditional
	CLEX 4: Overall effort	payment methods
		It takes your company a lot of efforts to get e-payment system to work
Perceived Trialability	TRIL 1: Technology access	Your company has proper access to the technology related to e-payment system before application
	TRIL 2:Service access	Your company has proper access to the services related to e-payment system before application
	TRIL 3:Try out opportunities	Your company has opportunities to try out the e-payment system before application
Perceived Observability	OBSR 1: Benefit information	Your company has proper information on the benefits of the e-payment system
	OBSR 2:Usage by others	There are lots of e-payment systems being used by other companies
	OBSR 3: Result apparentness	The result of applying e-payment would be apparent to you
	OBSR 4: Benefit understanding.	Benefits of e-payment application are easy to understand

related to individual perceptions were removed, and some constructs were still used from original terms by Rogers (1995). Table 1 shows the main variables, research hypotheses, and the corresponding items in the questionnaire.

A total of 22 items were used as 5-point Likert-type scaled questions with end points rating from "strongly agree" to "strongly disagree." The items for main constructs are presented as the following:

- **Relative advantage** is measured by six items, which indicate the degree of relative advantage to which the potential adopter perceives the online e-payment will bring into the company. Relative security is introduced since it is an essential factor to be considered (Asokan, Janson, & Waidner, 1997; Hui, 2001). The relative measures are compared to traditional payment methods. As Tornatzky and Klein (1982) mentioned the relative advantage is relative to whatever the innovation replaced, thus the perception of what the online e-payment innovation replaces is more relevant.

- **Compatibility** is measured by five items, which measure the degree to which the potential adopter perceives the online e-payment as compatible to the existing company practices and needs, as recommended by Rogers (1995).

- **Complexity** is measured by four items, which measure the degree to which a potential adopter perceives the online e-payment as relatively complex. Again the relative complexity is compared to traditional payment methods.

- **Trialability** is measured by three items, which measure the degree to which a potential adopter perceives the online e-payment as trialable. Within these items, "access to technology" and "access to services" were newly introduced, since they are essential

elements determining whether potential adopters can try out the innovation easily.

- **Observability** is measured by four items, which indicate the degree to which the result of adopting online e-payment is perceived to be visible to the potential adopter.

- **Adoption of online e-payment** as the dependent variable is measured by a binary measurement. Respondents would answer "yes" or "no" to identify their adoption status.

Since this research intended to collect the information from China, a Chinese version of instrument was developed through a back-translation process (Maxwell, 1996). To ensure the consistency of the instrument, the two versions have identical items and scales, but cultural and language factors were considered in translating items as well as the wording of the cover letter.

The research population was defined as commercial companies except online virtual companies that have the potential of applying online e-payment in China. The research sample was selected based on single stage simple random sampling (Saunders, Lewis, & Thornhill, 2000). A total of 900 sample companies were selected randomly from the list of China Stock Exchange Companies.

As this research examines hypotheses at the organizational level, the key informant method (Phillips, 1981) was used, in that the respondents of this research were chosen to be the senior managers of sample companies. One senior manager in each company was chosen, who is considered the representative of that company. This research employed the self-administered online questionnaire delivered via e-mail as an economical and efficient data collection technique. The online questionnaires were designed as Web pages and administered via e-mails; that is, a hyperlink of the online questionnaire was sent to respondents through e-mails so that respondents can access the questionnaire simply by clicking on a hyperlink and submitting their responses online. From the 900 e-mails that were sent out to the respondents, 136 were undeliverable due to failed remote mail host or invalid recipient name. By December 2002, 56 responses were received with 48 usable, and the response rate is 7.3%.

Validity and Reliability

Because this research has modified, the original instrument of Moore and Benbasat (1991) in the context of e-payment, the validity and the reliability need to be established again. Pilot interviews were conducted with two IS experts and then with six managers from Chinese businesses to ensure content validity and face validity of the instrument (Creswell, 1994). Some modifications were made based on the pilot interview for the final version of survey instrument.

To evaluate the construct validity, the confirmatory factor analysis (CFA) with Maximum Likelihood Estimation was performed using AMOS 4.01 (Arbuckle, 1999). In this research, the measurement model included five underlying latent constructs and their corresponding indicators. To assess the fit of the hypothesized underlying factor structure, several fit indices were examined. First, the chi-square (X^2) statistic divided by degrees of freedom (df) was used. Compared to chi-square, X^2/df is less sensitive to the sample sizes and indicates a better fit index (Bentler & Bonnett, 1980; Bhattacherjee, 2002). It is suggested that the ratio of less than three will indicate a good model fit (Kline, 1998). Moreover, two additional fit indices, comparative fit index (CFI) and non-normed fit index (NNFI), were employed. Both of these indices are robust to the sample sizes and are more appropriate to this study (Bhattacherjee, 2002). Normally, CFI and NNFI greater than 0.90 will indicate good model fit (Bentler & Bonnett, 1980). In addition, RMSR (root mean square residual) was also examined. RMSR is a measure of the average of fitted re-

siduals. In general, RMSRs around 0.05 indicate a good fit of the model to the data (Probst, 2003). RMSR is also useful to compare the fit of different models for the same data (Sharma, 1996).

To refine the instrument, factor loadings to each construct in the original instrument are examined. Items with factor loadings below 0.7 were eliminated (i.e., ADV 2, CLEX 2, CLEX 3, and OBSR 2). It is recommended that the measurement factor loadings exceed 0.70, so that each item is explained more by its hypothesized reflective construct than by error (Fornell & Larcker, 1981). Item ADV 2 is newly introduced in this study, which asks about respondent's perception of relative security of the e-payment system compared to the traditional payment methods. It is found that security of e-payment system tends to be independent of other aspects of relative advantage; that is, even if e-payment will demonstrate a certain level of advantage (such as enhanced efficiency) relative to the traditional payment methods, the security may still be a major concern to the respondents. In this sense, relative security may not be a proper indicator of the relative advantage construct. Items CLEX 2 and CLEX 3 examine respondent's perception of difficulties involved in maintaining and operating e-payment systems, respectively. The construct of complexity attempts to determine the potential adopter's perception on relative complexity of the e-payment systems compared to traditional payment. Non-adopters of e-payment may not be able to identify their perceptions of maintaining and operating e-payment. Therefore, they may give inadequate responses to these two questions. Item OBSR 2 examines potential adopter's perception on popularity of e-payment. Given that e-payment is a newly developed method of the payment in China and very few companies have actually adopted e-payment, respondents may have tended to consider e-payment as an unpopular innovation. In this sense, item OBSR 2 might give inconsistent responses compare to other related items.

Figure 2. Completely standardized solution for measurement model of refined scale. (Model fit: X²=197.709, df=125, X²/df=1.582, CFI=0.924, NNFI=0.907, RMSR=0.054. All factor loadings are significant at p=0.001 level.)

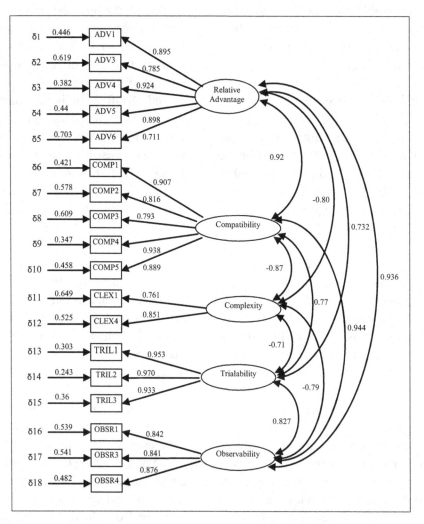

Confirmatory factor analysis was performed again with the refined instrument. Figure 2 gives the completely standardized solution of CFA for refined instrument. It is shown that all the factor loadings to the corresponding constructs are above 0.70. The fit indices also indicate a good model fit (X²/df=1.582, CFI=0.924, NNFI=0.907, RMSR= 0.054). To assess the convergent validity of the instrument, Fornell and Larcker (1981) have introduced a set of criteria: (1) all factor loadings

must be significant and exceed 0.70; (2) construct reliabilities must exceed 0.80; and (3) average variance extracted (AVE) by each construct must exceed the variance due to measurement error for that construct (i.e., AVE must exceed 0.50). As shown in Figure 2, all the factor loadings are above 0.70 and significant at the p = 0.001 level. As shown in Table 2, reliability of all the constructs is above 0.80. AVEs of constructs are all above 0.5. Therefore, the convergent validity of the instrument is confirmed. Moreover, Cronbach's alpha (Cronbach, 1990) is also calculated for each construct. As all the values are above 0.70, the internal consistencies of constructs are acceptable as recommended by Nunnally (1978).

To evaluate the discriminant validity of the instrument, Fornell and Larcker (1981) recommended that AVE for each construct should exceed the squared factor correlations between that construct and other constructs. As shown in the squared factor correlations matrix (see Table 2), squared factor correlations between relative advantage (ADV) and compatibility (COMP), and relative advantage (ADV) and observability (OBSR) have higher values than the corresponding AVEs. Moreover, squared factor correlation between compatibility (COMP) and complexity (CLEX) is higher than the AVE for complexity. This is mainly due to the high correlation between relative advantage, compatibility, and observability (correlations between each pair exceed 0.90). Likewise, correlation between compatibility and complexity is also high (r = -0.870).

Nevertheless, given indicators for these constructs were developed according to the theoretical framework of Rogers (1983, 1995) and based on the former established scales (Moore & Benbasat, 1991), it seems arbitrary to converge these constructs. As noted by Moore and Benbasat (1991), conceptual dimensionality should be distinguished from empirical dimensionality, in that constructs are conceptually different although they tend to be viewed identically by the respondents. For instance, a respondent who perceives e-payment to have high relative advantage tends to have a positive view on the compatibility of e-payment. Likewise, the respondent also tend to perceive that the result is highly visible. Moreover, a respondent who perceives e-payment to be compatible to his organization also tends to regard e-payment to be less complex. Therefore, it is not surprising to see high correlations between these constructs. As Bollen and Hoyle (1990) point out, high or perfect correlation is not a sufficient condition to claim that a concept is unidimensional rather than bidimensional. Therefore, in this research, they are retained as separate constructs in the analysis.

RESULTS AND DISCUSSION

Respondent Profiles and Their Adoption Status

Table 3 shows the information about respondents. A total of 48 usable responses were collected. Most of the responses were senior managers and all of them were in management positions. As sample companies were chosen randomly from companies

Table 2. Properties of refined instrument

Construct	Number of items	Cronbach's alpha	Construct reliability	AVE (Ave Var Ext)	Squared Factor Correlations				
					ADV	COMP	CLEX	TRIL	OBSR
ADV	5	0.919	0.939	0.757	1.000				
COMP	5	0.940	0.941	0.764	0.846	1.000			
CLEX	2	0.778	0.807	0.677	0.646	0.757	1.000		
TRIL	3	0.965	0.958	0.884	0.536	0.593	0.507	1.000	
OBSR	3	0.889	0.893	0.737	0.876	0.891	0.624	0.684	1.000

Notes: ADV= Relative advantage, COMP= Compatibility, CLEX= Complexity, TRIL= Trialability, OBSR= Observability.

Construct reliability$p_c = (\Sigma\lambda)^2/[(\Sigma\lambda)^2 + \Sigma var(\varepsilon)]$, AVE $= \Sigma\lambda^2/[\Sigma\lambda^2 + \Sigma var(\varepsilon)]$.

listed in stock exchange, the size and sector of them are varied. As shown in Table 4, about 33% of respondents (16/48) are e-payment adopters. Manufacturing and processing, and ICT/electronic companies represent a higher adoption rate (37% and 38%, respectively). Thus, more than half of the adopters are from finance and ICT/electronic sectors. The data analysis reveals that the online e-payment seems popular to those companies which are issuing, developing, or having direct access to related services and technologies. The company size of the e-payment adopters is also varied. Unsurprisingly, companies with larger sizes are more likely to be adopters in China.

As shown in Table 4, 44% of the adopters are large companies (with 250 or more employees). Thirty-one percent of the adopters are medium sized companies with 100 to 249 employees. This seems consistent with Rogers' (1995) argument that larger organizations are more innovative. Larger companies tend to have more resources and expertise, and have greater ability to afford failures and risks, so they are more likely to adopt new technologies (Brown, 1981).

Table 5 provides some information on types of e-payment instruments used in respondents' online systems. It is found that the credit card based method is employed as the major way for

Table 3. Respondent profile (N = 48)

	Number	Percentage
Job Title		
President/Chairman/MD	13	27
Financial manager	10	21
IT or IS Manager	13	27
Marketing and Sales Manager	9	19
IT or IS operator/maintainer	2	4
Other Managers	1	2
Number of Employees		
0-99	15	31
100-249	16	33
250-499	8	17
500 or more	9	19
Business Sectors		
Agriculture, Forest etc.	1	2
Construction, Mining	2	4
Manufacturing and Processing	14	29
Health and Medical	0	0
Petroleum and Chemical	2	4
Transportation Services	0	0
ICTs/Electronic	11	23
Wholesale/ Retail	6	13
Finance/services	10	21
Others	2	4

Table 4. Number of adopters by sector and company size

	Number	Percentage
Business Sectors		
Agriculture, Forest etc.	0	0
Construction, Mining	1	6
Manufacturing and Processing	6	37
Health and Medical	0	0
Petroleum and Chemical	0	0
Transportation Services	0	0
ICTs/Electronic	6	38
Wholesale/Retail	1	6
Finance/Services	2	13
Others	0	0
No. of Employees		
0-99	4	25
100-249	5	31
250-499	1	6
500 or more	6	38

online payment. 56% of the adopters have adopted a credit card based payment system. Electronic check, electronic currency, centralized account system, and smart card are less frequently adopted because these payment methods are newly introduced and not widely accepted. Less than one quarter of the adopters has adopted multipayment methods (see Table 5). Though this research is not able to explain "why" questions, it is thought that the technology and service availability may be a constraint that has limited Chinese companies to have more alternative payment solutions.

Table 5. Types of online e-payment method used by the adopters

	Number	Percentage
Payment instrument		
Credit Card Based	9	56
Debit Card Based	1	6
Electronic Cheque	4	25
Electronic Currency	3	19
Centralized Account System	3	19
Smart Card Based	0	0
Others	0	0
Multi instrument		
One	13	81
Two	2	13
Three or more	1	6

Adopters vs. Non-Adopters

An independent sample T-test was carried out with the adopters and non-adopters of e-payment to see whether the perception of the adopters and non-adopters over e-payment innovation are different (see Table 6). Not surprisingly, perceived innovation attributes are significantly different between adopters and non-adopters of e-payment systems. This confirms Rogers' (1983, 1995) argument and implies that these adopters of e-payment tend to have different levels of perceptions over e-payment's innovation characteristics. This could be a reason for the decision they have made for the adoption of e-payment.

Hypothesis Testing

The logistic regression model was used to test research hypotheses. Since the adoption of online e-payment is measured by binary choices of respondents (either adopted or not adopted), the logistic regression is an appropriate statistical technique to examine the relationship among innovation attributes and its adoption. Agresti (1996) suggested that the logistic regression model is the most popular model for binary data, and many researchers have used it to examine binary responses. For example, Chau and Tam (1997) employed logistic regression to examine the factors affecting the adoption of open systems. In their

work, the adoption of open systems was measured by a dichotomous variable (either adopted or not adopted), while independent variables were perceived factors affecting the adoption. Martins et al. (2004) employed logistics regression model in their study to examine the adoption of Internet in language schools. Given the similarity of this research to those works, the logistic regression technique was used for testing the hypotheses. Following a similar approach by Moore and Benbasat (1991), the average scores of the indicators for each innovation attribute were used to perform the logistic regression.

Field (2000) suggests that the appearance of multicollinearity may bias the result of logistic regression. Therefore, a multicollinearity test was carried out with the independent variables using SPSS. According to Myers (1990), a variance inflation factor (VIF) value greater than 10 is cause for concern. Menard (1995) suggests that a Tolerance Value below 0.1 will indicate a problem of collinearity. As shown in Table 7, the VIF for each innovation attributes are lower than 10 and tolerance levels are above 0.1. Therefore, collinearity poses no serious concern with the independent variables. Thus, a multiple logistic regression model deemed to be adequate for the hypotheses testing.

The result of multiple logistic regression analysis is shown in Table 8. Following the suggestion by Sharma (1996), the Likelihood ratio X^2 statistic

Table 6. Adopters vs. non-adopters

Attributes	Adopters (n= 16)		Non-adopters (n=32)		T-value	P-value of 2-tailed t-test
	Mean	S.D.	Mean	S.D.		
Relative Advantage	4.375	0.623	3.381	0.671	-4.950	.000
Compatibility	4.325	0.653	3.031	0.668	-6.370	.000
Complexity	3.000	0.966	3.891	0.606	3.917	.000
Trialability	4.229	0.664	3.000	1.040	-4.296	.000
Observability	4.000	0.609	2.781	0.721	-5.797	.000

Notes: Average score of indicators are used as the score of each attribute.

Table 7. Testing for multicollinearity

	Tolerance	VIF	ADV	COMP	CLEX	TRIL	OBSR
Relative Advantage	0.191	5.247	1.000				
Compatibility	0.157	6.386	0.874*	1.000			
Complexity	0.434	2.304	-0.697*	-0.743*	1.000		
Trialability	0.352	2.843	0.705*	0.771*	-0.619*	1.000	
Observability	0.187	5.356	0.857*	0.861*	-0.678*	0.778*	1.000

Notes: ADV=Relative advantage, COMP=Compatibility, CLEX=Complexity, TRIL=Trialability, OBSR=Observability. Average score of indicators are used as the score of each attribute.
* - significant at p=0.01 level

Table 8. Result of logistic regression analysis

Innovation Attributes	Coefficient	Wald Statistic	p (df=1)	Exp(B)	95% Conf. Interval for Exp(B)	
					Lower	Upper
Relative Advantage	-1.181	0.913	0.339	0.307	0.027	3.460
Compatibility	3.571	4.019	0.045	35.555	1.083	1167.281
Complexity	0.591	0.513	0.474	1.806	0.358	9.111
Trialability	-0.043	0.003	0.954	0.957	0.216	4.241
Observability	1.159	1.200	0.273	3.186	0.401	25.331

Notes: -2Log Likelihood: $X^2=30.836$ (df=42), p=0.8983; Change in -2Log Likelihood: $X^2 = 30.269$, (df=5), p<0.0005; Cox & Snell $R^2=0.468$; Negelkerke $R^2=0.650$.

(change in -2Log Likelihood) was employed to test the fit of the logistic regression model. The model chi-square is equal to 30.269 (df = 5), which is significant at the p = 0.0005 level. Moreover, deviance of the model (-2Log Likelihood) was also used to assess the model fit (Sharma, 1996). In this case, the chi-square statistic has a value of 30.836 (df = 42), which is not significant (p = 0.8983). Therefore, both tests indicate that the model fits the data well.

To examine the effect of innovation attributes on the adoption of online e-payment, the Wald statistic was used with null hypotheses (H_0) that probability of online e-payment adoption is independent of corresponding perceived innovation attribute. Within all the innovation attributes, only compatibility has a significant result (p = 0.045). To confirm the analysis, Exp(B) was also assessed. It is shown that 95% confidence interval for the Exp(B) of compatibility is above one (between 1.083 and 1167.281). This indicates that the change in compatibility is having a positive effect on the odds of company's e-payment adoption (odds = probability of adoption /1-probability of adoption). Therefore, only hypothesis 2 is supported. Thus, perceived compatibility of online e-payment is found to have significant positive influence on e-payment adoption. In this sense, to be compatible with previous ideas and practices will provide a familiar standard against which an innovation can be interpreted, thus uncertainty will be decreased (Rogers, 1995). According to Tornatzky and Klein (1982), compatibility is always a major concern of potential adopters. For Chinese enterprises, to apply a technology that is compatible with their existing situation and environment is always a wise step forward.

It is interesting to note that except perceived compatibility other innovation attributes (i.e., relative advantage, complexity, trialability, observability), which were suggested by prior studies as significant predictors of innovation adoption (Lee, 2004; Martins et al., 2004; Surry & Gustafson, 1994; Tornatzky & Klein, 1982), are not significant in this study. Although adopters and non-adopters tend to have different levels of perceptions over all the five innovation attributes (as shown in Table 6), only perceived compatibility is having significant effect on companies' adoption decision. The result suggests that as long as e-payment is compatible with their current practices, companies will adopt e-payment.

FUTURE RESEARCH

As this research attempts to explore the relationship between managers' attitudes towards an innovation and their influence on the company's adoption status, Rogers' theory is considered the most suitable approach for this purpose. However, to examine a broader range of factors, such as nonperceptive factors including environmental and structural variables and their influences on a company's technology adoption, other theoretical frameworks can be employed. One of them is the Technology-Organization-Environment (TOE) model developed by Tornatzky and Fleischer (1990). TOE advocates three aspects of a firm's context that are likely to influence the adoption and implementation of technological innovations, namely technological context, organizational context, and environmental context. For instance, Iacovou, Benbasat, and Dexter (1995) indicated that perceived benefits, organizational readiness, and external pressure are likely to affect the adoption of EDI by small businesses. Thong (1999) found out that not only the characteristics of decision maker but also other factors, namely IS characteristics, organizational characteristics, and environmental characteristics, can be primary determinants of ICT adoption in small firms. Kuan and Chau (2001) adopted the TOE framework to explore how perceived factors

such as direct benefits, financial cost, technical competence, industry pressure, and government pressure, influence the EDI adoption by small businesses. Based on the TOE framework, Zhu et al. (2004) identified six factors, namely, technology readiness, firm size, global scope, financial resources, competitive intensity, and regulatory environment, which contribute to the value of e-business at the firm level.

The technological context highlights the existing technology inside the firm, the accumulation of market technology, and the technological characteristics of the innovation. Typical constructs of technological context that have been used include characteristics of innovation (e.g., perceived benefits, complexity, compatibility) (Grover, 1993; Iacovou et al., 1995; Kuan & Chau, 2001; Thong, 1999), technical competence of the firm (Kuan & Chau, 2001; Thong, 1999), technology readiness of the firm (Iacovou et al., 1995; Zhu et al., 2004), and so forth. Given the rapid development of information technology and the increasingly integrated financial infrastructures, the technology is no longer the main obstacle of online e-payment development, even for developing countries like China. Companies are facing the choice of many competing payment solutions. However, concerns of cost effectiveness require the firm to adopt payment systems that are more compatible to their existing systems. Payment systems, which use most of the existing payment infrastructures, are more likely to be accepted by the vendors (O'Mahony et al., 2001).

Organizational context includes the various aspects of structural and management nature of the organization, such as firm size and scope, centralization, formalization, human resource quality, and so forth. Constructs used by researchers to measure organizational context include organizational readiness (Iacovou et al., 1995), management support (Grover, 1993; Ramamurthy, Premkumar, & Crum, 1999), organizational complexity (Damanpour, 1996), CEO's innovativeness and IS knowledge (Thong, 1999), firm size

(Damanpour, 1996; Grover, 1993; Thong, 1999; Zhu et al., 2004), financial resource (Iacovou et al., 1995; Kuan & Chau, 2001; Zhu et al., 2004), and so forth. For companies in which utilization of online e-payment is a necessity, organizational factors such as firm size, management support, and human resource quality could shape the readiness of companies to adopt online e-payment.

Environmental context consists of factors which form the external context of the organization, such as industry, competitors, and government policies. Constructs used to indicate environmental context include industry pressure (Iacovou et al., 1995; Kuan & Chau, 2001), government pressure (Kuan & Chau, 2001), competition (Grover, 1993; Ramamurthy et al., 1999; Thong, 1999; Zhu et al., 2004), regulatory environment (Zhu et al., 2004), customer characteristics (Ramamurthy et al., 1999), and so forth. For company's online e-payment adoption, environment factors seem to play a determinant role. First, given the fast growth of e-commerce, e-payment is almost a necessity to businesses. Without the utilization of e-payment, e-commerce is hardly to be realized by businesses (Goldfinger & Perrin, 2001). Second, unlike individual customers who tend to have more choices over adoption of e-payment without taking extra burdens, companies are either providers or users of e-payment. In order to survive the severe market competition, they tend to have less choice over whether or not to adopt e-payment.

It is suggested by this study that future research should be conducted to explore the effect of environmental and structural factors on online e-payment adoption. The TOE model can be one of the theoretical frameworks suitable for this purpose.

CONCLUSION AND IMPLICATIONS

This research aims to explore the relationship between managers' perceptions and the company's

online e-payment adoption. Based on the review of innovation adoption studies, Rogers' five innovation attributes, that is, relevant advantage, compatibility, complexity, trialability, and observability, are employed for the design of survey constructs and items related to online e-payment. Confirmatory factor analysis and Cronbach's alpha are used to refine the survey instrument and assess its validity and reliability.

An online questionnaire survey was conducted in P.R. China. Despite the low response rate and small sample size, findings generally reveal that adoption rate among respondents in China is still low (33%). The adopters in China tend to be in financial service and ICT sectors. Relative lack of technical services and expertise, weak technology infrastructure, and weak financial infrastructure could have led to the low adoption rate and lack of alternative e-payment solutions. A statistical test shows that adopters and non-adopters of e-payment tend to have different perceptions on innovation attributes of e-payment. It is believed that better understanding of influential factors and more insight into managers' perceptions will help to improve the current situation.

To test the research hypotheses, logistic regression model was employed. Results indicate that within all the innovation attributes, only the perceived compatibility is positively related with companies' online e-payment adoption. Chinese companies are more likely to adopt online e-payment, which is considered to be compatible with their commercial needs or existing practices. Moreover, as companies are sensitive to the compatibility of online e-payment when making adoption decisions, developers and vendors of online e-payment should take full consideration of the innovation compatibility to companies' current payment systems and commercial practices. Online e-payment, which is perceived as highly compatible with the existing systems, is more likely to be adopted by companies.

Although Rogers' (1983, 1995) innovation adoption framework is developed to generally predict the adoption of innovations according to potential adopter's perceptions of an innovation, the predictive power of the innovation attributes may vary with the nature of the particular innovation which is being studied. Moreover, the nature of potential adopters and the environment in which they make decisions should also be considered. Researchers should be aware of whether or not potential adopters have choice over the adoption of innovation. In this sense, a more comprehensive framework of Technology-Organization-Environment can be employed to e-payment adoption. The TOE model not only considers the technological characteristics of the innovation, but also the characteristics of the company and its external environment. Thus the TOE model is worth noting for future studies to form a more complete picture of what factors affect the adoption of online e-payment by companies.

Several limitations of this research need to be pointed out. First, the sample size is small and the response rate is low. Care should be exercised in interpreting the result and its generalizability. Second, although key informant method is deemed to be acceptable (Chau & Tam, 1997), the richness of the information of only one informant from each responding company may not be sufficient. Finally, the perceptions of online e-payment are based on a "one-off" survey. As the perceptions may change over time, a longitudinal approach to the measurement of attitudes is needed to more reliably measure the attitudes influencing e-payment adoption.

REFERENCES

Abrazhevich, D. (2001a). Classification and characteristics of electronic payment systems. In K. Bauknecht, S. K. Madria, & G. Pernul (Eds.), *Proceedings of EC-Web 2001* (pp. 81-90). Springer.

Abrazhevich, D. (2001b). Electronic payment systems: Issues of user acceptance. In *Proceedings of eBusiness and eWork 2001*. Venice, Italy: IOS Press.

Abrazhevich, D. (2001c). A survey of user attitudes towards electronic payment systems. In J. Vanderdonckt, A. Blandford, & A. Derycke (Eds.), *Proceedings of the Joint AFIHM-BCS Conference on Human-Computer Interaction IHM-HCI'2001* (vol. 2). Toulouse: Cepadues-Editions.

Adams, D. A., Nelson, R. R., & Todd, P. A. (1992). Perceived usefulness, ease of use, and usage of information technology: A replication. *MIS Quarterly, 16*(2), 227-247.

Agarwal, R., & Prasad, J. (1997). The role of innovation characteristics and perceived voluntariness in the acceptance of information technologies. *Decision Sciences, 28*(3), 557-582.

Agresti, A. (1996). *An introduction to categorical data analysis*. New York: John Wiley & Sons.

Arbuckle, J. L. (1999). *Amos version 4.01*. Chicago: SmallWaters Corp.

Asokan, N., Janson, P. A., & Waidner, M. (1997). The state of the art in electronic payment systems. *IEEE Computer, 28*(35), 28-35.

Bentler, P. M., & Bonnett, D. G. (1980). Significance tests and goodness of fit in the analysis of covariance structures. *Psychological Bulletin, 88*(3), 588-606.

Bhattacherjee, A. (2002). Individual trust in online firms: Scale development and initial test. *Journal of Management Information Systems, 19*(1), 211-241.

Bhattacherjee, A., & Premkumar, G. (2004). Understanding changes in belief and attitude toward information technology usage: A theoretical model and longitudinal test. *MIS Quarterly, 28*(2), 229-254.

Bollen, K. A., & Hoyle, R. H. (1990). Perceived cohesion: A conceptual and empirical examination. *Social Forces, 69*(2), 470-504.

Brown, L. A. (1981). *Innovation diffusion: A new perspective*. London: Methuen.

Buck, S. P. (1996). Electronic commerce: Would, could and should you use current Internet payment mechanisms. *Internet Research: Electronic Networking Applications and Policy, 6*(2/3), 5-18.

Chau, P. Y. K. (1996). An empirical assessment of a modified technology acceptance model. *Journal of Management Information Systems, 13*(2), 185-204.

Chau, P. Y. K., & Tam, K. Y. (1997). Factors affecting the adoption of open systems: An exploratory study. *MIS Quarterly, 21*(1), 1-21.

Cheng, J. M.-S., Sheen, G.-J., & Lou, G.-C. (2006). Consumer acceptance of the Internet as a channel of distribution in Taiwan: A channel function perspective. *Technovation, 26*(7), 856-864.

Chwelos, P., Benbasat, I., & Dexter, A. S. (2001). Research report: Empirical test of an EDI adoption model. *Information Systems Research, 12*(3), 304-321.

Creswell, J. W. (1994). *Research design: Qualitative and quantitative approaches*. London: Sage Publications.

Damanpour, F. (1996). Organizational complexity and innovation: Developing and testing multiple contingency models. *Management Science, 42*(5), 693-716.

Davis, F. D. (1989). Perceived usefulness, perceived ease of use and user acceptance of information technology. *MIS Quarterly, 13*(3), 319-340.

Davis, F. D. (1993). User acceptance of information technology: System characteristics, user perceptions and behavioral impacts. *International Journal of Man-Machine Studies, 38*, 475-487.

Downs, G. W., & Mohr, L. B. (1976). Conceptual issues in the study of innovation. *Administrative Science Quarterly, 21*(4), 700.

Field, A. (2000). *Discovering statistics using SPSS for windows*. London: SAGE.

Fishbein, M., & Ajzen, I. (1975). *Belief, attitude, intention and behavior: An introduction to theory and research*. Reading, MA: Addison-Wesley.

Fornell, C., & Larcker, D. F. (1981). Evaluating structural equation models with unobservable variables and measurement error. *Journal of Marketing Research, 18*(1), 39-50.

Goldfinger, C., & Perrin, J. (2001). *UNCTAD background paper: E-finance and small and medium-size enterprises (SMEs) in developing and transition economies*. Palais des Nations, Geneva.

Grover, V. (1993). An empirically derived model for the adoption of customer-based inter-organizational systems. *Decision Sciences, 24*(3), 603-640.

Harrison, D. A., Mykytyn, P. P., & Riemenschneider, C. K. (1997). Executive decisions about adoption of information technology in small business: Theory and empirical tests. *Information Systems Research, 8*(2), 171-195.

Harrison, T., & Waite, K. (2006). A time-based assessment of the influences, uses and benefits of intermediary Website adoption. *Information & Management, 43*(8), 1002-1013.

Henderson, R., & Divett, M. J. (2003). Perceived usefulness, ease of use and electronic supermarket use. *International Journal of Human-Computer Studies, 59*(3), 383-395.

Hui, D. (2001). *Why Hong Kong Internet users do not shop online: An empirical study*. Paper presented at the 1st International Conference on Electronic Business, Hong Kong.

Hung, S.-Y., Chang, C.-M., & Yu, T.-J. (2006). Determinants of user acceptance of the e-government services: The case of online tax filing and payment system. *Government Information Quarterly, 23*(1), 97-122.

Iacovou, C. L., Benbasat, I., & Dexter, A. S. (1995). Electronic data interchange and small organizations: Adoption and impact of technology. *MIS Quarterly, 19*(4), 465.

Karahanna, E., Straub, D. W., & Chervany, N. L. (1999). Information technology adoption across time: A cross-sectional comparison of pre-adoption and post-adoption beliefs. *MIS Quarterly, 23*(2), 183-213.

Kuan, K. K. Y., & Chau, P. Y. K. (2001). A perception-based model for EDI adoption in small business using technology-organization-environment framework. *Information & Management, 38*(8), 507-521.

Lee, T.-T. (2004). Nurses' adoption of technology: Application of Rogers' innovation-diffusion model. *Applied Nursing Research, 17*(4), 231-238.

Lewis, W., Agarwal, R., & Sambamurthy, V. (2003). Sources of influence on beliefs about information technology use: An empirical study of knowledge workers. *MIS Quarterly, 27*(4), 657-678.

Mantel, B. (2001). *E-money and e-commerce: Two alternative views of future innovations*: Federal Reserve Bank of Chicago.

Mantel, B., & McHugh, T. (2001). *Competition and innovation in the consumer e-payments market: Considering the demand, supply, and public policy issues*. Federal Reserve Bank of Chicago.

Mantel, B., & McHugh, T. (2002). *Evolving e-payment networks in the U.S.: The strategic, competitive and innovative implications*. Retrieved September 2, 2007, from http://www. chicagofed.org/paymentsystems/publications/E-Payment_Networks_Mantel_McHugh.pdf

Martins, C. B. M. J., Steil, A. V., & Todesco, J. L. (2004). Factors influencing the adoption of the Internet as a teaching tool at foreign language schools. *Computers & Education, 42*(4), 353-374.

Mathieson, K. (1991). Predicting user intentions: Comparing the technology acceptance model with the theory of planned behavior. *Information Systems Research, 2*(3), 173-191.

Maxwell, B. (1996). Translation and cultural adaptation of the survey instruments. In M. O. Martin & D. L. Kelly (Eds.), *Third International Mathematics and Science Study (TIMSS) Technical Report, Volume I: Design and Development*. Chestnut Hill, MA: Boston College.

Menard, S. (1995). *Applied logistic regression analysis*. Thousand Oaks, CA: Sage.

Min, H., & Galle, W. P. (2003). E-purchasing: Profiles of adopters and nonadopters. *Industrial Marketing Management, 32*(3), 227-233.

Moore, G. C., & Benbasat, I. (1991). Development of an instrument to measure the perceptions of adopting an information technology innovation. *Information Systems Research, 2*(3), 192-222.

Myers, R. (1990). *Classical and modern regression with applications* (2nd ed.). Boston: Duxbury.

Ngai, E. W. T., Poon, J. K. L., & Chan, Y. H. C. (2007). Empirical examination of the adoption of WebCT using TAM. *Computers & Education, 48*(2), 250-267.

O'Mahony, D., Peirce, M., & Tewari, H. (2001). *Electronic payment systems for e-commerce* (2nd ed.). Boston: Artech House.

Phillips, L. W. (1981). Assessing measurement error in key informant reports: A methodological note on organizational analysis in marketing. *Journal of Marketing Research, 16*, 395-415.

Pilioura, T. (1998). Electronic payment systems on open computer networks: A survey. In D. Tsichritzis (Ed.), *Electronic commerce objects.* Centre Universitaire d'Informatique, University of Geneva.

Porter, C. E., & Donthu, N. (2006). Using the technology acceptance model to explain how attitudes determine Internet usage: The role of perceived access barriers and demographics. *Journal of Business Research, 59*(9), 999-1007.

Premkumar, G., Ramamurthy, K., & Nilakanta, S. (1994). Implementation of electronic data interchange: An innovation diffusion perspective. *Journal of Management Information Systems, 11*(2), 157-186.

Probst, T. M. (2003). Development and validation of the job security index and the job security satisfaction scale: A classical test theory and IRT approach. *Journal of Occupational and Organizational Psychology, 76*, 451-467.

Ramamurthy, K., Premkumar, G., & Crum, M. R. (1999). Organizational and interorganizational determinants of EDI diffusion and organizational performance: A causal model. *Journal of Organizational Computing and Electronic Commerce, 9*(4), 253-285.

Rogers, E. M. (1983). *Diffusion of innovations* (3rd ed.). New York: Free Press.

Rogers, E. M. (1995). *Diffusion of innovations* (4th ed.). New York: Free Press.

Rogers, E. M., & Shoemaker, F. F. (1971). *Communications of innovations: A cross-cultural approach* (2nd ed.). New York: Free Press.

Saunders, M., Lewis, P., & Thornhill, A. (2000). *Research methods for business students* (2nd ed.). Harlow, UK: Prentice Hall.

Sharma, S. (1996). *Applied multivariate techniques.* New York: John Wiley & Sons.

Surry, D. W., & Gustafson, K. L. (1994). *The role of perceptions in the adoption of computer-based learning.* ERIC Clearinghouse on Information and Technology (ERIC Document Reproduction Service No. ED374788).

Teo, H. H., Wei, K. K., & Benbasat, I. (2003). Predicting intention to adopt interorganizational linkages: An institutional perspective. *MIS Quarterly, 27*(1), 1-31.

Thomas, W. I., & Znaniecki, F. (1927). *The Polish peasant in Europe and America.* New York: Knopf.

Thong, J. Y. L. (1999). An integrated model of information systems adoption in small businesses. *Journal of Management Information Systems, 15*(4), 187-214.

Tornatzky, L. G., & Fleischer, M. (1990). *The process of technological innovation.* Lexington, MA: Lexington Books.

Tornatzky, L. G., & Klein, K. J. (1982). Innovation characteristics and innovation adoption-implementation: A meta-analysis of findings. *IEEE Transactions on Engineering Management, 9*(1), 28-45.

Tung, L. L., & Rieck, O. (2005). Adoption of electronic government services among business organizations in Singapore. *The Journal of Strategic Information Systems, 14*(4), 417-440.

UNCTAD. (2001). *E-commerce and development report 2001.* Retrieved September 2, 2007, from http://r0.unctad.org/ecommerce/docs/edr01_en/edr01pt0_en.pdf

UNCTAD. (2002). *E-commerce and development report 2002.* Retrieved September 2, 2007, from http://r0.unctad.org/ecommerce/ecommerce_en/faq_en.htm

Venkatesh, V., & Brown, S. A. (2001). A longitudinal investigation of personal computers in homes: Adoption determinants and emerging challenges. *MIS Quarterly, 25*(1), 71-102.

Venkatesh, V., Morris, M. G., Davis, G. B., & Davis, F. D. (2003). User acceptance of information technology: Toward a unified view. *MIS Quarterly, 27*(3), 425-478.

Wonglimpiyarat, J. (2002). *The business strategies in payment innovations.* Paper presented at the 1st National Conference on Electronic Business, Thailand.

Zhu, K., Kraemer, K. L., Xu, S., & Derick, J. (2004). Information technology payoff in e-business environments: An international perspective on value creation of e-business in the financial services industry. *Journal of Management Information Systems, 21*(1), 17-54.

Chapter V
Internet Privacy Policies of the Largest International Companies in 2004 and 2006:
A Review of U.S. and Non-U.S. Companies

Alan R. Peslak
Penn State University, USA

Norbert Jurkiewicz
Penn State University, USA

ABSTRACT

This chapter is a review of Internet privacy policies of the world's largest companies. The report begins with a background on the right to privacy and privacy issues arising out of Internet usage. Attempts to regulate Internet privacy and self-regulatory effectiveness are also reviewed. The methodology for this study is to update and extend Internet privacy analysis by analyzing Web sites of the largest international companies (the Forbes International 100) for inclusion of fair information practices. In addition, a collection of consumer centered practices is defined and studied. The study was initially done in 2004 but the same companies were revisited and reviewed in 2006. Though there was some improvement in results over the approximately two year period, the general finding remains that within the Forbes International 100, fair information practices and consumer centered privacy policies are not being closely followed. It is also found that large U.S. firms are more likely to publish a privacy policy on their Web site than non-U.S. firms. Finally, if a large international firm does publish a privacy policy on its Web site, the level of compliance with fair information practices and consumer centered policies is not significantly different between U.S. and non-U.S. firms. Implications of the study for researchers and practitioners are reviewed.

INTRODUCTION

The growth in Internet usage and electronic commerce has resulted in an increased concern in the amount of information collected by corporate Web sites. Every day hundreds of millions of people throughout the world provide personal information over the Internet. Many personal data items are routinely submitted by, and captured from, users of corporate Web sites. The collection and use of this data has become the subject of controversy, and is the primary motivation for this study. The retention of this information, as well as its use both during and subsequent to initial transactions, is the subject of numerous studies by the government and other researchers. Inextricably bound to this issue is the concept of personal privacy, as well as how, and to what extent, this exchange and use of information affects individuals' privacy rights. On one hand, businesses and organizations can use the data to more efficiently provide goods and services to individuals. On the other hand, the collection and subsequent secondary use of the data can be viewed as a violation of individual privacy rights. The protections currently offered by most organizations are fair information practices (FIP), first detailed by the Organisation for Economic Co-operation and Development (OECD) in 1980. FIP are handled in the United States today via self-regulation with Federal Trade Commission (FTC) rules, which are expressed in an Internet privacy statement. European Union members are subject to specific regulations that generally include provisions similar to the FTC fair information practices, including *Regulation (EC) No 45/2001 of the European Parliament and of the Council of 18 December 2000* (The European Parliament and the Council of the European Union, 2000). A detailed list of many other countries privacy regulations is available from Laurant (2003), and generally all include fair information provisions. A review of Internet privacy statements and the protection provided by the top 100 organizations

in the world, as measured by *Forbes* magazine, is the subject of this chapter (Forbes Inc., 2004).

LITERATURE REVIEW

Privacy

The right to privacy has had a long history but was first clearly defined in the United States in 1890 by Warren and Brandeis as "the right to be left alone." Westin (1967) suggests that privacy in all cultures includes the need for seclusion and isolation but notes that there is a tendency to invade the privacy of others. Regulations are necessary to protect and maintain our right of privacy.

The right to privacy has a long history in Western culture but was also ratified as a worldwide principle by the United Nations in 1948. Specifically, Article 12 of the Universal Declaration of Human Rights states:

No one shall be subjected to arbitrary interference with his privacy, family, home or correspondence, nor to attacks upon his honour and reputation. Everyone has the right to the protection of the law against such interference or attacks. (United Nations General Assembly, 1948)

Against this backdrop of "universal" privacy rights has come the issue of personal data privacy in an era of massive data collection and retention.

Fair Information Practices

Privacy had been recognized as a significant issue in international electronic commerce as early as 1980 by the Organization for Economic Co-operation and Development (OECD). Specifically, the OECD is an organization with 30 member nations and relationships with 70 other countries that promotes "democratic government and the market economy" (OECD, 2005).

The OECD plays a prominent role in fostering good governance in the public service and in corporate activity. It helps governments to ensure the responsiveness of key economic areas with sectoral monitoring. By deciphering emerging issues and identifying policies that work, it helps policy-makers adopt strategic orientations. It is well known for its individual country surveys and reviews.

The OECD produces internationally agreed instruments, decisions and recommendations to promote rules of the game in areas where multilateral agreement is necessary for individual countries to make progress in a globalised economy. (OECD, 2005).

In their comprehensive document, the OECD outlined concepts that have come to be known as fair information practices.

Malman (2000) notes:

Each of the solutions to the privacy dilemma embrace all or at least some of a set of core principals about privacy rights that have come to be known as "Fair Information Practices". Despite considerable differences in cultural backgrounds and governance systems, there is a remarkable convergence around privacy principals. ... The most well known written form of the Fair Information Practices are the international guidelines published in 1980 by the Organization for Economic Cooperation and Development (OECD). The OECD *Recommendations Concerning and Guidelines Governing the Protection of Privacy and Transborder Flows of Personal Data* have played a significant role in framing privacy laws around the world. ... Conformity with Fair Information Practices requires that personal information must be:

- Obtained fairly and openly.
- Used only for the original specified purpose.
- Adequate, relevant and not excessive to purpose.
- Accurate and up to date.

- Accessible to the subject for review and correction of inaccuracies.
- Kept secure from unauthorized access or disclosure; and be subject to enforcement mechanisms.

The Federal Trade Commission (FTC) of the United States government began reviewing Internet privacy issues in the mid-1990s. After considerable discussion, the FTC issued core principles or Fair Information Practices that they believed should be followed by companies with active Internet sites. These Fair Information Practices were suggested to be self-regulatory and consisted of several principles: Notice, Choice, Access, Security, and Enforcement. As defined by the Federal Trade Commission in their 2000 report, the fair information practices were:

1. **Notice:** Data collectors must disclose their information practices before collecting personal information from consumers.
2. **Choice:** Consumers must be given options with respect to whether and how personal information collected from them may be used for purposes beyond those for which the information was provided.
3. **Access:** Consumers should be able to view and contest the accuracy and completeness of data collected about them.
4. **Security:** Data collectors must take reasonable steps to assure that information collected from consumers is accurate and secure from unauthorized use.
5. **Enforcement:** The use of a reliable mechanism to impose sanctions for noncompliance with these fair information practices as a critical ingredient in any governmental or self-regulatory program to ensure privacy online.

Although four core principles were noted, an unnumbered fifth element of Enforcement was noted as "critical" for an online privacy program.

This chapter will subsequently include all five variables.

This study reviews the specific fair information practices of Notice, Choice, Access, Security, and Enforcement, which are called for in both the U.S. FTC documents as well as the international standards proposed by the OECD. Table 1 matches the FTC FIP term with similar relevant language embodied in the OECD proclamation. The inclusion of these FIP can reasonably be expected to be included in all major international companies. As Malman (2000) noted, there is widespread international convergence on the concept of fair information practices. It is expected that the fair information practices as promulgated by the U.S. FTC would be followed by most international companies, since they are a subset of the fair information practices as originally proposed by the OECD.

Many international researchers have studied and supported the concepts of fair information practices in their studies. Smith, Milberg, and Burke (1996) examined individual concerns about the privacy practices of organizations. They identified four major areas of concern among individuals about their private information. These four areas of improper access, unauthorized secondary use, errors, and collection match the FTC fair information practices. Improper access directly maps to the FIP of Access. Unauthorized secondary use maps to the FIP of Choice. Individuals should have choice over how information collected from them is used, including uses for other than primary collection. Errors can be corrected only if the FIP of Access is allowed. Finally collection relates directly to Notice of information collected as well as Choice of providing the information and future uses of that information.

Milne and Culnan (2002) suggested that many past studies have measured content of policies but not Enforcement. This analysis extends prior analyses and includes analysis of Enforcement

Table 1. FIP in FTC and OECD (1980)

FTC FIP	FIP Inclusion in 1980 OECD Privacy Guidelines
Notice	The purposes for which personal data are collected should be specified not later than at the time of data collection and the subsequent use limited to the fulfillment of those purposes or such others as are not incompatible with those purposes and as are specified on each occasion of change of purpose.
Choice	There should be limits to the collection of personal data and any such data should be obtained by lawful and fair means and, where appropriate, with the knowledge or consent of the data subject.

Access	An individual should have the right:
	a. To obtain from a data controller, or otherwise, confirmation of whether or not the data controller has data relating to him;
	b. To have communicated to him, data relating to him
	    within a reasonable time;
	    at a charge, if any, that is not excessive;
	in a reasonable manner; and
	in a form that is readily intelligible to him;
	c. To be given reasons if a request made under subparagraphs(a) and (b) is denied, and to be able to challenge such denial; and
	d. To challenge data relating to him and, if the challenge is successful to have the data erased, rectified, completed or amended.

Security	Personal data should be protected by reasonable security safeguards against such risks as loss or unauthorised access, destruction, use, modification or disclosure of data.
Enforcement	A data controller should be accountable for complying with measures which give effect to the principles stated above. The draft Convention seeks to establish basic principles of data protection to be enforced by Member countries, Member countries should establish legal, administrative or other procedures or institutions for the protection of privacy and individual liberties in respect of personal data.

provisions. Culnan (1999) notes the importance of Security, another specific variable analyzed in this study. Green, France, Stepanek, and Borrus (2000) support the need for Enforcement.

The concept of fair information practices is not limited to the United States. The fair information practices are internationally supported. A review of the Laurant (2003) content shows many international countries include these provisions in their regulations. As an example, New Zealand passed an electronic commerce privacy act in 1993 including provisions for access, notice, purpose, disclosure of dissemination, and enforcement (Chung & Paynter, 2002). The United Kingdom passed a Data Protection Act in 1998 (Bath and North East Somerset Council, 2002) though most firms are not following this legislation (UMIST and the Office of the Information Commissioner, 2002). A Status of implementation of Directive 95/46 on the Protection of Individuals with regard to the Processing of Personal Data, which includes fair information practices provisions, shows that many European Union countries have passed legislation supporting this personal data protection directive including fair information practices (European Communities, 2004).

Internet Privacy

A number of researchers have examined Internet privacy. Laufer and Wolfe (1977) note the focus on disclosure of private information as a significant force in privacy research. This includes issues such as the psychological and social implications of information disclosure, when information will be disclosed, and the implications of that disclosure in the future. For example, individuals may be persuaded to provide personal information readily over the Internet to customize a purchase decision, but are unaware or would be reluctant to have this information used for other purposes in the future.

The importance of privacy concerns was investigated by O'Neill (2001) in an extensive study

of Internet users. O'Neill found that overall, 54% of the surveyed individuals were very concerned with security on the Internet and another 27% were somewhat concerned. Thus, a total of 81% were at least somewhat concerned with security on the Internet.

Marshall (1999) discusses the concept of Ogburn's cultural lag theory (rapid technological progress with inadequate development of ethical support for new technology). The rapid rise of the Internet and electronic commerce has not allowed the ethical support theory and implementation necessary to maintain a proper balance between the technology and individual rights. Sarathy and Robertson (2003) discussed the European and U.S. approaches to "digital privacy" and found that the United States has relied much more on self-regulation than Europe. The results of this self-regulation in the United States are poor (Culnan, 1999). With regard to privacy notices, Harris Interactive (2001) found that only 3% of respondents carefully read privacy policies of companies.

Many authors have noted the privacy issues and concerns associated with the Internet and electronic commerce. Ackerman, Cranor, and Reagle (1999) surveyed Internet users and found 87% were concerned with privacy over the Internet. Laufer and Wolfe (1977) saw Choice as one of the most important variables in balancing need for individual privacy and overall societal and economic benefits of information transfer. An individual needs to be able to choose "how, under what circumstances, and to what degree" their privacy whether in terms of information flow or relationships with the environment are disclosed and used.

Culnan and Armstrong (1999) summarize the many opportunities for personal data collection in B2C commerce transactions from registers and scanners, credit cards, and inventory databases, including credit history, online browsing patterns, purchase amounts, date and time of transactions, purchase locations, shipping and billing addresses, and any other information that customers are asked for and provide.

Mason (1986) developed a framework that indicated four major ethical issues that have arisen out of ubiquitous computers, databases, and information technology: PAPA—privacy, accuracy, property, and accessibility. These four concepts are included in the FTC fair information practices. Privacy is the overall concept behind all five fair information practices. Accuracy deals with the right to have all information correct and precise and the ability to change, if necessary. The FIPs of Notice and Choice are included. Property supports the issue that personal information and control thereof should remain in the hands of the provider. Personal information is property and should be treated accordingly. Finally, accessibility directly maps to the FIP of Access to information as well as the issues of unauthorized access through lack of Choice, Security breaches, or lack of Enforcement.

There have been a number of studies performed in the past that have analyzed Internet Web sites. Most of these studies have focused on random samples of commercial Web sites or a sample of some of the "most popular" Web sites. One of the first studies of Internet privacy policies was performed by the U.S. Federal Trade Commission in 1998. This first 1998 survey found that based on a random sample, only 15% of firms had privacy policies at all. The percentages of other variables showed extremely low compliance rates with Access and Security provisions and Enforcement not even measured. The "most popular" Web site survey showed higher compliance but still only 16% allowed Access to data and only 16% mentioned Security. Culnan (1999) performed a follow-up survey in 1999 with a random sample of the top 7,500 URLs and found improved results in many fair information practice categories, particularly Access, Security, and Notice. Notice was noted in 90% of Web sites reviewed and Access and Security were 40% and 46%, respectively.

The FTC itself performed a follow-up survey in the year 2000 and found much improved compliance vs. 1998. But the level of compliance was still not adequate for the FTC and they recommended legislation to require compliance with their fair information practices. That legislation never occurred. The first four FIP were measured and are compared with the 1998 survey results in Table 2. Some other variables were first measured in this survey including use of a third party seal, use of cookies, and opt-out features.

A survey was performed in 2002 by the Privacy and Freedom Foundation (Adkinson, Eisenrach, & Lenard, 2002) that for the most part confirmed the results of the FTC 2000 survey. Little change was seen in percentages of the random sample and the popular groups. Recent studies have included work by Ashrafi and Kuilboer (2005) and Schwaig, Kane, and Storey (2006). Ashrafi

Table 2. Percentage of companies whose privacy policies contained the fair information practices (Federal Trade Commission, 1998, 2000)

	FTC 1998 Random	FTC 1998 Popular	FTC 2000 Random	FTC 2000 Popular
Post Privacy Disclosure/ Information Practice Disclosure	15%	73%	88%	100%
Notice	54%	71%	55%	89%
Choice	33%	39%	71%	88%
Access	9%	10%	43%	83%
Security	15%	16%	55%	74%

and Kuilboer (2005) found that only 10% of the Fortune 500 privacy policies addressed 14 privacy issues developed by the authors. The authors focused on the FIP of Notice, Choice, Access, and Security and subcategories thereof. There was no exploration of Enforcement. Schwaig et al. (2006) approached the privacy policies from a somewhat different angle. They examined Fortune 500 companies and classified their privacy policies in one of four categories: mature, unconcerned, limited focus, and public relations. They suggest that due to limited compliance with FIP, Fortune 500 companies are primarily unconcerned about privacy (45%), offer limited protection (12%), or have the policies primarily only for public relations reasons (26%). It is suggest that only 16% have "mature," that is, fully developed, policies. The authors found that the top 100 companies had a "stronger degree of compliance" with FIP than the other Fortune 500 firms. The authors also note the need for longitudinal analysis.

METHODOLOGY

The overall research objective of the study was to examine the largest 100 international companies to determine privacy policy characteristics of the largest companies' Web sites across the world. The selection of companies was the Forbes magazine International 100. This study was performed in a two week period in April 2004. The methodology for the study closely followed prior methods of the FTC (1998, 2000), Culnan (1999), and Ackerman et al. (1999). All of the variables studied were extracted from the FTC 2000 report. The first determination was whether the organization posted a privacy policy on its Web site. The five fair information practices studied were: Notice, Choice, Access, Security, and Enforcement. In addition, a series of variables were extracted to separately analyze whether the sites included consumer centered procedures within their overall policy. Eight variables were studied, all of which were noted in the FTC report. Their consumer centered orientation followed the FTC report. In some cases, mention or disclosure is measured. Disclosure is seen as an important variable in many of the FTC survey questions. Disclosure is favorable and desired. The study was repeated in a two-week period in February 2006 with the same questions and the same company list. Due to one merger with another firm, 99 out of the 100 top companies from 2004 were restudied in 2006 to obtain direct comparisons. The eight variables and their meanings are shown in Table 3.

Table 3. Consumer centered variables (FTC, 2000)

Variable	Detailed Meaning
Post Privacy Policy	Does a firm have a privacy policy or not? It is suggested that absence of a policy is not a consumer centered approach.
How used	This is a measure of whether a company discloses in its privacy policy what it does with information collected. Disclosure is seen as a consumer centered policy.
In-out	Does the firm have a specific opt-in policy for information as opposed to requiring a specific opt-out or not mentioning at all?
Cookies	Is there specific mention of the use of cookies from their Web site? Mention is seen as favorable.
Seal	Is there a third party seal used on the site that independently verifies consumer centered policies?
Mention 3rd Parties	Is there a mention of what access external third parties may have to information? Mention is seen as favorable.
Sell to 3rd Parties	Is there inclusion of a provision that information is not sold to third parties?
Children	Is there any mention of children and specific policies related to children in their privacy policy? Mention is seen as favorable.

As a result of the literature review, six hypotheses were developed to test the levels of compliance with FIP and consumer centered practices.

Hypothesis 1. *Large International companies' Web sites are not consistently following the five fair information practices for online Internet sites.*

Hypothesis 2. *Large International companies' Web sites are not providing consumer centered privacy policies.*

Hypothesis 3. *Large U.S. International companies are more likely to include fair information practices than large non-U.S. International companies.*

Hypothesis 4. *Large U.S. International companies are more likely to have consumer centered policies than large non-U.S. International companies.*

Hypothesis 5. *If a privacy policy is posted, large U.S. International companies are more likely to follow fair information practices than large non-U.S. International companies.*

Hypothesis 6. *If a privacy policy is posted, large U.S. International companies are more likely to have consumer centered policies than large non-U.S. International companies.*

There were a series of 13 variables studied for each site (existence of policy, five fair information practices, and the seven noted consumer centered variables) that measured existence of a privacy policy, adherence to fair information practices for online Web sites, and other variables suggested to explore consumer centered privacy variables. Each of the Web sites was analyzed individually to determine observance of these variables. The authors carefully searched for privacy policies for each individual firm and manually recorded each of the variables for every Web site. The results were entered into Excel and then imported into and analyzed with SPSS 10.0 in 2004 and SPSS 14.0 in 2006.

RESULTS OF THIS STUDY

Hypothesis 1. *Large International companies' Web sites are not consistently following the five fair information practices for online Internet sites.*

Table 4 shows the number of the Forbes 100 International firms that followed the fair information practices in 2004. First, only 73% of the largest 100 firms posted a privacy policy at all. Twenty-seven of the world's largest companies did not have a privacy policy as a link from their home page. Including all 100 firms, only 57% provided Notice of what would be done with information collected from the Web site user. The next highest fair information practice followed was Security with 47 of the 100 firms including some mention of Security of information provided. Twenty-nine firms provided Access to information provided by users of the site and only 27 allowed Choice on what was to be done with the information provided. Finally, Enforcement was addressed by only 7 of the 100 firms. The 2006 data shown in the Revised 2006 Table 4 found that there was some overall improvement in all categories of fair information practices. Gains ranged from a 2.1% increase in including an enforcement provision to a 25.5% increase in allowing access to one's personal information. Overall, Table 5 shows the distribution of how many fair information practices each of the Forbes 100 included in 2004. Only 5 of the Forbes 100 had all five fair information practices. And only 16 had at least four or more. The revised 2006 table again shows that improvements were made in the two years and more firms followed more FIPs. But still 6 of the Forbes 100 included all five FIP and only 26 included four or more. Still, less than half included three or more. It is suggested that Hypothesis 1 is supported. Even though gains are being made, large International companies' Web sites are not consistently following the five fair information practices for online Internet sites.

In addition to studying fair information practices, this study also reviewed a series of eight other variables that attempted to determine the level of consumer centered nature of the Web sites. This review was an attempt to determine a resolution of the second hypothesis.

Hypothesis 2. *Large International companies' Web sites are not consistently providing consumer centered privacy policies.*

Table 6 reviews the 2004 results of this analysis. The table lists the percent of the top 100 firms that exhibited each of the noted variables. First, as noted, only 73 firms had a privacy statement at all. Only 56 firms explained how information collected from users of the site would be subsequently used. Only 5% of the firms have an opt-in choice where users must take a specific action to allow use of information. Others that have an opt-in or opt-out feature only allow for a decision to opt out. Their default is participation. Slightly more than one-half of the firms explicitly state they use cookies. There are third party privacy organizations that provide independent verification of Security and privacy policies, but only 5% of the Forbes 100 use these services. 60% of the firms do mention the use of information collected by external third parties. 13% do allow sale of

Table 4. Fair information practices overall results of the international 100 firms

FIP	% of all 100 firms
Post Privacy Policy	73.0%
Notice	57.0%
Choice	27.0%
Access	29.0%
Security	47.0%
Enforcement	7.0%

Table 4. Fair information practices overall results of the international 100 firms (Revised - 2006)

FIP	% of all 100 firms	2004	Increase/(Decrease)
Post Privacy Policy	78.8%	73.0%	5.8%
Notice	63.6%	57.0%	6.6%
Choice	39.4%	27.0%	12.4%
Access	54.5%	29.0%	25.5%
Security	63.6%	47.0%	16.6%
Enforcement	9.1%	7.0%	2.1%

Table 5. Number of fair information practices followed by number of Forbes 100

Number of FIP	Number of Companies	Number of Companies-2006	Number of Companies-2004	Difference
0	36	26	36	-10
1	13	9	13	-4
2	20	16	20	-4
3	15	22	15	7
4	11	20	11	9
5	5	6	5	1
Total	100	99	100	

information to third parties. The use of the Web site and collection of information from children is mentioned and usually excluded in 26 firms. The 2006-updated Table 6 exhibits only small favorable changes in these percentages.

Overall, it can be concluded that currently, the largest International Web sites do not consistently provide consumer centered privacy policies. They still often lack policies for children, information on how collected information will be used, and rarely require an opt-in provision. Third party seals are rare and more than a third do not provide any information about third party usage. Hypothesis 2 was supported. Large International companies'

Web sites are not providing consumer centered privacy policies.

Next, as noted, in 2004, 27 firms lacked a privacy policy altogether. Therefore, they publicly followed no fair information practices and had no consumer centered policies. This has remained relatively steady in 2006 with 22 of the remaining 99 firms without a privacy policy. Table 7 and Revised 2006 Table 7 examine the variables for those firms that had privacy polices. The conclusions reached in Hypotheses 1 and 2 remain unchanged. Though some variables are over 50%, many are well below with very few exhibiting a majority of the characteristics. The large international firms do not consistently follow fair information practices and the large firms do not consistently practice consumer centered privacy policies.

The next group of hypotheses and analyses examine the differences between large U.S. based international firms and large non-U.S. based firms. Hypotheses 3 through 6 examine the differences between these national groups to determine if U.S. firms are doing a better job of including, designing, and implementing online

Table 6. Consumer centered variables: Overall results of all international 100 firms

Variable	% Of All 100 Firms
Post Privacy Policy	73.0%
How used	56.0%
In-out	5.0%
Cookies	54.0%
Seal	6.0%
Mention 3rd Parties	60.0%
Sell to 3rd Parties	13.0%
Children	26.0%

Table 6. Consumer centered variables: Overall results of all international 100 firms (Revised – 2006)

Variable	% Of All 100 Firms
Post Privacy Policy	78.8%
How used	63.6%
In-out	7.0%
Cookies	70.7%
Seal	6.1%
Mention 3rd Parties	67.7%
Sell to 3rd Parties	7,1%
Children	34.3%

Table 7. Percent of firms with consumer centered variables based on those with privacy policies

Variable	% Of Those With Policies
How used	76.7%
Notice	78.1%
Choice	37.0%
In-out	6.9%
Cookies	74.0%
Access	39.7%
Security	64.4%
Enforcement	9.6%
Seal	8.2%
Mention 3rd Parties	82.2%
Sell to 3rd Parties	17.8%
Children	35.6%

Table 7. Percent of firms with consumer centered variables based on those with privacy policies (Revised – 2006)

Variable	% Of Those With Policies
How used	80.8%
Notice	74.4%
Choice	50.0%
In-out	9.0%
Cookies	83.3%
Access	67.9%
Security	73.1%
Enforcement	11.5%
Seal	7.7%
Mention 3rd Parties	80.8%
Sell to 3rd Parties	9.0%
Children	42.3%

privacy policies. The Forbes 100 dataset was stratified into two groups: 34 U.S. firms and 66 non-U.S. firms. The data were then separately analyzed. Standard cross tabulations were performed to determine the statistical significance of the differences found. Chi-square analysis was used for all dichotomous variables. All analyses used p < .05 for significance. Hypothesis 3 was first reviewed.

Hypothesis 3. *Large U.S. International companies are more likely to include fair information practices than large non-U.S. International companies.*

Table 8 presents the difference between U.S. firms and non-U.S. firms in 2004 for inclusion of each of the five fair information practices. Notice, Access, and Security all had about a 30 percentage point difference in inclusion for non-U.S. vs. U.S. firms. As an example, Access was included in 47% of U.S. firms' privacy policies but only 19% of non-U.S. firms. Enforcement provisions were mentioned in 18% of U.S. firms but only in 2% of non-U.S. firms. The only measure that was close was Choice, which was provided in 29% of U.S. firms vs. 26% for non-U.S. firms. It appears that there is a significant difference in U.S. vs. non-U.S. firms, but this assumption was statistically tested through Chi-square analysis. Table 6 also summarizes the significance of the differences (Chi-square p value) and finds that four of the five fair information practices Notice, Access, Security, and Enforcement showed significant (at p < .05) difference in privacy provisions of U.S. vs. non-U.S. large international Web sites. Only Choice was not statistically significant. In the updated 2006 analysis, there were some changes within the data but overall Hypothesis 3 was supported. Large U.S. International companies are more likely to include fair information practices than large non-U.S. International companies. In 2006, the inclusion of a privacy policy was still significantly less for non-U.S. based firms as well as the inclusion of an enforcement provision and notice provision. Both access and security for non-U.S. based firms increased significantly for non-U.S. based firms and the differences in these percentages are now not statistically significant

Table 8. Fair information practices in U.S. vs. non-U.S. firms based on all 100 firms

FIP	Overall	U.S.	Non-U.S.	Difference	Chi-square p value
Post Privacy Policy	73.0%	94.1%	63.6%	-30.5%	0.001
Notice	57.0%	79.4%	45.5%	-34.0%	0.001
Choice	27.0%	29.4%	25.8%	-3.7%	0.632
Access	29.0%	47.1%	19.7%	-27.4%	0.004
Security	47.0%	64.7%	37.9%	-26.8%	0.011
Enforcement	7.0%	17.7%	1.5%	-16.1%	0.002

at p < 0.05. Choice, however, improved dramatically in U.S. firms vs. non-U.S. firms and is now statistically significant at p < 0.008.

The next analysis examines the consumer centered variables in privacy policies to test the validity of Hypothesis 4.

Hypothesis 4. *Large U.S. International companies are more likely to have consumer centered policies than large non-U.S. International companies.*

In 2004 in nearly all cases (Table 9), there are large differences between the inclusion of consumer centered variables in U.S. Web sites vs. non-U.S. International Web sites. There is an unfavorable difference of 30% for non-U.S. firms in posting a privacy policy at all. Large unfavorable differences for international firms were recorded in posting how information was

used, use of privacy seal, mentioning third parties, and inclusion of provisions on children. Cookies were mentioned more often for U.S. firms. Specific mention of this variable is interpreted as more consumer centered than not because at least the variable is discussed and users of the site can determine how the firm handles this issue. On the other hand, inclusion of an opt-in provision was greater for international firms, and actual declarations that information is sold to third parties was less for international firms. In reviewing the significance of the difference, the opt-in provision was deemed not to be significant according to Chi-square tests. Likewise, sales of information to third parties were not significant. Table 9 also summarizes which firms (U.S. or non-U.S.) had p value significance vs. the others. The Revised 2006 analysis reflects no change in the significant variables. The results, and whether the variable was favorable for U.S. firms, non-U.S. firms, or

Table 8. Fair information practices in U.S. vs. non-U.S. firms based on all 100 firms (Revised – 2006)

FIP	Overall	U.S.	Non-U.S.	Difference	Chi-square p value
Post Privacy Policy	78.8%	93.9%	71.2%	-22.7%	0.007
Notice	58.6%	81.8%	47.0%	-34.8%	0.001
Choice	39.4%	57.6%	30.3%	-27.3%	0.008
Access	54.5%	60.6%	51.5%	-9.1%	0.261
Security	63.6%	72.7%	59.1%	-13.6%	0.134
Enforcement	9.1%	21.2%	3.0%	-18.2%	0.006

Table 9. Consumer-centered policies for U.S. vs. non-U.S. firms based on all 100 firms

Variable	Overall	U.S.	Non-U.S.	Difference	Chi-square p value
How used	56.0%	79.4%	43.9%	-35.5%	0.001
In-out	5.0%	2.9%	6.1%	3.1%	0.237
Cookies	54.0%	79.4%	40.9%	-38.5%	0.002
Seal	6.0%	17.7%	0.0%	-17.7%	0.001
Mention 3rd Parties	60.0%	85.3%	47.0%	-38.3%	0.001
Sell to 3rd Parties	13.0%	17.7%	10.6%	-7.0%	0.859
Children	26.0%	50.0%	13.6%	-36.4%	0.001

not significant, are shown in Table 10. Hypothesis 4 was supported. In more cases, large U.S. International companies are more likely to have consumer centered policies than large non-U.S. International companies.

The final set of hypotheses tested whether there was a significant difference in inclusion of fair information practices and consumer centered policies between U.S. and non-U.S. firms for firms that did have privacy policies posted.

Hypothesis 5. *If a privacy policy is posted, large U.S. International companies are more likely to have fair information practices than large non-U.S. International companies.*

The variances presented in Table 11 show that for firms in the Forbes 100 International, a larger percentage of U.S. firms have four of the five fair information practices promulgated by the FTC: Notice, Access, Security, and Enforcement. Choice is actually included in more non-U.S. firms' privacy policies than U.S. firms. But these results are generally not statistically significant. Only the variance in Enforcement provisions was found to be significant at p < 0.05. In 2006, both Choice and Enforcement are now statistically significant. But the other variables were not statistically significant. Therefore, Hypothesis 5

Table 10. Consumer-centered policy: Significant favorable variance U.S. vs. non-U.S. firm differences for all 100 firms

How used	U.S.
In-out	Not significant
Cookies	U.S.
Seal	U.S.
Mention 3rd Parties	U.S.
Sell to 3rd Parties	Not significant
Children	U.S.

p < .05 used

was rejected. If a privacy policy is posted, large U.S. International companies are *not* more likely to have fair information practices than large non-U.S. International companies. This difference however seems to be weakening.

Hypothesis 6. *If a privacy policy is posted, large U.S. International companies are more likely to have consumer centered policies than large non-U.S. International companies.*

Table 12 shows mixed results for Hypothesis 6 for 2004. Many variables show higher rates of consumer centered policies for U.S. firms, but other variables such as In-Out show higher rates

Table 9. Consumer-centered policies for U.S. vs. non-U.S. firms based on all 100 firms (Revised – 2006)

Variable	Overall	U.S.	Non-U.S.	Difference	Chi-square p value
How used	63.6%	81.8%	54.5%	-27.3%	0.006
In-out	7.1%	6.1%	7.6%	1.5%	0.571
Cookies	70.7%	84.8%	63.6%	-21.2%	0.023
Seal	6.1%	15.2%	1.5%	-13.7%	0.015
Mention 3rd Parties	67.7%	90.9%	56.1%	-34.8%	0.001
Sell to 3rd Parties	7.1%	6.1%	7.6%	1.5%	0.571
Children	34.3%	57.6%	22.7%	-34.9%	0.001

Table 11. FIP in U.S. vs. non-U.S. firms based on those firms that have privacy policies

FIP	Overall	U.S.	Non-U.S.	Difference	Chi-square p value
Notice	74.4%	87.1%	66.0%	-21.1%	0.031
Choice	50.0%	61.3%	42.6%	-18.7%	0.082
Access	67.9%	64.5%	70.2%	5.7%	0.388
Security	73.1%	77.4%	70.2%	-7.2%	0.332
Enforcement	11.5%	22.6%	4.3%	-18.3%	0.018

Table 11. FIP in U.S. vs. non-U.S. firms based on those firms that have privacy policies (Revised – 2006)

FIP	Overall	U.S.	Non-U.S.	Difference	Chi-square p value
Notice	78.1%	84.4%	71.4%	-13.0%	0.251
Choice	37.0%	31.3%	40.5%	9.2%	0.424
Access	39.7%	50.0%	31.0%	-19.1%	0.113
Security	64.4%	68.8%	59.5%	-9.2%	0.491
Enforcement	9.6%	18.8%	2.4%	-16.4%	0.016

for non-U.S. firms. Table 12 analyzes for significance, and finds that only Children and inclusion of a third party seal are significant variables at p < 0.05. With so many variables not significant and only two significant and favorable to U.S. firms, Hypothesis 6 was rejected. When viewed in 2006, both Seal and Children remain better for U.S. firms and now Mentioning of Third Parties and Selling to 3rd Parties are favorably statistically significant for U.S. firms. If a privacy policy is posted, large U.S. International companies are not more likely to have consumer centered policies than large non-U.S. International companies but now four of the seven variables are favorable to U.S. firms.

LIMITATIONS OF THE STUDY

The study provided interesting and useful results but, as with any study, there were limitations that must be recognized. The study analyzed the top international Web sites but only measured the results for the top 100 Web sites. The results cannot necessarily be extrapolated to all international Web sites. A more comprehensive study is necessary for this to be proven. This is a fruitful avenue for other researchers. In addition, although the five fair information practices enjoy widespread international acceptance as privacy related factors, other factors may be important and desirable for consumers' protection as well. A comprehensive study of consumer preferences and requirements could be undertaken to determine these. Finally, eight consumer centered variables were extracted from the FTC report and used as a measure of consumer centered policies. This source may include a U.S.-centric bias and may have lessened applicability in a world arena. A further analysis of these measures is appropriate and provides significant opportunities for further research. Work can be extended to analyze more international firms to see if these results are similar across a larger sampling of firms. In ad-

Table 12. U.S. vs. non-U.S. firms based on firms that have a privacy policy

Variable	Overall	U.S.	Non-U.S.	Difference	Chi-square p value
How used	76.7%	84.4%	69.1%	-15.3%	.171
In-out	6.9%	3.1%	9.5%	6.4%	.237
Cookies	74.0%	84.4%	64.3%	-20.1%	.242
Seal	8.2%	18.8%	0.0%	-18.8%	.004
Mention 3rd Parties	82.2%	90.6%	73.8%	-16.8%	.096
Sell to 3rd Parties	17.8%	18.8%	16.7%	-2.1%	.859
Children	35.6%	53.1%	21.4%	-31.7%	.006

Table 12. U.S. vs. non-U.S. firms based on firms that have a privacy policy (Revised – 2006)

Variable	Overall	U.S.	Non-U.S.	Difference	Chi-square p value
How used	80.8%	87.1%	76.6%	-10.5%	0.197
In-out	9.0%	6.5%	10.6%	4.2%	0.42
Cookies	83.3%	90.3%	78.7%	-11.6%	0.15
Seal	7.7%	16.1%	2.1%	-14.0%	0.034
Mention 3rd Parties	80.8%	96.8%	70.2%	-26.6%	0.003
Sell to 3rd Parties	9.0%	6.5%	10.6%	4.1%	0.42
Children	35.6%	53.1%	21.4%	-31.7%	0.006

dition, analysis can be performed on continental (Europe, Asia, etc.) and other subsegments of the data. Likewise, stratification by industry can be performed. The study used a limited literature review to determine current consumer centered issues. Other consumer centered variables may be viewed by others as more or less important. In other words, researchers may include or exclude other items in an analysis. This study should be rightly viewed as the start of an exploration of international Web site privacy policies and can be extended.

The two different time periods reviewed also provide some limitations to the analysis. Similar methods and personnel were used to collect data from both time periods but the increasing legal refinement has led to many more judgment calls in 2006 as to whether an FIP has been addressed. One area that was particularly troublesome was the

option of Choice. The authors took a strict definition of Choice from the FTC guidelines: "Choice - consumers must be given options with respect to whether and how personal information collected from them may be used for purposes beyond those for which the information was provided" (FTC, 2000). If there was no clear choice provided, then the policy was included as noncompliant.

CONCLUSION AND IMPLICATIONS

The results of analyzing the Forbes 100 International Web sites conclude that, for the most part, the largest International companies in the world do not follow fair information practices. Their privacy statements do not include by varying degrees the five principles of Notice, Access, Choice, Security, and Enforcement. Also, the firms do not generally follow consumer centered practices as measured by a series of defined variables. Generally, non-U.S. companies are less likely to have an Internet privacy policy and, as a result, are less likely to explicitly follow fair information practices or consumer centered policies. The non-U.S. firms that do have privacy policies do not differ significantly in their level of compliance with FIP relative to U.S. firms. In addition, the non-U.S. firms that do have privacy policies do not differ significantly in their level of consumer centered policies relative to U.S. firms. The results presented in this study confirm previous studies showing limited compliance with fair information practices, note the lack of consumer centered practices, and suggest further shortcomings in large international companies' privacy policies. Though some gains have been shown between 2004 and 2006, the conclusions first found in 2004 remain valid.

Overall, the study had three goals. First, it identified and analyzed current large international company Web sites to determine their level of compliance with generally recognized fair information practices, practices that protect and preserve consumers' privacy rights. In general, it was found that large international Web sites do not follow fair information practices and do not provide an acceptable level of protection of personal privacy for consumers. Ackerman et al. (1999) note that 87% of the individuals surveyed were concerned about privacy over the Internet. The ignoring of these concerns by large international firms prevents wider acceptance and use of the Internet as a marketing and consumer information tool. Gefen (2000) found that trust plays an extremely important role in electronic commerce. International firms should take necessary steps to adhere to fair information practices, increase consumer trust, improve their image, and as a result enhance their opportunities in electronic commerce.

The second goal was to determine whether there was general compliance with consumer centered policies on the part of large international companies. The study examined eight items from the FTC 2000 study and found a generally low level of consumer centered practices in the company Web site privacy policies. This should prove important to researchers who wish to further study either detailed privacy policies or a more extensive or diversified group of companies. Practitioners once again have opportunities for increased trust and improved marketing opportunities by addressing these consumer issues.

The final goal was to determine whether there were differences in levels of adherence to fair information practices and consumer centered policies in Internet privacy policies between U.S. and non-U.S. based firms. Generally, it was found that U.S. firms were more likely to have an explicit privacy policy than non-U.S. based firms. As a result of the lack of policies for many non-U.S. based firms, level of explicit adherence to fair information practices and consumer centered policies are higher among U.S. firms. When only firms that have privacy polices are included, levels of compliance are statistically equal. There is a clear message to practitioners. Non-U.S. based firms need to increase their inclusion of Internet privacy polices on their Web sites. In addition, all companies need to improve their levels of adherence to the noted FIP and consumer centered policies.

This work has contributed to the study of electronic commerce. First, the work extracted key factors to judge the overall privacy protection and consumer centered nature of company Web sites. These factors can be used as a framework to assess other Web sites as well as perform longitudinal studies. Second, the study is the first to consider and analyze U.S. vs. non-U.S. Web sites to determine relative differences between their privacy and consumer centered content. Finally, it was found that in many cases there are significant shortcomings in all large companies' Internet privacy policies. Self-regulation and/or international enforcement of regulations appear to be deficient. These findings can be used to target and address Internet privacy policy improvement and enforcement to improve consumer privacy as well as increase consumer trust.

REFERENCES

Ackerman, M., Cranor, L., & Reagle, J. (1999). Privacy in e-commerce: Examining user scenarios and privacy preferences. In *Proceedings of the 1st ACM Conference on Electronic Commerce* (pp. 1-8).

Adkinson, W., Eisenrach, J., & Lenard, T. (2002). *Privacy online: A report of the information practices and policies of commercial Web sites.* Retrieved September 2, 2007, from http://www.pff.org/publications/privacyonlinefinalael.pdf

Ashrafi, N. and Kuilboer, J. (2005). Online privacy policies: An empirical perspective on self-regulatory practices. *Journal of Electronic Commerce in Organizations, 3*(4), 61-74.

Bath and North East Somerset Council. (2002). *Data protection code of practice.* Retrieved September 2, 2007, from http://www.bathnes.gov.uk/dataprotection/data14.htm

Chung, W., & Paynter, J. (2002). Privacy issues on the Internet. In *Proceedings of the 35th Annual Hawaii International Conference on System Sciences* (pp. 2501-2509).

Culnan, M. (1999). *Georgetown Internet privacy policy survey: Report to the Federal Trade Commission.* Retrieved September 2, 2007, from http://www.msb.edu/faculty/culnanm/gipps/gipps1.pdf

Culnan, M., & Armstrong, P. (1999). Information privacy concerns, procedural fairness, and impersonal trust: An empirical investigation. *Organization Science, 10*(1), 104-115.

European Communities. (2004). *Status of implementation of Directive 95/46 on the Protection of Individuals with Regard to the Processing of Personal Data.* Retrieved September 2, 2007, from http://europa.eu.int/comm/internal_market/privacy/law/implementation_en.htm

The European Parliament and the Council of the European Union. (2000). Regulation (EC) No 45/2001 of the European Parliament and of the Council of 18 December 2000 on the protection of individuals with regard to the processing of personal data by the community institutions and bodies and on the free movement of such data. *Official Journal of the European Communities.* Retrieved September 2, 2007, from http://europa.eu.int/eur-lex/pri/en/oj/dat/2001/l_008/l_00820010112en00010022.pdf

Federal Trade Commission. (1998). *Privacy online: A report to Congress.* Retrieved September 2, 2007, from http://www.Federal Trade Commission.gov/reports/privacy3/priv-23a.pdf

Federal Trade Commission. (2000). *Privacy online: Fair information practices in the electronic marketplace, a report to Congress.* Retrieved September 2, 2007, from http://www.FederalTrade Commission.gov/reports/privacy2000/privacy2000.pdf

Forbes, Inc. (2004). *Forbes International 500.* Retrieved September 2, 2007, from http://www.forbes.com

Gefen, D. (2000). E-commerce: The role of familiarity and trust. *Omega, 28*(6), 725-737.

Green, H., France, M., Stepanek, M., & Borrus, A. (2000). Our four point plan. *Business Week, 3673,* 86.

Harris Interactive. (2001). *Privacy leadership initiative (PLI) privacy notices research final results.* Retrieved September 2, 2007, from http://www.FederalTradeCommission.gov/bcp/workshops/glb/supporting/harrris%20results.pdf

Laufer, R., & Wolfe, M. (1977). Privacy as a concept and social issue: A multidimensional developmental theory. *Journal of Social Issues, 33*(3), 22-42.

Laurant, C. (2003). *Privacy and human rights: An international survey of privacy laws and developments.* Retrieved September 2, 2007, from http://www.privacyinternational.org/survey/phr2003/countries/

Malman, S. (2000). Memes and corporate identities in the telecommunication sector. In *ITS 2000: The XIII Biennial Conference of the International Telecommunications Society.* Retrieved September 2, 2007, from http://www.its2000.org.ar/conference/malman.pdf

Mason, R. (1986). Four ethical issues of the information age. *MIS Quarterly, 10*(1), 5-12.

Marshall, K. (1999). Has technology introduced new ethical problems? *Journal of Business Ethics, 19*, 81-90.

Milne, G., & Culnan, M. (2002). Using the content of online privacy notices to inform public policy: A longitudinal analysis of the 1998-2001 U.S. Web surveys. *The Information Society, 18*(5), 345-359.

O'Neill, D. (2001). Analysis of Internet users' level of online privacy concerns. *Social Science Computer Review, 19*(1), 17-31.

Organisation for Economic Co-operation and Development. (1980). *OECD guidelines on the protection of privacy and transborder flows of personal data.* Retrieved September 2, 2007, from http://www.oecd.org/document/18/0,2340,en_2649_37441_1815186_1_1_1_37441,00.html

Organisation for Economic Co-operation and Development. (2005). *About OECD.* Retrieved September 2, 2007, from http://www.oecd.org/about/0,2337,en_2649_201185_1_1_1_1_1,00.html

Sarathy, R., & Robertson, C. (2003). Strategic and ethical considerations in managing digital privacy. *Journal of Business Ethics, 46*, 111-126.

Smith, H., Milberg, S., & Burke, S. (1996). Information privacy: Measuring individuals' concerns about organizational practices. *MIS Quarterly, 20*(2), 167-196.

UMIST and the Office of the Information Commissioner. (2002). *Study of compliance with the Data Protection Act of 1998 by UK based Websites.* Retrieved September 2, 2007, from http://www.co.umist.ac.uk/research/tech_reports/trs_2002_008_lam.pdf

United Nations General Assembly. (1948). *Universal Declaration of Human Rights.* Retrieved September 2, 2007, from http://www.un.org/Overview/rights.html

Warren, S., & Brandeis, L. (1890). The right to privacy. Retrieved September 2, 2007, from http://www.louisville.edu/library/law/brandies/privacy.html (Originally published in *Harvard Law Review, 4*(5).

Westin, A. (1967). *Privacy and freedom.* New York: Antheneum.

Chapter VI
Strength of Privacy Policy Statements and Consumer Trust

Dane K. Peterson
Missouri State Univesity, USA

David B. Meinert
Missouri State Univesity, USA

John R. Criswell II
Columbia College, USA

Martin D. Crossland
Oral Roberts University, USA

ABSTRACT

Privacy policy statements are one of the more commonly used techniques to alleviate consumers' concerns about information privacy which is generally considered one of the primary obstacles to the success of e-commerce. This exploratory study examined the willingness of individuals to provide various types of personal information given varying degrees of protection offered by privacy policy statements. The results demonstrated that the willingness to provide information to Web merchants increased as the level of privacy guaranteed by the statements increased. More interestingly, increasing levels of privacy promised by the statements had the greatest influence on individuals with prior familiarity with policy statements. The results also demonstrated that while most individuals were aware of privacy policy statements, less than half of the respondents had ever read a privacy statement.

INTRODUCTION

Increased Internet availability, reduced access costs, faster modem connections, greater process-ing power, and increased computer competence among consumers worldwide has created enormous growth potential for the rapidly expanding e-commerce industry (Kolsaker & Payne, 2002).

However the growth of e-commerce has been accompanied by an increased ability of Web merchants to gather, compile, and sell personal information about individual consumers without their consent (Kelly & Rowland, 2000). As a result, consumers' concerns regarding information privacy have become a major obstacle for many Web merchants as demonstrated by a survey reporting that information privacy was the main reason individuals were reluctant to engage in e-commerce transactions (Mercuri, 2005).

The emergence of Web site privacy policy statements in the late 1990s was a direct response to consumer concerns regarding information privacy. While privacy policy statements vary considerably in terms of protection afforded and enforcement, the intent is consistent—to increase consumer trust and, concomitantly, intention to consummate transactions via the Web. While privacy policy statements are ubiquitous, limited empirical research has been conducted to examine their impact on consumer trust. Use of privacy policy statements is a relatively new phenomenon, and examination of their use and implications is just beginning to be explored (Culnan, 1999; Grewal, Munger, Iyer, & Levy, 2003; Liu & Arnett, 2002; Luo & Najdawi, 2004; Miyazaki & Fernandez, 2000; Pennington, Wilcox, & Grover, 2003; Ranganathan & Ganapathy, 2002). To date, the literature on this topic has been limited to chronicling rates of utilization and variability in content and investigating the general impact of the presence or absence of such statements (Markel, 2005). The aim of this exploratory study was to develop further understanding of the efficacy of privacy policy statements to increase consumer trust. This study was intended to provide a preliminary understanding of the extent to which, if any, the strength (protection afforded) of privacy policy statements influences consumer willingness to provide personal information via the Web. As an exploratory study, three specific research questions were examined:

1. Do variations in the levels of protection provided by privacy policy statements influence consumer willingness to provide information?
2. What types of information are consumers willing to submit to Web sites given various levels of promised privacy?
3. Does *a priori* familiarity with privacy policy statements influence consumer willingness to provide information online?

By addressing these questions, this study aims to contribute to the knowledge and understanding of the efficacy of privacy policy statements. The findings, while considered preliminary given limitations in the scope of the study, should be of interest to both practitioners and academicians. The findings provide organizations employing privacy policy statements on their Web sites with greater insight into the influence of alternative forms of such statements. This is particularly true for those organizations whose Web sites are targeting younger, well-educated, and affluent consumers, the sampling frame utilized in this study. For academicians and other researchers, the findings demonstrate the potential for research on the relationship between privacy policy statements and consumer trust.

To address these research questions, this article reports the results of a survey designed to measure the impact of privacy policy statements on consumer willingness to provide varying types of information online. First, the article examines previous research to develop a basis for this investigation. This literature review necessarily examines findings related to consumer trust in e-commerce and methods for increasing consumer trust. The literature review is followed by a discussion of the levels of protection provided by privacy policy statements and the types of information typically requested by Web sites. Next, the purpose of the study is outlined in the context of the literature review. Third, a method section is presented that describes the data collection, sample, and the results. Following a discussion of the results, the limitations and opportunities for future research are addressed and the chapter concludes with a brief summary of the implications of the study.

LITERATURE REVIEW

The research questions noted in the Introduction were developed after reviewing research related to consumer trust in e-commerce, methods for increasing consumer trust, levels of protection provided by privacy policy statements, and types of information requested online. Background for the present study is provided via a review of the first two areas, while a discussion of the relevant research in the later two areas provides a context for the present study.

Consumer Trust in E-Commerce

Numerous studies have demonstrated that many potential customers are reluctant to engage in e-commerce transactions because of concerns about providing personal information through the Internet (Kolsaker & Payne, 2002; Miyazaki & Fernandez, 2001; Pavlou, Huigang, & Yajiong, 2007; Suh & Han, 2003). It has been estimated that $15 billion in e-commerce revenues for 2001 were unrealized due to a lack of consumer trust in either the ability or the intent of Web merchants to ensure that personal information would only be used in an acceptable manner (Sipior, Ward, & Ronglone, 2004).

Definition of Trust. A number of definitions of consumer trust have been suggested specifically with regard to e-commerce (e.g., Gefen & Heart, 2006; Lee & Turban, 2001; McKnight & Chevany, 2001). Most of the definitions of trust proposed within the realm of e-commerce share a number of common elements. One commonly cited definition defines trust as a consumer's willingness to rely on the

seller and take action in circumstances where such action makes the consumer vulnerable to the seller (Jarvenpaa, Tractinsky, & Saarinen, 1999). As in most definitions of trust, there is also an element of risk associated with the information submitted through the Internet. Consumers are vulnerable because they are dependent on Web merchants to use information in an acceptable manner. The definition also implies that consumers make their own subjective assessment of the risks involved in a particular e-commerce transaction. Finally, a consumer's actions are assumed to be the result of a rational decision making process.

Consumer Trust in E-Commerce Models. A variety of models on consumer trust in e-commerce have recently been proposed (Jarvenpaa et al., 1999; McKnight & Chervany, 2001; Lee & Turban, 2001; Limayem, Khalifa, & Frini, 2000; Liu, Marchewka, & Ku, 2004; Suh & Han, 2003; Tan & Thoen, 2001; Van Dyke, Midha, & Nemati, 2007). For the most part, these models share a number of common elements. For example, most models recognize that individual differences among consumers play a vital role in e-commerce trust. In general, consumers are assumed to differ in terms of their propensity to trust or their disposition to trust (Lee & Turban, 2001; McKnight & Chervany, 2002). The disposition or propensity to trust is likely influenced by consumers' awareness of Internet fraud and their past experiences regarding both the Internet and other situations involving risk. In addition to past experiences, individual differences in the willingness to engage in e-commerce transactions could also be the result of inherit differences in the inclination of individuals to take risks, such as a tendency to be risk averse or a risk seeker (Tan, 1999; Tan & Thoen, 2001).

The assumption that individuals differ in terms of their trust in e-commerce is supported by studies demonstrating individual differences with respect to gender (Metzger, 2006; Kolsaker

& Payne, 2002), amount of experience with the Internet (Corbitt, Thanasankit, & Han, 2003; Miyazaki & Fernandez, 2001), and cultural background (Jarvenpaa et al., 1999; Liu et al., 2004). In an attempt to examine the extent of individual differences, Sheehan (2000) developed a four category typology based on concerns about submitting personal information to Web sites. This study, based on 889 responses to an e-mail survey, indicated that only a small percentage of individuals could be classified in the extreme groups, "unconcerned" (16%) and "alarmed" (3%). The majority of individuals were classified in the middle two categories, "circumspect" (38%) and "wary" (43%). These results seem to imply that most individuals do not already have strong preconceived notions about the level of risk involved in providing personal information to Web merchants. Rather the results suggest that the specific attributes of a given Web site or Web merchant is likely to influence the decisions of most potential customers.

Another component that is common to most models on e-commerce trust is trust in the Internet system (Lee & Turban, 2001; McKnight & Chervany, 2002). It has been proposed that consumer trust in the Internet system is influenced by the perceived technical competence of the system, perceived performance level of the system, and the degree to which the consumer understands the Internet system (Lee & Turban, 2001). These perceptions of the trustworthiness of the Internet system are likely to be highly influenced by media reports. For instance, one frequently reported study conducted jointly by the Computer Security Institute and the FBI estimated the cost of system penetration by outsiders at over $7 billion annually (cited in Tribunlla, 2002).

The third and most investigated component of most models on e-commerce trust is trust in the Web merchant. Studies have shown that the size and reputation of a Web merchant greatly influences consumer trust (Jarvenpaa et al., 1999). It has also been demonstrated that the perceived ability,

integrity, and benevolence of a Web merchant influences consumer trust (Lee & Turban, 2001). This finding emphasizes that Web merchants must not only have good intentions, but also the perceived ability to protect personal information. Strength of authentication, nonrepudiation, confidentiality, privacy protection, and data integrity have all been shown to impact consumer trust in Internet Banking (Suh & Han, 2003).

Methods for Increasing Consumer Trust. To gain consumer trust, Web merchants must convince potential consumers that personal information obtained through e-commerce transactions will remain secure. To this end, Web merchants have employed a variety of security mechanisms to increase their perceived trustworthiness. These methods include seals of approval or third party certifications, quality and normalcy of Web site design, ratings or customer testimonials, endorsements by reference groups, and money-back guarantees (Ba & Pavlou, 2002; Corbitt et al., 2003; Grewal et al., 2003; Lee & Turban, 2001; Liu et al., 2004; Kimery & McCord, 2006; Pennington et al., 2003; Ranganathan & Ganapathy, 2002; Suh & Han, 2003; Tan, 1999). Since the effectiveness of these procedures have been reviewed in previous articles (Collier & Bienstock, 2006; Liu & Arnett, 2000; Ngai & Wat, 2002), a discussion of the effectiveness of the various security mechanisms will not be presented here.

One of the most widely used security mechanisms by Web merchants is a self-reported guarantee or a privacy policy statement. A privacy policy statement is a contractual commitment to consumers outlining how their personal information will be treated. Privacy policy statements represent one of the simpler and less expensive methods of increasing consumer confidence, which may account for their popularity. While it has been reported that seals of approval from third parties and rating systems based on consumer feedback do not significantly increase consumer trust (Lee & Turban, 2001; Pennington et al., 2003), the evidence suggests that posting a self-reported guarantee of compliance with e-commerce standards is an effective means of increasing consumer trust (Pennington et al., 2003; Ranganathan & Ganapathy, 2002). Privacy policy statements appear to be most beneficial to the Web merchants that have the greatest need to increase consumer trust (Grewal et al., 2003). These privacy policy statements were found to be much more useful for Web merchants that lacked name recognition than those with an established reputation.

Relevant Research

Although there is some evidence that privacy policy statements can be effective, these studies have only examined their effectiveness by comparing the presence vs. the absence of such statements on hypothetical Web sites. Prior studies have not taken into account the variation in the level of protection provided by the privacy policy statements currently posted on various Web sites. Therefore, little is known about how much protection Web merchants should guarantee in their privacy policy statements in order to enhance consumer trust. In addition, research on security mechanisms has largely ignored the type of information associated with online transactions. This study examined the willingness of individuals to provide various types of information based on varying levels of protection provided by privacy policy statements.

Levels of Protection. Studies examining the content of Web sites have found a remarkable amount of variability in the nature and types of privacy policy statements (Miyazaki & Fernandez, 2000; Liu & Arnett, 2002; Luo & Najdawi, 2004). These studies have reported that privacy policy statements vary in terms of their placement, length, and ease of reading. Most importantly, the statements vary in terms of the level of protection guaranteed (Liu & Arnett, 2002). Some

privacy policy statements are highly restrictive while others offer no real assurance of privacy. An example of a highly restrictive privacy policy statement might include a statement such as: "Under no circumstances will any information you provide to us over the Internet be released to any third party for any reason whatsoever" (4321net.com, 2002).

A less restrictive privacy policy statement might include language similar to the following excerpt from the Sun Microsystems privacy policy statement, "If you choose to provide us with your Personal Information on the Web, we may transfer that information, within Sun or to Sun's third party service providers, across borders and from your country or jurisdiction to other countries or jurisdictions around the world" (Sun Microsystems, 2001).

A third and least restrictive level of privacy statement does not provide any protection of personal information. In this scenario, the term privacy policy statement is a misnomer as the statement simply indicates that it is the intention of the Web merchant to share information collected on individuals with other organizations. Thus, these types of statements serve primarily as a means of protecting the Web site with respect to liability issues, as it is the intent of the Web site to share information on customers with other sources.

Types of Information Requested. Much of the research on e-commerce trust has focused on measures of consumers' beliefs, attitudes, and purchase intentions, without consideration for the types of information requested by the Web sites. As noted earlier, the inherent risk is associated with the type of personal information required. Thus, it seems likely that the type of information requested could affect beliefs concerning risk and thus the willingness or intentions of consumers to engage in e-commerce transactions. That is, consumers are likely to engage in e-commerce transactions when a certain threshold of trust is achieved or the level of perceived risk is acceptable. Most theories on risk take into account not only the perceived level of risk involved in a transaction or gamble, but also the stakes involved in the gamble (Tversky, 1995). Thus, it might be reasonable to assume that the trust threshold for engaging in e-commerce transactions varies depending on the potential loss or harm that could result from engaging in a specific transaction. Individuals may be likely to engage in e-commerce transactions when there is little to lose even if the level of trust is low. Conversely, if the perceived level of risk or potential loss or harm is substantial, there may be a reluctance to engage in e-commerce unless there is a high level of trust. It is likely that the perceived potential for loss or harm in e-commerce is dependent upon the type of personal information requested. Thus, whether a consumer engages in an e-commerce transaction is apt to depend not only on the level of trust, but also the potential loss associated with the type of personal information required.

There is enormous variability in the types of information requested by Web sites. Some Web sites require contact information before consumers are even allowed to access a Web site, and extensive personal information must be provided in order to complete a transaction (Sipior et al., 2004). At the other extreme, some Web sites make it possible for consumers to conduct transactions based on a limited amount of personal information submitted to the Web site using such techniques as buyer's authentication, confirmation and payment assurance, or nonrepudiation (Hoffman, Novak, & Peralta, 1999; Mercuri, 2005). Other Web sites may permit consumers to browse potential products and services and then print order forms that can be submitted using other modes of communication (e.g., telephone, conventional mail, or fax) (Miyazaki & Fernandez, 2000).

A preliminary review of Web sites suggests that most of the personal information requested by Web merchants can be classified as contact, biographical, or financial. Contact information includes such items as e-mail address, name,

mailing address, and telephone numbers. Contact information is of value to Web merchants for several reasons including creating mailing lists to publicize special promotions, products, or services offered by the Web merchant. However, contact information may also be sold by Web merchants to third parties. Consequently, many individuals are often reluctant to provide contact information to Web sites (Greiner, 2003).

Biographical information includes demographic data such as income, personal preferences, interests, and hobbies. Web merchants may use biographical information to profile customers, target future communications for marketing purposes, and customize Web pages for individual customers. Web sites may also use biographical information to market their site to advertisers by providing detailed information on visitors to their Web site (Liu et al., 2004). Because consumers are concerned that personal information may be sold to third parties, most individuals (90+ %) have refused to provide biographical information to a Web site on at least one occasion and many (approximately 40%) admitted in some instances to providing false information (Hoffman et al., 1999).

Financial information includes such items as credit card numbers and bank account numbers. Although consumers are obviously reluctant to provide financial information, this information is often viewed as necessary to complete an e-commerce transaction. However, numerous techniques such as buyer's authentication, confirmation and payment assurance, cryptography, digital signatures, nonrepudiation, and alternative payment methods can reduce the perceived risks associated with financial transactions (Hoffman et al., 1999; Kolsaker & Payne, 2002; Mercuri, 2005; Miyazaki & Fernandez, 2000). While such techniques may complicate the processing of orders for Web merchants, these procedures may reduce the perceived risk and increase consumer willingness to engage in e-commerce transactions.

PURPOSE OF THE STUDY

Research suggests that it would be advisable for Web merchants to post a privacy policy statement. However, there is little empirical evidence regarding the appropriate content of these statements. Therefore, this study examined the effects of varying levels of protection offered by privacy policy statements on the willingness of individuals to provide personal information. Recognizing that consumer privacy concerns are determined to some extent by what information is requested (Cespedes & Smith, 1993), it is necessary to examine the efficacy of privacy policy statements in the context of the information at risk. While information sensitivity varies from individual to individual, some information items or categories generate more privacy concerns than others. Therefore, a second objective of this study was to examine the main and interaction effects of types of information requested. To address this objective, when presenting the privacy policy scenarios, the effects of three information categories, contact, biographical, and financial, were examined.

Although privacy policy statements have become common, there is evidence suggesting that consumers may not be familiar with these statements (Westin & Maurici, 1998). It might be expected that with the increased popularity of e-commerce and the growing prevalence of privacy policy statements, more consumers at the present time would be aware of such statements. However, even though consumers may be aware of privacy policy statements, there is no guarantee that they read such statements. Research in the area of consumer behavior has demonstrated that customers frequently fail to read important and relevant information regarding transactions such as product warranties (Adler, 1994) or guarantees (Gore, 1995). Thus, although privacy policy statements are intended to increase consumer trust, if consumers are unaware or do not read the privacy policy statements, then the

statements provide dubious benefits. Therefore, this study also examined whether consumers had seen a privacy policy statement and whether they had read a privacy policy statement prior to participation in this study.

METHOD

Data Collection

Given the exploratory nature of this research and the need to present respondents with multiple scenarios (four forms of privacy policy statements times three types of information), a survey was selected over interviews (phone or person), mall intercepts, quasi-experimental or experimental design. A survey was selected over other methods to allow for detailed and consistent presentation of the descriptions for both privacy policy statements and information types. This format allowed respondents to compare and contrast descriptions, if necessary, to differentiate between the scenarios presented.

The survey provided the following definition of privacy policy statements. "A privacy policy statement explains a Web site's policy regarding the information that is provided online by users." Following the definition of a privacy policy statement, respondents were given examples of three levels of privacy (strong, moderate, and weak) that seem to typify many of the statements presented on Web sites. These examples were based on an examination of policy statements on over 75 Web sites. Table 1 contains the descriptions presented to respondents to differentiate between strong, moderate, and weak privacy policy statements. Abbreviated descriptions for the three types of privacy policy statements were utilized to minimize the risk of respondents misinterpreting lengthy or technically written statements. Although the hypothetical privacy statements used in this study were considerably more concise than those usually found on the Web, they captured the essence (i.e., level of protection) of what was found in a review of 75 such privacy statements.

Following the definition of each example of a privacy policy statement, respondents were asked to indicate their willingness to provide various types of information on a 6-point Likert scale, ranging from (1) "extremely unlikely" to (6) "extremely likely." The types of information requested were defined in the following manner for the respondents on the survey.

- **Contact information:** Request for e-mail address, name, mailing address, and telephone number.
- **Biographical information:** Request for demographic data, such as annual income, personal preferences, hobbies, and interests.
- **Financial information:** Request for credit card numbers, expiration date, bank account numbers, and so forth.

The decision to utilize broad information types reflected the breadth of information that can, and often is, collected via the Internet and the desire to avoid a lengthy survey instrument that could easily compromise the quality of responses and/or response rate.

Sample

The sample consisted of 261 students enrolled in graduate courses or non-credit professional courses offered through the College of Business Administration at one of two Midwestern state universities. To achieve a high response rate, the survey was administered during regularly scheduled class periods. Although participation was voluntary, nearly 100% of the enrolled students participated. While the validity of using students in behavioral research has been questioned (Alpert, 1967; Gordon, Slade, & Schmitt, 1986; Levitt, 1965), there are instances where they (students) are either good substitutes or surrogates for another population (Khera & Benson, 1970; LaTour, Champagne, & Behling, 1990; Remus, 1986) or by virtue of demographic profile, are representative of the target population under investigation. The latter instance was the primary justification for the use of graduate business students, specifically working professionals, in the present study. From its inception, the Internet and, to a large extent, e-commerce, has attracted substantially larger numbers of well educated and affluent consumers (Guglielmo, 1999). Consumers with more education and above average incomes continue to be more likely to use the Web and shop online (Enos, 2000; Kolettis, 2001).

Table 1. Descriptions of privacy policy statements examined

Type of Statement	Description Presented to Respondents
Strong	A strong privacy policy statement explains a Web vendor's policy concerning information that is provided by Web users and makes an explicit guarantee that they will not under any circumstances share the user's information with any other organization, company, or individual.
Moderate	A moderate privacy policy statement explains a Web vendor's policy concerning information that is provided by the Web users and also ensures that the information that is provided will remain confidential. It also provides limited sharing of information when the Web vendor believes that it is in the best interest of the customer, the Web vendor, or both.
Weak	A weak privacy policy statement explains a Web vendor's policy concerning information that is provided by the Web users, but does not offer any guarantee with respect to protecting personal information.

The present study relied on graduate students associated with business programs that have historically attracted working professionals. The profile of these students was consistent with the profile described above, as on average they are more educated and earn more than the general population. The average age of the graduate students was also very close to the median age (36 years old) of Internet users (Kolettis, 2001). While this convenience sample is not representative of all Internet users, it does represent a large segment of Internet users, one that is generally perceived to be more inclined to participate in e-commerce.

Findings

Table 2 summarizes the characteristics of the respondents. As illustrated in Table 2, most respondents connected to the Internet on a daily basis (84%). This compares favorably to national norms for Internet users as Kolettis (2001) re-

Table 2. Respondent profile: Demographics (n = 261)

Demographic Characteristic		
Age (years)		
Mean	35.7	
S	15.8	
Gender		
Male	113	(43.5%)
Female	147	(56.5%)
No Response	1	
Connect to Internet		
Daily	216	(84%)
Twice a Week	15	(5.8%)
Weekly	9	(3.5%)
Monthly	2	(0.7%)
Never	15	(5.8%)
No Response	4	(1.4%)
Provided An Email Address		
Yes	220	(84.3%)
No	41	(15.7%)
Awareness		
(Seen a Privacy Policy Statement)		
Yes	202	(77.4%)
No	59	(22.6%)
Familiarity		
(Read a Privacy Policy Statement)		
Yes	119	(45.6%)
No	142	(54.4%)

ported that 72% of women use the Web every day, while 87% of men are daily users. Almost the same percent had provided an e-mail address to a Web site (84.3%). Overall, the sample was somewhat younger and more educated than the general population, uses the Internet frequently, and most have previously provided personal information to a Web site. Consequently, the results must be generalized with caution. However, the sample would seem appropriate for a study aimed at determining the impact of privacy policy statements on the willingness of consumers to provide personal information to Web merchants.

As shown in Table 2, 77.4% of the 261 respondents had reported seeing a privacy policy statement. However, only 119, or 45.6%, indicated that they were familiar, or more specifically, had read, a Web site's privacy policy statement prior to the study.

The mean willingness to provide the various types of information for each level of privacy statement is presented in Table 3 by respondents' prior familiarity with policy statements. A 2 (previously familiar or read a statement vs. not familiar with private policy statements) X 3 (types of information) X 4 (privacy policy statements) mixed model ANOVA was conducted on the data. The overall mean willingness to provide information for individuals with prior familiarity of privacy statements was 2.81. The mean for respondents with no prior familiarity with privacy policy statements was 2.85. The ANOVA results indicated the difference between two groups was not significant ($F = 0.08$, $p = .775$).

The last row of Table 3 illustrates the differences in willingness to provide each of the three types of information requested. The ANOVA results revealed that the differences were significant ($F = 109.73$, $p < .001$). Posteriori pairwise comparison tests indicated that respondents were more willing to provide contact information than biographical information and more willing to

Table 3. Mean willingness to provide information to Web sites

Policy Statement	Type of Information Requested			Group Means	Grand Means
	Contact	Biographical	Financial		
Strong Policy					4.24
Familiar	4.81	4.27	4.19	4.44	
Not Familiar	4.50	4.05	3.80	4.10	
Moderate Policy					
Familiar	3.41	2.79	2.19	2.77	2.75
Not Familiar	3.35	2.72	2.17	2.75	
Weak Policy					
Familiar	2.51	2.00	1.47	2.00	2.08
Not Familiar	2.72	2.14	1.66	2.18	
No Policy	2.67	2.02	1.47	2.07	2.21
Familiar	3.11	2.29	1.68	2.36	
Not Familiar					
Grand Means	3.38	2.77	2.30		

Scale: (1) Extremely Unlikely to (6) Extremely Likely

provide biographical information than financial information.

The main effect for level of privacy offered by the policy statements is summarized in the last column of Table 3. The difference between the levels was significant ($F = 346.61$, $p < .001$). Posteriori pairwise comparison tests revealed that respondents were more likely to provide information given a strong privacy policy statement than a moderate statement. A moderate statement was significantly more effective than a weak statement and no policy statement. The difference between a weak and a no policy statement was not significant. As shown in the last column of Table 3, only for the strong policy statement was the mean above the midscale value of 3.5.

Perhaps the most interesting result was a significant interaction between prior familiarity with policy statements and the level of privacy offered by the statements ($F = 6.50$, $p < .001$). This interaction is illustrated in the next to last column of Table 3. Under conditions of a strong policy statement, respondents with previous familiarity of policy statements were more likely to provide information. In the presence of a moderate or weak policy statement, there were no significant differences for prior familiarity with policy statements. However, in the absence of a privacy policy statement, respondents with no prior familiarity with privacy statements were more likely to provide Web sites with personal information.

DISCUSSION

Not surprisingly, this study revealed that the willingness of individuals to provide information to Web merchants depends on the type of information requested. Respondents were more willing to provide contact than biographical information and likewise biographical rather than financial information. Given the inherent risk associated with these types of information, one would expect differences of this nature. These results suggest that alternative payment methods that do not require the submission of personal financial information may be extremely beneficial in overcoming one of the major obstacles faced by Web merchants.

The relative sensitivity of biographical information has implications for organizations that have, or plan to collect, such information for purposes of market segmentation or target marketing. The results suggest that consumers concerned about disclosing biographical information may opt to forgo providing any information, including contact, if the former information is a requirement. Future research is needed to demonstrate the necessity and potential value of differentiating between required and optional information either by category (e.g., biographical) or discrete element (e.g., home phone number).

The willingness to provide personal information varied depending on the level of privacy offered by the policy statements. As expected, respondents were most willing to provide information given a strong privacy statement. Moderate statements proved to be more effective than a weak or no policy statement. On the other hand, a weak privacy statement was no more effective than not providing any policy statement. Based on the mean responses for providing personal information, it appears that many Internet users, particularly younger, well educated, and affluent consumers, would be unwilling to provide personal information online, except when offered a strong privacy policy statement.

Overall, the willingness to provide personal information by individuals with prior familiarity of privacy statements differed very little from individuals with no prior familiarity with policy statements. However, this factor interacted with the level of privacy offered by the statements. Individuals with prior familiarity with policy statements were more likely to provide information with a strong statement and less likely to provide personal information when no policy statement was present. This would suggest that it is becoming increasingly important for Web merchants to provide not only a privacy policy statement on their Web site, but also make sure that the policy provides a strong guarantee of privacy. However, it is premature to suggest that broadening awareness of privacy policy statements among consumers and utilization of strong statements will significantly change behaviors. This finding may reflect a general concern or awareness of privacy related issues on the part of consumers as much as familiarity with privacy policy statements. It seems plausible to suggest that consumers concerned about privacy may have sought out information related to such policies or be more cognizant of their application.

One of the main goals of this study was to investigate the degree of prior awareness and familiarity with privacy policy statements. The findings indicate that while respondents were generally aware of privacy policy statements, most do not take the time to read them. This finding is noteworthy given the impact that such statements would purportedly have on consumer trust. If potential consumers do not read privacy policy statements, then even a strong guarantee of privacy will not be effective in terms of increasing confidence.

The success and growth of e-commerce is inextricably linked to consumer willingness to provide information to Web sites. The findings of this study, while preliminary, suggest that privacy policy statements have the potential to increase consumer trust and thus reduce one barrier to e-commerce. However, the findings suggest that privacy policy statements should have a strong guarantee of privacy in order to be effective. Most importantly, the value of a privacy policy statement may be most meaningful to those who are most likely to shop online. That is, consumers who take the time to read privacy policy statements may be the individuals most likely to engage in e-commerce transactions.

LIMITATIONS AND FUTURE RESEARCH

There are limitations to all research, and it is important to note those which may affect the results of this study. First, the sample size and target population were limited which brings into question the degree to which the findings can be generalized. As noted above, while the sample is representative of a significant percentage of Internet users, the findings may not be generalized to other distinct segments such as less educated and older consumers who are increasingly utilizing the Internet. Second, the hypothetical nature of the privacy policy statements used in this study may have seemed somewhat artificial to the respondents. Experimental or quasi-experimental research involving actual Web sites and privacy policy statements could be useful for replicating the results of this study. Third, the decision to reduce the granularity of the information types into three general categories rather than discrete data elements (e.g., credit card number, year of birth, blood type, social security number) may have impacted the results. Although some significant differences were noted using broad categories, it would be beneficial to extend these findings in a similar study using discrete data elements of varying sensitivity. Such research could potentially identify within category differences as well as validate the across group differences noted herein (e.g., contact vs. financial). Fourth, other variables may play a critical role in creating trust in addition to, or in combination with the privacy policy statement (Grewal et al., 2003). Factors such as reputation of the Web merchant, prior experience of the consumer, and an expectation for ongoing use of the Web site might impact consumers' perceptions concerning privacy policy statements and/or willingness to provide information. Similarly, further research is clearly needed to ascertain which individual variables might explain why consumers differ with respect to reading privacy policy statements. Also an understanding of the contextual factors relating to the likelihood that a privacy policy statement will be read could have an impact on the placement, text, and so forth of privacy policy statements.

Fundamentally, more research is needed to understand the impact of why the information is needed (context of the transaction), what information is collected, how it is collected online, and by whom the information is collected. A greater understanding of the main and interaction effects on consumer trust of why, what, how, and by whom information is collected could play a significant role in increasing future sales to current online shoppers and overcoming privacy related fears for those still reluctant to shop online.

SUMMARY

The steady increase in e-commerce sales figures and first-time online buyers demonstrates that consumers are becoming more willing to conduct business transactions via the Internet. However, growth in Internet based sales has lagged projections due in part to consumer concern over the privacy of personal data. The findings from this exploratory study imply that both the nature of information requested online and the degree of protection afforded by privacy policy statements influences consumer privacy concerns. There was also limited evidence to suggest that *a priori* familiarity of privacy policy statements may influence consumer behavior. In addition, the results of this study raise serious questions regarding the extent to which consumers read privacy policy statements. Research examining the validity of this finding, its impact on the efficacy of privacy policy statements, and procedures designed to increase the likelihood consumers will read privacy policy statements are clearly warranted.

The relatively homogeneous nature of the sample (younger, well-educated, affluent consumers) limits the generalization of the findings beyond this one, albeit the large segment of Internet users. However, while the findings should be characterized as preliminary and indicative only of a segment of Internet users, they demonstrate the research methodology employed in this study is appropriate for future research with more representative samples of Internet users. Future research efforts should systematically focus on the influence of why the information is needed (context of the transaction), what information is collected, how it is collected online and by whom the information is collected. Further study of these contextual factors will help determine the extent to which privacy policy statements can alleviate consumer concerns related to privacy and thus increase both Internet usage and participation in e-commerce. Clearly, more extensive research is needed to provide Web merchants with concrete evidence concerning the efficacy of alternative privacy policy statements on consumer trust.

REFERENCES

4321 Net. (2002, January 10). *Privacy statement and policy.* Retrieved September 3, 2007, from http://4321net.com/privacy_statement.htm

Adler, R. S. (1994). The last best argument for eliminating reliance from express warranties: "Real-world" consumers don't read warranties. *South Carolina Law Review, 45*(3), 429.

Alpert, B. (1967). Non-businessmen as surrogates for businessmen in behavioral experiments. *Journal of Business, 40*, 203-207.

Ba, S., & Pavlou, P. A. (2002). Evidence of the effect of trust building technology in electronic markets: Price premiums and buyer behavior. *MIS Quarterly, 26*(3), 243-269.

Cespedes, F.V., & Smith, H. J. (1993). Database marketing: New rules for policy and practice. *Sloan Management Review, 3,* 8-12.

Clausing, J. (1999). New privacy study says majority of sites provide warnings. *New York Times*, pp. 13-5.

Collier, J. E., & Bienstock, C. C. (2006). How do customers judge the quality of an e-tailer? *MIT Sloan Management Review, 48*(1), 35-40.

Corbitt, B. J., Thanasankit, T., & Han, Y. (2003). Trust and e-commerce: A study of consumer perceptions. *Electronic Commerce Research & Applications, 2*(3), 203-216.

Culnan, M. (1999). *Progress report to the Federal Trade Commission (FTC)* (funded by the Online Privacy Alliance). Retrieved September 3, 2007, from http://www.msb.edu/faculty/culnanm/gippshome.html

Enos, L. (2000). Net prices no lure for most e-shoppers. *Ecommerce Times*. Retrieved September 3, 2007, from http://www.ecommercetimes.com/story/4645.html

Fishbein, M., & Ajzen, I. (1975). *Belief, attitude, intention, and behavior: An introduction to theory and research.* Reading, MA: Addison-Wesley.

Gefen, D. (2002). Reflections on the dimensions of trust and trustworthiness among online consumers. *DATA BASE for Advances in Information Systems, 33*(3), 38-54.

Gefen, D., & Heart, T. (2006). On the need to include national culture as a central issue in e-commerce trust beliefs. *Journal of Global Information Management, 14*(4), 1-30.

Gordon, M. E., Slade, L. A., & Schmitt, N. (1986). The "science of the sophomore" revisited: From conjecture to empiricism. *Academy of Management Review, 11*(1), 191-277.

Gore, M. (1995). Read the fine print when selling guarantees. *Best Review, 95*(11), 64-65.

Grabner-Kraeuter, S. (2002). The role of consumers' trust in online-shopping. *Journal of Business Ethics, 39,* 43-50.

Greiner, L. (2003). Information requested is none of company's e-business. *Computing Canada, 29*(19), 19.

Grewal, D., Munger, J. L., Iyer, G. R., & Levy, M. (2003). The influence of Internet-retailing factors on price expectations. *Psychology & Marketing, 20*(6), 447-493.

Guglielmo, C. (1999). E-commerce: There to here. *Inter@Active Week, 6*(47), 106.

Hoffman, D. L., Novak, T. P., & Peralta, M. A. (1999). Information privacy in the marketspace: Implications for the commercial uses of anonymity on the Web. *The Information Society, 15,* 129-139.

Jarvenpaa, S. L., Tractinsky, N., & Saarinen, L. (1999). *Consumer trust in an Internet store: A cross-cultural validation.* Retrieved September 3, 2007, from http://www.ascusc.org/jcmc/vol5/issues2/jarvenpaaa.html

Kelly, E. P., & Rowland, H. C. (2000, May-June). Ethical and online privacy issues in electronic commerce. *Business Horizons*, pp. 3-12.

Khera, I. P., & Benson, J. D. (1970). Are students really poor substitutes for businessmen in behavioral research? *Journal of Marketing Research, 7,* 529-532.

Kimery, K. M., & McCord, M. (2006). Signals of trustworthiness in e-commerce: Consumer understanding of third-party assurance seals. *Journal of Electronic Commerce in Organizations, 4*(4), 52-74.

Kolettis, H. (2001). Who's caught in the Web? *Security Distributing & Marketing, 31*(11), 14.

Kolsaker, A., & Payne, C. (2002). Engendering trust in e-commerce: A study of gender-based concerns. *Marketing Intelligence & Planning, 20*, 206-214.

LaTour, M., Champagne, P. J., & Behling, R. (1990). Do students represent a viable source of data for researching business social responsibility and ethical issues? *The Journal of Computer Information Systems, 30*, 26-29.

Lee, M. K. O., & Turban, E. (2001). A trust model for consumer Internet shopping. *International Journal of Electronic Commerce, 6*(1), 75-91.

Levitt, T. (1965). *Industrial purchasing behavior.* Boston: Harvard University.

Limayem, M., Khalifa, M., & Frini, A. (2000). What makes consumers buy from Internet? A longitudinal study of online shopping. *IEEE Transactions on Systems, Man, and Cybernetics, 30*(4), 421-432.

Liu, C., & Arnett, K. (2000). Exploring the factors associated with Web site success in the context of electronic commerce. *Information & Management, 38*, 23-33.

Liu, C., & Arnett, K. (2002). An examination of privacy policies in Fortune 500 Web sites. *Mid-American Journal of Business, 17*(1), 13-22.

Liu, C., Marchewka, J. T., & Ku, C. (2004). American and Taiwanese perceptions concerning privacy, trust, and behavioral intentions in electronic commerce. *Journal of Global Information Management, 12*(1), 18-40.

Markel, M. (2005). The rhetoric of misdirection in corporate privacy-policy statements. *Technical Communication Quarterly, 14*(2), 197-214.

McKnight, D. H., & Chervany, N. L. (2001). What trust means in e-commerce customer relationships: An interdisciplinary conceptual typology. *International Journal of Electronic Commerce, 6*(2), 35-59.

Mercuri, R. T. (2005). Trusting in transparency. *Communications of the ACM, 48*(5), 15-19.

Metzger, M. J. (2006). Effects of site, vendor, and consumer characteristics on Web site trust and disclosure. *Communications Research, 33*(3), 155-179.

Miyazaki, A. D., & Fernandez, A. (2000). Internet privacy and security: An examination of online retailer disclosures. *Journal of Public Policy & Marketing, 19*(1), 54-61.

Ngai, E. W. T., & Wat, F. K. T. (2002). A literature review and classification of electronic commerce research. *Information & Management, 39*, 415-429.

Pavolou, P. A., Huigang, L., & Yajiong, X. (2007). Understanding and mitigating uncertainty in online exchange relationships: A principal-agent perspective. *MIS Quarterly, 31*(1), 105-136.

Pennington, R., Wilcox, H. D., & Grover, V. (2003). The role of system trust in business-to-consumer transactions. *Journal of Management Information Systems, 20*(3), 197-226.

Ranganathan, C., & Ganapathy, S. (2002). Key dimensions of business-to-consumer Web sites. *Information & Management, 39*, 457-465.

Remus, W. (1986). Graduate students as surrogates for managers in experiments on business decision making. *Journal of Business Research, 14*, 19-25.

Sheehan, K. B. (2000). Toward a typology of Internet users and online privacy concerns. *The Information Society, 18*, 21-32.

Sipior, J. C., Ward, B. T., & Rongione, N. M. (2004). Ethics of collecting and using consumer Internet data. *Information Systems Management, 21*(1), 58-66.

Suh, B., & Han, I. (2003). The impact of customer trust and perception of security control on the acceptance of electronic commerce. *International Journal of Electronic Commerce, 7*(3), 135-161.

Sun Microsystems. (2001, May 22). Sun online privacy policy. Retrieved September 3, 2007, from http://www.sun.com/privacy/

Tan, S. J. (1999). Strategies for reducing consumers' risk aversion in Internet shopping. *Journal of Consumer Marketing, 16*, 163-180.

Tan, Y., & Thoen, W. (2001). Toward a generic model of trust for electronic commerce. *International Journal of Electronic Commerce, 5*, 61-74.

Tribunalla, T. (2002, January). Twenty questions of e-commerce security. *The CPA Journal*, pp. 60-63.

Tversky, A. (1995). Weighing risk and uncertainty. *Psychological Review, 102*(2), 269-283.

Van Dyke, T. P., Midha, V., & Nemati, H. (2007). The effect of consumer privacy empowerment on trust and privacy concerns in e-commerce. *Electronic Markets, 17*(1), 68-81.

Westin, A., & Maurici, D. (1998). E-commerce and privacy: What net users want. *PriceWaterhouseCoopers*, p. 15.

Chapter VII
Seals on Retail Web Sites:
A Signaling Theory Perspective on Third–Party Assurances

Kathryn M. Kimery
Saint Mary's University, Canada

Mary McCord
University of Central Missouri, USA

ABSTRACT

Signaling theory provides the framework to address why third-party assurance (TPA) seals may not have the desired positive effect on consumer trust in online merchants. Based on identified antecedents of effective signaling, three research propositions are presented to explore (1) how reliably consumers are able to recall TPA seals on viewed retail Web sites, (2) how familiar consumers are with major TPA seals, and (3) how accurately consumers comprehend the assurances legitimately represented by the TPA seals. Results of this study of three major TPA seals (TRUSTe, BBBOnLine Reliability, and Veri-Sign) reveal that subjects have relatively poor notice and recall of TPA seals viewed on a Web site, have limited familiarity with TPA programs, and have incomplete and largely inaccurate understanding of the assurances represented by the TPA seals. These results suggest that TPA seals may not fulfill their potential to influence consumer trust in online merchants because the signals are not effectively noticed or accurately interpreted by consumers.

INTRODUCTION

According to recently reported consumer **sales** figures, business on the Internet continues to grow. U.S. nontravel, **electronic commerce** (EC) sales reached $102.1 billion in 2006, an increase of 24% from the previous year (comScore, 2007). During the same period, total retail **sales** in the U.S. increased only 6.3 % (CNBC, 2007). Jupiter-

Research predicts that U.S. business-to-consumer (B2C) **electronic commerce** will grow to $144 billion by the year 2010 (JupiterResearch, 2006). As a percentage of total retail sales, however, some have observed that electronic commerce growth has failed to meet early predictions (AICPA, 1998; Federal Trade Commission, 1998; Sivasailam, Kim, & Rao, 2002). B2C online sales still account for only 7% of adjusted total retail sales in the U.S. (excluding food, autos, and gas) (CNNMoney.com, 2006). Why many consumers are still choosing not to purchase online is certainly an issue worth exploring.

One explanation for consumer hesitancy to shop online put forth by electronic commerce researchers and industry practitioners alike is a lack of **trust** between consumers and online retailers (Gefen, 2000; Gefen, Karahanna, & Straub, 2003; Hoffman, Novak, & Peralta, 1999; McKnight, Kacmar, & Choudhury, 2004). In a major survey conducted by Forrester Research, almost two-thirds of respondents reported that they chose not to buy products online because of their concern about how their personal information would be used by online merchants (Portz, Strong, Busta, & Schneider, 2000). Using focus groups, a recent study found that consumers perceive three sources of online shopping risk related to the technology, the online merchant, and the products purchased (Lim, 2003). Further, some argue that the **trust** gap between consumers and online merchants is widening as the public becomes more aware of the information risks involved in Internet shopping (JupiterMedia, 2005; Perez, 2005). The **electronic commerce** marketplace is characterized by a high level of information asymmetry and a low level of personal interaction between consumers and merchants. As a result, it has proven difficult, especially during initial encounters, for consumers to determine which online merchants can be trusted to provide quality products or services, fulfill their orders accurately and promptly, and protect their personal and financial information.

One trust-building strategy employed by online merchants to help bridge the **trust** gap is to display **third-party assurance (TPA) seals** on their Web sites. These seals are visual **signals** to shoppers that an online merchant has met the specific **trust** standards put forward by a trust-assuring organization. Merchants who choose to participate in TPA programs do so with the expectation that displaying a TPA seal on their Web site will facilitate consumer trust and stimulate increased online **sales**.

The effectiveness of TPA seals for building consumer trust has received enthusiastic support from within the electronic commerce industry and the research community (ITSecurity, 2002; Luo, 2002; PublicEye, 2002; Schoder & Yin, 2000; Sivasailam et al., 2002). Unfortunately, empirical studies report, at best, an uncertain relationship between the display of TPA seals and consumer **trust** in Web merchants or decreased consumer concerns about online security or privacy risks (Kim, Steinfield, & Lai, 2004; Kimery & McCord, 2002; Mauldin & Arunachalam, 2002a, 2002b; Pennington, Wilcox, & Grover, 2003). If TPA seals are not effecting their intended impact on consumers' perceptions of online merchant trustworthiness, research is needed to help us understand why this is so. Signaling theory (Spence, 1973, 1974) provides a framework for understanding how signals of trustworthiness, like TPA seals, operate and may help clarify why TPA seals seem to be failing in their effort to build consumer trust in online merchants.

According to **signaling theory**, to function as an effective indicator of trustworthiness, a TPA seal must satisfy three requirements: (1) it must be perceived within the visual field of the merchant's Web site by the intended signal receiver, in this case, the online shopper; (2) its message must be accurately interpreted and comprehended by the receiver; and (3) it must be assessed as an honest and reliable indicator of the message it communicates. The current study focuses on accessing the first two of these requirements for effective signaling: signal perception and comprehension.

Using signaling theory as a foundation, this study explores how potential online shoppers perceive and comprehend TPA seals on unfamiliar retail Web sites. Results suggest that, as predicted, consumer perception and **recollection** of TPA seals viewed on unfamiliar retail Web sites is relatively low, consumer **familiarity** with major TPA seals is limited, and consumer **comprehension** of the trust-related assurances TPA seals represent is largely inaccurate and incomplete.

A brief summary of prior research on TPA seals, signaling theory, and the three major TPA seals examined in this study is presented next. Specific research propositions are then developed. This is followed by an explanation of the current study's methodology, data analysis, and results. Finally, implications of the results and directions for future research are discussed.

PRIOR RESEARCH

Trust

Trust has received considerable attention in the business and social science literature over the past few decades. Rousseau, Sitkin, Burt, and Camerer (1998) integrate common dimensions from various disciplines and define **trust** as "a psychological state comprising the intention to accept vulnerability based upon positive expectations of the intentions or behavior of another" (p. 395). Willingness of an individual to accept risks and uncertainty in an exchange with another party is based on the trustor's belief that the other party will behave in ways that are predictable and to the trustor's relative benefit. This view of trust as a cognitive balancing of expectations and perceived risks is consistent with a social exchange view on relationship development (Blau, 1969). Social exchange theory argues that people make rational choices about social relationships based primarily on the predicted future behaviors of others and suggests that expectations of a party's future behaviors are determined by an evaluation of that party's past behaviors, in conjunction with social cues regarding the intentions, capabilities, and values of the party (Blau, 1969).

The pivotal role of **trust** as a facilitator of commercial transactions and a foundation of business success is well documented. Trust has been shown to reduce perceptions of risk associated with transactions (Morgan & Hunt, 1994), enhance satisfaction with exchange outcomes (Anderson & Narus, 1990), and lead to longer, more committed buyer-seller relationships (Koehn, 2003). Trust has been characterized as the most precious asset any business can possess (Benassi, 1999; Zucker, 1986) and as a key determinant of successful buyer-seller relationships (Doney & Cannon, 1997; Ganesan, 1994).

Specifically related to B2C electronic commerce, considerable attention has been devoted to the losses associated with a lack of trust. The lack of consumer trust in online merchants has been highlighted by numerous authors as a critical barrier both to short-term success of individual online merchants and to the long-term growth of EC. It has been demonstrated in numerous studies that consumers are concerned about the trustworthiness and competence of online merchants and that these concerns are substantial enough to inhibit online spending (AICPA, 1998; Crowell, 2001; Hoffman et al., 1999). A 2005 study of 5,000 Internet users reveals that 32% of users are cautious about where they shop online and 14% restrict their spending online due to security concerns (Perez, 2005). The 2007 findings of the Digital Future Project, a multiyear cohort study underway at the University of Southern California, reveals that, while concerns about online shopping privacy have diminished slightly during the past two years, it remains at a very high level. Over 86% of respondents report some level of concern about the privacy of personal information they might provide to online merchants.

Over 46% are very or extremely concerned about privacy, and 53.1% are similarly very concerned about protection of their credit card information when they shop online (Center for Digital Future Project, 2007).

While **trust** is key for developing enduring and profitable relationships with customers in any arena, it is particularly relevant for **electronic commerce** (Metzger, 2006). Despite the growth in electronic commerce in recent years, consumers continue to perceive online shopping as inherently more risky than shopping through traditional face-to-face channels (Grabner-Kraeuter, 2002; Miyazaki & Fernandez, 2001; Sheehan & Hoy, 2000). Security issues involved with the transmittal of personal and financial information, the novelty of the mediating computer-based communications technology, unfamiliarity with many vendors on the Internet, and the lack of physical contact with both vendors and their products heighten the uncertainty associated with shopping online (Gefen et al., 2003; Pavlou & Gefen, 2005). Added to these factors, traditional social and legal controls have proven difficult to apply in e-commerce, because of the brief lifespan of some Internet businesses, the "virtuality" of online exchanges, rapidly evolving technologies, and the international locus of Internet-based operations (Grazioli & Jarvenpaa, 2000; Jarupunphol & Mitchell, 2002). Grabner-Kraeuter (2002) argues that trust is critical in overcoming resistance to buying online because trust acts as a coping mechanism for shoppers dealing with the uncertainty and complexity inherent in online shopping.

Empirical research in the electronic commerce domain has consistently found a positive relationship between perceived trustworthiness of an online merchant and a shopper's willingness to purchase. A field study by Hampton-Sosa and Koufaris (2005) reveals that trust in an online store is strongly associated with increased intention to purchase. Gefen et al. (2003) and Jarvenpaa, Tractinsky, and Vitali (2000) report similar findings. Kimery and McCord (2002) report a strong positive effect of consumer perceived **trust** in an online merchant and intention to purchase, mediated by both attitudes toward the merchant and perceived risk of the transaction.

Third-Party Assurance Seals

In an effort to reap the expected benefits of consumer trust, a growing number of Web-based merchants have adopted the use of one or more trust-enhancing mechanisms to ease shoppers' concerns about the risks associated with shopping online. Participating in one of the various TPA programs that have become available over the past decade or so and displaying the program's identifying seal on their Web sites is an increasingly common means of signaling merchants' trustworthiness to potential customers. A **TPA** seal is an icon or logo designed to identify a **trust** assurance program and communicate to consumers that the merchant has agreed to meet the program's standards, use a program-certified technology, or be bound in some way by certain procedures or third-party oversight. The seal on the Web site can be clicked by the consumer to reveal specific validation of the merchant's good-standing with the assuror and, possibly, additional disclosures related to the merchant's business practices, technology use, or prior performance. Figure 1 presents the seals of TRUSTe, VeriSign, and Better Business Bureau Online, three of the most common TPA seals.

While all assurance seals are designed to inform the shopper and to promote the seal-displaying merchant as a trustworthy party, the details of each seal's standards and assurances vary in both scope and focus. While some overlap between categories exists, three general assurance categories can be defined to clarify the underlying content of most of the seals:

1. **Privacy assurance:** Certifies that the merchant discloses and complies with privacy

Figure 1. Third-party assurance seals for TRUSTe, VeriSign, and Better Business Bureau Online

policies (i.e., TRUSTe and Better Business Bureau Online Privacy)

2. **Process assurance:** Certifies the merchant's compliance with the assuror's standards for internal business processes (i.e., WebTrust and Better Business Bureau Online Reliability)

3. **Technology assurance:** Certifies that specific technologies are employed by the merchant or the merchant's agents to enable secure or reliable order and payment handling (i.e., VeriSign, MasterCard Shop Smart, and Thawte)

Little is known empirically about the effectiveness of **TPA** seals as signals of trustworthiness. Few studies have directly tested the relationship between viewing TPA seals on retail Web sites and consumer perceptions of merchant trustworthiness. Those that have examined this relationship have not reported consistent findings. Metzger's (2006) results suggest that, contrary to expectations, the TRUSTe seal, alone or in combination with a strongly worded privacy policy, does not influence consumer trust in an online merchant or willingness to disclose personal information. Kim, Ferrin, and Rao (2004) and Houston and Taylor (1999) report similar results, that viewing TPA seals has no significant impact on enhancing trust or reducing privacy or security concerns about shopping online. Pennington et al. (2004) studied the impact of TPA seals, guarantees, and business ratings on consumer trust in an online merchant. They report no impact of the Better Business Bureau seal or BizRate ratings on increased

trust, although they did find a positive relationship between the display of merchant-provided guarantees and perceived trustworthiness of the merchant. In an experimental study involving three TPA seals—TRUSTe, Better Business Bureau Online, and VeriSign—Kimery and McCord (2002) could demonstrate no significant relationship between viewing any of the seals tested and consumer trust in an online merchant.

Other researchers have reported more positive results. Mauldin and Arunachalam (2002a) report that viewing an assurance seal on a Web site is related to reduced privacy concerns for shoppers. Interestingly, they find that it makes little difference whether the assurance is provided by a third-party or by the merchant itself. Kaplan and Nieschwietz (2003a, 2003b) report that viewing the WebTrust seal does have a positive effect on shoppers' expectations regarding merchant handling of information and order processing, and that the positive effect holds for both familiar and unfamiliar online merchants. Miyazaki and Krishnamurthy (2002) also find that viewing TPA seals, in this study, BBB Online and TRUSTe, has a positive influence on consumer attitudes toward Web merchants and, under conditions of higher perceived risk, may even influence the willingness to disclose personal information and purchase from the Web site. Finally, a recent study of eBay assurance seals (Square Trade, Power Seller, or Mask) by Nikitkov (2006) suggests that these seals positively influence consumer purchasing behavior at eBay. These seals are exclusive to eBay, however, and are not available to merchants doing business elsewhere on the Internet.

Signaling Theory

By design, TPA seals represent visual **signals** displayed by online merchants to communicate important information and social cues to consumers about the merchants' trustworthiness. This type of trust signal has been suggested as an important mechanism for building trust and facilitating exchanges between consumers and, in particular, unfamiliar e-merchants (Lynch, 2001; Pennington et al., 2004). **Signaling theory**, as developed in both natural and social science research, is concerned with the reliable and effective use of signals as part of human and animal interaction (Spence, 1973, 1974). A signal is an indicator—sign, artifact, or action—displayed by one party to communicate to others the existence of qualities, attributes, or intentions that may not be easily discernable without the signal. Signals are displayed with the intention of producing specific effects in the signal receiver's beliefs, attitudes, or behaviors. Signals are considered to be most useful in competitive environments, where there are mutual benefits, for signalers and signal receivers, associated with facilitating this communication and the desired outcomes.

The theory has its roots in the early writings of Veblen (1899) who first suggested that the overtly wasteful spending and trivial pastimes of wealthy members of society served as a signal of their status as elite and powerful individuals. To other wealthy individuals, this signal indicated that the signaler should be treated as a peer, while to individuals without the means to afford such "waste" of time and money, it indicated that the signaler should be treated with respect and deference. During the 1970s, signaling theory was formally defined and tested, primarily by researchers in the natural sciences. Zahavi (1975), a theoretical biologist, studied the elaborate status displays among certain animal species. He was the first to suggest that these displays are signals that convey information about hidden qualities of the signaler. The colorful, but heavy, tail of the male peacock,

for example, serves as a signal of its strength and status within a group of peacocks. The bigger the tail, the more dominant the peacock. Zahavi (1975) stated that the effective use of such signals accrue benefits—for the peacocks, genetically effective breeding pattern, and reduced physical conflict within the group—to both the signaler and the signal receivers.

Over the past three decades, other researchers, in fields of both natural and social sciences, have expanded and refined the theory (e.g., Guilford & Dawkins, 1993; Maynard-Smith & Harper, 2003). Signals have been classified based on how directly they are linked to the qualities they represent, costs associated with the signal displays, and the consequences of dishonest signaling. Of critical relevance to current research on **TPA** seals is the recognition that effective **signals** are those that communicate the sender's intended message, accurately and reliably, to the intended receivers. If a signal is not observed by the intended receiver, the signal has not been successful. If the meaning of a signal is not accurately interpreted by the receiver, the signal may deliver erroneous or incomplete information to the receiver, and, again, the signal is not successful. Without these essential prerequisites, signal observation and comprehension, a signal will not deliver its message effectively, nor will it produce the desired effects on the receiver's attitudes, beliefs, or behaviors.

Signaling theory provides a framework for examining why TPA seals may not exert a reliable and significant positive influence on consumer **trust** in online merchants. TPA seals are visual signals displayed on retail Websites to communicate a message about merchant trustworthiness. The object of the signal display is to establish and build consumer trust in the merchant and to overcome any trust-related hesitancy about making online purchases. **Signaling theory** clearly identifies two prerequisite antecedents to signal effectiveness: signal observation and **comprehension**. In the next section, we look more closely at prior research related specifically to these prerequisites of effective trust signaling and define research propositions to be evaluated in the current study.

Research Propositions

Recollection rate is used in the communication and marketing literature to describe the proportion of subjects who are able to accurately **recall** viewing a visual stimuli—image, logo, or other symbol—to which they have been exposed. Several electronic commerce researchers have reported the recollection rate of TPA seals displayed on Web sites, although there has been considerable variation in the nature of the study settings and manipulation. In Kovar, Burke, and Kovar's (2000) study of the WebTrust seal, all subjects were exposed to a seal-displaying Web site. Subjects had received prior instruction on the specific seal used in the study and were instructed to examine the Web site carefully and follow all links. Still, only minutes after viewing the Web site, only 58% of subjects could recall seeing the seal. In yet another study of the WebTrust seal, investigators again directed subjects to study a Web site carefully, to read all information displayed, to examine every page, and follow every link. Even with these directions, only 69% could recall the WebTrust seal on the Web site (Portz et al., 2000).

In studies with more naturalistic shopping simulations, lower seal recollection rates are typical. Lala, Arnold, Sutton, and Guan (2002) report that only 42% of their subjects could accurately recall whether the WebTrust seal was displayed on a Web site. More recently, in a study of multiple TPA seals, subjects were asked to search Web sites for specific product-related information, but without specific instruction to attend to other aspects of the Web sites (Moores, 2005). After completing the search task, subjects were asked to identify the TPA seals, if any, displayed on the Web sites. The recollection rates for seals in this

study ranged from a high of 42% for TRUSTe to a low of only 7.7% for the WebTrust seal.

Overall, even in cases when subjects are directly instructed to search for TPA seals or to click on every hyperlink, reported seal **recollection** rates have been below 70%. In more naturalistic settings, the recollection rates appear to be substantially lower. Poor attention to and low recollection of TPA seals on retail Web sites has been noted as a matter of concern for the electronic commerce industry and for researchers (Kaplan & Nieschwietz, 2003a, 2003b; Odom, Kumar, & Saunders, 2002; Portz et al., 2000). Kimery and McCord (2002) specifically question whether poor observation of TPA seals by subjects in their study was, at least, partly responsible for their inability to find a significant relationship between TPA seals and trust in the study's online merchant.

Signaling theory maintains that signals cannot effect their intended outcomes, if the signals are not observed by the intended receivers. Prior research suggests that seals tend to be overlooked on retail Web sites, and, in naturalistic study settings, recollection rates for TPA seals are likely to be below 50%, and, perhaps, considerably below that rate.

Proposition 1. *Online shoppers have limited ability to accurately recall TPA seals displayed on a merchant's Web site.*

Beyond recollection, it has also been suggested that online shoppers are simply not **familiar** with the seals or the assurances represented by the seals. Odom et al. (2002) report that consumers have limited recognition of most major TPA seals. Recognition is the most basic aspect of **familiarity** and signifies that a subject remembers seeing an image, in this case a TPA seal, at some time in the past (Odom et al., 2002). Their study presented subjects with five different TPA seals (VeriSign, TRUSTe, Good Housekeeping Seal Online, BBBOnLine, and WebTrust). Recognition of the seals ranged from a low of 3% for WebTrust to a high of 17% for the online Good Housekeeping Seal. The Odom study went on to collect self-reported perceptions of familiarity with the various TPA seals. The results are consistent with their recognition findings. Average familiarity ratings for the different seals ranged from a low of 1.04 (on a 5-point familiarity scale) for WebTrust to a high of 2.3 for the Good Housekeeping seal. Kim et al. (2004) asked subjects about their awareness of Web assurance seals in general. Their subjects report a relatively low mean awareness rating of 3.78, just above the midpoint on a 7-point scale.

Signaling theory identifies **comprehension** of signal meaning as a necessary antecedent to signal effectiveness. Using self-reports of familiarity with trust assurance programs and their identifying seals is one approach to accessing how confidently and accurately consumers are able to interpret the message conveyed by the TPA seals. Based on prior research, predicted consumer familiarity with TPA programs and their seals is expressed in Proposition 2.

Proposition 2. *Consumers have relatively little familiarity with TPA seals and the assurances they represent.*

Prior research also suggests that consumers tend to have little **comprehension** of the actual assurances represented by TPA seals. The report of a 1999 AT&T Labs survey cautioned that consumers frequently do not understand the content or mechanisms of Web assurances (Reagle & Cranor, 1999). Burke, Kovar, and Kovar (2001) report that viewing the WebTrust seal influences perceptions of an online merchant in areas unrelated to the actual assurances provided by WebTrust. They conclude that, despite the marketing and education efforts of the TPA sponsors, there is a significant gap between actual and perceived assurances represented by the WebTrust seal.

In another study of the WebTrust seal, Houston and Taylor (1999) report that seeing the seal makes online shoppers feel more assured about product quality, even though the seal does not warrant product quality. They suggest that consumers mistakenly perceive WebTrust as similar to an idealized Good Housekeeping Seal of Approval, promising general customer satisfaction with products and services. Portz et al. (2000) report similar incomplete and inaccurate interpretations of the WebTrust seal assurances and that accuracy of subject comprehension of assurances varied by assurance category. Only 28% of subjects correctly understood representations related to transaction integrity and only 44% correctly understood assurances related to business processes. Fifty-nine percent of the subjects incorrectly assumed that CPAs had approved the Web merchant's business practices, and 22% incorrectly believed that the TPA seal guaranteed them absolutely against fraudulent acts on the part of the merchant (Portz et al., 2000).

In a recent study, Moores (2005) reports that subjects are largely mistaken or uncertain about the meaning of TPA seals, their financial cost to merchants, the requirement for merchants to post privacy statements, requirements related to the collection and sharing of consumer information by merchants, and who assessed compliance with the practices assured by the TPA seals. He, also, reports that subjects were largely unaware that the assurances of the seals derive from third-party organizations, such as TRUSTe, the Association for Independent Certified Public Accountants, or the Better Business Bureau.

Drawing once again from signaling theory, we know that signal receivers must be able to accurately interpret and understand the intended signal message before any desired signal outcomes can be realized. Prior research suggests that online shoppers have a very limited understanding of the assurances represented by the TPA seals. Our expectations regarding consumer interpretation and comprehension of seal assurances are captured in Proposition 3.

Proposition 3. *Online shoppers have inaccurate and incomplete understanding of the assurances represented by TPA seals.*

CURRENT STUDY

TPA Programs

Three TPA seals—TRUSTe, BBBOnLine, and VeriSign—are employed in this study to evaluate the research propositions regarding seal recollection, familiarity, and comprehension. These three seals have been selected because of their dominance in each of the **TPA** categories—privacy assurance, process assurance, and technology assurance—and their prevalence in the electronic commerce industry and research literature. The Industry Standard (1999) identifies BBBOnLine, TrustE, and VeriSign as the three top TPA "brands." Luo (2002) describes these same seals as key examples of institutional mechanisms facilitating e-commerce transactions. In a report on TPA participation by Fortune 1000 companies, Sivasailam et al. (2002) include TRUSTe, BBBOnLine, and VeriSign as three of the four best-known TPA programs.

TRUSTe. Established in 1997, TRUSTe is an independent, nonprofit organization dedicated to promoting consumer confidence in e-commerce and facilitating the growth of the Internet as a safe marketplace. The organization addresses this goal by providing a seal of assurance for those Web merchants who agree to abide by the TRUSTe guidelines related to information privacy. TRUSTe guidelines require that: (1) a participating merchant prominently displays a privacy policy statement on their Web site; (2) consumers be allowed to choose whether or not their personal information is subject to secondary use by the merchant; (3) consumers have access to information collected about them; and (4) reasonable security measures be employed to maintain the privacy of personal information (TRUSTe, 2005). TRUSTe also accepts consumer privacy complaints regarding participating merchants and will work to resolve privacy-related problems. The TRUSTe organization can require the merchants modify their practices or change their posted privacy policy to maintain the right to display the TRUSTe seal. The TRUSTe organization claims that it is the most trust-invoking assurance program in existence, with approximately 1,300 participating companies and organizations. It has been identified by Neilsen NetRating surveys as the most prominent privacy-related TPA on the Web (TRUSTe, 2000). According to Cheskin Research (2000), the TRUSTe seal is the most trust-invoking TPA seal for U.S. Web users, followed by BBBOnLine and VeriSign TPA seals. More information on the TRUSTe program is available on the organization's Web site at www. TRUSTe.org.

BBBOnLine Reliability. This arm of the familiar Better Business Bureau (BBB) organization was launched in March of 1997 and is committed to creating greater trust and confidence in the Internet by providing assurances to consumers regarding online merchants' integrity and good business practices (Better Business Bureau, 2005; Sivasailam et al., 2002). The display of the BBBOnLine Reliability seal on a Web site is designed to assure consumers that the merchant: (1) is a member of their local Better Business Bureau; (2) pledges to meet the BBBOnLine Reliability standards for ethical online business practices; and (3) has agreed to resolve consumers' product- or service-related complaints using the BBB dispute resolution program. Companies who do not live up to these promises will lose the right to display the BBBOnLine seal. The Better Business Bureau (2005) reports that more than 24,000 Web sites display the BBBOnLine Reliability seal. More information regarding the BBBOnLine Reliability and other BBB-sponsored assurance programs is available at www.bbb.org.

VeriSign Secure Site. VeriSign, Inc., is a for-profit provider of e-commerce security-related services, including secure socket layer (SSL) server IDs for Web site authentication and encryption, payment handling services, and commercial Web site hosting services. Any online merchant who applies for and is granted a SSL server ID is permitted to display the VeriSign Secure Site seal. The VeriSign Secure Site seal is intended to assure online shoppers that a Web merchant is authentic, in that the merchant is who it claims to be, and further, that all financial transactions with the merchant's site are secured by SSL encryption. The VeriSign seal does not focus on the content of the site, the merchant's intentions toward reuse of customer personal or financial information, or the merchant's business practices. More information on VeriSign services and the VeriSign Secure Site seal is available at the company's Web site at www.VeriSign.com.

Study Setting

Subjects in this study are primarily college students from two midwestern U.S. universities. In EC-related research, college students are considered a valid pool from which to draw subjects because students are generally consistent with online shopping demographics (Jarvenpaa & Todd, 1996; OECD, 1999). Specifically, a recent study shows that the age group with the highest percentage of Internet users (74%) is 18 to 29 and that student status and years of education are the strongest independent predictors of Internet use (Lenhart, Horrigan, Rainie, Allen, Boyce, & Madden, 2003). Further, in a study using student and nonstudent Internet consumers, Pavlou and Fygenson (2006) found that the two groups do not differ significantly in terms of gender, age, education, income, Internet experience, or the study's outcome variables, which included intention to purchase from a Web site.

All subjects were given written instructions, which identified the procedures for the study and described the study scenario. The scenario explained to the subjects that they were to imagine buying a specific fondue pot requested as a wedding gift by a friend. It was recognized that product and price can influence the nature of how consumers make online purchase decisions online. The product, brand, and model of the target product were controlled by the scenario to ensure that all subjects would be examining the same products on the Web site and their attention would not be diverted by gift selection dilemmas. To reduce the possible influence of price comparison in the purchase decision making, the fondue pot was identified in the scenario as costing approximately $60-65, and the target product on the study Web site was priced at the low end of this range. The price-point for the item was set high enough to make the decision to buy a nontrivial matter and to create an impression of limited financial risk for subjects in the exercise. The instructions directed the subjects to assume that they had decided to definitely purchase the fondue pot, although they had not yet decided where or how to buy it.

After reading the instructions, subjects were directed to an online pretest survey form. The pretest questions focused on the subject's general disposition to trust, experience with online shopping, and other demographic variables. Following completion of the pretest, subjects were presented with one of four possible versions of the study's mock retail Web site. Each Web site was identical, with the sole exception of the TPA seal manipulation. Each site displayed the TRUSTe seal, the BBBOnLine Reliability seal, the VeriSign Secure Site seal, or no TPA seal at all. A partial depiction of the TRUSTe version of the study Web site is presented in Appendix A.

The Web sites were created by the authors to realistically mimic a retail Web site specializing in the sale of home products. The seals were prominently displayed on multiple pages of the Web site, including the home page, the product description pages, the shopping cart, and checkout page. To create a more natural shopping experience, subjects were given no specific instructions to follow all links or to look for, inspect, or click on TPA seals. To ensure that the subjects did fully complete the shopping task, however, the link to exit to the online post-test survey was not displayed on-screen until the target product was actually located and viewed by the subject. The post-test survey questioned subjects about, among other things, perceived trustworthiness of the online merchant. The post-test was followed by an online manipulation check questionnaire, which measured subjects' ability to accurately identify the seal on the Web site and their perceived level of familiarity with the displayed TPA seal. In addition, an open-ended question asked subjects to describe their comprehension of the assurances provided by the seal on the Web site. It was not possible for subjects to return to the merchant Web site once they had moved on to the post-test and manipulation check screens.

RESULTS

A total of 508 completed responses are included in this analysis, with 382 subjects exposed to Web sites containing one of the three TPA seals. Of the usable responses, roughly one-fourth were exposed to each Web site version (TRUSTe n = 137, BBB n = 122, VeriSign n = 114, no seal n = 139). Slightly more than half (55%) of all subjects were male, 95% were below the age of 30, and almost 98% were university students. The majority of the subjects were business majors (68.9%), with information systems being the most common major represented in the sample (27.3%).

Recollection

The three TPA seals (TRUSTe, BBBOnLine, and VeriSign) were graphically depicted on the manipulation check instrument. Subjects were asked to choose the seal they remembered seeing on the Web site. This question also included the response options "I did not see any of the above" and "I saw one of the above, but do not remember which." Responses to this question were compared with the seal actually displayed on the Web site. Recollection rates are presented in Table 1. Overall, slightly less than 57% of subjects were able to correctly recall the TPA seal displayed on the study Web site. Testing for comparison of proportions reveals that subjects were significantly less likely to accurately **recall** the BBBOnLine seal compared to both the TRUSTe seal ($z = -2.90$, significance < .01) and the VeriSign seal ($z = -3.45$, significance < .01). The difference in recollection rates between TRUSTe and VeriSign seals was not significant. The VeriSign seal enjoyed the highest recollection rate (66.7% correct), followed by TRUSTe (62.4% correct), and, finally, the BBBOnLine Reliability seal (44.3% correct).

Table 1. Seal recollection

| | **PRETEST** | | | **Total** |
	TRUSTe	**BBBOnLine**	**VeriSign**	
Inaccurate	50	68	38	156
	(37.6%)	(55.7%)	(33.3%)	(42.3%)
Accurate	83	54	76	213
	(62.4%)	(44.3%)	(66.7%)	(56.7%)
Total	133	122	114	369

Familiarity

Familiarity with the seal was captured both in terms of simple recognition of the seal ("Before participating in this study, had you ever seen or heard of this seal?") and perceived level of familiarity with the TPA program ("When you first saw the seal on the Web site, how familiar were you with the assurances that the seal represents?"). For the first question, subjects responded either "Yes," "No," or "I did not see a seal." The recognition results are presented in Table 2. Overall, 57% of subjects claimed that they had previously seen or heard of the TPA seal from the study Web site. Testing for comparison of proportions reveals that subjects had lower recognition of the BBBOnline seal compared to both the TRUSTe seal ($z = - -3.29$, significance $< .01$) and the VeriSign seal

($z = -2.02$, significance $< .05$). The difference in recognition between TRUSTe and VeriSign seals was not significant. The TRUSTe seal had the highest rate of recognition (67%), followed by VeriSign (57%), and BBBOnLine (40%).

Results of the subjects' self-reported level of **familiarity** with the assurances associated with the TPA seals are also presented in Table 2. Subjects responded to this question on a 5-point Likert-type scale with 1 anchored as "Very unfamiliar" and 5 anchored as "Very familiar." Overall, among subjects who did recall seeing a seal on the Web site, seal **familiarity** was fairly neutral with a mean of 3.05, only fractional above the midpoint of the scale. The TRUSTe seal was reported as having the highest mean level of familiarity (3.32), followed by the VeriSign seal (3.22), and, again lastly, by BBBOnLine (2.73). An ANOVA analysis reveals

Table 2. Recognition and familiarity

	Previous Exposure		Familiarity
Seal Viewed	**Yes**	**No**	**Mean**
TRUSTe	66 (67%)	33 (33%)	3.32
BBBOnLine Reliability	23 (40%)	35 (60%)	2.73
VeriSign	50 (57%)	38 (43%)	3.22
Total	139 (57%)	106 (43%)	3.05

Note: Responses of subjects who recalled seeing a seal. Column percentages are shown in parentheses.

Table 3. Post hoc tests of differences in mean familiarity

Test	Seal 1	Seal 2	Mean Difference	Sig.
Tukey HSD	TRUSTe	BBBOnLine	.59	.028*
	TRUSTe	VeriSign	.10	.953
	BBBOnLine	VeriSign	-.49	.109
Bonferroni	TRUSTe	BBBOnLine	.59	.033*
	TRUSTe	VeriSign	.10	.990
	BBBOnLine	VeriSign	-.49	.146

* α < 0.05 level of significance

that there are significant differences in the level of familiarity reported for the different seals ($f =$ 3.99, df = 3, $p < .008$). *Post hoc* tests, including the Tukey Honestly Significant Difference test and the Bonferroni test for multiple comparisons, indicate that the TRUSTe and the BBBOnLine seals have significantly different levels of familiarity. While there is a noticeable difference between VeriSign and BBBOnLine, this comparison does not meet the standards for significance. *Post hoc* test results are presented in Table 3.

Comprehension of Seal Assurances

Evaluating subject **comprehension** of seal assurances is based on the analysis of responses to an open-ended question, "If you saw a seal, what do you believe the seal represents about [the Web-based merchant]?" Content analysis was use to quantify the responses to this question. In content analysis, written statements are examined and explicit rules are used to make an objective analysis of their meaning. Content analysis is a qualitative technique that is particularly well suited to exploratory research and capturing information about subjective beliefs, attitudes, or perceptions of relationships (Neuman, 1994). Based on the two researchers' examination of responses to the open-ended question, a coding scheme of assurance categories was developed. Brief category descriptions, along with overall frequencies and response-rates for all seals are presented in Table 4. Each subject response could include multiple statements describing different types of seal assurances. Each statement was categorized individually, and, as a result, each subject response could potentially be coded into multiple categories. Multiple statements describing the same type of assurance were counted only once. The two principal researchers cross-coded responses from 90 subjects, approximately 15% of the total sample. Cross-coding validation resulted in an agreement rate of almost 97%. Differences in coding were discussed and resolved by the

researchers, and the remaining responses were independently coded by the two researchers.

The TRUSTe seal legitimately represents assurances that (1) the merchant will display a policy statement regarding information privacy, (2) the merchant will comply with that policy, (3) the customer will have an opportunity to provide input over how their personal information is reused by the merchant, (4) the customer will be given access to her own personal information, and (5) the merchant will use reasonable measures to protect customer privacy (TRUSTe, 2005). Considering each of these assurances individually, only 3% of subjects who recalled viewing the TRUSTe seal identified the existence of a privacy policy as one of the TRUSTe assurances, although a larger 13.5% correctly stated that compliance with the privacy policy was one of the TRUSTe assurances. Almost 7% of subjects believed that the seal indicated that the Web site was safe for personal information, which is consistent with the TRUSTe assurance that affiliated merchants will employ reasonable measures to ensure privacy of personal information. In addition, 7.5% of subjects recognized a linkage between the merchant and the TRUSTe organization, and 15.8% believed the seal indicates that the merchant is trustworthy. No subjects in this study identified that customers have input concerning how the merchant might reuse consumer personal information or that consumers have access to information kept about them. Some subjects mistakenly extended the TRUSTe assurances to include those not directly warranted by the TRUSTe seal. More than 19% of subjects believed the seal represents assurance of data encryption or financial data security (Response Categories 1 & 2). Almost 4% believed the merchant will not reuse consumer-provided information, 3% believed the Web merchant is authenticated, and 3% believed the seal attests to higher product or service quality.

The BBBOnLine Reliability seal certifies that the online merchant is a member of the local BBB organization, subscribes to the BBB ethi-

Table 4. Tabulation of comprehension response categories

#	Response Category	TRUSTe	BBB Reliability	VeriSign	TOTAL
1	Encrypted/secure site	21(15.8%)	16(13.0%)	**35(30.4%)**	72(19%)
2	Safe for financial info	7(3.8%)	2(1.6%)	**13(9.6%)**	22(5.8%)
3	Safe for personal info	**9(6.8%)**	2(1.6%)	**4(3.5%)**	15(4%)
4	Legitimate/authentic site	4(3.0%)	1(.9%)	**4(3.5%)**	9(2.3%)
5	Has privacy policy	**4(3.0%)**	4(3.3%)	11(9.6%)	19(5%)
6	Complies w/ privacy policy	**18(13.5%)**	4(3.3%)	5(4.4%)	27(7.1%)
7	Personal info. not shared	5(3.8%)	2(1.6%)	1(.9%)	8(2.1%)
8	Higher product or svc.quality	4(3.0%)	4(3.3%)	5(4.4%)	13(3.4%)
9	Generally trustworthy site	21(15.8%)	21(17.1%)	14(12.2%)	56(14.8%)
10	General positive comment	4(3.0%)	6(4.9%)	4(3.5%)	14(3.7%)
11	Affiliated w/ TPA program	**10(7.5%)**	**15(12.2%)**	5(4.4%)	30(7.9%)
12	Merchant wants customers to feel comfortable	3(2.3%)	6(4.9%)	10(8.7%)	19(5%)
13	Other assurance	3(2.3%)	5(4.0%)	3(2.6%)	11(2.9%)
14	Seal means nothing	2(1.5%)	6(4.9%)	4(3.5%)	12(3.1%)
15	Blank	41(30.4%)	45(35.4%)	25(21.6%)	111(29.4%
16	Did not see seal	2(1.5%)	4(3.1%)	1(<1%)	7(2%)
	Number of respondents recalling each seal type	135	127	116	378

Note: Category frequency as a percentage of subjects who recalled seeing each seal in parentheses. Bolded figures represent those perceptions judged to accurately reflect assurances provided by the TPA seals.

cal standards for business processes, and agrees to participate in BBB-sponsored resolution of consumer complaints (Better Business Bureau, 2005). More than 12% of subjects who reported seeing the BBB seal correctly stated that the seal reflects an association between the Web merchant and the BBB organization. Slightly more than 17% report that the BBBOnLine Reliability seal attests to the general trustworthiness of the merchant. None of the subjects identified that the merchant subscribes to a code of business ethics, or that the merchant is bound to resolve complaints via the Better Business Bureau's complaint resolution procedures. Other attributions made by subjects not specifically assured by the BBBOnLine Reliability seal include the belief that the Web site is encrypted and safe for personal or financial data

(16.2%), that the merchant has a privacy policy (3.31%), complies with the policy (3.3%), and that the merchant has higher product or service quality (3.3%). Almost 6% of subjects reported that the seal means nothing.

The VeriSign Secure Site seal is intended to assure online customers that a Web merchant is who it claims to be (authentication) and that all financial transactions with the merchant's site are secured by secure socket layer (SSL) encryption. The VeriSign seal does not focus on the content of the site, the merchant's intentions toward using customer information, or the merchant's business practices (VeriSign, 2002). The VeriSign Secure Site seal was correctly identified by 43.5% of subjects as certifying that the merchant operates a secure, encrypted Web site (Response Categories

1, 2, & 3). Approximately 3.5% correctly believed that the seal authenticates the merchant's identity. In addition, 4.4% of subjects stated that the seal indicates that the Web site employs VeriSign services. More than 12% of subjects believed the seal assures that the merchant is trustworthy. Subjects also identified assurances that are not legitimately warranted by VeriSign. Almost 9.6% of subjects mistakenly believed that the VeriSign seal assures that the merchant has a privacy policy. More than 4% of subjects inaccurately claimed the seal indicates that the merchant will comply with its privacy policy, and another 4.4% believed the seal assures higher product or service quality.

One approach to comparing the accuracy of TPA assurance comprehension is to calculate the percentage of subjects who are able to identify at least one valid assurance represented by the TPA seal. These results are summarized in Table 5. A chi-square analysis of these frequencies indicates that there is a highly significant difference between the three different TPA seals ($\chi^2 = 20.228$, df = 2, $p < .0001$). These figures reveal that subjects are more likely to be able to identify at least one valid

assurance represented by the VeriSign Secure Site seal than either the TRUSTe or the BBBOnLine seals. This is not totally consistent with subjects' prior exposure to the different TPA seals or self-reports of familiarity with the assurances associated with the TPA programs (Table 2).

DISCUSSION

These results indicate that suspicions by some in the **electronic commerce** research and practitioner community about poor consumer observation and **comprehension** of **TPA** seals may, in fact, be true. As predicted in Proposition 1, consumer attention to TPA seals on retail Web sites appears to be fairly casual, as evidenced by the low seal recollection rate among these subjects. Overall, subjects were unable to correctly identify the TPA seal from a merchant's Web site over 42% of the time. Accuracy varied based on the actual seal displayed, even though all seals were reproduced to the same scale and positioned in the same location on each version of the study Web site.

Table 5. Accurate perceptions of TPA assurances identified by subjects

SEAL	VALID TPA ASSURANCES	ANALYSIS CATEGORIES	COMPREHENSION ACCURACY*
TRUSTe	1. Has a privacy policy 2. Complies with policy 3. Reasonable security 4. Consumer input on use 5. Consumer access to info 6. Complaint resolution	1. Has a privacy policy 2. Complies with policy 3. Safe for personal info 4. Affiliated with TRUSTe	38 (28.1%)
BBB	1. Member of local BBB 2. Code of business ethics 3. Complaint resolution	1. Affiliated with BBB	15 (12.2%)
VeriSign	1. Encrypted site 2. Authentic site	1. Encrypted/secure site 2. Safe for financial info 3. Safe for personal info 4. Authentic site 5. Use VeriSign technology	51 (44%)

* Count (percentage) of subjects who were able to accurately identify at least one valid seal assurance.

Recollection rates range from a high of almost 67% for the VeriSign seal to a low of 44.26% for the BBBOnLine Reliability seal. This is particularly interesting given that several sources have described the BBBOnLine seal as benefiting from instant recognition, because of its association with the well-known BBB organization (Lucas, 2000). The Better Business Bureau (2005) itself claims that 90% of North Americans recognize the BBB logo. Clearly, given the poor recall of the seals after only a matter of minutes in this study, TPA seals do not adequately capture shoppers' attention or create a lasting impression in the minds of shoppers.

The ability of consumers to accurately recall specific TPA seals is likely to be influenced by consumer recognition of and familiarity with the TPA seals. Self-reports of prior exposure to and familiarity with seals in this study suggest that there is substantial variability in **familiarity** with the different seals. Sixty-seven percent of subjects claim to have had some previous exposure to the TRUSTe seal, and 57% claim to have heard of or seen the VeriSign seal prior to participating in this study. Both of these exposure rates are substantially higher than the 40% exposure rate subjects reported for the BBBOnLine Reliability seal. When questioned in more detail about their level of familiarity with the assurances provided by each seal, subjects' responses were fairly neutral. While subjects claimed familiarity with the TRUSTe and VeriSign seals slightly above the midpoint of the familiarity scale (3.32 and 3.22, respectively, on a 5-point scale), subjects judged the BBBOnLine Reliability seal to be more unfamiliar than familiar (2.73 on the same scale). These results are in keeping with the generally limited familiarity predicted in Proposition 2.

Low **familiarity** with the seals and their assurances presents a problem on two fronts. First, as demonstrated in this study's results, familiarity is clearly associated with notice and accurate recollection of displayed seals. The BBBOnLine Reliability seal had, by far, the lowest rate of rec-ollection, as well as the lowest reported familiarity. One strategy to improve notice and recall of seals on congested retail Web sites is to enhance consumers' awareness and familiarity with both the TPA seals and the organizations and assurances with which they are associated. On a second front, low general familiarity with TPA seals is associated with poor understanding of the specific assurances represented by the seals. To ensure that TPA seals signal the intended message regarding both the merchant and the assuring organization, it is imperative that both of these parties devote greater attention to building consumer familiarity with the TPA seals.

Looking at comprehension of TPA seal assurances in more detail, Proposition 3 predicted that consumers have poor **comprehension** of seal assurances. This prediction is supported by content analysis of subject responses to the open-ended question regarding specific assurances provided by the TPA seals. The subjects in this study demonstrate incomplete and, in some areas, highly inaccurate understanding of the seal assurances. One approach used to compare accuracy of assurance comprehension is to calculate the percentage of subjects who were able to correctly identify at least one assurance represented by each of the TPA seals. Based on this metric, the VeriSign seal assurances were the most accurately comprehended by the subjects in this study, with 44% of subjects stating that the seal certified that the site was encrypted and/or secure, that the merchant was legitimate, or that the site employed VeriSign technology or services. A key misunderstanding about the VeriSign seal is that it implies that the merchant maintains a privacy policy (9.6% of subjects). The TRUSTe seal is less well understood by subjects, even though it was of roughly equal familiarity to subjects. Only 28% of respondents who recalled seeing the seal correctly indicated that the seal certifies the existence of a privacy policy, merchant compliance with that policy, safety for personal information, or an affiliation between the Web site and the TRUSTe organization. The BBBOn-Line Reliability is, likewise, poorly understood by subjects. Fewer than 16% of subjects who recalled seeing the seal correctly indicated that the seal signals an affiliation between the Web merchant and the BBB organization. None of the other assurances represented by the BBBOnLine Reliability seal were identified accurately by subjects in this study.

Although only VeriSign assures encryption, a large percentage of subjects perceive all three seals as providing assurances that a site is encrypted or secure for financial information. For example, 19.6% of subjects incorrectly described the TRUSTe seal as warranting that the merchant Web site is encrypted or secure for financial transactions. Similarly, 14.6% of subjects believe that the BBBOnLine seal signifies that the Web site is secure or encrypted. It may be that subjects consider encryption an important aspect of being "assured," and therefore falsely attribute an assurance related to encryption to any seal displayed. If this is true, the assurance accuracy rate recorded for the VeriSign seal may be artificially inflated.

With the exception of the relatively high rate of accurate identification of the VeriSign seal with security and encryption, subjects do not demonstrate substantial knowledge about the legitimate representations of the TPA seals. For TRUSTe and BBBOnLine Reliability, two assurance seals that are considered to be among the most well-known and visible of all TPA programs, this indicates a serious gap between actual and consumer-perceived assurances of the TPA programs. Certainly, all of the TPA-sponsoring organizations want consumers to accurately understand the assurances that their seals represent and have employed various educational and marketing strategies to achieve this aim. The results of this study, unfortunately, suggest that these efforts have only been marginally effective in informing consumers about the TPA assurances.

Since all of the TPA-sponsoring organizations have expressed interest in building **trust** between consumers and online retailers, it is important to examine whether or not any of the TPA seals are perceived by consumers as assuring the trustworthiness of the displaying retailer. It is apparent that some subjects in this study do associate all three TPA seals, to one degree or another, with general trustworthiness of the Web merchant. The BBBOnLine Reliability was defined as indicating trustworthiness by more than 17.1% of subjects, while TRUSTe was considered as a sign of trustworthiness for almost 16% of subjects. The VeriSign seal was associated with trust in the merchant less frequently, by only 12.2% of subjects. These relatively low levels of consumer-perceived association between **TPA** seals and trustworthiness should stimulate a reappraisal by TPA-sponsoring organizations of how their programs are viewed by consumers and how they can, and should, modify their policies, practices, and standards to be more in line with their stated goals of building trust in online merchants and the electronic commerce marketplace.

Contributions and Implications

The results of this study are consistent with some prior research findings and tend to confirm a general feeling among some academicians and electronic commerce practitioners that **TPA** seals often go unnoticed by shoppers. The results also confirm suspicions that shoppers are largely unfamiliar with the TPA seals and have limited comprehension of the assurances represented. This research makes an important contribution, however, as one of the few reported studies that empirically captures how three of the most widely subscribed electronic commerce trust assurance programs—TRUSTe, VeriSign, and BBBOn-Line—are understood by consumers. Applying signaling theory as a framework, this study highlights two critical prerequisites for effective use of TPA seals as signals of trustworthiness.

First, online shoppers must observe the TPA seal on the Web site. Seals that go unnoticed have no opportunity to communicate any new information to an online shopper, and, as a result, have no opportunity to influence the shopper's attitudes toward the merchant or subsequent purchasing decisions. Second, online shoppers must comprehend the intended meaning of the signal; that is, they must have a clear understanding of the assurances represented by the TPA seals.

These results have practical implications for online merchants, as they make decisions about investing the significant financial and organizational resources required to participate in TPA programs. To maximize the potential return on such investments, they should ensure that their Web space is designed to maximize viewer attention to the TPA seals. Given that the seal's purpose is to influence the shopper's perception of the merchant's trustworthiness and, thereby, make it easier for the shopper to decide to purchase, the TPA seal should not be relegated to the order and check-out areas of the Web site. Shoppers should be exposed to the assurance seals as soon as possible upon entering the Web site. In addition, shoppers should be encouraged, via visual cues or text instructions, to click on the seal to reveal any linked seal explanations or company disclosures. If simple, well-written explanations are not available from the TPA provider, they should be produced by the merchant's own staff and linked to the seal.

These results also have important implications for organizations that sponsor TPA seal programs. Those responsible for producing or selecting seal graphics should concentrate their efforts on incorporating high-impact design elements. Size, color, and shape, in addition to location of the seal on the Web site, all influence the likelihood that viewers will observe and attend to the seal. **TPA** sponsors should also provide Web-ready documents containing details of their program standards, verifications of authenticity, as well as easy-to-read outlines of seal assurances to be linked to TPA seals on merchant Web pages. TPA sponsors also must bear the main responsibility for educating the Internet public about the assurances represented by the display of their seal on a participating merchant's Web site. They should clearly communicate how merchants earn the right to display their seal, the obligations of the merchant and of the TPA-sponsoring organization to the online consumer, the procedures for filing consumer complaints, and the repercussions to the merchant for violating the requirements put forth by the organization.

For researchers, these results may serve to inform ongoing work or stimulate new research efforts. Researchers involved in any study of the impact of TPA seals on consumer attitudes or behavior should be cognizant of the potential for poor attention to seals on real or mock Web sites. Similarly, it is likely that untrained subjects will have only limited understanding of the assurances that are represented by the TPA seals. Future research extensions of this study may include an examination of the possible impact of demographic and individual difference variables (i.e., disposition to trust, computer experience, or attitudes toward e-commerce) on seal recall, familiarity, and assurance comprehension. Also, future work may test the ability of TPA seals to influence the attitudes and behaviors of those subjects who do observe the displayed seals and comprehend the assurances they provide. Future research could also address some possible limitations of this study. First, while students may be regarded as an appropriate subject pool for studies of this kind, similar research could be undertaken using nonstudent subjects. This could be employed to consider the possible impact of age, income, or educational status on the outcome variables. A second modification could incorporate a more realistic simulation of financial risk for subjects involved in making online purchase decisions. Elevating the perception of transaction risk may motivate subjects to devote more attention to trust-enhancing mechanisms, including TPA trust signals.

CONCLUSION

This study demonstrates that, after browsing retail Web sites, consumers have difficulty noticing and accurately recalling TPA seals. Further, based on the subjects in this study, consumers' general level of familiarity with three common TPA seals—TRUSTe, BBBOnLine Reliability, and VeriSign—is still quite low. Perhaps most importantly, results indicate that consumer comprehension of the specific assurances associated with these seals is highly incomplete and inaccurate. **Signaling theory** suggests that TPA seals cannot be expected to fulfill their intended mission as signals of merchant trustworthiness, if the signal is not observed and comprehended by online shoppers. While these results highlight the need for more comprehensive marketing and education efforts on the part of TPA seal sponsors, it also suggests that more research should focus on understanding how consumers notice and attend to TPA seals, or other stimuli, on retail Web sites, and how the seals are perceived and interpreted by online shoppers.

REFERENCES

AICPA - American Institute of Certified Public Accountants (1998). *Electronic commerce assurance: Attitudes toward CPA WebTrust.* Retrieved September 5, 2007, from http://www.aicpa.org/Webtrust/yankel.htm

Anderson, J. C., & Narus, J. A. (1990). A model of distributor firm and manufacturer firm working partnerships. *Journal of Marketing, 54*(1), 42-58.

Benassi, P. (1999). TRUSTe: An online privacy seal program. *Communications of the ACM, 42*, 57-59.

Better Business Bureau. (2005). *BBBOnLine Reliability Program.* Retrieved September 5, 2007, from http://www.bbbonline.org/reliability/

Blau, P. (1964). *Exchange and power in social life.* New York: Wiley.

Burke, K., Kovar, S., & Kovar, B. (2001). Marketing WebTrust and managing consumer expectations. *Journal of Accounting and Finance Research, 9*(3), 62-72.

Center for Digital Future. (2007). *Online world as important to Internet users as real world? USC-Annenberg Digital Future Project finds major shifts in social communication and personal connections on the Internet.* Retrieved September 5, 2007, from http://www.digitalcenter.org/pdf/2007-Digital-Future-Report-Press-Release-112906.pdf

Cheskin Research. (2000). *Trust in the wired Americas.* Retrieved September 5, 2007, from http://www.cheskin.com

CNBC. (2007, January 16). *Retail sales growth seen moderating in '07: Trade groupers.* Retrieved September 5, 2007, from http://www.msnbc.msn.com/id/16652499/

CNNMoney.com. (2006, December 29). *Online holiday spending surges.* Retrieved September 5, 2007, from http://money.cnn.com/2006/12/29/news/economy/online_retail/?postversion=2006122910

comScore. (2007, January 3). *comScore Networks reports total non-travel e-commerce spending reaches $102 billion in 2006; up 24 percent versus 2005.* Retrieved September 5, 2007, from http://www.comscore.com/press/release.asp?press=1166

Crowell, W. (2001). Trust, the e-commerce difference. *Credit Card Manager, 14*(5), 80.

Doney, P., & Cannon, J. (1997). An examination of the nature of trust in buyer-seller relationship. *Journal of Marketing, 61*, 35-51.

Doney, P., Cannon, J., & Mullen, M. (1998). Understanding the influence of national culture on the development of trust. *Academy of Management Review, 23*(3), 601-620.

Federal Trade Commission. (1998). *Privacy online: A report to Congress, FTC's Consumer Response Center.* Washington, DC.

Ganesan, S (1994, April). Determinants of long-term orientation in buyer-seller relationships. *Journal of Marketing, 58*, 1-19.

Gefen, D. (2000). E-commerce: The role of familiarity and trust. *Omega, 28*(6), 725.

Gefen, D., Karahanna, E., & Straub, D. W. (2003). Trust and TAM in online shopping: An integrated model. *MIS Quarterly, 27*(1), 51-90.

Grabner-Kraeuter, S. (2002). The role of consumers' trust in online-shopping. *Journal of Business Ethics, 39*(1-2), 43-50.

Grazioli, S., & Jarvenpaa, S. (2000). Perils of Internet fraud: An empirical investigation of deception and trust with experienced Internet consumers. *IEEE Transactions on Systems, Man, and Cybernetics—Part A: Systems and Humans, 30*, 395-410.

Guilford, T., & Dawkins, M. (1993). Receiver psychology and the evolution of animal signals. *Animal Behavior, 42*, 1-14.

Hampton-Sosa, W., & Koufaris, M. (2005). The effect of Web site perceptions on initial trust in the owner company. *International Journal of Electronic Commerce, 10*(1), 55-81.

Hoffman, D., Novak, T., & Peralta, M. (1999). Building consumer trust online. *Communications of the ACM, 42*(4), 80-85.

Houston, R. W., & Taylor, G. K. (1999). Consumer perceptions of CPA WebTrust assurances: Evidence of an expectation gap. *International Journal of Auditing, 3*, 89-105.

ITSecurity. (2002, February 22). *First major post-9/11 privacy survey.* Retrieved September 5, 2007, from http://www.itsecurity.com/tecsnews/feb2002/feb260.htm

Jarupunphol, P., & Mitchell, C. (2002) E-commerce and the media—influences on security risk perceptions. In W. Cellary & A. Iyengar (Eds.), *Internet Technologies, Applications and Societal Impact: The 1st IFIP Workshop on Internet Technologies, Applications and Societal Impact*, Wroclaw, Poland (IFIP Conference Proceedings 232, pp. 163-173). Kluwer Academic.

Jarvenpaa, S., & Todd, P. (1996). Consumer reactions to electronic shopping on the World Wide Web. *International Journal of Electronic Commerce, 1*, 59-88.

Jarvenpaa, S. L., Tractinsky, N., & Vitale, M. (2000). Consumer trust in an Internet store. *Information Technology and Management Journal, 1*, 45-71.

Johnson, C., Delhagen, K., & Yuen, E. (2003). *US eCommerce overview: 2003 to 2008.* Forrester Research, Inc.

JupiterMedia. (2005). Accurate Web site visitor measurement crippled by cookie blocking and deletion, JupiterResearch finds. Retrieved September 5, 2007, from http://www.jupitermedia.com/corporate/releases/05.03.14-newjupresearch.html

JupiterResearch. (2006, February 6). *JupiterResearch forecasts online retail spending will reach*

$144 billion in 2010, a CAGR of 12% from 2005. Retrieved September 5, 2007, from http://www.jupitermedia.com/corporate/releases/06.02.06-newjupresearch.html

Kaplan, S. E., & Nieschwietz, R. J. (2003a). An examination of the effects of WebTrust and company type on consumers' purchase intentions. *International Journal of Auditing, 7,* 155-168.

Kaplan, S. E., & Nieschwietz, R. J. (2003b). A Web assurance services model of trust for B2C e-commerce. *International Journal of Accounting Information Systems, 4,* 95-114.

Kim, D. J., Steinfield, C., & Lai, Y. (2004). Revisiting the role of Web assurance seals in consumer trust. In *Proceedings of the 6th International Conference on Electronic Commerce, 60*(1), 280-287, Delft, The Netherlands.

Kimery, K., & McCord, M. (2002). Third-party assurances: Mapping the road to trust in eretailing. *Journal of Information Technology Theory and Applications (JITTA), 4*(2), 63-82.

Koehn, D. (2003). The nature and conditions for online trust. *Journal of Business Ethics, 43,* 3-19.

Kovar, S., Burke, K., & Kovar, B. (2000). Consumer responses to the CPA WebTrust assurance. *Journal of Information Systems, 14*(1), 17-25.

Lala, A., & Sutton, G. (2002). The impact of relative information quality of e-commerce assurance seals on Internet purchasing behavior. *International Journal of Accounting Information Systems, 3*(4), 237-253.

Lenhart, A., Horrigan, J., Rainie, L., Allen, K., Boyce, A., & Madden, M. (2003). *The ever-shifting Internet population: A new look at Internet access and the digital divide* (PEW Internet and American Life Project, No. 4162003). Retrieved September 5, 2007, from http://www.pewinternet.org/PPF/r/88/report_display.asp

Lewicki, R., & Bunker, B. (1996). Developing and maintaining trust in work relationships. In R. M. Kramer & T. R. Tyler (Ed.), *Trust in organizations: Frontiers of theory and research* (pp. 114-139). Thousand Oaks, CA: Sage.

Lim, N. (2003). Consumers' perceived risk: Sources versus consequences. *Electronic Commerce Research and Applications, 2,* 216-228.

Lucas, P. (2000). In search of a seal of approval. *Credit Card Management, 13*(5), 52-58.

Luo, X. (2002). Trust production and privacy concerns on the Internet: A framework based on relationship marketing and social exchange theory. *Industrial Marketing Management, 31*(2), 111-118.

Lynch, C. (2001). When documents deceive: Trust and provenance as new factors for information retrieval in a tangled Web. *Journal of the American Society for Information Science and Technology, 52*(1), 12-17.

Mauldin, E., & Arunachalam, V. (2002a). An experimental examination of alternative forms of Web assurance for business-to-consumer e-commerce. *Journal of Information Systems, 16*(1), 33-54.

Mauldin, E., & Arunachalam, V. (2002b). Reply to discussions of an experimental examination of alternative forms of Web assurance for business-to-consumer e-commerce. *Journal of Information Systems, 16*(1), 65-67.

Maynard-Smith, J., & Harper, D. (2003). *Animal signals.* Oxford, UK: Oxford University Press.

McKnight, D. H., Kacmar, C. J., & Choudhury, V. (2004). Shifting factors and the ineffectiveness of third party assurance seals: A two-stage model of initial trust in a Web business. *Electronic Markets, 14*(3), 252-266.

Metzger, M. (2006). Effects of site, vendor, and consumer characteristics on Web site trust and disclosure. *Communication Research, 33*(34), 155-179.

Miyazaki, A., & Fernandez, A. (2001). Consumer perceptions of privacy and security risks for online shopping. *Journal of Consumer Affairs, 36*, 28-49.

Miyazaki, A., & Krishnamurthy, S. (2002). Internet seals of approval: Effects on online privacy policies and consumer perceptions. *The Journal of Consumer Affairs, 36*(1), 28-49.

Moores, T. (2005). Do consumers understand the role of privacy seals in e-commerce? *Communications of the ACM, 48*(3), 86-91.

Morgan, R. M., & Hunt, S. D. (1994). The commitment-trust theory of relationship marketing. *Journal of Marketing, 58*(3), 20.

Neuman, W. L. (1994). *Social research methods* (2nd ed.). Boston: Allyn & Bacon.

Nikitkov, A. (2006). Information assurance seals: How they impact consumer purchasing behavior. *Journal of Information Systems, 20*(1), 1-17.

Odom, M. D., Kumar, A., & Saunders, L. (2002). Web assurance seals: How and why they influence consumers' decisions. *Journal of Information Systems, 16*(2), 231-250.

OECD. (1999). The economic and social impact of electronic commerce: Preliminary findings and research agenda. *Organisation for Economic Co-operation and Development*. Retrieved September 5, 2007, from http://www.oecd.org/dataoecd/3/12/1944883.pdf

Pavlou, P. A., & Fygenson, M. (2006). Understanding and predicting electronic commerce adoption: An extension of the theory of planned behavior. *MIS Quarterly, 30*(1), 115-143.

Pavlou, P. A., & Gefen, D. (2005). Psychological contract violation in online marketplaces: An-

tecedents, consequences, and moderating role. *Information Systems Research, 16*(4), 372-399.

Pennington, R., Wilcox, H., Dixon, & Grover, V. (2004). The role of system trust in business-to-consumer transactions. *Journal of Management Information Systems, 20*(3), 197-226.

Perez, J. C. (2005, June 24). Gartner: Security concerns to stunt e-commerce growth [Electronic version]. *ComputerWorld*. Retrieved September 5, 2007, from the IDG News Service database.

Portz, K., Strong, J. M., Busta, B., & Schneider, K. (2000). Do consumers understand what WebTrust means? *CPA Journal, 70*(10), 47.

PublicEye. (2002, March 30). Survey of 56,765 online shoppers suggests that many still use small e-tailers primarily for comparison shopping. *The Public Eye*. Retrieved September 5, 2007, from http://www.epubliceye.com/pr36.html

Reagle, J., & Cranor, L. F. (1999). The platform for privacy preferences. *Communications of the ACM, 42*(2), 48-55.

Rousseau, D. M., Sitkin, S. B., Burt, R. S., & Camerer, C. (1998). Not so different after all: A cross-discipline view of trust. *The Academy of Management Review, 23*(3), 393-404.

Schoder, D., & Yin, P. (2000). Building firm trust online. *Communications of the ACM, 43*, 73-79.

Sheehan, K., & Hoy, M. (2000). Dimensions of privacy concern among online consumers. *Journal of Public Policy & Marketing, 19*, 62-73.

Sivasailam, N., Kim, D., & Rao, H. R. (2002, May-June). What companies are(n't) doing about Web site assurance. *IEEE IT Professional*, pp. 33-40.

Spence, A. (1973). Job market signaling. *Quarterly Journal of Economics, 87*(3), 355-374.

Spence, A. (1974). *Market signaling: Informational transfer in hiring and related screening processes* (1st ed.). Cambridge, MA: Harvard University Press.

TRUSTe. (2005). *TRUSTe: Make privacy your choice.* Retrieved September 5, 2007, from http://www.truste.org/businesses/Web_privacy_seal.php

Veblen, T. (1899). *The theory of the leisure class.* New York: Macmillan.

Verisign. (2002). Retrieved September 5, 2007, from http://www.verisign.com

Zahavi, A. (1975). Mate selection: A selection for a handicap. *Journal of Theoretical Biology, 53*(1), 205-214.

Zucker, L. (1986). Production of trust: Institutional sources of economic structure: 1840-1920. In B. Staw & L. Cummings (Eds.), *Research in organizational behavior* (pp. 53-111). Greenwich, CT: JAI Press.

APPENDIX A: PARTIAL STUDY WEB SITE

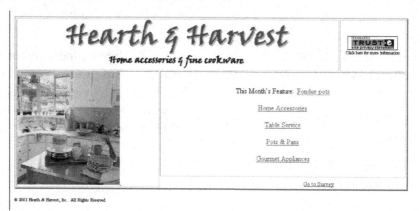

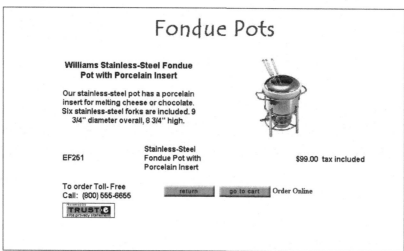

Chapter VIII

The King is Naked:
Discovering that Frequent Customers May Not be Your Best Friend

Luiz Antonio Joia
Brazilian School of Public and Business Administration-Getulio Vargas Foundation and Rio de Janeiro State University, Brazil

Paulo Sergio Sanz
Brazilian School of Public and Business Administration-Getulio Vargas Foundation, Brazil

ABSTRACT

The scope of this work is to explore the transaction profitability of frequent and sporadic buyers in the e-commerce arena. Evidence from relationship marketing literature stressing the impact of purchase frequency on customer profitability, as well as recent academic research challenging this approach and pointing out the importance of sporadic clients, are analyzed and presented. A single case study research methodology was chosen for this article, due to the exploratory facets associated with the subject and the industry under investigation. In order to gather relevant input to carry out this research, one of the largest retailing groups in Brazil was investigated. Conclusions are drawn showing that greater frequency of purchases does not necessarily translate into increased customer transaction profitability. Implications are presented, enabling practitioners and academics to grasp fully the real value of customers—both frequent and sporadic buyers—in order to develop coherent approaches for dealing with them adequately.

INTRODUCTION

Traditional marketing literature suggests that the benefits accrued from long-term relationships between firms and customers are greater than the returns reaped from short-term relationships. Conceptual evidence on this theory was collated from several researchers who have addressed the importance of retaining customers for corporate profitability (see, for instance: Kenny & Marshall,

2000; Kotler, 1999; McKenna, 1993; Peppers & Rogers, 1997; Reichheld, 2006; Reichheld & Sasser, 1990; Seybold, 1998).

Notwithstanding the perceived importance of frequent buyers, recent research has challenged this conventional approach, highlighting the fact that companies either fail to comprehend or assess correctly the true value associated with their customers, be they frequent or sporadic purchasers. This behavior may lead firms to make strategic mistakes as well as perpetuate managerial errors, such as high spending for retention of unprofitable customers or failing to perceive the importance of a high-value sporadic consumer (Dowling & Uncles, 1997; Reinartz & Kumar, 2000, 2002; Reinartz, Thomas, & Kumar, 2005; Schultz & Hayman, 1999).

The correct understanding of how to manage both frequent and sporadic buyers has assumed a truly important dimension, mainly in the **e-commerce** realm, due to the very high **churn rate** of customers in this arena. Reichheld and Shefter (2000) point out that up to 50% of consumers abandon an **e-retailing** company before the third year of their commercial relationship.

The impact of other issues related to the Internet regarding customer defection and transaction profitability is also relevant. The low **information asymmetry** generated by this technology makes customers far more aware of products and services, readily enabling them to search and locate where the best price can be found, thereby reducing **switching costs** (Smith, Bailey, & Brynjolfsson, 1999). According to Bakos (1997), if the **search cost** is low enough, buyers will tend to look for prices and products among all the available and potential sellers.

The scope of this research is to explore, in an empirical manner, the transaction profitability derived from sporadic and frequent customers in the home appliance **e-retailing** sector. The company analyzed is one of the largest retailing groups on the Brazilian market serving the major and minor appliance industry both through

conventional channels and via its Web site. Due to confidentiality issues, the name of the group was omitted from this chapter.

This study is divided into five sections. The first section identifies literature dealing with the relationship between customer retention and transaction profitability. The second section addresses the Brazilian environment with respect to Internet users and the e-commerce industry, comparing the latter to that of the U.S. The third section presents the research methodology used to gather and analyze data and discusses the criteria applied for categorizing clients according to their value to the company, as well as the inherent limitations of such criteria. In the fourth section, the evidence obtained is analyzed and the propositions about customer transaction profitability are tested. Finally, the last section summarizes and discusses the academic and managerial implications derived from the chapter's findings and also recommends further research tracks.

CUSTOMER RETENTION AND TRANSACTION PROFITABILITY

In relationship marketing literature, several authors have pointed out the beneficial impact of customer retention on corporate profitability. Kotler (1999) claims that the longer a client remains with a supplier, the more profitable this customer becomes. According to the aforementioned author, frequent buyers are more profitable for four main reasons: (a) they purchase more over the course of time; (b) the cost of serving a frequent client decreases with the passing of time; (c) satisfied consumers usually recommend the supplier favorably to others; and (d) frequent customers are less sensitive to price.

Day (1999) suggests that companies achieve higher profitability by building long-term relationships with their clients. Peppers and Rogers (1993) claim that there is only one way a business can guarantee its financial sustainability, namely by cultivating loyal and satisfied customers. These authors allege that the more purchases a consumer makes, the higher the profit margin obtained by the company. McKenna (1993) stresses this concept, stating that the development of strong ties with the customer is an effective way of leveraging the firm's competitive advantage.

Seybold (1998) ratifies these ideas, stating that when a company loses a client, it loses not only the potential profit that would be derived from this customer, but also the profits from the chain of consumers who hear the disgruntled customer's negative commentaries. Reichheld and Sasser (1990) declare that the loss of clients can have a greater impact on profitability than other traditional factors associated with a company's competitive advantage, such as market share and unit cost. According to these authors, the efficient management of customer retention is relevant in order to ensure that cumulative profits accrued from purchases made by clients supersede the investments made to acquire and retain them. In a later study, Reichheld and Teal (1996) state that businesses with a high rate of customer loss will face a difficult future, with reduced profits, slow growth, if any, and shorter life expectancy.

In view of the above, it is essential to assess the financial potential of all customers, in order to quantify their importance *vis-à-vis* corporate profitability. Kotler (1999) recommends the use of **LTV** (lifetime value) methodology, which depicts the total spending of customers within a specific product or service category, during their lives, irrespective of the company with which the business is transacted. According to Peppers and Rogers (1997), **LTV** represents the profit generated by clients minus the costs associated with their acquisition and retention, throughout the course of their relationship with a specific firm. Rust, Zeithmal, and Lemon (2000) point out that **LTV** is influenced by several factors, such as **cost of capital**, cross-selling, and word of mouth.

Stone (1984) suggests the use of recency, frequency, monetary value (RFM) metrics for classifying customers according to recency (time of most recent purchase), frequency (frequency/number of past purchases), and monetary value (ticket value per transaction). For the aforementioned author, the best customers, namely those who have the highest likelihood of buying again, are those who have purchased more recently, those who have purchased more frequently within a given time frame and those who have spent a sizeable sum of money.

These metrics seek to predict the financial potential of each consumer, according to the share-of-wallet concept, as the firm tries to increase its share in customer spending, rather than its share in the mass market (Sheth, Sisodia, & Sharma, 2000).

A relevant issue in customer retention is the acquisition cost. Relationship marketing theory often suggests that the cost of acquiring a new customer is five times greater than the cost involved in keeping an existing client satisfied. According to Goodman (1999), this metric originated from a study developed in 1984 by Technical Assistance Research Program (TARP), which sought to examine acquisition vs. retention cost in an automobile company in the U.S. Recent numbers from TARP suggest that the relationship between these two former variables can vary from 2:1 to 20:1, depending on the state of the economy and the industry analyzed (Goodman, 1999).

In the industry under scrutiny in this chapter, the acquisition cost is mainly concentrated in advertising, which belongs to the "Promotion" dimension of the traditional marketing mix (McCarthy, 1960). A report from CrossRoads (2001) indicates that the growth of advertising spending worldwide has been 30% greater than economic growth. According to this report, this pattern results from the belief companies have that continuous investment in advertising allows them to sustain their market share.

In marked contrast with the authors quoted, recent research has challenged the traditional methods adopted by most executives for retaining customers as well as the resulting managerial implications involved. Schultz and Hayman (1999) warn that if all the benefits accrued from customer retention claimed by firms were true, loyalty would not be so good for their clients, as they would be paying higher prices and advertising the company for free, in addition to receiving worse attention from the company.

Dowling and Uncles (1997) suggest that customer loyalty is probably a consequence of the industry within which the firm operates, as well as the power of brand name. According to them, investments in customer retention do not reap the desired benefits for the strategic positioning and brand equity of the company. Moreover, it is quite possible that these investments generate neither a significant rise in the number of frequent clients nor an increase in corporate profitability.

Some of the ideas of Dowling and Uncles (1997) tally with an empirical study conducted by Reinartz and Kumar (2000) in a catalog-based retailing company in the U.S. In this research, evidence was found which ran counter to some traditional concepts of relationship marketing, such as:

a. The relationship between customer lifetime and the corresponding firm's cumulative profitability was only verified, in a moderate way, with frequent higher-income clients—that is, merely a small percentage of all customers. Sporadic clients with higher incomes have higher LTV than those of frequent customers with lower incomes. The authors suggest that companies should not only focus on retaining clients—they must also develop effective tools to attract sporadic consumers.

b. The commercial transaction value diminishes during the course of the relationship between a company and its customers. Based on this statement, the notion that profits generated by frequent buyers always increase over the course of time is duly challenged.

c. As commercial transactions were analyzed individually, frequent customers were considered less profitable, both in terms of higher and lower income clients. In contrast with traditional relationship marketing literature, Reinartz and Kumar (2000) suggest that frequent buyers are more price-sensitive than sporadic purchasers.

d. The concept that servicing costs are lower for frequent customers was rejected. In order to back their theory, the authors used the ratio between mailing costs and customer revenues. The differences observed in the ratio between frequent and sporadic consumers were not statistically significant.

In a recent study, Reinartz and Kumar (2002) concluded that firms should not focus exclusively on their frequent clients. The above authors warn that mismanagement of customer retention can lead a company to make excessive investments in an attempt to retain unprofitable consumers, as well as undervalue the financial potential of sporadic buyers.

This issue is even more relevant when applied to **e-commerce**, where industry-specific characteristics influence customer defection and profitability. According to Smith et al. (1999), the reduced **information asymmetry** provided by electronic markets makes the customers more aware of their options, which leads to lower **search costs** for products and services. Bakos (1997) shows that if the **search cost** is low enough, buyers examine all products on offer and purchase the one that best suits their needs, resulting in decreased price premiums and customer profitability. Consequently, for customers, the decrease in **search cost** leads to lower **switching costs**, allowing them to change their allegiance to suppliers very easily.

THE SOCIAL AND ECONOMIC CONTEXT OF INTERNET USERS AND THE E-RETAILING INDUSTRY IN BRAZIL

Brazil is a federation with three levels of government:

- **Central:** Federal Government
- **Intermediary:** 27 states, plus the Federal District (Brasília, the capital of Brazil)
- **Local:** More than 5,500 municipalities with the constitutional status of autonomous members

The Federation was not created on a base-upward premise. Instead, it was based on consciousness about the perceived need to divide the unitary state. Furthermore, Brazil is a country with no significant cultural friction generated by differences of language, religion, or race. Most of the bibliography about Internet users addresses the **OECD** countries (OECD, 2002). Some developing countries, such as India, Brazil, Mexico, and so forth, use information technology in a very intensive way. This fact in itself may constitute a highly optimistic opportunity related to e-retailing initiatives. However, as these countries have large populations, absolute figures can lead the reader to misconceptions. If, for instance, one compares Canada and Brazil, it can be seen that while Brazil has almost the same number of Internet users as Canada, nearly 50% of the population of the latter is digitally included, whereas little more than 5% of the population of the former has access to the Internet (Joia, 2004).

The number of Internet users in Brazil is estimated at around 10 million. Thus, as stated earlier, it represents a very small percentage of the 180 million total population of a country whose GDP was close to US$588 billion in 2000 (Afonso, 2001; Neri, 2003). According to Afonso (2001), fixed-line telephones are the predominant option for Internet (62.5 million lines, of which

38.8 million are hard-wire and 23.7 are mobile cell phones). Individual services still only reach 39% of the population. Hence, reduced line access remains a limiting factor for Internet expansion, both for individual users and service providers. The high price for conventional telephone services represents another barrier in a country where the income per capita is around US$3,500 per year. Connections between the local and international **backbones** are still very expensive. Furthermore, **ISP**s do not offer local-line Internet connections in many small towns.

As may be imagined, the price of hardware is another obstacle to providing nationwide Internet access, since per-capita income in Brazil remains very low. Besides, the predominance of English-based content on Web sites limits accessibility to a very small percentage of the Brazilian population, namely those with the highest educational level. The lack of training, not just to deal with the Internet, but also to provide support to infrastructure as well as to develop new services and software is another obstacle in Brazil.

Furthermore, all of these issues constitute an environment that fosters digital inequalities. Most of these inequalities are merely the consequence of longstanding social and economic disparities in Brazil (Joia, 2004). Nonetheless, **e-retailing** sales grew by 80% in Brazil between the first six months of 2005 and the same period in 2006, totaling nearly US$1,750 million, according to figures released by the Brazilian Chamber of Electronic Commerce (E-bit, 2006), whereas the retailing industry as a whole in Brazil grew by only 11.8% during the same period, according to the Brazilian Institute of Geography and Statistics (IBGE, 2006). According to E-bit (2006), only 3.1% of the whole Brazilian population has made at least one online purchase to date. The average monthly income per household of these customers is US$1,674, and their average age is 35. More than 50% of these B2C consumers are male and 57% of them have an undergraduate degree.

Interestingly, when compared with the U.S., Brazil is in a slightly better position with regard to the **e-commerce** realm, according to data from the U.S. Census Bureau (2004) stating that e-retailing sales in the U.S. grew by 23.1% between the second quarter of 2003 and the second quarter of 2004, while the total retailing industry grew by 7.8% over the same period. Besides, e-commerce sales in the second quarter of 2004 in the U.S. accounted for 1.7% of total sales. As we have seen, the main problem in Brazil is not related to percentage figures (which are better than those in the U.S.). It has more to do with the absolute number of consumers on the Web, due to the heavy digital gap prevailing in Brazil.

RESEARCH METHODOLOGY

In order to gather relevant input to carry out this research, one of the largest retailing groups in Brazil was investigated. The firm's **database** was analyzed quantitatively to assess the transaction profitability derived from sporadic and frequent customers purchasing via the company's digital channel, namely its Web site. A single case research methodology was chosen for this chapter, due to the exploratory facets associated with the subject and the industry investigated, in order to reveal relevant and updated information for practitioners, executives, and academics.

This is an instrumental case study, where a particular object is examined in order to offer enhanced understanding about some question or theory (Eisenhardt, 1989; Stake, 1994). According to Yin (1994, pp. 40-41), a single case design is appropriate when it serves an innovative purpose, where an observer may gain access to a phenomenon that was previously inaccessible. In particular, this work presents two aspects that were previously inaccessible to scientific investigation, namely the real transaction profit margins of sporadic and frequent buyers (previous research merely estimated the profitability of

transactions) and transposition of the customer transaction profitability discussion to the Brazilian B2C arena.

Due to the characteristics of the products commercialized, namely major and minor home appliances (see Santos & Costa, 1997, for more information about this segment), this research is based on the premise that customers may only be considered frequent buyers if they make at least one purchase during every 12-month period. These are the same criteria adopted by the firm under analysis to categorize its frequent customers. The company was selected because it sells a broad range of products throughout the year, without seasonal variations in supply and demand. The analysis includes all customers who made purchases between the day the firm's Web site was inaugurated (July 1, 1999) and the day on which the data was extracted from the **database** (December 31, 2002).

The statistical tests that supported the conclusions drawn in this research were based on analysis of variance (**ANOVA**) and **linear regression** of the data collected, developed with a **significance level** of 5% ($\alpha = 0.05$), performed by **SPSS**. From a total of 149,062 customers, a sample of 14,906 buyers was selected at random (10% of the total), of which 10,421 were sporadic consumers and 4,482 were frequent purchasers.

The real value of all the monetary amounts involved in this research was calculated using the inflation rate during the 42 months under analysis (Rossi, 1997). The investigation conducted does not take into account customer acquisition costs, as the amounts for each specific client are not considered by the company under scrutiny.

The quantitative analysis dealt with the following selected attributes:

a. **Purchase frequency:** Number of purchases made by customers throughout their commercial relationship with the company via the Web site

b. **Average profit:** Average profit accrued from purchases made by clients throughout the course of their commercial relationship with the company via the Web site

c. **Average ticket:** Average value of purchases made by customers throughout their commercial relationship with the company via the Web site

Finally, as stated earlier, the customers were divided into two main groups: sporadic and frequent buyers. They were all classified according to their average ticket and segmented according to the **Pareto Analysis**, as suggested by Roos (cited in Chatzkel, 2002, p. 111) and Reinartz and Kumar (2000), as presented in Table 1.

Methodology Limitations

It is important to stress some limitations associated with the methodology adopted in this study. The first limitation refers to the premise that frequent customers of home appliances are clients who make at least one purchase during every 12-month period. The lack of literature clearly addressing the concept of how to define a frequent client within different industries led the authors to use the same criteria as those adopted by the firm under analysis. The second limitation is the fact that the data refer to the period between July 1999 and December 2002 (42 months), which might be considered a relatively short period of observation. Furthermore, customer segmentations other than the Pareto Analysis might have been taken into consideration. In fact, the customer's ticket value

was the major element considered for analyzing customer behavior in this virtual organization.

Another issue involves the research methodology chosen. A single case study presents considerable limitations in terms of generalization (**external validity**), especially in instrumental cases, where the analysis is restricted to the elements tested (in this case, anomalies in the transaction profitability of frequent customers). However, the firm under scrutiny revealed its profit margins for analysis, and this facet proved to be highly relevant and revealing as explained in the next section. The last important limitation is the impossibility of calculating total client profitability, since the costs of customer acquisition and retention are not computed by the firm under scrutiny. Consequently, this research deals exclusively with customer transaction profitability.

DATA ANALYSIS AND FINDINGS

As stated earlier, the researchers in this study were granted access to individualized transaction profit margins, discounting taxes and the **cost of capital** (financing taxes, credit card commissions, etc.), allowing them to calculate customer transaction profitability in a more reliable way than had been possible in previous research that sought to estimate the profitability of commercial transactions (see, for instance, Reinartz & Kumar, 2000, p. 23). In line with the empirical and theoretical background herein exposed, this work set out to test, quantitatively, four propositions concerning the profitability derived from sporadic and frequent customers in the e-retailing realm.

Table 1. Customer segmentation

Category	Description
Sporadic 20%	Sporadic consumers with the highest 20% average ticket
Sporadic 80%	Other sporadic consumers
Frequent 20%	Frequent customers with the highest 20% average ticket
Frequent 80%	Other frequent customers

Proposition 1. *The transaction profit of frequent customers increases as they purchase more frequently.*

Regressions were used to analyze the commercial transaction **mark-up** as dependent on the purchase frequency of each frequent customer in order to test this hypothesis. The regressions took the two segments of frequent customers into account (Pareto 20% and 80%). Table 2 summarizes this analysis, where the sign of the coefficient indicates the type of relationship between transaction profitability and purchase frequency (positive or negative).

From the regressions, it can be seen that the coefficient is negative (-6.18) for the segment of frequent customers with the highest average ticket (Pareto 20%), indicating an inverse relationship between transaction profit and customer purchasing frequency. In the other segment of frequent buyers (Pareto 80%), the coefficient is 0.34, indicating that transaction profitability increases slightly as more purchases are made by customers. In other words, this proposition cannot be supported for the frequent buyers with the highest average ticket (Pareto 20%).

Proposition 2. *The average ticket of frequent customers increases as they buy more frequently.*

Regressions were used to analyze the ticket value as dependent on the purchase frequency of each frequent client in order to test this hypothesis. The regressions took the two segments of frequent customers into account (Pareto 20% and 80%). Table 3 summarizes this analysis, where the sign of the coefficient indicates the type of relationship between ticket value and purchase frequency (positive or negative).

The coefficient is negative (-17.86) for the segment of frequent customers with the highest average ticket (Pareto 20%), indicating an inverse relationship between ticket value and customer purchasing frequency. In the other segment of frequent buyers (Pareto 80%), the coefficient is -0.02, indicating that the average ticket decreases only slightly as more purchases are made by clients. In other words, this proposition cannot be supported for all frequent customers using the digital sales channel of the firm investigated.

Proposition 3. *Frequent customers purchase more profitable products than sporadic consumers.*

For this test, the average **mark-up** of frequent and sporadic consumers within each segment (Pareto 20% and 80%) are compared. The analysis of variance is presented in Table 4.

Table 2. Regressions of transaction profitability as a function of purchase frequency

	R^2	Coefficients	Std Error	t Stat	P-value
Frequent 20%	0.74	-6.18	1.38	-4.46	< 0.01
Frequent 80%	0.56	0.34	0.12	2.76	< 0.05

Table 3. Regressions of average ticket as a function of purchase frequency

	R^2	Coefficients	Std Error	t Stat	P-value
Frequent 20%	0.63	-17.86	5.12	-3.48	< 0.05
Frequent 80%	0.51	-0.02	0.01	-2.49	< 0.05

Table 4. ANOVA: Average mark-up of frequent and sporadic customers

	Mark-up of Frequent Customers	Mark-up of Sporadic Customers	F Calc	P-value	F Crit
Pareto 20%	R$ 80.34	R$ 86.07	0.62	0.43	3.84
Pareto 80%	R$ 16.40	R$ 14.92	31.61	< 0.01	3.84

The low value of "F Calc" for the segment of buyers with the highest average ticket (Pareto 20%) indicates that the difference between averages is not significant. In the other segment of consumers (Pareto 80%), frequent clients present a higher transaction profit (R$16.40, approximately US$5.86) than the respective value associated with sporadic buyers (R$14.92, approximately US$5.33). Such evidence seems not to support Proposition 3, as the statement that frequent customers buy more profitable products than sporadic purchasers could not be verified for those consumers with the highest ticket value (Pareto 20%).

Proposition 4. *Frequent customers purchase more expensive products than sporadic buyers.*

For this test, the average tickets of frequent and sporadic consumers within each segment (Pareto 20% and 80%) are compared. The analysis of variance is presented in Table 5.

The high value of "F Calc" for all segments indicates that the difference between averages is significant. In the segment of buyers with the highest ticket (Pareto 20%), sporadic consumers present a higher average transaction value (R$455.43, approximately US$162.65) than the respective value associated with frequent customers

with the highest ticket (R$375.54, approximately US$134.12). This evidence led the researchers not to support Proposition 4, as the statement that frequent customers buy more expensive products than sporadic purchasers could not be verified for those consumers with the highest ticket value (Pareto 20% segment).

DISCUSSION AND FUTURE RESEARCH

The empirical evidence revealed by this study ratifies some of the findings presented by Reinartz and Kumar (2000), which was the main research stream used in the theoretical framework of this chapter. According to Campbell and Stanley (1963), the generalization of evidence transposed to different scenarios, populations, and moments is an important factor for improving the external validity of the research.

The following findings are presented in this chapter:

- The analysis of Proposition 1 showed that the profit associated with transactions made by frequent customers with the highest average ticket (Pareto 20%) decreases progressively over the course of their purchasing history.

Table 5. ANOVA: Average tickets of frequent and sporadic customers

	Ticket of Frequent Customers	Ticket of Sporadic Customers	F Calc	P-value	F Crit
Pareto 20%	R$ 375.54	R$ 455.43	34.05	< 0.01	3.84
Pareto 80%	R$ 126.62	R$ 103.71	449.61	< 0.01	3.84

This finding allows the researchers to challenge the contention that customer retention always enables firms to obtain a premium price, as suggested by relationship marketing theories (Brondmo, 2000; Day, 1999; Kotler, 1999; Peppers & Rogers, 1993; Reichheld & Teal, 1996).

- The test of Proposition 2 showed that the average ticket of frequent customers decreases as they purchase more frequently. This finding is directly opposed to some conceptual evidence from relationship marketing theories (Brondmo, 2000; Day, 1999; Kotler, 1999; Peppers & Rogers, 1993; Reichheld & Teal, 1996).

- The test of Proposition 3 showed that it is not true to say that frequent customers always purchase more profitable products than sporadic consumers, as stated in relationship marketing literature (Brondmo, 2000; Kotler, 1999; McKenna, 1993; Reichheld & Teal, 1996). This evidence cannot be supported for those consumers who purchase products with the highest average ticket (Pareto 20%).

- The test of Proposition 4 challenges traditional marketing literature, which contends that frequent customers always purchase more expensive products than sporadic consumers (Brondmo, 2000; Kotler, 1999; McKenna, 1993; Reichheld & Teal, 1996). This proposition cannot be supported for frequent buyers with the highest ticket value (Pareto 20%).

The evidence presented above does not invalidate the importance of frequent customers for firms. The key question seems to be to understand why and when transaction profitability associated with sporadic purchasers can be higher than that derived from frequent buyers. For traditional sales channels, this phenomenon might be explained by the increase in customer bargaining power (Porter, 1980). However, there is no possibility of price negotiation via the e-retailing channel of the company under analysis. In this case, the reduction of **information asymmetry** and increased access to market information afforded by the Internet could make it easier for frequent customers to reduce **transaction cost** and become aware of promotions (Bakos, 1997; Smith et al., 1999). Hence, it is important to investigate the anomalies revealed here in other sectors of e-retailing, in order to better understand the kind of factors that influence the transaction profitability of frequent and sporadic consumers on the Web. In other words, it would seem to be of paramount importance to analyze the influence of managerial practices on the transaction profitability of frequent and sporadic customers. Marketing and e-commerce literature abounds with innumerable managerial approaches associated with profitable relationships between firms and clients (see, for instance, Bakos, 1997; Brown, Tilton, & Woodside, 2002; Mitra & Lynch, 1996; Homburg, Workman, & Jensen, 2000; Kotha, Rajgopal, & Venkatachalam, 2004, to name but a few). Future research could replicate the quantitative methodology adopted here, and also include qualitative elements that convey to different marketing *praxis*. Following this line of reasoning, it is suggested that five practices accrued from relationship marketing literature should be tracked in further studies, as presented below:

a. **Supply of homogenous or differentiated products:** Alba, Lynch, Weitz, Janiszewski, Lutz, Sawyer, and Wood (1997) contend that price plays a highly relevant role when products are easily comparable. Consequently, utilization of differentiated products assures greater profitability for the retailer. Concomitantly, Lynch and Ariely (2000) point to empirical evidence showing that price sensitivity is reduced by offering differentiated products and increased by the supply of homogenous goods.

b. **Product dissemination strategy:** According to Mitra and Lynch (1996), dissemination of information not related to price favors a decision based on quality, thereby helping consumers select products which best suit specific desires and needs. Bakos (1997) adds that greater qualitative information transparency may mitigate the importance of price, thereby ensuring higher profitability for electronic retailers.

c. **Customizing communications with clients:** Conceptual evidence suggests that e-mail customization results in higher profitability for e-retailers (Chen & Sudhir, 2004). This tactic allows the implementation of differentiated offers, exploiting the individual potential of each consumer, respecting areas of interest, periods, and frequency of communication.

d. **Marketing orientation adopted:** To Day and Montgomery (1999), the more firms change the focus of their marketing approach from products to clients, the more they begin to gain full insight into the habits and needs of their consumers. Homburg et al. (2000) contend that a strategy geared to clients enables the companies to exploit their financial potential in an efficient way.

e. **Customer retention mechanisms:** According to Schouten and McAlexander (1995), one of the most important tactics for developing relationship marketing is based on the creation of communities of customers, gathering clients that share the same values and behavior patterns. Brown et al. (2002) show empirically how the construction of a solid structure of virtual communities represents an important source of profit in electronic retailing. For their part, Bolton, Kannan, and Bramlet (2000) point out that clients involved in loyalty programs pay little heed to negative evaluations of a given company *vis-à-vis* its competitors. Kotha et al. (2004) show a positive association between the market value of firms and the existence of relationship services, such as virtual communities and the personalization of Web sites.

Therefore, if it can be proven that the company under analysis does not take these critical success factors into consideration, it might be possible to understand why frequent customers are not performing better than sporadic buyers, thereby validating the marketing relationship theory via the Web.

In other words, qualitative analysis is needed in order to investigate whether the firm under analysis is complying with the best managerial *praxis* accrued from the marketing relationship theory developed for virtual organizations. It can be speculated that these anomalies might be the effects of managerial practices that are at odds with those one would expect to find in a world-class digital store. These are, undoubtedly, the next research tracks to be pursued.

REFERENCES

Afonso, J. R. (2001, April). E-government in Brazil: Experiences and perspectives. In *Forum of Federations,* Montreal, Canada.

Alba, J., Lynch, J., Weitz, B., Janiszewski, C., Lutz, R., Sawyer, A., & Wood, S. (1997). Interactive home shopping: Consumer, retailer, and manufacturers incentives to participate in electronic marketplaces. *Journal of Marketing, 61,* 38-53.

Bakos, J. Y. (1997). Reducing buyer search costs: Implications for electronic marketplaces. *Management Science, 43*(12), 1676-1692.

Bolton, R., Kannan, P., & Bramlet, M. (2000). Implications of loyalty program membership and service experiences for customer retention and value. *Journal of the Academy of Marketing Science, 28*(1), 95-108.

Brondmo, H. P. (2000). *The engaged customer. The new rules of Internet direct marketing.* New York: Harper Business.

Brown, S., Tilton, A., & Woodside, D. (2002). The case for on-line communities. *The McKinsey Quarterly, 1.*

Campbell, D. T., & Stanley, J. C. (1963). *Experimental and quasi-experimental designs for research.* Chicago: Rand McNally.

Chatzkel, J. (2002). A Conversation with Göran Roos. *Journal of Intellectual Capital, 3*(2), 96-117.

Chen, Y., & Sudhir, K. (2004). When shopbots meet emails: Implications for price competition on the Internet. *Quantitative Marketing and Economics, 2,* 233-255.

Crossroads. (2001). *A sector report: Consumer products.*

Day, G. (1999). *The market driven organization.* New York: Free Press.

Day, G., & Montgomery, D. (1999). Charting new directions for marketing [Special issue]. *Journal of Marketing, 63,* 3-13.

Dowling, G., & Uncles, M. (1997). Do customers loyalty programs really work? *Sloan Management Review, 38*(4), 71-82.

E-bit. (2004, August). *Web shoppers* (10th ed.). Retrieved September 5, 2007, from http://www.webshoppers.com.br/webshoppers.asp

Eisenhardt, K. M. (1989). Building theories from case study research. *Academy of Management Review, 14,* 532-550.

Goodman, J. (1999). *Basic facts on customer complaint behavior and the impact of service on the bottom line.* TARP.

Homburg, C., Workman, J., & Jensen, O. (2000). Fundamental changes in marketing organization: The movement toward a customer-focused organizational structure. *Journal of the Academy of Marketing Science, 28*(4), 459-478.

IBGE. (2004, November). *Monthly survey of commerce.* Retrieved September 7, 2007, from the Brazilian Institute of Geography and Statistics, http://www.ibge.gov.br/home/estatistica/indicadores/comercio/pmc

Joia, L. A. (2004). Bridging the digital divide: Some initiatives in Brazil. *International Journal of Electronic Government, 1*(3), 300-315.

Kenny, D., & Marshall, J. (2000, November-December). Contextual marketing: The real business of the Internet. *Harvard Business Review,* pp. 119-125.

Kotha, S., Rajgopal, S., & Venkatachalam, M. (2004). The role of online buying experience as a competitive advantage: Evidence from third-party ratings for e-commerce firms. *Journal of Business, 77*(2), 100-134.

Kotler, P. (1999). *How to create, win, and dominate markets.* New York: Free Press.

Lynch, J., & Ariely, D. (2000). Wine online: Search costs affect competition on price, quality, and distribution. *Marketing Science, 19*(1), 83-103.

McCarthy, E. J. (1960). *Basic marketing: A managerial approach.* R. D. Irwin.

McKenna, R. (1993). *Relationship marketing: Successful strategies for the age of the customer.* Cambridge: Perseus Publishing.

Mitra, A., & Lynch, J. (1996). Advertising effects on consumer welfare: Prices paid and liking for brands selected. *Marketing Letters, 7*(1), 19-29.

Neri, M. (2003). *Mapa da Exclusão Digital.* Retrieved September 7, 2007, from Centro de Políticas Sociais, EPGE/FGV, http://epge.fgv.br/portal/pesquisa/livros/2003.html

OECD. (2002). *Measuring the information economy 2002.* Retrieved September 7, 2007, from http://www.oecd.org/document/5/0,2340,en_2649_37409_2765701_1_1_1_37409,00.html

Peppers, D., & Rogers, M. (1993). *The one to one future: Building relationships one customer at a time.* New York: Doubleday.

Peppers, D., & Rogers, M. (1997). *Enterprise one to one: Tools for competing in the interactive age.* New York: Doubleday.

Porter, M. E. (1980). *Competitive strategy: Techniques for analyzing industries and competitors.* New York: Free Press.

Reichheld, F. (2006). *The ultimate question: Driving good profits and true growth.* Boston: Harvard Business School Press.

Reichheld, F., & Sasser, W. E. (1990, September-October). Zero defections: Quality comes to services. *Harvard Business Review*, pp. 105-111.

Reichheld, F., & Schefter, P. (2000, July-August). E-loyalty: Your secret weapon on the Web. *Harvard Business Review*, pp. 105-113.

Reichheld, F., & Teal, T. (1996). *The loyalty effect: The hidden force behind growth, profits, and lasting value.* Boston: Harvard Business School Press.

Reinartz, W., & Kumar, V. (2000). On the profitability of long-life customers in a noncontractual setting: An empirical investigation and implications for marketing. *Journal of Marketing, 64,* 17-35.

Reinartz, W., & Kumar, V. (2002, July). The mismanagement of customer loyalty. *Harvard Business Review*, pp. 86-94.

Reinartz, W., Thomas, J., & Kumar, V. (2005). Balancing acquisition and retention resources to maximize customer profitability. *Journal of Marketing, 69,* 63-79.

Rossi, J. W. (1997). A guide for present value models. *Institute of Applied Economic Research,* Text nº 482.

Rust, R. T., Zeithmal, V. A., & Lemon, K. N. (2000). *Driving customer equity: How customer lifetime value is reshaping corporate strategy.* New York: Free Press.

Santos, A. M., & Costa, C. S. (1997). General characteristics of retail in Brazil. *National Bank for Social and Economic Development, Setorial nº 5.*

Schouten, J., & McAlexander, J. (1995). Subcultures of consumption: An ethnography of the new bikers. *Journal of Consumer Research, 22*(1), 43-61.

Schultz, D., & Hayman, D. (1999, April). The two sides of loyalty. *Interactive Marketing.*

Seybold, P. B. (1998). *Customers.com: How to create a profitable business strategy for the Internet and beyond.* Auckland: Random House Publishing.

Sheth, J. N., Sisodia, R. S., & Sharma, A. (2000, Winter). The antecedents and consequences of customer-centric marketing. *Journal of the Academy of Marketing Science, 28*(2).

Smith, M. D., Bailey, J., & Brynjolfsson, E. (1999). Understanding digital markets: Review and assessment. In E. Brynjolfsson & B. Kahin (Eds.), *Understanding the digital economy: Data, tools, and research* (pp. 99-136). Cambridge, MA: MIT Press.

Stake, R. E. (1994). Case studies. In N. K. Denzin & Y. S. Lincoln (Eds.), *Handbook of qualitative research.* Thousand Oaks: Sage.

Stone, B. (1984). *Successful direct marketing methods* (3rd ed.). Lincolnwood: NTC Publishing.

U.S. Census Bureau. (2004, February). *Retail e-commerce sales in second quarter 2004*. Retrieved September 7, 2007, from the Department of Commerce News, http://www.census.gov/mrts/www/ecom.pdf

Yin, R. (1994). *Case study research: Design and methods*. Beverly Hills, CA: Sage.

Chapter IX
The Effect of Information Satisfaction and Relational Benefit on Consumer's Online Shopping Site Commitment

Chung-Hoon Park
Samsung SDS, Korea

Young-Gul Kim
KAIST, Korea

ABSTRACT

The critical determinant of consumers' commitment to online shopping sites is the information features on a given Web site because online shopping consumers cannot touch or smell the products as they usually do in traditional retail outlets. Customers have to base their judgments on the product information presented on the Web sites. To investigate the relationship between information features and consumers' loyalty to a Web site, we have developed two constructs affecting consumer's commitment to online shopping sites. The first construct indicates the consumer's overall evaluation of the online site and the second is the relational benefit of psychological perception about an online site. Results of the online survey with 1,278 Korean customers of online bookstores and ticketing services indicate that information quality, user interface quality, and security perceptions affect information satisfaction and relational benefit. These, in turn, are significantly related to each consumer's commitment to a site. Information satisfaction and relational benefit have a mediating role between online shopping sites' information service quality and site commitment. The effect of information satisfaction and relational benefit appear differently with online bookstores and ticketing services.

INTRODUCTION

As a new marketing channel, the Internet differs from the traditional retail formats in many ways.

A unique characteristic of online shopping is that consumers cannot touch or smell the products, as they might do in traditional retail outlets. Customers have to base their judgments on product information presented on the Web sites. That is, consumer purchases are mainly based on appearance such as pictures, images, quality information, and video clips of the product, and not on the actual experience (Hong, Thong, & Tam, 2005; Kolesar & Galbraith, 2000). Shopping at an online store is like shopping through a paper catalog because both involve mail delivery of the purchases and in both cases customers cannot touch or smell the items (Lighter & Eastman, 2002). So the promise of e-commerce and online shopping depends, to a great extent, on user interfaces and how people interact with computers (Griffith, Krampf, & Palmer, 2001, Hong et al., 2005). Moreover, the characteristics of information presentation, navigation, and order fulfillment in an interactive shopping medium are considered more important factors in building e-commerce trust than in traditional retailing (Alba, Lynch, Weitz, Janiszewski, Lutz, Sawyer, & Wood, 1997; Reynolds, 2000).

However, while the information content of Web sites is an important determinant of consumers' online shopping behavior, there is little empirical research on how the information features affect consumers loyalty to a Web based shopping site. Research conducted in a non-Western social context is limited. Therefore, this research addresses the important issue of how the information features affect consumers' loyalty to commercial Web sites and provides both theoretical and empirical analyses to explain consumers' commitment to an online site in a non-Western social context, especially Korea.

This study starts with the review of previous research of online shopping site attributes through information and explains how the information features affect consumers' commitment to commercial Web sites. Later we show how we have developed and validated a research model by collecting and analyzing Web survey data with Korean consumer respondents.

LITERATURE REVIEW

Many studies have looked into online shopping service attributes (Jarvenpaa & Todd, 1997; Liu & Arnett, 2000; Lohse & Spiller, 1998; Szmanski & Hise, 2000). These studies have classified the attributes of online stores into four categories: merchandise, customer service and promotions, navigation and convenience, and security. These studies have not recognized, however, that the information aspects of these service attributes result in consumer commitment to shopping Web sites. In this section, we therefore show, for each category of service attributes, the importance of information for achieving consumer Web site loyalty.

Merchandising includes product related characteristics such as assortment, variety, and product information. Rich product assortment can increase the probability that consumer needs will be met and satisfied. But not all products available in the merchant's catalog or real store are available online (Szymanski & Hise, 2000). According to Lohse and Spiller's (1997) study, big online stores are less effective than small stores at converting site traffic into sales because consumers have difficulty in finding the products they seek. It is argued that since a primary role of an online store is to provide price-related information and product information to help reduce consumers' search cost (Bakos, 1997), more extensive and higher quality information available online leads to better buying decisions and higher levels of consumer satisfaction (Lightner & Estman, 2002; Peterson, Balasubramanian, & Bronnenberg, 1997). Online shopping stores can offer hyperlinks to more extensive product information such as price comparison, product testimonials (e.g., book reviews at an online book store), and product demonstrations (e.g., software downloads).

The second attribute category for an online store is customer service and promotion. Customers want careful, continuous, useful communication, across geographic barriers (Lohse & Spiller, 1998). These attributes are frequently identified as a salient dimension to determine the store choice behavior in both online and offline stores (Jarvenpaa & Todd, 1997; Kolesar & Galbraith, 2000). Customer service includes sales clerk service for merchandise selection, answers to frequently asked questions, and credit, return, and payment policies. Customers want help with product selection, gift services, contact information for sales representatives, a FAQ section for speedy answers, and information about shipping and handling costs. Promotions involve advertising and sales events that attract customers such as frequent buyer schemes, lottery games, and product-related tips.

The third attribute category is navigation and convenience. This is related to the user interface of an online store (Szymanski & Hise, 2000). Store layout, organization features, as well as ease of use are considered in this category. Since the user interface of an online store influences the experience of consumers interacting with a retailer's product or service offering (Griffith et al., 2001), a well-designed user interface system may reduce consumers' cost of searching and the time required for information processing. That is, it will minimize the effort needed to perform choice and purchasing tasks (Hoque & Lohse, 1999). Online shopping is thought to be pleasurable and satisfying to consumers when the retailer sites are fast, uncluttered, and easy-to-navigate. Uncluttered and easy-to-navigate sites economize shopping time and the cognitive effort consumers expend figuring out how to shop effectively online (Szymanski & Hise, 2000). Moreover, general help functions might assist users to find a particular topic in the documentation. Help functions also include information about navigating the store or the use of ordering features like a shopping cart function. Most online shopping stores provide a product search engine, site map, and navigation

sequence guidance function to help consumers' searching and purchasing.

Finally, security of online transactions continues to dominate the discussions on e-commerce (Elliot & Fowell, 2000; Liao & Cheung, 2001; Szymanski & Hise, 2000). Consumers are concerned about disclosing their private and financial information (Malhotra, Kim, & Agarwal, 2004). While most online shopping sites provide personal information a privacy protection policy and guarantee for transaction security, they do not offer detailed information on how transaction and personal data are secured (Gauzente, 2004). Recent research suggests that consumer decisions to adopt e-commerce involve not only perceptions of the technology (e.g., perceived usefulness and ease of use, as mentioned above), but also beliefs about the e-vendors (Liu, Marchewka, Lu, & Yu, 2004; Yang & Fand, 2004). Similarly, the perceived risk of having one's personal identity or financial information stolen by hackers can deter Web site use. Thus, a lack of trust in the technical institutional environments surrounding the Web can also hinder e-commerce adoption (Liu et al., 2004; Malhotra et al., 2004). Web vendors must act purposefully to overcome consumer perceptions of uncertainty and risk by building trust both in their own Web sites and in the broader Internet environment.

Eventually, it can be seen that these four attributes of online shopping sites are about how to provide relevant information to meet consumers' needs for decision making in purchasing. Thus, the discussion about the critical factors in consumers' loyalty to online shopping store needs to be focused on the availability of information (Wolfinbarger & Gilly, 2001). The availability of information considers not only product or service information but also convenience and personalization for retaining customers. It depends on the degree to which information can be employed by consumers to predict their probable satisfaction with subsequent purchases. By cultivating their customer database and proactively offering desired information, a company is inviting a customer to come back (Srinivasan, Anderson, & Ponnavolu, 2002). Consequently, the success of online stores will be determined by the ability to tailor their information to meet the consumers' needs (DeLone & McLean, 2005). But, several factors determine the predictive value of the information with no one type of information to be uniformly valued by all consumers (Kolesar & Galbraith, 2000).

The basic requirement for inducing a consumer to become a customer of an online store and increasing the switching cost is to reduce the cost of information search and to maximize the predictability of product quality by providing tailored information to consumers (Bakos, 1991, 1997). Although the consumer may receive a tangible good at the end of the online transaction, the benefits to the consumer are not in the purchased good, which could have been obtained through alternative channels (Kolesar & Galbraith, 2000). Instead, the unique benefits to the consumer are in the performance of the online shopping transaction

itself such as saved time, increased convenience, and reduced risk of dissatisfaction (Wolfinbarger & Gilly, 2001).

RESEARCH MODEL AND HYPOTHESES

We have focused on the information features, provided by Web sites as consumer evaluation of online service quality and developed a research model of consumer's commitment to an online shopping store. Information quality dimensions have been adapted as antecedents from user information satisfaction in information service (IS) literature and site awareness from marketing literature. As dependent variables, we use site commitment from relationship marketing literature. As mediating variables to affect consumer's relational attitude, we introduce consumer information satisfaction and relational benefits. We describe the research model in Figure 1. Conceptualization of variables and hypotheses are explained.

Figure 1. Research model

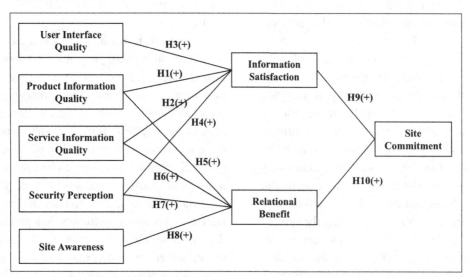

Information Satisfaction

Information satisfaction refers to consumers' dis/satisfaction with an overall information service encounter (Crosby & Stephens, 1987), which means navigating through Web pages and contents in an online service context. This is different from the overall satisfaction that refers to the consumers' overall evaluation of an organization based on all encounters and experiences with that particular organization (Jones & Suh, 2000). In this study, we have conceptualized information satisfaction as "an emotional reaction to the experience provided by the overall information service" (adapted from Westbrook et al., 1983).

According to the information systems literature, information quality and user interface quality are believed to affect user information satisfaction (DeLone & McLean, 2005; Wang & Strong, 1996). Information provided by the online store is divided into product information and service information. Product information includes product attribute information, consumer recommendations, evaluation reports, and so forth. Service information that most online stores provide includes membership information, FAQs, ordering and delivery information, and promotion.

To evaluate product and service information, we adopted six components of information quality from user information satisfaction research. They are relevancy, recency, sufficiency, playfulness, consistency, and understandability (DeLone & McLean, 2005; Moon & Kim, 2001; Wang & Strong, 1996). Information presented by online stores should support customer service and product search. Such information should be helpful and relevant in predicting the quality and utility of a product or service (Wolfinbarger & Gilly, 2001). To satisfy consumers' information needs, such information should be up-to-date in presenting products and services, sufficient to help consumers make a choice, consistent in representing and formatting the content, and easy to understand (McKinney, Yoon, & Zahedi, 2002;

Wang & Strong, 1996; Zhang, Keeling, & Pavur, 2000). Enjoyment, entertainment, and humor are important factors to form consumer's revisiting intention to Web sites (Childers, Carr, Peck, & Carson, 2001; Koufaris, 2002; O'Cass & Fenech, 2003). Therefore, playfulness is a salient factor in the presentation Web-based information.

H1: *There is a positive relationship between information satisfaction and product information quality.*

H2: *There is a positive relationship between information satisfaction and service information quality.*

User interface quality is related to system layout, navigation sequence, and convenience to search for a product or information, or simply to browse (Hong et al., 2004; McKinney et al., 2002; Molla & Licker, 2001; Szymanski & Hise, 2000). Since purchasing transaction can be adversely influenced by the poor online store design, it is essential to understand the effects of different layouts, and organizational, browsing, and navigation features on consumers' behavioral intentions (Hong et al., 2004; Lohse & Spiller, 1998). Online stores facilitate consumers' navigation by providing features such as search functions, guided navigation, and site maps. So in this research, we developed items corresponding to ease of navigation and convenience of searching for and ordering products as user interface quality measures.

H3: *There is a positive relationship between information satisfaction and user interface quality.*

Another important factor affecting information satisfaction in the Web environment is security. Consumers are concerned about online payment security, reliability, and the privacy policy of the online store (Gefen, 2000). So, security is a critical factor in acquiring and retaining consumers as online shopping service users. Basically, security concerns in e-commerce can be divided into concerns about user authentication and concerns about data and transaction security (Elliot & Fowell, 2000; Gauzente, 2004; Liu et al., 2004; Szymanski & Hise, 2000). According to prior research, as perception of security risk decreases, satisfaction with the information service of online stores is expected to increase.

H4: *There is a positive relationship between information satisfaction and security perception.*

Relational Benefit

In a traditional commercial service relationship, prior research has shown that relational benefit is an antecedent to building a long-term relationship (Gwinner, Gremmler, & Bitner, 1998; Patterson & Smith, 2001; Ravald & Gronroos, 1996). According to Gwinner et al. (1998), relational benefit is defined as "the benefit customers receive from long-term relationships above and beyond the core service performance." The literature suggests that an important part of relational benefit is the sense of reduced anxiety, trust, and confidence that customers experience. Trust is a key-mediating variable in relational exchanges (Garbarino & Johnson, 1999; Morgan & Hunt, 1994), and risk reduction is a key outcome of the service relationships (Berry, 1995). Although this sense of confidence and trust may be inextricably tied to the quality of the core service, it is perceived as the independent benefit of a long-term relationship (Ravald & Grönroos, 1996).

Based on the previous discussion of relational benefit, we focused on the role of risk reduction, minimization of information search and transaction cost, and cognitive consistency as part of the relational benefit in an online shopping context. Since consumer decision-making efficiency improves when the information processing task

is simplified and bounded (Sheth & Parvaytiyar, 1995), one would expect that consumers intend to maintain a relationship with the marketer to improve the consumer's future decision making. Consumers may be able to reduce information search and transaction cost by maintaining a relationship with a credible online store that satisfies their information needs.

H5: *There is a positive relationship between the product information quality and relational benefit.*

H6: *There is a positive relationship between the service information quality and relational benefit.*

Besides affecting consumers' evaluation of overall information service, as discussed earlier, assurance of security also plays an important role in trust forming by reducing the consumers' concerns about personal data abuse and vulnerability of transaction data (Liu et al., 2004). Consumers want detailed information on how their private and transaction data are secured (Elliot & Fowell, 2000). So, if the perceived level of security assurance meets consumer's expectations, a consumer may be willing to disclose her personal information and try to purchase with comfort.

H7: *There is a positive relationship between security perception and relational benefit.*

In the service marketing literature, an external source of information about a company, corporate image, reputation, and awareness were identified as important factors in the overall evaluation of the firm and its service (Zeithaml & Bitner, 1997). Apart from corporate image as a function of accumulated purchasing/consumption experience over time, most companies also provide external informational events (e.g., advertising or public relations) to attract new customers and keep existing customers (Andreassen & Lindestad, 1998).

We introduce site awareness as a perception by consumers about an online store that is based on external information events like advertising and word-of-mouth communication. It is defined as the "ability of a buyer to recognize or recall that a site is a member of a certain service category" (adapted from Aaker, 1991). This construct indicates consumers' perception of extrinsic information cues about an online store and is assumed to have an impact on customers' choice of a company when service attributes are difficult to evaluate.

H8: *There is a positive relationship between site awareness and relational benefit.*

As summarized, we expect consumers to perceive the relational benefits of an online store (i.e., on risk reduction, information searching, and transaction cost minimization), as a result of their evaluation of the information features of that online store.

Site Commitment

Commitment is an essential ingredient for a successful long-term relationship (Dwyer, Schurr, & Oh, 1987; Morgan & Hunt, 1994). Commitment has been defined as "an enduring desire to maintain a valued relationship" (Moorman, Zaltman, & Deshpande, 1992) or "a tendency to resist change" (Pritchard, Havitz, & Howard, 1999). It plays a key-mediating role in formation of consumers' loyalty and future behavioral intention (Garbarino & Johnson, 1999; Morgan & Hunt, 1994; Pritchard et al., 1999).

In the service marketing literature, service quality, perceived value, and satisfaction are considered as antecedents of commitment (Grönroos, 1990; Hocutt, 1998; Shemwell, Yavas, & Bilgin, 1998). That is, consumer's emotional and judgmental reaction to products or services is a key influential factor for consumers' commitment. The psychological benefit and trust are also essential ingredients for enhancing commitment

(Grönroos, 1990). They are validated to be more important than special treatment or social benefits in consumer relationships with service firms (Gwinner et al., 1998).

Based on the prior research, we expect information satisfaction and relational benefit to play a key role in forming consumers' site commitment to an online store. Information satisfaction indicates the consumer's overall evaluation of the online store's information service and relational benefit represents a cumulative psychological perception about the store.

H9: *There is a positive relationship between relational benefit and site commitment.*

H10: *There is a positive relationship between information satisfaction and site commitment.*

RESEARCH METHODOLOGY

When we developed the questionnaire, the multiple-item method was used, and each item was measured based on a 5-point Likert scale from "strongly disagree" to "strongly agree." All operational definitions of instrument are summarized in Appendix I. If possible, constructs that have already been used and validated by other researchers are adopted. Constructs that have not been used or developed previously are evaluated and adapted from the relevant literature as to how they might be operationalized and then were validated by pilot testing. The measurement items are shown in Appendix II.

Sampling and Data Collection

The unit of analysis in this study is the individual consumer who has experience with purchasing products at online stores. In deciding on the target online stores, we applied control to the several factors. Since the interest of this study is focused on investigating the relationship between information characteristics and consumer behavior, although price advantage and product quality are also important factors affecting consumer purchase behavior in online shopping, we decided to select the online bookstores that have a fixed price policy. It was documented that consumers do interact more online than off-line with this product category in Korea (KNSO, 2003). For the study, we selected three online bookstores in Korea with the highest sales volume. At these stores, price policy (e.g., no discount policy), delivery service, and payment process were similar.

To collect the consumer perception data, we built an online survey Web site that was hyper-linked to each target online bookstore—Kybo, Jongro, and Youngpung—and ticketing service—Ticketlink and Maxmovie—and conducted Web surveys during two months (from October to November 2003). The target subjects were Korean consumers who had memberships at the online bookstores and ticketing services. We asked for an ID number and password key-in at the beginning of the survey. We provided coupons or cybermoney as a reward for the survey participation in the form of gift vouchers for books and free ticket or bonus points at the online store. The survey period was from three to four weeks for each bookstore and ticketing service. The total

Table 1. Descriptive statistics of the respondent profile

Measure	Items	Frequency	Percent
Gender	Female	889	69.6
	Male	378	29.6
	Missing	11	0.8
Age	≤19	63	4.9
	20-29	891	69.7
	30-39	275	21.5
	≥40	35	2.7
	Missing	15	1.2
Occupation of Respondents	White collar employee	383	30.0
	Student	478	37.4
	Professional	181	14.2
	Self-employed	41	3.2
	Housewife	34	2.7
	Teacher	45	3.5
	Technical person	40	3.1
	Retired	18	1.4
	Missing	58	4.5
Time to use Internet	≤1 hour per a day	176	13.8
	2-5	837	65.5
	6-9	163	12.7
	≥10	75	5.9
	Missing	27	2.1
Purchase Frequency (during the last year)	≤2	456	35.7
	3~4	267	20.9
	5~6	187	14.6
	7~8	146	11.4
	≥9	216	16.9
	Missing	6	0.5

number of participants was 1,577. We excluded the cases of missing data (N = 161) and no membership ID number (N = 139), and finally used 1,278 samples for our analysis. For each site, the number of valid samples is 274 for Kybo, 171 for Jongro, 157 for Youngpung, 436 for Maxmovie, and 240 for Ticketlink.

Reliability and Validity of Instrument

Content validity defines how representative and comprehensive the items were in presenting the hypothesis. It is assessed by examining the process that was used in generating scale items (Straub, 1989). In this research, definitions of user interface quality, information quality, and security perception were developed based on the review of theory and research in information systems and other disciplines. Six items were selected for information quality, four items for user interface quality, and four items for security perception. For developing scales for site awareness, information satisfaction, relational benefit, and site commitment, we used the current marketing and service marketing literature. Four items were selected for site awareness, three items for information satisfaction, four items for relational benefit, and four items for commitment.

In this study, we follow Straub's (1989) processes of validating instruments to test construct validity in terms of convergent and discriminant validity. Convergent validity is the degree to which multiple attempts to measure the same concept are in agreement. For testing convergent validity, we evaluated the item-to-total correlation that is the correlation of each item to the sum of the remaining items. Items whose item-to-total correlation score was lower than 0.4 were dropped from further analysis.

Discriminant validity is the degree to which measures of different concepts are distinct. The discriminant validity of each construct was assessed by principal component factor analysis with VARIMAX rotation. As shown in Appendix III., the confirmatory factor analysis for independent variables yielded five distinct factors: user interface quality, product information quality, service information quality, security perception, and site awareness. Factor loadings for all variables were greater than 0.54 with no cross-construct loadings, indicating good discriminant validity. Together, the five observed factors accounted for 61% of the total variance.

To validate the appropriateness of the factor analysis, we applied several measures to the entire correlation matrix. Here, Bartlett's test of sphericity (p = 0.000) indicates the statistical probability that the correlation matrix has significant correlations among at least some of the variables, and the Kaiser-Meyer-Olkin measure of sampling adequacy (0.908) showed acceptable sampling adequacy (Hair, Anderson, Tatham, & Black, 1998, p. 99).

Next, we conducted the second factor analysis to investigate the distinctions among the dependent variables: information satisfaction, relational benefit, and site commitment. As shown in the table, factor loadings for the three variables were greater than 0.60 with no cross-construct loadings, and the three observed factors accounted for 64% of the total variance.

Internal consistency reliability is a statement about the stability of individual measurement items across replications from the same source of information. The Cronbach Alpha coefficient was used to assess reliability of the measures (Straub, 1991). As shown in Appendix III, reliability coefficients were acceptable for all constructs, ranging from 0.8687 for service information quality to 0.6712 for relational benefit. While all the reliability figures were higher than 0.6, the lowest acceptable limit for Cronbach's alpha suggested by Hair et al. (1998), variables with reliabilities lower than 0.8 deserve further refinement in future research.

Testing the Hypothesis

Hypotheses 1, 2, 3, and 4 examine the factors affecting information satisfaction. They are user interface quality, product information quality, service information quality, and security perception. Entering the variables in a single block, as shown in Table 2, we found that 39% of the variance in information satisfaction is explained by user interface quality, product information quality, service information quality, and security perception ($R^2 = 35.5\%$, F-value=176.513, $p<0.001$). At the 0.001 significance level, user interface quality and product information quality were significantly related to information satisfaction, while service information quality and security perception were found to affect information satisfaction at the 0.05 significance level.

Hypotheses 5, 6, 7, and 8 examine the factors affecting relational benefit. They are product information quality, service information quality, security perception, and site awareness. To investigate the hypotheses, entering the variables in a single block, we found that 31% of the variance for relational benefit is explained by product information quality, service information quality, security perception, and site awareness ($R^2 = 30.4\%$, F-value = 139.912, $p<0.001$). At the 0.001 significance level, product information quality, service information quality, and security perception were significantly related to relational benefit. Site awareness was also found to affect relational benefit at the 0.05 significance level.

Hypotheses 9 and 10 examine the links between both information satisfaction and relational benefit and consumer's site commitment. The result in Table 3 shows that information satisfaction and relational benefit explain 35% of the variance in site commitment ($R^2 = 35.9\%$, F-value = 359.024, $p<0.001$). At the 0.001 significance level, infor-

Table 2. Result of hypotheses tests

Model [a]	R^2	Adj. R^2	Std. β	t-value	VIF	Hypothesis result
(1) *Information Satisfaction* (INFSAT)						
INFSAT =UIQ + PIQ + SIQ + SEC +ε	0.357	0.355				
UIQ			0.301	10.453[b]	1.641	H1 was supported
PIQ			0.258	9.050[b]	1.609	H2 was supported
SIQ			0.122	4.222[b]	1.644	H3 was supported
SEC			0.053	2.059[c]	1.295	H4 was supported
(2) *Relational benefit* (BENEF)						
BENEF = PIQ + SIQ + SEC + SA + ε	0.306	0.304				
PIQ			0.175	6.264[b]	1.436	H5 was supported
SIQ			0.282	9.890[b]	1.489	H6 was supported
SEC			0.204	7.619[b]	1.306	H7 was supported
SA			0.064	2.576[c]	1.138	H8 was supported
(3) *Site Commitment* (COMMIT)						
COMMIT = INFSAT + BENEF + ε	0.360	0.359				
INFSAT			0.452	18.686[b]	1.164	H9 was supported
BENEF			0.261	10.780[b]	1.164	H10 was supported

a INFSAT, Information satisfaction; BENEF, Relational benefit; COMMIT, Site Commitment; UIQ, User interface quality; PIQ, Product Information quality; SIQ, Service Information quality; SEC, Security Perception; SA, Site awareness b p<0.001; c p<0.05 mation satisfaction and relational benefit were significantly related to site commitment.

Tests on Mediating Effect

According to Kenny (2001), the following three conditions must hold to support the mediating effect of a construct (see also Baron & Kenny, 1986):

1. The independent variable must have a significant association with the dependent variable.
2. The independent variable must have a significant association with the mediator.
3. When both the independent variable and the mediator variable are included as predictors, the mediator must have a significant effect on the dependent variable.

Complete mediation is supported when the beta coefficient for the independent variable in Condition 1 is significant, and the same coefficient in Condition 3 is not. Otherwise (still assuming all three conditions hold), partial mediation is supported (Baron & Kenny, 1986; Kenny, 1998). In Table 3, we report the results of the tests for mediation. The columns labeled (1), (2), (3), and (4) correspond to conditions 1 through 3. Mediation is indicated when all the beta coefficients, in columns (1), (2), and (3) are significant and the beta coefficients of mediators in column (4) are also significant. To assess the strength of the mediation, column (4) reports the beta coefficients for the independent variables when both they and the mediators are included.

The results Table 3 clearly support the notion that information satisfaction and relational benefit variables mediate the effect of user interface quality, product and service information quality, site awareness, and security perception on site commitment.

Consumer Commitment in Different Online Shopping Service

To examine whether the effect of online service type on the relationship between information satis-

Table 3. Testing the mediation effect of information satisfaction and relational benefit

	(1) IV → INFSAT		(2) IV → BENEF		(3) IV → COMMIT		(4) IV → COMMIT (Mediator included)	
	Std. β	t-value	Std. β	t-value	Std. β	t-value	Std. β	t-value
Independent variables [a] (IV):								
UIQ	0.301	10.453[b]	N/A	N/A	0.163	5.336[b]	0.027	0.908
PIQ	0.258	9.050[b]	0.175	6.264[b]	0.105	3.483[b]	-0.001	-0.043
SIQ	0.122	4.222[b]	0.282	9.890[b]	0.201	6.607[b]	0.124	4.315[b]
SEC	0.053	2.059[c]	0.204	7.619[b]	0.137	5.047[b]	0.090	3.533[b]
SA	N/A	N/A	0.064	2.576[c]	0.137	5.356[b]	0.089	3.741[b]
Mediators [a]:								
INFSAT							0.363	13.153[b]
BENEF							0.165	6.180[b]

a INFSAT, Information satisfaction; BENEF, Relational benefit; COMMIT, Site Commitment; UIQ, User interface quality; PIQ, Product Information quality; SIQ, Service Information quality; SEC, Security Perception; SA, Site awareness; b p<0.001; c p<0.05 faction and relational benefit and site commitment, we have conducted the stepwise regression analyses (Atuahene-Gima & Li, 2000). The procedure is as follows: First, the overall significance of a model comprising all antecedents and moderators is evaluated. Then, we add the interaction terms to the regression model and examine the increase in R^2. If the increase in R^2 is significant, it indicates the presence of the moderating effect. When this is the case, the individual interaction terms are then examined.

An equation for the moderated regression analyses and the results are presented in Table 4. Here, we note that since cross-product terms generally correlate strongly with their constituent variables, we used the residual centering method which uses residuals from regressing the cross-product term on its constituent variables to extract pure nonlinear terms. When the moderator is service type and the dependent variable is site commitment, we found that addition of the interaction terms with the antecedents to the regression equation yields a significant increase in R^2 (F change = 52.483, p < 0.001). In particular, it is noteworthy that information satisfaction appears to be more effective in case of the online

bookstore than for the online ticketing service ($\beta = 0.377$, p < 0.001). As the regression results shows, the intervention of relational benefit is more effective in increasing site commitment at online ticketing service than at online bookstore ($\beta = -0.390$, p < 0.01).

For more in-depth understanding of the moderating effects, we conducted two more regression analyses with the data set split into two; one was for the online bookstore and the other was only for the online ticketing service. The results of the separated regression analyses are also shown graphically in Figure 2. There are two lines in each graph, representing online bookstore and ticketing service. Also, each line has two values; one is the beta coefficient and the other is the intercept value from each regression analysis.

In the graph on the relationship between information satisfaction and site commitment, as information satisfaction increases, site commitment value for online bookstore increases steeply ($\beta = 0.550$). On the other hand, the line for online ticketing service is relatively flat ($\beta = 0.478$). Thus, we can confirm that the effect of information satisfaction on membership is contingent on online service type. The second graph on the relationship

Table 4. Results of stepwise regression analysis: Moderating effect of online service type

Model [a]	Std. β	t-value	R²	Adj. R²	ΔR²	df.	F-value	F Change
Full Model[#]			0.431	0.429	0.070	3/1271	192.510[b]	52.483[b]
Mediator Variables								
INFSAT	0.285	7.886[b]						
BENEF	0.409	11.330[b]						
Moderator Variables								
ST	0.300	2.616[c]						
Interaction Effects								
ST x BENEF (Residuals)	- 0.390	- 3.571[b]						
ST x INFSAT (Residuals)	0.377	3.378[b]						

a INFSAT, Information satisfaction; BENEF, Relational benefit; COMMIT, Site Commitment; ST, Service Type
b p < 0.001; c p < 0.05; #Model: COMMIT = INFSAT + BENEF + ST + ST x BENEF + ST x INFSAT + ε

Figure 2. Graphical representation of online service type's moderating effect

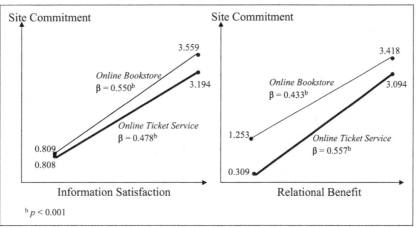

between relational benefit and site commitment, as relational benefit increases, site commitment value for online ticket service increases steeply ($\beta = 0.557$) and the line for online bookstore is relatively flat ($\beta = 0.433$).

We interpret that the product information and user interface, a relatively strong relationship with information satisfaction, is more important in consumers' decision making for repeat patronage at online bookstore than at online ticketing service. On the other hand, consumers who visit and purchase tickets at online ticketing service site consider security and service information related to event, checking tickets, and promotion as more important factors in decision making for repeat patronage than at online bookstore.

FINDINGS AND DISCUSSION

We found that a consumer's commitment to an online store is highly related to information satisfaction and relational benefit. At the same time, information satisfaction and relational benefit are significantly affected by product and service information quality, user interface quality, and security perception. These results imply that in-

formation of an online store is an important factor that affects each consumer's site loyalty.

We investigated the differential effect of product information and service information on both information satisfaction and relational benefit. Information satisfaction is affected more strongly by product information quality than by service information quality. Conversely, relational benefit is more strongly related to service information quality than to product information quality. These results may reflect the consumers' different perceptual weights to the information contents that online shopping stores provide. That is, in searching and purchasing, product information quality is a critical feature that affects the consumer. It is consistent with the prior discussion that the key benefit of e-commerce is organized and classified information, which enables consumers to reduce the costs of information search and processing (Alba et al., 1997; Bakos, 1991). Besides, consumers seem to consider service information quality as a more important factor in assessing the relational benefit of e-commerce in terms of reducing the transaction cost and risk.

The results show that information satisfaction and relational benefit are the significant factors affecting a consumer's site commitment in an online shopping context. This result is consistent with the prior research on commitment in the service context, which identifies satisfaction, trust, and relational benefits as antecedents of commitment (Garbarino & Johnson, 1999). Moreover, information satisfaction has a stronger effect on commitment, thus this result points out the important role of information satisfaction to building consumer commitment in an online shopping context relative to the real world service. The result of the mediation testing shows that the perception of shopping store attributes has an indirect effect on site commitment, as mediated by information satisfaction and relational benefit. A consumer's perception of an online store's attributes leads differently to information specific evaluation and relationship oriented evaluation so that both play a significant role in enhancing each consumer's commitment to the online store.

CONCLUSION AND FUTURE RESEARCH

As online shopping became increasingly common, there has been much research to explore the reasons behind this and ways to utilize it more effectively for commercial purposes. Most of the current research on consumer behavior in e-commerce takes either a technology-centered (i.e., the application of technology acceptance model or information system success model to e-commerce) or consumer-centered view (i.e., based on theory of reasoned action, transaction cost analysis, service quality measure). Among them, we reviewed the information aspects of an online shopping store. Different from the previous research, we have focused on the information quality dimension of online service in explaining the consumer relational behavior in e-commerce. As key mediating variables to predict consumer's behavioral intention to use online service, information satisfaction and relational benefit have been introduced. These are proven highly predictable

in describing consumers' relational behavior in e-commerce.

Although our findings provide meaningful implications for online stores, our study has several limitations. First, the use of self-reported scales to measure both independent and dependent variables suggests the possibility of a common method bias for the results. Second, although our model considers online store attributes as factors affecting consumer purchase behavior, since other factors such as price and promotion (e.g., loyalty program, price discount rate) were not included, we cannot explain the effect of price sensitivity and loyalty program on consumer purchase behavior with our model. Third, although this study has been conducted at the individual level of analysis, our sample data were collected from the customer-base of only three companies for online bookstore and two for online ticketing service. So we may not exclude the possibility that the lack of organizational variance may have affected our result.

The main contribution in this study is an empirical validation of consumer behavior in an online shopping context, and we investigated the perceptual difference of consumer's emotional and cognitive response to online shopping store attribute by comparative analysis between two different service types. Although much research on online store classification and its attribute has been conducted, little is known about the empirical evidence of consumer response to service attributes in a specific service type. So, academically, this study provides a seminal work for further research on various service categories in an online context and, practically, its results present the general guidance to develop the strategy of online shopping site design and operation for promoting consumers' revisiting and repeat patronage to each service category, respectively.

For future research, it is worthwhile to focus on the differences in consumer behavior according to product diversification and breadth of service domain. Moreover, it is also worthwhile to conduct comparative research on the differences of consumer behavior between off-line stores and online stores. Further study should also be conducted on consumers' relational behavior, and the differential effect of trust, commitment, and information satisfaction on purchasing behavior between relationship-oriented customers and transaction-oriented customers in an online shopping context (Garbarino & Johnson, 1999). As noted in the limitations of this study, we did not consider the factors such as price and promotion (e.g., loyalty program, price discount rate) that are also believed as important factors affecting consumers' choice and preference of e-commerce. To explain the effect of price sensitivity and loyalty program on consumer purchase behavior, it is worthwhile to test these constructs with our research model. The unit of analysis of this study is an individual level so that there is a limitation for applying the results to the company or online shopping site level. In Korea, there are many online shopping stores with a variety in range of categories—that is, computer and computer-related appliances, software, home electric appliances, electronic telecommunication equipment, music CDs, disks, videos, and musical instruments, travel arrangements and reservation services, beverage and health foods, cosmetics and perfumes, and clothes fashions miscellaneous goods. It can be assumed from the result of this study that the factors affecting consumer purchase behavior are different, depending on services or product categories that online stores provide.

Moreover, many attempts to develop e-satisfaction, e-SERVQUAL, or e-commerce metrics have been conducted (DeLone & McLean, 2004; Devaraj, Fan, & Kohli, 2002; Szymanski & Hise, 2000; McKinney et al., 2002). Our study may be applied to developing and validating e-commerce metrics that measure overall performance of online stores—that is, SERVQUAL metrics are used in measuring performance of the traditional service industry domain with a consumer point of view.

REFERENCES

Aaker, D. A. (1991). *Managing brand equity.* New York: The Free Press.

Alba, J., Lynch, J., Weitz, B., Janiszewski, C., Lutz, R., Sawyer, A., & Wood, S. (1997). Interactive home shopping: Consumer, retailer, and manufacturer incentives to participate in electronic marketplaces. *Journal of Marketing, 61*, 38-53.

Andreassen, T. W., & Lindestad, B. (1998). Customer loyalty and complex services. *International Journal of Service Industry Management, 9*(1), 7-23.

Atuahene-Gima, K., & Li, H. (2000). Marketing's influence tactics in new product development: A study of high technology firms in China. *Journal of Product Innovation Management, 17*, 451-470.

Bailey, J. E., & Pearson, S. W. (1983). Development of a tool for measuring and analyzing computer user satisfaction. *Management Science, 29*(5), 530-545.

Bakos, J. Y. (1991, September). A strategic analysis of electronic marketplaces. *MIS Quarterly*, pp. 295-310.

Bakos, J. Y. (1997). Reducing buyer search costs: Implications for electronic marketplaces. *Management Science, 43*(12), 1676-1692.

Baron, R. M., & Kenny, D. A. (1986). The moderator-mediator variable distinction in social psychological research: Conceptual, strategic, and statistical considerations. *Journal of Personality and Social Psychology, 51*(6), 1173-1182.

Berry, L. L. (1995). Relationship marketing of services-growing interest, emerging perspectives. *Journal of the Academy of Marketing Science, 23*(4), 236-245.

Childers, T. L., Carr, C. L., Peck, J., & Carson, S. (2001). Hedonic and utilitarian motivations for online retail shopping behavior. *Journal of Retailing, 77*, 511-535.

Crosby, L. A., & Stephens, N. (1987). Effects of relationship marketing on satisfaction, retention, and prices in the life insurance industry. *Journal of Marketing Research, 24*, 404-411.

DeLone, W., & McLean, E. R. (2004). Measuring e-commerce success: Applying the DeLone & McLean information systems success model. *International Journal of Electronic Commerce, 9*(1), 31-47.

Devaraj, S., Fan, Ming, & Kohli, Rajive (2002). Antecedents of B2C channel satisfaction and preference: Validating e-commerce metrics. *Information Systems Research, 13*(3), 316-333.

Dwyer, F. R., Schurr, P. H., & Oh, S. (1987). "Developing buyer-seller relationships," *Journal of Marketing, 51*, 11-27

Elliot, S., & Fowell, S. (2000). Expectations versus reality: A snapshot of consumer experiences with Internet retailing. *International Journal of Information Management, 20*, 323-336.

Garbarino, E., & Johnson, M. S. (1999). The different roles of satisfaction, trust, and commitment in customer relationships. *Journal of Marketing, 63*, 70-87.

Gauzente, C. (2004). Web merchants' privacy and security statement: How reassuring are they for customers? Two sided approach. *Journal of Electronic Commerce Research, 5*(3), 181-198.

Gefen, D. (2000). E-commerce: The role of familiarity and trust. *Omega, 28*(6), 725-737.

Griffith, D. A., Krampf, R. F., & Palmer, J. W. (2001). The role of interface in electronic commerce: Consumer involvement with print versus online catalogs. *International Journal of Electronic Commerce, 5*(4), 135-153.

Gronroos, C. (1990). Relationship approach to marketing in service contexts: The marketing and organizational behavior interface. *Journal Business Research, 20*, 3-11.

Gwinner, K. P., Gremmler, D. D., & Bitner, M. J. (1998). Relational benefits in services industries: The customer's perspective. *Journal of the Academy of Marketing Science, 26*(2), 101-114.

Hair, J. F., Jr., Anderson, R. E., Tatham, R. L., & Black, W. C. (1998). *Multivariate data analysis* (5th ed.). Upper Saddle River, NJ: Prentice Hall.

Hocutt, M. A. (1998). Relationship dissolution model: Antecedents of relationship commitment and the likelihood of dissolving a relationship. *International Journal of Service Industry Management, 9*(2), 189-200.

Hong, W., Thong, J. Y. L., & Tam, K. Y. (2005). The effects of information format and shopping task on consumers' online shopping behavior: A cognitive fit perspective. *Journal of Management Information Systems, 21*(3), 149-184.

Hoque, A. Y., & Lohse, G. L. (1999). An information search cost perspective for designing interfaces for electronic commerce. *Journal of Marketing Research, 36*(3), 387-394.

IMD World Competitiveness Center yearbook. (2005). Geneva, Switzerland: IMD Business School.

Jarvenpaa, S. L., & Todd, P. A. (1997). Consumer reactions to electronic shopping on the World Wide Web. *International Journal of Electronic Commerce, 1*(2), 59-88.

Jones, M. A., & Suh, J. (2000). Transaction-specific satisfaction and overall satisfaction: An empirical analysis. *Journal of Services Marketing, 14*(2), 147-159.

Kenny, D. A. (2001). *Mediation.* Retrieved September 7, 2007, from http://nw3.nai.net/~dakenny/mediate.htm

KNSO (Korea National Survey Office). (2003). *The annual results of e-commerce transaction survey in 2002*. Retrieved September 7, 2007, from http://www.nso.go.kr/eng/releases/e_suec0144.htm

Kolesar, M. B., & Galbraith, R. W. (2000). A services-marketing perspective on e-retailing: implications for e-retailers and directions for further research. *Internet Research, 10*(5), 424-438.

Koufaris, M. (2002). Applying the technology acceptance model and flow theory to online consumer behavior. *Information Systems Review, 13*(2), 205-223.

Liao, Z., & Cheung, M. T. (2001). Internet-based e-shopping and consumer attitudes: An empirical study. *Information and Management, 38*, 299-306.

Lightner, N. J., & Eastman, C. (2002). User preference for product information in remote purchase environment. *Journal of Electronic Commerce Research, 3*(3), 174-186.

Liu, C., & Arnett, K. P. (2000). Exploring the factors associated with Web site success in the context of electronic commerce. *Information and Management, 38*, 23-33.

Liu, C., Marchewka, J. T., Lu, J., & Yu, C.-S. (2004). Beyond concern: A privacy–trust- behavioral intention model of electronic commerce. *Information & Management, 42*, 127-142.

Lohse, G. L., & Spiller, P. (1998). Electronic shopping. *Communications of ACM, 41*(7), 81-89.

Malhotra, N. K., Kim, S. S., & Agarwal, J. (2004). Internet users' information privacy concerns (IUIPC): The construct, the scale, and a causal model. *Information Systems Research, 15*(4), 336-355.

McKinney, V., Yoon, K., & Zahedi, F. (2002). The measurement of Web-customer satisfaction: An expectation and disconfirmation approach. *Information Systems Review, 13*(3), 296-315.

Molla, A., & Licker, P. S. (2001). E-commerce systems success: An attempt to extend and re-specify the DeLone and McLean model of IS success. *Journal of Electronic Commerce Research, 2*(4), 131-139.

Moon, J.-W., & Kim, Y.-G. (2001). Extending the TAM for a World-Wide-Web context. *Information and Management, 38*, 217-230.

Moorman, C., Zaltman, G., & Deshpande, R. (1992). Relationships between providers and users of market research: The dynamics of trust within and between organizations. *Journal of Marketing Research, 29*, 314-328.

Morgan, R. M., & Hunt, S. D. (1994). The commitment-trust theory of relationship marketing. *Journal of Marketing, 58*, 20-38.

Nguyen, N., & Leblanc, G. (2001). Corporate image and corporate reputation in customers' retention decisions in services. *Journal of Retailing and Consumer Services, 8*, 227-236.

NIDA (National Internet Development Agency of Korea). (2004). *Survey on the computer and Internet usage*. Retrieved September 7, 2007, from http://www.nida.or.kr

O'Cass, A., & Fenech, T. (2003). Web retailing adoption: Exploring the nature of Internet users. *Journal of Retailing and Consumer Services, 10*, 81-94.

Patterson, P. G., & Smith, T. (2001). Relationship benefits in service industries: A replication in a southeast asian context. *Journal of Services Marketing, 15*(6), 425-443.

Peterson, R. A., Balasubramanian, S., & Bronnenberg, B. J. (1997). Exploring the implications of the Internet for consumer marketing. *Journal of the Academy of Management Science, 25*(4), 329-346.

Pinsonneault, A., & Kraemer, K. L. (1993). Survey research methodology in management information systems: An assessment. *Journal of Management Information Systems, 10*(2), 75-106.

Pritchard, M. P., Havitz, M. E., & Howard, D. R. (1999). Analyzing the commitment-loyalty link in service contexts. *Journal of the Academy of Management Science, 27*(3), 333-348.

Ratnasingham, P. (1998). The importance of trust in electronic commerce. *Internet Research, 8*(4), 313-321.

Ravald, A., & Gronroos, C. (1996). The value concept and relationship marketing. *European Journal of Marketing, 30*(2), 19-30.

Reynolds, J. (2000). eCommerce: A critical review. *International Journal of Retail & Distribution Management, 28*(10), 417-444.

Shemwell, D. J., Yavas, U., & Bilgin, Z. (1998). Customer-service provider relationships: An empirical test of a model of service quality, satisfaction, and relationship-oriented outcomes. *International Journal of Service Industry Management, 9*(2), 155-168.

Sheth, J. N., & Parvatiyar, A. (1995). Relationship marketing in consumer markets: Antecedents and consequences. *Journal of the Academy of Marketing Science, 23*(4), 255-271.

Straub, D. W. (1989). Validating instruments in MIS research. *MIS Quarterly, 13*(2), 147-169.

Srinivasan, S. S., Anderson, R., & Ponnavolu, K. (2002). Customer loyalty in e-commerce: An exploration of its antecedents and consequences. *Journal of Retailing, 78*, 41-50.

Szymanski, D. M., & Hise, R. T. (2000). E-satisfaction: An initial examination. *Journal of Retailing, 76*(3), 309-322.

Wang, R. Y., & Strong, D. M. (1996). Beyond accuracy: What data quality means to data consumers. *Journal of Management Information Systems, 12*(4), 5-34.

Westbrook, R. A., et al. (1983). Value-percept disparity: An alternative to the disconfirmation of expectations theory of consumer satisfaction. *Advances in Consumer Research, 10*, 256-261.

Wolfingbarger, M., & Gilly, M. C. (2001). Shopping online for freedom, control, and fun. *California Management Review, 43*(2), 34-55.

Yang, Z., & Fang, X. (2004). Online service quality dimensions and their relationships with satisfaction: A content analysis of customer reviews of securities brokerage services. *International Journal of Service Industry Management, 15*(3), 302-326.

Zeithaml, V. A., & Bitner, M. J. (1997). *Services marketing* (p. 114). Singapore: McGraw-Hill.

Zhang, X., Keeling, K. B., & Pavur, R. J. (2000). Information quality of commercial Web site home pages: An explorative analysis. In *Proceedings of the 21st International Conference on Information Systems*, Brisbane, Australia (pp. 164-175).

APPENDIX I: DEFINITIONS AND REFERENCES OF KEY CONSTRUCTS

Constructs	Definition	References
User interface quality	Customer perception of degree to convenience and user friendliness in using a Web site system	Szymanski and Hise, 2000; Griffith et al., 2001
Product Information Quality	Customer perception of the quality of information about product that is provided by a Web site (Relevancy, Recency, Sufficiency, Understandability, Consistency, Playfulness)	Wang et al., 1996; Delone and McLean, 1992; Bailey and Pearson, 1983
Service Information Quality	Customer perception of the quality of information about service that is provided by the Web site (Relevancy, Recency, Sufficiency, Understandability, Consistency, Playfulness)	Wang et al., 1996; Delone and McLean, 1992; Bailey and Pearson, 1983
Security Perception	Customer perceptions about the ability of an online store's controlling and safeguarding of transaction data from misappropriation or unauthorized alteration	Bailey and Pearson, 1983
Site awareness	The customer's ability to recognize or recall that a site is a member of a certain service category	Aaker, 1991
Information satisfaction	Emotional response to the experience provided by the overall information service	Westbrook, 1983
Relational benefit	Benefit customers receive from long-term relationships above and beyond core service performance	Gwwinner et al. 1998
Site commitment	An enduring desire to maintain a valued relationship with the site	Moorman et al., 1992

APPENDIX II: MEASUREMENTS OF INSTRUMENT OF KEY CONSTRUCTS

Construct	Items (anchors: strongly disagree/strongly agree)	Cronbach Alpha
Independent Variables		
User Interface Quality	1. This site is convenient to search for a book (ticket) 2. This site is convenient to order a book (ticket) 3. This site is easy to navigate wanted pages 4. This site is user friendly	0.7143
Product Information Quality	1. This site provides up-to-date book (ticket) information 2. This site provides sufficient book (ticket) information 3. This site presents book (ticket) information easy to understand 4. The book (ticket) information is consistent 5. The book (ticket) information is playful 6. The book (ticket) information is relevant	0.8216
Service Information Quality	1. This site provides up-to-date service information 2. This site provides sufficient service information 3. This site present service information easy to understand 4. The service information is consistent 5. The service information is playful 6. The service information is relevant	0.8680
Site awareness	1. Neighbors know this site very well 2. This site is very famous as an Internet bookstore (ticketing service) 3. This site is known through the advertising media (TV, newspaper, Internet, etc.)	0.6787
Security Perception	1. My private information is managed securely on this site 2. I am sure that payment information will be protected in this site 3. This site provides detailed information about security 4. *I am afraid that my private information will be used in an unwanted manner (R)*	0.7630
Mediators and Dependent Variable		
Information satisfaction	1. I am satisfied with the information service of this site compared to other shopping sites 2. Information service of this site satisfies my expectations 3. I am satisfied with the overall information service of this site	0.7690
Relational benefit	1. At this site, I am able to reduce the time to purchase wanted books (ticket) 2. At this site, I am able to reduce efforts to purchase wanted books (ticket) 3. At this site, I am able to purchase wanted books (ticket) that are hard to purchase at other stores 4. I will receive credible customer service from this site	0.6667
Site Commitment	1. I will not change my book (ticket) shopping site in the future 2. I will continuously purchase books (tickets) at this site in the future 3. I will recommend this site to other people 4. I will visit this site first when I want to buy books (tickets)	0.8765

Web site provides various types of information that evokes consumers' interest like humor, links to other sites of interest, and appetizer information, online games, gossips, and video clips. So this types of information, that we mean, is playful

APPENDIX III: CONSTRUCT VALIDITY AND RELIABILITY OF MEASURES

Construct	Item label	Eigen value	Factor loading	Item to total correlation	Cronbach alpha	Variance explained	Cumulative percentage
Independent Variables							
User interface quality	UIQ1	2.084	0.521	0.467	0.7143	9.5%	9.5%
	UIQ2		0.566	0.486			
	UIQ3		0.726	0.522			
	UIQ4		0.750	0.531			
Product Information Quality	PIQ1	3.348	0.570	0.480	0.8216	15.2%	24.7%
	PIQ2		0.783	0.672			
	PIQ3		0.714	0.647			
	PIQ4		0.622	0.586			
	PIQ5		0.644	0.536			
	PIQ6		0.696	0.608			
Service Information Quality	SIQ1	3.686	0.735	0.652	0.8680	16.8%	41.5%
	SIQ2		0.788	0.690			
	SIQ3		0.772	0.686			
	SIQ4		0.735	0.702			
	SIQ5		0.609	0.587			
	SIQ6		0.688	0.682			
Security Perception	SEC1	2.103	0.777	0.596	0.7630	9.5%	51%
	SEC2		0.795	0.636			
	SEC3		0.743	0.562			
Site awareness	SP1	1.916	0.772	0.509	0.6787	8.7%	59.7%
	SP2		0.811	0.538			
	SP3		0.673	0.432			
Mediators and Dependent Variable							
Information satisfaction	INFSAT1	2.115	0.801	0.605	0.7690	19.2%	19.8%
	INFSAT2		0.732	0.605			
	INFSAT3		0.796	0.610			
Relational benefit	BENEF1	2.078	0.653	0.444	0.6667	18.9%	38.1%
	BENEF2		0.656	0.472			
	BENEF3		0.749	0.416			
	BENEF4		0.666	0.471			
Site **Commitment**	COMMIT1	2.931	0.854	0.772	0.8765	26.6%	64.7%
	COMMIT2		0.823	0.774			
	COMMIT3		0.733	0.687			
	COMMIT4		0.748	0.714			

Chapter X
Online Shopping and Catalog Shopping:
Exogenous and Endogenous Antecedents of Consumers' Channel Choice

Maria Madlberger

Vienna University of Economics and Business Administration, Austria

ABSTRACT

Multichannel retailing can offer a wide range of synergies for retailers when their distribution channels accommodate consumer's preferences and their buying behavior. Among the large number of retail types, mail-order companies are well suited to benefit from electronic commerce. Not only can they use their infrastructure and experience with direct selling, but many mail-order companies also seek to use the Internet to attract new target groups to increase their typically small and narrow customer bases. Currently, we do not know enough about the antecedents of channel choices, especially in the mail-order sector. This chapter addresses this issue and draws special attention to exogenous (i.e., independent of the retailer) factors influencing online shopping behavior. These variables include perceived convenience and perceived security of online shopping in general and consumers' attitudes toward the catalog as the existing distribution channel. One endogenous factor, that is, attitude toward the online shop, is assumed to influence buying behavior at the online shop. To examine relationships between the catalog and the online shop, 2,363 consumers who are familiar with both distribution channels of a mail-order company were surveyed online. The structural equation model developed reveals that attitudes toward the printed catalog most strongly influence attitudes toward the online shop. Further, the analysis has shown that antecedents of buying behavior at the online shop are moderated by gender. Shopping behavior of men is influenced by their attitudes toward the catalog, while that of women is determined by their attitudes toward the online shop.

INTRODUCTION

Successful online retailers such as Amazon or eBay have become symbols of profitable e-com-merce activities. However, pure Internet players generated only 31% of total Internet sales in 2003, whereas multichannel retailers, that is, retailers that use online and off-line distribution channels simultaneously, account for 52% of Internet sales (Grosso, McPherson, & Shi, 2004). In the U.S., multichannel sales reached a level of $23.4 billion and a customer base of 55 million households in 2004. The top categories are apparel and accessories, home décor and furnishings, gifts, and men's and senior products (Multichannel Retailing on the Rise, 2005a). Academic research by Min and Wolfinbarger (2005) also shows that multichannel retailers have a higher market share and marketing efficiency than pure players.

One of the best known examples of multichannel retailing is the case of Tesco.com, which is one of the most successful electronic food retailers in the world (Madlberger, 2004). Tesco integrates its online distribution channel very strongly with its stores (Dawson, 2001). Also other retailers such as Sears, Gap, or Land's End demonstrate that synergies can be exploited when one organization has different distribution channels. Consequently, it is not surprising that today's e-commerce landscape, apart from a few exceptions, is largely dominated by multichannel retailers (Haeberle, 2003).

A recent study by the Financial Insight's 2006 U.S. Consumer Channel Preference Study revealed that consumers are heavy multichannel users in the financial sector. All distribution channels are important to them for different reasons (Each Delivery Channel, 2006). Similarly, studies on success factors in e-commerce have identified several synergies that facilitate online retailing for multichannel players. Retailers with a network of physical stores can achieve synergies in the form of lower costs, differentiation through value-added services, improved trust, and the possibility of extending product markets when they go online (Madlberger, 2006; Steinfield, Bouwman, & Adelaar, 2002). As Maltz, Rabinovich, and Sinha (2004) argue, brick and mortar stores benefit from their large experience in logistics handling. Moreover, multichannel retailers can spread their risks among several channels, which strengthens their financial standing.

Among traditional types of retailers, mail-order companies are in the best position to capitalize on synergies. These retailers are, in fact, considered to be well-suited for online business. This is also why most mail-order companies began to develop electronic marketing channels quite early in order to complement their catalog-based channels. For example, the apparel retailer Land's End launched its online shop as early as 1995 (Alptekinoglu & Tang, 2005). In addition, the target groups of many mail-order companies are stable but nondynamic and limited in size, which forces them to target new customer segments. The Internet could provide them with the opportunity to attract new customer segments and benefit from various synergies.

However, these synergies can only be turned into competitive advantages and financial gains if electronic retailers successfully respond to consumer needs. Hence, in addition to the analysis of potential synergy effects for multichannel retailers (Hansen & Madlberger, 2007), consumer behavior has to be taken into account. Besides the analysis of antecedents of online shopping, the distinction between influencing factors that are exogenous to the online shop and those that are endogenous (Monsuwé, Dellaert, & deRuyter, 2004) is critical. To gain insights into the antecedents of consumers' channel choices, the following two research questions are defined:

- Which exogenous factors influence consumers' attitudes toward a mail-order company's online shop as an endogenous factor?
- To what extent do their attitudes toward the online shop as an endogenous factor influence their buying behavior at that particular shop?

In order to answer these key questions, we have developed a structural equation model based on the theory of reasoned action as well as on findings from the literature on distribution channel choice. In particular, we address the role of exogenous factors (Monsuwé, Dellaert, & de Reytes, 2004). To test this model, we have conducted an empirical survey in cooperation with a mail-order company.

The chapter is organized as follows: First, we provide the theoretical basis of the research questions and discuss the literature used for the development of the model. The subsequent section focuses on the development of the model and explains the constructs, before the research design is outlined and the results of the structural equation model are presented. Ultimately, the results are discussed and conclusions are drawn from the findings.

MULTICHANNEL RETAILING AND MAIL-ORDER RETAILING

Distribution channels are a key research area in the context of retailing, marketing, and e-commerce (Coughlan, Anderson, Stern, & El-Ansary, 2001). Since the emergence of electronic commerce, research on consumers' channel choice has gained in attention and recognition from academia. Early research focused on channel choices between direct and retail-store-based channels (Alba, Lynch, Weitz, Janiszewski, Lutz, Sawyer, & Wood, 1997; Balasubramanian, 1998; Fain, 1994). With the increasing relevance of e-commerce and Web-based distribution channels, more research on channel choice was conducted (e.g., Alptekinoglu & Tang, 2005; Balabanis & Reynolds, 2001; Berman & Thelen, 2004; Coelho, Easingwood, & Coelho, 2003; Kaufman-Scarborough & Lindquist, 2002; Wallace, Giese, & Johnson, 2004).

Electronic commerce enables retailers to increase sales (Gabrielsson, Kirpalani, & Luostarinen, 2002). Companies often have multiple channels because they add channels incrementally to expand their businesses (Moriarty & Moran, 1990). Multichannel strategies are extremely complex and require a thorough examination of intra-organizational and environmental conditions. Distribution channels can behave in an undulating manner when they contract or expand, which may cause limitations to multichannel retailing in some industries (Gallaugher, 2002).

The retail sector comprises a large number of store types (Berman & Evans, 2001), differing in their range of goods, price levels, and store-related or Web site-related particularities. The largest differences exist between nonstore-based retailers, which do business through direct selling channels, and store-based retailers. Grosso, McPherson, and Shi (2004) provide a categorization framework of online retailers, distinguishing between online retailers with physical stores and those without physical outlets.

Retailers without physical stores are not a new phenomenon. They not only have a long history but also come in a variety of forms, for example, classic catalog mail-order businesses, party plan businesses, and television-based shopping channels. Direct selling has its roots in the U.S., where it originally resulted from the logistical needs to reach consumers in remote areas that did not have an adequate commercial infrastructure (Burton, 2000). Direct selling in Europe, meanwhile, has gained in popularity because many mail-order companies sell on credit and therefore offer clear advantages over most physical stores. Research on catalog shopping behavior has identified the main motivating factors for the choice for the traditional shopping catalog (Eastlick & Feinberg, 1999). Functional motivations (Sheth, 1983) include convenience (Eastlick & Feinberg, 1999; Jasper & Lan, 1992), range of goods (Reynolds, 1974), unique merchandise offerings (Januz, 1983), and a favorable price level (Korgaonkar, 1984). Arguing that also nonfunctional motives for catalog shopping are relevant, Eastlick and Feinberg (1999) discuss perceptions by the store clientele, promotions, and the reputation of the mail-order company.

Following Grosso, McPherson, and Shi's (2004) framework, mail-order companies that go online are classified as online retailers without physical stores. Compared with other types of retailing, mail-order business is most similar to electronic commerce. The main tasks the catalog fulfills are shifted to a Web site. Any processes that are related to ordering and distribution are equivalent in online and mail-order retailing. As mail-order companies are largely experienced with direct selling and possess an appropriate infrastructure for physical distribution, they are likely to have competitive advantages in online shopping also vis-à-vis store based retailers. From a logistics perspective, mail-order companies that run a Web shop are likely to have ship-to-one logistics, whereas store-based retailers usually opt for pallet-shipping logistics. As a consequence, the investment necessary to build up and maintain the online channel is much lower from a logistics perspective.

When mail-order companies go online, they can exploit a number of synergies, such as a wider range of goods, a higher degree of service person-alization, and enhanced opportunities for price variances, such as temporary price reductions or discounts, all of which cannot be obtained that easily in the catalog business alone. Synergies that are beneficial to store-based multichannel retailers, for example, cross-channel promotional opportunities, enhanced consumer confidence, or the opportunity to tap new customer segments (Madlberger, 2006), are available to mail-order companies as well. Xing and Grant (2006) state that it has not yet been clarified whether multichan-nel retailers or pure players can achieve a better customer service. But it is obvious that online mail-order companies have good opportunities to achieve a very high service level. Among the strategic alternatives proposed by Grosso, McPherson, and Shi (2004), mail-order companies operating online should turn out to be "efficiency machines" that generate large sales volumes.

However, as many classic mail-order companies typically attract only a small consumer segment, they rather belong to niche leaders.

An important issue for a multichannel retailer is consumers' channel choice. For a retailer, it is crucial not only to obtain knowledge about costs and benefits associated with different channels but also to develop an optimized channel architecture. Multichannel retailers should try to lure customers to the optimal channel instead of waiting for them to choose one (Myers, Pickersgill, & Van Metre, 2004). Schoenbachler and Gordon (2002) have developed a framework for analyzing potential antecedents of channel choice. They propose a research model that includes perceived risk, prior direct marketing experiences, motivation to buy from a channel, product category, and Web site design. Johnson, Yoo, Thee, Lennon, Jasper, and Damhorst (2006) empirically show that consum-ers who are time-pressed, dissatisfied with local offerings, unattached to their community, and unconcerned with financial security are more intensive multichannel shoppers than other con-sumer groups. Noble, Griffith, and Weinberger (2005) could reveal that different aspects of a purchase show a strong impact on consumers' channel choice. The Internet provides considerable value to consumers who search for information. In contrast, individuals who wish to possess a product prefer brick and mortar stores. As known from practice, almost two thirds of consumers search for products and product information on the Web and purchase products off-line. With increasing relevance of multichannel retailing, it becomes more and more necessary to use channel choice also as a customer segmentation criterion (Del Franco, 2006).

Multichannel shoppers are more profitable than single-channel shoppers as they tend to spend more money. The diminishing frontiers between online retailing and store-based retailing induce practitioners to refer to cross-channel retailing instead of multichannel retailing (Amato-Mc-

Coy, 2006; Blyth, 2006). Consumers are keen on multichannel interfaces that show an extremely high degree of integration and thus add value to them. A study by Shop.org shows the following cross-channel purchasing structure (see Table 1). As the numbers show, there is a large overlap between online and store customers as well as between catalog and online shoppers.

Van Birgelen, Jong, and de Ruyter (2006) investigated the intention to use a bank's off-line and online channel. They could show that consumers' behavioral intentions are strongly influenced by satisfaction with office-related performance factors for routine services. They also identified interaction effects between traditional and technology-mediated channel performance satisfaction levels. Of particular importance to multichannel retailers is the opportunity to increase customer loyalty. As Wallace, Glese, and Johnson (2004) empirically showed, multichannel retailing increases customer loyalty as it enables online retailers to improve their service level and thus customer satisfaction. Similarly, several academic researchers argue that the convergence of online and off-line retailing will play an important role in the near future (Dennis, Harris, & Sandhu, 2002; Enders & Jelassi, 2000; Kennedy & Coughlan, 2006; Oinas, 2002). In practice, however, only a third of UK multichannel retailers undertake cross-channel activities (Retailers Missing Opportunities, 2005b).

MODEL DEVELOPMENT

This survey focuses on channel-specific antecedents of buying behavior of a multichannel retailer's online shop. Previous studies on online shopping behavior have examined them in various contexts, focusing on the factors influencing online shopping behavior. For example, Gupta, Su, and Walter (2004) developed and tested an economic model that identifies channel characteristics and consumer risk profiles as antecedents. Also, the fit between information formats and shopping tasks influences shopping behavior on the Internet (Hong, Thong, & Tam, 2004). A key issue that has been discussed exhaustively in the literature is the role of trust in online shopping (Bhattacherjee, 2002; Reichheld & Schefter, 2000; Suh & Han, 2003).

A considerable body of previous research on online shopping behavior has drawn on the technology acceptance model (TAM) (Davis, 1989). For example, Gefen, Karahanna, and Straub (2003), Gefen (2000), and Lederer, Maupin, Sena, and Zhuang (2000) investigated TAM-based factors influencing online buying behavior. Pavlou (2003) added perceived risk to the model and regarded trust as a key independent variable. By taking into account perceived usefulness and perceived ease of use of a firm's online shop, TAM is related to factors that can be controlled by the retailer at least to some extent.

Table 1. Cross-channel purchasing relationships (Yellavalli, Holt, & Jandial, 2007)

Direction[1]	Percentage
Online ➔ Store	78%
Store ➔ Online	6%
Online ➔ Catalog	23%
Catalog ➔ Online	45%
Catalog ➔ Store	36%
Store ➔ Catalog	22%
[1] Reading example: 78% of online shoppers also buy through the retailer's physical stores.	

TAM is believed to be appropriate for explaining the acceptance of specific corporate information technologies (Monsuwé, Dellaert, & de Rugter, 2004), but is criticized for neglecting factors that go beyond the attributes of this special technology application (Moon & Kim, 2001). For this reason, Monsuwé, Dellaert, and de Rugter (2004) call for the consideration of exogenous variables in analyses of online shopping behavior. Exogenous factors are independent of a retailer's online shop and cannot be influenced by it. Similarly, Jarvenpaa and Todd (1997) point to the importance of investigating the relationship between perceived characteristics of Web shopping in general and user intentions. Although Monsuwé et al. (2004) recommend using these variables chiefly for investigations of online shopping in general, there is evidence suggesting that exogenous factors should be taken into account as well when analyzing the acceptance of a particular firm's online shop.

Of special relevance to channel choice behavior are the findings obtained by Noble, Goiffith, and Weinberger (2005). They conducted a survey in which they revealed that different channels are preferred for different phases of a purchase process. Information attainment is most strongly associated with the Internet and less related to physical stores and catalogs. Price comparisons are positively related to stores and negatively related to the Internet and catalogs. Assortment seeking turned out to show the strongest association again with the Internet, followed by the catalog and the physical stores.

A literature review by Chang, Cheoung, and Lai (2005) shows that previous research has focused on three different antecedents of online shopping: (1) perceived characteristics of the Web as a sales channel, (2) Web site and product characteristics, and (3) consumer characteristics. Several researchers have investigated how people's perceptions of Web characteristics in general influence their perceptions of an individual on-line shop. McKnight, Choudhury, and Kacmar (2002b) found that the risks associated with the Web negatively influence consumers' willingness to share personal information and their intention to purchase. Similarly, Burroughs and Sabherwal's (2002) work has revealed a significant influence of Internet security on purchasing behavior at an online store.

We are heading Monsuwé, Dellaert, and de Rugter (2004) call for integrating exogenous factors into the research design. As suggested by them, relevant exogenous factors that can influence online shopping behavior are consumer traits, situational factors, product characteristics, previous online shopping experiences, and trust in online shopping. Since the research model used in this chapter is an initial investigation of the impact of exogenous factors, we focus on those variables that emerge from the literature review as likely to be relevant. Therefore, we look at constructs related to previous online shopping experiences and trust in online shopping as consumers' perceptions of the attractiveness of online purchasing in general. As gender turned out to be a relevant sociodemographic factor, we investigate whether the suggested dependencies vary between men and women. The analysis does not account for situational factors, since this requires respondents to recall individual purchasing transactions. Also, product characteristics are not included in the model because the participating mail-order company sells products in a large number of categories with considerably different characteristics.

Previous online shopping experiences may be influenced by a variety of impressions, including, for example, product information, delivery terms, services offered, privacy, or visual appeal (Burke, 2002). Among these factors, perceived convenience and perceived security have turned out to be important factors in online shopping from the consumers' point of view (Ibbotson & Fahy, 2004). These factors are independent from a particular Web site's characteristics and are therefore not controllable by a single retailer. For this reason, we analyze perceived convenience and perceived security of online shopping as antecedents of consumers' attitudes toward an online shop. Previous research on online shopping has also revealed that attitudes toward one distribution channel influence attitudes toward another distribution channel (Balabanis & Reynolds, 2001; Kaufman-Scarborogh & Lindquist, 2002). Also, this factor is exogenous to the online shop but not exogenous to the retailer. Hence, we add attitudes toward the catalog as another exogenous antecedent of attitudes toward the online shop.

The endogenous factor, that is, the factor directly related to the online shop, is measured using the construct "attitude toward the online shop." Attitudes toward a particular technology are a key element of TAM, which regards this construct as a factor influencing people's intention to adopt a particular technology. As the focus of the study is on the importance of exogenous factors, we did not include the antecedents of attitudes toward the online shop (perceived usefulness, perceived ease of use).

The dependent variable is shopping behavior at the retailer's online shop. Unlike the TAM, we did not include intention to buy in the model but decided to look at actual behavior directly. We did this for two reasons. First, there is a strong relationship between the intention to display a particular behavior and the behavior itself, as previous research on the theory of reasoned action (TRA) (Ajzen & Fishbein, 1980) and the theory of planned behavior (TPB) (Ajzen, 1991) have shown. Second, the analysis focuses on consumers who are closely related to the retailer and so their intentions to buy can be expected to be very high.

Shopping behavior has many different facets. For commercial firms, parts of shopping behavior that directly influence monetary success are of special relevance. In addition, spending money is the ultimate and most consequent way of interacting with any kind of shop. Hence, shopping behavior in the research model is related to spending at the online shop.

So far, there has been no empirical evidence that attitudes toward a mail-order company's printed catalog influence shopping behavior at the

Figure 1. Research model

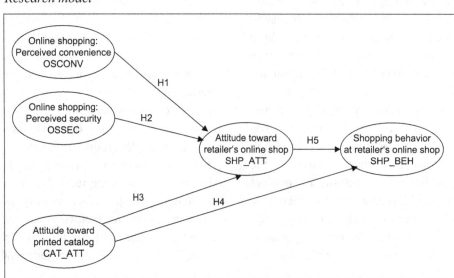

176

same retailer's online shop. The survey addresses this issue and investigates the influence of attitudes toward the catalog on shopping behavior at the online shop. On the basis of these considerations, we derive the research model summarized in Figure 1. In the following, the individual constructs and the related hypotheses are discussed.

Perceived Convenience of Online Shopping

Like traditional mail-order retailers, online shops argue that perceived convenience is one of the major advantages of direct selling compared with store-based shopping. Proponents of this argument hold that this convenience results from time savings. Serving consumers faced with increasing time constraints, they benefit from saving time that would otherwise be spent for driving to a store and back (Bhatnagar, Misra, & Rao, 2000). Indeed, time poverty has been identified as a key driver of online shopping (Eastlick & Feinberg, 1999). On the other hand, delays caused by long page loading times can negatively impact consumers' evaluation of a Web site (Dellaert & Kahn, 1999). Perceived convenience consists of several dimensions that can be characterized by their occurrence during the transaction phases. These include access and search convenience (Seiders, Berry, & Gresham, 2000) as well as time and place convenience (Kaufman-Scarborough & Lindquist, 2000). The latter denotes that there is no need to leave the present location to visit a shop. Also, a study by Torkzadeh and Dhillon (2002) reveals that perceived convenience is a key determinant of online shopping behavior. Based on these findings, we can conclude that perceived convenience of online shopping as an exogenous factor has a positive effect on attitudes toward the online shop.

H1: *The more convenient consumers perceive online shopping to be, the more positive will their attitudes toward the online shop be.*

Perceived Security of Online Shopping

Consumers' fear of security breaches and related risks has been a hurdle to the success of e-commerce for many years (Bhatnagar, Misia, & Rao, 2000). Perceived security is a twofold phenomenon. On the one hand, consumers evaluate the level of security of the Internet in general (exogenous factor), but on the other hand, trust in an individual vendor can influence buying behavior (Lee & Turban, 2001) as an endogenous factor. The second issue has been investigated in different contexts (Doney & Cannon, 1997; Hoffman, Novak, & Peralta, 1999; Jarvenpaa, Tractinsky, & Vitale, 2000; McKnight, Choudhury, & Kacmar, 2002a; Suh & Han, 2003). Previous research has found strong interrelations between trust and perceived security (Edwards, 2004; Lee & Turban, 2001). Yousafzai, Pallister, and Foxall (2003) argue that perceived security is an antecedent of trust. As the focus of this research is on exogenous variables characterized by perceived attributes of online shopping, the construct of perceived security rather than trust is used.

H2: *The more secure consumers perceive online shopping to be, the more positive will their attitudes toward the online shop be.*

Attitude Toward the Catalog

As the retailer's online shop is the virtual counterpart of the catalog-based distribution channel, an image transfer from the existing channel to the Web-based channel could take place, thus influencing attitudes toward the online shop. Consumers do not regard the Internet as an independent world separate from other shopping channels (Kaufman-Scarborogh & Lindquist, 2002). This claim is based on the findings by Balabanis and Reynolds (2001), who identified the store network of an apparel retailer as an important determinant of consumers' attitudes toward an

177

online shop. Similarly, Hansen (2005) found a significant influence of consumers' perceptions of the off-line channel on their attitudes toward the online shop. Hence, we conclude that people's attitudes toward the catalog positively influence their attitudes toward the online shop.

H3: *The more positive consumers' attitudes toward the catalog are, the more positive will their attitudes toward the online shop be.*

We also assume that consumers' attitudes toward the printed catalog as the complementary distribution channel directly influence shopping behavior at the online shop. Ahn, Ryu, and Han (2004) investigated the influence of off-line features, such as delivery and customer service, on the perceived usefulness of an online shop. However, a direct relationship between attitude toward one distribution channel and buying behavior at another channel has not been investigated yet, although there are indications that this relationship might be relevant. Consumers who are familiar with the printed catalog but are not experienced in using the Web site may decide to shop online irrespective of their attitudes toward the online shop. In addition, the existing distribution channel (i.e., the printed catalog) might be more prominent in the consumers' minds than the relatively new online shop. Hence, we assume that the more positive consumers' attitudes toward the printed catalog are, the more intensively will they buy from the online shop.

H4: *The more positive consumers' attitudes toward the catalog are, the more will they spend at the online shop.*

Attitude Toward the Online Shop

Attitude toward the online shop is the only endogenous factor influencing shopping behavior in the model. Yang and Lester (2004) and Lepkowska-White (2004) have empirically demonstrated that online buyers have a more positive attitude toward online shopping than nonbuyers. According to the theory of reasoned action (Ajzen & Fishbein, 1980) and Ajzen's (1991) theory of planned behavior, attitudes have a considerable impact on behavior (Churchill & Iacobucci, 2002). Therefore, we hypothesize that consumers' attitudes toward the online shop positively influence shopping behavior.

H5: *The more positive consumers' attitudes toward the online shop are, the more will they spend at the online shop.*

H3, H4, and H5 imply that consumers' attitudes toward the online shop can be assumed to directly influence shopping behavior as well as to mediate the influence of attitudes toward the catalog on shopping behavior. Hence, the model includes a mediational "triangle" with partial mediation (Venkatraman, 1989), as proposed in the models specified by Taylor and Todd (1995) and Pflughoeft, Ramamurthy, Soofi, Yasai-Ardekani, and Zahedi (2003).

RESEARCH METHODOLOGY

The consumer survey was carried out in cooperation with a major mail-order company in the German-speaking part of Europe and took place in the context of a master thesis under the author's supervision (Hummel, 2005). The cooperating company, henceforth "the retailer," had been doing catalog business successfully for many years before it established an online shop in the mid-1990s. The retailer issues a printed catalog twice a year with a volume of approximately 1,300 pages. In addition, several special catalogs are available. Describing the retailer by means of Coelho and Englewood's (2003) framework, we can say that the investigated shop is closely linked to its traditional distribution channel. The online shop is wholly owned by the retailer and is highly integrated. The retailer uses exclusively these two channels. The online shop comprises almost the same range of goods as the catalog and charges the same prices. Like the printed catalog, the online shop is divided into several product groups. The retailer offers a wide range of goods including the following product categories: apparel (ladies' wear, men's wear, children's wear, sportswear), furniture, consumer electronics, jewelry, sports and leisure, gardening, home improvement, cosmetics, toys and baby products, and car accessories.

All these categories are sold via the catalog and the online shop. The retailer uses the same logos and product photos online and in the printed catalog and has chosen a Web site design similar to the catalog design. Since the two channels are rather similar and do not target different consumer groups, they are classified as a monolithic channel system (Cespedes & Corey, 1990).

The online survey was conducted among the recipients of the retailer's newsletter in a period of one month in October and November 2004. A total of 35,000 subscribers of the retailer's free newsletter were contacted via e-mail and directed to the questionnaire. It is not necessary to be a customer of the company to receive the newsletter, but users have to register to be able to subscribe to the newsletter. Recipients are regularly informed via e-mail about promotions and special offers of

the retailer. Respondents were unable to access the questionnaire more than once. As an incentive for participation, a weekend trip was given away as a prize.

Before the survey was carried out, the questionnaire was revised by the retailer's marketing manager and two marketing assistants as well as the IT manager and two employees in the IT department. Next, the questionnaire was pretested by asking 12 undergraduate students to fill it out online. The questionnaire was not considerably changed after the pretest. Only minor adjustments in wording were necessary to ensure that the items would be interpreted correctly. Furthermore, a question concerning specific features of the online shop was removed, since it was not directly related to the model. This question was also eliminated to reduce the questionnaire's length. Finally, a status bar on each page indicated the completion progress of the questionnaire.

A total of 4,433 respondents answered the questionnaire, which corresponds to a response rate of 12.7%. Out of these, 2,070 incomplete questionnaires were eliminated, since they could not be used for model testing, which resulted in a sample of 2,363 completed questionnaires to be used for the analysis. A description of the sample's sociodemographic attributes is displayed in Table 2.

Table 2. Sample demographics (n = 2,363)

Gender		Age	
Male	34.2%	younger than 20 years	0.9%
Female	64.7%	20-29 years	16.4%
Education		30-39 years	32.2%
Primary school	5.2%	40-49 years	29.6%
Apprenticeship/vocational school	41.4%	50-59 years	16.2%
Secondary school	18.4%	60 years and older	4.7%
High school	24.7%		
University	10.3%		

As Table 2 shows, the sample contains a high proportion of female respondents, which can be put down to the similar gender distribution of the retailer's customers and its newsletter recipients. To some extent, the age structure of the sample also reflects the structure of the retailer's customers. However, the extremely small proportion of young users among the respondents (less than one percent) is striking for two reasons. First, the vast majority of young people below 20 years of age use the Internet regularly in the country where the study was conducted (Integral, 2006). Second, young people are usually more likely to participate in surveys than older persons. Both facts increase the probability that this age group participates in a survey. However, the age breakdown suggests differently, which can be explained by the structure of customers and prospective buyers of the mail-order company involved in the survey. Like many other mail-order companies, this retailer also has relatively few young customers. The educational level of the respondents is less biased. Although university graduates are a bit overrepresented, the educational structure is representative of the population of Internet users.

The respondents are very familiar with the Internet and online shopping. 53.7% have used the Internet for more than four years and 75.3% are online daily. The most popular purposes of Internet usage are information gathering (65.2% strongly agreed), banking (50.2%), and communicating (42.4%). 24.7% strongly agreed that they used the Internet for shopping purposes, while only 14.7% disagreed or strongly disagreed with this statement. Most respondents are also frequent online shoppers. 49.6% bought more than 10 times online last year and 30.3% bought online 5 to 10 times.

SCALE DEVELOPMENT

In order to test the research hypotheses discussed above, a set of scales has been developed for measuring the constructs, either derived from the literature or developed from scratch. The scales for perceived convenience were mainly adapted from Yang and Lester (2004), who investigated attitudes toward online shopping among online shoppers and nonshoppers. The perceived security items are derived from Hoffmann, Novak, and Peralata's (1999) study on consumer perceptions of online shopping and Miyazaki and Fernandez's (2001) research on privacy and security risks in online shopping. Attitudes toward the online shop were measured using and adapting the scales developed by Kim and Stoel (2004), who identified dimensions of Web site quality and satisfaction. The scales pertaining to attitudes toward the online shop were derived from Gehrt and Yan (2004) and Dholakia, Zhao, and Dholakia (2005). The former investigated factors influencing consumers' choice among online, catalog, and store channels, while the latter focused on channel choice between online shops and catalogs, taking into account catalog-specific aspects. Finally, online

Table 3. Reliabilities of constructs

Construct	Number of items	Cronbach alpha
OSCONV (perceived convenience of online shopping)	6	.863
OSSEC (perceived security of online shopping), reverse coded	6	.831
SHP_ATT (attitude toward online shop)	5	.851
CAT_ATT (attitude toward the printed catalog)	5	.819
SHP_BEH (shopping behavior at the online shop)	2	.614

Table 4. Factor loadings of the individual items

	Perceived convenience of online shopping (OSCONV)	Perceived security of online shopping (OSSEC)	Attitude toward the online shop (SHP_ATT)	Attitude toward the printed catalog (CAT_ATT)	Online shopping behavior (SHP_BEH)	Source of items
Online shopping 24 hours a day	.817					Young & Lester (2004)
Product and price comparison	.726					Young & Lester (2004)
Shopping independent for location	.772					Young & Lester (2004)
Time-saving	.688					Young & Lester (2004)
Convenient because of home delivery	.653					new
No time pressure	.812					new
Access to personal & payment data*		.653				Miyazaki & Fernandez (2001)
Security problems during payment*		.702				new
Data misuse for advertising purposes*		.776				Hoffman et al. (1999)
Trustworthiness of online shops		.676				new
Misuse of personal data*		.853				Hoffman et al. (1999)
Sharing of sensitive data with third parties*		.748				Hoffman et al. (1999)
Quick loading of shop			.763			Kim & Stoel (2004)
High image quality of shop			.790			new
User-friendliness of shop			.741			Kim & Stoel (2004)
Visually appealing design of shop			.736			Kim & Stoel (2004)
Up-to-date pages of shop			.644			new
Good design of catalog				.580		new
Easy and quick ordering from catalog				.697		Gehrt & Yan (2004)
Easy calculation of shopping amount				.676		new
Easy handling of returns				.746		Dholakia et al. (2005)
Confidential treatment of personal data				.726		Gehrt & Yan (2004)
Frequency of buying at online shop					.823	
Average annual spending at online shop					.849	new
Eigenvalue	6.446	3.293	2.183	1.387	1.184	
Variance Explained	.153	.137	.136	.117	.061	

* *reverse coded*

shopping behavior was measured using two items that capture the average frequency of buying from the online shop and the average amount of money spent there. All individual items and their sources are displayed in Table 4.

For item measurement, a 5-point Likert-type scale was used. It ranged from 1 (strongly agree) to 5 (strongly disagree). The constructs were the result of an exploratory factor analysis. In Table 3, the number of items used for each construct and their corresponding Cronbach Alpha values are presented.

Carrying out an exploratory factor analysis, we developed the constructs using formative items. Prior to this analysis, we ran the Kaiser-Meyer-Olkin test, which resulted in a value of 0.902, that is, above the recommended value of 0.90. Hence, data is considered appropriate for factor analysis. Subsequently, we applied the main component analysis with Varimax rotation. Only factors with Eigenvalues > 1 were used, which left us with five factors. The total explained variance is 60.39%. Table 4 shows the items and their sources, the constructs, and their factor loadings.

STUDY RESULTS

In order to analyze the antecedents of shopping behavior at the retailer's online shop, we calculated a structural equation model (SEM) using AMOS 5 (Arbuckle, 1999). Only fully completed questionnaires were used for the analysis.

Table 5 shows the standardized regression weights and their levels of significance obtained by the SEM. It indicates that all hypotheses, except for H2, are accepted. The asterisks denote the level of significance (see bottom of Table 5). All paths are significant at least at a 0.05 level. As the regression weight of H2, however, is close to zero, this hypothesis is rejected.

H1 assumed an influence of perceived convenience of online shopping (OS_CONV) on attitudes toward the online shop (SHP_ATT). This hypothesis is supported given the standardized regression coefficient of 0.198 with $p < .001$. H2 stated that attitudes toward the online shop (SHP_ATT) are influenced by perceived security of online shopping (OSSEC). The coefficient of -0.049 is highly significant but as this relationship is very weak, we reject H2. The next relationship investigated, posited by H3, pertains to the influence of attitudes toward the printed catalog (CAT_ATT) on attitudes toward the online shop (SHP_ATT). Here, the standardized regression coefficient amounts to 0.676 and is highly significant as well ($p < .001$). This value is, in fact, the highest in the whole model. H4 is also supported by the model with a coefficient of 0.118 and a p of <0.01. Finally, a relatively weak but still significant relationship is revealed by H5, which assumed that attitudes toward the online shop (SHP_ATT) influence buying behavior (SHP_BEH). The SEM procedure yields a standardized regression coefficient of 0.095 and a p level of 0.013.

Table 5. Results of the structural equation model

Hypothesis	Path	Regression weights	Significance	Hypothesis accepted/rejected
H1	OSCONV –> SHP_ATT	.198	***	accepted
H2	OSSEC –> SHP_ATT	-.049	**	rejected
H3	CAT_ATT –> SHP_ATT	.676	***	accepted
H4	CAT_ATT –> SHP_BEH	.118	**	accepted
H5	SHP_ATT –> SHP_BEH	.095	*	accepted
*** $p < .001$, ** $p < .01$, * $p < .05$, n.s. not significant				

In order to evaluate how well the model represents the real structure of the data, a series of fit indices is calculated using AMOS 5. In the following, those indices that have proved to be appropriate indicators in previous research are presented in Table 6 together with the values recommended in the academic literature (Anderson & Gerbing, 1984; Bentler, 1990; Brown & Cudek, 1993; Byrne, 2001; Hair, Anderson, Tatham, & Black, 1995). Being sensitive to large data sets, the Chi-square statistic is not used as an index of fit in this survey (Kline, 1998).

Table 6. Fit indices of the hypothesized model

Goodness of fit measure	Recommended value	Calculated value
GFI	.90 (Gefen et al., 2003)	.933
AGFI	.80 (Gefen et al., 2003)	.919
RMSEA	.08 (Brown & Cudek, 1993)	.055
Tucker-Lewis	.90 (Hair et al., 1995)	.913
NFI	.90 (Hair et al., 1995)	.911
CFI	.90 (Myerscough 2002)	.921

Table 7. Regression weights and hypotheses testing for the male sample

Male respondents (n = 809)				
Hypothesis	Path	Standardized regression weights	Significance	Hypothesis accepted/ rejected
H1	OSCONV –> SHP_ATT	.201	***	accepted
H2	OSSEC –> SHP_ATT	-.015	n.s.	rejected
H3	CAT_ATT –> SHP_ATT	.549	***	accepted
H4	CAT_ATT –> SHP_BEH	.213	***	accepted
H5	SHP_ATT –> SHP_BEH	.053	n.s.	rejected
*** p < .001, ** p < .01, * p < .05, n.s. not significant				

Table 8. Regression weights and hypotheses testing for the female sample

Female respondents (n = 1,528)				
Hypothesis	Path	Standardized regression weights	Significance	Hypothesis accepted/ rejected
H1	OSCONV –> SHP_ATT	.197	***	accepted
H2	OSSEC –> SHP_ATT	-.072	***	rejected
H3	CAT_ATT –> SHP_ATT	.725	***	accepted
H4	CAT_ATT –> SHP_BEH	.038	n.s.	rejected
H5	SHP_ATT –> SHP_BEH	.120	**	accepted
*** p < .001, ** p < .01, * p < .05, n.s. not significant				

As Table 6 shows, GFI, AGFI, and RMSEA comply with the recommended values. Also the baseline comparisons of the Tucker-Lewis index, the NFI, and the CFI exceed the 0.9 level. As a whole, the fit indices suggest a good fit of the model to the data.

In a next step, the influence of gender on the hypothesized model was analyzed. For this purpose, a multigroup analysis was performed (Byrne, 2001). The results are summarized in Table 7 for male respondents and Table 8 for female respondents. The total number of male and female respondents is lower than the total sample size, as 26 respondents did not indicate their gender and were thus excluded from the gender-specific analysis.

As shown in Table 7 and Table 8, tests of Hypotheses 1, 2, and 3 yield results consistent with the overall analysis. Women's attitudes toward the catalog influence their attitudes toward the online shop more strongly than those of men (regression weight of 0.735 compared with 0.549). Among women, attitudes toward the online shop are also influenced by perceived security to a higher extent. However, since the regression weight of 0.072 is still rather small, Hypothesis 2 is not accepted.

Concerning Hypotheses 4 and 5, significant differences between men and women can be observed. Hypothesis 4 is accepted for the male sample but rejected for the female sample. Hence, among men online shopping behavior is influenced by their attitudes toward the catalog but not by their attitudes toward the online shop. Conversely, Hypothesis 5 is rejected for the male sample but accepted for the female sample, suggesting that the opposite is true for women. Their online shopping behavior is influenced by their attitudes toward the online shop but not by their attitudes toward the catalog. This difference also explains the weaker significance level of Hypotheses 4 and 5 in the analysis of the whole sample.

DISCUSSION

The study investigated exogenous and endogenous antecedents of online shopping behavior of a multichannel retailer. As the results show, the most important factor influencing consumers' attitudes toward an online shop is their attitudes toward the catalog, which is a variable exogenous to the online shop. This result strengthens the assumption that image transfer effects are key determinants of consumers' attitudes toward an online sales channel. For an electronic retailer, this means that online and off-line distribution channels marketed under the same brand name should not be separated from each other. This result is consistent with the findings from several empirical studies (Balabanis & Reynolds, 2001; Kaufman-Scarborough & Lindquist, 2002), reporting that there are close links among distribution channels of a company. Since Internet buyers have a strong tendency to switch channels (Dholakia, Zhao, & Dholakia, 2005), brands can serve as anchors for retailers by building online loyalty and preventing customer switching (Chen & Hitt, 2002).

Among the other exogenous variables, perceived convenience of e-commerce has a significant influence on consumers' attitudes toward the online shop. Hence, consumers' general perceptions of the Internet as a shopping channel can have an impact on attitudes toward an individual online retailer. Consumers who regard online shopping as convenient have more favorable attitudes toward the online shop. As a large proportion of the consumers surveyed are also catalog shoppers, we conclude that convenience is an important factor for them. Convenience of online shopping can thus lead to more favorable attitudes toward the multichannel retailer's online shop among catalog shoppers and, eventually, toward online shopping.

Perceived security of online shopping does not seem to have any noteworthy effects on attitudes toward the online shop, with the relationship in the female sample slightly stronger than that for the male sample. People who believe that online shopping is secure do not view the shop more positively. This result is consistent with the findings by Salisbury, Pearson, Pearson, & Miller, (2001), who showed that perceived Web security does not influence consumers' intention to buy online. Also, the TAM-based research model by McCloskey (2004) reveals no significant impact of security concerns on buying behavior.

Notably, the antecedents of buying behavior at the retailer's online shop differ significantly for the two genders. This suggests that gender moderates the relationships between attitudes toward the catalog, attitudes toward the online shop, and buying behavior at the online shop. In the mediational triangle of the model, the paths resulting from the regression weights of men and women differ substantially. Gender differences in online shopping have been examined in numerous empirical studies, for example, Hansen (2005), Chang and Samuel (2004), and Rodgers and Harris (2003), all of which reveal that gender significantly influences various aspects of online shopping and related antecedents. Also, Eastlick and Feinberg (1994) have investigated differences between the two genders in the context of catalog shopping.

The present study reveals that men's attitudes toward the catalog are an important antecedent of purchasing behavior at the online shop, suggesting that attitudes become influential across channels among men. One explanation for this may be existing buying habits, for example, when consumers select products from the catalog and order them online. As Cheung and Limayem (2005) point out, habits are an important determinant of usage intentions. Catalog shoppers are used to the printed catalog and may regard it as the retailer's main distribution channel. However, this is only a speculative assumption that requires additional empirical evidence and cannot be confirmed by this study. The buying behavior of women, how-

ever, is determined by their attitudes toward the online shop rather than toward the catalog. Further research is needed to investigate the differences in buying patterns of men and women.

The results have several managerial implications for retailers: First, the study supports the notion that multichannel retailers can exploit synergies from their different distribution channels (Madlberger, 2006). If a positive attitude toward the printed catalog leads to a positive attitude toward the online shop, this fact is important for a mail-order company in a heterogeneous and complex online shopping environment. Even if a direct influence of attitudes toward the catalog on online buying behavior is only observed for men, attitudes toward the catalog are also indirectly relevant for women. The results imply, however, that marketing activities should be adapted to male and female target groups. Male customers of the retailer facilitating the survey mainly order electronics and men's wear but also ladies' wear and linens, whereas women order ladies' wear, linens, men's wear, and children's wear most frequently. Also sportswear and home textiles are ordered by female consumers in particular. Hence, for product categories that are chiefly of interest to men, an online catalog retailer should focus on creating positive attitudes toward the catalog. For categories that are mainly targeted at women, positive attitudes toward the online shop should be the goal. For both genders, perceived convenience of Internet shopping is relevant. Therefore, a retailer not only needs to offer a high level of convenience but is also dependent on consumers' general perceived convenience of Internet shopping. Consumers who have had bad experiences in this context might transfer these impressions to the online shop.

The model demonstrates that an online distribution channel strongly depends on the catalog business. This result is consistent with prior research on channel integration (e.g., Dennis, Hamis, & Sandhu, 2002; Enders & Jelassi, 2000; Oinas, 2002). The results stress the implication that it is essential to multichannel retailers to fully integrate their sales channels.

Similarly, as attitudes toward the printed catalog exert direct and indirect influences on online buying behavior, the majority of online customers are committed to the existing distribution channel. This appears to be a critical issue when mail-order companies want to attract new target groups, since attitudes toward the catalog seem to be a kind of gateway to the online shop. The retailer cannot rely on the possibility of the online shop attracting new consumers. In view of a very stable but narrow customer base with a small proportion of young and well educated people, the Internet would be a promising supplement to the traditional catalog business. Also in this respect, multichannel catalog retailers should put much effort on value-generating opportunities due to channel integration.

CONCLUSION AND LIMITATIONS

The results of this study have confirmed that an existing distribution channel has an influence on buying behavior at a retailer's online shop. This study is a first step toward understanding channel choices, particularly in the context of mail-order companies. It has several limitations that provide interesting avenues for future research in order to gain deeper insights into this topical issue in e-commerce.

Limitations of this study are twofold, pertaining to both the proposed model and the survey method. First, the proposed model is a very simplistic one given the high complexity of multichannel retailing. Some important variables have been left out that might play a key role in understanding consumer behavior in multichannel retailing.

Within the proposed model and its endogenous variable, antecedents of attitudes toward the online shop should be addressed in future studies. Research on TAM in an online shopping context is

an appropriate point of departure for this area and justifies the application of perceived usefulness and perceived ease of use. Additionally, factors that have turned out to be relevant for online shopping in prior research, such as trust in the retailer or the design of the online shop (Ahn et al., 2004), should be addressed. Also the mediating effect of attitude toward the online shop could be investigated more closely.

A key point that needs further attention is research on the reasons for the different antecedents of online buying behavior between men and women. Special attention should be paid to buying processes and buying patterns across channels. Habits might play a major role in this context and might moderate relationships as well (Cheung & Limayem, 2005).

In the context of exogenous variables, attitude toward the catalog is a key influencing factor. Therefore, antecedents of this variable should be investigated as well. A starting point could be the research by Duffy (2004) and Gehrt and Yan (2004). Attitudes and perceived characteristics of Internet shopping in general might considerably differ between experienced and inexperienced online shoppers, thus moderating the relationship between exogenous and endogenous variables. In addition, other exogenous variables, such as the perceived value of individualization or general online shopping patterns could be investigated. Finally, additional sociodemographic attributes could be included in the investigation.

Concerning the research methodology and the sample, it has to be stressed that the study was conducted in cooperation with one specific mail-order company, which limits the generalizability of the results. The respondents to the questionnaire are consumers who have subscribed to the retailer's newsletter and therefore have a certain relationship with the company. As most of the respondents are also customers, we do not gain insights into how other target groups behave and how the retailer could attract new customers. The study is restricted to the target group of one particular retailer, which limits the generalizability of the model to other retailers' customers, although most mail-order companies in the German-speaking world are faced with similar conditions and may thus draw conclusions from the above results. In order to obtain results that are more representative, the study should be replicated among a less specific group of consumers.

ACKNOWLEDGMENT

We thank the cooperating mail-order company that wants to be kept anonymous for participation and support of the survey. The management's engagement in the survey was essential for carrying out the investigation. The author is also very grateful to Michael Hummel, undergraduate student at the Vienna University of Economics and Business Administration. He assisted in preparing the questionnaire and collected data under the author's supervision.

REFERENCES

Ahn, T., Ryu, S., & Han, I. (2004). The impact of the online and offline features on the user acceptance of Internet shopping malls. *Electronic Commerce Research and Applications, 3*(4), 405-420.

Ajzen, I. (1991). The theory of planned behavior. *Organizational Behavior & Human Decision Processes, 50*(2), 179-211.

Ajzen, I., & Fishbein, M. (1980). *Understanding attitudes and predicting social behavior.* Englewood Cliffs, NJ: Prentice Hall.

Alba, J., Lynch, J., Weitz, B., Janiszewski, C., Lutz, R., Sawyer, A., & Wood, S. (1997). Interactive home shopping: Consumer, retailer, and manufacturer incentives to participate in electronic marketplaces. *Journal of Marketing, 61*(3), 38-53.

Alptekinoglu, A., & Tang, C.S. (2005). A model for analyzing multi-channel distribution systems. *European Journal of Operational Research, 163*(3), 802-824.

Amato-McCoy, D.M. (2006, November). Crossing channels. Chain Store Age, pp. 49-50.

Anderson, J.C., & Gerbing, D.W. (1984). The effect of sampling error on convergence, improper solutions, and goodness-of-fit indices for maximum likelihood confirmatory factor analysis. *Psychometrika, 49*(2), 155-173.

Arbuckle, J.L. (1999). *Amos User's Guide, Version 4.0.* Chicago: Smallwaters Cooperation.

Balabanis, G., & Reynolds, N.L. (2001). Consumer attitudes towards multi-channel retailer's Web sites: The role of involvement, brand attitude, Internet knowledge, and visit duration. *Journal of Business Strategies, 18*(2), 105-131.

Balasubramanian, S. (1998). Mail versus mall: A strategic analysis of competition between direct marketers and conventional retailers. *Marketing Science, 17*(3), 181-195.

Bentler, P.M. (1990). Comparative fit indexes in structural models. *Psychological Bulletin, 107*(2), 238-246.

Berman, B., & Evans, J.R. (2001). *Retail management: A strategic approach.* Upper Saddle River, NJ: Prentice Hall.

Berman, B., & Thelen, S. (2004). A guide to developing and managing a well-integrated multi-channel retail strategy. *International Journal of Retail & Distribution Management, 32*(2/3), 147-156.

Bhatnagar, A., Misra, S., & Rao, H.R. (2000). On risk, convenience, and lutesnet shopping behavior. *Communications of the ACM, 43*(11), 98-105.

Bhattacherjee, A. (2002). Individual trust in online firms: Scale development and initial tests. *Journal of Management Information Systems, 19*(1), 211-242.

Blyth, G. (2006, July 6). *Why we're still missing the cross-channel opportunity.* New Media Age, p. 15.

Brown, M.W., & Cudeck R. (1993). Alternative ways of assessing model fit. In K.A. Bollen & S. Long (Eds.), Testing structural equation models (pp. 136-162). Newbury Park, CA: Sage Publications.

Burke, R.R. (2002). Technology and the customer interface: What consumers want in the physical world and virtual store. *Journal of the Academy of Marketing Science, 30*(4), 411-432.

Burroughs, R.E., & Sabherwal, R. (2002). Determinants of retail electronic purchasing: A multi-period investigation. *Journal of Information System Operation Research, 40*(1), 35-56.

Burton, D. (2000). Postmodernism, social relations and remote shopping. *European Journal of Marketing, 36*(7/8), 792-810.

Byrne, B.M. (2001). *Structural equation modeling with AMOS.* Mahwah, NJ: Lawrence Erlbaum Associates.

Cespedes, F.V., & Corey, E.R. (1990). Managing multiple channels. *Business Horizons, 33*(3), 67-77.

Chang, J., & Samuel, N. (2004). Internet shopper demographics and buying behavior in Australia. *Journal of the Academy of Business, 5*(1/2), 171-176.

Chang, M.K., Cheung, W., & Lai, V.S. (2005). Literature derived reference models for the adoption of online shopping. *Information & Management, 42*(4), 543-559.

Chen, P.-Y., & Hitt, L.M. (2002). Measuring switching costs and the determinants of customer retention in Internet-enabled businesses: A study of the online brokerage industry. *Information Systems Research, 13*(3), 255-274.

Cheung, M.K., & Limayem, M. (2005, May). The role of habit and the changing nature of the relationship between intention and usage. In *Proceedings of the 13th European Conference of Information Systems*, Regensburg, Germany.

Churchill, G.A.J., & Iacobucci, D. (2002). *Marketing research: Methodological foundations.* Mason, OH: South-Western Publishing.

Coelho, I., Easingwood, C., & Coelho, A. (2003). Exploratory evidence of channel performance in signal vs. multiple channel stratregies. *International Journal of Detail & Distribution Management, 31*(11/12), 501-573.

Coughlan, A.T., Anderson, E., Stern, L.W., & El-Ansary, A.I. (2001). *Marketing channels.* Upper Saddle River, NJ: Prentice Hall.

Dawson, M. (2001). Land in Sicht. *Lebensmittelzeitung Spezial E-Business, 1*, 60-61.

Davis, F.D. (1989). Perceived usefulness, perceived ease of use, and user acceptance of information technology. *MIS Quarterly, 13*(3), 317-340.

Del Franco, M. (2006, February). The "C" is for channel. Multichannel Merchant, pp. 1-34.

Dellaert, B.G.C., & Kahn, B.E. (1999). How tolerable is delay? Consumer's evaluation of Internet Web sites after waiting. *Journal of Interactive Marketing, 13*(1), 41-54.

Dennis, C., Harris, L., & Sandhu, B. (2002). From bricks to clicks: Understanding the e-consumer. *Qualitative Market Research: An International Journal, 5*(4), 281-290.

Dholakia, R.R., Zhao, M., & Dholakia, N. (2005). Multichannel retailing. A case study of early experiences. *Journal of Interactive Marketing, 19*(2), 63-74.

Doney, P.M., & Cannon, J.P. (1997). An examination of the nature of trust in the buyer-seller relationship. *Journal of Marketing, 61*(2), 35-51.

Duffy, D.L. (2004). Using online retailing as a springboard for catalog marketing. *Journal of Consumer Marketing, 21*(3), 221-225.

Each Delivery Channel Has Its Own Strengths. (2006, December 18). Credit Union Executive Newsletter, p. 3.

Eastlick, M.A., & Feinberg, R.A. (1994). Gender differences in mail-catalog patronage motives. *Journal of Direct Marketing, 8*(2), 37-44.

Eastlick, M.A., & Feinberg, R.A. (1999). Shopping motives for mail catalog shopping. *Journal of Business Research, 45*(3), 281-290.

Edwards, L. (2004). Reconstructing consumer privacy protection on-line: A modest proposal. *International Review of Law Computers, 18*(3), 313-344.

Enders, A., & Jelassi, T. (2000). The converging business models of Internet bricks and clicks retailers. *European Management Journal, 18*(5), 542-550.

Fain, D. (1994). *Consumers navigating channels: Behavior motivations for direct vs. retail.* Unpublished manuscript, New York University.

Gabrielsson, M., Kirpalani, V.H.M., & Luostarinen, R. (2002). Multiple channel strategies in the European personal computer industry. *Journal of International Marketing, 10*(3), 73-95.

Gallaugher, J.M. (2002). E-commerce and the undulating distribution channel. *Communications of the ACM, 45*(7), 89-95.

Gefen, D., Karahanna, E., & Straub, D.W. (2003). Trust and TAM in online shopping: An integrated model. *MIS Quarterly, 27*(1), 51-90.

Gefen, D. (2000). E-commerce: The role of familiarity and trust. *Omega: The International Journal of Management Science, 28*(6), 725-737.

Gehrt, K.C., & Yan (2004). Situational, consumer, and retailer factors affecting Internet, catalog, and store shopping. *International Journal of Retail and Distribution Management, 32*(1), 5-18.

Grosso, C., McPherson, J., & Shi, C. (2004). Retailing: What's working online. *McKinsey Quarterly, 2005*(3), 18-20.

Gupta, A., Su, B., & Walter, Z. (2004). Risk profile and consumer shopping behavior in electronic and traditional channels. *Decision Support Systems, 38*(3), 347-367.

Haeberle, M. (2003). On-line retailing scores big. *Chain Store Age, 79*(7), 48.

Hair, J., Anderson, R.E., Tatham, R.L., & Black, W.C. (1995). *Multivariate data analysis with readings.* Englewood Cliffs, NJ: Prentice Hall.

Hansen, H.R., & Madlberger, M. (2007). Beziehungen zwischen dem Internet-Vertrieb und anderen Absatzwegen im Einzelhandel. In B.W. Wirtz (Ed.), *Handbuch Multi Channel Marketing,* Wiesbaden, Germany. Gabler.

Hansen, T. (2005). Understanding consumer online grocery behavior: Results from a Swedish study. *Journal of Euromarketing, 14*(3), 31-58.

Hoffman, D.L., Novak, T.P., & Peralta, M. (1999). Building consumer trust online. *Communications of the ACM, 42*(4), 80-85.

Hong, W., Thong, J.Y.L., & Tam, K.Y. (2004). The effects of information format and shopping task on consumers' online shopping behavior: A cognitive fit perspective. *Journal of Management Information Systems, 21*(3), 149-184.

Hummel, M. (2005). *E-commerce: Eine Sonderform des Versandhandels?* Unpublished master's thesis, Vienna University of Economics and Business Administration, Vienna, Austria.

Ibbotson, P., & Fahy, M. (2004). The impact of e-commerce on small Irish firms. *International Journal of Services Technology & Management, 5*(4), 317-331.

Integral. (2006). *Austrian Internet Monitor Internet-Entwicklung 3.* Quartal 2005. Retrieved September 7, 2007, from http://www.integral.co.at/dImages/AIM-C_3.%20Quartal2005.pdf

Januz, L.R. (1983). It's helpful to know who is purchasing through the mail. *Marketing News, 17,* 4.

Jarvenpaa, S.L., & Todd, P.A. (1997). Consumer reactions to electronic shopping on the World Wide Web. *International Journal of Electronic Commerce, 1*(2), 59-88.

Jarvenpaa, S.L., Tractinsky, N., & Vitale, M. (2000). Consumer trust in an Internet store. *Information Technology and Management, 1,* 45-71.

Jasper, C.R., & Lan, P.-N.R. (1992). Apparel catalog patronage: Demographic, lifestyle and motivational factors. *Psychology and Marketing, 9*(4), 275-296.

Johnson, K.K.P., Yoo, J.-J., Thee, J., Lennon, S., Jasper, C., & Damhorst, M.L. (2006). Multi-channel shopping: Channel use among rural consumers. *International Journal of Retail & Distribution Management, 34*(6), 453-466.

Kaufman-Scarborough, C., & Lindquist, J.D. (2002). E-Shopping in a Multiple Channel Environment. *Journal of Consumer Marketing, 19*(4/5), 333-350.

Kennedy, A., & Coughlan, J. (2006). Online shopping portals: An option for traditional retailers? *International Journal of Retail & Distribution Management, 34*(7), 516-528.

Kim, S., & Stoel, L. (2004). Apparel retailers: Website quality dimensions and satisfaction. *Journal of Retailing and Consumer Services, 11*(2), 109-117.

Kline, R.B. (1998). *Principles and practice of structural equation modeling.* New York: Guilford.

Korgaonkar, P.K. (1984). Consumer shopping orientations, non-store retailers, and consumers' patronage intentions: A multivariate investigation. *Journal of the Academy of Marketing Science, 12*(1), 11-22.

Lederer, A.L., Maupin, D.J., Sena, M.P., & Zhuang, Y. (2000). The technology acceptance model and the World Wide Web. *Decision Support Systems, 29*(3), 269-282.

Lee, M.K.O., & Turban, E. (2001). A trust model for consumer Internet shopping. *International Journal of Electronic Commerce, 6*(1), 75-91.

Lepkowska-White, E. (2004). Online store perceptions: How to turn browsers into buyers? *Journal of Marketing Theory & Practice, 12*(3), 36-47.

Madlberger, M. (2004). *Electronic retailing.* Wiesbaden, Germany: Deutscher Universitaetsverlag.

Madlberger, M. (2006). *Multi-channel retailing in B2C e-commerce.* In M. Khosrow-Pour (Ed.), Encyclopedia of e-commerce, e-government, and mobile commerce. Hershey, PA: Idea Group.

Maltz, A., Rabinovic, E., & Sinha, R. (2004). Logistics: The key on e-retail success. *Supply Chain Management Review, 1,* 56-63.

McCloskey, D. (2004). Evaluating electronic commerce acceptance with the technology acceptance model. *Journal of Computer Information Systems, 44*(2), 49-57.

McKnight, D.H., Choudhury, V., & Kacmar, C. (2002a). Developing and validating trust measures for e-commerce: An integrative typology. *Information Systems Research, 13*(3), 334-359.

McKnight, D.H., Choudhury, V., & Kacmar, C. (2002b). The impact of initial consumer trust on intentions to transact with a Web site: A trust building model. *Journal of Strategic Information Systems, 11*(3-4), 297-323.

Min, S., & Wolfinbarger, M. (2005). Market share, profit margin, and marketing efficiency of early movers, bricks and clicks, and specialists in e-commerce. *Journal of Business Research, 58*, 1030-1039.

Miyazaki, A.D., & Fernandez, A. (2001). Consumer perceptions of privacy and security risks for online shopping. *The Journal of Consumer Affairs, 35*(1), 27-44.

Monsuwé, T.P.Y., Dellaert, B.G.C., & deRuyter, K. (2004). What drives consumers to shop online? A literature review. *International Journal of Service Industry Management, 15*(1), 102-121.

Moon, J.W., & Kim, Y.-G. (2001). Extending the TAM for a World-Wide-Web context. *Information & Management, 38*(4), 217-230.

Moriarty, R., & Moran, U. (1990). Managing hybrid marketing systems. *Harvard Business Review, 68*(6), 146-155.

Multichannel Retailing on the Rise. (2005a, September). Chain Store Age, p. 20.

Myers, J.B., Pickersgill, A.D., & Van Metre, E.S. (2004). Steering customers to the right channels. *McKinsey Quarterly, 4*, 36-47.

Myerscough, M.A. (2002, August). Information systems quality assessment: Replicating Kettinger and Lee's USIF/SERVQUAL combination. In *Proceedings of the 8th Americas Conference on Information Systems, Dallas*, TX (pp. 1104-1115).

Noble, S.M., Griffith, D.A., & Weinberger, M.G. (2005). Consumer derived utilitarian value and channel utilization in a multi-channel retail context. *Journal of Business Research, 58*, 1643-1651.

Oinas, P. (2002). Towards understanding network relationships in online retailing. *International Review of Retail, Distribution & Consumer Research, 12*(3), 319-335.

Pavlou, P.A. (2003). Consumer acceptance of electronic commerce: Integrating trust and risk with the technology acceptance model. *International Journal of Electronic Commerce, 7*(3), 101-134.

Pflughoeft, K.A., Ramamurthy, K., Soofi, E.S., Yasai-Ardekani, M., & Zahedi, F. (2003). *Multiple conceptualizations of small business Web use and benefit. Decision Sciences, 34*(3), 467-512.

Reichheld, F., & Schefter, P. (2000). E-loyalty: Your secret weapon on the Web. *Harvard Business Review, 78*(4), 105-113.

Retailers Missing Opportunities to Sell More Products Via Online. (2005b, August 11). *New Media Age*, p. 9.

Reynolds, F.D. (1974). An analysis of catalog buying behavior. *Journal of Marketing, 38*(3), 47-51.

Rodgers, S., & Harris, M.A. (2003). Gender and E-Commerce: An Exploratory Study. *Journal of Advertising Research, 43*(3), 322-329.

Salisbury, W.D., Pearson, R.A., Pearson, A.W., & Miller, D.W. (2001). Perceived security and World Wide Web purchase intention. *Industrial Management & Data Systems, 101*(3/4), 165-176.

Schoenbachler, D.D., & Gordon, G.L. (2002). Multi-channel shopping: Understanding what drives channel choice. *The Journal of Consumer Marketing, 19*(1), 42-53.

Seiders, K., Berry, L.L., & Gresham, L.G. (2000). Attention, retailers! How convenient is your convenience strategy? *Sloan Management Review, 41*(3), 79-89.

Sheth, J.N. (1983). An integrative theory of patronage preference and behavior. In W.R. Darden & R.F. Lusch (Eds.), *Patronage behavior and retail management* (pp. 9-28). New York: Elsevier Science Publishing.

Steinfield, C., Bouwman, H., & Adelaar, T. (2002). The dynamics of click-and-mortar electronic commerce: Opportunities and management strategies. *International Journal of Electronic Commerce, 7*(1), 93-119.

Suh, B., & Han, I. (2003). The impact of customer trust and perception of security control on the acceptance of electronic commerce. *International Journal of Electronic Commerce, 7*(3), 135-162.

Taylor, S., & Todd, P.A. (1995). Understanding information technology usage: A test of competing models. *Information Systems Research, 6*(2), 144-176.

Torkzadeh, G., & Dhillon, G. (2002). Measuring factors that influence the success of Internet commerce. *Information Systems Research, 13*(2), 187-204.

Venkatraman, N. (1989). The concept of fit in strategy research: Toward verbal and statistical correspondence. *Academy of Management Review, 14*(3), 423-444.

Wallace, D.W., Giese, J.L., & Johnson, J.L. (2004). Customer retailer loyalty in the context of multiple channel strategies. *Journal of Retailing, 80*(4), 249-263.

Xing, Y., & Grant, D.B. (2006). Developing a framework for measuring physical distribution service quality of multi-channel and "Pure Player" Internet retailers. *International Journal of Retail & Distribution Management, 34*(4/5), 278-289.

Yang, B., & Lester, D. (2004). Attitudes toward buying online. *Cyber Psychology & Behavior, 7*(1), 85-91.

Yellavalli, B., Holt, D., & Jandial, A. (2007). *Retail multi-channel integration. delivering a seamless customer experience* (Infosys White Paper). Retrieved September 7, 2007, from http://www.infosys.com/supplychain/InfosysMCIWhitePaperfinal.pdf

Yousafzai, S.Y., Pallister, J.G., & Foxall, G.R. (2003). A proposed model of e-trust for electronic banking. *Technovation, 23*(11), 847-860.

Chapter XI
Digitizing Business Relationship:
Some Practical and
Theoretical Considerations

Jari Salo
University of Oulu, Finland

ABSTRACT

Companies are involved in different types of business relationships for various reasons. These include, but are not limited to, efficiency gains, innovation, and influencing other organizations. In the age of digitization, managers have witnessed new ways to manage business relationships, as the number of digital and electronic commerce tools has mushroomed. Business relationships digitization is an under-researched area, and therefore the purpose of this chapter is to illustrate how relationships are digitized and what managers as well as academics should know about this emerging phenomenon. With the help of an extensive literature review, this chapter presents an overview of basic features and types of digitized business relationships. The author outlines a model that tackles critical factors while digitizing business relationships. In addition, a case example depicting the digitization process of a business relationship is presented. The chapter concludes with a description of the contribution of the study and presents suggestions for further research.

INTRODUCTION

Business relationships have been the key focus of marketing studies particularly in the IMP-Group and also in various forms in marketing channel literature (see Wilkinson, 2001, for review). Business relationships are built up successively and gradually from one time limited contact between organizations to often very close, far-reaching exchange relationships. It should be pointed out that although business relationships may seem to be in a stable phase, they are in a constant state of flux. The development of business relationships through stages or cycles has been described in many publications (see, e.g., Dwyer, Shurr, & Oh, 1987; Ford, 1980; Wilson & Mummalaneni, 1986).

Both the popular and academic press has regularly written that the amount of business relationships that exist between buyers and sellers has decreased, but similarly the amount of trade contracted within existing business relationships has simultaneously increased (see, e.g., Bakos & Brynjolfsson, 1993; Matthyssens & Van den Bulte, 1994). Hence, the fact remains that in many cases, it is not profitable to play dozens or even hundreds of competing suppliers or customers against each other, but instead work directly with a few of them within a business relationship that is profitable for all parties. This is because as the number of possible partners increases, so do transaction costs (Clemons, Reddi, & Row 1993; Stump & Sriram, 1997). Thus, it is evident that existing business relationships are a vital area for research.

Still, not all existing business relationships are worth fighting for. To identify those relationships that are most profitable, academics and managers have come up with many evaluation schemes and tools that will be presented here. For a discussion on evaluating customers, see Fiocca (1982), and for suppliers, see Kraljic (1983) for examples. There are also studies that describe the evaluation of buyer-seller relationships (see Bensaou, 1999). Identification of the key relationships to be digitized is a pertinent aspect as it acts as a prerequisite for successful digitization.

Besides business relationship literature, the author employs the digitization discussion evolving in both academic and business presses (Fisher & Reibstein, 2001; Salo, 2006a; Sawhney, 1999). The term digitization is employed in many studies but left undefined (see, e.g., Ordanini & Pol, 2001). In this chapter, the term *digitization* refers

to the process of making information, business activities, for example, selling (Johnson & Bharadwaj, 2005), and offerings digital. Thus, business relationship digitization can be defined as the process of making information, business activities, and offerings related to exchange between two organizations digital (see Salo, 2006a).

An academically and managerially interesting research gap can be identified at the intersection of business relationship and digitization discussions. The author aims to fill part of this gap by identifying the means to digitize business relationships. To further elaborate, there is a growing interest in addressing this highly inconsistent and fragmented as well as expanding body of literature (see, e.g., Holland & Naudé, 2004; Kandampully, 2003; Reid & Plank, 2000). Furthermore, it is acknowledged here that digitization literature to date has addressed market and hierarchy governance mechanisms (see, e.g., Alba, Lynch, Weitz, Janiszewski, Lutz, Sawyer, & Wood, 1997; Grewal, Comer, & Mehta 2001) rather than business relationships. As stated, the focus here is on business relationships and how they are digitized. More specifically, what managers should know about this emerging field is also discussed. The chapter is organized as follows: A literature review of digitization, the benefits of relationship digitization, and the tools for digitization are presented followed by ideas on how to effectively select the right business relationships to be digitized. After that, the author shows possible steps to be taken when digitizing business relationship. The first three steps are based on a literature review. Business relationship digitization management issues are then illustrated with the help of a case study. The chapter concludes with implications and future research directions.

POSSIBILITIES OF DIGITIZATION

It is a well-known fact that digital tools can be harnessed in business relationships to yield extraordinary profits. Digitizing something refers to transferring data into digital form. Digital, in short, is the representation of data in digital (i.e., numerical) form, generally using a form of binary coding; binary is a method for representing characteristics or numeric values using a two state coding scheme (Emery, 1987). The two values of a binary digit, state or bit, are 1 and 0 (Breeding, 1992, p. 1). According to Breeding (1992), the digital form itself brings flexibility, reliability, and lower costs to various activities. Therefore, it is interesting to know what can be digitized, that is, made digital and exchanged between business parties. MIT professor Negroponte (1995) argued that everything could be digitized. However, it is suggested here that there are two basic types of knowledge components: tacit and explicit (see, e.g., Polanyi, 1966). When the information component is known (explicit), it can be more easily digitized. In short, if we do not know exactly how to do something or what something is, we can not digitize it. Therefore, as Mata, Fuerst, and Barney (1995) suggested, information technology skills (or EC skills) are the only sustainable competitive advantage due to the fact that they are hard to imitate.

VALUE OF DIGITIZATION

Digitization is valuable to an organization if it reduces costs or creates concrete benefits like increased sales. Costs of digitization are clearly accountable but the benefits are usually more unclear. Organizations can expect differential benefits from the digital tool adoption and these gains may vary from operational to strategic benefits besides opportunity ones (Sloane, 1994). Similar benefits were identified by Naudé, Holland, and Sudbury (2000) while researching electronic data interchange (EDI) implementation.

Costs of digitization emerge from different sources (Manecke & Schoensleben, 2004; Wang & Tsai, 2002). Among others, these include

investments in hardware, software, and skilled people (Howells & Wood, 1995). Moreover, if the needed software is created internally then costs are even higher.

As for the benefits of digitization, they largely depend on the business relationship characteristics. Business relationships can be characterized in many ways, for example, by looking at the products or services exchanged, processes conducted, and actors involved. Based on Choi, Whinston, and Stahl (1997), each of these three aspects can be either digitized or not. Thus, it can be argued that different types of business relationships require different types of digital infrastructures and tools for digitization.

By detailing the characteristics, we can provide an illustration of the characteristics of business relationships. For example a fully digital business relationship can be formed, without human intervention, if the product, process, and actors are digital. Fully digital business relationships are an effective option for software selling, leasing, or virtual Internet-based mobile phone operators as full digitization is possible. Furthermore, as the systems of two companies are integrated, data transmissions and transactions can be automated and information can be exchanged dynamically. In the case example, the price of transactions can be tied to the general price index with the help of an arithmetic formula and integrated to a company's enterprise resource planning (ERP) module. It is noted here that purely digital business relationships seldom exist, as usually the organization interacting is partly physical at the end.

Since transmissions are automatic and dynamic, human intervention is usually only needed when entering into a contract at the initiation of relationship digitization. In a nutshell, costs for transacting between business and customers can be lowered since the customer is served via a digital channel. An example could be a ring tone service provider that after establishing a business relationship with a telecommunication service provider supplies all the ring tones over an Internet connection in digital form without face-to-face interactions.

Benefits are less visible in situations where physical products are sold or procured but a lot of the internal as well as within business relationship administrative activities can be fully automated or digitized. Basically, the benefits of digitization can be summarized into eight main points: (1) reducing the amount of manual labor and mistakes (in the case of EDI, see Stern & Kaufmann, 1985), (2) possibility of increasing the volume of business with the help of EDI, Internet or extranet without a corresponding increase in labor costs (computers are handling more of the routine activities) (Ryssel, Ritter, & Gemünden, 2004; Salo, 2006a; Vlosky, Fontenot, & Blalock, 2000), (3) making informational and transactional activities more accurate and faster than before as it is possible to automatically and dynamically update databases and Web pages (Lancioni, Smith, & Oliva, 2000; Philip & Pedersen, 1997), (4) saving time on transmissions but also on the amount of time spent on the telephone and in face-to-face meetings and negotiations (Stern & Kaufmann, 1985), (5) providing managers with more time to take care of important activities, for example, new sales and strategy creation (Stern & Kaufmann, 1985), (6) reducing shortages of materials and number of production breaks as real-time and dynamically changing information flows to production (Carr & Smeltzer, 2002; Vlosky et al., 2000), (7) making R&D faster and more accurate as product development information flows both ways within resource and development (R&D) teams engaged in the relationship (Naudé et al., 2000; Stauffert, 1991), and (8) strengthening existing business relationships through investments in digital tools and thus reducing uncertainties relating to the market and technology (Naudé et al., 2000; Ryssel et al., 2004; Stern & Kaufmann, 1985).

TOOLS FOR DIGITIZING BUSINESS RELATIONSHIPS

Now, with an understanding of what digitization is, it is easier to proceed to describe digital systems. Digital tools or systems are usually based on a combination of computers, software, and telecommunication networks. Together, these provide the digital infrastructure for a company. There are many systems that form the digital infrastructure, and they all need to be integrated within a business relationship. These systems provide the means to communicate in business relationships; for example, EDI represents the simplest solution where information transmissions can be conducted over private lines or the Internet. EDI is one of the oldest digital tools, but it is effective for repeated, similarly occurring information transmissions, for example, daily orders and overnight money settlements (see, e.g., Emmelhainz, 1993; Mukhopadhaya, 1998). Another more information rich communication and transaction solution is the extranet, in which connections are usually carried out over a secured Internet connection (Radosevich, 1997). In a more complex system setting, first or second generation ERP systems can be integrated over a secured Internet line with the help of EAI or Web services (see, e.g., Bond, Genovese, Miklovic, Wood, Zrimsek, & Rayner, 2000). These acronyms and their definitions, as well as some source material related to these systems are presented in Table 1.

Table 1 depicts some of the most commonly used tools for digitization and their usage as well as indicating sources for more information on each solution. Hasselbring (2000) and Salo (2006b) provide further information on how to integrate digital infrastructures inside and between organizations. All in all, it is visible that digitization and further automatization of activities, such as ordering, invoicing, and warehouse management, enables efficiency and innovation gains to be realized within business relationships. The question to be answered is which relationships should be digitized?

CHERRY PICKING THE BUSINESS RELATIONSHIPS TO BE DIGITIZED

It can be stated that those relationships that are suitable for digitization should be digitized. This is easier said than done. Suitability depends mainly

Table 1. Tools for creating and integrating digital infrastructures within business relationships

Digital tool	Purpose	Source of information
Electronic Data Interchange (EDI)	Standard protocols are used to share information among participating companies through computer-to-computer exchange of electronic documents relating to purchasing, selling, shipping, receiving, inventory control, financial, and other activities.	Stern and Kaufmann (1985) Emmelhainz (1993) Archer and Yuan (2000)
Electronic Data Interchange over secured internet (I-EDI)	Similar to EDI but over a secured Internet connection. Usually cheaper and has higher scalability than EDI. Identical to Web-based EDI.	Angeles (2000) Garcia-Dastuge and Lambert (2003)
Extranet	An extranet is usually built to communicate and exchange information with customers, suppliers, and other important third parties. In a technical sense, an extranet is formed when an organization permits outsiders access to their internal TCP/IP networks like the intranet. It is often less costly than the previous tools. Can be used to deliver more information rich material than EDI.	Radosevich (1997) Vlosky et al. (2000)
First generation Enterprise Resource Planning (ERP1) system	Total automation of the procurement process, from the point where an employee places an order, through the internal approval process, and right to eventual fulfillment with the help of different software modules. May include human resource management, payroll activities, and other financial documentation modules.	Krapf (1999) Hodge (2002) Motwani, Mirchandani, Madan, and Gunasekaran (2002) Al-Mashari, Al-Mudimigh, and Zairi (2003)
Second generation Enterprise Resource Planning (ERP2) system	Similar to ERP1 but extended beyond one organization to include inter-organizational parties. Provides a tool for managers to visualize inter-organizational processes. In practice it is hard to differentiate between first and second generation systems.	Gardiner, Hanna, and LaTour (2002) Hodge (2002)
Enterprise Application Integration (EAI)	Used as an enabler application between applications that are otherwise incompatible. Achieves application integration through four layers: connectivity, transportation, translation, and process automation.	Whiting (2003) Themistocleous and Irani (2002) Linthicum (2000)
Web services	Can be used universally to standardize communication between applications in order to connect systems, business partners, and customers cost-effectively through the World Wide Web. Enables easier and faster integration with trading partners. Usually less expensive than EAI but only suitable for small organizations.	Prokein and Faupel (2006) Curbera, Duftler, Khalaf, Nagy, Mukhi, and Weerawarana (2002), Chen, Chen, and Shao (2003), Whiting (2003)
ERP adapters	Some ERP software houses provide adapters that enable integration between their ERP system and competitors' ERP systems. Provides real-time information retrieval and update.	Stoer, Nienhaus, Birkeland, and Menkhaus (2003)
Customer Relationship Management system (CRM)	Used to manage information regarding a customer relationship between a customer and a seller. Usually seen as an effective way to manage a large base of B2C relationships (e.g., in the banking industry).	Wilson, Daniel, and McDonald (2002) Zablah, Bellenger, and Johnston (2004)

continued on following page

Table 1. continued

Digital tool	Purpose	Source of information
Supply Chain Management system (SCM)	Usually used to manage information and material flows between a manufacturer and a retailer. Retailing industry specific solutions are labeled efficient consumer response (ECR) solutions.	Lancioni (2000) Lancioni et al. (2000)
Mobile technologies (WLAN, PDA, RFID, M-CRM)	Can be used to mobilize various activities including sales force automation (SFA), order pick-ups, and other information and transaction flows between business parties. Warehouse and logistic processes are made less costly and more accurate. M-CRM encompasses customer relationship management via handheld devices such as a mobile or hybrid phone.	Salo (in press) Sinisalo, Salo, Karjaluoto, and Leppäniemi (in press) Aungst and Wilson (2005) Balasubramanian, Peterson, and Järvenpää (2002) Lefebvre, Lefebvre, Bendavid, Fosso, and Wamba (2006)
Intelligent agents	Intelligent agents can interpret information and identify events based on some logical rule. Based on this, the individuals who have access to the system can make more accurate decisions regarding, for example, production, calls for bids, and logistic services. Limited access could be given to customers so that they could see, e.g., in which phase of production their order is. May be used to coordinate business information in business networks.	Liu, Turban, and Matthew (2000) Papazoglou (2001)

on the purpose of the relationship. If a relationship is used to procure something, the decision regarding digitization can be based, for example, on Kraljic's portfolio (Kraljic, 1983). He identifies four items in relation to the digitization decision; they are dealt with here.

Leverage items with high profit impact and low complexity could be acquired through digital means. Usually, these are raw materials or others that are relatively easily bought digitally and sometimes even delivered digitally (e.g., the software components). In those relationships, the usages of tools to digitize activities and thereby gain efficiency are key issues. Strategic items with high profit impact and high complexity should not be bought digitally straight away. One might use digital tools to evaluate and compare available solutions, but these items should not be bought digitally as high complexity is involved (high need or market uncertainty). Strategic item could be a new saw mill acquired by an integrated paper mill. Thus, traditional procurement styles

are more appropriate. Routine items with low profit impact and low complexity are first to be procured automatically and digitally as they are easy to acquire digitally. Examples of routine items are office supplies. Bottleneck items with low profit impact and high complexity can be evaluated and acquired digitally. These could be, for example, antennas needed for mobile phones. During periods with relatively low supply but high demand, a more personal procurement style based on existing trust and commitment between parties is needed as one might receive special treatment if the other party is more willing to favor your company instead of others. Thus, the use of digital business relationships in procurement seems to depend on what and how many times something is procured.

If a relationship is used to sell something, the view is similar to the profit impact and complexity presented in Kraljic's portfolio (Kraljic, 1983), but instead of looking into procurement costs, we must consider selling costs, customer demands, and complexity. Selling costs are dependent on customer demands; for example, some customers want free service and additional price reductions while others will buy a solution without any price reductions or additional service. In addition, some customers consider price to be the only meaningful indicator while others regard other factors like quality as parallel to price. Thus, selling and digitization of activities is dependent on these contingencies. These contingencies are presented in an insightful way in Fiocca's two-step portfolio (Fiocca, 1982). In the first step, customers are classified into four groups based on the difficulty of managing the account and the strategic importance of the account. These four groups are key-difficult, non-key difficult, key-easy, and non-key easy. The groups are briefly dealt with here in relation to digitization.

The key-difficult group has high complexity and high importance and thus it is not suitable to be digitized as it requires speed, rich information, and a personal touch while handling the selling situation. The non-key difficult group has high complexity but low importance, and thus it might be helpful to attempt to lower the difficulty by providing buying assistance for customers over the Internet or another secure connection. In addition, one might negotiate long-term contracts in order to both lower the difficulty and increase the importance of the items. An example of this could be a forest industry valve producer who provides Internet-based services (e.g., brochures and ordering possibility) for their customers. The key-easy group has low complexity and high importance, and thus it is a candidate for digitized interaction. As it is an important account, it would make operations with customers easier as one might use less costly ways of communicating and transacting. The non-key easy group has low complexity and importance. Thereby, all communications and transactions should be digital with these type of accounts as they represent a challenge when using administrative and selling budgets in a meaningful way. This could include targeting those costs to

more profitable customer groups in which more profit could be yielded.

After step one, accounts are further categorized into nine groups based on the customers' business attractiveness and relative relationship importance. It can be stated that those accounts with high business attractiveness should be taken care of through personal means as they are at risk of being lost if handled with digital tools. Those that have little attractiveness and low relationship importance should be taken care of with digital tools, that is, in some way changing the logic to digital relationship type. This could be done, for example, by providing additional benefits if the customer engages in a relationship.

If a relationship is used for innovation, that is, R&D and knowledge transfers, digital infrastructure should be developed in a way that fosters innovation and does not hinder it. Digital tools should be easy to use and information rich (see Daft & Lengel, 1984 for definition). However, if R&D activities are critical to a company or a strategic alliance, then social interaction might be the only way to gain results. New product development teams have been using Internet-based R&D applications and other product development software for a long time (Smith, 2004). This is because digital tools have their limitations, which are most visible when information rich activities are handled. It should be noted here that business relationships are part of business networks and thus relationship connections to other network members must be considered when digitizing business relationships (see, e.g., Salo & Alajoutsijärvi, 2003). For example, in the U.S. and the UK, major retailers are successfully pushing their supplier networks to adopt RFID systems to enhance warehouse control and speed up inventory turnover and by doing so driving all extra costs out of logistical systems.

It is evident from the above that those business relationships that require a lot of routine activities can be easily digitized, as can those that have a relatively low profit impact in general. Those are the ones with high costs but low benefit levels. Business relationships that are strategically important and require a personal touch need to remain traditional or only partially digitized. Examples of the former solution are relationships between a manufacturer and a supplier of largely available raw material (e.g., sawmill and forest owner or steel mill and iron concentrate provider) while examples of the latter solution are relationships between a service provider and a client (e.g., advertising agency client relationships and consulting agency and client relationships).

BUSINESS RELATIONSHIP DIGITIZATION

After the appropriate buyer-seller relationship is identified, digitization is initiated. Management teams from both sides of a business relationship gather, and digitization is initiated by mapping the pertinent information and transaction flows between parties. Each of the activities, its owner, and the channel in which it is conducted is charted. These flows and activities are dependent on the relationship characteristics mentioned before. The case example at the end of this section provides an empirical illustration of characteristics, activities, transaction and information flows, digital tools, and relationship digitization.

Internal digital infrastructure is employed within a company or an organization but, when it is partially opened up for external connections with business relationship parties, we can talk about relationship specific digital infrastructure. This requires that both sides have matching digital infrastructures. Ryssel et al. (2004) suggests that when business relationship-specific systems are integrated with internal systems, more benefits are created, also known as value. Thus, the formation of this relationship specific digital infrastructure together with the relationship counterpart is one of the important decisions regarding business relationship digitization, after the relationship

to be digitized has been selected and flows have been charted. The digital tools presented above in Table 1 act as the basic building blocks of digitized business relationships. After the digital infrastructure has been acquired or formed from the existing hardware and software, digital activities are initiated through the developed digital infrastructure. Most commonly, orders, warehouse information, and invoices are handled digitally. The following list, based on the previous literature review, illustrates the phases of business relationship digitization:

1. Select appropriate business relationship (see Bensaou, 1999; Fiocca, 1982; Kraljic, 1983 for advice).
2. Map transaction and information flows.
3. Form the required relationship specific digital infrastructure (see, e.g., Salo, 2006a).
4. Initiate digital activities.
5. Follow up, reorganize, and digitize more activities if needed.

The most crucial phase is clearly selecting the right partner, that is, the one that is willing and with whom your company has a long-term relationship, as it is in those relationships that efficiency gains are sought. If we are dealing with an innovative R&D type of relationship, then more two-way interactive, information-rich digital tools are needed to provide an almost natural interaction environment.

METHODOLOGY

The author uses conceptual analysis and logical reasoning as the main research and analysis tool. In the empirical part of the study, the author deploys methods that can be described as qualitative in nature. The author employs the case study method because with the use of a case study method, it is possible to receive detailed and rich information from one focal phenomenon (Woodside & Wilson, 2003).

A case study is applicable to situations in which researchers require deeper understanding, solid contextual sense, and provocation toward theory building (Bonoma, 1985; Eisenhardt, 1989). More specifically, this case is a business relationship composed of two companies interacting with each other. Case selection is an important phase in case study research, and therefore the literature is full of advice on how to select cases (Eisenhardt, 1989; Perry, 1998; Pettigrew, 1989; Romano, 1989). Still, the decision as to how many and which cases are selected is left to the researcher (Romano, 1989). The author conducted a single pilot case study to form a preliminary conceptualization of business relationship digitization. The choice undoubtedly influences the generalizability of the results of the study (Eisenhardt, 1989). Therefore, the choice of this case study means that this study does not aim

at statistical generalization based on hypothesis testing but attempts to provide explorative ideas that can be tested later in a large scale quantitative survey. In the chosen case, companies the author conducted 11 in-depth interviews with semistructured interview questions (see Arksey & Knight, 1999). Table 2 provides a detailed illustration of the interview data.

The tape-recorded interviews were transcribed to text processing software. The interviewees were asked if there were mistakes in the transcribed text. Minor changes were made to some of the texts. After that, the author read the text many times to get familiar with the material in order to start data analysis. The author also used documents, minutes of meetings, industry reports, and plant visits to triangulate the respondents' answers in order to validate the research results (Yin, 1989). This is called data triangulation to differentiate it from other triangulation forms, for example,

Table 2. Interview data

Company Z	Type of contact	Date, Duration of interview and transcribed pages
Purchasing Manager	Telephone calls, e-mail correspondence, and interview	November 24, 2003, 1h 40min,17 pages
Business IT Manager	Telephone calls and interview	March 15, 2004, 1h 30 min, 25 pages
IT Manager	Telephone calls, e-mail correspondence, and interview	March, 24, 2004, 1h 45 min, 18 pages
Technology Advisor	Telephone calls, e-mail correspondence, interview, and plant tour	March 17, 2004, 1h, 45 min, 21 pages
Production Planner	Telephone calls and interview	March 17, 2004, 1h 59 min, 30 pages
Product Manager	Telephone calls and interview	March 17, 2004, 1h 59 min, 30 pages
Company Q		
CEO	Telephone calls, e-mail correspondence, plant visit, and interview	November 17, 2003, 2h 10min, 37 pages
Production Manager	Interview and plant tour	November 17, 2003, 1h 30 min, 13 pages
CIO	Telephone calls and interview	November 18, 2003, 1h 45min, 23 pages
Production specialist	Interview and plant tour	November, 17, 2003, 1h 10 min, 13 pages
CFO	Telephone call and interview	November 18, 2003, 1h 55min , 20 pages

theoretical triangulation (Patton, 1987). After that, the author presented analyzed data in the form of a case story, which is a common form of case reporting (Yin, 1989, pp. 106-107). The identities of the case companies or the informants are not revealed in the study for confidentiality reasons. Next, we move on to the empirical illustration of business relationship digitization in the steel industry context.

DESCRIPTION OF Z-Q BUSINESS RELATIONSHIP DIGITIZATION

Steel mills all over the globe from China to the U.S. are trying to find organizational structure and customer solutions that provide a unique competitive advantage. As a part of these ongoing efforts to streamline operations and find new solutions, steel mills have made their internal operations as automatic and computerized as possible. In addition, they have begun production of hardened and light steel solutions as new elements in their offering that they provide to customers, who are always demanding more value from metal solutions.

Since these changes in business logic were not seen as superior enough, the steel mills started to look for efficiencies and innovation from outside their own competence sphere (i.e., from steel engineering service suppliers). This example reports a case study of one business relationship from the steel industry that depicts the ways digital tools are employed sequentially to increase efficiencies and speed up innovation. Company Z is a large European steel maker and company Q is a large steel engineering service provider.

The History of the Z-Q Business Relationship

Company Z has had a long and trustful business relationship with the parent company of Q for 40 years; the relationship with Q is about 10 years

old. As Z and the parent company of Q have many business relationships between them, the Z-Q relationship was chosen to be partly digitized as there were many routine activities in the relationship and almost the same product is exchanged constantly.

In brief, Q provides hardening services for Z while the parent company focuses on heavy steel objects and welding activities. After the individual steel plates and components are hardened by Q, they are further processed by Z and then sold to their customers as part of their steel solutions. These solutions can vary from part of an oil rig to steel plates manufactured for military usage in mine clearance vehicles. Z and the parent company of Q had been negotiating for years to start hardening activities. After successful negotiations, Q was established by the parent company to provide hardening services for Z. Z provided technical assistance and also helped in R&D issues related to steel metallurgy. When the business relationship was initiated most of Q's product was sold to Z, but today sales are divided over a large customer base. From this point on, the author focuses on the interfacing processes between Z and Q and attempts to distinguish the changes made in the process that enabled both organizations to work more productively.

Inefficiencies at the Initiation of the Business Relationship

When the business relationship was initiated, many of the traditional order-to-delivery processes were manual and physical. Most of the documents were paper based, and phoning and faxing were used regularly for interaction. In production, information was input manually into the hardening machines and test reports were paper based. Moreover, many of the documents needed to be checked again and again at different phases of production. A lot of labor was needed for the administrative work, and as we know by now, this usually only adds costs and decreases the value received by the end customer. As many of the processes related to getting the order to production were manual and physical, it caused delays in production and cost over-runs on some occasions. Due to these facts, the order-to-delivery process was extremely laborious with multiple manual phases, repetition of the same actions and many information gaps. Because of these problems, measures were taken, as the business relationship was perceived to be valuable for both of the companies. The problems mentioned were addressed with a sequential development program. As a result of the program, many of the difficulties were solved.

Increasing Efficiency with Digital Tools

There were several meetings and negotiations to start dealing with the problems. The first real steps toward solving the problems were taken by Q when they acquired an ERP software that among other things allowed it to receive Z's orders over a secured Internet connection in digitized form. This is known as an extranet solution. After an order arrives to Q's ERP system, it automatically informs production employees via e-mail of the new order. A parallel e-mail is received by Q's production manager.

This adoption of technology by Q signaled to Z that Q is willing to make the adaptations necessary to their business relationships to serve Z even better than before. This investment into digital tools decreased the hassle surrounding order processing. Later, Z signaled to Q by increasing orders that the relationship would continue to grow in the future.

Besides orders, Q and Z have had problems with pricing mainly because it involves a lot of manual repetition as similar products are sold over time. At the end of 2004, Q adopted a new pricing module for ERP and made considerable changes to routines and pricing policies. After the adoption of the extra module, products that already had predetermined prices are now priced and checked automatically and digitally. If an order arrives that contains steel products that are non-standardized (e.g., small or oversized), the order e-mail is forwarded to the production manager who, depending on the order size, solely or together with the CEO defines and inputs the price information required. To sum up, these changes have reorganized and streamlined previously manual and physical process phases into automatic and digitally assisted ones that are cheaper and easier to control by both of the parties.

The newest addition to the business relationship is the mobile solution based on WLAN (Wi-Fi) architecture and smart mobile handsets. This mobile solution enables Q to transmit hardening information and test reports directly to Z's systems. Moreover, Z can more easily inform their production and salespeople about Q's capacity changes. Previously, reports were written on paper, input into a system, printed, and then sent to Z's administration who filed it. Now the mobile system enables information to be input directly to a PDA which updates Q's ERP system and provides, for example, e-mail notification to Z about the new reports, which are essential for the documentation of the steel solutions delivered to customers.

Besides making essential reporting activities easier, the new mobile system enables Z to pinpoint changes in the hardening capacity of Q that helps Z to sell more steel solutions as they can promise products to customers faster and close deals sooner than before (see Salo, 2006a). In the beginning of the business relationships, a hardening capacity check was manual and information received by Z's sales department was usually too outdated to reliably act upon and thus information needed to be rechecked and this took time and extra effort. Figure 1 provides an illustration of the currently employed digital tools in the Z-Q business relationship.

To reach the current phase highlighted in Figure 1, several decisions had to be made by both companies. In a nutshell, these were choosing a business relationship, mapping the information and transaction flows, and digitizing those flows where possible. Both organizations made changes to existing procedures and routines by making the information and transaction gaps smaller and even forcing them to close. This would have not been possible without the warm and trustful relationship between the parties. Most importantly, adoption of specific digital tools and mobile technologies has made the business relationship more effective and efficient. Altogether, investments into new technology and changes made to work practices have clearly generated extra sales and benefits for both parties.

DISCUSSION

The previous section presented some ways of integrating business relationships and the digitization phenomenon. The author illustrated how business advantage could be gained using business relationships with the help of the presented digital tools. It is suggested that efficiencies and innovations might be gained in business relationships while employing digital tools such as I-EDI,

ERP 1/2, extranet, RFID, and mobile solutions. After discussing benefits, the stages of selecting a digitizable business relationship were discussed. Those stages were identified as dependent of the nature of buyer-seller relationship. The nature was identified as varying according to the purpose of the relationship, that is, whether it is used for procurement, selling, or innovation. The author then highlighted the importance of knowing the context of digitization. In short, this means that managers must be aware of what the product exchanged within the business relationship is, what activities are carried, and what structure within the relationship upholds these processes. Based on the theoretical insights presented and empirical findings that emerged from the case study, Figure 2 was composed to depict some possible factors that may influence the digitization of business relationships.

It is suggested in the preliminary framework that business relationship digitization is affected positively by the various antecedents and the accelerating factors while it is hindered by the inhibitors. The antecedents or prerequisites should have existed long before the digital tools are adopted. Depending on how beneficial (i.e., valuable) the relationship is for both parties, the antecedents

Figure 1. Digital tools employed in the Z-Q business relationship

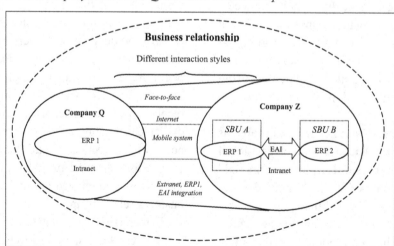

may be positive or negative thus further reinforcing inhibiting or accelerating elements. Within the studied relationship, we identified antecedents such as a close business relationship, existing trust and commitment, willingness to adopt digital tools within business relationships, and clear benefit allocation both inside and between companies which were similar to those identified in theory (see, e.g., Clemons et al., 1993; Ryssel et al., 2004). These antecedents may facilitate the digitization process. Salo (2006a) presents a more elaborated analysis of the business relationship digitization process in the steel industry context.

Further validation is needed to be absolutely sure of the results, how the factors overlap, and how their confounding effects play out. The aim of future work is to find out mutually exclusive and collectively exhaustive factors and their elements.

To sum up, selecting a business relationship that might yield more profits if digitized is the first managerial task when moving towards digitized business relationships. Then, managers from both sides should be actively involved in mapping the transaction and communication flows between business parties. After that, appropriate digital tools are integrated into the business relationship. This selection depends on existing digital tools and those that are required by the identified flows. Needed digital tools can be procured or developed internally. In the best case, IT specialists are only needed for a couple of months to integrate systems. After digital infrastructure deployment, digital activities are initiated; old and new systems should run in parallel for a couple of months to avoid unnecessary mistakes (see a warning example in Laudon & Traver, 2002, p. 670). Finally, the last stage of the first digitization cycle is to monitor existing digital activities and if needed reorganize as well as plan for further digitization operations.

Figure 2. Preliminary framework of factors that seem to influence business relationship digitization

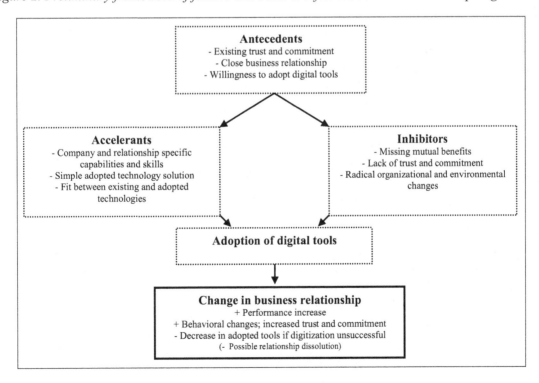

Overall, it can be stated that this manuscript is beneficial to both managers and academics. The following practical issues are investigated and discussed: (1) How to successfully select business relationships to be digitized, (2) How to identify the right digital tools to be employed while digitizing a business relationship, and (3) How and to what extent business relationships should be made digital. These questions also guide business relationship researchers into valuable future research areas.

CONCLUSION

The major contributions of this chapter are the identification of the tools and selection criteria for digitizing business relationships that are provided to help managers to understand and manage the business relationship digitization process. For academics, we have provided and conceptualized business relationships and the impacts brought by digitization in a novel way. Our results underscore the pertinent aspect of relationship selection as well as the mapping of critical transactional and informational flows in the business relationship. This study also provided a description of the factors affecting business relationship digitization and suggested ways for managers to grasp and tackle the emerging phenomenon. Factors that were seen to influence digitization were divided into antecedents, accelerants, inhibitors, adoption, and decision. These factors were built from various characteristics.

The chapter is rather theoretical in nature and this should be considered as a limitation of the chapter although the author provided an illustrative case example. Nevertheless, it is emphasized that solid theoretical contribution usually provides understandable managerial insights.

Although marketing and management researchers have long recognized that successful implementation of strategy decisions, for example, digitization, is key for value creation within and across companies, the theoretical and empirical understanding of this issue remains limited. Therefore, further studies are needed with an emphasis on selecting the right business relationships and activity flows to be digitized. A large scale quantitative study in the future would be advisable to test some of the emerging relationships between various proposed factors impacting digitization. In addition, more research is necessary to develop a solid framework that describes business relationship digitization. Preliminary work conducted by Salo in (2006a) is a stepping stone in the right direction. To conclude, more research is needed to crystallize the field of business relationship digitization and the factors and their elements influencing it. Managers have already embraced digital tools and especially mobile technologies. It is the researcher's endeavor to capture the impacts of these tools on business on a more broad scope. Hopefully, this chapter has provided some interesting insights into the art of digitizing business relationships or inter-organizational relationships and provides new research ideas for scholars around the world.

AUTHOR'S NOTE

An earlier version of this chapter was published by IGI Global in the *Journal of Electronic Commerce in Organizations, 4*(4), 75-93, under the title "Business Relationship Digitization: What We Need to Know before Embarking on Such Activities?"

REFERENCES

Alba, J.J., Lynch, J., Weitz, B., Janiszewski, C., Lutz, R., Sawyer, A., & Wood, S. (1997, July). Interactive home shopping: Consumer, retailer, and manufacturer intensives to participate in electronic marketplaces. *Journal of Marketing, 61*, 38-53.

Al-Mashari, M., Al-Mudimigh, A., & Zairi, M. (2003). Enterprise resource planning: A taxonomy of critical factors. *European Journal of Operational Research, 146*(2), 352-364.

Angeles, R. (2000). Revisiting the role of Internet-EDI in the current electronic commerce scene. *Logistics Information Management, 13*(1), 45-57.

Archer, N., & Yuan, Y. (2000). Managing business-to-business relationships throughout the e-commerce procurement life cycle. *Internet Research: Electronic Networking Applications and Policy, 10*(5), 385-395.

Arksey, H., & Knight, P. (1999). *Interviewing for social scientists.* London: Sage Publications.

Aungst, S.G., & Wilson, D.T. (2005). A primer for navigating the shoals of applying wireless technology to marketing problems. *Journal of Business & Industrial Marketing, 20*(2), 59-69.

Bakos, J.Y., & Brynjolfsson, E. (1993). Information technology, incentives, and the optimal number of suppliers. *Journal of Management Information Systems, 10*(2), 37-53.

Balasubramanian, S., Peterson, R.A., & Järvenpää, S.L. (2002). Exploring the implications of m-commerce for markets and marketing. *Journal of the Academy of Marketing Science, 30*(4), 348-361.

Bensaou, M. (1999). Portfolios of buyer-supplier relationships. *Sloan Management Review, 40*(4), 35-44.

Bond, B., Genovese, Y., Miklovic, D., Wood, N., Zrimsek, B., & Rayner, N. (2000, October). *ERP is dead—Long live ERP 2.* Gartner Group, RAS Services.

Bonoma, T. (1985). Case research in marketing: Opportunities, problems and a process. *Journal of Marketing Research, 22*(2), 199-208.

Breeding, K. (1992). *Digital design fundamentals* (2nd ed.). Prentice Hall.

Carr, A.S., & Smeltzer, L.R. (2002). The relationship between information technology use and buyer-seller relationships: An exploratory analysis of the buying firm's perspective. *IEEE Transactions on Engineering Management, 49*(3), 293-304.

Chen, M., Chen, A.N., & Shao, B.M. (2003). The implications and impacts of Web services to electronic commerce research practices. *Journal of Electronic Commerce Research, 4*(4), 128-139.

Choi, S.-Y., Whinston, A.B., & Stahl, D.O. (1997). *The economics of electronic commerce.* Indianapolis: Macmillan Technical Publishing.

Clemons, E.K., Reddi, S., & Row, M.C. (1993). The impact of IT on the organization of economic activity: The "move to the middle" hypothesis. *Journal of Management Information Systems, 10*(2), 9-35.

Curbera, F., Duftler, M., Khalaf, R., Nagy, W., Mukhi, N., & Weerawarana, S. (2002). Unraveling the Web services Web: An introduction to SOAP, WSDL, and UDDI. *IEEE Internet Computing, 6*(2), 86-93.

Daft, R.L., & Lengel, R.H. (1984). Information richness: A new approach to manager information processing and organization design. In B. Staw & L.L. Cummings (Eds.), *Research in organizational behavior.* Greenwich: JAI Press.

Dwyer, F.R., Shurr, P., & Oh, S. (1987). Developing buyer-seller relationships. *Journal of Marketing, 51*(2), 1-25.

Eisenhardt, K.M. (1989). Building theories from case study research. *Academy of Management Review, 14*(4), 532-550.

Emery, J. (1987). *Management information systems the critical strategic resource*. Oxford University Press.

Emmelhainz, M. (1993). *EDI: A total management guide*. Van Nostrand Reinhold.

Fiocca, R. (1982). Account portfolio analysis for strategy development. *Industrial Marketing Management, 11*(1), 53-62.

Fisher, M., & Reibstein, D.J. (2001). Technology-driven demand: Implications for the supply chain. In J. Wind & V. Mahajan (Eds.), *Digital marketing* (pp. 285-309). John Wiley.

Ford, D. (1980). The development of buyer-seller relationships in industrial markets. *European Journal of Marketing, 14*(5/6), 339-354.

Garcia-Dastuge, S., & Lambert, D. (2003). Internet-enabled coordination in supply chain. *Industrial Marketing Management, 32*(2), 251-263.

Gardiner, S., Hanna, J., & LaTour, M. (2002). ERP and the reengineering of industrial marketing processes. A prescriptive overview for the new-age marketing manager. *Industrial Marketing Management, 31*(4), 357-365.

Grewal, R., Comer, J.M., & Mehta, R. (2001, July). An investigation into the antecedents of organizational participation in business-to-business electronic markets. *Journal of Marketing, 65*, 17-33.

Hasselbring, W. (2000). Information system integration. *Communications of the ACM, 43*(6), 33-38.

Hodge, G. (2002). Enterprise resource planning in textiles. *Journal of Textile and Apparel, Technology and Management, 2*(3), 1-8.

Holland, C.P., & Naudé, P. (2004). The metamorphosis of marketing into an information handling problem. *Journal of Business & Industrial Marketing, 19*(3), 165-166.

Howells, J., & Wood, M. (1995). Diffusion and management of electronic data interchange: Barriers and opportunities in the UK pharmaceutical and health industries. *Technology Analysis and Strategic Management, 7*(4), 371-387.

Johnson, D.S., & Bharadwaj, S. (2005). Digitization of selling activity and sales force performance: An empirical investigation. *Journal of the Academy of Marketing Science, 33*(1), 3-18.

Kandampully, J. (2003). B2B relationships and networks in the Internet age. *Management Decision, 41*(5), 443-451.

Kraljic, P. (1983). Purchasing must become supply management. *Harvard Business Review, 61*(5), 109-117.

Krapf, E. (1999). Can businesses find common ground for e-commerce. *Business Communications Review, 29*(4), 43-46.

Lancioni, R. (2000). New developments in supply chain management for the millennium: Determining supplier and buyer effect on inventory performance. *Industrial Marketing Management, 29*(1), 1-6.

Lancioni, R., Smith, M., & Oliva, T. (2000). The role of the Internet in supply chain management. *Industrial Marketing Management, 29*(1), 45-56.

Laudon, K.C., & Traver, C.G. (2002). *E-commerce: Business, technology, society*. Addison-Wesley.

Lefebvre, L.A., Lefebvre, E., Bendavid, Y., Fosso, S., & Wamba, H. (2006, January). RFID as enabler of B-to-B e-commerce and its impact on business processes: A pilot study of a supply chain in the retailing industry. In *Proceedings of the Hawaii International Conference on System Sciences (HICSS-39)*. Retrieved September 10, 2007, from http://www.computer.org/portal/site/ ieeecs/

Linthicum, D. (2000). *Enterprise application integration*. Boston: Addison-Wesley.

Liu, S, Turban, E., & Matthew, K. (2000). Software agents for environmental scanning in electronic commerce. *Information Systems Frontiers, 2*(1), 85-98.

Manecke, N., & Schoensleben, P. (2004). Cost and benefit of Internet-based support of business processes. *International Journal of Production Economics, 87*(3), 213-229.

Mata, F.J., Fuerst, W.L., & Barney, J.B. (1995). Information technology and sustained competitive advantage: A resource-based analysis. *MIS Quarterly, 19*(4), 487-504.

Matthyssens, P., & Van den Bulte, C. (1994). Getting closer and nicer partnerships in the supply chain. *Long Range Planning, 27*(1), 71-83.

Motwani, J., Mirchandani, D., Madan, M., & Gunasekaran, A. (2002). Successful implementation of ERP projects: Evidence from two case studies. *International Journal of Production Economics, 75*(1-2), 83-96.

Mukhopadhyay, T. (1998). How to win with electronic data interchange in information technology and industrial competitiveness. In C. Kemerer (Ed.), *How IT shapes competition* (pp. 91-106). Boston: Kluwer Academic Publishers.

Naudé, P., Holland, C., & Sudbury, M. (2000). The benefits of IT-based supply chains: Strategic or operational? *Journal of Business-to-Business Marketing, 7*(1), 45-67.

Negroponte, N. (1995). *Being digital.* Random House.

Ordanini, A., & Pol, A. (2001). Infomediation and competitive advantage in B2B digital marketplaces. *European Management Journal, 19*(3), 276-285.

Papazoglou, M. (2001). Agent-oriented technology in support of e-business. *Communications of the ACM, 44*(4), 71-77.

Patton, M.Q. (1987). *Qualitative evaluation and research methods.* Sage Publications.

Perry, C. (1998). Process of case study methodology for postgraduate research in marketing. *European Journal of Marketing, 32*(9/10), 785-802.

Pettigrew, A.M. (1989). Context and action in the transformation of the firm. *Journal of Management Studies, 24*(6), 649-670.

Philip, G., & Pedersen, P. (1997). Inter-organizational information systems: Are organizations in Ireland deriving strategic benefits from EDI? *International Journal of Information Management, 17*(5), 337-357.

Polanyi, M. (1966). *The tacit dimension.* Doubleday & Company.

Prokein, O., & Faupel, T. (2006, January). Using Web service for intercompany cooperation: An empirical study within the German industry. In *Proceedings of the Hawaii International Conference on System Sciences (HICSS-39).* Retrieved September 10, 2007, from http://www.computer. org/portal site/ieeecs/

Radosevich, L. (1997). Early adopters hail extranet benefits, dodge pitfalls. *InfoWorld, 19*(23), 65-66.

Reid, D.A., & Plank, R.E. (2000). Business marketing comes of age: A comprehensive review of the literature. *Journal of Business-to-Business Marketing, 7*(2/3), 9-178.

Romano, C. (1989). Research strategies for small business: A case study. *International Small Business Journal, 7*(4), 35-43.

Ryssel, R., Ritter, T., & Gemünden, H.G. (2004). The impact of information technology deployment on trust, commitment and value creation in business relationships. *Journal of Business & Industrial Marketing, 19*(3), 197-207.

Salo, J. (2006a). *Business relationship digitalization: A case study from the steel processing industry* (pp. 1-296). Oulu University Press, Oulu, Finland. Retrieved September 10, 2007, from http://herkules.oulu.fi/isbn9514282396/isbn9514282396.pdf

Salo, J. (2006b). IT-enabled integration of business relationship in the steel industry context. In B. Walters & Z. Tang (Eds.), *IT-enabled strategic management: Increasing returns for the organization* (pp. 275-294). Hershey, PA: Idea Group Publishing.

Salo, J. (in press). Mobile technology usage in business relationships. In M. Khosrow-Pour (Ed.), *Encyclopedia of information science and technology* (2nd ed.). Hershey, PA: Idea Group Publishing.

Salo, J., & Alajoutsijärvi, K. (2003, September 4-6). Strained business relationships. In *Proceedings of the 19th IMP Conference on Managing in Networks*, Lugano, Switzerland (pp. 1-10). Retrieved September 10, 2007, from http://www.impgroup.com

Sawhney, M. (1999, September). Let's get vertical. *Business 2.0.*

Sinisalo, J., Salo, J., Karjaluoto, H., & Leppäniemi. M. (in press). Management of mobile customer relationships: Underlying issues and opportunities. *Business Process Management Journal.*

Sloane, A. (1994). *Computer communications: Principles and business applications.* Maidenhead: McGraw-Hill.

Smith, P. (2004). Accelerated product development: Techniques and traps. In K.B. Kahn (Ed.), *The PDMA handbook of new product development* (2nd ed., pp. 173-187). John Wiley.

Stauffert, T. (1991). *Informationstechnik und Abhängigkeit.* Frankfurt a.M. Verlag Peter Lang.

Stern, L., & Kaufmann, P. (1985). Electronic data interchange in selected consumer goods industries: An interorganizational perspective. In R.D. Buzzell (Ed.), *Marketing in an electronic age* (pp. 52-73). Boston: Harvard Business School Press.

Stoer, M., Nienhaus, J., Birkeland, N., & Menkhaus, G. (2003). IT infrastructure for supply chain management in company networks with small and medium-sized enterprises. In *Proceedings of the International Conference on Enterprise Information Systems*, France.

Stump, R., & Sriram, V. (1997). Employing information technology in purchasing: Buyer-supplier relationships and size of the supplier base. *Industrial Marketing Management, 26*(2), 127-136.

Themistocleous, M., & Irani, Z. (2002). Towards a novel framework for the assessment of enterprise application integration packages. In *Proceedings of the 36th Hawaii International Conference on Systems Sciences.* Retrieved September 10, 2007, from http://www.computer.org/ portal /site/ieeecs/

Vlosky, R.P., Fontenot, R., & Blalock, L. (2000). Extranets: Impacts on business practices and relationships. *Journal of Business & Industrial Marketing, 15*(6), 438-457.

Wang, J.C., & Tsai, K.H. (2002). Factors in Taiwanese firms' decisions to adopt electronic commerce: An empirical study. *World Economy, 25*(8), 1145-1167.

Whiting, R. (2003). A win-win combination? *Information Week.* Retrieved September 10, 2007, from http://www.informationweek.com. story/IWK20030314S0001

Wilkinson, I. (2001). A history of network and channels thinking in marketing in the 20th century. *Australasian Journal of Marketing, 9*(2), 23-53.

Wilson, H., Daniel, E., & McDonald, M (2002). Factors for success in customer relationship management (CRM) systems. *Journal of Marketing Management, 18*(1-2), 193-219.

Wilson, D.T., & Mummalaneni, V. (1986). Bonding and commitment in buyer-seller relationships: A preliminary conceptualisation. *Journal of Industrial Marketing & Purchasing, 1*(3), 44-58.

Woodside, A., & Wilson, E.J. (2003). Case study research methods for theory building. *Journal of Business & Industrial Marketing, 18*(6/7), 493-508.

Yin, R. (1989). *Case study research*. Sage Publications.

Zablah, A.R, Bellenger, D.N., & Johnston, W.J. (2004). An evaluation of divergent perspectives on customer relationship management: Towards a common understanding of an emerging phenomenon. *Industrial Marketing Management, 33*(6), 475-489.

Chapter XII

Understanding the Impact of Wireless Local Area Networks on Users and Assessing User Satisfaction with Wireless Local Area Networks

Leida Chen
Creighton University, USA

Ravi Nath
Creighton University, USA

Jonathan Cowin
Creighton University, USA

ABSTRACT

Recently, wireless local area network (WLAN) has gained increasing popularity. WLAN equipment manufacturers and practitioners claimed that WLAN had brought dramatic improvements in the forms of productivity gains and attainment of convenience, flexibility, mobility, and time saving to organizations and their employees. However, very little academic research has been conducted to verify these claims and further our understanding of this new phenomenon. By surveying end users and managers, this study investigates the impact of WLAN on users and their work. User satisfaction with WLAN is also assessed. This chapter presents the findings from the study along with a discussion on recent development and future trends of WLAN. Finally, recommendations to researchers, managers, WLAN technology providers, and equipment manufacturers are also provided.

INTRODUCTION

Growth in nomadic computing is driven by the incessant advances in wireless and mobile technologies and the business need for mobility. Nomadic computing refers to an environment where nomad users have access to computing resources, communication capabilities, and services that are transparent, integrated, convenient, and adaptive (Kleinrock, 2001). Industry experts are predicting a growing trend of a new way of doing business based on wireless and mobile technologies—mobile commerce (m-commerce). While many wireless technologies promise to revolutionize the conduct of business, organizations often fail to make a business case for investing in these technologies (Goldman, 2001; Use tech as a tool, 2002). In addition, the rapid technological innovations in this field have left many IT managers still trying to sort out the different technology platforms and the type of business applications that these technologies would effectively support. Many questions remain to be answered in the area of nomadic computing providing researchers with ample research opportunities as outlined by Lyytinen and Yoo (2002).

It is imperative to understand the business value of nomadic computing. Balasubramanian, Peterson, and Jarvenpaa (2002) suggested that mobile technologies relax spatial and/or temporal constraints of activities. For example, with mobile technologies, a worker in the field can check e-mail at any time. Without the technologies, this activity would be limited by both spatial and temporal constraints (i.e., One can only check e-mail when she is at a location where a computer and a network connection is present). In the same vein, Chen and Nath (2003) proposed a model that helps managers determine the value of mobile and wireless applications. The model stipulates that the value of mobile and wireless applications is a function of the user's immediacy of information needs and user mobility.

Even though a national nomadic information environment (NIE) is somewhat possible by using services provided by various national wireless providers, many small pockets of NIEs have emerged and they continue to grow. Most of these NIEs with limited geographic reach serve employees within the organization's physical boundaries. Open standards such as wireless fidelity (Wi-Fi) and bluetooth allow organizations to develop these NIEs with relative ease and low costs. Data and information can be shared seamlessly between different devices and networks within a limited geographic area. Such NIEs are often referred to as wireless local area networks (WLAN). Many organizations have adopted the IEEE802.11b and IEEE802.11g technology, two of the Wi-Fi standards, to provide wireless access to users within a local geographical area (e.g., a building, campus, airport, coffee shop, and hotel). According to the 2001 NOP World-Technology study (2001), the market penetration of WLAN in the U.S. reached 10% in 2000, and users credited WLAN with attainment of convenience, flexibility, mobility, time saving, and productivity gains. A more recent study conducted as part of the PEW Internet and American Life Project showed that 17% of Internet users have logged on the net using a wireless device such as Internet-connected mobile phones and WiFi-enabled laptops (Rainie, 2004). While IEEE802.11b and IEEE802.11g are the most popular WLAN solutions among U.S. businesses today, newer technology solutions (e.g., IEEE802.11a and IEEE802.11i) are promising higher data speed and enhanced security in the near future (Funk, 2005). There also exists a significant potential for WiFi technology in the consumer market. By 2009, according to Datacomm Research Company, WLAN equipment sales will triple in terms of number of units sold primarily due to their growing use in home entertainment applications (LAN Product News, 2005).

In the case of WLAN, while user mobility is limited to a small geographical area (e.g., an office or a building), it supports a wide range of immediacy of information needs. Therefore, while WLAN delivers important business value to organizations, the value proposition can be amplified if user mobility is extended beyond organizational boundaries. That is, if the spatial constraints are relaxed. New developments to overcome the range limitation of WiFi are also under way. Another promising technology, WiMax, supported by the WiMax Forum consisting of over 200 industry members, is designed to have a bandwidth of 40 Mbps over a five-mile range (Wright, 2005).

Most research efforts in WLAN have been devoted to technical issues. For example, Xu and Walke's (2001) study examined the design issues of self-organizing broadband wireless networks. Hsu, Qian, and Ilyas (2003) proposed and analyzed two algorithms for establishing ad hoc WLANs. In another study, Lehr and McKnight (2003) compared the technical standards of 3G and WiFi, two competing technology standards for broadband wireless Internet access, and recommended a complementary strategy that allowed both standards to coexist. At the same time, there is dearth of empirical research dealing with the impact of WLAN on users and their work environment. Most of the evidence in support of WLAN is anecdotal and conceptual (e.g., Keane, 2002; Malladi & Agrawal, 2002; McGarvey, 2002). Therefore, there is a need for a systematic, scientific, and empirical investigation that evaluates the user and work benefits of WLAN. Specifically, the proposed research seeks to investigate the impact (benefits and risks) of WLAN on users from both the end user's and IT manager's perspectives. These findings will provide an unbiased assessment of WLAN benefits and risks and, perhaps, corroborate the claims made by practitioners and equipment manufacturers. Furthermore, understanding users' perception of WLAN is crucial to technology providers and equipment manufacturers as this knowledge can guide and help them in designing user-centric products and services. Also, the findings of this study should provide insights to academicians

and practitioners in this evolving area of nomadic computing.

This research attempts to answer the following research questions:

- **Research question 1:** *What are the underlying constructs explaining the impact of WLAN on users?*
- **Research question 2:** *What are the perceived benefits and risks of WLAN to users?*
- **Research question 3:** *What factors are related to user satisfaction with WLAN?*

WIRELESS LAN

The last few years have witnessed the emergence of a wide range of portable devices, including portable PCs, PDAs, handheld computers, and handsets. Many of these devices have wireless capabilities that are either embedded or attached. At the same time, the workforce is becoming increasingly mobile (Daniel, 2000). To increase the agility of an organization, employees need to have access to core corporate information from anywhere and at anytime. As a result, organizations often find themselves in need to extend their existing network to places that cannot be economically reached with cables (Singer, 2001). WLANs offer organizations a flexible and cost-effective alternative. They are especially useful in situations where real time information access is desired and physical network wiring is infeasible (Malladi & Agrawal, 2002). Today, WLANs are gaining popularity for the following reasons. First, WLAN technologies, especially WiFi, have reached maturity. The technical standard has received broad industry support, hence a high level of interoperability can be expected from WLAN products from different vendors. Furthermore, the speed of WLAN as defined by 802.11x wireless Ethernet standards has improved to be comparable to the bandwidth of wired LAN with relative reliability. Finally, the costs of WLAN equipment have decreased dramatically to make it financially feasible for many organizations to adopt them (Conover, 2000). As a result, significant growth in the WLAN market was witnessed in the last few years. Besides home and office wireless networks, many retail and service businesses have created "WiFi hot spots" to provide wireless Internet access to their customers (OECD, 2003).

As mentioned earlier, WLANs offer several benefits to organizations. First, WLAN can help improve employee productivity, which leads to cost savings for organizations. For example, a health care organization is achieving savings of $1,000 a day, per pharmacist, by delivering timely information to the pharmacists' handheld devices via an in-house WLAN (Keane, 2002). Furthermore, by providing employees with vital information from anywhere and at anytime, employees can be more proactive and react more quickly to business problems and opportunities. At Carlson hotels, managers use WLAN to access all the information they need to manage the properties in real-time on PocketPCs. As a result, managers can quickly spot any problems or opportunities at their hotel and react to them (McGarvey, 2002). Also, a number of high-end hotels are improving customer service by experimenting with undesked staff who can check guests in in the lobby, parking lot, or conference room (McGarvey, 2002). Several major stadiums are bringing wireless point-of-sale (POS) to customers' seats in order to generate more sales (Baldwin, 2002). When combined with voice over IP (VoIP) technology, WLANs can transmit voice conversations, giving WiFi users access to the corporate telephone system wirelessly with reduced costs (Wang, Liew, & Li, 2005). In summary, anecdotal evidences suggest that WLANs provide users with convenience, mobility, and flexibility at work. They also help reduce costs and enhance the level of service for organizations.

In spite of many benefits that WLAN applications can provide, they do have their weaknesses.

First, WLAN lacks the security, reliability, range, and bandwidth that most users are accustomed to from wired LAN (Stanley, 2002). An investigation by *BusinessWeek* (Green, Rosenbush, Crockett, & Holmes, 2003) identified a number of challenges faced by WLAN technology including unclear standards, spotty security, limited range, hidden costs, and the lack of inter-operability. One of the most widely cited problems with WLAN is security. The nature of the radio transmission technology used in WLANs inevitably opens the possibility of eavesdropping, masquerading, and unauthorized use by hackers (Elliott & Phillips, 2004, p. 416; Regan, 2003). IT professionals are also facing many complications during the implementation of WLAN due to their lack of experience in this new technical area. This problem is worsened further by the emergence of a wide range of wireless devices (Shapland, Gavurlin, & Chartoff, 2002). The conflict between the capacity of the WLAN and the growing number of organizational applications makes the management of WLANs more difficult. The problem is especially pronounced when a firm uses VoIP over its WLANs. Network managers are finding out that only a few VoIP stream sessions can be supported simultaneously without affecting the performance of WLANs (Wang et al., 2005). In addition to the technical difficulties, it is still too early for organizations to determine the real return on investment (ROI) of WLAN, and many organizations are seeing little usage of WLAN by users after its implementation (OECD, 2003). Also, the uncertainty about the direction of WLAN technologies and government regulations governing the use of WLAN is leading to hesitation on the part of organizations in making sizable investment in WLAN projects (Markoff, 2002).

THEORETICAL DEVELOPMENT

The body of MIS literature over the last few decades offers many studies on the adoption of new media such as personal computer networks (e.g., Nath, 1988; Lucas & Spitler, 2000; Remenyi & Money, 1991), the Internet (e.g., Alba, Lynch, Weitz, Janiszewski, Lutz, Sawyer, & Wood, 1997; Chen, Gillenson, & Sherrell, 2003; Jarvenpaa & Todd, 1997), and Intranets (e.g., Lai, 2001; Phelps & Mok, 1999). While each has its unique characteristics, the media in these studies, notably LANs, the Internet, and intranets bear remarkable resemblance with WLAN.

A common theme found in literature on the adoption of new media is user satisfaction. Many research projects were dedicated to the evaluation of user satisfaction with media and the search for the determinants of user satisfaction with media. User satisfaction was identified as one of the measures for IS success by DeLone and McLean (1992). It has been widely used as the single measure of IS success due to (1) its high degree of face validity, (2) availability of reliable instruments for measure, and (3) conceptual weakness and unavailability of other measures. Much research has contributed to the development of an instrument for measuring user satisfaction (e.g., Bailey & Pearson, 1983; Doll & Torkzadeh, 1988; Ives, Olson, & Baroudi, 1983; Palvia, 1996; Phelps & Mok, 1999; Woodroof & Burg, 2002).

Another common theme found in this body of literature was risk. While each new medium had obvious benefits to users and organizations, the benefits were often coupled with risks that were disruptive. Identifying risks of new media is crucial as it prompts organizations to reevaluate their decisions to adopt the new medium and proactively develop ways to address these risks. As Phelps and Mok (1999) found with intranets, these risks were often not limited to technical risks. Business risks and organizational risks were found to be more complex and persistent. Based on the observations outlined above, this study intends to investigate the benefits and risks associated with WLAN and their relationship with user satisfaction.

The nascence of this field is also reflected by the lack of theories specifically designed to address issues in ubiquitous computing environments such as WLANs. Classic frameworks such as the technology acceptance model (TAM) and innovation diffusion theory (IDT) are often applied to study the adoption of new technologies. Venkatesh and Davis (2000) later proposed and validated a theoretical extension of TAM, TAM2, by including constructs related to social influence processes (subjective norm, voluntariness, and image) and cognitive instrumental processes (job relevance, output quality, result demonstrability, and perceived ease of use). Nevertheless, these theories tend to be too general in nature and fail to address the issues uniquely relevant to the technology under study (Legris, Ingham, & Collerette, 2003). Studies employing these theories often have to extend the models to include constructs unique to the technology under study (e.g., Chen et al., 2004; Devaraj, Fan, & Rajiv, 2002). In addition, these theories require researchers to utilize a confirmatory research design. In the case of WLAN, little empirical research on its impact on users exists; therefore, an exploratory approach is employed by this study.

There is limited literature that addresses some of the issues under study here. Lyytinen and Yoo's (2002) framework provides a broad view of NIE. This framework was used to understand the research implications of NIE for IS researchers. The framework for NIE stipulates that the three key drivers that influence and enable both nomadic computing infrastructure and services are mobility, digital convergence, and mass scale. As the users move away from a stationary computing environment to a NIE, the need for mobility has enormous impact on the design of devices, content, and networks. Second, digital convergence refers to open standards that allow heterogeneous devices and networks to share information seamlessly. Finally, mass scale is reflected by the wide availability of NIE at a global level and the high usage level demonstrated by users, and mass scale is essential to the attainment of true mobility and digital convergence. These three interweaving factors influence the design and deployment of NIE infrastructure and services. Based on this framework, Lyytinen and Yoo (2002) generated eight research themes for NIE. They are individual-level services, infrastructure for individual level, team-level services, infrastructure for team level, organizational-level services, infrastructure for organizational level, interorganizational-level services, and infrastructure for interorganizational level. The eight research themes are by and large applicable to WLAN. This study attempts to address one of the eight themes, individual-level services, especially the question of what impact WLAN has on users through the three aforementioned research questions. A more recent study by Lyytinen, Varshney, Ackerman, Davis, Avital, Robey, Sawyer, and Sorensen (2004) laid out more detailed research directions for researchers interested in studying NIE. The study suggested that researchers explore the application, network, data, security, and privacy issues relevant to NIE in order to understand the impact of NIE. Based on this recommendation, this study will focus on WLAN's potential impact on operational efficiency, decision-making effectiveness, collaboration and communication, network service quality, privacy, and data security, from the perspectives of both users and network managers.

Jessup and Robey (2002) underscored the importance of social issues when studying ubiquitous computing environments. They claimed that new technologies, such as wireless technology, that enable mobile work environments would inevitably cause social consequences. Researchers should conduct three levels of social analysis: individual, team, and organization. This study again focuses on one aspect of the individual level of social analysis by addressing the impact of WLANs on users' quality of work life.

The existing literature outlined above offers this study some general directions. While un-derstanding the magnitude of value delivered by WLAN is important, it is even more critical to identify the areas from which the value comes. Equally important is the identification of factors that are preventing WLAN from realizing its full potential. This study will expand existing research by delving into these questions. An exploratory research design is utilized for this study.

RESEARCH METHODOLOGY

Questionnaire Development

In order to develop questionnaire items that measure the impact, both benefits and risks, a multistage approach was undertaken. In stage one, the existing literature on WLAN was synthesized. Table 1 summarizes the WLAN impact areas and the supporting literature. These areas encompass issues such as the quality of the user's work life, operational efficiency, decision-making effectiveness, collaboration and communication, network service quality, privacy, and data security. From this information, an initial list of statements indicating the potential impact of WLAN on users was created. Each item was phrased so that it can be rated using a 5-point Likert scale (1 = strongly disagree; 5 = strongly agree). In the next stage, this list of items was shown to several WLAN users and three IT managers responsible for WLAN in their organizations. They were asked to comment on the completeness of these items and suggest additions, deletions, and modifications. Feedback from these two groups (users and managers) resulted in significant revisions to the initial list of items. To further refine the list, two faculty members in IT, independently, reviewed this list and provided their feedback. As a result of this process, 23 items were retained to gauge the impact of WLAN on end users. These items are listed in Table 2.

User satisfaction is a key construct that has been widely used in IS literature as a surrogate

Table 1. Underlying areas, description, and sources

Underlying Area	Description	Sources
Operational Efficiency	WLAN has been accredited for improving operational efficiency by reducing the time and costs for data entry, information search, and execution.	NOP World-Technology, 2001; Keane, 2002; Malladi & Agrawal, 2002
Decision-Making Effectiveness	WLAN has been accredited for reducing information float so that the right information can be accessed by the right person at the right time to make decisions.	Sweeney, 2000; McGarvey, 2002; Green, 2003
Collaboration and Communication	WLAN has been accredited for improving connectivity between workers for collaboration and communication.	NOP World-Technology, 2001; Wang et al., 2005
Network Service Quality	WLAN is considered slower, less reliable, and harder to use than the wired LAN.	Sweeney, 2000; Malladi & Agrawal, 2002; Shapland et al., 2002; Cantwell, 2003; Wang et al., 2005
Privacy and Security	WLAN is considered less secure than the wired LAN leading to users' privacy and security concerns.	Stanley, 2002; Green, 2003; Regan, 2003; Elliott & Phillips, 2004
Quality of Work Life	WLAN has been accredited for improving user mobility and flexibility and making working anywhere anytime possible.	Jessup & Robey, 2002; Cantwell, 2003

Table 2. WLAN user impact items

Compared to wired LAN

I1. WLAN is more convenient for the user.
I2. WLAN gives the user more mobility.
I3. WLAN allows the user to be more flexible at work.
I4. WLAN has made the user's life easier at work.
I5. WLAN improves collaboration among users.
I6. WLAN improves organizational knowledge sharing.
I7. WLAN improves organizational communication.
I8. WLAN improves the user's productivity.
I9. WLAN allows the user to reduce errors at work.
I10. WLAN allows the user to connect other handheld devices to the network more easily.
I11. WLAN saves the user time at work.
I12. WLAN improves the user's operational efficiency.
I13. WLAN reduces paperwork for the user.
I14. WLAN improves the user's decision-making capability.
I15. WLAN allows the user to better serve customers.
I16. WLAN allows the user to access up-to-date information.
I17. WLAN allows the user to be more proactive.
I18. WLAN is slower than wired LAN.
I19. WLAN is NOT as reliable as wired LAN.
I20. WLAN is NOT as easy to use as wired LAN.
I21. WLAN is NOT as secured as wired LAN.
I22. I am more concerned about my privacy on WLAN
I23. I am concerned about someone intercepting information if I use WLAN at work.

measure for system success (DeLone & McLean, 1992). This research intends to identify factors that are related to user satisfaction with WLAN. To ascertain user satisfaction with WLAN, five items developed by Phelps and Mok (1999) within the context of Intranet user satisfaction were adapted for the WLAN environment. This set of statements was chosen over other user satisfaction instruments as it is designed specifically for a network environment. Other measures are most suitable to end-user computing satisfaction (e.g., Bailey & Pearson, 1983; Doll & Torkzadeh, 1988; Ives et al., 1983). The five items are:

- The extent to which the user intended to use WLAN for work.
- Whether the user would recommend co-workers to use WLAN.
- The user's perception of whether implementing WLAN represented a positive move for the organization.
- The user's perception of whether he was better or worse off using WLAN.
- The user's overall satisfaction with WLAN.

Once again, each of the five items was measured using a 5-point Likert scale (1 = strongly disagree; 5 = strongly agree).

It is well established that there is usually a discrepancy in the perceived benefits and risks between IT professionals (who design and implement the system) and end users (who use the system). It is worthwhile to investigate the magnitude of this discrepancy within the context of WLAN. Therefore, the same set of questions measuring the perceived benefits and risks of WLAN were administered to both IT professionals and end users. The two sets of responses will be compared to measure the degree of discrepancy.

Two separate questionnaires, one for WLAN users and one for network administrators, were developed. In addition to the relevant items dis-cussed above, each questionnaire had a section that elicited demographic information regarding the respondent and the WLAN in the respondent's organization.

Data Collection Procedure

Data collection posed a greater challenge than the authors expected. Besides the fact that only a small percentage of firms had implemented WLAN, many organizations remained secretive about their WLAN use due to security reasons. The data collection process began with identifying a number of organizations that had adopted WLAN. This information was obtained through direct contact with key persons of organizations in a major Midwestern metropolitan area. WLAN users in 14 organizations with WLAN were identified. The IS or business managers of these organizations, who worked directly with WLAN, were then contacted. They were asked whether their organizations would be willing to participate in this study. 14 organizations agreed to participate in this study. The 14 organizations include two higher education institutions, two computer hardware manufacturers, two communications companies, two transportation companies, a consulting firm, a computer software company, a consumer product manufacturer, a health care organization, a law firm, and a wireless service firm. Upon receiving their permission, questionnaires were sent to the contact person of each organization. The contact person was responsible for distributing the questionnaires to WLAN users and network managers at her organization. Completed questionnaires were returned directly to the authors by the respondents using postage-paid envelopes provided by the researchers. Respondents were assured that the information collected would be kept confidential. A total of 200 user surveys and 50 network manager surveys were distributed. Note that in many organizations, there were multiple network managers in charge

Table 3. User and WLAN profile

User Profile		
Gender	n	%
Male	51	77.3
Female	15	22.7
Age	n	%
25 – 34	25	37.9
35 – 44	25	37.9
45 – 54	16	24.2
Frequency of WLAN use at Work	n	%
1 (Not at All)	2	3.0
2	18	27.3
3	22	33.3
4	12	18.2
5 (Very Frequently)	12	18.2
Applications Using WLAN	n*	%
E-mail	52	78.8
Corporate data access	44	66.7
Internet and WWW	49	74.2
Data input	39	59.1
Data processing	25	37.9
File sharing	30	45.5
Calendaring/Scheduling	36	54.5
Other	9	13.6

* Multiple responses were provided.

WLAN Profile		
WLAN Coverage	n	%
Corporate-Wide	3	21.4
Building-Wide	4	28.6
Department-Wide	1	7.1
Workgroup-Wide	2	14.3
Not Reported	4	28.6
Areas Using WLAN	n**	%
Information Technology	10	71.4
Sales and Marketing	6	42.9
Human Resources	4	28.6
Accounting	5	35.7
Finance	6	42.9
Manufacturing	4	28.6
Customer Services	5	35.7
Supply Chain Management	4	28.6
Legal	3	21.4
Research and Development	5	35.7
Other	2	14.3

continued on following page

Table 3. continued

** A WLAN can cover multiple functional areas.		
# of WLAN Users	n	%
Less than 25	3	21.4
25 – 99	2	14.3
100 – 499	0	0
500 – 999	4	28.6
1000 or more	1	7.1
Not Reported	4	28.6
Length of Time Using WLAN	n	%
Less than 6 months	0	0
6 months – 1 year	3	21.4
1 year – 2 years	3	21.4
2 years – 3 years	2	14.3
Over 3 years	2	14.3
Not Reported	4	28.6

of WLANs. 66 user responses and 10 network manager responses were complete and thus, usable for this study.

ANALYSIS AND RESULTS

User Profile

Table 3 shows the profiles of end users and WLANs in their organizations. Note that the studied organizations represent a broad spectrum of industries with WLAN usage in many functional areas within an organization. Not surprisingly, in 10 of the 14 organizations, the IT group is using WLAN while other areas such as sales and marketing and finance are not too far behind. Also, given the newness of the technology, a majority of the WLANs have been implemented during the past three years. With respect to WLAN users, they use WLAN for a myriad of applications such as e-mail, Internet, corporate data access, data input and processing, and calendaring and scheduling.

Factor Analysis

The 23 WLAN impact items shown in Table 1 were factor analyzed to identify the underlying constructs (factors). One important issue in factor analysis is the case-to-variable ratio. Stevens (1986) recommends a ratio of 5:1 to guarantee a robust and reliable factor analysis procedure. However, researchers such as Fuller and Swanson (1992) have utilized ratios as low as 2:1. In our analysis, the case-to-variable ratio is roughly 3:1 (66 users and 23 variables). This ratio is adequate given the suggested ratio guidelines but one needs to be cautious in interpreting the results. Principal components analysis was used to extract the initial factors and the number of factors was determined by using the eigenvalue-greater-than-one criterion (Kaiser, 1974). Table 4 shows the initial statistics for the five factors with eigenvalues greater than one.

Note that the 5-factor solution explains nearly 67% of the variation. Next, to obtain the most meaningful configuration of the 5-factors, several orthogonal rotation methods were tried. Varimax

Table 4. Eigen values and percentage variation explained

Factor	Eigenvalue	% Variance
1	7.65	33.3
2	2.48	10.8
3	2.10	9.1
4	1.88	8.2
5	1.38	6.0
	Total	67.4%

rotation yielded the most interpretable and meaningful factors. Table 5 shows the matrix of final factor loadings. A cutoff value of 0.40 was chosen to bond an item to a factor. Numbers exceeding 0.40 in absolute value are bolded in Table 5. An examination of the factor loadings matrix revealed that while most items bonded with only one factor, four items (I1, I6, I8, and I18) bonded with two factors as their factor loadings exceeded 0.40. In these instances, it was decided to assign the item to the factor with the highest loading. A thorough and careful examination of the items associated with each of the five factors (see Table 5) leads us to describe the five factors as follows:

- **Factor 1:** The seven items in this factor primarily deal with enhancing users' efficiency, reducing errors and paperwork, saving time, improving decision making, and allowing the user to be more proactive. In light of this, this factor is named "efficiency and effectiveness (EE)."
- **Factor 2:** Items bonding with this factor reflect how WLAN enhances users' work lives by providing mobility, flexibility, convenience, and making user more productive. Thus, this factor is named "quality of work life (QW)."
- **Factor 3:** All three items in this factor focus on improved communication, collaboration, and knowledge sharing among co-workers. Therefore, this factor is called "collaboration and communication (CC)."

- **Factor 4:** Items in this factor pertain to information security and privacy issues. This factor is named "security and privacy (SP)."
- **Factor 5:** Items in this factor address issues of WLAN reliability, speed, and ease-of-use. Thus, this factor is named "wireless network quality (NQ)."

The five user impact factors, the associated items, and their mean and standard deviation are reported in Table 6. The score for each factor is computed by averaging values of items comprising the factor across all cases. Note that "quality of work life (QW)" has the highest mean value (4.03), followed by "communication and collaboration (CC)" (3.34) and "efficiency and effectiveness (EE)" (3.24). The remaining two factors "security and privacy (SP)" and "wireless network quality (NQ)" have lower scores of all the factors (2.78 and 2.61, respectively). This means users do not find the quality of the WLAN to be better than that of the wired network. Also, the security and privacy issues concerns are pretty much the same as they would be in a non-WLAN environment. The main benefits of wireless networks lie in how untethered network access enhances users' quality of work vis-à-vis convenience, mobility, and the ability to access information anywhere. Furthermore, WLANs provide a platform that is highly conducive to communication, collaboration, and information sharing. In sum, WLAN

Table 5. Matrix of factor loadings

Item			Factors		
	Factor 1	Factor 2	Factor 3	Factor 4	Factor 5
I9	0.682	-0.113	0.338	-0.099	0.016
I11	0.747	0.343	0.260	-0.005	0.012
I12	0.770	0.378	0.214	-0.038	-0.084
I13	0.816	0.081	0.217	0.077	0.019
I14	0.782	0.032	0.277	-0.095	0.134
I16	0.762	0.220	-0.106	0.108	-0.024
I17	0.714	0.355	0.067	0.131	0.141
I1	0.168	0.566	0.023	-0.028	0.419
I2	0.117	0.756	-0.008	0.032	-0.017
I3	0.078	0.717	0.353	0.094	0.073
I4	0.367	0.630	0.364	0.195	0.103
I8	0.478	0.556	0.284	0.076	0.085
I15	0.343	0.649	0.106	0.176	0.077
I5	0.164	0.226	0.779	0.030	0.011
I6	0.437	0.034	0.774	0.120	-0.035
I7	0.350	0.294	0.649	-0.034	0.101
I21	-0.098	-0.041	0.094	0.820	-0.094
I22	0.102	0.083	0.016	0.891	0.044
I23	0.059	0.206	-0.015	0.802	0.099
I10	0.260	0.230	-0.236	-0.141	0.399
I18	0.225	-0.464	0.132	0.125	0.671
I19	-0.088	0.018	0.085	0.068	0.869
I20	-0.056	0.318	-0.014	-0.021	0.734

Table 6. Factors and associated items

		Mean	SD
Factor 1: Efficiency and Effectiveness (EE)		3.24	0.82
I9	WLAN allows me to reduce errors at work.	2.82	0.82
I11	WLAN saves me time at work.	3.36	1.12
I12	WLAN improves my operational efficiency.	3.55	1.04
I13	WLAN reduces paperwork.	3.08	1.09
I14	WLAN improves my decision-making capability.	2.92	1.01
I16	WLAN allows me to access up-to-date information.	3.62	1.05
I17	WLAN allows me to be more proactive.	3.35	0.97
Factor 2: Quality of Work Life (QW)		4.03	0.63
I1	WLAN is more convenient.	4.08	0.90
I2	WLAN gives me more mobility.	4.74	0.44
I3	WLAN allows me to be more flexible at work.	4.17	0.87
I4	WLAN has made my life easier at work.	3.74	0.97
I8	WLAN improves my productivity.	3.76	0.86
I15	WLAN allows me to better serve my customers.	3.67	0.95

continued on following page

Table 6. continued

Factor 3: Collaboration and Communication (CC)		3.34	0.78
I5	WLAN improves collaboration among co-workers.	3.47	0.92
I6	WLAN improves organizational knowledge sharing.	3.24	0.91
I7	WLAN improves organizational communication.	3.32	0.88
Factor 4: Security and Privacy (SP)		2.78	0.93
I21*	WLAN is as secured as wired LAN.	2.59	1.14
I22*	I am not more concerned about my privacy on WLAN than on wired LAN.	2.82	1.10
I23*	I am not concerned about someone intercepting information if I use WLAN at work.	2.92	1.06
Factor 5: Wireless Network Quality (NQ)		2.61	0.73
I10	WLAN allows me to connect other handheld devices to the network more easily.	3.09	1.00
I18*	WLAN is as fast as wired LAN.	1.95	1.00
I19*	WLAN is as reliable as wired LAN.	2.41	0.99
I120*	WLAN is as easy to use as wired LAN.	3.00	1.23

*. The item is negatively worded in the questionnaire.

tends to make users more effective in what they do and also improve their operational efficiency.

Satisfaction with WLAN

Five indicators of users' affinity with WLAN adapted from Phelps and Mok (1999) are considered. Table 7 shows the mean and standard deviation of the five items. Note that the mean for each measure is over 3.00 reflecting a reasonable degree of agreement with each item. Next, to ascertain the degree of relationship between the five WLAN impact factors and the five satisfaction measures, correlation coefficients between the factors and measures were calculated. They are shown in the second panel of Table 6. As the correlation table shows, efficiency and effectiveness (EE), quality of work life (QW), and collaboration and communication (CC) correlate significantly with all user satisfaction items. Wireless network quality (NQ) correlates significantly with two items: the extent to which the user intends to use WLAN for work and the user's overall satisfaction with WLAN.

Security and privacy (SP), however, only correlates significantly with one user satisfaction item: the user's perception of whether implementing WLAN represents a positive move for the organization. These findings suggest that IT managers need to focus on improving the benefits related to EE, QW, and CC that are brought by WLAN in order to enhance overall end-user experience. Nevertheless, while the correlations between the SP and NQ factors and the majority of the user satisfaction items were not statistically significant, we should not underestimate and ignore WLAN security, privacy, and quality issues. User perceptions are reflections of their actual experiences and thus their satisfaction with WLAN will only be negatively affected when episodes of security breach, invasion of privacy, and/or deteriorated wireless network quality occur.

IT Manager Perspectives

Scores for the five WLAN impact factors were calculated for IT managers. Figure 1 shows a com-

Table 7. User satisfaction with WLAN

User Satisfaction Items	Mean	SD
US1: I intend to use WLAN for my work.	3.88	0.92
US2: I would recommend other staff to use WLAN.	3.85	0.97
US3: The introduction of WLAN has been a positive move for my organization.	3.94	0.89
US4: I am better off with WLAN.	3.70	0.94
GUS: Overall, I am satisfied with the WLAN in my organization.	3.62	0.97

parison of the mean scores of these factors for IT managers and users. Note that IT managers' scores are higher than those of WLAN users for each of the five factors. For "wireless network quality (NQ)," the mean for IT managers is statistically significantly higher than that for users (t = 2.96; p = 0.004) at the 0.01 level of significance. For the other four factors, the two groups (managers and users) do not differ significantly.

SUMMARY AND CONCLUSION

This research identified five constructs underlying the impact of WLAN on users: efficiency and effectiveness, quality of work life, collaboration and communication, security and privacy, and wireless network quality. In addition, users felt that WLAN improved their quality of work life, enhanced work efficiency and effectiveness, and lead to better collaboration and communication. With respect to the issue of security and privacy, and the quality of the wireless network environment, users were somewhat neutral.

The analysis further indicated that users were fairly positive with their experiences with WLAN as measured by their intention to use it, whether they will recommend it to others, whether WLAN is a positive move for the organization, whether they are better off with WLAN, and the overall

Figure 1. WLAN impact scores for users and IT managers

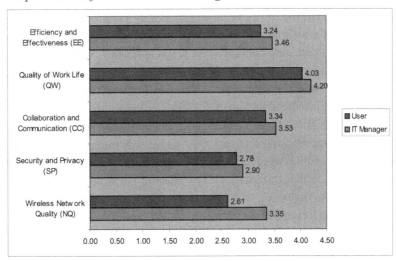

satisfaction with the WLAN. Also, three of the five impact factors (efficiency and effectiveness, quality of work life, and collaboration and communication) had statistically significant relationships with each of the five satisfaction indicators. The other two factors (security and privacy, and wireless network quality) did not correlate significantly across all satisfaction measures—indicating that there is something to be desired when it comes to network quality, security, and privacy aspects of a wireless environment.

For organizations, the findings of this study can help in designing new business processes that account for the benefits of untethered computing. For IT managers, these findings can serve as a guide in educating WLAN users on the benefits and perils of wireless environment. For wireless technology providers and equipment manufacturers, the findings of this study should help in better understanding the needs of their customers in order for them to develop customer-centric products and services in the future.

There are several implications for practice of these research findings. First, even though the overall experiences of the WLAN users are positive, network managers must be proactive in educating users regarding the business benefits of the wireless environment that include improved user efficiency, decision making, quality of work life, and communication and collaboration. Hopefully, more informed users would use the wireless environment more readily and with less hesitation. Second, IT managers need to address concerns of wireless security and user privacy. As wireless technology becomes more pervasive, security and privacy concerns will continue to be at the top of the list of issues needing attention. Once again, wireless computing with appropriate security measures that meet and exceed the needs of the nomadic users are warranted. Third, users expect reliable and efficient wireless networks, and IT managers must make every effort to deliver such an infrastructure.

RECENT DEVELOPMENT AND FUTURE TRENDS OF WLAN

In the past year, wireless network technology has expanded rapidly, with much more innovation expected in the future. Numerous managers and IT directors have cited productivity gains as a direct result of WLAN implementation. In a survey conducted by Gartner, 44% of companies surveyed reported that their primary reason for switching to WLAN technology was to increase productivity (Breidenbach, 2006). Growth of WLAN technology has been slowed due to the various competing technologies as well as the cost of implementing systems. Moreover, questions continue to arise regarding the security of WLANs (Hamblen, 2006).

Questions regarding the security of WLAN technology have impeded the growth of WLAN infrastructures. Security issues in WLAN technology come about from wireless hotspots or unsecured network areas (Potter, 2006). Two areas for security improvement have been identified: security to protect network operations and portable device security. Strong security mechanisms available in these areas remain low. This becomes increasingly problematic as an additional 460 million new wireless devices are expected to be available by 2010. These statistics point to a data centered security mechanism, which could generate a significant portion of WLAN security revenue if a suitable technology reveals itself (PACE, 2006).

Among the most exciting new developments in WLAN, Voice Over WLAN (VoWLAN) technologies are starting to be widely adopted. Companies like Aruba™ are searching for ways to seamlessly integrate Wi-Fi and cellular networks using Voice over Internet Protocol while following the 802.11e standard for handling voice and video traffic (Cox, 2006). Nevertheless, the versatility of WLAN also causes it to suffer from spectrum saturation: Wi-Fi phones, video coupled with standard WLAN service will saturate the network and drastically reduce performance (Bort, 2006). Traditionalists in the field of telecommunications advocate LAN technology over its wireless counterpart. WLAN is currently not competitive in speed with LAN Ethernet technology, and its high percentage bandwidth use makes it much more expensive to maintain.

In the field of wireless communication, several new technologies have emerged recently. Most notable is Wi-Max, which relies on the 802.16 standard. Wi-Max offers great scalability, performance, reduced per user cost, and a maximum range of 31 miles. Wi-Max is currently compatible with foreign technologies while offering high performance and scalability (Axner, 2006). Used currently as a backhaul for wireless hotspots, it is predicted by many that Wi-Max, an alternative to Wi-Fi, might end up being marketed as a complement to Wi-Fi technology (Choi, Muller, Kopeck, & Makarsky, 2006). In addition to Wi-Max, mobile application security system (MASS) has emerged as a security mechanism independent from the mobile framework, favorable due to the small window it allows for malicious data to enter a network (Floyd, 2006).

IMPLICATIONS FOR FUTURE RESEARCH

This study represents an important step towards a better understanding of the impact of WLAN on users and organizational work. For IS researchers, this study provides insights into the role of WLAN within the realm of nomadic computing. These findings can serve as a guide for future research studies in this evolving and dynamic field of wireless computing. The five underlying factors of WLAN impact on users can be considered as key variables in future investigations. Additional studies are also recommended to examine the relationship between organizational computing needs and nomadic computing environments.

Besides considering the impact of network facilities as this study has done, future studies should also take into account the impact of devices and applications. This will help answer questions such as which mobile solutions are appropriate for corporate decision-making tasks. Thus, in sum this research sets forth important initial directives for future research in nomadic computing.

LIMITATIONS

One limitation of this study is the relatively low case-to-variable ratio. The case-to-variable ratio for this study is roughly 3. While prior exploratory studies with similar case-to-variable ratio have proven to produce valid results, it is recommended that the findings of this study be interpreted with caution. Another limitation of this study is that it only focuses on user perceptions of the benefits and risks of WLAN. WLAN's impact on organizations is not included in this study. In order to obtain a clearer picture of the roles of nomadic computing environments such as WLANs in today's organization, it is recommended that future studies examine the impact of WLANs on organizations by including constructs such as costs, management issues, and security measures. This will offer network managers valuable insights on how to utilize nomadic computing technologies to maximize their benefits to organizations.

REFERENCES

Alba, J., Lynch, J., Weitz, B., Janiszewski, C., Lutz, R., Sawyer, A., & Wood, S. (1997). Interactive home shopping: Consumer, retailer, and manufacturer incentives to participate in electronic marketplaces. *Journal of Marketing, 61*, 38-53.

Axner, D.H. (2006). Does WiMax have the right stuff? *Business Communications Review, 36*(7), 58-62.

Bailey, J.E., & Pearson, S.W. (1983). Development of a tool for measuring and analyzing computer user satisfaction. *Management Science,* 530-545.

Balasubramanian, S., Peterson, R.A., & Jarvenpaa, S.L. (2002). Exploring the implications of m-commerce for markets and marketing. *Journal of the Academy of Marketing Science, 30*(4), 348-361.

Baldwin, H. (2002). Sell where you want, when you want. *Mbusiness,* pp. 29-30.

Bort, J. (2006, October 23). Wireless LANs not for all. *The New Data Center,* p. 68.

Breidenbach, S. (2006, October 9). The Wi-Fi divide. *Network World,* pp. 47-50.

Cantwell, E. (2003). In-building wireless: How to keep a signal when you're indoors. *Wireless Business & Technology, 3*(3), 12-14.

Chen, L., Gillenson, M.L, & Sherrell, D.L. (2004). Consumer acceptance of virtual stores: A theoretical model and critical success factors for virtual stores. *Data Base, 32*(2), 8-31.

Chen, L., & Nath, R. (2004). A framework for mobile business applications. *International Journal of Mobile Communications.*

Choi, Y.B., Muller, J., Kopeck, C.V., & Makarsky, J.M. (2006). Corporate wireless LAN security: Threats and an effective security assessment framework for wireless information assurance. *International Journal of Mobile Communications, 4*(3), 267-291.

Conover, J. (2000, August 7). Anatomy of IEEE 802.11b wireless. *Network Computing,* pp. 96-100.

Cox, J. (2006, November 13). Aruba to unify Wi-Fi and cellular voice. *Network World,* p. 34.

Daniel, D. (2000, November 24). Wired on wirelessness: No strings. *Computing Canada,* pp. 18-19.

DeLone, W.H., & McLean, E.R. (1992). Information systems success: The quest for the dependent variable. *Information Systems Research, 3*(1), 60-95.

Devaraj, S., Fan, M., & Rajiv, K. (2002). Antecedents of B2C channel satisfaction and preference: Validating e-commerce metrics. *Information Systems Research, 13*(3), 316-335.

Doll, W.J., & Torkzadeh, G. (1988). The measurement of end-user computing satisfaction. *MIS Quarterly, 12*(2), 259-274.

Elliott, G., & Phillips, N. (2004). *Mobile commerce and wireless computing systems* (1st ed., p. 416). Essex, UK: Pearson Education Limited.

Floyd, D. (2006, April). Mobile application security system (MASS). *Bell Labs Technical Journal,* pp. 191-198.

Fuller, A.L., & Swanson, E.G. (1992). Information centers as organizational innovations. *Journal of Management Information Systems, 9*(1), 47-68.

Funk, P. (2005). 802.11i secures wireless LANs. *Network World, 22*(12), 39.

Goldman, C. (2001). Data on aisle six! *Overland Park, 18*(17), 11A-15A.

Green, H., Rosenbush, S., Crockett, R.O., & Holmes, S. (2003). Wi-Fi means business. *Businessweek,* pp. 86-92.

Hair, J.F., Anderson, R.E., Tatham, R.L., & Grablowsky, B.J. (1984). *Multivariate data analysis.* New York: Macmillan Publishing Co.

Hamblen, M. (2006, December 18). Wireless LANs reach round 2. *ComputerWorld,* p. 10.

Hsu, S., Qian, L., & Ilyas, M. (2003). An analytic study of two probabilistic models for establishing ad hoc WLANs. *Information Technology and Management, 4*(1), 55-67.

Ives, B., Olson, M., & Baroudi, J. (1983). The measurement of user information satisfaction. *Communications of the ACM, 26*(10), 785-793.

Jarvenpaa, S.L., & Todd, P.A. (1997). Consumer reactions to electronic shopping on the World Wide Web. *International Journal of Electronic Commerce, 1*(2), 59-88.

Jessup, L.M., & Robey, D. (2002). The relevance of social issues in ubiquitous computing environments. *Communications of the ACM, 45*(12), 88-91.

Keane, B. (2002). Lowering health care costs out-of-the-box. *Wireless Business & Technology, 2*(2), 36-38.

Kaiser, H.F. (1974). An index of factorial simplicity. *Psychometrika, 39*, 31-36.

Kleinrock, L. (2001). Breaking loose. *Communications of the ACM, 44*(9), 41-45.

LAN Product News. (2005). Wireless LAN equipment shipment to triple within 5 years. *LAN Product News.* Retrieved September 11, 2007, from http://cuhsl.creighton.edu/login?url=http:// search.epnet.com.cuhsl.creighton.edu/login. aspx?direct=true&db=buh&an=16475413

Legris, P., Ingham, J., & Collerette, P. (2003). Why do people use information technology? A critical review of the technology acceptance model. *Information & Management, 40*(3), 191-206.

Lehr, W., & McKnight, L.W. (2003). Wireless Internet access: 3G vs. WiFi? *Telecommunications Policy, 27*, 351-370.

Lia, V.S. (2001). Intraorganizational communication with intranets. *Communications of the ACM, 44*(7), 95-100.

Lucas, H.C., & Spitler, V. (2000). Implementation in a world of workstations and networks. *Information & Management, 38*, 119-128.

Lyytinen, K., Varshney, U., Ackerman, M.S., Davis, G., Avital, M., Robey, D., Sawyer, S., & Sorensen, C. (2004). Surfing the next wave: Design and implementation challenges of ubiquitous computing environments. *Communications of AIS, 13*, 697-716.

Lyytinen, K., & Yoo, Y. (2002). Research commentary: The next wave of nomadic computing. *Information Systems Research, 13*(4), 377-388.

Malladi, R., & Agrawal, D.P. (2002). Current and future applications of mobile and wireless networks. *Communications of the ACM, 45*(10), 144-146.

Markoff, J. (2002). Military seeks to restrict wireless. *San Francisco Chronicle*, pp. B1, B4.

McAdam, R. (2000). The implementation of reengineering in SMEs: A grounded study. *International Small Business Journal, 18*(4), 29-45.

McGarvey, R. (2002). Hospitality checks out wireless. *Mbusiness*, 18-23.

Nath, R. (1988). Local area networks: The network managers' perspective. *Information & Management, 14*(4), 175-181.

NOP World-Technology. (2001). *Wireless LAN benefit study* (CISCO Thought Leadership Series). Retrieved September 11, 2007, from http://newsroom.cisco.com/dlls/tln/WLAN_study.pdf

OECD. (2003). Overview of wireless LANs. *OECD Papers, 3*(9), 7-11.

PACE. (2006, November). WLAN security weak in most businesses. *PACE*, p. 4.

Palvia, P.C. (1996). A model and instrument for measuring small business user satisfaction with information technology. *Information & Management, 31*(3), 151-163.

Phelps, R., & Mok, M. (1999). Managing the risks of intranet implementation: An empirical study of user satisfaction. *Journal of Information Technology, 14*, 39-52.

Potter, B. (2006). Wireless hotspots: Petri dish of wireless security. *Communications of the ACM, 49*(6), 51-56.

Rainie, L. (2004). The rise of wireless connectivity and our latest findings: A PIP data memo. *Pew Internet and American Life Project.* Retrieved September 11, 2007, from http://www.usabilityviews.com/uv007099.html

Regan, K. (2003, January). Wireless LAN security: Things you should know about WLAN security. *Network Security*, 7-9.

Remenyi, D., & Money, A. (1991). A user-satisfaction approach to IS effectiveness measurement. *Journal of Information Technology, 6*, 162-175.

Shapland, E., Gavurlin, S., & Chartoff, M. (2002). Making wireless LANs work for you. *Business Communications Review*, pp. 30-34.

Singer, T. (2001). Wireless LANs come of age. *Plant Engineering, 44*, 46, 48.

Stanley, R.A. (2002). Wireless LAN risks and vulnerabilities (White Paper). *Information Systems Audit and Control.*

Stevens, J. (1986). *Applied multivariate statistics for the social sciences.* Hillsdale, NJ: Lawrence Erlbaum.

Sweeney, T. (2000, November 13). Wireless LANs almost ready for widescale adoption. *Informationweek.com*, pp. 286-292.

Use tech as a tool. (2002). *Men's Health*, p. 64.

Wang, W., Liew, S.C., & Li, V.O.K. (2005). Solutions to performance problems in VoIP over a 802.11 wireless LAN. *IEEE Transactions on Vehicular Technology, 54*(1), 366-384.

Woodroof, J., & Burg, W. (2003). Satisfaction/dissatisfaction: Are users predisposed? *Information & Management, 40*(4), 317-324.

Wright, M. (2005). WiMax wireless broadband. *EDN, 50*(7), 44-50.

Xu, B., & Walke, B. (2001). Design issues of self-organizing broadband wireless networks. *Computer Networks, 37*(1), 73-81.

Chapter XIII
An Exploratory Study of "Killer Applications" and Critical Success Factors in M-Commerce

Gordon Xu
University of Auckland, New Zealand

Jairo A. Gutiérrez
University of Auckland, New Zealand

ABSTRACT

This research deals with two aspects of mobile commerce (m-commerce); namely killer applications and critical success factors. After compiling significant information from the related literature, a Delphi panel was assembled by selecting a group of experts who has significant knowledge about m-commerce and wireless communications. The panel was requested to comment on a number of m-commerce issues and scenarios gleaned from the literature review, and members of the panel also were asked to indicate which issues were more important and which of the presented scenarios were more likely. Three separate rounds of the Delphi survey were carried out and the final results indicated that the short message service (SMS) and a killer portfolio were the two most likely killer applications of m-commerce. Additionally, four factors—convenience, ease of use, trust, and ubiquity—were identified as the most important to m-commerce success. According to the Delphi results and the experts' comments, the highlighted features of the killer applications were found to match the most significant critical success factors as voted by the panel.

INTRODUCTION

Many experts proclaim that the decade of mobile commerce (m-commerce) has arrived. There are hundreds of millions of regular mobile subscribers in the world, and there is potential for many more, but m-commerce seems to hesitate to move forward. China Mobile (Hong Kong), one of the world's largest mobile phone carriers, stated in its 2002 annual report that the corporation is facing increased pressure from flagging average revenue per user (ARPU) per month and minutes of usage (MOU) per user per month. In fact, these same pressures have been taking place in the U.S., Europe, Korea, Australia, New Zealand, and elsewhere. A key obstacle to the progress of m-commerce is a lack of appropriately defined killer applications. To promote m-commerce, there should be less focus on increasing the speeds of wireless data networks now and more on developing compelling applications (Diercks, 2001). Also, in order to help mobile providers to avoid following the same old disastrous road of the e-commerce providers in 2000, critical success factors for m-commerce need to be defined in order to help launch new mobile services.

Therefore, one of the main objectives of this research is to discover and define the likely killer applications in m-commerce from the expansion of current e-commerce applications in a mobile setting and innovative ideas from researchers and practitioners. Hopefully, a set of well-defined killer applications will drive m-commerce from its current limited acceptance to a new, more progressive level. Second, the research attempts to discover and explore the critical success factors that will encourage the uptake of mobile as opposed to conventional e-commerce services. The likely critical success factors will indicate a new way to conduct m-commerce. In addition, it also will attempt to demonstrate links between these two aspects and to highlight the commonness between them.

The findings provided by the research will help vendors, carriers, providers, content partners, and investors in the creation of compelling value for users, based on the following research questions:

1. What are the likely killer applications in m-commerce?
2. What are the critical success factors that will make m-commerce successful?
3. What are the common factors that killer applications and critical success factors share?

LITERATURE REVIEW

Although there are many definitions of the term *mobile commerce*, in this research, m-commerce is simply referred to as *electronic commerce* that uses a mobile device over wireless telecommunication networks.

Table 1. M-commerce application framework (Seen, 2000, p. 150)

CATEGORY	APPLICATIONS	
	Passive (self-activated)	**Active (user-activated)**
Transaction management	Tolls, payments, automatic updates	Shopping
Digital content delivery	E-mail, short messages	Information browsing, directory services, video
Telemetry services	Status monitoring, interactive marketing, smart messaging	Stock quotations, appliance management

Classification of M-Commerce Applications

There is potentially an unlimited number of m-commerce applications (Varshney, 2001; Varshney & Vetter, 2002), which leads to a demand for classification, since currently, it is almost impossible to cover the whole range of potential m-commerce products and services (Lehner &Watson, 2001). Senn (2000) classifies m-commerce applications into three main categories: transaction management, digital content delivery, and telemetry services (see Table 1). Varshney and Vetter (2002) developed a more detailed class of m-commerce applications roughly categorized by m-commerce business models based on mobile characteristics. The applications are classified into 11 categories, as shown in Table 2. Yuan and Zhang

(2003) argue that value propositions in m-commerce which define the relationship between seller offerings and buyer purchases by identifying how the seller achieves the buyer's needs (Clarke, 2001) originate from mobility and location awareness and are contrary to Internet-based e-commerce. Therefore, they group various m-commerce applications based on these value propositions into six categories, as shown in Table 3.

Possible Killer Apps in M-Commerce

The concept of killer application could be interpreted in a number of ways, ranging from applications that are adopted rapidly on a broad scale to ones that directly generate the highest revenues for the service providers (Anckar & D'Incau, 2002).

Table 2. Classes of m-commerce applications (Varshney & Vetter, 2002, p. 187)

Class of Applications	Details	Examples
Mobile financial applications	Applications where mobile device becomes a powerful financial medium	Banking, brokerage, and payments for mobile users
Mobile advertising	Applications turning the wireless infrastructure and devices into a powerful marketing medium	User specific and location sensitive advertisements
Mobile inventory management	Applications to reduce the amount of inventory needed by managing in-house and inventory-on-move	Location tracking of goods, boxes, troops, and people
Product locating and shopping	Applications helping to find the location of product and services	Finding the location of a new/used car of certain model, colour and optional features
Proactive service management	Applications attempting to provide users information on services they may need in very-near-future	Transmission of information related to aging (automobile) components to vendors
Wireless re-engineering	Applications for improving the quality of business services using multicast support of wireless infrastructure	Instant claim-payments by insurance companies
Mobile auction or reverse auction	Applications allowing users to buy or sell certain items using multicast support of wireless infrastructure	Airlines competing to buy a landing time slot during runway congestion
Mobile entertainment services & games	Applications providing the entertainment services to users on per event or subscription basis	Video-on-demand, audio-on-demand, and interactive games
Mobile office	Applications providing the complete office environment to mobile users any where any time	Working from traffic jams, airport, and conferences
Mobile distance education	Applications extending distance/virtual education support for mobile users every where	Taking a class using streaming audio and video
Wireless data centre	Applications providing large amounts of stored data to mobile users for making ""intelligent" decisions	Detailed information on one or more products can be downloaded by vendors

Table 3. Value propositions and applications for m-commerce (Yuan & Zhang, 2003, p. 43)

Value Propositions	Applications
Ubiquitous communication	✓ Mobile voice communication ✓ Short message service (SMS) ✓ E-mail ✓ Voice mail and video mail
Emergency and time critical information services	✓ Emergency call service ✓ Personal medical services ✓ Notification, reminder, and alert service ✓ Airline schedule information ✓ Stock market information ✓ Weather information ✓ Headline news ✓ Crisis alert
Location-sensitive service	✓ Wide or short-range navigation ✓ Nearby facilities/services locating ✓ Accompanying tour guide ✓ Local transportation information ✓ Local service directory assistant
Pocket e-Wallet	✓ Integrated personal identification ✓ Impulsive purchase ✓ Micro-payment ✓ Banking ✓ Electronic coupons ✓ Intelligent home automation
Portable entertainment	✓ Mobile video player ✓ TV/Radio ✓ Music ✓ Sports scores ✓ Gaming ✓ Gambling ✓ Lottery
Improving productivity of mobile workforce	✓ Remote connection to back office ✓ Mobile job assignment/scheduling/dispatch ✓ Mobile personal organizer ✓ Mobile collaboration ✓ Mobile videoconferencing

An appropriate definition of killer application in this research is an application or a service that creates compelling value and that reaches widespread popularity among large numbers of users. Following its success as a killer application of the wired Internet, some researchers seem to agree that e-mail services will become an initial killer wireless application for m-commerce (Ghosh & Swaminatha, 2001; Kannan, Chang & Whinston, 2001). Some authors argue that 2.5G and 3G services probably have been overestimated, whereas 2G services have been underestimated (Birch, 2002). This argument can be proved by today's successful story of SMS. Other researchers are likely to be interested in mobile financial applications that could be the possible killer applications of m-commerce and mobile devices that become a business tool, replacing banks, ATMs, and credit cards, and offering value-added services such as micropayments (Varshney & Vetter, 2002). They believe that mobile payments will be the next killer application for the mobile Internet (Van Blokland, 2004), since, in their view, payment functionality integrated into a mobile device is compelling (Elkington, Viner, Tokuda & Ortiz, 2001). Location-based services

(LBS) also are touted by some researchers as the killer application for m-commerce (Clarke, 2001; Darling, 2001; Rockhold, 2001). Finniear (2003) argues that the use of location-based services to optimize business processes and performance is the basis for the killer application most likely to create large premium revenue. Some analysts say that music is a strong candidate to become a killer application, because mobile devices will take over from the Sony Walkman and integrate the enormous popular success of online music (Bhushan & Subbarao 2001; Young, 2000). But Dijck (2001) argues that there is no real added value for the consumer, especially the person who already has many little gadgets which allow him or her to carry around music. It seems that there is no easy consensus. "Since there is no single killer application, vendors must support a range of applications" (Brodsky, 2003, p. 1). Accordingly, Carlson, Dickson, Jelassi, Vogel, and Walden (2001) point to various types of combinations of m-commerce products and services, which are listed in Table 4. Buellingen and Woerter (2004) argue that not all services likely are to be in demand at the same time or uniformly over mobile

or fixed networks. Additionally, Bhushan and Subbarao (2001) suggest the killer applications will vary widely from region to region and from one business domain to another. Therefore, it is helpful to think of a killer application as an ever-evolving continuum of different applications with certain characteristics that make them inherently valuable (Coley, 2002). Figure 1, adapted from Buellingen and Woerter (2004), depicts a roadmap for discovering the possible killer applications of m-commerce.

Critical Success Factors for M-Commerce

Critical success factors (CSFs) are sought by every organization. The concept was first introduced by Rockart (1979, p. 85) for defining chief executives' information needs. He defines critical success factors as follows:

Critical success factors thus are, for any business, the limited number of areas in which results, if they are satisfactory, will ensure successful competitive performance for the organization.

Figure 1. Diffusion of mobile services (Buellingen & Woerter, 2004, p. 1406)

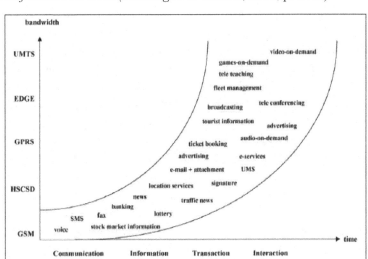

Table 4. Combinations of m-commerce products and services (Adapted from Carlson et al., 2001)

Type of Combinations	Description
Killer Cocktail	A mix in which the components cannot be distinguished [Nokia]
Killer Pizza	A mix in which the components can be distinguished
Killer Bouquet	A set of components for which the aggregate is more than the sum of its parts [The Mobile Commerce Research Centre]
Killer Soup	The more ingredients you put in, the better it gets – an operator will be needed for stirring
Killer Fondue	As for the killer soup, but no operator is needed for stirring

They are the few key areas where "things must go right" for the business to flourish. If results in these areas are not adequate, the organization's efforts for the period will be less than desired. (Rockart, 1979)

This opinion or concept has been accepted and cited by many scholars (Averweg & Erwin, 1999; Boynton & Zmud, 1984; Butler & Fitzgerald, 1999; Feindt, Jeffcoate & Chappell, 2002; Guimaraes, Gupta & Rainer, 1999; Kanji & Wallage, 2000; Munro & Wheeler, 1980). Earlier literature about critical success factors for m-commerce addresses many aspects, including technology, social, and business factors. The wireless application protocol (WAP) seems to be one of the most popular m-commerce technical standards to enable m-commerce anytime, anywhere. Thus, reviewing critical factors of WAP adoption will provide some ways to identify the critical success factors for m-commerce. Hung, Ku, and Chang (2003) built a model based on the theory of planned behavior (TPB) and innovation diffusion theory (IDT) in order to understand WAP adoption behavior. 3G is another important technology for m-commerce. The success factors in Odegaard's (2001) article, "Solving the M-Maze," are as follows:

- The KIS effect: keep it simple.
- The KIP effect: keep it personal.
- Flexible finance.

- Partner for profit.
- Integrate to accumulate.

Buellingen and Woerter (2004) argue that factors related to broadband services and complex applications will become more and more important with regard to ever-evolving mobile services. They point out that prices of services and terminals, the quality of transmission, and coverage are critical success factors of previous GSM-based mobile communications. Today, however, transmission rate, data protection, integrity of communication, transmission security and reliability, user-friendliness, the design of the man-engine-interface, and personalization have become critical success factors for advanced mobile technologies.

Charles, Monodee, and Nurek (2000) report very different findings. According to their research, in their six critical success factors for m-commerce (integrity of the WAP interface, availability of technology, availability of WAP infrastructure, interoperability, security, and speed and efficiency), there is only one significant factor. "Security was indeed the major concern of the respondents" (Charles et al., 2000, p. 32). Siau and Shen (2003) also believe that there is one factor for m-commerce success. "Customer trust is crucial for the growth and success of mobile commerce" (Siau & Shen, 2003, p. 94). They suggest that extending initial trust formation to continuous trust development could sustain customer trust

Table 5. Critical success factors for mobile payments (Antovski & Gusev, 2003, p.97)

Factor	Features
Ease of use	Few clicks, intuitive, flexibility, performance, installing/download
Security	Privacy, confidentiality, integrity, authentication, verification/non-repudiation
Comprehensiveness	Transferability, divisibility, standardization
Expenses	Set-up fees, transaction fees, subscription fees
Technical acceptability	Integration effort, interoperability, scalability, remote access, performance

in m-commerce, and that technology trust and vendor trust are equally important in securing customer trust (Siau & Shen, 2003).

In Arthur D. Little's (2001) research, these value propositions are extended to key success factors in m-commerce, which offers the advantage of being available anywhere at anytime. The main factors are the following:

- **Convenience:** Powerful and small-sized mobile terminals offer users an opportunity to use the right services anywhere at anytime. Compared to e-commerce, m-commerce really is about convenience (Smith, 2002).
- **Localization:** Locating a user with a mobile device adds significant value for m-commerce over conventional e-commerce via user satisfaction.
- **Personalization:** The mobile device will not become a shared utility and can have the unique identity of its user. Creating end-user customized services is crucial for optimizing interaction paths of providers and customers.
- **Ubiquity and timeliness:** Mobile terminals offer users access to real-time information from any location via always-on technology.
- **Customer ownership:** Mobile devices are suited for person-to-person (P2P) marketing strategies, which derive from a comprehensive customer database.

- **Pricing:** Pricing structures must be easy to understand.
- **Simple:** Since there is limited display space on mobile devices, the content must be clear and simple. The learning effort for a user must be reduced.

Other researchers enumerate success factors in some typical m-commerce services, as well. For example, Antovski and Gusev (2003) summarize critical success factors for mobile payments in Table 5.

In terms of the successful NTT DoCoMo's i-Mode service, Sadeh (2002) summarizes the success ingredients as authentication, billing infrastructure, and always-on technology. He says that "by providing convenience to its customers through an easy-to-use packet-switched solution that brings together a critical mass of reasonably priced services, i-Mode was able to achieve nearly instantaneous success, leaving many other operators in the dust" (Sadeh, 2002, p. 203). Dholakia and Rash (2004) argue that an m-portal which connects end users and service providers is a key element for the success of m-commerce. The importance of m-portals can be seen in the experience of the successful i-Mode platform of NTT DoCoMo. Integration and partnering are two primary key success factors for m-portals. Furthermore, Barnes and Huff (2003) combine TAM and the theory of reasoned action (TRA) in order to develop a model which could be applied to the case of i-Mode to help understand its success. They conclude their findings about the success of i-Mode in Japan by emphasizing the importance of a trusted, branded, useful, easy-to-use, holistic package of services and the value of investment and leveraging of technological infrastructure.

RESEARCH APPROACH

The Delphi technique[1] (hereafter referred to as the Delphi) is, in the authors' view, the most suitable methodology for this type of exploratory research and is used to gather data. Mobile commerce is still in its infancy, and it is too new to have adequate historical data. In their book, *The Delphi Method: Techniques and Applications*, Linstone and Turoff (1975, p. 3) present the following definition of the Delphi:

Delphi may be characterized as a method for structuring a group communication process so that the process is effective in allowing a group of individuals, as a whole, to deal with a complex problem.

The Delphi has proved to be an accepted research tool in the information systems field (Bacon & Fitzgerald, 2001; Brancheau, Janz & Wetherbe, 1996; Lai & Chung, 2002; Nambisan, Agarwal & Tanniru, 1999; Peffers & Tuunanen, 2005; Schmidt, Lyytinen, Keil & Cule, 2001). Galliers (1992) points out that the Delphi is "clearly of significant benefit in the rapidly changing world of information systems" (p. 156), including m-commerce. M-commerce employs many uncertain mobile technologies which are updated constantly and unpredictably. This leads to an unlimited number of m-commerce applications, and even more new applications will come in the near future. Moreover, the high complexity of m-commerce itself means that achieving success is complicated. These opinions support the use of the Delphi for this m-commerce study. Furthermore,

Linstone and Turoff (1975) described some situations which are suited to the technique, and this study shares the following similar characteristics to those discussed:

- The problem does not lend itself to precise analytical techniques but can benefit from subjective judgments on a collective basis.
- The participants that are needed to contribute to the study of a complex problem have little history of adequate information (no historical data exist, or past data are inappropriate for a new situation) and may represent various experiences or expertise.
- The heterogeneity of the participants must be preserved in order to ensure validity of the results.

Rowe and Wright (2001) state that one of the conditions for the use of the Delphi is when expert judgment is necessary and the use of statistical methods is inappropriate (either impractical or impossible).

In fact, the Delphi does not provide more accurate assessments, judgments, or forecasts than other methods (Rowe, Wright & Bolger, 1991; Woudenberg, 1991). Gordon (1994) claims that it may be no more accurate than any expert, single or composite, but no better way exists to gather and synthesize opinions than the Delphi.

Since the Delphi technique recommends making use of heterogeneous experts who have knowledge of the topic being investigated (Hasson, Keeney & McKenna, 2000; Rowe & Wright, 2001; Rowe et al., 1991), a great deal of attention must be given to the selection of participants (Gordon, 1994). Thus, potential participants must be experts in wireless communications, m-commerce, or e-commerce. For this study, panel members were selected based on their expertise. Some attendees of the 2004 IEEE New Zealand Wireless Workshop and the Future of Mobile Technology Forum at the University of Auckland were invited to participate; others members were recruited based on their knowledge or experience as evidenced by journal publications or nomination by peers. The panel was comprised of male and female panelists and included academic researchers and industry practitioners. Also, the research narrowed down the scope to the New Zealand context. Recent research points out the fact that the current mobile market in New Zealand is a duopoly of Vodafone and Telecom Mobile with 3.1 million subscribers between them, and the mobile penetration rate is around 75% (Budde, 2004). Cell phones are becoming a necessary part of Kiwi users' lives. Furthermore, IDC forecasts that both cellular revenue and subscribers in New Zealand will continue to grow to 3.5 million subscribers, or 82% of the population, by 2008 (Buckley & Wanklyn, 2004). Of the 66 potential participants from the initial invitation, 10 experts participated in all rounds (see Table 6). The number of participants meets Armstrong's (cited in Rowe & Wright, 2001) suggestion about the ideal Delphi group size comprised of 5 to 20 members.

This research was limited to 3 rounds rather than being left open-ended, which is in accordance with Rowe and Wright's (2001) suggestions. Round one of the Delphi tried to shake down the key variables. It removed the ones which were believed to be obviously unsuitable and elicited new ideas from the panelists. The results of round one were collected to generate more appropriate issues for the next round.

In round 2, all the issues identified and proposed in the first round were consolidated into a list of scenarios and fed back to the panel, which consisted of the participants who had answered the round-one questionnaire. In the second round, the panel was asked to rank and rate these newly generated issues, and the panelists had to provide comments about why they ranked them as they did. A Likert scale, which was designed to examine how strongly subjects agreed or disagreed with statements (Cavana, Delahaye & Sekaran, 2001), was employed. Furthermore, a four-point response scale rather than an odd total of possible response points (5-point or 7-point response scale) was used in this study, as recommended by Linstone and Turoff (1975). For example, the study asked panelists about the importance of each factor to make m-commerce successful with a 4-point scale, including (1) unimportant, (2) slightly important, (3) important, and (4) very important. Alternatively, it asked the possibility of it being a killer

Table 6. Position/occupations of the round one panel

Positions/Occupations	Number of People	Percentage
Practitioners		
Director	1	10%
Leader of m-commerce strategy and implementation	1	10%
Propositions Manager	3	30%
Subtotal of Practitioners	**5**	**50%**
Academics		
Associate Professor	3	30%
Senior Lecturer	1	10%
Lecturer	1	10%
Subtotal of Academics	**5**	**50%**
Total	**10**	**100%**

Table 7. Likely "killer applications" sorted by ranking scores

Order of Likelihood	Issue No.	"Killer Application"/Issue	Ranking Score
1	G	Short Text Messaging (SMS)	125
2	N	"Killer" Portfolio	117
3	F	Mobile E-Mail	103
4	L	Mobile Music	100
5	B	Micropayment	99
6	K	Mobile Gaming	84
7	D	Mobile Top-up Transaction	82
8	H	Location-based Information Service	80
9	I	Information Alerts Service	72
10	A	Basic Banking Services	67
11	O	No "Killer App" At All	65
12	M	Mobile Video	62
13(14)	E	Mobile Shopping/Booking	54
13(14)	J	Mobile Advertising (M-Advertising)	54
15	C	Financial Alerts Service	36

Table 8. Critical success factors sorted by ranking scores

Order of Importance	Factor No.	Critical Success Factor	Ranking Score
1	a	Convenience	129
2	b	Ease of Use	126
3	l	Trust	117
4	i	Ubiquity	106
5	e	Security	97
6	j	Improvement of Bandwidth	92
7	f	Crystal-clear Pricing	91
8	d	More Powerful Devices	83
9	g	Personalization	80
10	h	Battery Life	79
11	k	Handset Look/Design	77
12	c	Location-sensitive	67

application by using (1) unlikely, (2) somewhat likely, (3) likely, and (4) very likely. The results of round two were recorded in a ranked list of issues with comments about each item.

In the final round 3, a similar procedure was repeated. The ranked list with all anonymous comments was sent back to the panel. The panelists then were asked to reconsider their own rankings and revise any of their scores as they wished. The purpose of this round was to seek an agreement of opinions and for dissenting views to be confirmed.

Figure 2. Four critical success factors of m-commerce

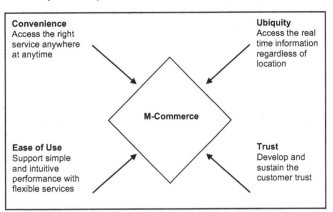

RESULTS OF THE DELPHI STUDY

There are 2 sets of ranking systems in this study: one for ranking 15 killer applications of m-commerce and the other for ranking the 12 critical success factors of m-commerce. Through the ranking systems, the most likely applications and issues and the important factors for m-commerce can be defined.

Table 7 shows the ranking scores of the Delphi study for all potential killer applications and issues. It sorts them in descending order in order to view them from the most likely to the least likely killer applications and issues as ranked by the panel. Short text messaging (SMS) and killer portfolio, which were voted by the panel in the top two positions, are the most likely killer applications of m-commerce. Furthermore, these two killer applications are obvious, as there was quite a significant difference (of 14 points) between the second position and third.

The critical success factors ranking scores were also sorted in descending order, from the most important factors to the least important factors, as shown in Table 8. According to the selections of the panel, 4 factors—convenience, ease of use, ubiquity, and trust—are the most important for m-commerce success.

DISCUSSION

According to the results from the Delphi study, SMS and a killer portfolio are the two most likely killer applications in m-commerce. SMS is an enabler service with many m-commerce applications and services based on it. On the other hand, SMS is the simplest application—users feel it is easy to use, and providers feel it is easy to launch due to its low cost. A killer portfolio is designed to satisfy customer needs. One expert in the panel stated that many people have lots of different reasons or requirements for using m-commerce; therefore, a killer portfolio might provide them with a convenient mechanism in their specific situations. Furthermore, in terms of the analysis of the Delphi study, killer applications not only have to provide a compelling value to the customer but also must be simple and easy to offer by the providers. In Table 7, the top likely killer application, SMS, already has been there, and it is really simple and inexpensive for both customers and suppliers. At the bottom of the rankings, other listed applications are definitely more complicated than SMS. There are not just more complex but there are also additional technical issues for these applications; for example, the mobile service provider and operator has to invite and cooperate with third parties (e.g., banks and

Figure 3. Relationships between "killer applications" and critical success factors in m-commerce

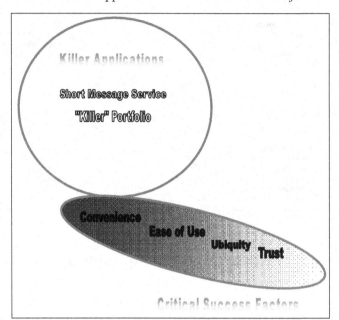

merchants) in order to launch them. This could increase the uncertainty of successfully launching and providing a new service to the customer. Thus, this study suggests that the combination of applications for a killer portfolio first must focus on selecting the most basic and simplest applications. For example, SMS could be the first option to be built into a killer portfolio.

According to the findings of the study, 4 factors from the given list will drive m-commerce to succeed: convenience, ease of use, trust, and ubiquity (see Figure 2). The most important reason for people to own a mobile is the convenience it provides; this extends to its use as an m-commerce device. M-commerce services must be simple and intuitive; otherwise, users will get frustrated and not adopt them. Trust is a very important factor for all forms of e-commerce, and it is crucial for the growth and success of m-commerce. Ubiquity is another important factor for all mobile services in which people need access anytime and anywhere. This last factor highly correlates to convenience; moreover, according to the analysis, the other 3

factors are linked to convenience, as well. Once again, the findings seem to confirm that m-commerce is really about convenience.

Some features of the identified killer applications are revealed in this study. SMS has four features: (1) it provides ubiquitous communication; (2) it is a bearer service for other applications; (3) it is the simplest form of m-commerce; and (4) it is a cost-effective service. The killer portfolio has two features: (1) it is a combination of m-commerce applications; and (2) it meets and satisfies the customer's needs. Due to these features, both of the nominated killer applications really serve the purpose of convenience. Second, SMS as a ubiquitous communication service meets the ubiquity factor of m-commerce. Third, because of its simplicity, SMS is definitely easy to use. A killer portfolio has its own combination features. Therefore, if it includes SMS as its basic component, it also might have SMS features. As a result, there are three common factors between killer applications and the critical success factors of m-commerce; namely, convenience, ubiquity, and ease of use. This relationship is illustrated in Figure 3.

A killer application can be seen as an entity, while critical success factors can be considered its projection. Accordingly, if people are doubtful about the existence of killer applications, critical success factors also might prove elusive. Furthermore, if a killer application cannot be defined clearly, its projection and critical success factors might be vague, as well. If a killer application already has been identified, then the factors that drive m-commerce success can be figured out, based on its features. This also can be reversed: critical success factors might be assumed first, and then a killer application of m-commerce that has these factors as its features can be developed. Since, at the moment, the killer applications of m-commerce are not well defined, the shadow of the critical success factors in Figure 3 is of varied intensity—the dark part (e.g., convenience) indicates that the factors meet the features of likely killer applications. However, the bright part (e.g., trust) shows that the factors definitely cannot relate to the killer applications. To sum up, killer applications and critical success factors do have a strong relationship, and in order to help m-commerce succeed, both of them must be well defined.

CONCLUSION

This research has contributed to the m-commerce field by exploring the most likely killer applications and the critical success factors of mobile commerce and by highlighting the relationship between them.

Some suggestions for future study are outlined here: first, this research topic could be extended to a wider area (multinational or even global context). This might overcome a geographic bias in the current study. Second, other research methodologies can be applied to this topic in order to do further research with a larger population.

Perhaps a survey can be conducted to reflect potential m-commerce users' opinions. Third, integrating some basic and useful applications into a killer portfolio could add more value to an m-commerce service and, hence, attract more users. Finally, a further research project might focus on discovering relationships among each of the critical success factors of m-commerce.

REFERENCES

Anckar, B., & D'Incau, D. (2002). Value-added services in mobile commerce: An analytical framework and empirical findings from a national consumer survey. In *Proceedings of the 35th Annual Hawaii International Conference on System Sciences*.

Antovski, L., & Gusev, M. (2003). *M-payments*. Proceedings of 25th International Conference Information Technology Interfaces ITI 2003, 95-100.

Averweg, U.R., & Erwin, G.J. (1999). Critical success factors for implementation of decision support systems in South Africa. *Proceedings of the 32nd Hawaii International Conference on System Sciences* (pp. 1-10).

Bacon, C.J., & Fitzgerald, B. (2001). A systemic framework for the field of information systems. *ACM SIGMIS Database 32*(2), 46-67.

Barnes, S.J., & Huff, S.L. (2003). Rising sun: iMode and the wireless Internet. *Communications of the ACM 46*(11), 79-84.

Bhushan, N., & Subbarao, V. (2001). *Mobile commerce: Killer applications, infosys*. Retrieved from http://www.ebusinessforum.gr/content/downloads/mcommerce.pdf

Birch, D.G.W. (2002). *Emerging models for mobile commerce, consult hyperion*. Retrieved from http://www.ebusinessforum.gr/content/downloads/mCommerce.pdf

Boynton, A.C., & Zmud, R.W. (1984). An assessment of critical success factors. *Sloan Management Review 25*(4), 17-27.

Brancheau, J.C., Janz, B.D., & Wetherbe, J.C. (1996). Key issues in information systems management: 1994-95 SIM delphi results. *MIS Quarterly 20*(2), 225-242.

Brodsky, I. (2003). *M-commerce trials and tribulations: It may finally be time for mobile commerce to hit its stride—Frequencies, American's network*. Retrieved from http://www.findarticles.com/p/articles/mi_m0DUJ/is_2003_Nov_1/ai_110928131

Buckley, A., & Wanklyn, C.T. (2004). *Prepaid subscribers curb New Zealand cellular services market growth*. IDC. Retrieved from http://www.idcresearch. co.nz/PressRelease_Mobile0404.pdf

Budde, P. (2004). *Telecoms highlights in New Zealand*. Retrieved from http://www.budde.com.au/paulsdesk/paulsAnalysis.html

Buellingen, F., & Woerter, M. (2004). Development perspectives, firm strategies and applications in mobile commerce. *Journal of Business Research 57*(12), 1402-1408.

Butler, T., & Fitzgerald, B. (1999). Unpacking the systems development process: An empirical application of the CSF concept in a research context. *Journal of Strategic Information Systems 8*(4), 351-371.

Carlson, C., Dickson, G., Jelassi, T., Vogel, D., & Walden, P. (2001). Mobile commerce: Core issues, products and services. *Proceedings of the 14th Bled Electronic Commerce Conference*, Bled, Slovenia.

Cavana, R.Y., Delahaye, B.L., & Sekaran, U. (2001). *Applied business research: Qualitative and quantitative methods*. Milton, Queensland, Australia: John Wiley & Sons.

Charles, L., Monodee, F., & Nurek, T. (2000). *The critical success factors for m-commerce*. Rondebosch: University of Cape Town.

Clarke, I., III. (2001). Emerging value propositions for m-commerce. *Journal of Business Strategies, 18*(2), 133-148.

Coley, B. (2002). *Enabling the killer application*. Texas Instruments Incorporated. Retrieved from http://focus.ti.com/pdfs/vf/wireless/killerapps.pdf

Darling, A. (2001). Waiting for the m-commerce explosion. *Telecommunications International, 35*(2), 34-38.

Dholakia, N., & Rash, M. (2004). Configuration m-commerce portals for business success. In N. Shi (Ed.), *Mobile commerce applications* (pp. 76-93). Hershey, PA: Idea Group Publishing.

Diercks, R. (2001). Will m-commerce live up to the hype? *Wireless Internet Magazine, 1*(1). Retrieved March 2001, from http://www.wirelessinternetmag.com/news/0104/0104_research_hype.htm

Dijck, P.V. (2001). *Making money the wireless way, commentary & society*. Retrieved from http://www.evolt.org/article/Making_money_the_wireless_way/25/5439/?format

Elkington, H., Viner, N., Tokuda, R., & Ortiz, M. (2001). *Mobile payments: Killer app or paper tiger?* London: The Boston Consulting Group.

Feindt, S., Jeffcoate, J., & Chappell, C. (2002). Identifying success factors for rapid growth in SME e-commerce. *Small Business Economics, 19*(1), 51-62.

Finniear, L. (2003). When will we see an LBS killer app? *Geospatial Solutions, 13*(2), 58.

Galliers, R.D. (1992). Choosing information systems research approaches. In R. Galliers (Ed.),

Information systems research: Issues, methods and practical guidelines (pp. 144-162). Oxford: Blackwell Scientific Publications.

Ghosh, A.K., & Swaminatha, T.M. (2001). Software security and privacy risks in mobile e-commerce. *Communications of the ACM, 44*(2), 51-57.

Gordon, T.J. (1994). *The Delphi method.* American Council for the United Nations University (AC/UNU) Millennium Project. Retrieved from http://www.futurovenezuela.org/_curso/5-delphi.pdf

Guimaraes, T., Gupta, Y.P., & Rainer Jr., R.K. (1999). Empirically testing the relationship between end-user computing problems and information centre success factors. *Decision Sciences, 30*(2), 393-413.

Hasson, F., Keeney, S., & McKenna, H. (2000). Research guidelines for the delphi survey technique. *Journal of Advanced Nursing, 32*(4), 1008-1015.

Hung, S.Y., Ku, C.Y., & Chang, C.M. (2003). Critical factors of WAP services adoption: An empirical study. *Electronic Commerce Research and Applications, 2*(1), 42-60.

Kanji, G.K., & Wallage, W. (2000). Business excellence through customer satisfaction. *Total Quality Management, 11*(7), 979-998.

Kannan, P.K., Chang, A.M., & Whinston, A.B. (2001). Wireless commerce: Marketing issues and possibilities. In *Proceedings of the 34th Annual Hawaii International Conference on System Sciences* (pp. 1-6).

Lai, V.S., & Chung, W. (2002). Managing international data communications. *Communications of the ACM, 45*(3), 89-93.

Lehner, F., & Watson, R.T. (2001). *From e-commerce to m-commerce: Research directions.* Regensburg, Germany: University of Regensburg.

Retrieved from http://www.ebusinessforum.gr/content/downloads/ResearchDirections.pdf

Linstone, H.A., & Turoff, M. (1975). *The delphi method: Techniques and applications.* Ontario: Addison-Wesley.

Little, A.D. (2001). *Key success factors for m-commerce.* Vienna: Arthur D. Little Int. GmbH.

Munro, M.C., & Wheeler, B.R. (1980). Planning, critical success factors, and management information requirements. *MIS Quarterly, 4*(4), 27-38.

Nambisan, S., Agarwal, R., & Tanniru, M. (1999). Organizational mechanisms for enhancing user innovation in information technology. *MIS Quarterly, 23*(3), 365-395.

Odegaard, P. (2001). Solving the m-maze. *Global Telecoms Business, 58*, 42.

Peffers, K., & Tuunanen, T. (2005). Planning for IS applications: A practical, information theoretical method and case study in mobile financial services. *Information & Management, 42*(3), 483-501.

Rockart, J.F. (1979). Chief executives define their own data needs. *Harvard Business Review, 57*(2), 81-93.

Rockhold, J. (2001). The business of where. *Wireless Review, 18*, 14-18.

Rowe, G., & Wright, G. (2001). Expert opinions in forecasting: The role of the delphi technique. In J.S. Armstrong (Ed.), *Principles of forecasting: A handbook for researchers and practitioners* (pp. 125-144). Norwell, MA: Kluwer Academic Publishers.

Rowe, G., Wright, G., & Bolger, F. (1991). Delphi: A reevaluation of research and theory. *Technological Forecasting and Social Change, 39*(3), 235-251.

Sadeh, N. (2002). *M-commerce: Technologies, services, and business models.* New York: John Wiley & Sons.

Schmidt, R., Lyytinen, K., Keil, M., & Cule, P. (2001). Identifying software project risks: An international delphi study. *Journal of Management Information Systems, 17*(4), 5-36.

Senn, J.A. (2000). The emergence of m-commerce. *Computer, 33*(12), 148-150.

Siau, K., & Shen, Z. (2003). Building customer trust in mobile commerce. *Communications of the ACM, 46*(4), 91-94.

Smith, B. (2002). Under the radar. *Wireless Week, 8*, 38-39.

Van Blokland, A. (2004). Killer apps from Do-CoMo and KDDI. *J@pan Inc., 53*, 6

Varshney, U. (2001). Location management support for mobile commerce applications. *Proceedings of the 1ˢᵗ International Workshop on Mobile Commerce* (pp. 1-6).

Varshney, U., & Vetter, R. (2002). Mobile commerce: Framework, applications and networking support. *Mobile Networks and Applications, 7*(3), 185-198.

Woudenberg, F. (1991). An evaluation of delphi. *Technological Forecasting and Social Change, 40*(2), 131-150.

Young, S. (2000, December 11). E-commerce (a special report): Buying in—In search of the killer app: As mobile commerce gets going, the question everybody wants to know is a simple one: What will get consumers to flock to it? *Wall Street Journal*, p. R.8.

Yuan, Y., & Zhang, J.J. (2003). Towards an appropriate business model for m-commerce. *International Journal of Mobile Communications, 1*(1/2), 35-56.

ENDNOTE

[1] The name of Delphi technique was drawn humorously from the site of the Greek oracle at Delphi where necromancers foretold the future using hallucinogenic vapors and animal entrails.

This work was previously published in the Journal of Electronic Commerce in Organizations, Vol. 4, Issue 3, edited by M. Khosrow-Pour, pp. 63-79, copyright 2006 by IGI Publishing, formerly known as Idea Group Publishing (an imprint of IGI Global).

Chapter XIV
E–Commerce and Sales Taxes in the United States:
Adequacy, Fairness, and Management

Christopher G. Reddick
The University of Texas at San Antonio, USA

ABSTRACT

This chapter examines the relationship between electronic commerce and the U.S. state sales and use tax system. A framework is used in this study of a high-quality tax system and it is applied to taxing electronic commerce sales. The first part of this chapter analyzed nine principles of an effective tax system, and divided these principles into the categories of adequacy of revenue, fairness of revenue, and management of revenue. In the second part of this chapter, these principles are tested to determine what impact electronic commerce taxation has on an effective revenue system. The results of these initial tests suggest that taxation of electronic commerce was associated with fairness in the tax system. In particular, the results suggested that states that had fairer tax systems were more likely to rely less on a sales tax and more on taxing Internet access. Management and adequacy of the revenue systems of states were not found to have a significant bearing on taxing electronic commerce. These results reinforce the existing public finance and legal theories which argue that the sales tax is not a fair revenue stream, and it should be re-evaluated especially in light of the contentious issue of taxing electronic commerce.

INTRODUCTION

Taxing of electronic commerce is one of the most pressing tax policy issues U.S. state governments face in the 21st century. This chapter examines how electronic commerce affects the sales tax system and its adherence to the standards of a high-quality tax system. This study uses several principles to devise measures of revenue capacity, or the ability of state governments to have a high degree of adequacy, fairness, and management in their revenue system. Revenue capacity is different from tax capacity; the latter represents the ability of a government entity to finance its public services (Berry & Fording, 1997). Revenue capacity is broader, encompassing not just state revenue raising ability, but the management of the revenue system and equity issues.

This study attempts to discern how states deal with taxing electronic commerce, particularly if they have a high-quality revenue system. Specifically, areas such as taxing Internet access, having a state sales tax, taxing digital downloads, and participation in the Streamlined Sales Tax Project (SSTP) are examined. (The SSTP is an effort created by state governments to simplify and modernize sales and use tax collection and administration.)

The study is notably different from existing empirical work in that it examines how the taxing of electronic commerce affects revenue capacity. This chapter qualitatively applies nine principles of an effective tax system, dividing them into the categories of adequacy of revenues, fairness of revenues, and management of revenues to the taxation of electronic commerce. These three categories are then tested quantitatively to determine the impact that taxing electronic commerce has on revenue capacity. The key question asked is: *For states that are less reliant on taxing electronic commerce sales, will they have higher levels of revenue capacity?*

Taxing Electronic Commerce and Information Systems (IS) Research

A common argument for not taxing Internet sales is that the Internet is viewed by some as an infant industry which requires protection. In information systems (IS) research, we would like to know whether taxing Internet sales would lead to less use of this communication media because of the higher price. There are potentially positive spillover effects arising from the size of the Internet. The idea is that aiding the Internet early will yield large benefits to future generations (Goolsbee &

Zittrain, 1999). Furthermore, as the number of Internet transactions rise, the value of Internet commerce rises as well. There is some empirical evidence that supports a ban on taxing Internet sales in the short run (Goolsbee & Zittrain, 1999) and other evidence suggesting that it makes no difference to sales if Internet access is taxed (Bruce, Deskins, & Fox, 2004).

Another common argument in favor of banning taxes on the Internet relates to a "digital divide" in Internet access in America. The Internet and other information technologies are more prevalent among wealthier people than among lower income individuals (Bruce et al., 2004). Therefore, taxing Internet sales will affect the poor more than the rich in the United States. Lower income individuals will not have as much Internet access to take advantage of purchasing online and potentially avoiding paying sales tax. These two arguments are especially pertinent to IS research, and are explored in more detail later in this chapter.

This chapter is divided into three parts. The first part of the study looks at how the existing system of sales taxation adheres to the standards of a high-quality revenue system, and how electronic commerce affects this relationship. The second part of the study uses the information presented in the first part to build hypotheses and test relationships of how the presence of electronic commerce and taxation affects the revenue capacity of states. The third part presents recommendations, limitations, and avenues for future research on taxing electronic commerce sales.

PRINCIPLES OF HIGH-QUALITY STATE TAX SYSTEM APPLIED TO SALES TAXES ON ELECTRONIC COMMERCE

There are nine principles of a high-quality state tax system that can be applied to the taxing of electronic commerce. The comparison is based upon criteria outlined in the 1992 document entitled "Principles of a High-Quality State Revenue System" prepared by the Foundation for State Legislatures and the National Conference of State Legislators (NCSL, 1992). The nine principles have been placed into three groups, representing key issues that state governments face in revenue capacity. These groups are adequacy, fairness, and management of revenues. The principles and their impact on taxing electronic commerce sales are summarized in Table 1. Each of the principles is discussed as well as applications to taxing electronic commerce sales.

Adequacy of Revenue

The principles under this group include 1, 2, and 3. Principle 1 of a high-quality tax system is that the state revenue system should be complementary. For example, different rates and filing requirements across jurisdictions increase the costs of taxpayer compliance. State and local governments should cooperate to avoid a patchwork of rate structures across the state since a revenue system that minimizes complexity eases compliance costs and improves efficiency of revenue collection. Many

Table 1. Comparing principles of high-quality tax system and taxing of electronic commerce

Category	Principle	Is principle found in taxing electronic commerce sales? (Yes or No)	Key Literature
Adequacy	1. Elements that are complementary in state and local finances	No	Brunori (2001)
	2. Revenue reliable manner, i.e., stability, certainty, and sufficiency	No	Bruce and Fox (2001a, 2001b); Cline and Neubig (1999); Goolsbee and Zittrain (1999)
	3. Relies on a balanced variety of revenue sources	No	Mikesell (2001); Bruce and Fox (2001a)
Fairness	4. Treats taxpayers equitably	No	McLure (2002a, 2002b)
	5. Responsive to international and interstate competition	No	Hellerstein (1998); Bruce et al. (2003)
	6. Accountable to taxpayers	No	Due and Mikesell (1994); Mikesell (2004); Cornia et al. (2004)
Management	7. Facilitates taxpayer compliance	No	McLure (2002a, 2002b); Due and Mikesell (1994)
	8. Simple to administer	No	McLure (2000, 2002b)
	9. Minimize its involvement in spending decisions	No	Fox and Murray (1997); Goolsbee (2000); Cornia et al. (2004)

state sales taxes have separate local rates piggy backed on top of state rates, adding complexity to an already complicated system.

How does Principle 1 apply to electronic commerce and the sales tax? When calculating potential tax liability, it is not just the 45 different sales taxes that must be taken into account; there are other numerous local rates that must be applied. Local government's use of sales taxes indicates there are about 7,500 jurisdictions that have a general sales tax program authorized by 34 states (Ward & Sipior, 2004). This wide variation makes it extremely complicated when collecting the sales and use taxes, especially on electronic commerce purchases (Brunori, 2001). Principle 1 is clearly violated if there is an effort to tax electronic commerce without simplification of all the tax rates.

Principle 2 deals with the revenue system producing revenue in a reliable manner. This involves stability, certainty, and sufficiency of the tax system. There should be stability in that the amount of revenue collected should be relatively constant over time and not subjected to unpredictable fluctuations. A diversified revenue structure with a broad tax base tends to be more stable than an undiversified structure with a narrow tax base. Certainty implies that the number and types of tax changes will be kept to a minimum. Individuals should not be subjected to frequent changes in tax rates and bases because frequent changes interfere with their economic choices and the ability to make long-term financial plans and decisions. In this principle, sufficiency means that a high-quality revenue system produces enough revenue to finance the level of services that the state chooses to provide.

In taxing electronic commerce, revenue collected in a reliable manner is being eroded because of remote sales. This makes the necessity of taxing electronic commerce especially important in order to produce additional tax revenue in tight economic times (GAO, 2000). As Bruce and Fox

(2001a, 2001b) note, the economic losses from not taxing electronic commerce will be substantial in the near future. They estimate that by 2011, states will lose anywhere from 2.6% to 9.9% of their total state tax collections to electronic commerce. Other research indicates that revenue losses will be much lower because research does not distinguish between business to business e-commerce the largest portion of e-commerce (Victor & Jih, 2006). For instance, Cline and Neubig (1999) found revenue losses for 1998 to be only one-tenth of 1% of total sales tax revenue. Goolsbee and Zittrain (1999) estimated that revenue loss in 1998 was less than one quarter of 1% of sales tax revenue and by 2003, losses would be less than 2% of total sales tax revenue. Some argue that once the issues of trust and risk of using the Internet have been resolved, electronic commerce will begin to have real tax implications for states (Clay & Strauss, 2000).

Principle 3 is that a high-quality revenue system should rely upon a diverse and balanced range of sources. One goal of a revenue system is economic neutrality, to prevent the distortion of individual and business behavior. If reliance is divided among numerous sources and their bases are broad, rates can be kept low in order to minimize their impact on behavior. A broad base tax system helps meet the goal of diversification because it spreads the burden of the tax among more payers. States should attempt to avoid excessive reliance on any single revenue source.

The taxing of electronic commerce partly violates Principle 3 because many states rely heavily on the sales tax. However, the important question for this study is whether the taxation of electronic commerce is causing a narrowing of the tax base. For example, the sales tax base equaled 51.4% of the state's personal income in 1979, but has fallen to 42% in 2000 (Mikesell, 2000, 2001). The narrowing of the sales tax base is attributed to three major factors (Yang & Poon, 2001). The first is remote sales, including electronic commerce, catalogue and telephone sales, and cross-state shopping, all of which have been expanding greatly in recent years. The second factor is the shift in consumption patterns towards greater consumption of services (exempt from taxes in most states) and less consumption of goods. Third, continued legislative exemptions have narrowed the base in essentially every state. As a result, states have responded to the narrowing tax base by raising rates (Bruce & Fox, 2001a). For instance, the median sales tax rate increased across states from 3.25% in 1970 to 5.3% in 2003. The existing evidence shows that there is an increased reliance on the sales tax and the narrowing of its base. Both of these factors can partly be attributed to the loss of tax revenue from electronic commerce sales.

Fairness of Revenue

The principles under this group include 4, 5, and 6. Principle 4 refers to the fairness of revenue category. A high-quality tax system treats taxpayers equitably. This is measured by horizontal equity and vertical equity. Horizontal equity requires that individuals in similar circumstances have similar tax burdens. Vertical equity refers to the distribution of tax burdens among people in different circumstances. Reliance on sales taxes tends to make state and local revenue systems regressive and a high-quality tax system should minimize regressivity.

Not taxing electronic commerce sales makes the sales tax even more regressive for low-income groups since their effective rate is higher for them. Therefore, Principle 4 is violated because of electronic commerce and the sales tax lacks horizontal equity. Higher income groups have greater Internet access and will more easily be able to avoid paying sales taxes than lower income groups making their effective rate lower (McLure, 2002b). McLure (2002a) believes that it is unfair to exempt electronic commerce purchases, which

are disproportionately made by the relatively affluent, while taxing purchases from local vendors are made disproportionately by the less affluent, increasing the regressivity of the sales tax.

Principle 5 is that a high-quality tax system should be responsive to interstate and international economic competition. If there are different sales tax rates between states, economic distortions are created because businesses will locate in jurisdictions where they have the least tax burden. Therefore, states are under increased pressure to make revenue systems a tool for economic development. The problem is that tax breaks can erode tax bases. A state that imposes a tax burden far different from that of its neighboring states runs a risk of hurting its local economy. Therefore, taxes should provide similar treatment for all industries and all firms within a given industry and state.

The taxing of electronic commerce violates Principle 5 since the current sales tax system provides some economic incentives for businesses to locate in jurisdictions where their customers have the least tax burden. Taxing electronic commerce has not provided an additional problem since it has existed before the Internet because of mail order and phone retailers. However, the rise of the Internet has exasperated this problem in terms of competition and the economic distortions that it creates. This tax wedge affects location decisions of businesses that face paying use taxes (Bruce, Fox, & Murray, 2003). The tax wedge between local and remote purchases occurs when citizens can buy locally and pay sales tax, or they can buy remotely and more often than not avoid paying sales or use tax on the purchase. The tax differential can amount to a discount of up to 10%. Sales taxes encourage firms to locate their production facilities in the lowest tax rate states to evade use taxes (Cornia, Sjoquist, & Walters, 2004).

For example, Amazon.com has admitted that one of the reasons for its location in the state of Washington is to limit the percentage of sales on which it must collect taxes. In addition, Walmart. com claimed that it was a separate online entity from its "brick and mortar" Wal-mart Stores Inc. Therefore, Walmart.com asserted that it did not have to collect sales taxes on online transactions with customers within states where Wal-Mart Stores Inc. maintains retail stores, which is every state in the United States (Cockfield, 2002). Firms are required to collect sales tax in states where operations exist because of nexus, or having a physical presence. Therefore, Wal-Mart, being in 50 states, should be obligated to collect sales tax in all applicable states for its Internet operations. In addition, Barnes and Noble avoided this issue by organizing BN.com as a separate entity, so only its warehouses and management (initially in the states of New York and New Jersey) were counted as taxable locales. Traditional nexus rules are based upon concepts of territory and the physical presence of the taxpayer in the state. However, such an approach makes little sense since the Internet has no geographic borders (Hellerstein, 1998).

Principle 6 is that a high-quality tax system should be accountable to taxpayers. Tax laws should be explicit and not hidden, proposed changes should be well publicized in advance to stimulate debate. Lawmakers have a responsibility to ensure that policy produces the intended effect and does so at a reasonable cost.

The sales tax system violates Principle 6 in the taxation of electronic commerce. In the existing system, most taxpayers are not aware that they must pay taxes on remote sales which does not make it accountable to taxpayers. This is probably why taxpayer compliance is only around 1% for use taxes (Due & Mikesell, 1994). The greatest problem is that taxpayers do not understand what the use tax is and how it fits into the overall tax system (Cornia et al., 2004). In addition, the existing literature argues that direct collection from consumers of the use tax is not feasible (Mikesell, 2001).

Management of Revenue

The principles under this group include 7, 8, and 9. Principle 7 fits into the management of revenue category, arguing that a high-quality tax system facilitates taxpayer compliance. It does this by avoiding a maze of taxes, forms, and filing requirements. The reduction in complexity helps taxpayers understand the tax system and reduces the costs of compliance. It is important for the taxpayer to feel that the system is fair because taxpayer compliance is largely voluntary (Reddick, 2006).

The sales tax system and electronic commerce violates the transparency requirement because it is dependent upon the business having a physical presence, or nexus, in the purchaser's state (McLure, 2002a). If this is not the case, it is incumbent upon the consumer to remit what is called a use tax to the taxing authority. However, most people are not aware that if they do not pay a sales tax on a remote purchase, they are responsible for remitting the corresponding use tax to their taxing authority (Cornia et al., 2004; Due & Mikesell, 1994). In addition, the exemptions for food and services also makes the sales tax system more complicated and higher statutory rates are required to cover these exemptions (Mikesell, 2001, 2004). The vendor has the complicated task of trying to figure out what is taxable and what is not taxable, all of which increases compliance costs. Differing state exemptions for digital downloads and taxing Internet access are other problems that violate the transparency requirement (McLure, 2002b).

Principle 8 is that a high-quality tax system which is easy to administer reduces the likelihood of errors and facilitates fairness. Poor tax administration will mean that tax burdens are distributed among taxpayers in ways the law did not intend. If the tax system is administered fairly, individuals and businesses are more likely to pay their respective share of the tax burden.

Therefore, a fair tax system should increase taxpayer compliance.

Electronic commerce diminishes fairness since individuals can choose to purchase items online to avoid paying sales taxes. This significantly diminishes tax fairness and equity in administration (McLure, 2002b). For instance, determining who should remit the tax for tangible goods is a manageable problem. The goods must be shipped to a location, which is a reasonable approximation of where it will be used, and the opportunities for businesses and consumers to behave in ways that minimize their taxes are not that burdensome. Digital goods, by contrast, are not subject to similar constraints. Even if the sellers of such goods decided to collect sales tax, buyers could conceivably have the digital product shipped to an Internet location and pay for the product with a credit card whose billing address listed a state without a sales tax. The anonymity of Internet transactions seriously complicates both tax administration and tax compliance, if taxes are based on the destination of sales or the source of income (McLure, 2000).

Principle 9 is that a high-quality tax system minimizes its involvement in spending decisions and makes involvement explicit. For example, tax deductions, credits, and exemptions shift tax burdens from a favored set of taxpayers to less favored taxpayers. For this reason, the costs should be explicit or transparent and should be reviewed annually.

The taxing of electronic commerce favors online purchases over main street vendors (Fox & Murray, 1997). Research shows that differences in sales tax rates along state borders cause consumers to switch their purchases from the higher to lower tax jurisdictions (CBO, 2003). Goolsbee (2000) found that the probability of buying something online decreases as the local sales tax rate rises. Specifically, this author found that controlling for demographic characteristics and applying existing tax rates to the Internet reduces the number of buyers online by 20 to 25% and reduces sales

by 25 to 30%. There appears to be tax sensitivity of consumers that could have a negative impact on electronic commerce. However, taxing electronic commerce would have a positive impact on taxpayer equity (McLure, 2002a).

The application of taxing electronic commerce and the nine principles of high-quality taxation reveal that this system fails on all counts. It is the existence of the sales tax that creates the problem, but it is exacerbated with taxing electronic commerce. These nine principles are used to test the impact that taxing electronic commerce has on revenue capacity. A model is created in the next part of this chapter that tests the relationship among the nine principles. Principles 1 to 3 examine adequacy of revenue, Principles 4 to 6 examine fairness of the revenue system, and Principles 7 to 9 examine the impact of management on the revenue system. However, before this chapter specifies the hypothesis and models, there is a brief examination of the existing empirical studies on the taxation of electronic commerce to see how this study fits into the literature.

TAXING ELECTRONIC COMMERCE SALES AND STATE GOVERNMENT REVENUE CAPACITY

There are several empirical studies that examine the impact of electronic commerce taxation on Internet sales, Internet access, and digital downloads (see Table 2). These studies can be divided into either consumers and taxing electronic commerce sales or state governments and taxing Internet sales. Both will be reviewed.

Consumers and Taxing Electronic Commerce

Taxing Internet Access. Bruce et al. (2004) examine the effect that Internet access taxation has on Internet access rates. Their empirical results showed that taxing Internet access does not have

Table 2. Existing empirical studies on taxing electronic commerce

Consumers and Taxing Electronic Commerce	Existing Empirical Studies	State Governments and Taxing Electronic Commerce	Existing Empirical Studies
a. Taxing Internet Access	Bruce et al. (2004)	a. Participation in SSTP	Cornia et al. (2004); Cameron (2004)
b. Taxing Internet Sales	Goolsbee and Zittrain (1999); Goolsebee (2000); Vijayasarathy (2001); Alm and Melnik (2005)	b. Taxing Internet Access, Downloads, Internet Sales	Nesbary (2000); Best and Teske (2002)

a statistically significant effect on Internet access rates. The strongest impact was from income, with Internet access rising as the individual's income rose.

Taxing Internet Sales. Using public opinion data from Forrester, a market research firm, Goolsbee and Zittrain (1999) did an analysis of consumer behavior and taxing Internet sales. First, they found that aggressive enforcement of taxes on Internet commerce raised only a small amount of revenue in the short term. Second, enforcing taxes on Internet sales disproportionately benefited higher income and highly educated people, but this effect lessened substantially because of the proliferation of the Internet. Third, the costs of complying with taxes on Internet commerce were unlikely to be very large for most online transactions. Finally, there are positive externalities or spillover effects of the Internet that should be considered before aggressively applying taxes.

In the literature on consumers' reaction to taxing Internet sales, Goolsbee (2000) conducted an empirical analysis on how local taxation affects the decision of consumers to buy goods over the Internet. Controlling for individual characteristics, consumers living in places with higher tax rates are significantly more likely to buy online. The magnitude of the tax effect suggests that applying existing sales taxes to the Internet might reduce the number of online buyers by as much as 24%.

Vijayasarathy (2002) examined whether the shopping orientations of consumers would change their behavior as a result of sales taxes being charged for online purchases. The survey results indicated that charging sales tax would not have a negative impact on online shopping.

Finally, Alm and Melnik's (2005) study attempted to determine the impact of sales taxes on the probability of online shopping. Their results indicated that sales taxes typically have a positive and statistically significant impact on the probability of consumers buying online. For instance, a 1% change in the tax price reduces the probability of buying online by roughly 0.5%, which is one fourth the size of Goolsbee's (2000) estimates. In addition, the probability of online purchases tends to be greater for higher income groups and lower for most minorities, which is similar to Goolsbee and Zittrain's (1999) finding.

State Governments and Taxing Electronic Commerce

Participation in the SSTP. Cornia et al. (2004) explored the hypothesis that if the sales and use tax structures are simplified, then remote vendors would voluntarily collect and remit the sales tax if it was in their commercial interests. These authors conducted a simulation, and their results revealed that large firms without nexus would prefer a voluntary system to a mandatory collection system, but participation would hinge on the compensation level for compliance set by the state.

In another study on this issue, Cameron (2004) attempted to identify state characteristics that increased the likelihood of participation in the SSTP. This author found three factors being supported: the more business vitality the less likely to participate in the SSTP; the higher the technological innovation of the state, the less likely to participate in the SSTP; and the greater the reliance on the sales tax, the more likely to participate in the SSTP.

Taxing Internet Access, Downloads, and Internet Sales. Nesbary (2000) tested a model that examined the impact of taxation of goods and services sold over the Internet, taxation of Internet access fees, and taxation of digital downloads from the Internet. This author tested these as dependent variables against fiscal, organizational, and demographic factors as predictor variables. Overall, the results did not show significant relationships among these common factors that were perceived to be associated with taxing Internet sales.

In a similar line of inquiry, Best and Teske (2002) examine the impact of interest groups and political and economic factors and found that they were correlated with adoptions of taxing Internet access and digital downloads. Their study was similar to the Nesbary study; however, Best and Teske found some significant relationships. The results of their models indicate that interest groups are extremely influential in state decisions to tax Internet sales.

This study is different from the existing empirical work because it focuses on testing whether electronic commerce taxation is associated with being a high revenue capacity state. This has not been previously modeled in the literature. It fits into the existing empirical studies outlined in Table 2 on state governments and electronic commerce taxation. The following section formally outlines the hypotheses tested in this study that are derived from some of these empirical studies.

Hypotheses

In order to examine the impact that revenue capacity has on the taxation of electronic commerce, four groups of hypotheses are tested. These hypotheses will be briefly mentioned followed by a detailed discussion of how each is specified. It should be noted that this study does not outline all 32 tests conducted here as hypotheses, but mentions the most important ones showing their impact on electronic commerce and revenue capacity.

Adequacy of Revenue

Hypothesis 1a: *State governments that tax Internet access will have more adequate revenue capacity.*

Hypothesis 1b: *State governments that do not have a sales tax will have more adequate revenue capacity.*

Hypothesis 1c: *State governments that tax Internet downloads will have more adequate revenue capacity.*

Hypothesis 1d: *State governments that do not participate in the SSTP will have more adequate revenue capacity.*

Fairness of Revenue

Hypothesis 2a: *State governments that tax Internet access will have a fairer tax system.*

Hypothesis 2b: *State governments that do not have a sales tax will have a fairer tax system.*

Hypothesis 2c: *State governments that tax digital downloads will have a fairer tax system.*

Hypothesis 2d: *State governments that do not participate in the SSTP will have a fairer tax system.*

Management of Revenue

Hypothesis 3a: *State governments that tax Internet access will have a greater ability to manage their revenue system.*

Hypothesis 3b: *State governments that do not have a sales tax will have a greater ability to manage their revenue system.*

Hypothesis 3c: *State governments that tax digital downloads will have a greater ability to manage their revenue system.*

Hypothesis 3d: *State governments that do not participate in the SSTP will have a greater ability to manage their revenue system.*

Revenue Capacity

Hypothesis 4a: *State governments that tax Internet access will increase their overall revenue capacity (or adequate revenue capacity, fair tax system, and better management of revenues).*

Hypothesis 4b: *State governments that do not have a sales tax will increase overall revenue capacity.*

Hypothesis 4c: *State governments that tax digital downloads will increase overall revenue capacity.*

Hypothesis 4d: *State governments that do not participate in the SSTP will increase overall revenue capacity.*

Hypotheses 1 to 4 examine the impact of electronic commerce variables on the adequacy of revenue, fairness of revenue, management of revenue, and overall revenue capacity. For instance, in Hypothesis 1a, the existing empirical research has investigated the relationship between taxing Internet access and electronic commerce (Best &

Teske, 2002; Bruce et al., 2004; Nesbary, 2000). For Hypothesis 1b, the reaction of government of having a sales tax on electronic commerce has been investigated by Nesbary (2000) and Best and Teske (2002). For Hypothesis 1c, taxing digital downloads has also been examined by the above authors. Finally, for Hypothesis 1d there is existing research on the relationship of the SSTP and electronic commerce (Cameron, 2004; Cornia et al., 2004; Swain & Hellerstein, 2005). These hypotheses can be operationalized with data measuring state revenue capacity.

Revenue Capacity Dependent Variables

The following section discusses the dependent variables used in this study to test the impact of revenue capacity on electronic commerce taxation. In order to measure the impact that the electronic commerce variables have on revenue capacity, data were compiled from *Governing Magazine* (Barrett, Greene, Mariani, & Sostek, 2003). They collected data in 2003 on the nine previously mentioned principles of high-quality tax systems and narrowed them down into four measures of state revenue capacity, which are:

1. **Adequacy of revenue:** Several issues are measured here. Does the state have adequate revenues currently and for the foreseeable future to provide reasonable support for the programs the legislature has historically seen fit to fund? Is there a balanced, multitax approach that does not overly rely on any one tax? Is the state experiencing budget shortfalls that can be attributed to a weakness in tax revenues? Are there long-term trends that call into question the ability of the current tax system to deliver sufficient revenue down the road? Are there structural issues that make it particularly difficult to deal with obvious tax problems?

2. **Fairness of revenue:** This measures such issues as: Are similar taxpayers taxed similarly, and as a result is the broadest possible base being taxed at the lowest possible rates? Is the system overly regressive? How thoroughly does the state tax services? Do the sales tax on goods have a broad base with a minimum of unnecessary exemptions? Does the state's taxes avoid excessive exemptions and deductions that are not mean-tested? Is there anything extremely unfair about the state's approach to corporate taxes?

3. **Management of revenue:** This measures such issues as: Does the state have adequate resources and management capacity to optimize voluntary compliance, find and get taxes from those who do not voluntarily comply, and do this with optimal efficiency for both the state and its taxpayers? How accurate have its revenue estimates been and assessments of the impact of tax changes over time? Does the state engage in studies of its tax system and use them to create better policy? Does it have good information and data to facilitate understanding of the tax system? What is the quality of human resources? Is there high turnover, lack of training, lack of workforce planning, or many line budget cuts? To what extent has the state engaged in taxpayer education efforts and taken steps to improve customer relations?

4. **Revenue capacity:** This measures the adequacy, fairness, and management of the state revenue system. This variable is compiled by adding up the values for each of the three above mentioned categories for each of the states and dividing them by three to get an overall revenue capacity score (to be discussed more thoroughly later in this chapter).

The *Governing Magazine* rating methodology consisted of a general outline of the elements that contribute to adequacy, fairness, and management through interviews and document reviews to determine how successful states had been establishing them. For example, *Governing Magazine* staff conducted interviews with heads of the revenue departments or designated officials in most states. Interviews were conducted with tax experts and documents were evaluated that shed further light on the state revenue systems were evaluated. A four star rating system was devised:

- **Four stars:** The state has done very well in the area under consideration and generally has at least one or two elements that make it stand out from the other states in a positive way.
- **Three stars:** Although there is in general room for improvement, the state is essentially performing well. This means that the structure of the state is such that in the near future the revenue streams will be adequate.
- **Two stars:** The state could continue to function as it currently does into the near future. However, there are clear elements to the tax system that would benefit from change.
- **One star:** The area under review needs some kind of dramatic reform. Alteration at the margins will not be enough to fix the state's tax problems.

Some of the states, which had four stars for adequacy of their revenue system included Delaware, New Mexico, North Dakota, and Wyoming (Table 3). Hawaii was the only state that had four stars for fairness of the revenue system. For management capacity of the revenue system, four stars were reported for Delaware, Florida, Michigan, Minnesota, Missouri, and Washington. In the revenue capacity variable (which is the average of the three scores for each state) the highest score was 3.7, reported for the state of Delaware, out of a maximum attainable score of four.

The lowest scores for revenue adequacy can also be found in Table 3. Some of the states with

Table 3. State revenue capacity and taxing electronic commerce issues. Sources: (a) Barrett et al. (2003) and (b) CCH (2004)

State	Adequacy of Revenue[a] (Max 4 Stars)	Fairness of Revenue[a] (Max 4 Stars)	Management of Revenue[a] (Max 4 Stars)	Revenue Capacity (Max 4 Stars)	Tax Internet Access[b] (1=Tax Internet Access)	Sales Tax[b] (1=Sales Tax)	Tax Downloads[b] (1=Tax Downloads)	SSTP[b] (1=SSTP)
Alabama	1	1	2	1.3	0	1	1	0
Alaska	1	3	2	2.0	0	0	0	0
Arizona	2	2	2	2.0	0	1	1	0
Arkansas	2	2	2	2.0	0	1	0	1
California	1	2	2	1.7	0	1	0	0
Colorado	1	2	2	1.7	0	1	1	0
Connecticut	2	2	2	2.0	1	1	1	0
Delaware	4	3	4	3.7	0	0	0	0
Florida	1	1	4	2.0	0	1	0	0
Georgia	3	2	2	2.3	0	1	0	0
Hawaii	3	4	2	3.0	0	1	1	0
Idaho	3	2	3	2.7	0	1	1	0
Illinois	2	1	2	1.7	0	1	1	0
Indiana	3	2	3	2.7	0	1	1	1
Iowa	3	2	2	2.3	0	1	0	1
Kansas	2	2	3	2.3	0	1	1	1
Kentucky	2	2	2	2.0	0	1	0	1
Louisiana	2	2	2	2.0	0	1	1	0
Maine	2	2	3	2.3	0	1	1	0
Maryland	2	2	3	2.3	0	1	0	0
Massachusetts	2	2	3	2.3	0	1	0	0
Michigan	2	2	4	2.7	0	1	1	0
Minnesota	2	2	4	2.7	0	1	1	1
Mississippi	2	2	1	1.7	0	1	1	0
Missouri	2	2	4	2.7	0	1	0	0
Montana	1	3	2	2.0	0	0	0	0
Nebraska	2	2	3	2.3	0	1	1	1
Nevada	1	1	1	1.0	0	1	0	1
New Hampshire	2	2	3	2.3	0	0	0	0
New Jersey	2	2	3	2.3	0	1	0	0
New Mexico	4	3	1	2.7	1	1	1	0
New York	2	2	3	2.3	0	1	1	0
North Carolina	2	2	3	2.3	0	1	0	1
North Dakota	4	3	2	3.0	1	1	1	1
Ohio	2	2	3	2.3	1	1	1	1

continued on following page

Table 3. continued

State	Adeq-uacy of Revenue[a] (Max 4 Stars)	Fairness of Revenue[a] (Max 4 Stars)	Manag-ement of Revenue[a] (Max 4 Stars)	Revenue Capacity (Max 4 Stars)	Tax Internet Access[b] (1=Tax Internet Access)	Sales Tax[b] (1=Sales Tax)	Tax Down-loads[b] (1=Tax Downloads)	SSTP[b] (1=SSTP)
Oklahoma	2	2	2	2.0	0	1	0	1
Oregon	1	3	3	2.3	0	0	0	0
Pennsylvania	3	2	2	2.3	0	1	0	0
Rhode Island	2	2	2	2.0	0	1	0	0
South Carolina	2	2	2	2.0	0	1	0	0
South Dakota	3	3	3	3.0	1	1	1	1
Tennessee	1	1	2	1.3	0	1	1	1
Texas	1	1	3	1.7	1	1	1	1
Utah	3	2	3	2.7	0	1	1	1
Vermont	3	3	2	2.7	0	1	0	1
Virginia	2	2	2	2.0	0	1	0	0
Washington	1	2	4	2.3	0	1	1	1
West Virginia	2	2	2	2.0	0	1	1	1
Wisconsin	2	3	3	2.7	1	1	1	0
Wyoming	4	2	2	2.7	0	1	1	1

low revenue adequacies included Alabama and Nevada. In total, there were 11 states with only one star for adequacy of the revenue system. For fairness of the revenue system, there were six states with only one star—Alabama, Florida, Illinois, Nevada, Tennessee, and Texas. For the management capacity variable there were three states with only one star, being Mississippi, Nevada, and New Mexico.

In order to measure the impact of electronic commerce and taxation on revenue capacity, an index was composed using the scores obtained from *Governing Magazine*. One star is worth one point, two stars is two points, and so forth. The average score for the 50 states was just over two points for adequacy and fairness and just over two and one half points for management capacity (Table 4). Two points indicates that the state could continue to function at its current level, but there are structural changes that could be beneficial to the current tax system.

Total revenue capacity is also measured, which is compiled by adding the adequacy, fairness, and management scores and dividing this score by three to get an overall value out of four. This study used the score for each of the adequacy, fairness, and management of revenues variables for each state government to create an overall revenue capacity score (Table 4). Therefore, if a state did well on each of these scores, this would be reflected in the overall revenue capacity score. A limitation of using this four star rating system is that there are only four choices; this reduces the precision of the dependent variables, and this should be kept in mind when interpreting the results. Variability of the ratings could come from a number of factors that may not be captured in the models presented here. The following section discusses the independent variables that are used to explain state government revenue capacity.

Table 4. Descriptive statistics of variables. Sources: Barrett et al. (2003); b CCH (2004); c Bruce and Fox (2001a); d Governing Magazine (2003); and NA = Not Applicable

	N	Minimum	Maximum	Mean	Predicted Impact
Adequacy of Revenue[a]	50	1.00	4.00	2.12	NA
Fairness of Revenue[a]	50	1.00	4.00	2.10	NA
Management of Revenue[a]	50	1.00	4.00	2.52	NA
Revenue Capacity Index	50	1.00	3.67	2.25	NA
Tax Internet Access[b]	50	0.00	1.00	0.14	+
Sales Tax[b]	50	0.00	1.00	0.90	-
Tax Downloads[b]	50	0.00	1.00	0.54	+
Streamlined Sales Tax Project[b]	50	0.00	1.00	0.40	-
Sales Tax % State Revenue[c]	50	0.00	62.60	32.08	-
Sales Tax Base % Personal Income[c]	50	0.00	109.20	44.42	+
% Households with Internet Access[d]	50	36.10	64.10	50.23	+
State Retail Sales % of U.S.[d]	50	0.18	10.69	2.00	-

Predictor Variables

The electronic commerce independent variables are reported in Table 4. Internet access is used as a predictor of revenue capacity, and it has been modeled in prior research on taxing Internet sales (Best & Teske, 2002). The results in Table 4 indicate that 14%, or seven states, tax Internet access. In accordance with the Internet Tax Freedom Act (ITFA) of 1998, these states represent only those that were able to tax Internet access before it was banned by Congress. There are 90%, or 45 states, that have a sales tax, and this variable has also been studied in the literature on taxing electronic commerce (Bruce et al., 2004; Nesbary, 2000). In addition, 54% of the states tax digital downloads. Best and Teske (2002) incorporated digital downloads in their models of taxation of Internet sales. Finally, there were 20 states in 2003 that had adopted the provisions of the SSTP. Cameron (2004) examined the impact on state participation in the SSTP from business and economic conditions of the state and found

an empirical connection; therefore, it should be included in the models.

In addition to the electronic commerce variables, this research has controlled for the amount of sales tax collected as a percent of total state revenue. This variable can be used to demonstrate how dependent a state is on sales taxes. Existing literature indicates that the sales tax base is narrowing (Mikesell, 2001). States that have a smaller base would greatly benefit from taxing electronic commerce. Therefore, a measure of this is the state tax base as a percentage of personal income. In addition, this research uses the amount of household Internet access as a predictor variable. States that have higher Internet access are more likely to be concerned about collecting taxes on Internet sales. The state's retail sales, as a percentage of total retail sales, is used to measure the dependence of the state on the retail industry. Higher state dependence on retail sales indicates a greater need to collect sales taxes. The following section presents the models that are tested to determine the impact of taxing electronic commerce on revenue capacity.

Models

The models used in this study test four different types of revenue capacity issues. The results are initially suggestive of some correlations. The first dependent variable measures how adequate revenues are for the state. The second dependent variable examines fairness of the state revenue system. The third dependent variable tests state management of the revenue system. The final dependent variable is a revenue capacity index, a combination of the three measures.

It is anticipated that taxing Internet access will have a positive impact on the revenue capacity dependent variables because states will be able to collect more tax revenue from these fees. (The direction of predicted causality for all of the independent variables is shown in Table 4.) Existing work has indicated a relationship between taxing Internet access and sales tax reliance (Best & Teske, 2002). However, other empirical studies have found no relationship between Internet access and taxing electronic commerce (Bruce et al., 2004; Nesbary, 2000).

If the state has a sales tax, negative coefficients are anticipated for the capacity variables since the state may be more dependent upon this tax compared to other forms of taxation such as income taxes. As discussed in the first part of this chapter, there has been a tendency for state governments to raise their sales tax rate, and electronic commerce is one cause of a decreased sales tax base. In terms of the principles mentioned in the first part of this chapter, the sales tax and electronic commerce fails in terms of providing adequate revenue (exemptions to the base and loss of sales tax revenues from electronic commerce), fairness (it is a regressive tax, more so with electronic commerce), and management (nexus rules make it difficult for vendor compliance).

If the state taxes digital downloads, it is an indication that the state will have a higher capacity score because of a more balanced revenue system. This is associated with the fairness principle in that digital downloads should be taxed similarly to purchases made off-the-shelf. Fairness would decrease since consumers would choose to purchase more digital downloads. Management capacity would be applicable because it would make compliance more difficult sorting between what is taxable and not taxable.

In addition, states that have implemented the SSTP initiative should experience a negative impact on revenue capacity since they are trying to over-ride the physical presence rules of the *Quill* decision. This implies that they are more dependent upon sales taxes. This is related to adequacy principle in that these states are not getting enough revenue from the sales tax because of the loss in tax revenues from electronic commerce sales. Second, fairness is not achieved since consumers that purchase online can escape the sales tax. Finally, management capacity is impaired since there is the compliance costs associated with vendors and consumers trying to discern what is taxable.

Some of the other predictor variables should also be briefly mentioned. One of them is the state sales tax as a percentage of state revenue. This is anticipated to have a negative impact on capacity. A higher sales tax base as a percentage of personal income is anticipated to increase revenue capacity. Household Internet access should increase revenue capacity because it represents a greater threat to taxing remote sales and an increased need to diversify revenue sources. A high level of dependence by the state on retail sales should decrease revenue capacity.

Results

The results of the models of adequacy of revenue, fairness of revenue, management of revenue, and revenue capacity are illustrated in Table 5. Ordinary least squares (OLS) regression is the appropriate statistical procedure to use when working with a continuous dependent variable. The results from the OLS regressions of the rev-

E-Commerce and Sales Taxes in the United States: Adequacy, Fairness, and Management

Table 5. Regressions of adequacy, fairness, management, and revenue capacity tested against taxing electronic commerce issues

Independent Variables	Adequacy of Revenue			Fairness of Revenue			Management of Revenue			Revenue Capacity Index		
	Beta	t-statistic	Significant	Beta	t-statistic	Significant	Beta	t-statistic	Significant	Beta	t-statistic	Significant
Constant	1.72	(1.52)	0.14	1.55	(2.39)**	0.02	0.21	(0.18)	0.85	1.16	(1.75)	0.09
Tax Internet Access	0.22	(1.58)	0.12	0.30	(2.76)***	0.01	-0.10	(-0.68)	0.50	0.20	(1.43)	0.16
State Sales Tax	0.16	(0.71)	0.48	-0.39	(-2.23)**	0.03	-0.04	(-0.16)	0.87	-0.09	(-0.41)	0.68
Tax Downloads	-0.03	(-0.19)	0.85	-0.04	(-0.31)	0.76	0.22	(1.36)	0.18	0.09	(0.56)	0.58
Streamlined Sales Tax Project	0.00	(0.01)	0.99	-0.11	(-1.04)	0.31	0.19	(1.26)	0.22	0.05	(0.37)	0.71
State Sales Tax % State Revenue	-0.45	(-2.16)**	0.04	-0.52	(-3.16)***	0.00	0.06	(0.26)	0.79	-0.45	(-2.12)**	0.04
Sales Tax Base % Personal Income	0.49	(2.23)**	0.03	0.72	(4.19)***	0.00	-0.23	(-1.00)	0.32	0.47	(2.08)**	0.04
% Households with Internet Access	0.02	(0.14)	0.89	0.23	(2.09)**	0.04	0.36	(2.39)**	0.02	0.31	(2.10)**	0.04
State Retail Sales % of U.S.	-0.31	(-2.09)**	0.04	-0.25	(-2.19)**	0.03	0.22	(1.43)	0.16	-0.17	(-1.10)	0.28
Model Diagnostics												
F-statistic		(2.59)**	0.02		(7.31)***	0.00		(1.78)*	0.10		(2.15)**	0.05
Adjusted-R²		0.41			0.71			0.30			0.36	
N		50			50			50			50	

Notes: ** *significant at 0.05 level; and* *** *significant at 0.01 level.*

enue adequacy variable suggest no statistically significant coefficients for the taxing of electronic commerce variables. Other results show that as state sales tax as a percent of revenue increase, there will be a decrease in adequacy of revenue by about half of a point. Second, as the tax base increases there will be a rise in adequacy of state revenue by half of a point. Third, as state retail sales tax rises, there will be a decrease in adequacy by one third of a point. The adjusted-R^2 for the adequacy model was 0.41, and the F-statistic suggested that the model as a whole was statistically significant.

The second capacity variable tested was the fairness of the state revenue system, and this model suggests more robust results than the adequacy variable (Table 5). The results of the regression suggest that states that tax Internet access will increase fairness of their tax system by around one third of a point. Second, for states that have a sales tax, which implies the ability to tax Internet sales, fairness decreases by over one third of a point. Third, as sales tax revenue increases as a percentage of revenue, the fairness of the revenue system will decrease by around half of a point. Forth, as the sales tax base of the state rises, fairness increases by over two thirds of a point. An increase in household Internet access means that fairness will increase by about one fifth of a point. Finally, an increase in retail sales tax will decrease fairness by a quarter of a point. The adjusted-R^2 for this model was significantly higher than the previously mentioned adequacy model, suggesting that two thirds of the variance is explained by fairness.

The third capacity variable examined was management capacity (Table 5). The only predictor of management capacity was household Internet access, which increased by one third of a point. This would suggest that wealthier states have greater ability to access the Internet, having more resources devoted to management of their revenue system.

The last OLS regression model is a combination of the previously mentioned capacity variables (Table 5). First, an increase in sales tax revenue as a percentage of state revenue will decrease revenue capacity by almost half a point. Second, as the tax base rises, the revenue capacity will increase by half of a point. Third, Internet access increases capacity by one third of a point. The results for the revenue capacity variable, however, do not show any significant impact from taxing electronic commerce.

The overriding message from the empirical results suggests some initial support only for Hypothesis 2 of the impact of electronic commerce tax variables on revenue fairness. If a state has a sales tax, there will be a decrease in revenue fairness. In addition, those states that tax Internet access will increase the fairness of the revenue system.

The following section concludes by providing an assessment as to why fairness is the most important predictor of taxing electronic commerce and discusses some policy recommendations and limitations of this research.

CONCLUSION

This chapter has demonstrated how the existing sales tax system compares to the principles of a high-quality revenue system. The key contribution of this study is looking at the impact of electronic commerce on revenue capacity; in contrast to the existing empirical work which has focused on consumers' reaction to electronic commerce taxation or the socio-economic and political factors that influence electronic commerce taxation.

The first part of this chapter showed that when it comes to taxing Internet sales the existing sales tax system violates all nine principles in areas broadly defined as adequacy, fairness, and management of the state revenue system. In adequacy of revenues, some states have incurred significant revenue losses because of remote sales. These losses are estimated to be in the range of one to 10 percent. In addition, losses are compounded by the sales tax base shrinking, partly because electronic commerce is no longer the dominant revenue source for states. In the fairness of revenue system category, the sales tax is already a regressive tax. The taxing of Internet sales makes it even more so, because those that are more affluent have greater Internet access. Finally, management of revenues is difficult since vendors are not required to collect sales taxes on remote purchases (but they can volunteer to do so) unless they have a physical presence or nexus within the purchaser's state. On the one hand, businesses want to avoid charging sales taxes to customers because it represents a discount for customers and an increase in the vendor's profits. On the other hand, the public is generally not aware that they are required to pay the use tax if it is not collected by vendors. This explains the low consumer compliance rate.

The second part of this chapter tested several models that examined the impact of electronic commerce on state revenue capacity; it essentially tested the nine principles of a high-quality tax system outlined in the first part of this chapter. The results suggested that the most important determinant of taxing electronic commerce was the fairness of the state revenue system. Referring back to the first part of this chapter, only Principles 4 to 6 (fairness of the revenue system) of a high quality revenue system were supported in the empirical results. There was some initial evidence that fairness decreases when states have a sales tax and it increases when states tax Internet access. These quantitative results are similar to those reported by existing public finance and legal scholars (McLure, 2002a, 2002b; Mikesell, 2001). Indeed, with the narrowing of the sales tax base, there has been a shift away from the sales tax as the dominant revenue source for state governments (Mikesell, 2004).

Long Term and Short Term Policy Recommendations

Some long term and short term policy recommendations for the taxing of electronic commerce sales are outlined in this section. One long term solution is for state and local governments that now depend on sales tax revenues to substitute other taxes such as income taxes (Litan & Rivlin, 2001; Reddick & Coggburn, 2006). If the decline in the sales tax base accelerates because of a rapid increase in electronic commerce sales, some or many jurisdictions may be tempted to act on their own, replacing the revenue with other sources. Another long term solution is for the federal government to reduce its dependence on income taxes in favor of a national sales tax or value added tax. Since the federal government can tax sales wherever they occur, a federal sales or value added tax would automatically solve the problem of treating electronic commerce and other remote sales equally. However, with the general antitax sentiment in the United States, this may be a difficult sell for politicians in the short term (Mikesell, 2001).

Because it is not very likely that there will be a major overhaul of the tax systems of state governments or the federal government in the near future, what can be done in the short-term? One possible solution is for states to be more aggressive in the enforcement of collecting use taxes owed by consumers. What often gets confused is that the sales tax is not owed if the firm does not have nexus, or a physical presence, in the state where the Internet purchaser resides. When this is the case, the consumer is required to remit the use tax to his state taxing authority. Two approaches are used for collecting use taxes from consumers. The first approach is the individual income tax reporting booklet that is mailed to taxpayers with filing instructions. The second approach is a use tax reporting line on the state income tax return itself, with instructions on how the owed amount would be computed. In 2003, 19 of 38 states provided information for taxpayers to report use tax obligations on their individual state income tax return, and another eight provide information about the use tax in the individual income tax booklets (Manzi, 2003). The consumer participation rates for use tax compliance are extremely low at around 1.5%. However, states such as Maine, Michigan, and North Carolina have been more successful and have achieved compliance rates moderately above that level.

Limitations of this Study

There are some limitations to this study that should be mentioned. First, the four star rating system cannot capture many factors that could possibly influence revenue capacity because it is limited to a small number of categories. Second, this study has conducted 32 tests (4 dependent variables times 8 independent variables) with a sample size of 50. As a result, the chances of including errors are greater with such a small sample size. Therefore, the findings should be viewed as suggestive, and not definitive. Third, there also is the limitation of using secondary data in the analysis of the impact of electronic commerce on revenue capacity since the four-star rating system is a subjective measure. However, this study is different from existing work in that it combines both qualitative research (how taxing electronic commerce compares against nine principles of an effective revenue system) and quantitative research (testing these principles with a model of how electronic commerce affects revenue capacity).

Future research could examine citizens' perceptions concerning the taxing of electronic commerce. There is much written on state government's reaction to taxing electronic commerce; however, more needs to be known about citizens' perception of taxing Internet sales. The existing literature indicates that politically it is very difficult to find enough common ground among 45 states and 36 local governments on

streamlining their sales tax systems through the SSTP (Cornia et al., 2004). Discerning what public support exists for taxing electronic commerce should provide some indication of the extent of reform politicians could achieve by addressing this important tax issue.

REFERENCES

Alm, J., & Melnik, M.I. (2005). Sales taxes and the decision to purchase online. *Public Finance Review, 33*(2), 184-212.

Barrett, K., Greene, R., Mariani, M., & Sostek, A. (2003). The way we tax: A 50 state report. *Governing Magazine, 16*(5), 20-97.

Berry, W.D., & Fording, R.C. (1997). Measuring state tax capacity and effort. *Social Science Quarterly, 78*(1), 158-166.

Best, S., & Teske, P. (2002). Explaining state Internet sales taxation: New economy, old-fashion interest group politics. *State Politics and Policy Quarterly, 2*(1), 37-51.

Bruce, D., Deskins, J., & Fox, W.F. (2004). Has Internet access taxation affected Internet use? *Public Finance Review, 32*(2), 131-147.

Bruce, D., & Fox, W.F. (2001a). *State and local sales tax revenue losses from e-commerce: Updated estimates.* Knoxville, TN: Center for Business and Economic Research.

Bruce, D., & Fox, W.F. (2001b). E-commerce and local finance: Estimates of direct and indirect sales tax losses. *Municipal Finance Journal, 22*(3), 24-47.

Bruce, D., Fox, W., & Murray, M. (2003). To tax or not to tax? The case of electronic commerce. *Contemporary Economic Policy, 21*(1), 25-40.

Brunori, D. (2001). *State tax policy: A political perspective.* Washington, DC: The Urban Institute Press.

Cameron, A.C. (2004). Factors leading to state participation in the streamlined sales tax project. *Journal of Public Budgeting, Accounting, & Financial Management, 16*(4), 80-108.

CCH. (2004). *CCH Tax Research Network*. Riverwoods, IL: CCH Incorporated.

Clay, K., & Strauss, R.P. (2000). Trust, risk, and electronic commerce: 19th century lessons for the 21st century. *State Tax Notes, 19*, 1701-1710.

Cline, R.J., & Neubig, T.S. (1999). *Masters of complexity and bearers of great burden: The sales tax system and compliance costs for multistate retailers* (Tech. Rep.). Ernst and Young Economics Consulting and Quantitative Analysis.

Cockfield, A.J. (2002). Walmart.com: A case study of entity isolation. *State Tax Notes, 25*, 633-701.

Congressional Budget Office. (CBO). (2003). *Economic issues in taxing Internet and mail-order sales*. Washington, DC: Congress of the United States Congressional Budget Office.

Cornia, G.C., Sjoquist, D.L., & Walters, L.C. (2004). Sales and use tax simplification and voluntary compliance. *Public Budgeting & Finance, 24*(1), 1-31.

Due, J.F., & Mikesell, J.L. (1994). *Sales taxation: State and local structure and administration* (2nd ed.). Washington, DC: Urban Institute Press.

Fox, W.F., & Murray, M. (1997). The sales tax and electronic commerce: So what's new? *National Tax Journal, 50*(3), 573-592.

General Accounting Office (GAO). (2000). *Sales taxes: Electronic commerce growth presents challenges; Revenue losses are uncertain*. Washington, DC: United States General Accounting Office.

Goolsbee, A. (2000). In a world without borders: The impact of taxes on Internet commerce. *Quarterly Journal of Economics, 115*(2), 561-576.

Goolsbee, A., & Zittrain, J. (1999). Evaluating the costs and benefits of taxing Internet commerce. *National Tax Journal, 52*(3), 413-428.

Governing Magazine. (2003). *State and Local Source Book 2003*. Washington, DC: Congressional Quarterly Press.

Hellerstein, W. (1998). Electronic commerce and the future of state taxation. In D. Brunori (Ed.), *The future of state taxation* (pp. 207-222). Washington, DC: The Urban Institute Press.

Litan, R.E., & Rivlin. A.M. (2001). *Beyond the dot.coms: The economic promise of the Internet*. Washington, DC: Brookings Institution Press.

Manzi, N. (2003). *Use tax collection on income tax returns in other states* (Policy Brief). Minnesota House of Representatives Research Department.

McLure, C.E. (2000). The taxation of electronic commerce: Background and proposal. In N. Imparato (Ed.), *Public policy and the Internet: Privacy, taxes, and contract* (pp. 49-113). Stanford: Hoover Institution Press.

McLure, C.E. (2002a). Thinking straight about the taxation of electronic commerce: Tax principles, compliance problems, and Nexus. *NBER/Tax Policy & the Economy, 16*(1), 115-140.

McLure, C.E. (2002b). Sales and use taxes on electronic commerce: Legal, economic, administrative, and political issues. *The Urban Lawyer, 34*(2), 487-520.

Mikesell, J.L. (2000). Remote vendors and American sales and use taxation: The balance between fixing the problem and fixing the tax. *National Tax Journal, 53*(4), 1273-1285.

Mikesell, J.L. (2001). The threat to state sales taxes from e-commerce: A review of the principal issues. *Municipal Finance Journal, 22*(3), 48-60.

Mikesell, J.L. (2004). The prospects for general sales taxation in American state and local government finance: Challenges for a fiscal workhorse unready for the new millennium. *Journal of Public Budgeting, Accounting, & Financial Management, 16*(1), 63-79.

National Conference of State Legislatures (NCLS). (1992). *Principles of a high-quality state revenue system*. Washington, DC: National Conference of State Legislatures. Retrieved September 12, 2007, from http://www.ncsl.org

Nesbary, D. (2000). The taxation of Internet commerce. *Social Science Computer Review, 18*(1), 17-39.

Reddick, C.G. (2006). A consumer's perspective on the use tax and electronic commerce. *Journal of Internet Commerce, 5*(1), 23-43.

Reddick, C.G., & Coggburn, J.D. (2006). E-commerce and the future of the American sales tax system. In H.A. Frank (Ed.), *Handbook of public financial management* (pp. 179-206). Boca Raton, FL: CRC Press/Taylor and Francis Publishers.

Swain, J.A., & Hellerstein, W. (2005). The political economy of the streamlined sales and use tax agreement. *National Tax Journal, 58*(3), 605-619.

Victor, C., & Jih, W-J. (2006). Fair or not? The taxation of e-commerce. *Information Systems Management, 23*(1), 68-72.

Vijayasarathy, L.R. (2002). Internet taxation, privacy and security: Opinions of the taxed and legislated. *Quarterly Journal of Electronic Commerce, 3*(1), 53-71.

Ward, B.T., & Sipior, J.C. (2004). To tax or not to tax e-commerce: A United States perspective. *Journal of Electronic Commerce Research, 5*(3), 172-180.

Yang, J., & Poon, W. (2001). Taxable base of Internet commerce. *Municipal Finance Journal, 22*(3), 70-80.

Chapter XV
Gender and E–Commerce Adoption Barriers:
A Comparison of Small Businesses in Sweden and Australia

Robert MacGregor
University of Wollongong, Australia

Lejla Vrazalic
University of Wollongong in Dubai, UAE

ABSTRACT

Previous research has shown that gender plays a role in the use of information technology by small businesses and that differences exist between the ways in which male and female small business owners/managers perceive information technology, including e-commerce. However, our understanding of whether gender is important in relation to e-commerce adoption barriers is limited. This chapter examines whether differences exist in how male and female owners/managers of small businesses in regional areas in Sweden and Australia perceive e-commerce adoption barriers. The results of a survey of more than 450 small businesses are presented and indicate that, although both male and female owners/managers agree on the key reasons for not adopting e-commerce, they assign different priorities these reasons. In Sweden, male owner/managers are more concerned about the technical complexities of implementing e-commerce, while females assign a higher importance to the unsuitability of e-commerce. In Australia, the situation is reverse. The results have implications for e-commerce adoption programs and initiatives.

INTRODUCTION

One question that inevitably seems to be raised in most areas of business research is the ques-tion of gender. In the area of small business, the past 20 years has seen a shift away from the traditional male-dominated economy that centred on manufacturing, towards a more service and retail-based economy that has seen a substantial increase in the participation of females (Cox, 1999; Teltscher, 2002). Not only has there been a rise in the participation of females in the workforce, but the advent of affordable technology has led to a more flexible method of work and a greater global participation by the workforce. In small business in particular, these changes have led to a greater 'equality' in the makeup of the workforce (Singh, 2001; Teltscher, 2002). Studies (Brisco, 2002; Schmidt & Parker, 2003) have shown that in some areas of the small business sector, female participation is as high as 70% with over one third of small businesses in several Asian countries owned/managed by females.

The development of technology has been substantial over the last two decades. For the small business sector, principal among the changes has been the use of the Internet and e-commerce in the day-to-day running of the business. E-commerce involves the application of Web-based information technologies towards automating business processes, transactions, and workflows, and buying and selling information, products, and services using computer networks (Kalakota & Whinston, 1997). For small businesses, e-commerce is seen as a major source of competitive advantage, allowing them to both reach customers on a global level as well as compete with larger businesses within that global marketplace. Governments worldwide have recognised this potential and created various funding schemes and initiatives to facilitate e-commerce adoption in small businesses.

Despite government support for e-commerce adoption by small businesses, it is mainly the larger businesses that have reaped the benefits of this technology (Riquelme, 2002). In contrast, the rate of e-commerce adoption in the small business sector has remained relatively low (Magnusson, 2001; Poon & Swatman, 1998; Van Akkeren & Cavaye, 1999). This sluggish pace of e-commerce diffusion into small businesses has been attrib-

uted to various barriers or impediments that are faced by these organisations. A number of different e-commerce adoption barriers have been documented in research studies (Lawrence, 1997; Purao & Campbell, 1998; Quayle, 2002; Riquelme, 2002; Van Akkeren & Cavaye, 1999). At the same time, a number of studies (Butler, 2000; Rodgers & Harris, 2003; Sexton, Johnson, & Hignite, 2002) have compared the use of e-commerce by males and females. Our study is concerned with the effects of gender on e-commerce adoption barriers, specifically.

This chapter will present the findings of two studies undertaken in Sweden and Australia to examine the differences in how e-commerce barriers are perceived by male and female small business owners/managers. The chapter begins by examining the nature of small businesses and identifying features that are unique to the sector in order to set the context for the study. This is followed by a literature review of e-commerce adoption barriers and relevant gender studies. The research methodology is subsequently presented and followed by the statistical analysis of the results. In the final part of the chapter, the results are discussed and conclusions are drawn.

Small Business

There are numerous definitions of what constitutes a small business. These are primarily based on two factors: the number of employees in the organisation and the annual revenue. In Australia, the Australian Bureau of Statistics defines a small business as an organisation which employs less than 20 individuals. By contrast, in Sweden a business is deemed small if it has fewer than 50 employees (Gustafsson, Klefsjo, Berggren, & Granfors-Wellemets, 2001). This is in line with the European Union definition which classifies organisations with 10 to 49 employees as being in the small business category. Since this study involves both Sweden and Australia, for comparative purposes, the European definition is used.

It is important to note that small businesses are not simply scaled down versions of large businesses (Wynarczyk, Watson, Storey, Short, & Keasey, 1993). Although size is a major distinguishing factor, small businesses have a number of other unique features that set them apart from larger organisations. Small businesses are more risky ventures with higher rates of failure (DeLone, 1988; Hill & Stewart, 2000). They maintain inadequate transaction records (Miller & Besser, 2000; Tetteh & Burn, 2001) and suffer from a short-range management perspective (Bunker & MacGregor, 2000; Welsh & White, 1981). Small businesses are also 'resource poor' and more reluctant to invest in information technology (Walczuch, Van Braven, & Lundgren, 2000). As a result, there is a lack of technical knowledge in small businesses (Martin & Matlay, 2001).

Other studies (Bunker & MacGregor, 2000; Murphy, 1996; Reynolds, Savage, & Williams, 1994) have examined the differences in management styles between large and small businesses. These studies have shown that among other characteristics, small businesses tend to have a management team often consisting only of one or two individuals; they are strongly influenced by the owner and the owner's personal idiosyncrasies; they have little control over their environment (Westhead & Storey, 1996; Hill & Stewart, 2000); and they have a strong desire to remain independent (Dennis, 2000; Drakopolou-Dodd, Jack, & Anderson, 2002).

Although it is beyond the scope of this chapter to determine the impact of these unique small business characteristics on e-commerce adoption, it can be argued that the typical traits of a small business have some bearing on their use of e-commerce technology. This is most noticeable in the literature pertaining to e-commerce adoption barriers.

E-COMMERCE ADOPTION BARRIERS

E-commerce has been widely touted as an opportunity for small businesses to gain instant access to global markets and customers (Coviello & McAuley, 1999). However, the pace of e-commerce diffusion in the small business sector has been sluggish. The reasons for this are diverse and have been examined in various studies as inhibitors or barriers that prevent small businesses from adopting and, subsequently, fully reaping the benefits of e-commerce.

Amongst the reasons found by previous studies are the high costs and complexity of implementation, resistance to change, lack of resources, security concerns, and the unsuitability of e-commerce to the small business. The results of previous research in this area have been summarised in Table 1.

Having examined the nature of small businesses and some of the reasons why small businesses do not use e-commerce, we will now turn to previous research into the role of gender in small businesses.

GENDER AND GENERAL OWNERSHIP/MANAGEMENT OF SMALL BUSINESS

The role of gender in small businesses has been studied from a number of different perspectives. These will be discussed in some detail in order to show how the gender affects various facets of small business at both the macro and the micro levels.

Ownership/Management Statistics and Movement into the Small Business Sector

A number of previous studies (Brooksbank, 2000; Carter, 2000; Reynolds et al., 1992) have suggested

Table 1. Summary of e-commerce adoption barriers in small businesses

Barriers to E-Commerce Adoption	Related Literature
High cost of implementation; Internet technologies too expensive to implement	Riquelme (2002) Van Akkeren & Cavaye (1999) Purao & Campbell (1998) Lawrence (1997) Iacovou et al. (1995)
E-commerce is too complex to implement	Fielding (1996) Quayle (2002)
Small businesses require short-term ROI and e-commerce is long-term	Lawrence (1997) McGowan & Madey (1998)
Resistance to change because of the fear of new technology amongst employees	Van Akkeren & Cavaye (1999) Lawrence (1997)
Preference for and satisfaction with traditional manual methods (phone, fax, etc.)	Lawrence (1997) Venkatesan and Fink (2002)
Lack of technical skills and IT knowledge amongst employees; Lack of computer literate/ specialised staff	Riquelme (2002) Van Akkeren and Cavaye (1999) Lawrence (1997) Iacovou et al. (1995) Quayle (2002) Damsgaard and Lyytinen (1998)
Lack of time to implement e-commerce	Van Akkeren and Cavaye (1999) Lawrence (1997) Walczuch et al. (2000)
E-commerce not deemed to be suited to the way the organisation does business or the way our clients do business	Poon and Swatman (1997) Hadjimonolis (1999) Iacovou, Benbasat, and Dexter (1995)
E-commerce not deemed to be suited to the products/services	Poon and Swatman (1997) Hadjimonolis (1999)
E-commerce perceived as a technology lacking direction	Lawrence (1997)
Lack of awareness about business advantages/opportunities e-commerce can provide	Iacovou et al. (1995) Quayle (2002)
Lack of available information about e-commerce	Lawrence (1997)
Concern about security of e-commerce	Riquelme (2002) Van Akkeren and Cavaye (1999) Purao and Campbell (1998) Hadjimonolis (1999) Quayle (2002)
Lack of critical mass amongst customers, suppliers, and business partners	Hadjimonolis (1999)
Heavy reliance on external consultants (often considered by small businesses to be inadequate) to provide necessary expertise	Van Akkeren and Cavaye (1999) Lawrence (1997)
Lack of e-commerce standards	Tuunainen (1998) Robertson and Gatignon (1986)

that the primary motivation for moving into the small business sector is the desire to become self-employed. An examination of the UK labour force figures for the 1990s (Labour Force Survey, 1990-1999) shows that while the growth in self-employment for males was 4.73%, the growth in self-employment for females was 19.06%. Studies by Nillson (1997), Brush and Hisrich (1999), and Sandberg (2003) have provided similar figures in Europe, the U.S., and Scandinavia. While the early studies (Goffee & Skase, 1985; Hisrich & Brush, 1986) concentrated on the motivational comparisons between males and females, studies by Brush (1997), Buttner and Moore (1997), and Carter and Cannon (1992) found that females saw becoming self-employed within the small business sector as a means of circumventing the 'glass ceiling.'

Finance and Finance Availability

A study of 600 UK small and medium enterprises (SMEs) (Carter & Rosa, 1998) found that males were more likely to make use of bank loans and overdrafts than females in order to finance their business. Indeed, females were less likely to use or rely on financial institutional arrangements including cheaper sources of finance (such as extended supplier credit) than were their male counterparts. This same study found that female owner/managers used less start-up capital (33%) than males, resulting in fewer employees and long-term disadvantages in terms of their business being able to grow.

Aside from the use of financial instruments, studies (Carter, 2000; Carter & Rosa, 1998; Sandberg, 2003) have also shown that the ability to access finance often differs between male and female small business owner/managers. Many of these studies have concluded that while financial institutions may have a nondiscriminatory policy, the application of those policies often prejudice against women through stereotyping.

Management Style

An examination of the literature surrounding gender differences and management style in the small business sector provides differing and disparate results. Early studies (Maupin, 1990; Powell, 1993) suggested that there were few real differences in leadership styles between men and women. However, studies by Johnson and Storey (1993) found female owner/managers less confident, less aggressive, and lacking in problem solving abilities compared to male owner/managers. Other more recent studies (McGregor & Tweed, 2001; Verheul, Risseeuw, & Bartelse, 2002) found that female managers of small business were more comfortable with giving instructions to staff through informal conversation than were their male counterparts. Indeed, while the male managers stressed the role and use of power, female managers stressed the importance of interpersonal communication. These studies also showed that female managers were more likely to hire external expertise and were more inclined to develop business strategies that were specific to their particular business than were their male counterparts.

A recent study of small businesses in Sweden (Sandberg, 2003) showed that female managers paid more attention to business-to-business links and strategic alliances than did males. The study also showed that female managers were more mindful of both their customers and their staff than were male managers. Similar findings were reported in a study carried out on New Zealand small businesses (McGregor & Tweed, 2001).

Networking

Previous research (DeWine & Casbolt, 1983; Smeltzer & Fann, 1989) suggests that male networks are often far more informal than female networks. More recent studies (Brush, 1997; Carter, 2000; Carter & Rosa, 1998; Sandberg,

2003) support these earlier findings adding that females appear to be less welcome in social business networks often resulting in a reduced ability to use network partners to gain finance or attract technical or marketing assistance. This stands out in contrast to females having better interpersonal communication skills.

Business Types

Female owned/managed small businesses are usually smaller in size than organisations owned/managed by men. These differences in size often translate into differences in turnover and long-term growth potential for the business (Loscocco et al., 1991; Loscocco & Leicht, 1993). Kalleberg and Berg (1987) also found that many female owned/managed small businesses were in less innovative sectors of the market compared to male owned/managed small businesses.

Success/Failure

While there are well documented gender-based differences in the approach to business and business management (see above), studies comparing male success to female success, or indeed male failure to female failure, have found no real differences in the likelihood of success or failure dependent on gender (Kolsaker & Payne, 2002; Labich, 1994; Perry, 2002).

IT Adoption and Use

A number of early studies (Gilroy & Desai, 1986; Meier & Lambert, 1991) found that males were less anxious about using computer technology than females. Yet, according to Gebler (2000), in the year 2000, female Internet users exceeded male users. The implications of this event are significant considering the previous research into the use of the Internet by females. Shade (1998) and Sheehan (1999) both found that females were more concerned with privacy and security issues and subsequently more cautious about using the Internet for online shopping and trading. Presumably, the same concerns would apply to female business owners considering e-commerce adoption. Kolsaker and Payne (2002) refuted these studies by finding no significant differences between the genders in relation to Internet privacy and security. It should be noted, however, that their study followed the surge of female users after 2000, while the studies by Shade (1998) and Sheehan (1999) preceded the widespread use of the Internet by females.

Although the gap between male and female Internet adoption rates has disappeared resulting in a more gender-balanced use of the Internet, differences remain in how the Internet is actually used. For example, Akhter (2003) found that men were still more likely to use the Internet for shopping than women. This would suggest that males may be more open to e-commerce adoption as business owners because they are more willing to adopt the technology as consumers. However, empirical evidence of such a trend is not available. Although our knowledge of gender differences in relation to *Internet* adoption as users and consumers is broad, our understanding of gender differences in relation to *e-commerce* adoption as business owners is scarce and inadequate. The exception is a study of e-commerce and teleworking in 112 Spanish small businesses by Perez, Carnicer, and Sanchez (2002). The authors found that small businesses with female managers were significantly more concerned with the difficulty of using the technology than were their male counterparts. The study also cited cost of the technology and changes to work procedures as being of more concern to female managers.

Our study aims to add to the literature about gender and small business presented above by comparing the male and female perceptions of e-commerce adoption barriers in Swedish and Australian small businesses. The following section provides an overview of the research which was undertaken to address this aim.

RESEARCH METHODOLOGY

The study examined the role and effects of gender from three viewpoints. The first was to determine whether there were any significant gender-based differences in relation to business characteristics such as the age of the business, the size of the business, the market focus, and alliance membership. The second was to determine whether there were any gender-based differences in how e-commerce adoption barriers were perceived. The third was to determine whether there were any gender-based differences in the how the e-commerce adoption barriers were grouped or prioritised.

A survey instrument was developed to collect data from small business owners/managers in Sweden and Australia as part of a larger study into e-commerce adoption. Sweden and Australia were selected due to their similarities in terms of economic development (OECD ranking) as well as their level of Internet penetration (above 50%), thus enabling comparisons to be made. Respondents were asked about the age of the business (less than a year, 1-2 years, 3-5 years, 6-10 years, 11-20 years, more than 20 years); the size of the business (0 employees, 1-9 employees, 10-19 employees, 20-49 employees, 50-199 employees); the market focus (local, regional, national, international); the business sector (industrial, service, retail, finance); and whether the business was part of any alliances, amongst other things. The responses were then analysed using two-tailed t-tests in order to determine associations between gender and the business characteristics listed above.

Ten of the most commonly occurring barriers to e-commerce adoption from Table 1 were

Figure 1. Question about barriers to e-commerce adoption used in survey

Our organisation does not use e-commerce because:	Rating				
E-commerce is not suited to our products/ services.	1	2	3	4	5
E-commerce is not suited to our way of doing business.	1	2	3	4	5
E-commerce is not suited to the ways our clients (customers and/or suppliers) do business.	1	2	3	4	5
E-commerce does not offer any advantages to our organisation.	1	2	3	4	5
We do not have the technical knowledge in the organisation to implement e-commerce.	1	2	3	4	5
E-commerce is too complicated to implement.	1	2	3	4	5
E-commerce is not secure.	1	2	3	4	5
The financial investment required to implement e-commerce is too high for us.	1	2	3	4	5
We do not have time to implement e-commerce.	1	2	3	4	5
It is difficult to choose the most suitable e-commerce standard with so many different options available.	1	2	3	4	5

23. This question relates to the reasons why your organisation is not using e-commerce. Below is a list of statements indicating possible reasons. Based on your opinion, please rank each statement on a scale of 1 to 5 to indicate how important it was to your decision NOT to use e-commerce, as follows:

1 = the reason was very unimportant to your decision not to use e-commerce

2 = the reason was unimportant to your decision not to use e-commerce

3 = the reason was neither unimportant nor important to your decision not to use e-commerce

4 = the reason was important to your decision not to use e-commerce

5 = the reason was very important to your decision not to use e-commerce

identified based on previous research. A series of six in-depth interviews with small businesses in Australia were undertaken to determine whether the barriers were applicable and complete. All of the identified barriers were found to applicable and no additional barriers were forthcoming. Based on the six in-depth interviews, a question was developed to collect data about e-commerce adoption barriers. Respondents who had not adopted e-commerce were asked to rate the importance of each barrier to their decision not to adopt e-commerce using a standard 5-point Likert scale (as shown in Figure 1). The Likert scale responses were assumed to posses the characteristics of an interval measurement scale for data analysis purposes.

A total of 1,170 surveys were distributed by post to randomly selected businesses in the Varmland region in Sweden, while 160 surveys were administered by phone in the Illawarra region in Australia. A sample of regional small businesses was selected due to the minimal amount of research available into regional small businesses. The survey administration method was chosen owing to previous research showing that a mail survey is more appropriate in Scandinavian countries, compared to Australia where response rates to mail surveys were low. Consequently, a telephone survey was administered in Australia to ensure a higher response rate.

RESULTS AND ANALYSIS

The results of the survey will be discussed separately for each country first before being compared in a subsequent section.

Sweden

A total of 313 responses were received from Swedish small businesses representing a 26.8% response rate. Of those, 86% were from male owned/managed small businesses, representing the majority of the respondent group. The percentage of female respondents is substantially lower than in previous studies (Carter, 2000; Nillson, 1997; Sandberg, 2003) that reported up to 25% of small businesses were female owned/managed. One possible explanation is that these earlier studies were conducted in capital cities, whereas the current study was conducted in a regional city.

A series of two-tailed t-tests were undertaken to assess whether there were any associations between gender and various business characteristics. The results indicated that associations exist between gender and business size, and gender and market focus. This is shown in Table 2.

Of the responses received from Swedish small businesses, 40% indicated that they were non-adopters of e-commerce. A series of two-tailed t-tests was then applied to these responses to determine whether there were any significant differences between the ratings of e-commerce barriers by male and female owners/managers. Table 3 provides the findings.

An examination of Table 3 shows that for the Swedish respondents, there were no significant gender differences in the way that e-commerce barriers were perceived. This suggests that the male and female owners/managers of small businesses that had not adopted e-commerce have comparable views about e-commerce barriers.

Finally, factor analysis was used to determine the groupings and priorities of e-commerce bar-

Table 2. Associations between gender and business characteristics - Sweden

Factor	Mean Male	N Male	Mean Female	N Female	t-value	p
Business Size	2.65	268	1.96	45	3.888	<.005
Market Focus	2.06	268	1.58	45	3.184	<.05

Table 3. Gender differences in the perception of barriers to e-commerce adoption: Sweden

Barriers	Mean Male	N Male	Mean Female	t value	Significance
E-commerce is not suited to our products/ services	2.74	108	2.65	.193	.847
E-commerce is not suited to our way of doing business	2.63	108	2.53	.213	.832
E-commerce is not suited to the ways our clients (customers and/or suppliers) do business	2.59	108	2.29	.602	.548
E-commerce does not offer any advantages to our organisation	2.39	108	2.12	.576	.566
We do not have the technical knowledge in the organisation to implement e-commerce	2.59	108	2.65	-.125	.901
E-commerce is too complicated to implement	1.98	108	1.94	.096	.923
E-commerce is not secure	2.07	108	2.00	.175	.862
The financial investment required to implement e-commerce is too high for us	2.29	108	1.94	.781	.436
We do not have time to implement e-commerce	2.46	108	2.24	.470	.639
It is difficult to choose the most suitable e-commerce standard with so many different options available	2.32	108	2.18	.301	.764

riers by males and females, in order to examine whether gender differences existed.

The results of the Kaiser-Meyer-Olkin MSA (.872 for males, .721 for females) and Bartlett's test of Sphericity ($\chi^2 = 578$, $p = .000$ for males, $\chi^2 = 578$, p = .000 for females) indicated that the data sets satisfied the assumptions for factorability. Principle Components Analysis was chosen as the method of extraction in order to account for maximum variance in the data using a minimum number of factors. A two-factor solution was extracted with Eigenvalues of 4.594 and 1.436 for males and 1.435 and 5.906 for females. This

was supported by an inspection of the Scree Plots. These two factors accounted for 70.994% of the total variance in males and 81.575% in females. These results are summarised in Table 4.

The two resulting components were rotated using the Varimax procedure and a simple structure was achieved as shown in the rotated component matrix (Table 5). Two components were identified in each gender group.

The results of the Swedish study presented above show that e-commerce barriers are grouped according to two distinct factors by male and female small business owners/managers in Sweden.

Table 4. Total variance explained (barriers): Sweden

Component	Rotation Sums of Squared Loadings					
	Eigenvalue		% of Variance		Cumulative %	
	Males	Females	Males	Females	Males	Females
1	4.954	1.435	55.04	15.95	55.04	15.95
2	1.436	5.906	15.96	65.63	71.00	81.58

Table 5. Rotated component matrix (barriers): Sweden

	Component 1: Too Difficult		Component 2: Unsuitable	
	Males	Females	Males	Females
E-commerce is not suited to our products/services.			.631	.914
E-commerce is not suited to our way of doing business.			.672	.929
E-commerce is not suited to the ways our clients (customers and/or suppliers) do business.			.739	.904
E-commerce does not offer any advantages to our organisation.			.655	.906
We do not have the technical knowledge in the organisation to implement e-commerce.	.717	.591		
E-commerce is too complicated to implement.	.850	.909		
E-commerce is not secure.	.838	.779		
The financial investment required to implement e-commerce is too high for us.	.784	.787		
We do not have time to implement e-commerce.	.746	.785		
It is difficult to choose the most suitable e-commerce standard with so many different options available.	.764	.850		

These factors have been termed 'Too Difficult' and 'Unsuitable.' The 'Too Difficult' factor is related to the barriers which make e-commerce complicated to implement, including barriers such as the complexity of e-commerce implementation techniques, the difficulty in deciding which standard to implement because of the large range of e-commerce options, the difficulty of obtaining funds to implement e-commerce, the lack of technical knowledge, and the difficulty of finding time to implement e-commerce. The 'Unsuitable' factor is related to the perceived unsuitability of e-commerce to small businesses. The barriers in this group include the unsuitability of e-commerce to the organisation's products/services, its way of doing business, and its client's way of doing business, as well as the lack of perceived advantages of e-commerce implementation. These results will be discussed further in subsequent sections. We will now examine the results from the Australian study.

Australia

Of the 160 responses received in Australia, 102 (or 64%) were from male owned/managed small businesses. Similarly to the Swedish context, the majority of the respondents in Australia were male owner/managers.

A series of two-tailed t-tests were undertaken to determine whether any associations existed between gender and business characteristics. Unlike Sweden (where two associations were found) there were no associations between the gender of the owner/manager and business characteristics in Australia.

Of the responses received from Australian small businesses, almost 85% indicated that they were non-adopters of e-commerce. A series of two-tailed t-tests was then applied to these responses to determine whether there were any significant differences between the ratings of e-commerce barriers by male and female owners/managers. Table 6 provides the findings.

Table 6. Gender differences in the perception of barriers to e-commerce adoption: Australia

Barriers	Mean Male	Mean Female	t value	Significance
E-commerce is not suited to our products/ services	3.57	2.75	-2.963	.004
E-commerce is not suited to our way of doing business	3.64	3.04	-2.288	.024
E-commerce is not suited to the ways our clients (customers and/or suppliers) do business	3.46	3.43	-.079	.937
E-commerce does not offer any advantages to our organisation	3.45	3.02	-1.624	.107
We do not have the technical knowledge in the organisation to implement e-commerce	3.06	3.18	.386	.700
E-commerce is too complicated to implement	2.90	3.24	1.137	.257
E-commerce is not secure	2.86	2.80	-.199	.843
The financial investment required to implement e-commerce is too high for us	2.88	2.92	.141	.888
We do not have time to implement e-commerce	2.88	3.27	1.369	.173
It is difficult to choose the most suitable e-commerce standard with so many different options available	2.58	2.84	.914	.362

Table 7. Total variance explained (barriers): Australia

Component	Rotation Sums of Squared Loadings					
	Eigenvalue		% of Variance		Cumulative %	
	Males	Females	Males	Females	Males	Females
1	2.738	4.440	27.378	44.403	27.378	44.403
2	3.635	2.586	36.351	25.861	63.730	70.264

Table 6 indicates that male and female owners/managers differed on the perception of two barriers related to suitability ('e-commerce is not suited to our products/ services' and 'e-commerce is not suited to our way of doing business').

Finally, factor analysis was used to determine the groupings and priorities of e-commerce barriers by males and females, in order to examine whether gender differences existed.

The results of the Kaiser-Meyer-Olkin MSA (.784 for males and .786 for females) and Bartlett's Test for Sphericity ($\chi^2 = 415$, p = .000 for males, $\chi^2 = 313$, p = .000 for females) indicated that both sets of data satisfied the assumptions of factor-

ability. Principle components analysis was chosen as the method of extraction in order to account for maximum variance in the data using a minimum number of factors. For both males and females, a two-factor solution was extracted with Eigenvalues 3.635 and 2.738 for males and 4.440 and 2.586 for females. The Eigenvalues accounted for 63.730% of variance for males and 70.264% for females. These are summarised in Table 7.

The two resulting components were rotated using the Varimax procedure and a simple structure was achieved as shown in the rotated component matrix (Table 8).

Similar to the Swedish respondents, both male and female small business owners/managers

Table 8. Rotated component matrix (barriers): Australia

	Component 1: Too Difficult		Component 2: Unsuitable	
	Males	Females	Males	Females
E-commerce is not suited to our products/ services.			.902	.884
E-commerce is not suited to our way of doing business.			.896	.926
E-commerce is not suited to the ways our clients (customers and/or suppliers) do business.			.886	.922
E-commerce does not offer any advantages to our organisation.			.855	.732
We do not have the technical knowledge in the organisation to implement e-commerce.	.774	.758		
E-commerce is too complicated to implement.	.820	.885		
E-commerce is not secure.	.591	.765		
The financial investment required to implement e-commerce is too high for us.	.749	.739		
We do not have time to implement e-commerce.	.717	.790		
It is difficult to choose the most suitable e-commerce standard with so many different options available.	.668	.816		

grouped e-commerce barriers around suitability factors and implementation factors. The following section will discuss the results.

DISCUSSION

The results of the two-tailed t-tests to determine associations between gender and other business characteristics showed that in Sweden, gender was associated with the size and the market focus of the business. Several studies (Carter, 2000; Loscooco & Leicht, 1993; Sonfield, Lussier, Corman, & McKinney, 2000) found that female owned/managed small businesses were usually smaller in terms of staff than male owned/managed small businesses. Nillson (1997), Brush and Hisrich (1999), and Sandberg (2003) have also shown that the growth in self-employed females was significantly higher than for males. Table 2 supports these studies by indicating that female respondents in Sweden tended to have smaller staff levels than male counterparts. This suggests that micro businesses in regional Sweden may be predominantly owned by women. There was no corresponding finding for Australia.

In terms of market focus, the data in Sweden suggest that male owned/managed small businesses are more likely to focus on national or international markets, while female owned/managed small businesses are focusing on local and regional markets. One immediate response to this difference would be that male and female owned/managed small businesses are involved in different business sectors, however, the data do not support this conclusion.

Despite previous research indicating that male owned/managed small businesses were more likely to engage in some form of alliance (Carter, 2000; Smeltzer & Fann, 1989; Sandberg, 2003), the results of our study do not indicate any associations between gender and alliance membership.

One of the aims of the study was to determine whether the rating of importance of e-commerce adoption barriers differed depending on the gender of the owner/manager. In Sweden, this was not the case. There were no significant differences for any of the barriers between male and female owned/managed businesses. By comparison, an examination of the Australian data (see Table 6) shows that two barriers ('e-commerce is not suited to our products/services' and 'e-commerce is not suited to our way of doing business') showed a significant difference. In both cases, those respondents that had a male owner/manager rated these barriers as more important that those businesses with female owner/managers.

However, comparing the means of the ratings between Sweden and Australia shows an interesting result. Unlike Sweden, where the mean ratings of barriers by both male and female respondents were low, Australian small businesses generally rated the barriers as important (mean of 3 or more). This is in line with the low rate of e-commerce adoption found in the Australian sample (15%), where these barriers clearly play a more important role.

The results of the Factor Analysis show that while both the Swedish and Australian respondents grouped adoption barriers as either 'too difficult' or 'unsuitable,' their relative importance differed. In Sweden, female owner/managers assigned a higher priority to barriers related to the suitability of e-commerce to their organisation. By contrast, male respondents placed a higher emphasis on the complexities (difficulties) associated with e-commerce implementation. In Australia, female respondents prioritised the complex nature of e-commerce as a barrier, while men were more concerned about suitability (which is in line with the findings from the two-tailed t-test above). It should be noted, however, that in the Australian context, the differences between males and females in terms of emphasis are less pronounced.

The results of the Swedish study appear to disagree with previous research which suggested

that males were less anxious about computing technology (Perez et al., 2002; Rodgers & Harris, 2003; Singh, 2001). The Swedish results presented in this chapter imply the opposite, with males reporting difficulties associated with e-commerce as a more important adoption barrier. A number of explanations are possible. Simon (2001) found that females tended to be 'less enthralled by technology than males' (Simon, 2001, p. 30) and used a more comprehensive information processing scheme when making decisions about technology. In a similar vein, Singh (2001) proposed that females use the Internet as a tool for carrying out activities and not as a technology that must be mastered. Both Simon (2001) and Singh (2001) appear to be suggesting that females are more likely to consider Internet technologies, including e-commerce, in relation to their suitability for a particular activity. In contrast, males view Internet technologies simply as tools which require time, effort, and resources to learn and implement.

The Australian results (which are the reverse of the Swedish findings) are in line with previous research (Gilroy & Desai, 1986; Meier & Lambert, 1991) showing that males were less anxious about using computer technology than females and thus less concerned about technical implementation issues. An alternate explanation may be provided by a recent study carried out by the authors (MacGregor & Vrazalic, 2007) which suggested that approaches to cluster development and networking may be one of the 'keys' to apparent differences between Swedish and Australian small businesses and their priorities for barriers to e-commerce adoption. Briefly, this study suggested that heavy government involvement in the networking and cluster development process in Sweden, particularly by male owned/managed small businesses, may actually have reduced the 'unsuitability' concerns, whereas less government involvement and less cluster development in Australia by male owned/managed small businesses has maintained that concern.

LIMITATIONS

It should be noted that the study presented here has several limitations. The choice of variables selected for the study is somewhat problematic because of the complex nature of adoption barriers which change over time. Furthermore, according to Sohal and Ng (1998), the views expressed in the surveys are of a single individual from the responding organisation, and only those interested in the study are likely to complete and return the survey. Where mail surveys are used, there is also the risk of not knowing whether the intended person actually completed the survey, despite clear instructions from the authors requesting that this person should be the primary owner of the small business only. Also, only a small number of female primary owners responded to the survey which implies the necessity to undertake further research with more female owners in order to verify the results presented here. This study was carried out in regional areas. It can be argued that the results may be generalisable to similar regional areas in other countries with the same characteristics as Sweden and Australia. However, additional research is clearly required to determine whether this is the case. Finally, this is a quantitative study, and further qualitative research is required to gain a better understanding of the key issues.

CONCLUSION AND IMPLICATIONS

Our primary aim in the chapter was to expand our understanding of the role of gender in e-commerce adoption and adoption barriers specifically. The approach used to do this involved several types of statistical analyses on data collected from small businesses located in regional areas in Sweden and Australia. The economic and technological development of both countries being similar, it was possible to compare the results of the two studies in order to draw parallels and highlight areas of divergence.

The results were somewhat mixed, with some similarities and some differences between small businesses in the two locations. In Sweden, an association was found between the gender of the owner/manager and business size, as well as market focus. Female respondents tended to own/manage smaller businesses, and found most of their customer base in local/regional areas. There were no such associations in Australia.

Where gender and e-commerce barriers are concerned, Australian small businesses owned/managed by males rated barriers related to the unsuitability of e-commerce as statistically more significant, compared to their female counterparts. This would suggest that, where the suitability of e-commerce was concerned, males in Australian regional small businesses were more concerned than females. This was supported by further tests which drew out the underlying factors based on which male and female owners/managers grouped e-commerce barriers. While both Australian and Swedish respondents grouped e-commerce barriers around two factors (suitability and complexity), in Australia male respondents emphasised the unsuitability of e-commerce, while in Sweden men prioritised difficulties associated with implementing e-commerce. This suggests that, in Sweden, male owned/managed small businesses would benefit from additional technical support with e-commerce implementation, while their Australian counterparts first need to be convinced that e-commerce is suitable and beneficial to their organisation. These findings are aligned with the overall adoption rate in the two locations. Australian small businesses in regional areas had alarmingly low adoption rates and it can be argued that this is because the majority of small business owners (who tend to be male) need to be persuaded that e-commerce is an appropriate business strategy for their organisation. Therefore, in Australia, government initiatives to promote e-commerce adoption should target male owned/managed small businesses with strategies that promote the suitability of e-commerce to their businesses and help them determine the value of e-commerce to their organisation. The same should be done for female owners/managers in Sweden, possibly leading to higher adoption and participation rates in e-commerce.

REFERENCES

Akhter, S.H. (2003). Digital divide and purchase intention: Why demographic psychology matters? *Journal of Economic Psychology, 24*, 321-327.

Brisco, R. (2002). Turning analog women into a digital workforce: Plugging women into the new Asia economy. *Digital Divide Network*. Retrieved September 12, 2007, from http://www.digitaldividenetwork.org

Brooksbank, D. (2000). Self employment and small firms. In S. Carter & D. Jones-Evans (Eds.), *Enterprise and small business: Principles, policy and practice*. London: FT Prentice Hall.

Brush, C.G. (1997). Women's entrepreneurship. In *Proceedings of the OECD Conference on Women Entrepreneurs in Small and Medium Enterprises*. Paris: OECD.

Brush, C.G., & Hisrich, R. (1999). Women owned businesses: Why do they matter? In Z. Acs (Ed.), *Are small firms important? Their role and impact*. Boston: Kluwer Academic Publishers.

Bunker, D.J., & MacGregor, R.C. (2000). Successful generation of information technology (IT) requirements for small/medium enterprises (SMEs): Cases from regional Australia. In *Proceedings of SMEs in a Global Economy*, Wollongong, Australia (pp. 72-84).

Butler, D. (2000). Gender, girls and computer technology: What's the status now? *Clearing House, 73*(4), 225-229.

Buttner, E.H., & Moore, D.P. (1997, January). Women's organisational exodus to entrepreneur-

ship: Self reported motivations and correlates with success. *Journal of Small Business Management*, pp. 34-47.

Carter, S. (2000). Improving the numbers and performance of women-owned businesses: Some implications for training and advisory services. *Education & Training, 42*(4/5), 326-333.

Carter, S., & Cannon, T. (1992). *Women as entrepreneurs*. London: Academic Press.

Carter, S., & Rosa, P. (1998). The financing of male and female owned businesses. *Entrepreneurship and Regional Development, 10*(3), 225-241.

Coviello, N., & McAuley, A. (1999) Internationalisation and the smaller firm: A review of contemporary empirical research. *Management International Review, 39*(3), 223-240.

Cox, B. (1999, June 8). Gender gap narrows, changing landscape for e-commerce. *Internetnews*. Retrieved September 12, 2007, from http://www.internetnews.com

DeLone, W.H. (1988). Determinants for success for computer usage in small business. *MIS Quarterly, 12*(1), 51-61.

Dennis, C. (2000). Networking for marketing advantage. *Management Decision, 38*(4), 287-292.

DeWine, S., & Casbolt, D. (1983). Networking: External communication systems for female organisational members. *Journal of Business Communication, 20*, 57-67.

Drakopoulou-Dodd, S., Jack, S., & Anderson, A.R. (2002). Scottish entrepreneurial networks in the international context. *International Small Business Journal, 20*(2), 213-219.

Gebler, D. (2000, October 6). Rethinking e-commerce gender demographics. *E-Commerce Times*. Retrieved September 12, 2007, from http://www.ecommercetimes.com

Gilroy, F., & Desai, H. (1986). Computer anxiety: Sex, race and age. *International Journal of Man-Machine Studies, 25,* 711-719.

Goffee, R., & Skase, R. (1985). *Women in charge: The experience of female entrepreneurs.* London: Allen & Unwin.

Gustafsson, R., Klefsjo, B., Berggren, E., & Granfors-Wellemets, U. (2001). Experiences from implementing ISO 9000 in small enterprises: A study of Swedish experiences. *The TQM Magazine, 13*(4), 232-246.

Hadjimonolis, A. (1999). Barriers to innovation for SMEs in a small less developed country (Cyprus). *Technovation, 19*(9), 561-570.

Hill, R., & Stewart, J. (2000). Human resource development in small organisations. *Journal of European Industrial Training, 24*(2/3/4), 105-117.

Hisrich, R., & Brush, C.G. (1986). *The woman entrepreneur: Starting, financing and managing a successful new business.* Lexington: Lexington Books.

Iacovou, C.L., Benbasat, I., & Dexter, A.S. (1995). Electronic data interchange and small organisations: Adoption and impact of technology. *MIS Quarterly, 19*(4), 465-485.

Johnson, S., & Storey, D. (1993). Male and female entrepreneurs and their businesses. In S. Allen & C. Truman (Eds.), *Women in business: Perspectives on women entrepreneurs.* London: Routledge.

Kalakota, R., & Whinston, A. (1997). *Electronic commerce: A manager's guide.* Reading, MA: Addison-Wesley.

Kalleberg, A.L., & Berg, I. (1987). *Work and industry.* New York: Plenum Press.

Kolsaker, A., & Payne, C. (2002). Engendering trust in e-commerce: A study of gender-based concerns. *Marketing Intelligence & Planning, 20*(4/5), 206-214.

Labich, K. (1994). Why companies fail. *Fortune, 14,* 52-68.

Lawrence, K.L. (1997). Factors inhibiting the utilisation of electronic commerce facilities in Tasmanian small- to medium-sized enterprises. In *Proceedings of the 8th Australasian Conference on Information Systems,* Adelaide, Australia (pp. 587-597).

Loscocco, K.A., & Leicht, K.T. (1993). Gender, work-family linkages and economic success among small business owners. *Journal of Marriage and the Family, 55,* 875-887.

MacGregor, R.C., & Vrazalic, L. (in press). Small business clusters and their role in prioritising barriers to e-commerce adoption: A study of two approaches to cluster development. *International Journal of Electronic Marketing and Retailing.*

Martin, L.M., & Matlay, H. (2001). 'Blanket' approaches to promoting ICT in small firms: Some lessons from the DTI ladder adoption model in the UK. *Internet Research: Electronic Networking Applications and Policy, 11*(5), 399-410.

Maupin, R. (1990). Sex role identity and career success of certified public accountants. *Advances in Public Interest Accounting,* pp. 97-105.

McGregor, J., & Tweed, D. (2001). Gender and managerial competence: Support for theories of androgyny. *Women in Management Review, 16*(6), 279-286.

Meier, S.T., & Lambert, M.E. (1991). Psychometric properties and correlates of three computer aversion scales. *Behaviour Research Methods, Instruments and Computers, 23*(1), 9-15.

Miller, N.L., & Besser, T.L. (2000). The importance of community values in small business strategy formation: Evidence from rural Iowa.

Journal of Small Business Management, 38(1), 68-85.

Murphy, J. (1996). *Small business management.* London: Pitman.

Nillson, P. (1997). Business counselling services directed towards female entrepreneurs: Some legitimacy dilemmas. *Entrepreneurship and Regional Development, 9*(3), 239-258.

Perez, M.P., Carnicer, M.P.L., & Sanchez, A.M. (2002). Differential effects of gender perceptions of teleworking by human resources managers. *Women in Management Review, 17*(6), 262-275.

Perry, S.C. (2002). A comparison of failed and non-failed small businesses in the United States: Do men and women use different planning and decision making strategies? *Journal of Developmental Entrepreneurship, 7*(4), 415-428.

Poon, S., & Swatman, P. (1997). The Internet for small businesses: An enabling infrastructure. In *Proceedings of the 5th Internet Society Conference* (pp. 221-231).

Poon, S., & Swatman, P.M.C. (1998, June 8-10). Small business Internet commerce experiences: A longitudinal study. In *Proceedings of the 11th International Bled Electronic Commerce Conference*, Bled, Slovenia.

Powell, G.N. (1993). *Women and men in management.* Newbury Park: Sage Publications.

Purao, S., & Campbell, B. (1998, August 14-16). Critical concerns for small business electronic commerce: Some reflections based on interviews of small business owners. In *Proceedings of the Association for Information Systems Americas Conference*, Baltimore (pp. 325-327).

Quayle, M. (2002). E-commerce: The challenge for UK SMEs in the 21st century. *International Journal of Operations and Production Management, 22*(10), 1148-1161.

Reynolds, W., Savage, W., & Williams, A. (1994). *Your own business: A practical guide to success.* ITP.

Riquelme, H. (2002). Commercial Internet adoption in China: Comparing the experience of small, medium and large business. *Internet Research: Electronic Networking Applications and Policy, 12*(3), 276-286.

Rodgers, S., & Harris, M.A. (2003). Gender and e-commerce: An exploratory study. *Journal of Advertising Research, 43*(3), 322.

Sandberg, K.W. (2003). An exploratory study of women in micro enterprises: Gender related difficulties. *Journal of Small Business and Enterprise Development, 10*(4), 408-417.

Schmidt, R.A., & Parker, C. (2003). Diversity in independent retailing: Barriers and benefits - The impact of gender. *International Journal of Retail and Distribution Management, 31*(8), 428-439.

Sexton, R.S., Johnson, R.A., & Hignite, M.A. (2002). Predicting Internet/e-commerce use. *Internet Research, 12*(5), 402-410.

Shade, L.R. (1998). A gendered perspective on access to the information infrastructure. *The Information Society, 14*, 33-44.

Sheehan, K. (1999). An investigation of gender differences in online privacy concerns and resultant behaviour. *Internet Marketing*, pp. 159-173.

Simon, S.J. (2001). The impact of culture and gender on Web sites: An empirical study. *The DATA BASE for Advances in Information Systems, 32*(1), 18-37.

Singh, S. (2001). Gender and use of the Internet at home. *New Media & Society, 3*(4), 395-415.

Smeltzer, L.R., & Fann, G.L. (1989, April). Gender differences in external networks of small business owner/managers. *Journal of Small Business Management*, 25-32.

Sohal, A.S., & Ng, L. (1998). The role and impact of information technology in Australian business. *Journal of Information Technology, 13*(3), 201-217.

Sonfield, M., Lussier, R., Corman, J., & McKinney, M. (2001). Gender comparisons in strategic decision making: An empirical analysis of the entrepreneurial strategy matrix. *Journal of Small Business Management, 39*(2), 165-173.

Teltscher, S. (2002). *E-Commerce and Development Report 2002.* United Nations Conference on Trade and Development.

Tetteh, E., & Burn, J. (2001). Global strategies for SME-business: Applying the SMALL framework. *Logistics Information Management, 14*(1-2), 171-180.

Tuunainen, V.K. (1999). Opportunities of effective integration of EDI for small businesses in the automotive industry. *Information & Management, 36*(6), 361-375.

Van Akkeren, J., & Cavaye, A.L.M. (1999, December 1-3). Factors affecting entry-level Internet technology adoption by small business in Australia: An empirical study. In *Proceedings of the 10th Australasian Conference on Information Systems*, Wellington, New Zealand.

Venkatesan, V.S., & Fink, D. (2002). Adoption of Internet technologies and e-commerce by small and medium enterprises (SMEs) in Western Australia. In *Proceedings of the Information Resource Management Association International Conference* (pp. 1136-1137).

Verheul, I., Risseeuw, P., & Bartelse, G. (2002). Gender differences in strategy and human resource management. *International Small Business Journal, 20*(4), 443-476.

Walczuch, R., Van Braven, G., & Lundgren, H. (2000). Internet adoption barriers for small firms in The Netherlands. *European Management Journal, 18*(5), 561-572.

Welsh, J.A., & White, J.F. (1981, July-August). A small business is not a little big business. *Harvard Business Review*, 18-32.

Westhead, P., & Storey, D.J. (1996). Management training and small firm performance: Why is the link so weak? *International Small Business Journal, 14*(4), 13-24.

Wynarczyk, P., Watson, R., Storey, D.J., Short, H., & Keasey, K. (1993). *The managerial labour market in small and medium sized enterprises.* London: Routledge.

Chapter XVI
Personas of E–Commerce Adoption in Small Businesses in New Zealand

Nabeel Al-Qirim

College of Information Technology, United Arab Emirates University, UAE

ABSTRACT

Focus group methodology is introduced in this article as one appropriate methodology to study the impact of technological innovation factors on e-commerce (EC) adoption in small businesses (SMEs) in New Zealand. The research results suggested two emerging issues pertaining to EC adoption in SMEs in this research. First, SMEs would not invest their scant resources on perceived risky advanced EC initiatives. In adopting simple EC technologies such as Web pages and e-mail, factors like cost and compatibility were found not hindering the adoption decision. On the other hand, the proposed drivers to adopt these simple technologies were not highly significant as such. Second, the SMEs retained a particular view about advancing their simple EC initiatives. They envisaged that advancing their EC initiatives, such as adopting full-blown and interactive Web sites, will give more weight to the impact of the different factors in this research on their adoption decisions of EC. The gulf between the current adoption and usage levels and the envisaged advanced EC initiatives seemed to be increasing further, suggesting the weakness of the EC phenomenon in SMEs in this research. The research portrays a path where such gaps could be addressed, and hence, this path should guide the SMEs in advancing their EC initiatives. Implications arising from this research with respect to theory and to practice are discussed in this research.

IMPLICATIONS IN E-COMMERCE RESEARCH IN SMALL BUSINESSES

Historically, in review of IS research in small to medium-sized enterprises (SMEs) (Blili & Ray-mond, 1993; Cragg & King, 1992, 1993; Jansen, 1998; Levy, Powell & Yetton, 1998; Reimensch-neider & Mykytyn, 2000; Soh, Yap & Raman, 1992; Thong, 1999; Thong, Yap & Raman, 1994), it was observed that these studies kept referring to three recurring themes concerning technology adoption and use in SMEs. First, SMEs face different technological, managerial, organizational, and environmental challenges which always would challenge their existence in the marketplace. Second, the central organizational structure and decision making in SMEs usually reflects the personality of the business manager, who is usually the owner, as well. In comparison with large enterprises, the third theme pointed to the laggardness of the SME sector in adopting or using IS strategically in business.

Globalization effect and rapid technological and environmental changes which surround the SMEs always have exerted tremendous pressure on their scant resources and have challenged their existence in the long term. The previous literature suggested the same and pointed to the fact that SMEs run their businesses on a day-by-day basis and, hence, opted not to adopt long-term plans or strategies as such. Therefore, it was not surprising when the previous researchers suggested the incompleteness of most of the IS initiatives in SMEs.

It was expected that the recent emergence of electronic commerce (EC) in the early 1990s would bridge such a historical void between large and small enterprises. Features of the Internet, such as its openness, unified standards, interoperability, and global interconnectedness, provide unprecedented opportunities to SMEs in order to network, to expand in scope, and to increase their market shares. The vision of gaining access to global and interconnected networks and of achieving seamless integration across disparate/legacy systems seemed to be possible for most of the SMEs in the world. However, in review of EC research in SMEs (Table 1), the results seemed to be disappointing, as well. This literature pointed to the following difficulties:

Table 1. Determinants of EC adoption in SMEs

	Factors	Found significant	Found insignificant	Found most significant
	Technological			
1	Relative advantage	1, 2, 3, 4, 5, 7, 8, 9, 12, 14, 15, 16, 18		
2	Compatibility	2, 4, 15, 16, 17, 18		
3	Complexity	3	5	
	Organizational			
1	Top management support	4		
2	Organizational readiness (size) (cost/financial and technical resources)	1, 4, 5, 7, 8, 9, 10, 12, 17	4	1, 5,9
3	Information intensity and product characteristics	12, 14, 15	4, 18	
4	Managerial time		4	
	Environmental			
1	Industry pressure (competition)	1, 5, 6, 7, 8, 9, 10, 12, 16(-)	4, 13, 18	1, 9
2	Government pressure	1, 5, 6		1
3	Consumer readiness	10, 12, 16(-)		
4	Support from technology vendors	12, 19		

1. Grandon and Pearson (2004) found that only a small number of studies focused on the adoption and use of EC in SMEs.

2. SMEs are laggards in adopting or in using EC more strategically in business (Abell & Lim 1996; Abell & Black, 1997; Adam & Deans, 2000; Deloitte, 2000; Grandon & Pearson, 2004; MOED, 2000a, 2000b; Poon, 2000; Poon & Swatman, 1995, 1997, 1998, 1999a, 1999b; PWHC, 1999; Teo, Tan & Buk, 1998).

3. The available empirical research that focuses on success factors of EC (e.g., Web sites) is anecdotal, exploratory in nature, and does not provide sufficient insights into the combinations of these factors (Liu & Arnett, 2000).

In explaining the third point, Drew (2003) found that SMEs in England are placing EC at the center of their technology and corporate strategies and plan to use it as a means of transformational change. However, Peet, Brindley, and Ritchie (2002) found that European firms, including England, are at the early stages of adopting EC and that their Web sites lack interactivity and are limited to text-based content. They warned that unless the growing digital EC divide, even between Europe and the U.S., is bridged, this could lead to disastrous effects, especially on European SMEs. In contrast, recent research found that, in reality, few SMEs adopted EC in the U.S. (Grandon & Pearson, 2004). This research indicated that SMEs establish Web sites primarily to advertise and to promote their business rather than to conduct EC as such. Such anecdotal views across different research studies in England, Europe, and the U.S. bring further gloom to the EC adoption phenomenon in SMEs.

In NZ, a survey-based research covering the countries of the Asia Pacific Economic Cooperation (APEC) (PWHC, 1999), painted a gloomy picture of EC uptake and use by NZ SMEs. Findings from the Deloitte (2000) survey indicate a lack of knowledge among NZ SMEs about EC and its applications. Despite the high adoption rates of e-mail, domain names, and Web sites, NZ businesses were lagging behind other countries in the use of EC in business and in the adoption of EC technology in general (Deloitte, 2000). In spite of the different perceived advantages, the Internet was used mainly as a communication tool, and Web sites were used for publishing organizational information only. They were rarely used in conducting commercial transactions. Electronic commerce was viewed as strategically important within SMEs but even more so within larger organizations, specifically in the financial services sector (Deloitte, 2000).

A survey research by the NZ Government (MOED, 2000b) showed that nearly one in four NZ firms (23%) included in the survey were engaged to some extent with the export of goods or services, with larger firms more likely to be exporters than smaller ones. More than 50% of firms with 20 or more employees were exporters. The business sectors most likely to include exporting firms were information and communication technology (45%), manufacturing (38%), and business services (27%). Longitudinal research in NZ suggested the same and found that although the number of firms with Web sites had increased from 8.8% to 63.4% in only one year, most of these Web sites have provided lists of products and services (Chapple, 2002). Only 20% of these sites could take orders, with only one in 12 taking payments online.

According to this literature review, conducting more EC research in SMEs could shed more light on the gloom that surrounds the EC phenomenon in SMEs. These disappointing findings raise the importance of focusing on other important contextual influences besides the technological ones (i.e., organizational, environmental, etc.) when investigating the EC adoption phenomenon in SMEs.

Therefore, this research attempted to provide answers to the following research questions: What are the different contextual factors that could influence EC adoption and success in SMEs? How can these factors influence EC adoption and success in SMEs in New Zealand (NZ)? The first question has a theoretical implication and, hence, is aimed at developing a theoretical framework for EC adoption in SMEs. The second question attempted to achieve two objectives. The first one aimed at investigating the significance of the developed research model on EC adoption in SMEs, and the second objective endeavored to provide different interpretations and rich insights pertaining to the EC adoption phenomenon in SMEs in NZ. Whether the EC initiatives in NZ SMEs were successful or not were among the objectives of this research.

Achieving the previous objectives is of importance to SME/EC researchers, professionals, and policymakers in different countries in the world interested in EC in SMEs in general and in SMEs in NZ specifically, as both the market structure and the economy in NZ are quite unique. Such uniqueness stems from several facts: 84% of the NZ sector is dominated by micro-enterprises that employ only up to five employees (MOED, 2000a); the country is geographically isolated, and time differences separate NZ from the rest of the developed countries in the northern hemisphere specifically; the population of NZ is relatively small (~4 million), dominated mostly by low- to average-income families; and more than one-third of the population resides in the Auckland region (~1.2 million) alone (NZStat,1999). Therefore, it was expected that such constraints would limit the growth of EC in businesses in general and in SMEs specifically in NZ. This argument would be discussed further upon completing the research analysis.

For the purpose of this research, small business EC is defined as "the use of Internet technology and applications to support business activities of a small firm" (Poon, 1999)—in order to streamline business processes and activities for the purpose of developing successful business models and of

delivering end-to-end services to online customers and businesses.

The approaches followed by this research in answering the previous questions and in achieving the research objectives were based on adopting the technological innovation theories as a reference theoretical framework here to develop the research model and on the focus group (FG) methodology as the main vehicle for data collection and analysis. The research analysis, discussion, and conclusion progress accordingly.

THEORETICAL E-COMMERCE ADOPTION FRAMEWORK

In review of the technological innovation literature, it was observed that Rogers' (1983, 1995) innovation diffusion theory (IDT) appears to be the one most researchers have accepted for identifying perceived critical characteristics of innovations (Iacovou, Benbasat & Dexter, 1995; Moore & Benbasat, 1991, 1996; Premkumar & Roberts, 1999; Thong, 1999). Rogers' (1995) characteristics of technological innovations (relative advantage, compatibility, complexity, observability, trialability) have been hypothesized by different researchers in order to influence the attitude of potential adopters in a number of studies on IS adoption or rejection (Moore & Benbasat, 1996; Tornatzky & Klein, 1982). However, the same researchers who endorse Rogers' (1995) model argued that Rogers' (1995) model should be blended with other contexts/factors in order to provide a more holistic adoption model.

In line with this argument and following a review of the technological innovation (IS) adoption research in SMEs (Premkumar & Roberts, 1999; Rogers, 1995; Thong, 1999; Thong & Yap, 1995, 1996), the following factors emerged as potential determinants of EC adoption in SMEs: (1) technological context—relative advantage, cost, and compatibility; (2) organizational context—size and information intensity; (3) individual context—manager-owner (CEO) factors, manager's innovativeness, and manager's IS knowledge; and (4) environmental context—competition, external support from technology vendors, and pressure from suppliers or buyers. However, the direct extension of these factors to EC adoption research was not a straightforward process, as EC introduced unique features pertaining to its technologies (security, privacy, loss of intimate interactions, spam, viruses, culture, cyber law, cross-border trade, taxation, tariff, globalization, etc.). Earlier studies were confirming this contention in that the facilitation factors for adopting innovations vary according to the innovation type (Swanson, 1994).

Therefore, the previous factors were revisited in light of recent EC research (Table 1) in order to develop EC factors that are as close as possible to the previously depicted factors in SMEs.

According to this literature review of EC, the researcher maintained the same IS determinants indicated previously as potential determinants of EC adoption in SMEs but replaced the manager's IS knowledge with the manager's EC involvement and the information intensity with the information intensity of products and services. These changes were found to be more relevant to EC than IS. Earlier literature (Table 1) pointed to information intensity as more of an intraorganizational factor which pertains to an intensive internal information-processing environment (i.e., ticketing), which emphasizes the need for IS (not EC) in order to enhance the efficiency and the effectiveness of information processing and distribution. EC could

assist SMEs in streamlining the whole selling and delivery processes or at least in supplementing the selling of the physical products at different levels (Poon, 2000; Teo et al., 1998). Poon and Swatman (1998, 1999a) emphasized the manager's involvement as more vital to EC success than the IS knowledge perspective. They indicated a lack of the formal IS or EC training among the managers of the different SMEs. This finding has been suggested by EC research in small businesses in NZ (Deloitte, 2000). Table 2 shows the different research factors in the EC adoption framework in this research.

In order to extend an understanding of these determinants, it was decided to evaluate each in a focus group (FG) context.

RESEARCH METHODOLOGY: SETTING THE STAGE

Focus group research is a process of obtaining possible ideas or solutions to a problem from a group of participants by discussing it (Aaker et al., 1998), (Blackburn & Stokes, 2000; Bloor et al., 2001; Stewart & Shamdasani, 1990). One important emphasis in this method is on the results of group interaction when focused on a series of topics introduced by a discussion leader (moderator not the researcher) (Aaker, Kumar & Day, 1998; Blackburn & Stokes, 2000; Morgan, 1997, 1998). An FG can throw light on the normative understanding upon which groups draw to reach their collective judgment and can provide a valu-

Table 2. A theoretical framework of EC adoption in SMEs

Innovation characteristics:		**The Environment:**	
i.	Relative advantage	i.	Competition from other companies in the business (Rivalry)
ii.	Compatibility	ii.	External pressure from Suppliers/buyers
iii.	Cost	iii.	External Support from Technology vendors
Individual characteristics:		**Organisational characteristics:**	
i.	CEO's EC innovativeness	i.	Information intensity of products and services
ii.	CEO's EC involvement		

able resource for documenting the complex and varying processes through which group norms and meanings are shaped, elaborated, and applied (Bloor, Frankland, Thomas & Robson, 2001).

An FG is extremely flexible (Morgan, 1998), and researchers suggested its use as one viable tool in implementing IS research (Clarke, 1999a, 1999b, 2001). FG research plays a major part as the principal data source and as an ancillary method alongside and complementing other methods—pre-pilot work to provide a contextual basis for survey design; a contemporary extension of survey and other methods to provide interpretative aid to survey findings; and a method of communicating findings to research subjects for the objective of creating further discussions and, hence, discovering new insights (Bloor et al., 2001). In this research, the FG methodology was used as the principal data source in order to confirm/refute the importance of the different factors in the adoption model (Table 1) (i.e., irrelevant, positively, negatively). The exploratory focus here is stressed as well.

Some proponents of FG research have extended their arguments about its strength in order to indicate that FG methodology can yield rich data on group norms similar to long periods of ethnographic fieldwork (Bloor et al., 2001). Depending on the research purpose, FG can be relatively structured with specific questions asked or very unstructured (Fontana & Frey, 1994 in Blackburn & Stokes, 2000). For example, the objectives of FG research are similar to unstructured in-depth interviews (e.g., case studies), but the moderator plays a more passive role than an interviewer does (Morgan, 1997; Stewart & Shamdasani, 1990).

Strengths and Weaknesses of FG Research

One of the strongest advantages of FG methodology is that it offers participants more stimulation than an interview (one-on-one), as it involves more than one participant and leads to the creation of new ideas and more meaningful comments (Aaker et al., 1998; Blackburn & Stokes, 2000). The security of being in a crowed encourages some participants to speak out, and a relatively large amount of information can be gathered in a short period of time at a relatively small cost. Such psychological security derived from group membership may be particularly relevant to researching owner-managers in SMEs, as they would be more relaxed and more open about their views in a group of peers rather than on an interview (Blackburn & Stokes, 2000).

On the other hand, FG research does have reported weaknesses (Blackburn & Stokes, 2000; Bloor et al., 2001; Morgan, 1997; Stewart & Shamdasani, 1990). Therefore, the researcher and the moderator prior to conducting the session addressed the following concerns:

1. Responses in a group may be contaminated by the opinions of other group members. Therefore, the moderator attempted to ensure equal and fair discussions among the different participants by inviting and involving each participant in the FG to posit an opinion and to share in the ongoing discussions.

2. It is to be expected that abnormal experiences will be silenced, and hence, the moderator should play a vital role in involving everybody in the discussions and in allowing for the different facts to emerge and to be discussed in the session.

3. It may be difficult to assemble six, eight, or 10 participants if they were of a difficult type to recruit, such as executives (e.g., very busy managers)—one of the challenges in this research which resulted in having a limited number of participants in the FG.

4. FG research members are not representative of a large population (a limitation which is addressed next).

5. It should be recognized that the amount of direction provided by the moderator

does influence the types and quality of the data obtained from the group. Thus, the moderator made sure that his engagement in the session was limited to the previous instructions and guidelines and to avoiding expressing any opinions or giving too many directions during the session.

Data Analysis, Validity, and Generalizability

This research relied on two sources of evidence: namely, from interviewing the managers of SMEs in an FG setting and from visiting the Web sites of the participating SMEs in the session in order to validate the interviewees' responses concerning the adoption and usage of their Web sites. Further e-mail and telephone communications were conducted with the participants in order to get further details about their organizations or to clarify some of the their responses in the FG session.

Data analysis in this research consisted of examining, categorizing, and tabulating the evidence guided by the factors in the research model (Yin, 1994). The original objectives and design of this research were based on such factors, which, in turn, reflected a set of research questions, reviews of the literature, and new insights. Research reporting on the analysis of data collected by FG research is scarce, and indeed, this may be the least developed part of the FG methodology (Blackburn & Stokes, 2000). However, Morgan (1998) suggested two basic approaches for analyzing data from FGs: ethnographic summary or systematic coding through content analysis. The amount of analysis and its level of detail and rigor, however, depend on the purpose of the research. As the bulk of this research was based on a developed set of determinants extended from the innovation theories and backed by EC research in SMEs, holistic content analysis was not necessary, and hence, adopting Morgan's (1998) first method of analysis, ethnographic summary is represented

here by using narrative techniques backed by quotes from the participants' responses concerning the different factors, as they were discussed in the FG session.

In ensuring issues of internal validity (the accuracy of information and whether it matched reality), an investigator needs to develop a sufficiently operational set of measures in order to collect data (Yin, 1994). In order to meet the test of validity, this research conducted an extensive literature review and developed an adoption model based on this literature. Relying on this constructed theoretical framework further assured that the interpretations and justifications made were accurate and objective. It should be emphasized that the research results and conclusions came about as a result of the different discussions among the different participants in the FG of the different factors in the research model. These conflicting or agreeing views in the FG session have assisted this research in making accurate and valid conclusions. Shifting the power from the researcher and his or her analytical tools to the participants in order to confirm or refute the research conclusions represented the strongest point in FG research (Blackburn & Stokes, 2000). This approach should eliminate any subjectivity or bias at the researcher's side during data analysis. In addition, employing a neutral moderator to lead the FG session has reduced further the subjectivity effect in data analysis and has constrained the role of the researcher to an observant only. It could be argued here that subjectivity is an absolute term here and cannot be eliminated completely. One should not forget that even the moderator brings his or her own set of beliefs and biases to the FG setting. Overall, it could be agreed that the contribution of FG in reducing the effect of subjectivity is well noted when compared with other methodologies.

The fail-safe feature of the aforementioned procedure in collecting data from the interviews (Figure 1) is preferred among FG researchers, as it facilitates a balanced and a multi-faceted coverage of the research topic (Bloor et al., 2001). This procedure compared what the SMEs really knew about EC with what they answered in the confirmatory stage, leading either to confirming the findings or to raising implications alongside the different factors. The different sources of evidence discussed previously and contacting the participants on several occasions to validate their responses further strengthened the validity of the research results. To further substantiate the participants' responses, direct quotes from their discussions were included in the report. Finally, participants were given the opportunity to review a draft of the final report and to reflect on the report's findings and on their responses.

In discussing the generalizability of the research results, Yin (1994) indicated that this process is not automatic. A theory must be tested through replication of the findings in a second or even a third FG; where the theory has specified that the same results should occur, the results might be accepted for a much larger number of similar cases. Although this was noted as a limitation in this research, it was hoped that this initial research, using FG research, would produce interesting insights and, hence, lay the foundation for undertaking more FGs by any future research. This task will be implemented in the next phase of this project.

STEPS IN CONDUCTING FOCUS GROUP RESEARCH

FG literature suggests following five stages in implementing FG research: planning, recruiting, moderating, analyzing, and reporting. A group of 6 to 10 or 12 (Blackburn & Stokes, 2000; Clarke, 1999b; Stewart & Shamdasani, 1990) or even up to 14 (Bloor et al., 2001) have become customary in FG research.

According to the Ministry of Economic Development (MOED) (2000a), NZ SMEs are defined as enterprises which employ 19 or less

full-time (working 30 hours or more per week) equivalent and working proprietors plus half the number of part-time employees and working employees (FTEs). Small enterprises are defined as those employing 0 to 5 FTEs (often called micro-businesses) and medium-sized enterprises as those employing 6 to 19 FTEs. Other areas (e.g., Europe and the U.S.) define their SMEs as having a much larger number of employees (500 or less). Therefore, selecting a range of 100 FTEs and less was found adequate for comparison purposes with NZ SMEs (Cameron & Massey, 1999; Igbaria, Zinatelli & Cavaye, 1998). This makes comparison possible between the research results of this study and those of similar studies in different countries.

From a sample of 324 SMEs selected randomly from the North Shore Telephone Business Directory, 26 showed interest in joining the FG session. Accordingly, 16 SMEs agreed to attend the FG, and eventually, 10 confirmed their attendance. However, only six attended the FG session (Table 3). Having 6 participants in the FG session was quite adequate, and earlier FG research in small business endorsed the same (Blackburn & Stokes, 2000). Blackburn and Stokes (2000) suggested that groups over 8 are less manageable. The different SMEs were complete strangers. Researchers have favored group of strangers, as they are more likely to express taken-for-granted opinions and experiences (Bloor et al., 2001; Stewart & Shamdasani, 1990). Not all the participants were native English speakers, which influenced the transcription (quotes) quality of some of their conversations (those were transcribed as spoken by those participants). The participants came from different businesses in the market; however, most of them were engaging more in business-to-business (B2B) relationships than in business-to-consumer (B2C) ones.

After identifying and defining the research problems and questions and the FG participants, the third step involved identifying the moderator (facilitator) for the FG sessions. The moderator is the key to assuring that a group discussion goes smoothly. The researcher selected a moderator who was a senior lecturer in the School of Education and Social Sciences, Auckland University of Technology, for his apability to run group discussions. However, the moderator had no prior experience with EC. Several meetings took place with the moderator in order to explain the FG agenda, content, scenario, and implementation. He showed keen interest in and enthusiasm for undertaking the moderator role. In order to reduce the effect of moderator biases on the FG, the researcher had to work closely with him during the preparation and post-interview phases in order to avoid skewing the outcomes of the session.

The session took place at one of the conference facilities at Auckland University of Technology. The meeting lasted from 5:30 P.M. to 10:20 P.M. The session started with snacks, and there were several breaks so the participants could sustain the long FG session. Such informal social interaction encourages a relaxed atmosphere (Blackburn & Stokes, 2000). The participants completed a basic demographic questionnaire (blinded) about their organizations before starting the FG session

(Table 4). The participants varied in terms of the industries to which they belonged, the annual turnover, and their sophistication with technology and computers. However, they all had been in the marketplace for a long time and were managed by the owner. All of the participants were senior executives and owners of the business, except for participant F, who was the chief technology officer of that company.

The researcher took the role of the observer in the FG session. The session was videorecorded, notes were taken by the researcher, and a printout of discussion notes (written by the moderator) on an electronic whiteboard copier was obtained. The moderator used this whiteboard to show the different factors in the research model and the views of the participants. These tools were used to capture data from participants and to assist during the data analysis phase.

ANALYSIS, RESULTS, AND IMPLICATIONS

A big decision in investing in a Web site is the need to publicize the Web site, ... it is like a grain of

Table 3. Business details and models of the different participants in the FG session

Participants					
A	**B**	**C**	**D**	**E**	**F**
Manufacturing (Greenhouse automation tools)	Importer and manufacturer of industrial Diamond tools.	Wholesale/ Retail (Fire arms and ammunitions)	Manufacturer, Wholesale/ Online retail (Tourism videos, CDs, DVDs about NZ)	Construction	IT & Communications Services (Develop integrated electronic security systems)
Business Models					
B2B	**B2B**	**B2B/B2C**	**B2B/B2C**	**B2B**	**B2B**
Manufacturing (greenhouse automation tools)	Importer and manufacturer of industrial diamond tools.	Wholesale/ retail (fire arms and ammunitions)	Manufacturer, wholesale/ online retail (tourism videos, CDs, DVDs about NZ)	Construction	IT and communications services (develop integrated electronic security systems)

Table 4. Demographic details about the different participants in the FG session

Organisational details	Participants					
	A	**B**	**C**	**D**	**E**	**F**
The number of personal computers (terminals) at your organisation.	8	5	2	2	9	15
The number of computer servers at your organisation.	1	1	0	0	2	2
Do you have a local area network (LAN)	Yes	Yes	No	No	Yes	Yes
The total number of staff who have access to the Internet	5	1	2	2	5	15
The title of the person attending the FG meeting	Manager	Director	Managing director	Managing director	Director	Chief technology officer
Is the organisation managed by the owner or one of the owners	Yes	Yes	Yes	Yes	Yes	Yes
Mention the number of full-time equivalent staff (FTEs) in your business	5	4	2	2	7	20
What was your annual turnover last financial year (approximately, in NZ$)	500,000	800,000	400,000	320,000	600,000	1.5 Million
Age of the business	4	11	50	13	18	50

sand in the beach and no one will be able to find your Web site unless you submit the URL to the different search engines, which requires lots of time and money and we have to keep on doing it and this is important to attract and to lead customers to our Web site. (Participant A in the FG)

Relative Advantage

In a review of the participants' responses concerning the adopted EC technologies, it was observed that their adoption of EC was limited to adopting e-mail (internal and external) and Web sites. This is summarized in Table 4, together with the participants' responses about advantages and reported disadvantages. The SMEs described their Web site initiatives as simple and named such Web sites passive initiatives. The SMEs named their advanced EC initiatives interactive EC, such as using full products and services online, receiving and

fulfilling queries and orders online, interacting online with their buyers, and collecting payments online. Some of the participants discussed using other EC technologies, such as Internet banking and credit card payment (Table 5).

All of the participants emphasized the importance of having a Web presence, and then the cost element is weighed against the expected benefits from EC. Some of the participants adopted the Web site mainly as an advertising medium, as an address of the company, or as an image enhancement tool. Some of the participants emphasized that their Web sites were pushed to a further level of sophistication and/or will undergo ongoing development and enhancements (mostly technological). However, Participant E indicated that it is the nature of the business that dictates the sophistication of the Web site, and they are planning to develop their customer-service-based Web site further but were not sure when the company

Table 5. Adopted EC technologies by SMEs in the FG

	Adopting companies	Advantages/Applications	Reported disadvantages/Non-adopters
Internal email	A, E, F	Convenient, efficient, transfer of documents, and communication across remote offices.	No network, few employees, all on one site and no need for it, can shout, and impersonal.
External email	All	Convenient, efficient, formal mean, cheaper than fax/tel., record management of correspondence, legitimate use of informal language and open 24 hours 7 days a week.	Viruses, spam, employee's misuse.
Web page (simple)	All	Becoming the yellow pages on the Internet, image enhancement and simple electronic company brochure.	
Web page (more than Internet presence)	A, D, E	Nature of the business facilitates having detailed Web site, outreach to international markets and product catalogues.	Lazy, large product range to put into Web site, needs big learning curve, needs continuous update and expensive to retain (marketing it through traditional media and search engine).
Internet banking	A, D, E	Convenience, fast and efficient payments of accounts, 24X7, monitoring financial and transactions movements conducted by the accountant, and up to date financial information.	Lazy to do it, security threats, lack of signature (needs two managers to sign the checks).
Credit card payment	D	Facilitates Internet sales in comparison with the paper system.	Fear and perceived security threats and misusing the credit card number by the merchant nationally or/and internationally. However, credit card companies are responsible for any damage pertaining to fraudulent activities over the Internet. Eventually all the companies indicated that this is only a perceived threat.

will do that. Participant C indicated, "There is a long learning curve involved in developing the Web sites, and learning from their mistakes takes a lot of time and effort." Participant D's company sold videocassettes, CDs, and DVDs about NZ tourist destinations and scenery. These were more attractive to international market customers, and therefore, the company provided an online transaction processing and payment tool on its Web site in order to allow international customers to shop and buy online.

Low vs. High EC Capability

...Generally if you are adopting a technology, it is definitely an advantage to the business. However, being a leader in adopting new and emerging tech-nologies is highly risky and possibly disadvantageous to the business due to financial commitments and risks ... payback, technology risk ... choosing the wrong platform or technology. Adopting email and Web page is not risky and everybody is using it in business. (Participant F in the FG)

The participants also emphasized the need to make a clear distinction between low and high EC capability. All of the participants emphasized that they were positioned at the low level of the EC capability continuum. Issues relating to strategic and interactive EC initiatives (high EC capability), such as providing full details about their products and services online, buying and configuring state-of-the-art EC infrastructure, and collecting payments online, were not represented in the cases.

All of the participants retained a solid opinion that all the benefits as well as the risks are at the high levels of EC.

Intangible Benefits

When the participants were asked if they were witnessing any real tangible benefits from their EC initiatives, the participants indicated that it would be quite difficult to quantify such advantages. Except for participants A and D, the participants were not witnessing real tangible benefits. They viewed having an online presence as a must; otherwise, they feared being left alone behind other leaders in adopting EC. Participant F commented, "I think of the moment we all adopt email and Web pages, that's why such initiatives are not that expensive up to this point … you can choose not to open your email or Web page. I am talking about the next point such as adopting interactive Web sites where the big decision will take place."

Business/Product Specifics and International Opportunities

Participant D commented, "You think about the Internet as an international marketer, it is marvellous for NZ, because our big problems have always been being a long way from our markets." Participant D, for instance, develops and sells online videos, CDs, and DVDs that include promotional information about tourism in NZ. These were highly attractive to international tourists interested in visiting NZ. The Internet offered participant A's business different opportunities. He commented, "Wider exposure to the world through the Internet and increase our market share and profits … take advantage of exchange rates mainly conducted in U.S. dollars by credit card payments … and greater profit margins over the Internet due to the absence of the Goods and Services Tax (GST)."

Standard Products

The Internet was a logical extension to the business of Participant D in selling standard products such as videos, CDs, and DVDs to online buyers. The other participants agreed on the fact that the business model of Participant D was more appropriate to the online environment. The participants commented that their businesses were quite different and that there were no prior guidelines or EC models to follow or any assurances that what they would invest in, in terms of advanced EC initiatives, would yield satisfactory returns. These aspects point to product specifics, which, in turn, point to industry specifics pertaining to the business of the different participants. Such specifics meant that the products of certain industries were more suitable to the Internet than others.

Misconceptions and Driving EC Forward

Participant D criticized Participant C and other participants for using excuses such as they do not have the time or the resources to adopt EC. Participant C responded, "I am only saying they are a factor (among other factors), I am in the business of selling what I sell. … I am not in the business of … eBusiness as such. I can go on quite nicely as I am in the moment without going any deeper (engaging in EC)." Participant D commented, "It is interesting some of the things we discussed so far … I am just hearing what are two negatives coming through … and it is on the basis of cost or time component and maybe reservation or nervousness about that technology and how it is used … the way I always worked is that ignorance can be a wonderful thing because you can find people to do it for you provided you can justify it otherwise I think you can get sucked into yourself." Participant C commented, "That is right if you are looking at its benefits from your market (product) … your market and my market are probably quite different." Participant D commented, "I do not need to understand the in/out of technology to sell it … but what it can do for me (business driving technology not the other way around). … I understand video but I do not understand DVD or CD but I know I can sell them and I can make programmes (EC) to sell them." It was clear from this discussion that the SMEs would need to understand how to use and drive technology to their benefits.

Cost

Cost-Benefit Analysis and Uncertainty

The moderator asked the participants, "What is stopping you from progressing to the high levels of EC?" The participants responded by confirming that unless EC proves to be feasible and financially justifiable, they would not take the jump into advanced EC initiatives. The participants emphasized that progressing to more advanced EC projects and initiatives requires huge investment, time, and effort and, above all, possesses high-risk elements (small NZ market scope in comparison with the U.S. and international markets and opportunities are vague to them). Most of the participants perceived going to the high EC arena as a dark area and stressed the need for help from experts in the field (business analysts, consultants) to bridge the existing gap between their lack of detailed knowledge about EC and their businesses and how to exploit EC opportunities to their benefits. Achieving low-level EC capability, such as establishing a Web page or an online catalogue, was not expensive and was quite affordable, as noted by all participants.

Compatibility

Readiness for the Internet

When asked about the compatibility or acceptability of the technology to their internal value system, beliefs, work style with clients, and internal technological systems in place, the participants indicated that such issues did not impede their adoption decision of EC. All of the participants indicated that business people in NZ have no aversion to technology. Participant B commented, "No … there is no reason for it to have anything against technology." However, the participants re-emphasized in the session that it is when they advance to more sophisticated EC initiatives that incompatibility issues may emerge as major barriers to EC adoption. The participants raised legal concerns and other fears relating to contract enforceability, security, and the lack of the ink signatures as major impediments over the Internet.

Information Intensity of Products and Services

When the participants were asked about the impact of the information part of their products on their adoption decision of EC and whether their products were suitable to be offered on the Internet, they all replied favorably and positively. However, Participant A indicated, "Most of our sales are done through distributors, so I think going to a shopping trolley type of situation is not appropriate for my business. On the other hand, we have small number of products, which means we can handle the whole range of products on our Web site very easily … our products are high-tech (greenhouse automation products) which makes the Internet suitable medium for our products. However, they need a lot of support, which we can provide through the Internet quite cheaply." Thus, Participant A envisaged their products to be appropriate for the Internet in the long term. The preceding argument points to the product/industry specifics discussed earlier.

Participant C sells firearms through its retail outlet and through a network of dealers nationwide. Participants B and C envisaged that they could include a catalogue of their products on the

Web site. Participant C commented, "I will say that if I wanted to sell directly over the Internet, all our products are suitable to sell," but he was not doing it, because the owner raised issues concerning firearms licensing over the Internet; but he indicated that "other firearms retailers are doing it online," which makes it a possibility for his business, as well.

Industry/Product Specifics

Thus, SMEs with high information-content products (e.g., software, technical manuals, drawings, catalogues) that could be sold/offered on the Internet were more likely to adopt EC (e.g., Participant D) than others. However, each company has its own product specifics, which, in turn, points to industry-specific issues, as discussed earlier.

However, what could be synthesized from the previous analysis is that EC could be used more effectively to supplement the selling of the participants' products and services, even if they could not be digitized. The reluctance of some of the participants in doing that were attributed to reasons ranging from a lack of knowledge about EC opportunities and benefits to situations where participants showed lack of interest in exploring EC opportunities (lazy, as indicated by Participant C).

Competition and the International Opportunities

It was suggested from discussions with the different participants around this factor that none of them retained an open eye on their competitors as such, and therefore, the effect of competition on their adoption decision of EC was not critical. Most of the participants were at the low levels of EC (passive and simple EC initiatives), and they indicated that all their competitors were at a similar position. Participant D commented, "We have been always looking for an innovative way of using technology in the business but usually

not forced into it, I will do it whether my competitors have it or not … this is the way I am." This response points to the innovative role of this CEO in adopting EC. E-commerce provided Participant D as well as their competitors with new international opportunities and, indeed, enlarged their slice in the global market share over the Internet. But knowing the share of their competitors or monitoring them as such was not represented in the case of Participant D, who commented, "I do not know … all what I know is that I make better sales than in the past and they (competitors) might be too."

Rationalizing EC Adoption in NZ SMEs

Except for Participants A and D, none of the SMEs pointed to international opportunities. Thus, providing international opportunities to NZ SMEs would assist them in combating the geographical isolation and the time difference that separates NZ from the rest of the world. On the other hand, the same findings point to another perspective. The small market scope and potential of the local NZ market (e.g., small population 3.8M, scattered major cities dominated by low-income families1) may not motivate many local SMEs to embrace EC. Interestingly, most of the participants in the FG envisaged utilizing EC more strategically in their businesses in order to gain a more strategic edge over their competitors in the near future. On the other hand, this perspective showed the weakness of their current EC initiatives.

External Support from Technology Vendors

Approaches in Developing EC in NZ SMEs

Participant D considered itself lucky, since many university graduates and students surrounded their business and helped them to create their Web site at a very low cost. Participant A hosts its own Web site on its own local server. It was lucky, as its ISP turned out to be a neighbor, and all that it took for Participant A to connect to the Internet was a cable from its building to the ISP. Although such features appeared to encourage adoption among Participants A and D, they were concerned, as it could suggest that the EC initiatives of both participants were circumstantial. If IT students did not surround the business of Participant D, it could be argued that Participant D would not have progressed to this level with its Web site. If the ISP were not a neighbor to Participant A, it could be argued that Participant A might not have insourced its Web server. Such approaches have been criticized by EC research in SMEs as being unprofessional in having strategic EC initiatives (Walczuck, Braven & Lundgren, 2000).

In discussing the experiences of the participants with technology vendors and consultants, Participant A indicated that he faced a conflict with his Web site. "We had a Web site produced professionally and we really did not like it in terms of the appearance and the designer did not want to change it … in the end we did it ourselves from scratch!" Except for Participant D, all the participants retained negative perceptions about technology vendors and consultants in NZ. Participant F endorsed the same points raised by Participant E in terms of the high services costs charged by technology vendors and raised suspicions about their capability to solve problems, and he perceived the same negative perceptions about Web developers.

Pressure from Suppliers and Buyers

When the participants were requested to comment on the impact of their buyers on their adoption decision of EC, they all indicated that their buyers would influence their adoption decision positively and significantly. It is their customers that drive their businesses. Participant A commented, "All

our overseas buyers communicate with us through email only … it's essential, fast and cheap and its great. … While in NZ most of our clients are farmers and some of them communicate with us by email." As for the impact of suppliers on their adoption of EC, most of the participants indicated that their suppliers have no effect on their adoption decision.

CEO Innovativeness

When the participants were requested to comment on the innovative role of the CEO on EC adoption, they all indicated that in small businesses, the CEO is the main person behind almost if not all of the different initiatives in the company.

When the participants were requested to comment on their personal experience in adopting EC, Participant F commented, "The CEO actively engaged in the conversation of the subject, … came up with ideas of his own and sought feedback." On the other hand, the participants pointed to other aspects of the CEO which could impede adoption. The participants indicated that factors such as fear of technology and an older CEO might resist change and vote against the adoption of EC and, hence, negatively affect the adoption decision. Participant A commented, "I think familiarity with technology or fear from technology is one aspect … possibly age, younger manager is probably more ready to adopt technology … but not in our case (laughing)."

CEO Involvement

The participants indicated that in small businesses, the CEO not only is involved in the adoption decision but also in the whole EC project (e.g., selecting suppliers, supervising the project). His role is vital in the small business, and he or she may not be necessarily involved in every aspect of the EC project (as pointed out by Participant F), but he or she is there in vital stages.

DISCUSSION AND CONCLUSION

Adopting Simple or Sophisticated EC

This research proposed an EC adoption model and attempted to investigate its importance using an FG made up of 6 participants representing 6 SMEs in NZ. The FG research provided rich insights and unveiled intertwined and sometimes conflicting views among the participants about the different proposed determinants of EC adoption in this research. Confirming the importance or triviality of these determinants was based on the participants' unanimous consensus about the impact of these factors on their adoption decision of EC. In comparison with other methodologies, this consensus among the participants in the FG pointed to the uniqueness and the importance of the FG methodology. This consensus has increased further the validity of the research results.

According to the previous research analysis, Table 6 summarizes the views of the participants alongside the low and the envisaged EC initiatives with respect to the different factors in the research model. As can be seen from the last column in Table 6, both the technological innovation theories and the EC research were used to substantiate or refute the research findings.

Weak EC Phenomenon in SMEs in NZ

The FG results (Table 6) showed two main perspectives pertaining to EC adoption in SMEs in the FG session. First, at the low levels of EC adoption and use, none of the challenging factors, such as cost and compatibility, seemed to impede EC adoption in the FG. On the other hand, none of the suggested drivers, such as relative advantage, pressure from suppliers, buyers, and competitors, appeared to encourage adoption. These findings were supported by research studies, as shown in

Table 6. However, these findings seemed to contradict some of the findings in recent EC research in SMEs (Table 1), which found that most of the factors influence EC adoption significantly and positively. Such differences across the literature and the research findings suggested the uniqueness of the adoption phenomenon in SMEs in NZ in that such limited significance led to a conclusion that EC adoption and use in SMEs in the FG were not that extensive as such and that such initiatives did not exceed the adoption of simple e-mail and Web sites. Most of the SMEs called their Web sites passive (Web pages). This is one significant finding in this research, and future research should consider investigating different forms of Web sites at different sophistication levels (e.g., information-based, transaction-based, end-to-end services, etc.).

The exception was Participant D, who sold standard products and collected money online from international clients interested in buying videocassettes and CDs about NZ scenery and tourist places. Participant A sold a lot of its products in overseas markets and, hence, opted to have a detailed and rich information-based Web site in order to encourage overseas clients to do business with him. This driver has motivated Participant A to add more functionalities to his Web site (i.e., software downloads), but that did not include the online transaction feature like Participant D.

Finally, a significant finding in this research was the emergence of the envisaged advanced and futuristic EC initiatives (e.g., interactive Web sites). Most of the participants kept relating their responses to these anticipated initiatives in the future (Table 6). It was at the envisaged advanced EC initiatives that the participants stressed the importance of EC to their businesses and the significance of the different factors on their adoption decision of EC. At that level of sophistication, the participants emphasized cost and compatibility as major deterrents. It was clear that all the participants retained positive

Table 6. The views of the different participants about EC adoption factors

Sl./No.	Context	Influence EC adoption (+: positively), (-: negatively), (I: irrelevant)	EC research that supports the research findings/argument
1	**Technological context**		
a	Relative advantage: - Current low EC initiatives - Envisaged high EC initiatives	(+) (+); Could be highly significant	Not significant advantages (Poon & Swatman, 1997, 1998, 1999a; Walczuch et al., 2000)
b	Cost: - Current low EC initiatives - Envisioned high EC initiatives	(-); But not significant as such (-); Could be highly significant	No significant costs (Poon & Swatman, 1998; Walczuch et al., 2000)
c	Compatibility: - Current low EC initiatives - Envisioned high EC initiatives	(+); But not significant as such (-); Could be highly significant	Significant incompatibilities (Teo et al., 1998; Thong, 1999 ; Walczuch et al., 2000)
2	**Organisational context**		
a	Information Intensity - Current low EC initiatives - Envisioned high EC initiatives	(+); But not significant as such (+); Could be highly significant	Not significant (Teo et al., 1998; Thong & Yap, 1995, 1996)
3	**Environmental context**		
a	Buyers' pressure Suppliers' pressure	(+) (I)	Not significant (Premkumar & Roberts, 1999)
b	Competitors: - Current low EC initiatives - Envisioned high EC initiatives	(+); But not significant as such (+); Could be highly significant	Not significant (Teo et al., 1998; Thong, 1999; Thong & Yap, 1995,1996)
c	Support from technology vendors: - Current low EC initiatives - Envisioned high EC initiatives	(-); Important (-); Could be highly significant	Not significant (Delone, 1988; Premkumar & Roberts, 1999; Raymond, 1985)
4	**Individual context**		
a	Manager's innovativeness	(+)	Significant (Thong, 1999; Thong & Yap, 1995, 1996)
b	Manager's involvement	(+)	Important Poon and Swatman (1997, 1998, 1999a)

views and enthusiasm about EC advantages and opportunities in the long term and pointed to the strategic importance of being in the EC field earlier on in order not to be left out when EC becomes ubiquitous in the future.

Theoretical Significance and Implications

It was observed that the research findings across the factors supported in part the views of the EC literature (Tables 1 and 6). For example, research found that barriers concerning the adaptation of business processes were hardly expressed among adopters and non-adopters of EC in SMEs (Walczuch et al., 2000), where most of the SMEs use EC on an experimental level and are not concerned with process adaptation. Poon and Swatman (1997, 1998, 1999a) and Walczuch, et al. (2000) observed that although the relative advantage factor was important to the adoption decision of EC, the reported advantages by SMEs were mere perceptions and intangible benefits (e.g., online presence/brochure, e-mail communications). Cost was indicated as an unimportant factor to the adoption decision of simple EC initiatives in this research, and the literature supported the same. Information intensity of products, pressure from suppliers and buyers, and competition were highlighted by this research and the literature as unimportant determinants of EC adoption.

However, two observations were made from Table 6:

1. **Compatibility:** Unlike the literature view (Teo et al., 1998; Thong, 1999; Walczuch et al., 2000), it was observed that the participants in the FG indicated that EC was compatible with them, which supported most of the research in Table 1. However, the participants envisaged that this factor could play a negative role in the future, when they attempt to adopt advanced EC initiatives.
2. **Support:** Support from technology vendors seemed to impede the adoption decision of EC in SMEs in NZ.

The research findings and the previous observations may reveal key cultural perspectives pertaining to the adoption culture of EC in SMEs in NZ. For example, as opposed to the literature, NZ SMEs viewed EC as compatible with them. The negative effect of technology vendors on EC adoption needs to be resolved in order for EC to succeed in NZ SMEs.

Crossing the EC Chasm: Implications for Practice

The main issue that this research attempted to address during the FG sessions was to understand the reluctance of the participating SMEs from moving to the interactive EC initiatives. This has been answered in part in the aforementioned product/industry specifics and the uniqueness of the NZ perspective. However, the participants suggested the existence of a divide between their current simple EC initiatives and the envisaged sophisticated ones. They highlighted this divide as risky and as a grey area and stressed the need for help from experts in the field to show them how to cross this EC divide. Even Participant D stressed this perspective as well. All the participants stressed that at the advanced levels of EC, most of the benefits as well as the risks would challenge their EC initiatives. Factors such as cost, compatibility, competition, technology vendors, suppliers, and buyers could play a crucial role in the success of such advanced initiatives (Table 6). However, at the current stage, most of the participants were not willing to progress any further in the direction of advancing their EC initiatives. The uniqueness of NZ SMEs stressed the need for not blaming the SMEs for being reluctant to move a head with their EC initiatives.

Accordingly, it is suggested that the following implications arising from this research could be of importance to SMEs, professionals, researchers, and policymakers in SMEs in NZ and elsewhere:

1. Findings from cases A and D highlighted the importance of providing international opportunities to SMEs in order to increase their chances to adopt EC. Thus, increasing the awareness of SMEs about international EC opportunities and business models could further increase the chances for adopting EC.

2.   The adoption decision could be encouraged further, if the SME's awareness about EC opportunities (as a technology and as a business enabler) were enhanced. Thus, promoting EC opportunities and knowledge not just to online businesses but also to brick-and-mortar SMEs as a vehicle for supplementing the selling of physical products and services could further increase the chances for EC success in SMEs.

3.   A tacit argument here contends that EC might not be the magical solutions for many of the SMEs, and hence, rationalizing EC adoption criteria among the SMEs was emphasized in this research. This assertion points to the uniqueness of the NZ SME's context (e.g., geographical isolation, time differences with most of the northern hemisphere, and small market scope dominated by low-income families. However, this should not prevent NZ SMEs from exploring EC opportunities first before making their final decision whether to accept or to reject EC. According to Rogers (1995), reaching this stage of appraising the appropriateness of the technological innovation to the organization's business represented an innovative approach, even if the potential adopter decided not to adopt the innovation eventually.

4.   There was some evidence to suggest that the attitude toward EC among some of the participants was not critical (i.e., lazy to consider EC). Such a perspective led to a conclusion that SMEs would adopt EC minimally and to a level where they would not endanger their scant resources (time and money) on perceived risky advanced EC initiatives. SMEs that belonged to this category were not willing to expedite their EC learning curves and to move to advanced EC initiatives. Therefore, most of the initiatives of the participants were initial, not strategic, and not costly.

5.   Deepening our understanding about product specifics, as highlighted in this research, could lead to more insights pertaining to the diffusion and the success of EC across various industries. Another issue discussed in this research was the EC business models of participating SMEs (B2B and B2C). Some of the appropriate EC technologies for B2B-type interrelationships, such as extranet, EDI, XML, and ERP, were not represented in the SMEs in this research. This finding further confirmed the laggardness of the B2B SMEs (at least in adopting EC). Expanding on these issues by increasing the number of participating SMEs (adopting different EC) in any future FG could assist in identifying more accurate EC adoption patterns across the different SMEs, maybe at the national level.

6.   An interesting insight in this research was represented by the emergence of the participants' views concerning the envisaged EC initiatives in the future. These views could help researchers, professionals, and policymakers to help low-adopting SMEs to move from their current positions to the envisaged ones by addressing the deterrents and motivators in this research. However, such perceptions concerning the envisaged EC initiatives need to be substantiated further. This task could be achieved by any future research which focuses on SMEs that have adopted advanced EC initiatives.

Finally, providing a comprehensive regulatory framework by the government and perhaps by other interested parties in EC in general and in NZ SMEs specifically that could govern and address the different deterrents and motivators in this research (e.g., security, privacy, standards, online practices, legal issues, taxation, payments, copyright, social wellfarism, etc.) could assist the SMEs to bridge this electronic divide between them and EC. Introducing and exploring the impact of other macro and micro forces which could influence EC adoption in SMEs could yield more insights pertaining to EC adoption in SMEs.

Personas of EC Adoption

In conclusion, this research introduced the following framework (Figure 1) to summarize the main issues found in this research. At the low EC initiatives, the participants reported little benefits from their limited initiatives. The participants pointed to their Web site initiatives as being simple passive Web sites and did not exceed the online brochureware presence (not interactive). The participants also highlighted the advanced EC initiatives. Accordingly, dividing the Web site initiatives into low (Web pages) and advanced (interactive Web sites) is quite logical in this research. The views of the participants alongside the passive and the envisaged interactive EC initiatives were shown in Figure 1. The reported impediments and accelerators were shown as well in the middle of Figure 1. The reported EC divide is represented in Figure 1 as a phase of transformation and innovativeness. The transformation phase was needed to bridge the impediments shown in Figure 1. The participants noted the importance of receiving help from experts in the field in order to bridge this divide. The emphasis in this phase was on reaching a level where the SME's business could drive the EC technology, not the opposite. The EC initiatives of most of the participants (passive) were driven by technology only, and hence, they were not integrated with internal processes and systems in place in SMEs. These findings seemed to support earlier research that found that barriers concerning the adaptation of business processes were hardly expressed among adopters and non-adopters of the Internet in SMEs (Walczuch et al., 2000), where most of the SMEs use EC on an experimental level and are not concerned with process adaptation. Of course, bridging this divide

requires an innovative CEO in order to elevate the business to that level of sophistication in EC. According to Figure 1, several personas of EC adoption were suggested:

1. **Early Innovators:** Some of the participants (e.g., Participant D) would grasp the EC learning curve faster than others, driven mostly by aspects pertaining to their products and to international opportunities (or if their products could attract high national demand) and to businesses that emerged purely from the Internet side. Such aspects could provide the sufficient motivation for these SMEs to progress rapidly with their EC initiatives and to catch up with the EC learning curve more quickly. The technological innovation literature indicated that firms for whom an innovation is most profitable become early adopters (Davies, 1979). In order to capture such an opportunity would require an alert and innovative manager. Innovation champions inside the adopting firm (i.e., CEO) would increase the chances of adoption earlier on (Attewell, 1992). The straight line means here a faster adoption decision (not a linear relationship)

2. **Innovators:** Other participants who do not enjoy all these motivating aspects (e.g., Participant A) highlighted in point (1), still were considered innovators but would take a slower path in adopting EC and in catching up with the EC learning curve. SMEs who realized that EC was not advantageous to them (e.g., Participant F) ultimately may opt to not adopt it.

3. **Laggards:** SMEs with little interest (uncritical) in EC may take a longer learning curve in order to further their EC initiatives.

4. Finally, SMEs who realize that EC is not advantageous to them (e.g., Participant F) ultimately may opt to not adopt it.

Limitations and Future Research

Including more participants from SMEs in New Zealand in any future research could further endorse the previously suggested personas. It is important to expand on the envisaged advanced EC initiatives, which is emphasized as a limitation in this research. This research had one participant (D) that could represent this level of advanced EC initiatives. However, Participant D was criticized for not using professional expertise in developing its Web site. Participant D admitted this and emphasized the need for experts to show him how to further expand his EC initiative. It seems that this participant was reluctant to spend

further resources on such expensive experts and opted to resort to students and cheaper recent graduates. Future focus group research could consider introducing more participants from the envisaged high EC initiatives and investigating their responses with respect to these perceptions. This is the scope of the next phase of this research. Another important issue to consider and address is whether technology vendors could provide adequate EC services to SMEs. The participants in this research already have questioned their capabilities.

This research introduced important determinants of EC adoption in SMEs in New Zealand and provided rich descriptions of accelerators

Figure 1. An EC-progression path for SMEs

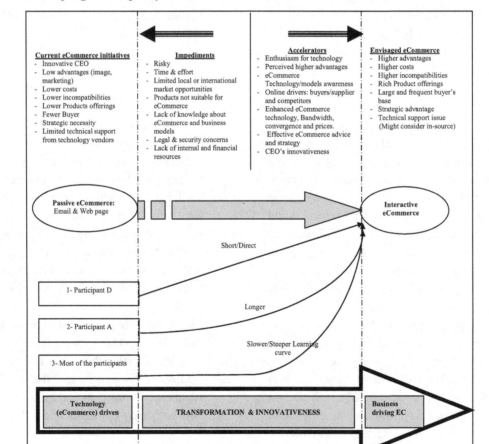

and impediments to the adoption decision of EC. The research also pointed to future research. Thus, addressing these factors by researchers, professionals, and policymakers alongside the two adoption perspectives previously discussed could contribute significantly to the success of EC in SMEs in New Zealand and elsewhere. Although obtaining data from 6 participants was viewed as acceptable by the focus group literature, concluding the most significant factors on EC adoption was not possible in this research. Undertaking more focus groups or a large survey could introduce more generalizable results. This research pointed to other limitations and stressed the need for more research in order to address these limitations.

REFERENCES

Aaker, D., Kumar, V., & Day, G. (1998). *Marketing research* (6th ed.). New York: John Wiley & Sons.

Abell, W., & Black, S. (1997). *Business use of the Internet in New Zealand: A follow-up study.* Retrieved August 8, 2000, from http://www.scu.edu.au/ausweb96/business/abell/paper.htm

Abell, W., & Lim, L. (1996). *Business use of the Internet in New Zealand: An exploratory study.* Retrieved August 8, 2000, from http://www.scu.edu.au/ausweb96/business/abell/paper.htm

Attwell, P. (1992). Technology diffusion and organisational learning: The case of business computing. *Organisational Science, 3*(1), 1-19.

Beatty, R.C., Shim, J.P., & Jones, M.C. (2001). Factors influencing corporate Web site adoption: A time-based assessment. *Information & Management, 38*, 337-354.

Blackburn, R., & Stokes, D. (2000). Breaking down the barriers: Using focus groups to research small and medium sized enterprises. *International Small Business Journal, 19*(1), 44-67.

Blili, S., & Raymond, L. (1993). Information technology: Threats and opportunities for small and medium-sized enterprises. *International Journal of Information Management, 13*, 439-448.

Bloor, M., Frankland, J., Thomas, M., & Robson, K. (2001). *Focus groups in social research.* London: Sage Publications.

Cameron, A., & Massey, C. (1999). *Small and medium sized enterprises: A New Zealand perspective.* Auckland: Addison Wesley Longman New Zealand.

Chang, M.K., & Cheung, W. (2001). Determinants of the intention to use Internet/WWW at work: A confirmatory study. *Information & Management, 39*, 1-14.

Chapple, I. (2002, August 14). Small firms drag feet with Internet. *The New Zealand Herald.* Retrieved August 14, 2002, from http://www.nzherald.co.nz/storyprint.cfm?stotyID=2347435

Chwelos, P., Benbasat, I., & Dexter, A. (2001). Research report: Empirical test of an EDI adoption model. *Information Systems Research, 12*(3), 304-321.

Clarke, R. (1999a). *Appropriate research methods for electronic commerce.* Retrieved March 16, 2000, from http://www.anu.edu.au/people/Roger.Clarke/ResMeth.html

Clarke, R. (1999b). Focus groups. Retrieved July 25, 2002, from http://www.xamax.com.au/Res/FocusGrps.html

Clarke, R. (2001). *If eBusiness is different then so is research in eBusiness.* Retrieved July 25, 2002, from http://www.anu.edu.au/people/Roger.Clarke/EC/EBR0106.html

Cragg, P., & King, M. (1992). Information systems sophistication and financial performance of small engineering firms. *European Journal of Information Systems, 1*(6), 417-426.

Davies, S. (1979). *The diffusion of process innovations*. Cambridge: Cambridge University Press.

Deloitte Touche Tohmatsu. (2000). *Deloitte e-business survey: Insights and issues facing New Zealand business*. Retrieved August 8, 2000, from http://www.deloitte.co.nz/images/acrobat/survey.pdf

Doolin, B., Mcleod, L., McQueen, B., & Watton, M. (2003). Internet strategies for establishing retailers: Four New Zealand case studies. *Journal of Information Technology Cases and Applications, 5*(4), 3-19.

Drew, S. (2003). Strategic use of e-commerce by SMEs in the east of England. *European Management Journal, 21*(1), 79.

Grandon, E., & Pearson, J.M. (2004). E-commerce adoption: Perceptions of managers/owners of small and medium sized firms in Chile. *Communications of the Association for Information Systems, 13*, 81-102.

Iacovou, C., Benbasat, I., & Dexter, A. (1995, December). Electronic data interchange and small organisations: Adoption and impact of technology. *MIS Quarterly*, 465-485.

Igbaria, M., Zinatelli, N., & Cavaye, A. (1998). Analysis of information technology success in small firms in New Zealand. *International Journal of Information Management, 18*(2), 103-119.

Jansen, A. (1998). Technology diffusion and adoption in small, rural firms. In T. Larsen, & E. McGuire (Eds.), *Information systems innovation and diffusion: Issues and directions* (pp. 345-372). Hershey, PA: Idea Group Publishing.

Kuan, K., & Chau, P. (2001). A perception-based model of EDI adoption in small businesses using technology-organization-environment framework. *Information & Management, 38*, 507-521.

Kula, V., & Tatoglu, E. (2003). An exploratory study of Internet adoption by SMEs in an emerging market economy. *European Business Review, 15*(5), 324-333.

Levy, M., Powell, P., & Yetton, P. (1998). SMEs and the gains from IS: From cost reduction to value added. *IFIP WG8.2 and WG8.6 Joint Working Conference on Information Systems: Current Issues and Future Changes*, Helsinki, Finland. Retrieved June 5, 2000, from http://www.bi.no/dep2/infomgt/wg82-86/proceedings/Table-of-contents.htm

Liu, C., & Arnett, P. (2000). Exploring the factors associated with Web sites success in the context of electronic commerce. *Information and Management, 38*, 23-33.

Macgregor, R., & Vrazlaic, L. (2004). Don't be an island. *Computerworld*. Retrieved March 30, 2004, from http://www.compuetworld.com.au/pp.php?id=588458220&taxid=14

Mehrtens, J., Cragg, P., & Mills, A. (2001). A model of Internet adoption by SMEs. *Information & Management, 39*, 165-176.

Mirchandani, A.A., & Motwani, J. (2001, Spring). Understanding small business electronic commerce adoption: An empirical analysis. *Journal of Computer Information Systems*, 70-73.

MOED (Ministry of Economic Development). (2000a). *SMEs in New Zealand: Structure and dynamics, firm capability team, update report*. Retrieved May 5, 2000, from http://www.MOED.govt.nz/gbl/bus_dev/smes2/index.html#TopOfPage

MOED (Ministry of Economic Development). (2000b). *Electronic commerce in New Zealand: A survey of business use of the Internet information technology*. Policy Group Competition and

Enterprise branch. Retrieved May 16, 2001, from http://www.ecommerce.govt.nz/ecat/resources/index.html

Moore, G., & Benbasat, I. (1991). Development of an instrument to measure the perceptions of adopting an information technology innovation. *Information Systems Research, 2*(3), 192-221.

Moore, G., & Benbasat, I. (1996). Integrating diffusion of innovations and theory of reasoned action models to predict utilisation of information technology by end-users. In K. Kautz, & J. Pries-Heje (Eds.), *Diffusion and adoption of information technology* (pp. 132-146). London: Chapman & Hall.

Morgan, L. (1997). *Focus groups as qualitative research* (2nd ed.). Thousand Oaks, CA: Sage Publications.

Morgan, L. (1998). *The focus group guidebook: Focus group kit volume 1.* Thousand Oaks, CA: Sage Publications.

NZStat (Statitics New Zealand). (1999, March). *Income of persons (final): Year ended March 1999.* Retrieved November 9, 2002, from http://www.stats.govt.nz

NZStat (Statitics New Zealand). (2001). *A report on the Post-Enumeration Survey 2001.* Retrieved November 9, 2002, from http://www.stats.govt.nz/domino/external/pasfull/

Peet, S., Brindley, C., & Ritchie, B. (2002). The European Commission and SME support mechanisms for e-business. *European Business Review, 14*(5), 335-341.

Poon, S. (1999). Small business and Internet commerce: What are the lessons learned? In F. Sudweeks, & C. Romm (Eds.), *Doing business on the Internet: Opportunities and pitfalls* (pp. 113-124). London: Springer-Verlag.

Poon, S. (2000). Business environment and Internet commerce benefits—A small business

perspective. *European Journal of Information Systems, 9*, 72-81.

Poon, S., & Swatman, P. (1995). The Internet for small businesses: An enabling infrastructure for competitiveness. Retrieved June 27, 2000, from http://inet.nttam.com

Poon, S., & Swatman, P. (1997) Internet-based small business communication. *International Journal of Electronic Commerce, 7*(2), 5-21.

Poon, S., & Swatman, P. (1998) A combined-method study of small business Internet commerce. *International Journal of Electronic Commerce, 2*(3), 31-46.

Poon, S., & Swatman, P. (1999a). An exploratory study of small business Internet commerce issues. *Information & Management, 35*, 9-18.

Poon, S., & Swatman, P. (1999b). A longitudinal study of expectations in small business Internet commerce. *International Journal of Electronic Commerce, 3*(3), 21-33.

Premkumar, G., & Roberts, M. (1999). Adoption of new information technologies in rural small businesses. *The International Journal of Management Science (OMEGA), 27*, 467-484.

PWHC (PriceWaterhouseCoopers). (1999). *SME electronic commerce study* (TEL05/97T). Retrieved April 10, 2000, from http://apec.pwcglobal.com/sme.html

Reimenschneider, C., & Mykytyn, P. (2000). What small business executives learned about managing information technology. *Information & Management, 37*, 257-269.

Rogers, E. (1983). *Diffusion of innovation.* New York: The Free Press.

Rogers, E. (1995). *Diffusion of innovation.* New York: The Free Press.

Santarelli, E., & D'Altri, S. (2003). The diffusion of e-commerce among SMEs: Theoretical implications and empirical evidence. *Small Business Economics, 21*(3), 273.

Soh, P., Yap, S., & Raman, S. (1992). Impact of consultants on computerisation success in small business. *Information & Management, 22*, 309-313.

Stewart , D., & Shamdasani, P. (1990). *Focus groups: Theory and practice.* Newbury Park, CA: Sage Publications.

Swanson, E.B. (1994). Information systems innovation among organisations. *Management Science, 40*(9), 1069-1092.

Teo, T., Tan, M., & Buk, W. (1998). A contingency model of Internet adoption in Singapore. *International Journal of Electronic Commerce, 2*(2), 95-118.

Thong, J. (1999). An integrated model of information systems adoption in small business. *Journal of Management Information Systems, 15*(4), 187-214.

Thong, J., & Yap, C. (1995). CEO characteristics, organisational, characteristics and information technology adoption in small business. *Omega, International Journal of Management Sciences, 23(*4), 429-442.

Thong, J., & Yap, C. (1996). Information technology adoption by small business: An empirical study. In K. Kautz, & J. Pries-Heje (Eds.), *Dif-*

fusion and adoption of information technology (pp. 160-175). London: Chapman & Hall.

Thong, J., Yap, S., & Raman, K. (1994). Engagement of external expertise in information systems implementation. *Journal of Management Information Systems, 11*(2), 209.

Tornatzky, L., & Klein, K. (1982). Innovation characteristics and innovation adoption implementation: A meta-analysis of findings. *IEEE Transactions on Engineering Management, 29*(11), 28-45.

Walczuch, R., Braven, G., & Lundgren, H. (2000). Internet adoption: Barriers for small firms in the Netherlands. *European Management Journal, 18*(5), 561-572.

Yin, R. (1994). *Case study research design and methods.* Thousand Oaks, CA: Sage Publications.

Zhu, K., Kraemer, K., & Xu, S. (2003). Electronic business adoption by European firms: A cross-country assessment of the facilitators and inhibitors. *European Journal of Information Systems, 12*(4), 251.

ENDNOTE

[1]   Average taxable income is $NZ 24,251 (year ending 1999) (NZStat, 1999).

This work was previously published in the Journal of Electronic Commerce in Organizations, Vol. 4, Issue 3, edited by M. Khosrow-Pour, pp. 18-45, copyright 2006 by IGI Publishing, formerly known as Idea Group Publishing (an imprint of IGI Global).

Chapter XVII
Motivators for IOS Adoption in Denmark

Helle Zinner Henriksen
Copenhagen Business School, Denmark

ABSTRACT

Organizational adoption of innovations does not always follow easily comprehendible patterns. This is often the case with interorganizational information systems (IOS), where adoption is dependent on attributes related both to the organization and to its environment. The present study operationalizes the Tornatzky and Fleischer (1990) model for organizational adoption in order to investigate reasons for adoption and non-adoption among businesses in the Danish steel and machinery industry. This particular industry segment had been subject to massive information campaigns focusing on the benefits of IOS in the form of EDI from business associations. The study suggests that environmental and organizational attributes rather than technological attributes are the main determining forces for adoption of EDI.

INTRODUCTION

Why do some organizations adopt a technological innovation that is announced to yield both operational and strategic benefits, while others hesitate or decide not to adopt? This question is highly relevant, especially in the case of interorganizational information systems (IOS), due to the great importance of IOS in transforming industries, value chains, and markets. Surprisingly, few Danish organizations have adopted IOS, in spite

of their relevant technical capabilities and their high degree of IT usage. From this perspective, the reluctance to adopt IOS appears to be even more irrational and incomprehensible. The phenomenon of organizations lagging behind adoption of IT, regardless of their capabilities to do so, is well known (Harrison, Mykytyn, & Riemenschneider, 1997). What is missing are sensible explanations for this situation.

Small companies dominate the Danish business sectors. About two-thirds of the approximately 50,000 companies within the industrial sector has less than 10 employees. National and international industry and trade associations have created a number of awareness campaigns and have focused on creating advantageous conditions for the small and medium-sized enterprises (SMEs) to enable them to adopt IT, especially IOS such as EDI. The aims of these campaigns were to assist the companies in reducing or eliminating work routines and to support them in a market characterized by increased competition. The technological development has led to an increase in quality and functionality and a decrease in cost of hardware and software (Harrison et al., 1997). The traditional technological barriers for organizational adoption of IOS, therefore, might not play the same dominant role as it did earlier. This new situation makes it highly relevant to examine explanatory factors for IOS adoption among SMEs, which traditionally have relatively fewer resources allocated to IS acquisitions than larger companies (Lai & Guynes, 1997).

In order to find an explanation for the puzzling situation of the limited IOS adoption and diffusion among Danish SMEs, a survey was conducted. The survey addressed SMEs in the Danish steel and machinery industry. The main reason for choosing this particular sector was the fact that business associations had targeted information campaigns toward this sector prior to the inception of the study.

ADOPTION OF INNOVATIONS

Adoption can be viewed as having or not having an innovation (Tornatzky & Fleischer, 1990), or it can be viewed as using the innovation vs. not having it (Rogers, 1995). Adoption, according to Rogers (1995), is "a decision to make full use of an innovation as the best course of action available and rejection is a decision not to adopt an innovation." Rogers' (1995) definition does not distinguish between adoption and use of the innovation. In this article, the core understanding of the term adoption is having vs. not having (Tornatzky & Fleischer, 1990) rather than not having vs. using (Rogers, 1995). Consequently, measures related to effects of adoption of the innovation are not considered. The important point relevant to this study is that some dividing line is crossed when the adopters decide to invest resources necessary to accommodate the effort to change (Kwon & Zmud, 1987).

Tornatzky and Fleischer (1990) suggested that three explanatory contexts influence the process by which innovations are adopted in organizations. These three contexts are the organizational

Figure 1. The Tornatzky and Fleischer (1990) model for adoption

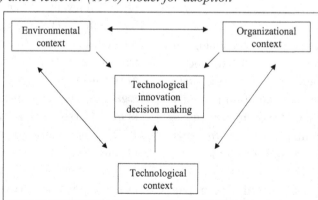

context, the environmental context, and the technological context.

The three explanatory contexts depicted in Figure 1 were operationalized for this study of the Danish steel and machinery industry.

OPERATIONALIZATION OF THE RESEARCH MODEL

In this study, the adoption-decision variables in relation to IOS adoption are related mainly to secondary innovation attributes. Downs and Mohr (1976) distinguished between primary and secondary innovation attributes. Primary attributes are considered to be invariant across settings and organizations (e.g., company size), which can be measured fairly objectively. Secondary attributes are based on subjective characteristics; for example, complexity and relative advantage. The perception of secondary attributes is assumed to be influenced by characteristics of both the particular setting as well as individuals involved in the adoption of an innovation. The measures applied in the present survey are subjective in the sense that they are perceived and interpreted by the responder.

The Organizational Context

Tornatzky and Fleischer (1990) suggest that an organization provides a rich source of formal and informal structures and processes that either constrain or facilitate the adoption of innovations. Generally, profitability and improved performance have been found to be motivators for adoption of IS (Attewell, 1992). Performance improvements (Clark & Stoddard, 1996), accurate exchange of business information (Srinivasan, Kekre, & Mukhopadhyay, 1994), and benefits related to integration of EDI (Massetti & Zmud, 1996; Premkumar, Ramamurthy, & Nilakanta, 1994) are among the themes that have been studied in the

IS literature. Direct savings are rarely reported in IOS studies (Cox & Ghoneim 1996; O'Callaghan & Turner, 1995). Indirect savings, on the other hand, often are explored. These savings can be related to reduction in the workforce due to less rekeying of data and a decreased need for manual storing of documents, lower inventory costs, and shortened duration of transactions (O'Callaghan & Turner, 1995). The following six propositions were operationalized for the organizational context.

The first proposition examines how expected savings have influenced the motivation to adopt IOS.

Proposition O1. *Prospects of future savings motivate IOS adoption.*

Tornatzky and Fleischer (1990) focus on human resources in relation to the organizational context. IS studies have included issues such as adequate education (Kurnia & Johnston, 2000) and employees' IS knowledge (Thong, 1999). The EDI literature has focused to a limited extent on issues related to work environment and human resources. Swatman and Swatman (1992) suggest that adoption of EDI may lead to organizational restructuring involving staff retraining due to changing work functions. Especially training of employees has been found to be one of the major determinants for SMEs gaining benefits from EDI adoption (O'Callaghan & Turner, 1995; Raymond & Bergeron, 1996). Proposition O2 focuses on the perception that adoption of IOS will create better work conditions for employees, which will lead to more independent job functions for employees.

Proposition O2. *The assumption that IOS will create a better work environment motivates adoption.*

Proposition O3 focuses on re-training due to changes in staff functions, as described by Swatman and Swatman (1992).

Proposition O3. *The assumption that IOS will benefit from the development and utilization of human resources motivates adoption.*

Proposition O4 focuses on the often-claimed benefit of EDI related to the elimination of redundant rekeying of data and elimination of manual control of data (O'Callaghan & Turner, 1995).

Proposition O4. *The assumption that IOS eliminates trivial work motivates adoption.*

Most IOS adoption studies have focused on commodities and standardized products such as aircraft parts (Choudhury, Hartzel & Konsynski, 1998), hospital supplies (Steinfield, Kraut, & Plummer, 1995), and office supplies (Jelassi & Figon, 1994). Research has especially shown a high level of adoption of EDI in the automotive industry (Tuunainen, 1998) and in the grocery sector (Andersen, Juul, Henriksen, Bjorn-Andersen, & Bunker, 2000). Commodities and standardized products characterize both of these sectors. Even though EDI is useful for exchanging business information, regardless of the item being a commodity or something highly specific, the EDI literature and practice so far have mainly concentrated on commodities. In order to investigate whether or not the type of business activities influences the motivation for EDI adoption, the following proposition was formulated.

Proposition O5. *The decision maker's awareness that the company's business activities are well suited for IOS motivates adoption.*

Iacovou, Benbasat, and Dexter (1995) directly referred to organizational readiness for EDI. The study related organizational readiness to the level of financial and technological resources. Lai and Guynes (1997) referred to employees' positive attitudes to organizational change. One aspect, which has been seen as a factor for organizational readiness for EDI adoption, is related to whether

adopters are EDI initiators or followers (Swatman & Swatman, 1992). Companies that are persuaded or directly forced to adopt EDI are not well prepared for EDI and, consequently, might not immediately, if ever, reap the full benefits of EDI. This led to the formulation of proposition O6.

Proposition O6. *The assumption that companies consider themselves to be well prepared for IOS motivates adoption.*

The Environmental Context

The environmental context is the arena in which the organization conducts its business (Tornatzky & Fleischer, 1990). The environmental context comprises the organization's competitors, its access to resources, and its dealings with government agencies. Three IS studies, which included the environmental context in their survey instrument, focused on competition (Kurnia & Johnston, 2000; Thong, 1999). A number of studies suggests that adoption of EDI could lead to improved competitiveness (Chatfield & Bjorn-Andersen, 1997), new business opportunities (Jelassi & Figon, 1994), and changes in interfirm processes and politics (Lee, Clark, & Tam, 1999). The following five propositions were operationalized for the environmental context. Proposition E1 is related directly to possible improved competitiveness due to IOS adoption.

Proposition E1. *The prospect of improving the company's competitiveness motivates IOS adoption.*

Proposition E2 is related to the strategic alliances between business partners for the purpose of maintaining a competitive edge (Chau & Tam, 1997).

Proposition E2. *The prospect of increasing the company's market share motivates IOS adoption.*

IOS adoption often relates to power and pressure, which relates to the obligation of a firm to adopt an innovation in order to stay on good terms with its customers or suppliers (Hart & Saunders, 1998). Hart and Saunders (1998) explored the different ways to exert power in relation to business partners. They distinguished between persuasive and coercive power. Iacovou, et al. (1995) distinguished between competitive pressures and imposition by trading partners. Bergeron and Raymond (1992) included the benefits from strategic repositioning of the firm due to implementation of EDI in their survey. Pressure related to imposition of business partners (Iacovou et al., 1995) was operationalized in Proposition E3, which is related to the knowledge that EDI is being used among business partners.

Proposition E3. *The knowledge that several business partners already use IOS motivates adoption.*

Proposition E4 is related to a situation in which the company is subject to persuasive power (Hart & Saunders, 1998). The company is not directly forced to adopt IOS, but business partners may take steps, such as informing about IOS benefits and offering assistance in relation to the adoption and implementation process.

Proposition E4. *The fact that IOS has been recommended by others motivates adoption.*

Proposition E5 is related to direct pressure from business partners. Pressure can take different dimensions, ranging from promises to threats (Iacovou et al., 1995). Promises include rewards, such as rebates due to IOS usage, and threats include sanctions, such as suspension of the partnership.

Proposition E5. *The fact that the company is put under pressure to use IOS motivates adoption.*

The Technological Context

The technological context comprises both the internal and external technologies relevant to the firm. It includes current practices and equipment internal to the firm as well as the pool of available technologies external to the firm. Decisions to adopt a technology depend on what is available as well as how the available technology fits the firm's current technology. Tornatzky and Fleischer (1990) call attention to the fact that not all innovations are relevant to all industries. The following four propositions were operationalized for the technological context. Proposition T1 is related to managers' perception of the importance of the technical level of IOS. Instead of specifically investigating issues related to standards, means for transportation, or prospect of integration, this opinion data item was kept in very general terms.

Proposition T1. *A reasonable technical level of IT solutions motivates adoption.*

Proposition T2 is directly related to price. A theoretical reference to T2 is the relative advantage of IOS adoption (Rogers, 1995) or cost-benefit considerations.

Proposition T2. *A reasonable price level of IT solutions motivates adoption.*

None of the reviewed studies concerning adoption of IOS specifically included issues related to the threat of technological marginalization due to reluctance to adopt a technological innovation. The included studies were rich in examples of economic marginalization in the sense that non-adoption, for example, could lead to weakened competitive advantages. The adoption and diffusion theory, on the other hand, is rich in examples related to the issue of technological marginalization (Attewell, 1992; Rogers, 1995).

The first perspective is related to the situation in which the potential adopter is in a neutral position toward the innovation, per se. However, mere knowledge that not having the innovation might exclude the company from being up-front might serve as a motivator for adoption. The threat of being a laggard (Rogers, 1995) with respect to adoption was formulated in Proposition T3.

Proposition T3. *A feeling of being left behind with respect to IOS motivates adoption.*

Proposition T4 is directly related to the fads and fashion phenomenon presented by Abrahamson (1996). Though researchers do not perceive IOS as new and interesting, this might not be the case for practitioners. Innovation is a relative term, which is conditioned by the perception of the potential adopter (Rogers, 1995).

Proposition T4. *The assumption that IOS is new and interesting motivates adoption.*

RESEARCH METHOD

A postal questionnaire was used for collection of survey data for this study. The questionnaire was sent to the management of 917 manufactures and wholesalers in the steel and machinery sector in Denmark. A total of 252 responses were received, out of which 247 were included in the analysis, resulting in a response rate of 27.4%. The response rate was approximately equal to the response rate of other similar studies (Chau, 2001).

The methods of principal components and exploratory factor analysis, which are often used in similar studies, are based on a matrix of Pearson's correlation coefficients, and therefore, data should satisfy the assumptions for these statistical methods (Hatcher & Stepanski, 1994). However, it can be argued that Likert scales are merely manifestations of ordered categories (Siegel & Castellan, 1988), and therefore, the requirement of at least an interval scale for the Pearson correlation coefficient is not met. Based on the previously mentioned considerations, it was decided to use non-parametric methods of analysis for this study. The main objective of the statistical analysis was to uncover the patent priorities of the responders with respect to adoption of IOS. Here, patent priority refers to the manifest, face-value expressions of the responders.

Two preliminary steps were used to identify the factors motivating or demotivating adoption of EDI. First, Fischer's exact two-sided test was applied to identify those items that were strongly related to one of the three levels of adoption: adoption, planning to adopt, and non-adoption. Fischer's exact test was chosen, because many cell counts in the two-by-two tables were relatively small. Second, data were analyzed by applying the technique of graphical models using the DIGRAM software application (Kreiner, 2001). This technique made it possible to analyze the relationships between all the items taken together and the respective levels of adoption. Logistic regression analysis was chosen as the final step in the search for patent priorities. The independent explanatory items for logistic regression analysis

Table 1. Cronbach's coefficient alpha for the three constructs

Context	Adopters	Planners	Non-adopters
Organizational	0.76	0.72	0.82
Environmental	0.70	0.74	0.82
Technological	0.52	0.34	0.49

were the items that were identified either by the two-way tables using Fischer's exact tests and/or through the exploratory analysis using graphical models.

Similar to other adoption studies (Moore & Benbasat, 1991) multi-item indicators were used for the opinion data items concerning the motivation for adoption. Seven-point Likert scales ranging from *fully agree* to *strongly disagree* were used. Due to the limited number of responders, it was necessary to collapse the seven-point scales to binary scales. These binary scales were constructed to reflect agreement and disagreement with the adoption items in question.

If the construct scales are not reliable, it may not make sense to perform additional analyses. An analysis of Cronbach's coefficient alpha was performed, based on the operationalization of the three constructs: organizational context, en-

vironmental context, and technological context given adoption status.

Generally, the lower acceptable limit for summed scales traditionally is considered to be 0.70 (Nunnally, 1978). The constructs for the organizational context and the environmental context showed an acceptable reliability level independent of adoption status (cf. Table 1). On the other hand, the operationalization of the technological context is below the generally acceptable reliability level, independent of adoption status.

Exploratory Analysis of Opinion Data Items Related to the Three Adoption Levels

Based on the results from Fischer's exact test, it was found that six items were strongly related to adoption. Four items were found to be of

Table 2. Opinion data items identified for inclusion in the binary logistic regression

Proposition	Fischer's Exact			Graphical modeling			Items for inclusion		
	A	**P**	**N**	**A**	**P**	**N**	**A**	**P**	**N**
T1		*	*						
T2		**	**					+	+
O1	***		***	←		←	+		+
O5	**		***			←	+		+
O2				←			+		
O3									
O4	**		***				+		+
O6	***		***				+		+
E1		***	***					+	+
E2		***	***	←	←	←	+	+	+
E3	***		***	←		←	+		+
E5									
T3	***						+		
T4				←				+	
E4		**			←	←	+		+

Legend: A = adopter, P = planner, N = non-adopter,
* = p <= 0.050, ** = p <= 0.010, *** = p <= 0.001,
← = p <=0.05, + = item for inclusion in the binary logistic regression analysis.

Table 3. Summary results of the logistic regression analysis given the status indicator

Status	Parameter	Maximum Likelihood Estimates			Odds Ratio Estimates		
		Estimate	Pr > ChiSq		Point estimate	95% Wald Confidence Limits	
Adopter	Intercept	-1.2413	0.0004				
	O6, yes	0.5958	0.0546		3.292	0.977	11.097
	E3, yes	1.1872	0.0008		10.744	2.700	42.747
Planners	Intercept	-1.5351	0.0073				
	E2, yes	1.1998	<.0001		11.019	3.492	34.764
	E4, yes	-1.2237	0.0327		0.087	0.009	0.817
Non-adopters	Intercept	-2.2777	0.0011				
	O6, yes	-1.1409	0.0147		0.102	0.016	0.639
	E2, yes	-1.4475	0.0026		0.055	0.008	0.363
	E3, yes	-1.9272	0.0015		0.021	0.002	0.229

Table 4. Hosmer and Lemeshow Goodness-of-Fit Test

Status	Chi-Square	DF	PR > ChiSq
Adopters	4.3804	2	0.1119
Planners	0.1637	2	0.9214
Non-adopters	1.5645	4	0.8152

importance for planners, and nine items were of importance for non-adopters. The exploratory multivariate analysis suggests that four opinion data items had a causal relationship with adoption. For planners, there were causal relationships with three opinion data items. Finally, for non-adopters, five causal relationships were found.

Binary Logistic Regression Analysis for Adopters, Planners, and Non-Adopters

Binary logistic regression analyses were performed in order to estimate the explanatory power and strength of the adoption motivators summarized in Table 3 for these dependent variables: adopter, planner, and non-adopter. The stepwise forward selection method was selected

for the logistic regression analysis procedures. The level of inclusion and exclusion was set at the 5% level, as recommended by Hosmer and Lemeshow (1989).

Table 4 shows that for adopters, planners, and non-adopters, the Hosmer and Lemeshow (1989) goodness-of-fit tests are all greater than 5%, which supports the fit of the model. For more details concerning the statistical analysis, see Henriksen (2002).

DISCUSSION OF RESULTS

Propositions related to the technological context were not found to influence the motivation for adoption for any of the responders, regardless of the level of adoption. One reason could be that the opinion data items were not well defined. As shown in the Cronbach's coefficient alpha test, the construct of the technological context was not well defined for any of the three adoption levels.

For adopters and non-adopters, the opinion data items related to the organizational context and environmental context were found to explain motivation for IOS adoption or non-adoption. For planners, the opinion data related to the environmental context were found to explain the motivation for IOS adoption. In the following section, a closer look at the significance of each of the explanatory opinion data items for each of the adoption levels are presented.

Factors Motivating Adoption

Two factors were found to motivate IOS adoption. The two propositions—O6: "The assumption that companies considering themselves to be well prepared for IOS are more likely to adopt"; and E3: "The knowledge that several business partners already use IOS motivates adoption"—could not be rejected.

One could argue that proposition O6 ("The assumption that companies considering themselves to be well prepared for IOS are more likely to adopt") from a managerial point of view comprises all of the organizational context opinion items. When a company states that it is well prepared for EDI adoption, the implication is that the remaining organizational context items in some way or another are covered.

Another interpretation supporting the outcome of the analysis is related to the nature of the social system (Rogers, 1995). If the prevailing attitude in the social system is that IOS adoption is the norm, then companies are likely to perceive themselves as being ready for adoption. Finally, the importance of organizational readiness could be a result of the influence from change agents' promotional efforts that through campaigns have informed about the innovation. The importance of proposition O6, according to this interpretation,

is influenced by social processes and communication about the innovation. If this interpretation is accepted, then the knowledge that several business partners already use IOS (proposition E3) supports even more strongly the notion of a social process attitude toward adoption.

Among the environmental context opinion data items, proposition E3 appears to be the most important statement. The awareness that business partners already use IOS induces the potential adopters to perceive adoption as the norm. Another interpretation of the importance of proposition E3 for adopters can be supported by the exponential diffusion curve (Attewell, 1992). Adoption according to this view becomes more and more attractive, when more and more people have adopted the innovation. This is especially the case when interorganizational attributes are related to an innovation, where critical mass is important for benefits to accrue from the investment (Markus, 1987).

One aspect that is important to consider when interpreting the priorities indicated by the adopters is that their responses reflect an ex-post evaluation. The two propositions, O6 and E3, that were found to be statistical significant in the logistic regression analysis are less concrete and of a more general nature than the rest of the propositions comprising the organizational context and the environmental context. Instead of specifically replying that the motivation for adoption was related, for example, to concrete attributes, the motivation is expressed in more general and more vague terms.

Factors Motivating Companies Planning to Adopt IOS

Two factors were found to motivate companies to adopt IOS. Propositions E2 ("The prospect of increasing the company's market share motivates adoption") and E4 ("The fact that IOS has been recommended by others motivates adoption") could not be rejected.

For planners, the determining factors motivating IOS adoption are related solely to the environmental context. Here, it should be noted that planners do not consider recommendations from others to be of great importance. This indicates that recommendations from other businesses and from business associations are of little importance, when businesses decide to adopt IOS. This appears to be contrary to the variables determining adoption defined by Rogers (1995). As mentioned in relation to adopters, the variables related to the nature of the social systems and change agents' promotion efforts were used as a suitable framework for understanding why these particular propositions were relevant to adopters.

One interpretation is that rationality rather than social processes drives the motivation for IOS adoption among the responders that indicated that they plan to adopt. One reason could be that planners, compared to adopters, indicated contemporary adoption preferences contrary to the adopters who expressed an ex-post evaluation of their motivation for adoption. The planners, in contrast to the adopters, indicated more concrete motivation priorities. This suggests that the planners, independent of recommendations from change agents and norms in the social system, consider adoption of IOS to improve the organization's strategic performance, thereby leading to increased market shares.

Factors Causing a Non-Adopting Attitude toward IOS

Three factors were found to cause a non-adopting attitude toward IOS. Propositions O6 ("The assumption that companies considering themselves to be well prepared for IOS are more likely to adopt"), E2 ("The prospect of increasing the company's market share motivates adoption"), and E3 ("The knowledge that several business partners already use IOS motivates adoption") could not be rejected.

The environmental context seemed to be the dominant explanatory factor for responders remaining as non-adopters. However, one opinion data item related to the organizational context also was found to be a significant explanatory factor for non-adopters. Proposition O6 was found to be of major importance for adopters. Non-adopters, on the other hand, stated that they did not consider organizational readiness to be of any importance with respect to IOS adoption. A similar pattern was found in relation to proposition E3. This opinion data item was of major importance for adopters, whereas it had no relevance for non-adopters. However, there might be some logical explanation for this inconsistency of preferences among the two levels of adoption—what makes good sense for adopters and planners does not appear to make sense for non-adopters. Common for all opinion data items for non-adopters was their disagreement with all of these statements. One explanation for non-adopters not finding IOS attractive at all might be related to the attributes of the non-adopting companies included in the analysis sample. The non-adopters generally were small, independent companies. Such companies are believed to have limited power to initiate an IOS partnership, and, most likely, they are allotted the role of an IOS follower. Generally, it is found that followers do not derive the same benefits as initiators (Swatman & Swatman, 1992). Operational and strategic gains from IOS adoption for small companies, therefore, might be limited. This is also the case in relation to the five innovation attributes defined by Rogers (1995). The relative advantage of IOS for small adopters is limited in relation to the efforts required to set up an IOS solution with very few business partners.

In relation to adopters, it was argued that a possible reason for adopters indicating that organizational readiness was a motivator for IOS adoption could be found in the nature of the social system and the change agents' promotion efforts. According to the non-adopters, organizational readiness was not important. One interpretation of this outcome is that non-adopters did not consider themselves to be addressees of the IOS campaigns launched by change agents. Pedagogical intervention (Eckhoff, 1983; Henriksen, 2002), therefore, might be of limited value for companies that postpone or reject adoption of IOS. Additionally, the social system, to which they perceive themselves to belong, may not attach much value to IOS.

The two opinion data items concerning the environmental context, which resulted from the logistic regression analysis for non-adopters, were related to a possible increase of the company's market share due to IOS adoption and the awareness that several business partners were using IOS. Proposition E3 was considered as the mildest form of pressure leading to IOS adoption among the 15 opinion data items. This external community pressure did not influence non-adopters. A rational interpretation might be that non-adopters did not expect to reach a critical mass of business partners using IOS. An interpretation guided by social processes could be that non-adopters simply do not identify themselves with IOS adopters. Therefore, there is no basis for an imitation process. With respect to proposition E2, it could be argued that if the non-adopters thought that IOS adoption was likely to increase their market share, they would probably already have adopted IOS.

To sum up, it looks like the non-adopters think that they can do fine without this innovation. Therefore, they do not agree with or show any sign of enthusiasm with respect to any of the defined motivators for IOS adoption.

CONCLUDING REMARKS

About 16% of the companies in the Danish steel and machinery industry had adopted IOS in the form of EDI at the time of the survey. The national rate of EDI adoption for all industries was about 15% (Henriksen, 2002). Given the claimed strategic and operational advantages companies can derive from IOS adoption, this low level of adoption is difficult to understand. In the reported survey, 15 propositions related to a mix of operational and strategic benefits of IOS were tested, based on data from 247 Danish companies in the steel and machinery industry. The objective of the study was to uncover the patent priorities of the responders. Based on the analysis, it was found that organizational and environmental attributes rather than technological attributes determined IOS adoption in this particular sector. Pressure and organizational readiness were found both to be the primary motivating factors for IOS adoption and also for rejection of the innovation.

One of the lessons learned from the study is that there is a discrepancy in the way an innovation is presented by business associations and the way it is perceived in the business community. The business associations representing the steel and machinery industry communicated the innovation as a means for improving competitive advantage. However, businesses belonging to the categories of planners and non-adopters did not share this viewpoint. Planners did not follow the recommendations of others, but they did view IOS as a competitive tool (e.g., a means for increasing their market share). What is remarkable in this survey is that what made adopters accept the innovation was exactly what influenced non-adopters not to adopt. Non-adopters disagreed with the notion that organizational readiness or pressure would influence their decisions to adopt. For both planners and non-adopters, the opinion data item related to increase of market share was one of the patent priorities. However, non-adopters did not indicate that this would influence their decision to adopt.

It is surprising that the responders did not pay much attention to the technological attributes as promoters or inhibitors of adoption. One reason could be that the awareness campaigns on EDI, after all, have demystified the technological dimension of EDI. Another explanation might be that the technological attributes related to an innovation determine the rate of adoption to a lesser extent than IS researchers normally expect.

REFERENCES

Abrahamson, E. (1996). Management fashion. *The Academy of Management Review, 21*, 254-285.

Andersen, K. V., Juul, N. C., Henriksen, H. Z., Bjorn-Andersen, N., & Bunker, D. (2000). *Business-to-business e-commerce, enterprises facing a turbulent world.* Copenhagen: DJØF Publishers.

Arunachalam, V. (1995). EDI: An analysis of adoption, uses, benefits and barriers. *Journal of Systems Management,* 60-64.

Attewell, P. (1992). Technology diffusion and organizational learning: The case of business computing. *Organization Science, 3*, 1-19.

Bergeron, F., & Raymond, L. (1992). The advantages of electronic data interchange. *Database, 23*, 19-31.

Chatfield, A. T., & Bjorn-Andersen, N. (1997). The impact of IOS-enabled business process change on business outcomes: Transformation of the value chain of Japan airlines. *Journal of Management Information Systems, 14*, 13-40.

Chau, P. Y. K. (2001). Inhibitors to EDI adoption in small businesses: An empirical investigation. *Journal of Electronic Commerce Research, 2*, 1-19.

Chau, P. Y. K., & Tam, K. Y. (1997, March). Factors affecting the adoption of open systems: An exploratory study. *MIS Quarterly,* 1-21.

Choudhury, V., Hartzel, K. S., & Konsynski, B. R. (1998, December). Uses and consequences of electronic markets: An empirical investigation in the aircraft parts industry. *MIS Quarterly,* 471-507.

Clark, T., & Stoddard, D. B. (1996). Interorganizational business process redesign: Merging technological and process innovation. *Journal of Management Information Systems, 13*, 9-28.

Cox, B., & Ghoneim, S. (1996). Drivers and barriers to adopting EDI: A sector analysis of UK industry. *European Journal of Information Systems, 5*, 24-33.

Downs, G. W., & Mohr, L. B. (1976). Conceptual issues in the study of innovation. *Administrative Science Quarterly, 21*, 700-714.

Eckhoff, T. (1983). *Statens styringsmuligheter—Særlig i ressurs- og miljøspørsmål.* Oslo: Tanum-Norli.

Harrison, D. A., Mykytyn, P. P., & Riemenschneider, C. K. (1997). Executive decisions about adoption of information technology in small business: Theory and empirical tests. *Information Systems Research, 8*, 171-195.

Hart, P., & Saunders, C. (1998). Emerging electronic partnerships: Antecedents and dimensions of EDI use from the supplier's perspective. *Journal of Management Information Systems, 14*, 87-111.

Hatcher, L., & Stepanski, E. (1994). *A step-by-step approach to using the SAS system for univariate and multivariate statistics.* Cary: SAS Institute.

Henriksen, H. Z. (2002). *Performance, pressures, and politics: Motivators for adoption of interorganizational information systems.* Copenhagen: Samfundslitteratur. Retrieved October 2003, from http://www.hellezinnerhenriksen.info/publications.html#PhD.

Hosmer, D. W., & Lemeshow, S. (1989). *Applied logistic regression.* New York: John Wiley and Sons.

Iacovou, C. L., Benbasat, I., & Dexter, A. S. (1995, December). Electronic data interchange and small organizations: Adoption and impact of technology. *MIS Quarterly,* 465-485.

Jelassi, T., & Figon, O. (1994). Competing through EDI at Brun Passot: Achievements in France. *MIS Quarterly, 18,* 337.

Kreiner, S. (2001). *Introduction to DIGRAM and SCD* [working paper]. Copenhagen: Department of Biostatistics, University of Copenhagen.

Kurnia, S., & Johnston, R.B. (2000). The need of a processual view of inter-organizational systems adoption. *Journal of Strategic Information Systems, 9,* 295-319.

Kwon, T. H., & Zmud, R. W. (1987). Unifying the fragmented models of information systems implementation. In R. J. Boland, & R. A. Hirschheim (Eds.), *Critical issues in information systems research* (pp. 227-251). John Wiley & Sons.

Lai, V. S., & Guynes, J. L. (1997). An assessment of the influence of organizational characteristics on information technology adoption decision: A discriminative approach. *IEEE Transactions on Engineering Management, 44,* 146-157.

Lee, H. G., Clark, T., & Tam, K. Y. (1999). Research report: Can EDI benefit adopters? *Information Systems Research, 10,* 186-195.

Markus, L. M. (1987). Toward a "critical mass" theory of interactive media. Universal access, interdependence and diffusion. *Communication Research, 14,* 491-511.

Massetti, B., & Zmud, R. W. (1996, September). Measuring the extent of EDI usage in complex organizations: strategies and illustrative examples. *MIS Quarterly,* 331-345.

Moore, G. C., & Benbasat, I. (1991). Development of an instrument to measure the perceptions of adopting an information technology innovation. *Information Systems Research, 2,* 192-222.

Nunnally, J. C. (1978). *Psycometric theory.* New York: McGraw-Hill.

O'Callaghan, R., & Turner, J. A. (1995). Electronic data interchange—Concepts and issues. In H. Krcmar, N. Bjorn-Andersen, & R. O'Callaghan (Eds.), *EDI in Europe: How it works in practice* (pp. 1-19). John Wiley & Sons.

Premkumar, G., Ramamurthy, K., & Nilakanta, M. (1994). Implementation of electronic data interchange: An innovation diffusion perspective. *Journal of Management Information Systems, 11,* 157-177.

Raymond, L., & Bergeron, F. (1996). EDI success in small and medium-sized enterprises: A field study. *Journal of Organizational Computing and Electronic Commerce, 6,* 161-172.

Rogers, E. M. (1995). *Diffusion of innovations.* The Free Press.

Siegel, S., & Castellan, N. J. (1988). *Nonparametric statistics for the behavioral sciences.* Boston: McGraw-Hill.

Srinivasan, K., Kekre, S., & Mukhopadhyay, T. (1994). Impact of electronic data interchange technology on JIT shipments. *Management Science, 40,* 1291-1304.

Steinfield, C., Kraut, R., & Plummer, A. (1995). The impact of interorganizational networks on buyer-seller relationships. *Journal of Computer-Mediated Communication, 1*(3).

Swatman, P. M. C., & Swatman, P. A. (1992). EDI system integration: A definition and literature survey. *The Information Society, 8,* 169-205.

Thong, J. Y. L. (1999). An integrated model for information systems adoption in small businesses. *Journal of Management Information Systems, 15,* 187-214.

Tornatzky, L. G., & Fleischer, M. (1990). *The process of technological innovation.* Lexington Books.

Tuunainen, V.K. (1998). Opportunities of effective integration of EDI for small businesses in the automotive industry. *Information & Management, 34,* 361-375.

This work was previously published in the Journal of Electronic Commerce in Organizations, Vol. 4, Issue 2, edited by M. Khosrow-Pour, pp. 25-39, copyright 2006 by IGI Publishing, formerly known as Idea Group Publishing (an imprint of IGI Global).

Compilation of References

4321 Net. (2002, January 10). *Privacy statement and policy.* Retrieved September 3, 2007, from http://4321net.com/privacy_statement.htm

Aaker, D. A. (1991). *Managing brand equity.* New York: The Free Press.

Aaker, D., Kumar, V., & Day, G. (1998). *Marketing research* (6th ed.). New York: John Wiley & Sons.

Abecker, A., Tellmann, R., & Grimm, S. (2001). *Analysis of B2B standards and systems* (Project: SSWS - Semantic Web Enabled Web Services, IST-2001-37134).

Abell, W., & Black, S. (1997). *Business use of the Internet in New Zealand: A follow-up study.* Retrieved August 8, 2000, from http://www.scu.edu.au/ausweb96/business/abell/paper.htm

Abell, W., & Lim, L. (1996). *Business use of the Internet in New Zealand: An exploratory study.* Retrieved August 8, 2000, from http://www.scu.edu.au/ausweb96/business/abell/paper.htm

Abrahamson, E. (1996). Management fashion. *The Academy of Management Review, 21,* 254-285.

Abrazhevich, D. (2001a). Classification and characteristics of electronic payment systems. In K. Bauknecht, S. K. Madria, & G. Pernul (Eds.), *Proceedings of EC-Web 2001* (pp. 81-90). Springer.

Abrazhevich, D. (2001b). Electronic payment systems: Issues of user acceptance. In *Proceedings of eBusiness and eWork 2001.* Venice, Italy: IOS Press.

Abrazhevich, D. (2001c). A survey of user attitudes towards electronic payment systems. In J. Vanderdonckt, A. Blandford, & A. Derycke (Eds.), *Proceedings of the Joint AFIHM-BCS Conference on Human-Computer Interaction IHM-HCI'2001* (vol. 2). Toulouse: Cepadues-Editions.

Ackerman, M., Cranor, L., & Reagle, J. (1999). Privacy in e-commerce: Examining user scenarios and privacy preferences. In *Proceedings of the 1st ACM Conference on Electronic Commerce* (pp. 1-8).

Adams, D. A., Nelson, R. R., & Todd, P. A. (1992). Perceived usefulness, ease of use, and usage of information technology: A replication. *MIS Quarterly, 16*(2), 227-247.

Adkinson, W., Eisenrach, J., & Lenard, T. (2002). *Privacy online: A report of the information practices and policies of commercial Web sites.* Retrieved September 2, 2007, from http://www.pff.org/publications/privacyonlinefinalael.pdf

Adler, R. S. (1994). The last best argument for eliminating reliance from express warranties: "Real-world" consumers don't read warranties. *South Carolina Law Review, 45*(3), 429.

Afonso, J. R. (2001, April). E-government in Brazil: Experiences and perspectives. In *Forum of Federations,* Montreal, Canada.

Agarwal, R., & Prasad, J. (1997). The role of innovation characteristics and perceived voluntariness in the acceptance of information technologies. *Decision Sciences, 28*(3), 557-582.

Agresti, A. (1996). *An introduction to categorical data analysis.* New York: John Wiley & Sons.

Ahn, T., Ryu, S., & Han, I. (2004). The impact of the online and offline features on the user acceptance of Internet shopping malls. *Electronic Commerce Research and Applications, 3*(4), 405-420.

AICPA - American Institute of Certified Public Accountants (1998). *Electronic commerce assurance: Attitudes toward CPA WebTrust.* Retrieved September 5, 2007, from http://www.aicpa.org/Webtrust/yankel.htm

Ajzen, I. (1991). The theory of planned behavior. *Organizational Behavior & Human Decision Processes, 50*(2), 179-211.

Ajzen, I., & Fishbein, M. (1980). *Understanding attitudes and predicting social behavior.* Englewood Cliffs, NJ: Prentice Hall.

Akhter, S.H. (2003). Digital divide and purchase intention: Why demographic psychology matters? *Journal of Economic Psychology, 24*, 321-327.

Alba, J., Lynch, J., Weitz, B., Janiszewski, C., Lutz, R., Sawyer, A., & Wood, S. (1997). Interactive home shopping: Consumer, retailer, and manufacturers incentives to participate in electronic marketplaces. *Journal of Marketing, 61*, 38-

Alm, J., & Melnik, M.I. (2005). Sales taxes and the decision to purchase online. *Public Finance Review, 33*(2), 184-212.

Al-Mashari, M., Al-Mudimigh, A., & Zairi, M. (2003). Enterprise resource planning: A taxonomy of critical factors. *European Journal of Operational Research, 146*(2), 352-364.

Alpert, B. (1967). Non-businessmen as surrogates for businessmen in behavioral experiments. *Journal of Business, 40*, 203-207.

Alptekinoglu, A., & Tang, C.S. (2005). A model for analyzing multi-channel distribution systems. *European Journal of Operational Research, 163*(3), 802-824.

Amato-McCoy, D.M. (2006, November). Crossing channels. Chain Store Age, pp. 49-50.

Anckar, B., & D'Incau, D. (2002). Value-added services in mobile commerce: An analytical framework and empirical findings from a national consumer survey. In *Proceedings of the 35th Annual Hawaii International Conference on System Sciences.*

Andersen, K. V., Juul, N. C., Henriksen, H. Z., Bjorn-Andersen, N., & Bunker, D. (2000). *Business-to-business e-commerce, enterprises facing a turbulent world.* Copenhagen: DJØF Publishers.

Anderson, J. C., & Narus, J. A. (1990). A model of distributor firm and manufacturer firm working partnerships. *Journal of Marketing, 54*(1), 42-58.

Anderson, J.C., & Gerbing, D.W. (1984). The effect of sampling error on convergence, improper solutions, and goodness-of-fit indices for maximum likelihood confirmatory factor analysis. *Psychometrika, 49*(2), 155-173.

Andreassen, T. W., & Lindestad, B. (1998). Customer loyalty and complex services. *International Journal of Service Industry Management, 9*(1), 7-23.

Angeles, R. (2000). Revisiting the role of Internet-EDI in the current electronic commerce scene. *Logistics Information Management, 13*(1), 45-57.

Antovski, L., & Gusev, M. (2003). *M-payments.* Proceedings of 25th International Conference Information Technology Interfaces ITI 2003, 95-100.

Arbuckle, J.L. (1999). *Amos User's Guide, Version 4.0.* Chicago: Smallwaters Cooperation.

Archer, N., & Yuan, Y. (2000). Managing business-to-business relationships throughout the e-commerce procurement life cycle. *Internet Research: Electronic Networking Applications and Policy, 10*(5), 385-395.

Arksey, H., & Knight, P. (1999). *Interviewing for social scientists.* London: Sage Publications.

Arunachalam, V. (1995). EDI: An analysis of adoption, uses, benefits and barriers. *Journal of Systems Management,* 60-64.

Ashrafi, N. and Kuilboer, J. (2005). Online privacy policies: An empirical perspective on self-regulatory practices. *Journal of Electronic Commerce in Organizations, 3*(4), 61-74.

Asokan, N., Janson, P. A., & Waidner, M. (1997). The state of the art in electronic payment systems. *IEEE Computer, 28*(35), 28-35.

Athaide, G.A., Stump, R.L., & Joshi, A.W. (2003). Understanding new product co-development relationships in technology-based, industrial markets. *Journal of Marketing Theory and Practice, 11*(3), 46-58.

Attewell, P. (1992). Technology diffusion and organizational learning: The case of business computing. *Organization Science, 3*, 1-19.

Atuahene-Gima, K., & Li, H. (2000). Marketing's influence tactics in new product development: A study of high technology firms in China. *Journal of Product Innovation Management, 17*, 451-470.

Aubert, B., Rivard, S., & Patry, M. (1994, December 14-17). Development of measures to assess dimensions of IS operation transactions. In *Proceedings of the International Conference on Information Systems,* Vancouver, Canada (Vol. 15, pp. 13-26).

Aungst, S.G., & Wilson, D.T. (2005). A primer for navigating the shoals of applying wireless technology to marketing problems. *Journal of Business & Industrial Marketing, 20*(2), 59-69.

Averweg, U.R., & Erwin, G.J. (1999). Critical success factors for implementation of decision support systems in South Africa. *Proceedings of the 32nd Hawaii International Conference on System Sciences* (pp. 1-10).

Axner, D.H. (2006). Does WiMax have the right stuff? *Business Communications Review, 36*(7), 58-62.

Ba, S., & Pavlou, P. A. (2002). Evidence of the effect of trust building technology in electronic markets: Price premiums and buyer behavior. *MIS Quarterly, 26*(3), 243-269.

Bacon, C.J., & Fitzgerald, B. (2001). A systemic framework for the field of information systems. *ACM SIGMIS Database 32*(2), 46-67.

Bailey, J. E., & Pearson, S. W. (1983). Development of a tool for measuring and analyzing computer user satisfaction. *Management Science, 29*(5), 530-545.

Bakos, J. Y. (1991, September). A strategic analysis of electronic marketplaces. *MIS Quarterly*, pp. 295-310.

Bakos, J. Y. (1997). Reducing buyer search costs: Implications for electronic marketplaces. *Management Science, 43*(12), 1676-1692.

Bakos, J.Y., & Brynjolfsson, E. (1993). Information technology, incentives, and the optimal number of suppliers. *Journal of Management Information Systems, 10*(2), 37-53.

Balabanis, G., & Reynolds, N.L. (2001). Consumer attitudes towards multi-channel retailer's Web sites: The role of involvement, brand attitude, Internet knowledge, and visit duration. *Journal of Business Strategies, 18*(2), 105-131.

Balasubramanian, S. (1998). Mail versus mall: A strategic analysis of competition between direct marketers and conventional retailers. *Marketing Science, 17*(3), 181-195.

Balasubramanian, S., Peterson, R.A., & Jarvenpaa, S.L. (2002). Exploring the implications of m-commerce for markets and marketing. *Journal of the Academy of Marketing Science, 30*(4), 348-361.

Baldwin, H. (2002). Sell where you want, when you want. *Mbusiness*, pp. 29-30.

Bandyopadhyay, S., Barron, J. M., & Chaturvedi, A. R. (2005). Competition among sellers in online exchanges. *Information Systems Research, 16*, 47-60.

Barnes, S.J., & Huff, S.L. (2003). Rising sun: iMode and the wireless Internet. *Communications of the ACM 46*(11), 79-84.

Baron, J.P., Shaw, M.J., & Bailey, A.D., Jr. (2000). Web-based e-catalog systems in B2B procurement. *Communications of the ACM, 43*(5), 93-100.

Baron, R. M., & Kenny, D. A. (1986). The moderator-mediator variable distinction in social psychological research: Conceptual, strategic, and statistical considerations. *Journal of Personality and Social Psychology, 51*(6), 1173-1182.

Barrett, K., Greene, R., Mariani, M., & Sostek, A. (2003). The way we tax: A 50 state report. *Governing Magazine, 16*(5), 20-97.

Bath and North East Somerset Council. (2002). *Data protection code of practice.* Retrieved September 2, 2007, from http://www.bathnes.gov.uk/dataprotection/data14.htm

Beatty, R.C., Shim, J.P., & Jones, M.C. (2001). Factors influencing corporate Web site adoption: A time-based assessment. *Information & Management, 38*, 337–354.

Benassi, P. (1999). TRUSTe: An online privacy seal program. *Communications of the ACM, 42*, 57-59.

Beneventano, D., & Magnani, S. (2004). A framework for the classification and the reclassification of electronic catalogs. *ACM Symposium on Applied Computing.*

Beneventano, et al. (2004). A Web service based framework for the semantic mapping amongst product classification schemas. *Journal of Electronic Commerce Research, 5*(2).

Bensaou, M. (1999). Portfolios of buyer-supplier relationships. *Sloan Management Review, 40*(4), 35-44.

Bentler, P. M., & Bonnett, D. G. (1980). Significance tests and goodness of fit in the analysis of covariance structures. *Psychological Bulletin, 88*(3), 588-606.

Bentler, P.M. (1990). Comparative fit indexes in structural models. *Psychological Bulletin, 107*(2), 238-246.

Bergeron, F., & Raymond, L. (1992). The advantages of electronic data interchange. *Database, 23*, 19-31.

Berman, B., & Evans, J.R. (2001). *Retail management: A strategic approach.* Upper Saddle River, NJ: Prentice Hall.

Berman, B., & Thelen, S. (2004). A guide to developing and managing a well-integrated multi-channel retail strategy. *International Journal of Retail & Distribution Management, 32*(2/3), 147-156.

Berry, L. L. (1995). Relationship marketing of services-growing interest, emerging perspectives. *Journal of the Academy of Marketing Science, 23*(4), 236-245.

Berry, W.D., & Fording, R.C. (1997). Measuring state tax capacity and effort. *Social Science Quarterly, 78*(1), 158-166.

Best, S., & Teske, P. (2002). Explaining state Internet sales taxation: New economy, old-fashion interest group politics. *State Politics and Policy Quarterly, 2*(1), 37-51.

Better Business Bureau. (2005). *BBBOnLine Reliability Program.* Retrieved September 5, 2007, from http://www.bbbonline.org/reliability/

Bhattacherjee, A. (2002). Individual trust in online firms: Scale development and initial test. *Journal of Management Information Systems, 19*(1), 211-241.

Bhattacherjee, A., & Premkumar, G. (2004). Understanding changes in belief and attitude toward information technology usage: A theoretical model and longitudinal test. *MIS Quarterly, 28*(2), 229-254.

Bhushan, N., & Subbarao, V. (2001). *Mobile commerce: Killer applications, infosys.* Retrieved from http://www.ebusinessforum.gr/content/downloads/mcommerce.pdf

Birch, D.G.W. (2002). *Emerging models for mobile commerce, consult hyperion.* Retrieved from http://www.ebusinessforum.gr/content/downloads/mCommerce.pdf

Blackburn, R., & Stokes, D. (2000). Breaking down the barriers: Using focus groups to research small and medium sized enterprises. *International Small Business Journal, 19*(1), 44–67.

Blau, P. (1964). *Exchange and power in social life.* New York: Wiley.

Blili, S., & Raymond, L. (1993). Information technology: Threats and opportunities for small and medium-sized enterprises. *International Journal of Information Management, 13*, 439–448.

Bloor, M., Frankland, J., Thomas, M., & Robson, K. (2001). *Focus groups in social research.* London: Sage Publications.

Blyth, G. (2006, July 6). *Why we're still missing the cross-channel opportunity.* New Media Age, p. 15.

Bollen, K. A., & Hoyle, R. H. (1990). Perceived cohesion: A conceptual and empirical examination. *Social Forces, 69*(2), 470-504.

Bolton, R., Kannan, P., & Bramlet, M. (2000). Implications of loyalty program membership and service experiences for customer retention and value. *Journal of the Academy of Marketing Science, 28*(1), 95-108.

Bond, B. (1990). Sales & marketing—A fundamental difference. *Telephone Engineer & Management, 94*(8), 188-189.

Bond, B., Genovese, Y., Miklovic, D., Wood, N., Zrimsek, B., & Rayner, N. (2000, October). *ERP is dead—Long live ERP 2.* Gartner Group, RAS Services.

Bonoma, T. (1985). Case research in marketing: Opportunities, problems and a process. *Journal of Marketing Research, 22*(2), 199-208.

Bort, J. (2006, October 23). Wireless LANs not for all. *The New Data Center*, p. 68.

Böttcher, S., & Groppe, S. (2003). *Automated data mapping for cross enterprise data integration.*

Boynton, A.C., & Zmud, R.W. (1984). An assessment of critical success factors. *Sloan Management Review 25*(4), 17-27.

Brack, K. (2000). Your e-options. *Industrial Distribution, 89*(7), 54-58.

Brancheau, J.C., Janz, B.D., & Wetherbe, J.C. (1996). Key issues in information systems management: 1994-95 SIM delphi results. *MIS Quarterly 20*(2), 225-242.

Breeding, K. (1992). *Digital design fundamentals* (2nd ed.). Prentice Hall.

Breidenbach, S. (2006, October 9). The Wi-Fi divide. *Network World*, pp. 47-50.

Brisco, R. (2002). Turning analog women into a digital workforce: Plugging women into the new Asia economy. *Digital Divide Network*. Retrieved September 12, 2007, from http://www.digitaldividenetwork.org

Brodsky, I. (2003). *M-commerce trials and tribulations: It may finally be time for mobile commerce to hit its stride—Frequencies, American's network.* Retrieved from http://www.findarticles.com/p/articles/mi_m0DUJ/is_2003_Nov_1/ai_110928131

Brondmo, H. P. (2000). *The engaged customer. The new rules of Internet direct marketing.* New York: Harper Business.

Brooksbank, D. (2000). Self employment and small firms. In S. Carter & D. Jones-Evans (Eds.), *Enterprise and small business: Principles, policy and practice.* London: FT Prentice Hall.

Brown, L. A. (1981). *Innovation diffusion: A new perspective.* London: Methuen.

Brown, M.W., & Cudeck R. (1993). Alternative ways of assessing model fit. In K.A. Bollen & S. Long (Eds.), Testing structural equation models (pp. 136-162). Newbury Park, CA: Sage Publications.

Brown, S., Tilton, A., & Woodside, D. (2002). The case for on-line communities. *The McKinsey Quarterly, 1.*

Bruce, D., & Fox, W.F. (2001a). *State and local sales tax revenue losses from e-commerce: Updated estimates.* Knoxville, TN: Center for Business and Economic Research.

Bruce, D., & Fox, W.F. (2001b). E-commerce and local finance: Estimates of direct and indirect sales tax losses. *Municipal Finance Journal, 22*(3), 24-47.

Bruce, D., Deskins, J., & Fox, W.F. (2004). Has Internet access taxation affected Internet use? *Public Finance Review, 32*(2), 131-147.

Bruce, D., Fox, W., & Murray, M. (2003). To tax or not to tax? The case of electronic commerce. *Contemporary Economic Policy, 21*(1), 25-40.

Brunori, D. (2001). *State tax policy: A political perspective.* Washington, DC: The Urban Institute Press.

Brush, C.G. (1997). Women's entrepreneurship. In *Proceedings of the OECD Conference on Women Entrepreneurs in Small and Medium Enterprises.* Paris: OECD.

Brush, C.G., & Hisrich, R. (1999). Women owned businesses: Why do they matter? In Z. Acs (Ed.), *Are small firms important? Their role and impact.* Boston: Kluwer Academic Publishers.

Buck, S. P. (1996). Electronic commerce: Would, could and should you use current Internet payment mechanisms. *Internet Research: Electronic Networking Applications and Policy, 6*(2/3), 5-18.

Buckley, A., & Wanklyn, C.T. (2004). *Prepaid subscribers curb New Zealand cellular services market growth.* IDC. Retrieved from http://www.idcresearch. co.nz/PressRelease_Mobile0404.pdf

Budde, P. (2004). *Telecoms highlights in New Zealand.* Retrieved from http://www.budde.com.au/paulsdesk/paulsAnalysis.html

Buellingen, F., & Woerter, M. (2004). Development perspectives, firm strategies and applications in mobile commerce. *Journal of Business Research 57*(12), 1402-1408.

Bunduchi, R. (2005). Business relationships in Internet-based electronic markets: The role of goodwill trust and transaction costs. *Information Systems Journal, 15*, 321-341.

Bunker, D.J., & MacGregor, R.C. (2000). Successful generation of information technology (IT) requirements for small/medium enterprises (SMEs): Cases from regional Australia. In *Proceedings of SMEs in a Global Economy*, Wollongong, Australia (pp. 72-84).

Burgel, O., & Murray, G.C. (2000). The international market entry choices of start-up companies in high-technology industries. *Journal of International Marketing, 8*(2), 33-63.

Burke, K., Kovar, S., & Kovar, B. (2001). Marketing WebTrust and managing consumer expectations. *Journal of Accounting and Finance Research, 9*(3), 62-72.

Burke, R.R. (2002). Technology and the customer interface: What consumers want in the physical world and virtual store. *Journal of the Academy of Marketing Science, 30*(4), 411-432.

Burroughs, R.E., & Sabherwal, R. (2002). Determinants of retail electronic purchasing: A multi-period investigation. *Journal of Information System Operation Research, 40*(1), 35-56.

Burton, D. (2000). Postmodernism, social relations and remote shopping. *European Journal of Marketing, 36*(7/8), 792-810.

Butler, D. (2000). Gender, girls and computer technology: What's the status now? *Clearing House, 73*(4), 225-229.

Butler, T., & Fitzgerald, B. (1999). Unpacking the systems development process: An empirical application of the CSF concept in a research context. *Journal of Strategic Information Systems 8*(4), 351-371.

Buttner, E.H., & Moore, D.P. (1997, January). Women's organisational exodus to entrepreneurship: Self reported motivations and correlates with success. *Journal of Small Business Management*, pp. 34-47.

Byrne, B.M. (2001). *Structural equation modeling with AMOS*. Mahwah, NJ: Lawrence Erlbaum Associates.

Cameron, A., & Massey, C. (1999). *Small and medium sized enterprises: A New Zealand perspective*. Auckland: Addison Wesley Longman New Zealand.

Cameron, A.C. (2004). Factors leading to state participation in the streamlined sales tax project. *Journal of*

Public Budgeting, Accounting, & Financial Management, 16(4), 80-108.

Campbell, D. T., & Stanley, J. C. (1963). *Experimental and quasi-experimental designs for research*. Chicago: Rand McNally.

Campbell, N.C.G. (1985). An interaction approach to organizational buying behavior. *Journal of Business Research, 13*(1), 35-49.

Cantwell, E. (2003). In-building wireless: How to keep a signal when you're indoors. *Wireless Business & Technology, 3*(3), 12-14.

Carlson, C., Dickson, G., Jelassi, T., Vogel, D., & Walden, P. (2001). Mobile commerce: Core issues, products and services. *Proceedings of the 14th Bled Electronic Commerce Conference*, Bled, Slovenia.

Carr, A.S., & Smeltzer, L.R. (2002). The relationship between information technology use and buyer-seller relationships: An exploratory analysis of the buying firm's perspective. *IEEE Transactions on Engineering Management, 49*(3), 293-304.

Carter, S. (2000). Improving the numbers and performance of women-owned businesses: Some implications for training and advisory services. *Education & Training, 42*(4/5), 326-333.

Carter, S., & Cannon, T. (1992). *Women as entrepreneurs*. London: Academic Press.

Carter, S., & Rosa, P. (1998). The financing of male and female owned businesses. *Entrepreneurship and Regional Development, 10*(3), 225-241.

Cavana, R.Y., Delahaye, B.L., & Sekaran, U. (2001). *Applied business research: Qualitative and quantitative methods*. Milton, Queensland, Australia: John Wiley & Sons.

Cavusoglu, H., Raghunathan, S., & Mishra, B. (2002). Optimal design of information technology security architecture. *International Conference on Information Systems, 23*, 749-756.

CCH. (2004). *CCH Tax Research Network*. Riverwoods, IL: CCH Incorporated.

Center for Digital Future. (2007). *Online world as important to Internet users as real world? USC-An-*

nenberg *Digital Future Project finds major shifts in social communication and personal connections on the Internet*. Retrieved September 5, 2007, from http://www.digitalcenter.org/pdf/2007-Digital-Future-Report-Press-Release-112906.pdf

Cespedes, F.V., & Corey, E.R. (1990). Managing multiple channels. *Business Horizons, 33*(3), 67-77.

Cespedes, F.V., & Smith, H.J. (1993). Database marketing: New rules for policy and practice. *Sloan Management Review, 3*, 8-12.

Chandler, A.D. (1977). *The visible hand: The managerial revolution in American business*. Cambridge, MA: Belknap Press.

Chang, J., & Samuel, N. (2004). Internet shopper demographics and buying behavior in Australia. *Journal of the Academy of Business, 5*(1/2), 171-176.

Chang, M.K., & Cheung, W. (2001). Determinants of the intention to use Internet/WWW at work: A confirmatory study. *Information & Management, 39*, 1–14.

Chang, M.K., Cheung, W., & Lai, V.S. (2005). Literature derived reference models for the adoption of online shopping. *Information & Management, 42*(4), 543-559.

Chapple, I. (2002, August 14). Small firms drag feet with Internet. *The New Zealand Herald*. Retrieved August 14, 2002, from http://www.nzherald.co.nz/storyprint.cfm?stotyID=2347435

Charles, L., Monodee, F., & Nurek, T. (2000). *The critical success factors for m-commerce*. Rondebosch: University of Cape Town.

Chatfield, A. T., & Bjorn-Andersen, N. (1997). The impact of IOS-enabled business process change on business outcomes: Transformation of the value chain of Japan airlines. *Journal of Management Information Systems, 14*, 13-40.

Chatzkel, J. (2002). A Conversation with Göran Roos. *Journal of Intellectual Capital, 3*(2), 96-117.

Chau, P. Y. K. (1996). An empirical assessment of a modified technology acceptance model. *Journal of Management Information Systems, 13*(2), 185-204.

Chau, P. Y. K. (2001). Inhibitors to EDI adoption in small businesses: An empirical investigation. *Journal of Electronic Commerce Research, 2*, 1-19.

Chau, P. Y. K., & Tam, K. Y. (1997). Factors affecting the adoption of open systems: An exploratory study. *MIS Quarterly, 21*(1), 1-21.

Chen, L., & Nath, R. (2004). A framework for mobile business applications. *International Journal of Mobile Communications*.

Chen, L., Gillenson, M.L, & Sherrell, D.L. (2004). Consumer acceptance of virtual stores: A theoretical model and critical success factors for virtual stores. *Data Base, 32*(2), 8-31.

Chen, M., Chen, A.N., & Shao, B.M. (2003). The implications and impacts of Web services to electronic commerce research practices. *Journal of Electronic Commerce Research, 4*(4), 128-139.

Chen, P.-Y., & Hitt, L.M. (2002). Measuring switching costs and the determinants of customer retention in Internet-enabled businesses: A study of the online brokerage industry. *Information Systems Research, 13*(3), 255-274.

Chen, Y., & Sudhir, K. (2004). When shopbots meet emails: Implications for price competition on the Internet. *Quantitative Marketing and Economics, 2*, 233-255.

Cheng, J. M.-S., Sheen, G.-J., & Lou, G.-C. (2006). Consumer acceptance of the Internet as a channel of distribution in Taiwan: A channel function perspective. *Technovation, 26*(7), 856-864.

Cheskin Research. (2000). *Trust in the wired Americas*. Retrieved September 5, 2007, from http://www.cheskin.com

Cheung, M.K., & Limayem, M. (2005, May). The role of habit and the changing nature of the relationship between intention and usage. In *Proceedings of the 13th European Conference of Information Systems*, Regensburg, Germany.

Chiang, K., & Dholakia, R.R. (2003). Factors driving consumer intention to shop online: An empirical investigation. *Journal of Consumer Psychology, 13*(1-2), 177-183.

Childers, T. L., Carr, C. L., Peck, J., & Carson, S. (2001). Hedonic and utilitarian motivations for online retail shopping behavior. *Journal of Retailing, 77*, 511-535.

Chin, W. W., Marcolin, B. L., & Newsted, P. R. (2003). A partial least squares latent variable modeling approch for measuring interaction effects: Results from a Monte Carlo simulation study and voice mail emotion/adoption study. *Information Systems Research, 14*, 189-217.

Choi, S.-Y., Whinston, A.B., & Stahl, D.O. (1997). *The economics of electronic commerce.* Indianapolis: Macmillan Technical Publishing.

Choi, Y.B., Muller, J., Kopeck, C.V., & Makarsky, J.M. (2006). Corporate wireless LAN security: Threats and an effective security assessment framework for wireless information assurance. *International Journal of Mobile Communications, 4*(3), 267-291.

Choudhury, V., Hartzel, K. S., & Konsynski, B. R. (1998, December). Uses and consequences of electronic markets: An empirical investigation in the aircraft parts industry. *MIS Quarterly,* 471-507.

Chow, S., & Holden, R. (1997). Toward an understanding of loyalty: The moderating role of trust. *Journal of Managerial Issues, 9*, 275-298.

Christiaanse, E., & Venkatraman, N. (2002). Beyond sabre: An empirical test of expertise exploitation in electronic channels. *MIS Quarterly, 26*(1), 15-39.

Chung, W., & Paynter, J. (2002). Privacy issues on the Internet. In *Proceedings of the 35th Annual Hawaii International Conference on System Sciences* (pp. 2501-2509).

Churchill, G.A.J., & Iacobucci, D. (2002). *Marketing research: Methodological foundations.* Mason, OH: South-Western Publishing.

Chwelos, P., Benbasat, I., & Dexter, A. (2001). Research report: Empirical test of an EDI adoption model. *Information Systems Research, 12*(3), 304–321.

Clark, J., & DeRose, S. (1999). XML path language (XPath) version 1.0. Retrieved September 1, 2007, from http://www.w3c.org/TR/xpath

Clark, T. H., & Lee, H. G. (2000). Performance, interdependence and coordination in business-to-business electronic commerce and supply chain management. *Information Technology and Management, 1*(1-2), 85-105.

Clark, T., & Stoddard, D. B. (1996). Interorganizational business process redesign: Merging technological and process innovation. *Journal of Management Information Systems, 13*, 9-28.

Clarke, I., III. (2001). Emerging value propositions for m-commerce. *Journal of Business Strategies, 18*(2), 133-148.

Clarke, R. (1999a). *Appropriate research methods for electronic commerce.* Retrieved March 16, 2000, from http://www.anu.edu.au/people/Roger.Clarke/ResMeth.html

Clarke, R. (1999b). Focus groups. Retrieved July 25, 2002, from http://www.xamax.com.au/Res/FocusGrps.html

Clarke, R. (2001). *If eBusiness is different then so is research in eBusiness.* Retrieved July 25, 2002, from http://www.anu.edu.au/people/Roger.Clarke/EC/EBR0106.html

Clausing, J. (1999). New privacy study says majority of sites provide warnings. *New York Times,* pp. 13-5.

Clay, K., & Strauss, R.P. (2000). Trust, risk, and electronic commerce: 19th century lessons for the 21st century. *State Tax Notes, 19*, 1701-1710.

Clemons, E.K., Reddi, S., & Row, M.C. (1993). The impact of IT on the organization of economic activity: The "move to the middle" hypothesis. *Journal of Management Information Systems, 10*(2), 9-35.

Cline, R.J., & Neubig, T.S. (1999). *Masters of complexity and bearers of great burden: The sales tax system and compliance costs for multistate retailers* (Tech. Rep.). Ernst and Young Economics Consulting and Quantitative Analysis.

CNBC. (2007, January 16). *Retail sales growth seen moderating in '07: Trade groupers.* Retrieved September 5, 2007, from http://www.msnbc.msn.com/id/16652499/

CNNMoney.com. (2006, December 29). *Online holiday spending surges.* Retrieved September 5, 2007, from http://money.cnn.com/2006/12/29/news/economy/online_retail/?postversion=2006122910

Cockfield, A.J. (2002). Walmart.com: A case study of entity isolation. *State Tax Notes, 25*, 633-701.

Cohendet, P., Llerena, P., & Marengo, L. (2000). Is there a pilot in the evolutionary firm? In N. Foss & V. Mahnke (Eds.), *Competence, governance, and entrepreneurship: Advances in economic strategy research* (pp. 95-115). New York: Oxford University Press.

Coley, B. (2002). *Enabling the killer application.* Texas Instruments Incorporated. Retrieved from http://focus.ti.com/pdfs/vf/wireless/killerapps.pdf

Collier, J. E., & Bienstock, C. C. (2006). How do customers judge the quality of an e-tailer? *MIT Sloan Management Review, 48*(1), 35-40.

comScore. (2007, January 3). *comScore Networks reports total non-travel e-commerce spending reaches $102 billion in 2006; up 24 percent versus 2005.* Retrieved September 5, 2007, from http://www.comscore.com/press/release.asp?press=1166

Congressional Budget Office. (CBO). (2003). *Economic issues in taxing Internet and mail-order sales.* Washington, DC: Congress of the United States Congressional Budget Office.

Conover, J. (2000, August 7). Anatomy of IEEE 802.11b wireless. *Network Computing,* pp. 96-100.

Corbitt, B. J., Thanasankit, T., & Han, Y. (2003). Trust and e-commerce: A study of consumer perceptions. *Electronic Commerce Research & Applications, 2*(3), 203-216.

Cornia, G.C., Sjoquist, D.L., & Walters, L.C. (2004). Sales and use tax simplification and voluntary compliance. *Public Budgeting & Finance, 24*(1), 1-31.

Coughlan, A.T., Anderson, E., Stern, L.W., & El-Ansary, A.I. (2001). *Marketing channels.* Upper Saddle River, NJ: Prentice Hall.

Coviello, N., & McAuley, A. (1999) Internationalisation and the smaller firm: A review of contemporary empirical research. *Management International Review, 39*(3), 223-240.

Cox, B. (1999, June 8). Gender gap narrows, changing landscape for e-commerce. *Internetnews.* Retrieved September 12, 2007, from http://www.internetnews.com

Cox, B., & Ghoneim, S. (1996). Drivers and barriers to adopting EDI: A sector analysis of UK industry. *European Journal of Information Systems, 5*, 24-33.

Cox, J. (2006, November 13). Aruba to unify Wi-Fi and cellular voice. *Network World*, p. 34.

Cragg, P., & King, M. (1992). Information systems sophistication and financial performance of small engineering firms. *European Journal of Information Systems, 1*(6), 417–426.

Creswell, J. W. (1994). *Research design: Qualitative and quantitative approaches.* London: Sage Publications.

Crosby, L. A., & Stephens, N. (1987). Effects of relationship marketing on satisfaction, retention, and prices in the life insurance industry. *Journal of Marketing Research, 24*, 404-411.

Crossroads. (2001). *A sector report: Consumer products.*

Crowell, W. (2001). Trust, the e-commerce difference. *Credit Card Manager, 14*(5), 80.

Culnan, M. (1999). *Georgetown Internet privacy policy survey: Report to the Federal Trade Commission.* Retrieved September 2, 2007, from http://www.msb.edu/faculty/culnanm/gipps/gipps1.pdf

Culnan, M. (1999). *Progress report to the Federal Trade Commission (FTC)* (funded by the Online Privacy Alliance). Retrieved September 3, 2007, from http://www.msb.edu/faculty/culnanm/gippshome.html

Culnan, M., & Armstrong, P. (1999). Information privacy concerns, procedural fairness, and impersonal trust: An empirical investigation. *Organization Science, 10*(1), 104-115.

Curbera, F., Duftler, M., Khalaf, R., Nagy, W., Mukhi, N., & Weerawarana, S. (2002). Unraveling the Web services Web: An introduction to SOAP, WSDL, and UDDI. *IEEE Internet Computing, 6*(2), 86-93.

Daft, R.L., & Lengel, R.H. (1984). Information richness: A new approach to manager information processing and organization design. In B. Staw & L.L. Cummings (Eds.), *Research in organizational behavior.* Greenwich: JAI Press.

Dai, Q., & Kauffman, R. J. (2001, January). Business models for Internet-based e-procurement systems and B2B electronic markets: An exploratory assessment. In *Proceedings of the 34th Hawaii International Conference on Systems Sciences*, Maui.

Damanpour, F. (1996). Organizational complexity and innovation: Developing and testing multiple contingency models. *Management Science, 42*(5), 693-716.

Daniel, D. (2000, November 24). Wired on wirelessness: No strings. *Computing Canada*, pp. 18-19.

Daniel, T. A., & McInerney, M. L. (2005). E-commerce and the "reluctant" small business owner: How technology is changing the business model for small and medium-sized enterprises (SMEs). *The International Journal of Applied Management and Technology, 3*, 183-206.

Darling, A. (2001). Waiting for the m-commerce explosion. *Telecommunications International, 35*(2), 34-38.

Davies, S. (1979). *The diffusion of process innovations.* Cambridge: Cambridge University Press.

Davis, F. D. (1989). Perceived usefulness, perceived ease of use and user acceptance of information technology. *MIS Quarterly, 13*(3), 319-340.

Davis, F. D. (1993). User acceptance of information technology: System characteristics, user perceptions and behavioral impacts. *International Journal of Man-Machine Studies, 38*, 475-487.

Dawson, M. (2001). Land in Sicht. *Lebensmittelzeitung Spezial E-Business, 1*, 60-61.

Day, G. (1999). *The market driven organization.* New York: Free Press.

Day, G., & Montgomery, D. (1999). Charting new directions for marketing [Special issue]. *Journal of Marketing, 63*, 3-13.

Del Franco, M. (2006, February). The "C" is for channel. Multichannel Merchant, pp. 1-34.

Dellaert, B.G.C., & Kahn, B.E. (1999). How tolerable is delay? Consumer's evaluation of Internet Web sites after waiting. *Journal of Interactive Marketing, 13*(1), 41-54.

Deloitte Touche Tohmatsu. (2000). *Deloitte e-business survey: Insights and issues facing New Zealand business.* Retrieved August 8, 2000, from http://www.deloitte.co.nz/images/acrobat/survey.pdf

DeLone, W., & McLean, E. R. (2004). Measuring e-commerce success: Applying the DeLone & McLean information systems success model. *International Journal of Electronic Commerce, 9*(1), 31-47.

DeLone, W.H. (1988). Determinants for success for computer usage in small business. *MIS Quarterly, 12*(1), 51-61.

DeLone, W.H., & McLean, E.R. (1992). Information systems success: The quest for the dependent variable. *Information Systems Research, 3*(1), 60-95.

Dennis, C. (2000). Networking for marketing advantage. *Management Decision, 38*(4), 287-292.

Dennis, C., Harris, L., & Sandhu, B. (2002). From bricks to clicks: Understanding the e-consumer. *Qualitative Market Research: An International Journal, 5*(4), 281-290.

Devaraj, S., Fan, M., & Rajiv, K. (2002). Antecedents of B2C channel satisfaction and preference: Validating e-commerce metrics. *Information Systems Research, 13*(3), 316-335.

DeWine, S., & Casbolt, D. (1983). Networking: External communication systems for female organisational members. *Journal of Business Communication, 20*, 57-67.

Dholakia, N., & Rash, M. (2004). Configuration m-commerce portals for business success. In N. Shi (Ed.), *Mobile commerce applications* (pp. 76-93). Hershey, PA: Idea Group Publishing.

Dholakia, R.R., Zhao, M., & Dholakia, N. (2005). Multichannel retailing. A case study of early experiences. *Journal of Interactive Marketing, 19*(2), 63-74.

Dholakia, U. M., & Rego, L. (1998). What makes commercial Web pages popular? An empirical investigation of Web page effectiveness. *European Journal of Marketing, 32*, 724-736.

Diercks, R. (2001). Will m-commerce live up to the hype? *Wireless Internet Magazine, 1*(1). Retrieved

March 2001, from http://www.wirelessinternetmag. com/news/0104/0104_research_hype.htm

Dijck, P.V. (2001). *Making money the wireless way, commentary & society.* Retrieved from http://www. evolt.org/article/Making_money_the_wireless_way/ 25/5439/?format

Doan, A. (2003). *Ontology matching: A machine learning approach.*

Doll, W.J., & Torkzadeh, G. (1988). The measurement of end-user computing satisfaction. *MIS Quarterly, 12*(2), 259-274.

Doney, P., & Cannon, J. (1997). An examination of the nature of trust in buyer-seller relationship. *Journal of Marketing, 61*, 35-51.

Doney, P., Cannon, J., & Mullen, M. (1998). Understanding the influence of national culture on the development of trust. *Academy of Management Review, 23*(3), 601-620.

Doney, P.M., & Cannon, J.P. (1997). An examination of the nature of trust in the buyer-seller relationship. *Journal of Marketing, 61*(2), 35-51.

Doolin, B., Mcleod, L., McQueen, B., & Watton, M. (2003). Internet strategies for establishing retailers: Four New Zealand case studies. *Journal of Information Technology Cases and Applications, 5*(4), 3–19.

Dorloff, F.-D., Schmitz, V., & Leukel, J. (2002). Coordination and exchange of XML catalog data. In *Proceedings of the 5th International Conference on E-Commerce Research (ICER-5).*

Dowling, G., & Uncles, M. (1997). Do customers loyalty programs really work? *Sloan Management Review, 38*(4), 71-82.

Downs, G. W., & Mohr, L. B. (1976). Conceptual issues in the study of innovation. *Administrative Science Quarterly, 21*(4), 700.

Dozier, R. (2000, January 18). Federal Reserve changes priced services fee [Editorial]. *Journal Record*, p. 1.

Drakopoulou-Dodd, S., Jack, S., & Anderson, A.R. (2002). Scottish entrepreneurial networks in the international context. *International Small Business Journal, 20*(2), 213-219.

Drew, S. (2003). Strategic use of e-commerce by SMEs in the east of England. *European Management Journal, 21*(1), 79.

Due, J.F., & Mikesell, J.L. (1994). *Sales taxation: State and local structure and administration* (2nd ed.). Washington, DC: Urban Institute Press.

Duffy, D.L. (2004). Using online retailing as a springboard for catalog marketing. *Journal of Consumer Marketing, 21*(3), 221-225.

Dunbar, A.E., & Phillips, J.D. (2001). The outsourcing of corporate tax function activities. *The Journal of the American Taxation Association, 23*(2), 35-50.

Dwyer, F. R., Schurr, P. H., & Oh, S. (1987). "Developing buyer-seller relationships," *Journal of Marketing*, Vol. 51, 11-27

Each Delivery Channel Has Its Own Strengths. (2006, December 18). Credit Union Executive Newsletter, p. 3.

Eastlick, M.A., & Feinberg, R.A. (1994). Gender differences in mail-catalog patronage motives. *Journal of Direct Marketing, 8*(2), 37-44.

Eastlick, M.A., & Feinberg, R.A. (1999). Shopping motives for mail catalog shopping. *Journal of Business Research, 45*(3), 281-290.

E-bit. (2004, August). *Web shoppers* (10th ed.). Retrieved September 5, 2007, from http://www.webshoppers.com. br/webshoppers.asp

Eckhoff, T. (1983). *Statens styringsmuligheter—Særlig i ressurs- og miljøspørsmål.* Oslo: Tanum-Norli.

eCl@ss (2004). eCl@ss White Paper, V0.6. Retrieved September 1, 2007, from http://www.eclass.de

Edwards, L. (2004). Reconstructing consumer privacy protection on-line: A modest proposal. *International Review of Law Computers, 18*(3), 313-344.

Eisenhardt, K. M. (1989). Building theories from case study research. *Academy of Management Review, 14*, 532-550.

Elia, E., Lefebvre, L., & Lefebvre, E. (2007). Focus of B2B electronic commerce initiatives and related benefits in manufacturing SMEs. *Journal of Information Systems and E-Business Management, 5*, 1-23.

Elkington, H., Viner, N., Tokuda, R., & Ortiz, M. (2001). *Mobile payments: Killer app or paper tiger?* London: The Boston Consulting Group.

Elliot, S., & Fowell, S. (2000). Expectations versus reality: A snapshot of consumer experiences with Internet retailing. *International Journal of Information Management, 20*, 323-336.

Elliott, G., & Phillips, N. (2004). *Mobile commerce and wireless computing systems* (1st ed., p. 416). Essex, UK: Pearson Education Limited.

Emery, J. (1987). *Management information systems the critical strategic resource.* Oxford University Press.

Emmelhainz, M. (1993). *EDI: A total management guide.* Van Nostrand Reinhold.

Enders, A., & Jelassi, T. (2000). The converging business models of Internet bricks and clicks retailers. *European Management Journal, 18*(5), 542-550.

Enos, L. (2000). Net prices no lure for most e-shoppers. *Ecommerce Times.* Retrieved September 3, 2007, from http://www.ecommercetimes.com/story/4645.html

European Communities. (2004). *Status of implementation of Directive 95/46 on the Protection of Individuals with Regard to the Processing of Personal Data.* Retrieved September 2, 2007, from http://europa.eu.int/comm/internal_market/privacy/law/implementation_en.htm

Evans, J. R., & Laskin, R. L. (1994). The relationship marketing process: A conceptualization and application. *Industrial Marketing Management, 23*, 439-452.

Fain, D. (1994). *Consumers navigating channels: Behavior motivations for direct vs. retail.* Unpublished manuscript, New York University.

Federal Trade Commission. (1998). *Privacy online: A report to Congress.* Retrieved September 2, 2007, from http://www.Federal Trade Commission.gov/reports/privacy3/priv-23a.pdf

Federal Trade Commission. (2000). *Privacy online: Fair information practices in the electronic marketplace, a report to Congress.* Retrieved September 2, 2007, from http://www.FederalTrade Commission.gov/reports/privacy2000/privacy2000.pdf

Feindt, S., Jeffcoate, J., & Chappell, C. (2002). Identifying success factors for rapid growth in SME e-commerce. *Small Business Economics, 19*(1), 51-62.

Field, A. (2000). *Discovering statistics using SPSS for windows.* London: SAGE.

Finniear, L. (2003). When will we see an LBS killer app? *Geospatial Solutions, 13*(2), 58.

Fiocca, R. (1982). Account portfolio analysis for strategy development. *Industrial Marketing Management, 11*(1), 53-62.

Fishbein, M., & Ajzen, I. (1975). *Belief, attitude, intention and behavior: An introduction to theory and research.* Reading, MA: Addison-Wesley.

Fishbein, M., & Ajzen, I. (1975). *Belief, attitude, intention, and behavior: An introduction to theory and research.* Reading, MA: Addison-Wesley.

Fisher, L. (1976). *Industrial marketing.* London: Business Books Limited.

Fisher, M., & Reibstein, D.J. (2001). Technology-driven demand: Implications for the supply chain. In J. Wind & V. Mahajan (Eds.), *Digital marketing* (pp. 285-309). John Wiley.

Floyd, D. (2006, April). Mobile application security system (MASS). *Bell Labs Technical Journal*, pp. 191-198.

Forbes, Inc. (2004). Forbes International 500. Retrieved September 2, 2007, from http://www.forbes.com

Ford, D. (1980). The development of buyer-seller relationships in industrial markets. *European Journal of Marketing, 14*(5/6), 339-354.

Fornell, C., & Larcker, D. F. (1981). Evaluating structural equation models with unobservable variables and measurement error. *Journal of Marketing Research, 18*(1), 39-50.

Fox, W.F., & Murray, M. (1997). The sales tax and electronic commerce: So what's new? *National Tax Journal, 50*(3), 573-592.

Fuller, A.L., & Swanson, E.G. (1992). Information centers as organizational innovations. *Journal of Management Information Systems, 9*(1), 47-68.

Funk, P. (2005). 802.11i secures wireless LANs. *Network World, 22*(12), 39.

Gabrielsson, M., Kirpalani, V.H.M., & Luostarinen, R. (2002). Multiple channel strategies in the European personal computer industry. *Journal of International Marketing, 10*(3), 73-95.

Gallaugher, J.M. (2002). E-commerce and the undulating distribution channel. *Communications of the ACM, 45*(7), 89-95.

Galliers, R.D. (1992). Choosing information systems research approaches. In R. Galliers (Ed.), *Information systems research: Issues, methods and practical guidelines* (pp. 144-162). Oxford: Blackwell Scientific Publications.

Gal-Or, E., & Ghose, A. (2005). The economic incentives for sharing security information. *Information Systems Research, 16*, 186-208.

Ganesan, S (1994, April). Determinants of long-term orientation in buyer-seller relationships. *Journal of Marketing, 58*, 1-19.

Garbarino, E., & Johnson, M. S. (1999). The different roles of satisfaction, trust, and commitment in customer relationships. *Journal of Marketing, 63*, 70-87.

Garcia-Dastuge, S., & Lambert, D. (2003). Internet-enabled coordination in supply chain. *Industrial Marketing Management, 32*(2), 251-263.

Gardiner, S., Hanna, J., & LaTour, M. (2002). ERP and the reengineering of industrial marketing processes. A prescriptive overview for the new-age marketing manager. *Industrial Marketing Management, 31*(4), 357-365.

Gauzente, C. (2004). Web merchants' privacy and security statement: How reassuring are they for customers? Two sided approach. *Journal of Electronic Commerce Research, 5*(3), 181-198.

Gebauer, J., & Scharl, A. (1999). Between flexibility and automation: An evaluation of Web technology from a business process perspective. *Journal of Computer-Mediated Communication, 5*(2). Retrieved September 1, 2007, from http://jcmc.indiana.edu/

Gebler, D. (2000, October 6). Rethinking e-commerce gender demographics. *E-Commerce Times.* Retrieved September 12, 2007, from http://www.ecommercetimes.com

Gefen, D. (2000). E-commerce: The role of familiarity and trust. *Omega: The International Journal of Management Science, 28*(6), 725-737.

Gefen, D. (2002). Customer loyalty in e-commerce. *Journal of the Association for Information Systems, 3*, 27-51.

Gefen, D. (2002). Reflections on the dimensions of trust and trustworthiness among online consumers. *DATA BASE for Advances in Information Systems, 33*(3), 38-54.

Gefen, D., & Heart, T. (2006). On the need to include national culture as a central issue in e-commerce trust beliefs. *Journal of Global Information Management, 14*(4), 1-30.

Gefen, D., Karahanna, E., & Straub, D. W. (2003). Trust and TAM in online shopping: An integrated model. *MIS Quarterly, 27*(1), 51-90.

Gehrt, K.C., & Yan (2004). Situational, consumer, and retailer factors affecting Internet, catalog, and store shopping. *International Journal of Retail and Distribution Management, 32*(1), 5-18.

General Accounting Office (GAO). (2000). *Sales taxes: Electronic commerce growth presents challenges; Revenue losses are uncertain.* Washington, DC: United States General Accounting Office.

Gengatharen, D., & Standing, C. (2005). A framework to assess the factors affecting success or failure of the implementation of government-supported regional e-marketplaces for SMEs. *European Journal of Information Systems, 14*, 417-433.

Ghosh, A.K., & Swaminatha, T.M. (2001). Software security and privacy risks in mobile e-commerce. *Communications of the ACM, 44*(2), 51-57.

Gilroy, F., & Desai, H. (1986). Computer anxiety: Sex, race and age. *International Journal of Man-Machine Studies, 25*, 711-719.

Goffee, R., & Skase, R. (1985). *Women in charge: The experience of female entrepreneurs.* London: Allen & Unwin.

Goldfinger, C., & Perrin, J. (2001). *UNCTAD background paper: E-finance and small and medium-size enterprises (SMEs) in developing and transition economies.* Palais des Nations, Geneva.

Goldman, C. (2001). Data on aisle six! *Overland Park, 18*(17), 11A-15A.

Goodman, J. (1999). *Basic facts on customer complaint behavior and the impact of service on the bottom line.* TARP.

Goolsbee, A. (2000). In a world without borders: The impact of taxes on Internet commerce. *Quarterly Journal of Economics, 115*(2), 561-576.

Goolsbee, A., & Zittrain, J. (1999). Evaluating the costs and benefits of taxing Internet commerce. *National Tax Journal, 52*(3), 413-428.

Gordon, M. E., Slade, L. A., & Schmitt, N. (1986). The "science of the sophomore" revisited: From conjecture to empiricism. *Academy of Management Review, 11*(1), 191-277.

Gordon, T.J. (1994). *The Delphi method.* American Council for the United Nations University (AC/UNU) Millennium Project. Retrieved from http://www.futuro-venezuela.org/_curso/5-delphi.pdf

Gore, M. (1995). Read the fine print when selling guarantees. *Best Review, 95*(11), 64-65.

Governing Magazine. (2003). *State and Local Source Book 2003.* Washington, DC: Congressional Quarterly Press.

Grabner-Kraeuter, S. (2002). The role of consumers' trust in online-shopping. *Journal of Business Ethics, 39*(1-2), 43-50.

Grabowski, H., Lossack, R., & Weißkopf, J. (2002). *Datenmanagement in der produktentwicklung* [Data management in product developmet]. Hanser.

Grandon, E., & Pearson, J. M. (2004). E-commerce adoption: Perceptions of managers/owners of small and medium sized firms in Chile. *Communications of the Association for Information Systems, 13*, 81-102.

Grazioli, S., & Jarvenpaa, S. (2000). Perils of Internet fraud: An empirical investigation of deception and trust with experienced Internet consumers. *IEEE Transactions on Systems, Man, and Cybernetics—Part A: Systems and Humans, 30*, 395-410.

Green, H., France, M., Stepanek, M., & Borrus, A. (2000). Our four point plan. *Business Week, 3673,* 86.

Green, H., Rosenbush, S., Crockett, R.O., & Holmes, S. (2003). Wi-Fi means business. *Businessweek,* pp. 86-92.

Greiner, L. (2003). Information requested is none of company's e-business. *Computing Canada, 29*(19), 19.

Grewal, D., Munger, J. L., Iyer, G. R., & Levy, M. (2003). The influence of Internet-retailing factors on price expectations. *Psychology & Marketing, 20*(6), 447-493.

Grewal, R., Comer, J.M., & Mehta, R. (2001, July). An investigation into the antecedents of organizational participation in business-to-business electronic markets. *Journal of Marketing, 65,* 17-33.

Griffin, A. (1997). The effect of project and process characteristics on product development cycle time. *Journal of Marketing Research, 34*(1), 24-36.

Griffith, D. A., Krampf, R. F., & Palmer, J. W. (2001). The role of interface in electronic commerce: Consumer involvement with print versus online catalogs. *International Journal of Electronic Commerce, 5*(4), 135-153.

Gronroos, C. (1990). Relationship approach to marketing in service contexts: The marketing and organizational behavior interface. *Journal Business Research, 20,* 3-11.

Grönroos, C. (1994). From marketing mix to relationship marketing: Towards a paradigm shift in marketing. *Management Decision, 32,* 4-20.

Grosso, C., McPherson, J., & Shi, C. (2004). Retailing: What's working online. *McKinsey Quarterly, 2005*(3), 18-20.

Grover, V. (1993). An empirically derived model for the adoption of customer-based inter-organizational systems. *Decision Sciences, 24*(3), 603-640.

Guglielmo, C. (1999). E-commerce: There to here. *Inter@Active Week, 6*(47), 106.

Guilford, T., & Dawkins, M. (1993). Receiver psychology and the evolution of animal signals. *Animal Behavior, 42*, 1-14.

Guimaraes, T., Gupta, Y.P., & Rainer Jr., R.K. (1999). Empirically testing the relationship between end-user computing problems and information centre success factors. *Decision Sciences, 30*(2), 393-413.

Gupta, A., Su, B., & Walter, Z. (2004). Risk profile and consumer shopping behavior in electronic and traditional channels. *Decision Support Systems, 38*(3), 347-367.

Gustafsson, R., Klefsjo, B., Berggren, E., & Granfors-Wellemets, U. (2001). Experiences from implementing ISO 9000 in small enterprises: A study of Swedish experiences. *The TQM Magazine, 13*(4), 232-246.

Gwinner, K. P., Gremmler, D. D., & Bitner, M. J. (1998). Relational benefits in services industries: The customer's perspective. *Journal of the Academy of Marketing Science, 26*(2), 101-114.

Hadjimonolis, A. (1999). Barriers to innovation for SMEs in a small less developed country (Cyprus). *Technovation, 19*(9), 561-570.

Haeberle, M. (2003). On-line retailing scores big. *Chain Store Age, 79*(7), 48.

Hair, J. F., Jr., Anderson, R. E., Tatham, R. L., & Black, W. C. (1998). *Multivariate data analysis* (5th ed.). Upper Saddle River, NJ: Prentice Hall.

Hamblen, M. (2006, December 18). Wireless LANs reach round 2. *ComputerWorld*, p. 10.

Hampton-Sosa, W., & Koufaris, M. (2005). The effect of Web site perceptions on initial trust in the owner company. *International Journal of Electronic Commerce, 10*(1), 55-81.

Handschuh, Schmid, & Stanoevska-Slabeva (1997). The concept of a mediating electronic product catalog. *Electronic Markets Journal, 7*(3).

Hansen, H.R., & Madlberger, M. (2007). Beziehungen zwischen dem Internet-Vertrieb und anderen Absatzwegen im Einzelhandel. In B.W. Wirtz (Ed.), *Handbuch Multi Channel Marketing*, Wiesbaden, Germany. Gabler.

Hansen, T. (2005). Understanding consumer online grocery behavior: Results from a Swedish study. *Journal of Euromarketing, 14*(3), 31-58.

Harris Interactive. (2001). *Privacy leadership initiative (PLI) privacy notices research final results.* Retrieved September 2, 2007, from http://www.FederalTradeCommission.gov/bcp/workshops/glb/supporting/harrris%20results.pdf

Harrison, D. A., Mykytyn, P. P., & Riemenschneider, C. K. (1997). Executive decisions about adoption of information technology in small business: Theory and empirical tests. *Information Systems Research, 8*(2), 171-195.

Harrison, T., & Waite, K. (2006). A time-based assessment of the influences, uses and benefits of intermediary Website adoption. *Information & Management, 43*(8), 1002-1013.

Hart, P., & Saunders, C. (1998). Emerging electronic partnerships: Antecedents and dimensions of EDI use from the supplier's perspective. *Journal of Management Information Systems, 14*, 87-111.

Hartzell, D.J, Pittman, R.H., & Downs, D.H. (1994). An updated look at the size of the U.S. real estate market portfolio. *The Journal of Real Estate Research, 9*(2), 197-212.

Hasselbring, W. (2000). Information system integration. *Communications of the ACM, 43*(6), 33-38.

Hasson, F., Keeney, S., & McKenna, H. (2000). Research guidelines for the delphi survey technique. *Journal of Advanced Nursing, 32*(4), 1008-1015.

Hatcher, L., & Stepanski, E. (1994). *A step-by-step approach to using the SAS system for univariate and multivariate statistics.* Cary: SAS Institute.

Heide, J.B., & John, G. (1992). Do norms matter in marketing relationships? *Journal of Marketing, 56*(2), 32-35.

Heide, J.B., & Miner, A.S. (1992). The shadow of the future: Effects of anticipated interaction and frequency of contact on buyer-seller cooperation. *Academy of Management Journal, 35*(2), 265-292.

Hellerstein, W. (1998). Electronic commerce and the future of state taxation. In D. Brunori (Ed.), *The future of state taxation* (pp. 207-222). Washington, DC: The Urban Institute Press.

Henderson, R., & Divett, M. J. (2003). Perceived usefulness, ease of use and electronic supermarket use. *International Journal of Human-Computer Studies, 59*(3), 383-395.

Henriksen, H. Z. (2002). *Performance, pressures, and politics: Motivators for adoption of interorganizational information systems.* Copenhagen: Samfundslitteratur. Retrieved October 2003, from http://www.hellezinner-henriksen.info/publications.html#PhD.

Hentrich, J. (2001). *B2B-Katalog-Management.* Galileo Business.

Hill, R., & Stewart, J. (2000). Human resource development in small organisations. *Journal of European Industrial Training, 24*(2/3/4), 105-117.

Hill, R.W. (1972). The nature of industrial buying decisions. *Industrial Marketing Management, 2*(10), 45-55.

Hill, R.W. (1973). *Marketing technological products to industry.* Oxford: Pergamon Press.

Hisrich, R., & Brush, C.G. (1986). *The woman entrepreneur: Starting, financing and managing a successful new business.* Lexington: Lexington Books.

Hocutt, M. A. (1998). Relationship dissolution model: Antecedents of relationship commitment and the likelihood of dissolving a relationship. *International Journal of Service Industry Managment, 9*(2), 189-200.

Hodge, G. (2002). Enterprise resource planning in textiles. *Journal of Textile and Apparel, Technology and Management, 2*(3), 1-8.

Hoffman, D. L., Novak, T. P., & Peralta, M. A. (1999). Information privacy in the marketspace: Implications for the commercial uses of anonymity on the Web. *The Information Society, 15*, 129-139.

Hoffman, D.L., Novak, T.P., & Peralta, M. (1999). Building consumer trust online. *Communications of the ACM, 42*(4), 80-85.

Holland, C.P., & Naudé, P. (2004). The metamorphosis of marketing into an information handling problem. *Journal of Business & Industrial Marketing, 19*(3), 165-166.

Hollensen, S., & Grünbaum, N.N. (2003). A holistic model for coordinating supplier and customer relationships. In *Proceedings of the 19th Imp-Conference*, Lugano, Switzerland.

Homburg, C., Workman, J., & Jensen, O. (2000). Fundamental changes in marketing organization: The movement toward a customer-focused organizational structure. *Journal of the Academy of Marketing Science, 28*(4), 459-478.

Homse, E. (1981). *An interaction approach to marketing and purchasing strategy.* Unpublished doctoral dissertation, University of Manchester, Institute of Science and Technology.

Hong, W., Thong, J. Y. L., & Tam, K. Y. (2005). The effects of information format and shopping task on consumers' online shopping behavior: A cognitive fit perspective. *Journal of Management Information Systems, 21*(3), 149-184.

Hoque, A. Y., & Lohse, G. L. (1999). An information search cost perspective for designing interfaces for electronic commerce. *Journal of Marketing Research, 36*(3), 387-394.

Hosmer, D. W., & Lemeshow, S. (1989). *Applied logistic regression.* New York: John Wiley and Sons.

Houston, R. W., & Taylor, G. K. (1999). Consumer perceptions of CPA WebTrust assurances: Evidence of an expectation gap. *International Journal of Auditing, 3*, 89-105.

Howells, J., & Wood, M. (1995). Diffusion and management of electronic data interchange: Barriers and opportunities in the UK pharmaceutical and health industries. *Technology Analysis and Strategic Management, 7*(4), 371-387.

Hsu, S., Qian, L., & Ilyas, M. (2003). An analytic study of two probabilistic models for establishing ad hoc WLANs. *Information Technology and Management, 4*(1), 55-67.

Hui, D. (2001). *Why Hong Kong Internet users do not shop online: An empirical study.* Paper presented at the 1st International Conference on Electronic Business, Hong Kong.

Hummel, M. (2005). *E-commerce: Eine Sonderform des Versandhandels*? Unpublished master's thesis, Vienna University of Economics and Business Administration, Vienna, Austria.

Hung, S.-Y., Chang, C.-M., & Yu, T.-J. (2006). Determinants of user acceptance of the e-government services: The case of online tax filing and payment system. *Government Information Quarterly, 23*(1), 97-122.

Hung, S.Y., Ku, C.Y., & Chang, C.M. (2003). Critical factors of WAP services adoption: An empirical study. *Electronic Commerce Research and Applications, 2*(1), 42-60.

Iacovou, C. L., Benbasat, I., & Dexter, A. S. (1995). Electronic data interchange and small organizations: Adoption and impact of technology. *MIS Quarterly, 19*(4), 465.

Ibbotson, P., & Fahy, M. (2004). The impact of e-commerce on small Irish firms. *International Journal of Services Technology & Management, 5*(4), 317-331.

IBGE. (2004, November). *Monthly survey of commerce.* Retrieved September 7, 2007, from the Brazilian Institute of Geography and Statistics, http://www.ibge.gov.br/home/estatistica/indicadores/comercio/pmc

Igbaria, M., Zinatelli, N., & Cavaye, A. (1998). Analysis of information technology success in small firms in New Zealand. *International Journal of Information Management, 18*(2), 103–119.

IMD World Competitiveness Center yearbook. (2005). Geneva, Switzerland: IMD Business School.

Integral. (2006). *Austrian Internet Monitor Internet-Entwicklung 3.* Quartal 2005. Retrieved September 7, 2007, from http://www.integral.co.at/dImages/AIM-C_3.%20Quartal2005.pdf

ITSecurity. (2002, February 22). *First major post-9/11 privacy survey.* Retrieved September 5, 2007, from http://www.itsecurity.com/tecsnews/feb2002/feb260.htm

Ives, B., Olson, M., & Baroudi, J. (1983). The measurement of user information satisfaction. *Communications of the ACM, 26*(10), 785-793.

Jansen, A. (1998). Technology diffusion and adoption in small, rural firms. In T. Larsen, & E. McGuire (Eds.), *Information systems innovation and diffusion: Issues and directions* (pp. 345–372). Hershey, PA: Idea Group Publishing.

Januz, L.R. (1983). It's helpful to know who is purchasing through the mail. *Marketing News, 17*, 4.

Jarupunphol, P., & Mitchell, C. (2002) E-commerce and the media—influences on security risk perceptions. In W. Cellary & A. Iyengar (Eds.), *Internet Technologies, Applications and Societal Impact: The 1ˢᵗ IFIP Workshop on Internet Technologies, Applications and Societal Impact*, Wroclaw, Poland (IFIP Conference Proceedings 232, pp. 163-173). Kluwer Academic.

Jarvenpaa, S. L., & Todd, P. A. (1997). Consumer reactions to electronic shopping on the World Wide Web. *International Journal of Electronic Commerce, 1*(2), 59-88.

Jarvenpaa, S. L., & Tractinski, N. (1999). Consumer trust in an Internet store: A cross-cultural validation. *Journal of Computer-Mediated Communication, 5*(2). Retrieved September 1, 2007, from http://jcmc.indiana.edu/

Jarvenpaa, S. L., Tractinsky, N., & Saarinen, L. (1999). *Consumer trust in an Internet store: A cross-cultural validation.* Retrieved September 3, 2007, from http://www.ascusc.org/jcmc/vol5/issues2/jarvenpaaa.html

Jasper, C.R., & Lan, P.-N.R. (1992). Apparel catalog patronage: Demographic, lifestyle and motivational factors. *Psychology and Marketing, 9*(4), 275-296.

Jelassi, T., & Figon, O. (1994). Competing through EDI at Brun Passot: Achievements in France. *MIS Quarterly, 18*, 337.

Jessup, L.M., & Robey, D. (2002). The relevance of social issues in ubiquitous computing environments. *Communications of the ACM, 45*(12), 88-91.

Jeusfeld, M. (2004, February 12-14). Integrating product catalogs via multi-language ontologies. In W. Hasselbring (Ed.), *Enterprise Application Integration 2004, Proceedings of the GI-/GMDS Workshop on Enterprise Application Integration (EAI-04)*, Oldenburg, Germany.

John, G. (1984, August). An empirical investigation of some antecedents of opportunism in a marketing channel. *Journal of Marketing Research, 21, 278-289.*

John, G., & Reve, T. (1982). The reliability and validity of key informant data from dyadic relationships in marketing channels. *Journal of Marketing Research, 19*(4), 517-525.

John, G., & Weitz, B. (1989). Salesforce compensation: An empirical investigation of factors related to use of salary versus incentive compensation. *Journal of Marketing Research, 26*, 1-14.

Johnson, C., Delhagen, K., & Yuen, E. (2003). *US eCommerce overview: 2003 to 2008.* Forrester Research, Inc.

Johnson, D.S., & Bharadwaj, S. (2005). Digitization of selling activity and sales force performance: An empirical investigation. Journal of the Academy of Marketing Science, 33(1), 3-18.

Johnson, K.K.P., Yoo, J.-J., Thee, J., Lennon, S., Jasper, C., & Damhorst, M.L. (2006). Multi-channel shopping: Channel use among rural consumers. *International Journal of Retail & Distribution Management, 34*(6), 453-466.

Johnson, S., & Storey, D. (1993). Male and female entrepreneurs and their businesses. In S. Allen & C. Truman (Eds.), *Women in business: Perspectives on women entrepreneurs.* London: Routledge.

Joia, L. A. (2004). Bridging the digital divide: Some initiatives in Brazil. *International Journal of Electronic Government, 1*(3), 300-315.

Jones, M. A., & Suh, J. (2000). Transaction-specific satisfaction and overall satisfaction: An empirical analysis. *Journal of Services Marketing, 14*(2), 147-159.

Joseph, V. B., Cook, R. W., & Javalgi, R. G. (2001). Marketing on the Web: How executives feel, what businesses do. *Business Horizons, 44*, 32-40.

Judd, C.M., & McClelland, G.H. (1989). *Data analysis: A model-comparison approach.* New York: Harcourt Brace Jovanovich.

JupiterMedia. (2005). Accurate Web site visitor measurement crippled by cookie blocking and deletion, JupiterResearch finds. Retrieved September 5, 2007, from http://www.jupitermedia.com/corporate/releases/05.03.14-newjupresearch.html

JupiterResearch. (2006, February 6). JupiterResearch forecasts online retail spending will reach $144 billion in 2010, a CAGR of 12% from 2005. Retrieved September 5, 2007, from http://www.jupitermedia.com/corporate/releases/06.02.06-newjupresearch.html

Kaiser, H.F. (1974). An index of factorial simplicity. *Psychometrika, 39*, 31-36.

Kalakota, R., & Whinston, A. (1997). *Electronic commerce: A manager's guide.* Reading, MA: Addison-Wesley.

Kalleberg, A.L., & Berg, I. (1987). *Work and industry.* New York: Plenum Press.

Kandampully, J. (2003). B2B relationships and networks in the Internet age. *Management Decision, 41*(5), 443-451.

Kanji, G.K., & Wallage, W. (2000). Business excellence through customer satisfaction. *Total Quality Management, 11*(7), 979-998.

Kannan, P.K., Chang, A.M., & Whinston, A.B. (2001). Wireless commerce: Marketing issues and possibilities. In *Proceedings of the 34th Annual Hawaii International Conference on System Sciences* (pp. 1-6).

Kaplan, S. E., & Nieschwietz, R. J. (2003a). An examination of the effects of WebTrust and company type on consumers' purchase intentions. *International Journal of Auditing, 7*, 155-168.

Kaplan, S. E., & Nieschwietz, R. J. (2003b). A Web assurance services model of trust for B2C e-commerce. *International Journal of Accounting Information Systems, 4*, 95-114.

Karahanna, E., Straub, D. W., & Chervany, N. L. (1999). Information technology adoption across time: A cross-sectional comparison of pre-adoption and post-adoption beliefs. *MIS Quarterly, 23*(2), 183-213.

Kassarjian, H. H. (1977). Content analysis in consumer research. *Journal of Consumer Research, 4*, 8-18.

Kaufman-Scarborough, C., & Lindquist, J.D. (2002). E-Shopping in a Multiple Channel Environment. *Journal of Consumer Marketing, 19*(4/5), 333-350.

Keane, B. (2002). Lowering health care costs out-of-the-box. *Wireless Business & Technology, 2*(2), 36-38.

Kelly, E. P., & Rowland, H. C. (2000, May-June). Ethical and online privacy issues in electronic commerce. *Business Horizons*, pp. 3-12.

Kennedy, A., & Coughlan, J. (2006). Online shopping portals: An option for traditional retailers? *International Journal of Retail & Distribution Management, 34*(7), 516-528.

Kenny, D. A. (2001). Mediation. Retrieved September 7, 2007, from http://nw3.nai.net/~dakenny/mediate.htm

Kenny, D., & Marshall, J. (2000, November-December). Contextual marketing: The real business of the Internet. *Harvard Business Review*, pp. 119-125.

Khera, I. P., & Benson, J. D. (1970). Are students really poor substitutes for businessmen in behavioral research? *Journal of Marketing Research, 7*, 529-532.

Kim, D. J., Steinfield, C., & Lai, Y. (2004). Revisiting the role of Web assurance seals in consumer trust. In *Proceedings of the 6th International Conference on Electronic Commerce, 60*(1), 280-287, Delft, The Netherlands.

Kim, S., & Stoel, L. (2004). Apparel retailers: Website quality dimensions and satisfaction. *Journal of Retailing and Consumer Services, 11*(2), 109-117.

Kimery, K. M., & McCord, M. (2006). Signals of trustworthiness in e-commerce: Consumer understanding of third-party assurance seals. *Journal of Electronic Commerce in Organizations, 4*(4), 52-74.

Kimery, K., & McCord, M. (2002). Third-party assurances: Mapping the road to trust in eretailing. *Journal of Information Technology Theory and Applications (JITTA), 4*(2), 63-82.

Klein, S. (1989). A transaction cost explanation of vertical control in international markets. *Academy of Marketing Science Journal, 17*(3), 253-260.

Kleinrock, L. (2001). Breaking loose. *Communications of the ACM, 44*(9), 41-45.

Kline, R.B. (1998). *Principles and practice of structural equation modeling*. New York: Guilford.

KNSO (Korea National Survey Office). (2003). The annual results of e-commerce transaction survey in 2002. Retrieved September 7, 2007, from http://www.nso.go.kr/eng/releases/e_suec0144.htm

Koehn, D. (2003). The nature and conditions for online trust. *Journal of Business Ethics, 43*, 3-19.

Kolesar, M. B., & Galbraith, R. W. (2000). A services-marketing perspective on e-retailing: implications for e-retailers and directions for further research. *Internet Research, 10*(5), 424-438.

Kolettis, H. (2001). Who's caught in the Web? *Security Distributing & Marketing, 31*(11), 14.

Kolsaker, A., & Payne, C. (2002). Engendering trust in e-commerce: A study of gender-based concerns. *Marketing Intelligence & Planning, 20*, 206-214.

Komiak, S., Wang, W., & Benbasat, I. (2005). Trust building in virtual salespersons versus in human salespersons: Similarities and differences. *e-Service Journal, 4*.

Korgaonkar, P., & O'Leary, B. (2006). Management, market, and financial factors separating winners and losers in e-business. *Journal of Computer-Mediated Communication, 11*(4). Retrieved September 1, 2007, from http://jcmc.indiana.edu/vol11/issue4/korgaonkar.html

Korgaonkar, P.K. (1984). Consumer shopping orientations, non-store retailers, and consumers' patronage intentions: A multivariate investigation. *Journal of the Academy of Marketing Science, 12*(1), 11-22.

Kotha, S., Rajgopal, S., & Venkatachalam, M. (2004). The role of online buying experience as a competitive advantage: Evidence from third-party ratings for e-commerce firms. *Journal of Business, 77*(2), 100-134.

Kotler, P. (1999). *How to create, win, and dominate markets*. New York: Free Press.

Koufaris, M. (2002). Applying the technology acceptance model and flow theory to online consumer behavior. *Information Systems Review, 13*(2), 205-223.

Kovar, S., Burke, K., & Kovar, B. (2000). Consumer responses to the CPA WebTrust assurance. *Journal of Information Systems, 14*(1), 17-25.

Kraljic, P. (1983). Purchasing must become supply management. *Harvard Business Review, 61*(5), 109-117.

Krapf, E. (1999). Can businesses find common ground for e-commerce. *Business Communications Review, 29*(4), 43-46.

Kreiner, S. (2001). *Introduction to DIGRAM and SCD* [working paper]. Copenhagen: Department of Biostatistics, University of Copenhagen.

Kuan, K. K. Y., & Chau, P. Y. K. (2001). A perception-based model for EDI adoption in small business using technology-organization-environment framework. *Information & Management, 38*(8), 507-521.

Kula, V., & Tatoglu, E. (2003). An exploratory study of Internet adoption by SMEs in an emerging market economy. *European Business Review, 15*(5), 324–333.

Kurnia, S., & Johnston, R.B. (2000). The need of a processual view of inter-organizational systems adoption. *Journal of Strategic Information Systems, 9*, 295-319.

Kwon, T. H., & Zmud, R. W. (1987). Unifying the fragmented models of information systems implementation. In R. J. Boland, & R. A. Hirschheim (Eds.), *Critical issues in information systems research* (pp. 227-251). John Wiley & Sons.

Labich, K. (1994). Why companies fail. *Fortune, 14*, 52-68.

Lai, V. S., & Guynes, J. L. (1997). An assessment of the influence of organizational characteristics on information technology adoption decision: A discriminative approach. *IEEE Transactions on Engineering Management, 44*, 146-157.

Lai, V.S., & Chung, W. (2002). Managing international data communications. *Communications of the ACM, 45*(3), 89-93.

Laios, L., & Moschuris, S. (1999). An empirical investigation of outsourcing decisions. *Journal of Supply Chain Management, 35*(1), 33-42.

Lala, A., & Sutton, G. (2002). The impact of relative information quality of e-commerce assurance seals on Internet purchasing behavior. *International Journal of Accounting Information Systems, 3*(4), 237-253.

Lam, Y. S., Shankar, V., Erramilli, M. K., & Murthy, B. (2004). Customer value, satisfaction, loyalty, and switching costs: An illustration from a B-to-B service context. *Journal of the Academy of Marketing Science, 32*, 293-311.

LAN Product News. (2005). Wireless LAN equipment shipment to triple within 5 years. *LAN Product News.* Retrieved September 11, 2007, from http://cuhsl.creighton.edu/login?url=http://search.epnet.com.cuhsl.creighton.edu/login.aspx?direct=true&db=buh&an=16475413

Lancioni, R. (2000). New developments in supply chain management for the millennium: Determining supplier and buyer effect on inventory performance. *Industrial Marketing Management, 29*(1), 1-6.

Lancioni, R., Smith, M., & Oliva, T. (2000). The role of the Internet in supply chain management. *Industrial Marketing Management, 29*(1), 45-56.

LaTour, M., Champagne, P. J., & Behling, R. (1990). Do students represent a viable source of data for researching business social responsibility and ethical issues? *The Journal of Computer Information Systems, 30*, 26-29.

Laudon, K.C., & Traver, C.G. (2002). *E-commerce: Business, technology, society.* Addison-Wesley.

Laufer, R., & Wolfe, M. (1977). Privacy as a concept and social issue: A multidimensional developmental theory. *Journal of Social Issues, 33*(3), 22-42.

Laurant, C. (2003). *Privacy and human rights: An international survey of privacy laws and developments.* Retrieved September 2, 2007, from http://www.privacy-international.org/survey/phr2003/countries/

Lawrence, K.L. (1997). Factors inhibiting the utilisation of electronic commerce facilities in Tasmanian small- to medium-sized enterprises. In *Proceedings of the 8th Australasian Conference on Information Systems*, Adelaide, Australia (pp. 587-597).

Lawson-Body, A. (2003, August 4-6). An instrument for measuring the effect of trusted electronic inter-organizational relationships on customer loyalty. In *Proceedings of the 2003 Americas Conference on Information Systems (AMCIS 2003)*, Tampa, Florida.

Lawyer, K. (1967, June). *Product characteristics as a function in marketing* [Speech]. London: Polytechnic School of Management Studies.

Lederer, A.L., Maupin, D.J., Sena, M.P., & Zhuang, Y. (2000). The technology acceptance model and the World Wide Web. *Decision Support Systems, 29*(3), 269-282.

Lee, H. G., Clark, T., & Tam, K. Y. (1999). Research report: Can EDI benefit adopters? *Information Systems Research, 10*, 186-195.

Lee, M. K. O., & Turban, E. (2001). A trust model for consumer Internet shopping. *International Journal of Electronic Commerce, 6*(1), 75-91.

Lee, T.-T. (2004). Nurses' adoption of technology: Application of Rogers' innovation-diffusion model. *Applied Nursing Research, 17*(4), 231-238.

Lefebvre, L.A., Lefebvre, E., Bendavid, Y., Fosso, S., & Wamba, H. (2006, January). RFID as enabler of B-to-B e-commerce and its impact on business processes: A pilot study of a supply chain in the retailing industry. In *Proceedings of the Hawaii International Conference on System Sciences (HICSS-39)*. Retrieved September 10, 2007, from http://www.computer.org/portal/site/ieeecs/

Legris, P., Ingham, J., & Collerette, P. (2003). Why do people use information technology? A critical review of the technology acceptance model. *Information & Management, 40*(3), 191-206.

Lehner, F., & Watson, R.T. (2001). *From e-commerce to m-commerce: Research directions.* Regensburg, Germany: University of Regensburg. Retrieved from http://www.ebusinessforum.gr/content/downloads/ResearchDirections.pdf

Lehr, W., & McKnight, L.W. (2003). Wireless Internet access: 3G vs. WiFi? *Telecommunications Policy, 27,* 351-370.

Lenhart, A., Horrigan, J., Rainie, L., Allen, K., Boyce, A., & Madden, M. (2003). *The ever-shifting Internet population: A new look at Internet access and the digital divide* (PEW Internet and American Life Project, No. 4162003). Retrieved September 5, 2007, from http://www.pewinternet.org/PPF/r/88/report_display.asp

Lepkowska-White, E. (2004). Online store perceptions: How to turn browsers into buyers? *Journal of Marketing Theory & Practice, 12*(3), 36-47.

Levenburg, N., & Klein, H. (2006). Delivering customer services online: Identifying best practices of medium-sized enterprises. *Information Systems Journal, 16,* 135-147.

Levenburg, N., & Magal, S. (2005). Applying importance-performance analysis to evaluate e-business strategies among small firms. *eService Journal, 3.*

Levitt, T. (1965). *Industrial purchasing behavior.* Boston: Harvard University.

Levy, M., Powell, P., & Yetton, P. (1998). SMEs and the gains from IS: From cost reduction to value added. *IFIP WG8.2 and WG8.6 Joint Working Conference on Information Systems: Current Issues and Future Changes*, Helsinki, Finland. Retrieved June 5, 2000, from http://www.bi.no/dep2/infomgt/wg82-86/proceedings/Table-of-contents.htm

Lewicki, R., & Bunker, B. (1996). Developing and maintaining trust in work relationships. In R. M. Kramer & T. R. Tyler (Ed.), *Trust in organizations: Frontiers of theory and research* (pp. 114-139). Thousand Oaks, CA: Sage.

Lewin, J. E., & Johnston, W. J. (1997). Relationship marketing theory in practice: A case study. *Journal of Business Research, 39,* 23-31.

Lewis, W., Agarwal, R., & Sambamurthy, V. (2003). Sources of influence on beliefs about information technology use: An empirical study of knowledge workers. *MIS Quarterly, 27*(4), 657-678.

Li, F., & Williams, H. (1999). Interfirm collaboration through interfirm networks. *Information Systems Journal, 9,* 103-115.

Lia, V.S. (2001). Intraorganizational communication with intranets. *Communications of the ACM, 44*(7), 95-100.

Liao, Z., & Cheung, M. T. (2001). Internet-based e-shopping and consumer attitudes: An empirical study. *Information and Management, 38,* 299-306.

Lightner, N. J., & Eastman, C. (2002). User preference for product information in remote purchase environment. *Journal of Electronic Commerce Research, 3*(3), 174-186.

Lim, N. (2003). Consumers' perceived risk: Sources versus consequences. *Electronic Commerce Research and Applications, 2,* 216-228.

Limayem, M., Khalifa, M., & Frini, A. (2000). What makes consumers buy from Internet? A longitudinal study of online shopping. *IEEE Transactions on Systems, Man, and Cybernetics, 30*(4), 421-432.

Linstone, H.A., & Turoff, M. (1975). *The delphi method: Techniques and applications.* Ontario: Addison-Wesley.

Linthicum, D. (2000). *Enterprise application integration.* Boston: Addison-Wesley.

Litan, R.E., & Rivlin. A.M. (2001). *Beyond the dot.coms: The economic promise of the Internet.* Washington, DC: Brookings Institution Press.

Little, A.D. (2001). *Key success factors for m-commerce.* Vienna: Arthur D. Little Int. GmbH.

Lituchy, T. R., & Rail, A. (2000). Bed and breakfasts, small inns, and the Internet: The effect of technology on the globalization of small businesses. *Journal of International Marketing, 8,* 86-97.

Liu, C., & Arnett, K. (2000). Exploring the factors associated with Web site success in the context of electronic commerce. *Information & Management, 38,* 23-33.

Liu, C., & Arnett, K. (2002). An examination of privacy policies in Fortune 500 Web sites. *Mid-American Journal of Business, 17*(1), 13-22.

Liu, C., Marchewka, J. T., & Ku, C. (2004). American and Taiwanese perceptions concerning privacy, trust, and behavioral intentions in electronic commerce. *Journal of Global Information Management, 12*(1), 18-40.

Liu, C., Marchewka, J. T., Lu, J., & Yu, C.-S. (2004). Beyond concern: A privacy–trust- behavioral intention model of electronic commerce. *Information & Management, 42,* 127-142.

Liu, S, Turban, E., & Matthew, K. (2000). Software agents for environmental scanning in electronic commerce. *Information Systems Frontiers, 2*(1), 85-98.

Lohse, G. L., & Spiller, P. (1998). Electronic shopping. *Communications of ACM, 41*(7), 81-89.

Lombard, M., & Ditton, T. (1997). At the heart of it all: The concept of presence. *Journal of Computer-Mediated Communication, 3*(2). Retrieved September 1, 2007, from http://jcmc.indiana.edu/

Loscocco, K.A., & Leicht, K.T. (1993). Gender, work-family linkages and economic success among small business owners. *Journal of Marriage and the Family, 55,* 875-887.

Lucas, H.C., & Spitler, V. (2000). Implementation in a world of workstations and networks. *Information & Management, 38,* 119-128.

Lucas, P. (2000). In search of a seal of approval. *Credit Card Management, 13*(5), 52-58.

Luo, X. (2002). Trust production and privacy concerns on the Internet: A framework based on relationship marketing and social exchange theory. *Industrial Marketing Management, 31*(2), 111-118.

Lynch, C. (2001). When documents deceive: Trust and provenance as new factors for information retrieval in a tangled Web. *Journal of the American Society for Information Science and Technology, 52*(1), 12-17.

Lynch, J., & Ariely, D. (2000). Wine online: Search costs affect competition on price, quality, and distribution. *Marketing Science, 19*(1), 83-103.

Lynch, P.D., Kent, R.J., & Srinivasan, S.S. (2001). The global Internet shopper: Evidence from shopping tasks in twelve countries. *Journal of Advertising Research, 41*(3), 15-23.

Lyytinen, K., & Yoo, Y. (2002). Research commentary: The next wave of nomadic computing. *Information Systems Research, 13*(4), 377-388.

Lyytinen, K., Varshney, U., Ackerman, M.S., Davis, G., Avital, M., Robey, D., Sawyer, S., & Sorensen, C. (2004). Surfing the next wave: Design and implementation challenges of ubiquitous computing environments. *Communications of AIS, 13,* 697-716.

Macgregor, R., & Vrazlaic, L. (2004). Don't be an island. *Computerworld.* Retrieved March 30, 2004, from http://www.compuetworld.com.au/pp.php?id=5884582 20&taxid=14

MacGregor, R.C., & Vrazalic, L. (in press). Small business clusters and their role in prioritising barriers to e-commerce adoption: A study of two approaches to cluster development. *International Journal of Electronic Marketing and Retailing.*

MacNeil, I.R. (1974). The many futures of contracts. *Southern California Law Review, 47*, 691-816.

Madlberger, M. (2004). *Electronic retailing*. Wiesbaden, Germany: Deutscher Universitaetsverlag.

Madlberger, M. (2006). *Multi-channel retailing in B2C e-commerce*. In M. Khosrow-Pour (Ed.), Encyclopedia of e-commerce, e-government, and mobile commerce. Hershey, PA: Idea Group.

Malhotra, N. K., Kim, S. S., & Agarwal, J. (2004). Internet users' information privacy concerns (IUIPC): The construct, the scale, and a causal model. *Information Systems Research, 15*(4), 336-355.

Malladi, R., & Agrawal, D.P. (2002). Current and future applications of mobile and wireless networks. *Communications of the ACM, 45*(10), 144-146.

Malman, S. (2000). Memes and corporate identities in the telecommunication sector. In *ITS 2000: The XIII Biennial Conference of the International Telecommunications Society*. Retrieved September 2, 2007, from http://www.its2000.org.ar/conference/malman.pdf

Maltz, A. (1993). Private fleet use: A transaction cost model. *Transportation Journal, 32*, 46-53.

Maltz, A., Rabinovic, E., & Sinha, R. (2004). Logistics: The key on e-retail success. *Supply Chain Management Review, 1*, 56-63.

Manecke, N., & Schoensleben, P. (2004). Cost and benefit of Internet-based support of business processes. *International Journal of Production Economics, 87*(3), 213-229.

Mantel, B. (2001). *E-money and e-commerce: Two alternative views of future innovations*: Federal Reserve Bank of Chicago.

Mantel, B., & McHugh, T. (2001). *Competition and innovation in the consumer e-payments market: Considering the demand, supply, and public policy issues*. Federal Reserve Bank of Chicago.

Mantel, B., & McHugh, T. (2002). *Evolving e-payment networks in the U.S.: The strategic, competitive and innovative implications*. Retrieved September 2, 2007, from http://www.chicagofed.org/paymentsystems/publications/E-Payment_Networks_Mantel_McHugh.pdf

Manzi, N. (2003). *Use tax collection on income tax returns in other states* (Policy Brief). Minnesota House of Representatives Research Department.

Markel, M. (2005). The rhetoric of misdirection in corporate privacy-policy statements. *Technical Communication Quarterly, 14*(2), 197-214.

Markoff, J. (2002). Military seeks to restrict wireless. *San Francisco Chronicle*, pp. B1, B4.

Markus, L. M. (1987). Toward a "critical mass" theory of interactive media. Universal access, interdependence and diffusion. *Communication Research, 14*, 491-511.

Marron, P.J., Lausen, G., & Weber, M. (2003). Catalog integration made easy. In *Proceedings of the ICDE 2003*, Bangalore.

Marshall, K. (1999). Has technology introduced new ethical problems? *Journal of Business Ethics, 19*, 81-90.

Martin, L.M., & Matlay, H. (2001). 'Blanket' approaches to promoting ICT in small firms: Some lessons from the DTI ladder adoption model in the UK. *Internet Research: Electronic Networking Applications and Policy, 11*(5), 399-410.

Martins, C. B. M. J., Steil, A. V., & Todesco, J. L. (2004). Factors influencing the adoption of the Internet as a teaching tool at foreign language schools. *Computers & Education, 42*(4), 353-374.

Mason, R. (1986). Four ethical issues of the information age. *MIS Quarterly, 10*(1), 5-12.

Massetti, B., & Zmud, R. W. (1996, September). Measuring the extent of EDI usage in complex organizations: strategies and illustrative examples. *MIS Quarterly*, 331-345.

Mata, F.J., Fuerst, W.L., & Barney, J.B. (1995). Information technology and sustained competitive advantage: A resource-based analysis. *MIS Quarterly, 19*(4), 487-504.

Mathieson, K. (1991). Predicting user intentions: Comparing the technology acceptance model with the theory of planned behavior. *Information Systems Research, 2*(3), 173-191.

Matthyssens, P., & Van den Bulte, C. (1994). Getting closer and nicer partnerships in the supply chain. *Long Range Planning, 27*(1), 71-83.

Mauldin, E., & Arunachalam, V. (2002a). An experimental examination of alternative forms of Web assurance for business-to-consumer e-commerce. *Journal of Information Systems, 16*(1), 33-54.

Mauldin, E., & Arunachalam, V. (2002b). Reply to discussions of an experimental examination of alternative forms of Web assurance for business-to-consumer e-commerce. *Journal of Information Systems, 16*(1), 65-67.

Maupin, R. (1990). Sex role identity and career success of certified public accountants. *Advances in Public Interest Accounting,* pp. 97-105.

Maxwell, B. (1996). Translation and cultural adaptation of the survey instruments. In M. O. Martin & D. L. Kelly (Eds.), *Third International Mathematics and Science Study (TIMSS) Technical Report, Volume I: Design and Development.* Chestnut Hill, MA: Boston College.

Maynard-Smith, J., & Harper, D. (2003). *Animal signals.* Oxford, UK: Oxford University Press.

McAdam, R. (2000). The implementation of reengineering in SMEs: A grounded study. *International Small Business Journal, 18*(4), 29-45.

McCabe, D.L. (1987). Buying group structure: Constriction at the top. *Journal of Marketing, 51*(4), 89-98.

McCarthy, E. J. (1960). *Basic marketing: A managerial approach.* R. D. Irwin.

McCloskey, D. (2004). Evaluating electronic commerce acceptance with the technology acceptance model. *Journal of Computer Information Systems, 44*(2), 49-57.

McGarvey, R. (2002). Hospitality checks out wireless. *Mbusiness,* 18-23.

McGregor, J., & Tweed, D. (2001). Gender and managerial competence: Support for theories of androgyny. *Women in Management Review, 16*(6), 279-286.

McKenna, R. (1993). *Relationship marketing: Successful strategies for the age of the customer.* Cambridge: Perseus Publishing.

McKinney, V., Yoon, K., & Zahedi, F. (2002). The measurement of Web-customer satisfaction: An expectation and disconfirmation approach. *Information Systems Review, 13*(3), 296-315.

McKnight, D. H., & Chervany, N. L. (2001). What trust means in e-commerce customer relationships: An interdisciplinary conceptual typology. *International Journal of Electronic Commerce, 6*(2), 35-59.

McKnight, D. H., Kacmar, C. J., & Choudhury, V. (2004). Shifting factors and the ineffectiveness of third party assurance seals: A two-stage model of initial trust in a Web business. *Electronic Markets, 14*(3), 252-266.

McKnight, D.H., Choudhury, V., & Kacmar, C. (2002a). Developing and validating trust measures for e-commerce: An integrative typology. *Information Systems Research, 13*(3), 334-359.

McKnight, D.H., Choudhury, V., & Kacmar, C. (2002b). The impact of initial consumer trust on intentions to transact with a Web site: A trust building model. *Journal of Strategic Information Systems, 11*(3-4), 297-323.

McLure, C.E. (2000). The taxation of electronic commerce: Background and proposal. In N. Imparato (Ed.), *Public policy and the Internet: Privacy, taxes, and contract* (pp. 49-113). Stanford: Hoover Institution Press.

McLure, C.E. (2002a). Thinking straight about the taxation of electronic commerce: Tax principles, compliance problems, and Nexus. *NBER/Tax Policy & the Economy, 16*(1), 115-140.

McLure, C.E. (2002b). Sales and use taxes on electronic commerce: Legal, economic, administrative, and political issues. *The Urban Lawyer, 34*(2), 487-520.

Mehrtens, J., Cragg, P., & Mills, A. (2001). A model of Internet adoption by SMEs. *Information & Management, 39,* 165–176.

Meier, S.T., & Lambert, M.E. (1991). Psychometric properties and correlates of three computer aversion scales. *Behaviour Research Methods, Instruments and Computers, 23*(1), 9-15.

Menard, S. (1995). *Applied logistic regression analysis.* Thousand Oaks, CA: Sage.

Mercuri, R. T. (2005). Trusting in transparency. *Communications of the ACM, 48*(5), 15-19.

Metzger, M. (2006). Effects of site, vendor, and consumer characteristics on Web site trust and disclosure. *Communication Research, 33*(34), 155-179.

Mikesell, J.L. (2000). Remote vendors and American sales and use taxation: The balance between fixing the problem and fixing the tax. *National Tax Journal, 53*(4), 1273-1285.

Mikesell, J.L. (2001). The threat to state sales taxes from e-commerce: A review of the principal issues. *Municipal Finance Journal, 22*(3), 48-60.

Mikesell, J.L. (2004). The prospects for general sales taxation in American state and local government finance: Challenges for a fiscal workhorse unready for the new millennium. *Journal of Public Budgeting, Accounting, & Financial Management, 16*(1), 63-79.

Miller, N.L., & Besser, T.L. (2000). The importance of community values in small business strategy formation: Evidence from rural Iowa. *Journal of Small Business Management, 38*(1), 68-85.

Milne, G., & Culnan, M. (2002). Using the content of online privacy notices to inform public policy: A longitudinal analysis of the 1998-2001 U.S. Web surveys. *The Information Society, 18*(5), 345-359.

Min, H., & Galle, W. P. (2003). E-purchasing: Profiles of adopters and nonadopters. *Industrial Marketing Management, 32*(3), 227-233.

Min, S., & Wolfinbarger, M. (2005). Market share, profit margin, and marketing efficiency of early movers, bricks and clicks, and specialists in e-commerce. *Journal of Business Research, 58*, 1030-1039.

Mirchandani, A.A., & Motwani, J. (2001, Spring). Understanding small business electronic commerce adoption: An empirical analysis. *Journal of Computer Information Systems*, 70–73.

Mitra, A., & Lynch, J. (1996). Advertising effects on consumer welfare: Prices paid and liking for brands selected. *Marketing Letters, 7*(1), 19-29.

Miyazaki, A. D., & Fernandez, A. (2000). Internet privacy and security: An examination of online retailer disclosures. *Journal of Public Policy & Marketing, 19*(1), 54-61.

Miyazaki, A., & Fernandez, A. (2001). Consumer perceptions of privacy and security risks for online shopping. *Journal of Consumer Affairs, 36*, 28-49.

Miyazaki, A., & Krishnamurthy, S. (2002). Internet seals of approval: Effects on online privacy policies and consumer perceptions. *The Journal of Consumer Affairs, 36*(1), 28-49.

Miyazaki, A.D., & Fernandez, A. (2001). Consumer perceptions of privacy and security risks for online shopping. *The Journal of Consumer Affairs, 35*(1), 27-44.

MOED (Ministry of Economic Development). (2000a). *SMEs in New Zealand: Structure and dynamics, firm capability team, update report.* Retrieved May 5, 2000, from http://www.MOED.govt.nz/gbl/bus_dev/smes2/index.html#TopOfPage

MOED (Ministry of Economic Development). (2000b). *Electronic commerce in New Zealand: A survey of business use of the Internet information technology.* Policy Group Competition and Enterprise branch. Retrieved May 16, 2001, from http://www.ecommerce.govt.nz/ecat/resources/index.html

Molla, A., & Licker, P. S. (2001). E-commerce systems success: An attempt to extend and respecify the DeLone and McLean model of IS success. *Journal of Electronic Commerce Research, 2*(4), 131-139.

Monsuwé, T.P.Y., Dellaert, B.G.C., & deRuyter, K. (2004). What drives consumers to shop online? A literature review. *International Journal of Service Industry Management, 15*(1), 102-121.

Moon, J.-W., & Kim, Y.-G. (2001). Extending the TAM for a World-Wide-Web context. *Information and Management, 38*, 217-230.

Moore, G. C., & Benbasat, I. (1991). Development of an instrument to measure the perceptions of adopting an information technology innovation. *Information Systems Research, 2*(3), 192-222.

Moore, G., & Benbasat, I. (1996). Integrating diffusion of innovations and theory of reasoned action models to predict utilisation of information technology by end-users. In K. Kautz, & J. Pries-Heje (Eds.), *Diffusion and adoption of information technology* (pp. 132–146). London: Chapman & Hall.

Moores, T. (2005). Do consumers understand the role of privacy seals in e-commerce? *Communications of the ACM, 48*(3), 86-91.

Moorman, C., Zaltman, G., & Deshpande, R. (1992). Relationships between providers and users of market research: The dynamics of trust within and between organizations. *Journal of Marketing Research, 29*, 314-328.

Morgan, L. (1997). *Focus groups as qualitative research* (2nd ed.). Thousand Oaks, CA: Sage Publications.

Morgan, L. (1998). *The focus group guidebook: Focus group kit volume 1.* Thousand Oaks, CA: Sage Publications.

Morgan, R. M., & Hunt, S. D. (1994). The commitment-trust theory of relationship marketing. *Journal of Marketing, 58*, 20-38.

Moriarty, R., & Moran, U. (1990). Managing hybrid marketing systems. *Harvard Business Review, 68*(6), 146-155.

Motwani, J., Mirchandani, D., Madan, M., & Gunasekaran, A. (2002). Successful implementation of ERP projects: Evidence from two case studies. *International Journal of Production Economics, 75*(1-2), 83-96.

Mukhopadhyay, T. (1998). How to win with electronic data interchange in information technology and industrial competitiveness. In C. Kemerer (Ed.), *How IT shapes competition* (pp. 91-106). Boston: Kluwer Academic Publishers.

Muldoon, K. (2000). *How to profit through catalog marketing.* NTC Business Books.

Multichannel Retailing on the Rise. (2005a, September). Chain Store Age, p. 20.

Munro, M.C., & Wheeler, B.R. (1980). Planning, critical success factors, and management information requirements. *MIS Quarterly, 4*(4), 27-38.

Murphy, J. (1996). *Small business management.* London: Pitman.

Myers, J.B., Pickersgill, A.D., & Van Metre, E.S. (2004). Steering customers to the right channels. *McKinsey Quarterly, 4*, 36-47.

Myers, R. (1990). *Classical and modern regression with applications* (2nd ed.). Boston: Duxbury.

Myerscough, M.A. (2002, August). Information systems quality assessment: Replicating Kettinger and Lee's USIF/SERVQUAL combination. In *Proceedings of the 8th Americas Conference on Information Systems, Dallas, TX* (pp. 1104-1115).

Nambisan, S., Agarwal, R., & Tanniru, M. (1999). Organizational mechanisms for enhancing user innovation in information technology. *MIS Quarterly, 23*(3), 365-395.

Nath, R. (1988). Local area networks: The network managers' perspective. *Information & Management, 14*(4), 175-181.

National Conference of State Legislatures (NCLS). (1992). *Principles of a high-quality state revenue system.* Washington, DC: National Conference of State Legislatures. Retrieved September 12, 2007, from http://www.ncsl.org

Naudé, P., Holland, C., & Sudbury, M. (2000). The benefits of IT-based supply chains: Strategic or operational? *Journal of Business-to-Business Marketing, 7*(1), 45-67.

Negroponte, N. (1995). *Being digital.* Random House.

Nelson, P. (2001). Advertising as information. *Journal of Political Economy, 82*(4), 729-754.

Neri, M. (2003). *Mapa da Exclusão Digital.* Retrieved September 7, 2007, from Centro de Políticas Sociais, EPGE/FGV, http://epge.fgv.br/portal/pesquisa/livros/2003.html

Nesbary, D. (2000). The taxation of Internet commerce. *Social Science Computer Review, 18*(1), 17-39.

Neuman, W. L. (1994). *Social research methods* (2nd ed.). Boston: Allyn & Bacon.

Ngai, E. W. T., & Wat, F. K. T. (2002). A literature review and classification of electronic commerce research. *Information & Management, 39*, 415-429.

Ngai, E. W. T., Poon, J. K. L., & Chan, Y. H. C. (2007). Empirical examination of the adoption of WebCT using TAM. *Computers & Education, 48*(2), 250-267.

Nguyen, N., & Leblanc, G. (2001). Corporate image and corporate reputation in customers' retention decisions in services. *Journal of Retailing and Consumer Services, 8*, 227-236.

NIDA (National Internet Development Agency of Korea). (2004). *Survey on the computer and Internet usage.* Retrieved September 7, 2007, from http://www.nida.or.kr

Nikitkov, A. (2006). Information assurance seals: How they impact consumer purchasing behavior. *Journal of Information Systems, 20*(1), 1-17.

Nillson, P. (1997). Business counselling services directed towards female entrepreneurs: Some legitimacy dilemmas. *Entrepreneurship and Regional Development, 9*(3), 239-258.

Noble, S.M., Griffith, D.A., & Weinberger, M.G. (2005). Consumer derived utilitarian value and channel utilization in a multi-channel retail context. *Journal of Business Research, 58*, 1643-1651.

NOP World-Technology. (2001). *Wireless LAN benefit study* (CISCO Thought Leadership Series). Retrieved September 11, 2007, from http://newsroom.cisco.com/dlls/tln/WLAN_study.pdf

Nouwens, J., & Bouwman, H. (1995). Apart together in electronic commerce: The use of information and communication technology to create network organizations. *Journal of Computer-Mediated Communication, 1*(3). Retrieved September 1, 2007, from http://jcmc.indiana.edu/

Noy, N.F., & Musen, M.A. (1999). SMART: Automated support for ontology merging and alignment. In *Proceedings of the 12th Banff Workshop on Knowledge Acquisition, Modeling, and Management*, Banff, Alberta, Canada.

Noy, N.F., & Musen, M.A. (2000). PROMPT: Algorithm and tool for automated ontology merging and alignment. In *Proceedings of the 17th National Conference on Artificial Intelligence (AAAI-2000)*, Austin, TX.

Nunnally, J. C. (1978). *Psycometric theory.* New York: McGraw-Hill.

NZStat (Statitics New Zealand). (1999, March). *Income of persons (final): Year ended March 1999.* Retrieved November 9, 2002, from http://www.stats.govt.nz

O'Callaghan, R., & Turner, J. A. (1995). Electronic data interchange—Concepts and issues. In H. Krcmar, N. Bjorn-Andersen, & R. O'Callaghan (Eds.), *EDI in Europe: How it works in practice* (pp. 1-19). John Wiley & Sons.

O'Cass, A., & Fenech, T. (2003). Web retailing adoption: Exploring the nature of Internet users. *Journal of Retailing and Consumer Services, 10*, 81-94.

O'Mahony, D., Peirce, M., & Tewari, H. (2001). *Electronic payment systems for e-commerce* (2nd ed.). Boston: Artech House.

O'Neill, D. (2001). Analysis of Internet users' level of online privacy concerns. *Social Science Computer Review, 19*(1), 17-31.

Odegaard, P. (2001). Solving the m-maze. *Global Telecoms Business, 58*, 42.

Odom, M. D., Kumar, A., & Saunders, L. (2002). Web assurance seals: How and why they influence consumers' decisions. *Journal of Information Systems, 16*(2), 231-250.

OECD. (1999). The economic and social impact of electronic commerce: Preliminary findings and research agenda. *Organisation for Economic Co-operation and Development.* Retrieved September 5, 2007, from http://www.oecd.org/dataoecd/3/12/1944883.pdf

OECD. (2002). *Measuring the information economy 2002.* Retrieved September 7, 2007, from http://www.oecd.org/document/5/0,2340,en_2649_37409_2765701_1_1_1_37409,00.html

OECD. (2003). Overview of wireless LANs. *OECD Papers, 3*(9), 7-11.

Oerlemans, L.A.G., & Meeus, M.T.H. (2001). R&D cooperation in a transaction cost perspective. *Review of Industrial Organization, 18*(1), 77-90.

Oinas, P. (2002). Towards understanding network relationships in online retailing. *International Review of Retail, Distribution & Consumer Research, 12*(3), 319-335.

Olson, G. (2000, May). An overview of B2B integration. *Enterprise Application Integration Journal, 4.*

Omelayenko, B., & Fensel, D. (2001a, August 5). A layered integration approach for product descriptions in B2B e-commerce. In *Proceedings of the Workshop on E-Business & the Intelligent Web at the 17th International Joint Conference on Artificial Intelligence (IJCAI-2001)*, Seattle, WA.

Omelayenko, B., & Fensel, D. (2001b, July 7-10). An analysis of B2B catalogue integration problems. In *Proceedings of the International Conference on Enterprise Information Systems (ICEIS-2001)*, Setúbal, Portugal.

Ordanini, A., & Pol, A. (2001). Infomediation and competitive advantage in B2B digital marketplaces. *European Management Journal, 19*(3), 276-285.

Organisation for Economic Co-operation and Development. (1980). *OECD guidelines on the protection of privacy and transborder flows of personal data.* Retrieved September 2, 2007, from http://www.oecd.org/document/18/0,2340,en_2649_37441_1815186_1_1_1_37441,00.html

Organisation for Economic Co-operation and Development. (2005). *About OECD.* Retrieved September 2, 2007, from http://www.oecd.org/about/0,2337,en_2649_201185_1_1_1_1_1,00.html

Otim, S., & Grover, V. (2006). An empirical study on Web-based services and customer loyalty. *European Journal of Information Systems, 15*, 527-541.

PACE. (2006, November). WLAN security weak in most businesses. *PACE*, p. 4.

Palvia, P.C. (1996). A model and instrument for measuring small business user satisfaction with information technology. *Information & Management, 31*(3), 151-163.

Papazoglou, M. (2001). Agent-oriented technology in support of e-business. *Communications of the ACM, 44*(4), 71-77.

Park, S.-Y., & Yun, G. W. (2004). The effect of Internet-based communication systems on supply chain management: An application of transaction cost analysis. *Journal of Computer-Mediated Communication, 10*(1). Retrieved September 1, 2007, from http://jcmc.indiana.edu/

Patterson, P. G., & Smith, T. (2001). Relationship benefits in service industries: A replication in a southeast asian context. *Journal of Services Marketing, 15*(6), 425-443.

Patton, M.Q. (1987). *Qualitative evaluation and research methods.* Sage Publications.

Pavlou, P. A., & Fygenson, M. (2006). Understanding and predicting electronic commerce adoption: An extension of the theory of planned behavior. *MIS Quarterly, 30*(1), 115-143.

Pavlou, P. A., & Gefen, D. (2005). Psychological contract violation in online marketplaces: Antecedents, consequences, and moderating role. *Information Systems Research, 16*(4), 372-399.

Pavlou, P.A. (2003). Consumer acceptance of electronic commerce: Integrating trust and risk with the technology acceptance model. *International Journal of Electronic Commerce, 7*(3), 101-134.

Payan, J. M., & McFarland, R. G. (2005). Decomposition influence strategies: Argument structure and dependence as determinants of the effectiveness of influence strategies in gaining channel member compliance. *Journal of Marketing, 69*, 66-79.

Peet, S., Brindley, C., & Ritchie, B. (2002). The European Commission and SME support mechanisms for e-business. *European Business Review, 14*(5), 335–341.

Peffers, K., & Tuunanen, T. (2005). Planning for IS applications: A practical, information theoretical method and case study in mobile financial services. *Information & Management, 42*(3), 483-501.

Pennington, R., Wilcox, H. D., & Grover, V. (2003). The role of system trust in business-to-consumer transactions. *Journal of Management Information Systems, 20*(3), 197-226.

Pennington, R., Wilcox, H., Dixon, & Grover, V. (2004). The role of system trust in business-to-consumer transactions. *Journal of Management Information Systems, 20*(3), 197-226.

Peppers, D., & Rogers, M. (1993). *The one to one future: Building relationships one customer at a time.* New York: Doubleday.

Peppers, D., & Rogers, M. (1997). *Enterprise one to one: Tools for competing in the interactive age.* New York: Doubleday.

Perez, J. C. (2005, June 24). Gartner: Security concerns to stunt e-commerce growth [Electronic version]. *ComputerWorld.* Retrieved September 5, 2007, from the IDG News Service database.

Perez, M.P., Carnicer, M.P.L., & Sanchez, A.M. (2002). Differential effects of gender perceptions of teleworking by human resources managers. *Women in Management Review, 17*(6), 262-275.

Perry, C. (1998). Process of case study methodology for postgraduate research in marketing. *European Journal of Marketing, 32*(9/10), 785-802.

Perry, S.C. (2002). A comparison of failed and non-failed small businesses in the United States: Do men and women use different planning and decision making strategies? *Journal of Developmental Entrepreneurship, 7*(4), 415-428.

Peterson, R. A., Balasubramanian, S., & Bronnenberg, B. J. (1997). Exploring the implications of the Internet for consumer marketing. *Journal of the Academy of Management Science, 25*(4), 329-346.

Pettigrew, A.M. (1989). Context and action in the transformation of the firm. *Journal of Management Studies, 24*(6), 649-670.

Pflughoeft, K.A., Ramamurthy, K., Soofi, E.S., Yasai-Ardekani, M., & Zahedi, F. (2003). *Multiple conceptualizations of small business Web use and benefit. Decision Sciences, 34*(3), 467-512.

Phelps, R., & Mok, M. (1999). Managing the risks of intranet implementation: An empirical study of user satisfaction. *Journal of Information Technology, 14,* 39-52.

Philip, G., & Pedersen, P. (1997). Inter-organizational information systems: Are organizations in Ireland deriving strategic benefits from EDI? *International Journal of Information Management, 17*(5), 337-357.

Phillips, L. W. (1981). Assessing measurement error in key informant reports: A methodological note on organizational analysis in marketing. *Journal of Marketing Research, 16,* 395-415.

Pilioura, T. (1998). Electronic payment systems on open computer networks: A survey. In D. Tsichritzis (Ed.), *Electronic commerce objects.* Centre Universitaire d'Informatique, University of Geneva.

Pinckney, B. (2000). New law helps banks break barriers. *Capital District Business Review, 27*(3), 20.

Pinsonneault, A., & Kraemer, K. L. (1993). Survey research methodology in management information systems: An assessment. *Journal of Management Information Systems, 10*(2), 75-106.

Polanyi, M. (1966). *The tacit dimension.* Doubleday & Company.

Poon, S. (1999). Small business and Internet commerce: What are the lessons learned? In F. Sudweeks, & C. Romm (Eds.), *Doing business on the Internet: Opportunities and pitfalls* (pp. 113–124). London: Springer-Verlag.

Poon, S. (2000). Business environment and Internet commerce benefit: A small business perspective. *European Journal of*

Poon, S., & Swatman, P. (1995). The Internet for small businesses: An enabling infrastructure for competitiveness. Retrieved June 27, 2000, from http://inet.nttam.com

Poon, S., & Swatman, P. (1997) Internet-based small business communication. *International Journal of Electronic Commerce, 7*(2), 5–21.

Poon, S., & Swatman, P. (1997). The Internet for small businesses: An enabling infrastructure. In *Proceedings of the 5th Internet Society Conference* (pp. 221-231).

Poon, S., & Swatman, P. (1998) A combined-method study of small business Internet commerce. *International Journal of Electronic Commerce, 2*(3), 31–46.

Poon, S., & Swatman, P. (1999a). An exploratory study of small business Internet commerce issues. *Information & Management, 35,* 9–18.

Poon, S., & Swatman, P. (1999b). A longitudinal study of expectations in small business Internet commerce. *International Journal of Electronic Commerce, 3*(3), 21–33.

Poon, S., & Swatman, P.M.C. (1998, June 8-10). Small business Internet commerce experiences: A longitudinal study. In *Proceedings of the 11ᵗʰ International Bled Electronic Commerce Conference*, Bled, Slovenia.

Porter, C. E., & Donthu, N. (2006). Using the technology acceptance model to explain how attitudes determine Internet usage: The role of perceived access barriers and demographics. *Journal of Business Research, 59*(9), 999-1007.

Porter, M. E. (1980). *Competitive strategy: Techniques for analyzing industries and competitors.* New York: Free Press.

Porter, M. E. (2001). Strategy and the Internet. *Harvard Business Review, 79*, 63-78.

Portz, K., Strong, J. M., Busta, B., & Schneider, K. (2000). Do consumers understand what WebTrust means? *CPA Journal, 70*(10), 47.

Potter, B. (2006). Wireless hotspots: Petri dish of wireless security. *Communications of the ACM, 49*(6), 51-56.

Poulovassilis & Brien (1998). A general formal framework for schema transformation. *Data & Knowledge Engineering, 28*, 47-71.

Powell, G.N. (1993). *Women and men in management.* Newbury Park: Sage Publications.

Premkumar, G., & Roberts, M. (1999). Adoption of new information technologies in rural small businesses. *The International Journal of Management Science (OMEGA), 27*, 467–484.

Premkumar, G., Ramamurthy, K., & Nilakanta, M. (1994). Implementation of electronic data interchange: An innovation diffusion perspective. *Journal of Management Information Systems, 11*, 157-177.

Pritchard, M. P., Havitz, M. E., & Howard, D. R. (1999). Analyzing the commitment-loyalty link in service contexts. *Journal of the Academy of Management Science, 27*(3), 333-348.

Probst, T. M. (2003). Development and validation of the job security index and the job security satisfaction scale: A classical test theory and IRT approach. *Journal of Occupational and Organizational Psychology, 76*, 451-467.

Prokein, O., & Faupel, T. (2006, January). Using Web service for intercompany cooperation: An empirical study within the German industry. In *Proceedings of the Hawaii International Conference on System Sciences (HICSS-39)*. Retrieved September 10, 2007, from http://www.computer.org/portal site/ieeecs/

PublicEye. (2002, March 30). Survey of 56,765 online shoppers suggests that many still use small e-tailers primarily for comparison shopping. *The Public Eye.* Retrieved September 5, 2007, from http://www.epubliceye.com/pr36.html

Purao, S., & Campbell, B. (1998, August 14-16). Critical concerns for small business electronic commerce: Some reflections based on interviews of small business owners. In *Proceedings of the Association for Information Systems Americas Conference*, Baltimore (pp. 325-327).

PWHC (PriceWaterhouseCoopers). (1999). *SME electronic commerce study* (TEL05/97T). Retrieved April 10, 2000, from http://apec.pwcglobal.com/sme.html

Quantz, J., & Wichmann, T. (2003). *E-business-standards in Germany.* Research project commissioned by the German Federal Ministry of Economics final report (short version).

Quayle, M. (2002). E-commerce: The challenge for UK SMEs in the 21st century. *International Journal of Operations and Production Management, 22*(10), 1148-1161.

Radosevich, L. (1997). Early adopters hail extranet benefits, dodge pitfalls. *InfoWorld, 19*(23), 65-66.

Rafaeli, S., & Sudweeks, F. (1997). Networked interactivity. *Journal of Computer-Mediated Communication, 2*(4). Retrieved September 1, 2007, from http://jcmc.indiana.edu/

Rainie, L. (2004). The rise of wireless connectivity and our latest findings: A PIP data memo. *Pew Internet and American Life Project.* Retrieved September 11, 2007, from http://www.usabilityviews.com/uv007099.html

Ramakrishnan, A. (2000). *Leveraging the power of UNSPSC for business intelligence* (White Paper).

Ramamurthy, K., Premkumar, G., & Crum, M. R. (1999). Organizational and interorganizational determinants of EDI diffusion and organizational performance: A causal model. *Journal of Organizational Computing and Electronic Commerce, 9*(4), 253-285.

Ranganathan, C., & Ganapathy, S. (2002). Key dimensions of business-to-consumer Web sites. *Information & Management, 39*, 457-465.

Ratnasingham, P. (1998). The importance of trust in electronic commerce. *Internet Research, 8*(4), 313-321.

Ravald, A., & Gronroos, C. (1996). The value concept and relationship marketing. *European Journal of Marketing, 30*(2), 19-30.

Raymond, L., & Bergeron, F. (1996). EDI success in small and medium-sized enterprises: A field study. *Journal of Organizational Computing and Electronic Commerce, 6*, 161-172.

Reagle, J., & Cranor, L. F. (1999). The platform for privacy preferences. *Communications of the ACM, 42*(2), 48-55.

Reddick, C.G. (2006). A consumer's perspective on the use tax and electronic commerce. *Journal of Internet Commerce, 5*(1), 23-43.

Reddick, C.G., & Coggburn, J.D. (2006). E-commerce and the future of the American sales tax system. In H.A. Frank (Ed.), *Handbook of public financial management* (pp. 179-206). Boca Raton, FL: CRC Press/Taylor and Francis Publishers.

Regan, K. (2003, January). Wireless LAN security: Things you should know about WLAN security. *Network Security*, 7-9.

Reichheld, F. (2006). *The ultimate question: Driving good profits and true growth*. Boston: Harvard Business School Press.

Reichheld, F. F., & Schefter, P. (2000). Your secret weapon on the Web. *Harvard Business Review, 78*, 105-113.

Reichheld, F., & Sasser, W. E. (1990, September-October). Zero defections: Quality comes to services. *Harvard Business Review*, pp. 105-111.

Reichheld, F., & Schefter, P. (2000). E-loyalty: Your secret weapon on the Web. *Harvard Business Review, 78*(4), 105-113.

Reichheld, F., & Teal, T. (1996). *The loyalty effect: The hidden force behind growth, profits, and lasting value.* Boston: Harvard Business School Press.

Reid, D.A., & Plank, R.E. (2000). Business marketing comes of age: A comprehensive review of the literature. *Journal of Business-to-Business Marketing, 7*(2/3), 9-178.

Reimenschneider, C., & Mykytyn, P. (2000). What small business executives learned about managing information technology. *Information & Management, 37*, 257–269.

Reinartz, W., & Kumar, V. (2000). On the profitability of long-life customers in a noncontractual setting: An empirical investigation and implications for marketing. *Journal of Marketing, 64*, 17-35.

Reinartz, W., & Kumar, V. (2002, July). The mismanagement of customer loyalty. *Harvard Business Review*, pp. 86-94.

Reinartz, W., Thomas, J., & Kumar, V. (2005). Balancing acquisition and retention resources to maximize customer profitability. *Journal of Marketing, 69*, 63-79.

Remenyi, D., & Money, A. (1991). A user-satisfaction approach to IS effectiveness measurement. *Journal of Information Technology, 6*, 162-175.

Remus, W. (1986). Graduate students as surrogates for managers in experiments on business decision making. *Journal of Business Research, 14*, 19-25.

Renner, et al. (2001). Specification BMEcat, Version 1.2. Retrieved September 1, 2007, from http://www.bmecat.org/Download/BMEcatV12e.pdf

Retailers Missing Opportunities to Sell More Products Via Online. (2005b, August 11). *New Media Age*, p. 9.

Reynolds, F.D. (1974). An analysis of catalog buying behavior. *Journal of Marketing, 38*(3), 47-51.

Reynolds, J. (2000). eCommerce: A critical review. *International Journal of Retail & Distribution Management, 28*(10), 417-444.

Reynolds, W., Savage, W., & Williams, A. (1994). *Your own business: A practical guide to success.* ITP.

Rindfleisch, A., & Moorman, C. (2003). Interfirm cooperation and customer orientation. *Journal of Marketing Research, 67,* 421-436.

Ring, P.S., & Van de Ven, A.H. (2000). Formal and informal dimensions of transactions. In A.H. Van de Ven, H.L. Angle, & M.S. Poole (Eds.), *Research on the management of innovation: The Minnesota studies* (pp. 171-192). Oxford: Oxford University Press.

Riquelme, H. (2002). Commercial Internet adoption in China: Comparing the experience of small, medium and large business. *Internet Research: Electronic Networking Applications and Policy, 12*(3), 276-286.

Rockart, J.F. (1979). Chief executives define their own data needs. *Harvard Business Review, 57*(2), 81-93.

Rockhold, J. (2001). The business of where. *Wireless Review, 18,* 14-18.

Rodgers, S., & Harris, M.A. (2003). Gender and E-Commerce: An Exploratory Study. *Journal of Advertising Research, 43*(3), 322-329.

Rogers, E. (1983). *Diffusion of innovation.* New York: The Free Press.

Rogers, E. (1995). *Diffusion of innovation.* New York: The Free Press.

Rogers, E. M., & Shoemaker, F. F. (1971). *Communications of innovations: A cross-cultural approach* (2nd ed.). New York: Free Press.

Romano, C. (1989). Research strategies for small business: A case study. *International Small Business Journal, 7*(4), 35-43.

RosettaNet. (2004). RosettaNet technical dictionary: RNTD Specification v4.0. Retrieved September 1, 2007, from http://www.rosettanet.org

Rossi, J. W. (1997). A guide for present value models. *Institute of Applied Economic Research,* Text n° 482.

Rousseau, D. M., Sitkin, S. B., Burt, R. S., & Camerer, C. (1998). Not so different after all: A cross-discipline view of trust. *The Academy of Management Review, 23*(3), 393-404.

Rowe, G., & Wright, G. (2001). Expert opinions in forecasting: The role of the delphi technique. In J.S.

Armstrong (Ed.), *Principles of forecasting: A handbook for researchers and practitioners* (pp. 125-144). Norwell, MA: Kluwer Academic Publishers.

Rowe, G., Wright, G., & Bolger, F. (1991). Delphi: A reevaluation of research and theory. *Technological Forecasting and Social Change, 39*(3), 235-251.

Rowley, J., & Dawes, J. (2000). Disloyalty: A closer look at non-loyals. *Journal of Consumer Marketing, 17,* 538-549.

Rust, R. T., Zeithmal, V. A., & Lemon, K. N. (2000). *Driving customer equity: How customer lifetime value is reshaping corporate strategy.* New York: Free Press.

Ryssel, R., Ritter, T., & Gemünden, H.G. (2004). The impact of information technology deployment on trust, commitment and value creation in business relationships. *Journal of Business & Industrial Marketing, 19*(3), 197-207.

Sadeh, N. (2002). *M-commerce: Technologies, services, and business models.* New York: John Wiley & Sons.

Salam, A. F., Lakshmi, I., & Srikantan, R. (2001). Relationship marketing and B2B e-commerce. *ICIS.*

Salo, J. (2006a). *Business relationship digitalization: A case study from the steel processing industry* (pp. 1-296). Oulu University Press, Oulu, Finland. Retrieved September 10, 2007, from http://herkules.oulu.fi/isbn9514282396/isbn9514282396.pdf

Salo, J. (2006b). IT-enabled integration of business relationship in the steel industry context. In B. Walters & Z. Tang (Eds.), *IT-enabled strategic management: Increasing returns for the organization* (pp. 275-294). Hershey, PA: Idea Group Publishing.

Salo, J. (in press). Mobile technology usage in business relationships. In M. Khosrow-Pour (Ed.), *Encyclopedia of information science and technology* (2nd ed.). Hershey, PA: Idea Group Publishing.

Salo, J., & Alajoutsijärvi, K. (2003, September 4-6). Strained business relationships. In *Proceedings of the 19th IMP Conference on Managing in Networks,* Lugano, Switzerland (pp. 1-10). Retrieved September 10, 2007, from http://www.impgroup.com

Sandberg, K.W. (2003). An exploratory study of women in micro enterprises: Gender related difficulties. *Journal of Small Business and Enterprise Development, 10*(4), 408-417.

Santarelli, E., & D'Altri, S. (2003). The diffusion of e-commerce among SMEs: Theoretical implications and empirical evidence. *Small Business Economics, 21*(3), 273.

Santos, A. M., & Costa, C. S. (1997). General characteristics of retail in Brazil. *National Bank for Social and Economic Development, Setorial n° 5*.

Sarathy, R., & Robertson, C. (2003). Strategic and ethical considerations in managing digital privacy. *Journal of Business Ethics, 46*, 111-126.

Saunders, M., Lewis, P., & Thornhill, A. (2000). *Research methods for business students* (2nd ed.). Harlow, UK: Prentice Hall.

Sawhney, M. (1999, September). Let's get vertical. *Business 2.0*.

Sawyers, A. (1996). 1979 oil shock meant recession for U.S., depression for autos. *Automotive News, 70*(5666), 140-144.

Schmidt, R., Lyytinen, K., Keil, M., & Cule, P. (2001). Identifying software project risks: An international delphi study. *Journal of Management Information Systems, 17*(4), 5-36.

Schmidt, R.A., & Parker, C. (2003). Diversity in independent retailing: Barriers and benefits - The impact of gender. *International Journal of Retail and Distribution Management, 31*(8), 428-439.

Schoder, D., & Yin, P. (2000). Building firm trust online. *Communications of the ACM, 43*, 73-79.

Schoenbachler, D.D., & Gordon, G.L. (2002). Multi-channel shopping: Understanding what drives channel choice. *The Journal of Consumer Marketing, 19*(1), 42-53.

Schouten, J., & McAlexander, J. (1995). Subcultures of consumption: An ethnography of the new bikers. *Journal of Consumer Research, 22*(1), 43-61.

Schultz, D., & Hayman, D. (1999, April). The two sides of loyalty. *Interactive Marketing*.

Seiders, K., Berry, L.L., & Gresham, L.G. (2000). Attention, retailers! How convenient is your convenience strategy? *Sloan Management Review, 41*(3), 79-89.

Senn, J.A. (2000). The emergence of m-commerce. *Computer, 33*(12), 148-150.

Sexton, R.S., Johnson, R.A., & Hignite, M.A. (2002). Predicting Internet/e-commerce use. *Internet Research, 12*(5), 402-410.

Seybold, P. B. (1998). *Customers.com: How to create a profitable business strategy for the Internet and beyond*. Auckland: Random House Publishing.

Shade, L.R. (1998). A gendered perspective on access to the information infrastructure. *The Information Society, 14*, 33-44.

Shapland, E., Gavurlin, S., & Chartoff, M. (2002). Making wireless LANs work for you. *Business Communications Review*, pp. 30-34.

Sharma, S. (1996). *Applied multivariate techniques*. New York: John Wiley & Sons.

Sheehan, K. (1999). An investigation of gender differences in online privacy concerns and resultant behaviour. *Internet Marketing*, pp. 159-173.

Sheehan, K. B. (2000). Toward a typology of Internet users and online privacy concerns. *The Information Society, 18*, 21-32.

Sheehan, K., & Hoy, M. (2000). Dimensions of privacy concern among online consumers. *Journal of Public Policy & Marketing, 19*, 62-73.

Shemwell, D. J., Yavas, U., & Bilgin, Z. (1998). Customer-service provider relationships: An empirical test of a model of service quality, satisfaction, and relationship-oriented outcomes. *International Journal of Service Industry Management, 9*(2), 155-168.

Sheth, J. N., & Parvatiyar, A. (1995). Relationship marketing in consumer markets: Antecedents and consequences. *Journal of the Academy of Marketing Science, 23*(4), 255-271.

Sheth, J. N., Sisodia, R. S., & Sharma, A. (2000, Winter). The antecedents and consequences of customer-centric marketing. *Journal of the Academy of Marketing Science, 28*(2).

Sheth, J.N. (1983). An integrative theory of patronage preference and behavior. In W.R. Darden & R.F. Lusch (Eds.), *Patronage behavior and retail management* (pp. 9-28). New York: Elsevier Science Publishing.

Siau, K., & Shen, Z. (2003). Building customer trust in mobile commerce. *Communications of the ACM, 46*(4), 91-94.

Siegel, S., & Castellan, N. J. (1988). *Nonparametric statistics for the behavioral sciences.* Boston: McGraw-Hill.

Simon, S.J. (2001). The impact of culture and gender on Web sites: An empirical study. *The DATA BASE for Advances in Information Systems, 32*(1), 18-37.

Singer, T. (2001). Wireless LANs come of age. *Plant Engineering, 44,* 46, 48.

Singh, S. (2001). Gender and use of the Internet at home. *New Media & Society, 3*(4), 395-415.

Sinisalo, J., Salo, J., Karjaluoto, H., & Leppäniemi. M. (in press). Management of mobile customer relationships: Underlying issues and opportunities. *Business Process Management Journal.*

Sipior, J. C., Ward, B. T., & Rongione, N. M. (2004). Ethics of collecting and using consumer Internet data. *Information Systems Management, 21*(1), 58-66.

Sivasailam, N., Kim, D., & Rao, H. R. (2002, May-June). What companies are(n't) doing about Web site assurance. *IEEE IT Professional*, pp. 33-40.

Sloane, A. (1994). *Computer communications: Principles and business applications.* Maidenhead: McGraw-Hill.

Smeltzer, L.R., & Fann, G.L. (1989, April). Gender differences in external networks of small business owner/managers. *Journal of Small Business Management*, 25-32.

Smith, A. (1776). *The wealth of nations.* London: W. Strahau & T. Cadell.

Smith, B. (2002). Under the radar. *Wireless Week, 8,* 38-39.

Smith, H., Milberg, S., & Burke, S. (1996). Information privacy: Measuring individuals' concerns about organizational practices. *MIS Quarterly, 20*(2), 167-196.

Smith, J. B. (1997). Selling alliances: Issues and insights. *Industrial Marketing Management, 26,* 149-161.

Smith, M. D., Bailey, J., & Brynjolfsson, E. (1999). Understanding digital markets: Review and assessment. In E. Brynjolfsson & B. Kahin (Eds.), *Understanding the digital economy: Data, tools, and research* (pp. 99-136). Cambridge, MA: MIT Press.

Smith, P. (2004). Accelerated product development: Techniques and traps. In K.B. Kahn (Ed.), *The PDMA handbook of new product development* (2nd ed., pp. 173-187). John Wiley.

Soh, P., Yap, S., & Raman, S. (1992). Impact of consultants on computerisation success in small business. *Information & Management, 22,* 309–313.

Sohal, A.S., & Ng, L. (1998). The role and impact of information technology in Australian business. *Journal of Information Technology, 13*(3), 201-217.

Son, J.-Y., Narasimhan, S., & Riggins, J. F. (2000). Factors affecting the extent of electronic cooperation between firms: Economic and sociological perspectives. *ICIS.*

Sonfield, M., Lussier, R., Corman, J., & McKinney, M. (2001). Gender comparisons in strategic decision making: An empirical analysis of the entrepreneurial strategy matrix. *Journal of Small Business Management, 39*(2), 165-173.

Spence, A. (1973). Job market signaling. *Quarterly Journal of Economics, 87*(3), 355-374.

Spence, A. (1974). *Market signaling: Informational transfer in hiring and related screening processes* (1st ed.). Cambridge, MA: Harvard University Press.

Srinivasan, K., Kekre, S., & Mukhopadhyay, T. (1994). Impact of electronic data interchange technology on JIT shipments. *Management Science, 40,* 1291-1304.

Srinivasan, S. S., Anderson, R., & Ponnavolu, K. (2002). Customer loyalty in e-commerce: An exploration of its antecedents and consequences. *Journal of Retailing, 78,* 41-50.

Stake, R. E. (1994). Case studies. In N. K. Denzin & Y. S. Lincoln (Eds.), *Handbook of qualitative research.* Thousand Oaks: Sage.

Stanley, R.A. (2002). Wireless LAN risks and vulnerabilities (White Paper). *Information Systems Audit and Control.*

Stauffert, T. (1991). *Informationstechnik und Abhängigkeit.* Frankfurt a.M. Verlag Peter Lang.

Steinfield, C., Bouwman, H., & Adelaar, T. (2002). The dynamics of click-and-mortar electronic commerce: Opportunities and management strategies. *International Journal of Electronic Commerce, 7*(1), 93-119.

Steinfield, C., Chan, A., & Kraut, R. E. (2000). Computer mediated markets: An introduction and preliminary test of market structure effects. *Journal of Computer-Mediated Communication, 3*. Retrieved September 1, 2007, from http://www.ascusc.org/jcmc/vol5/issue3/steinfield.html

Steinfield, C., Kraut, R., & Plummer, A. (1995). The impact of interorganizational networks on buyer-seller relationships. *Journal of Computer-Mediated Communication, 1*(3).

Stern, L., & Kaufmann, P. (1985). Electronic data interchange in selected consumer goods industries: An interorganizational perspective. In R.D. Buzzell (Ed.), *Marketing in an electronic age* (pp. 52-73). Boston: Harvard Business School Press.

Stevens, J. (1986). *Applied multivariate statistics for the social sciences.* Hillsdale, NJ: Lawrence Erlbaum.

Stewart , D., & Shamdasani, P. (1990). *Focus groups: Theory and practice.* Newbury Park, CA: Sage Publications.

Stoer, M., Nienhaus, J., Birkeland, N., & Menkhaus, G. (2003). IT infrastructure for supply chain management in company networks with small and medium-sized enterprises. In *Proceedings of the International Conference on Enterprise Information Systems*, France.

Stone, B. (1984). *Successful direct marketing methods* (3rd ed.). Lincolnwood: NTC Publishing.

Straub, D. W. (1989). Validating instruments in MIS research. *MIS Quarterly, 13*(2), 147-169.

Street, C. T., & Meister, D. B. (2004). Small business growth and internal transparency: The role of information systems. *MIS Quarterly, 28*, 473-506.

Stump, R., & Sriram, V. (1997). Employing information technology in purchasing: Buyer-supplier relationships and size of the supplier base. *Industrial Marketing Management, 26*(2), 127-136.

Suh, B., & Han, I. (2003). The impact of customer trust and perception of security control on the acceptance of electronic commerce. *International Journal of Electronic Commerce, 7*(3), 135-161.

Suh, B., & Han, I. (2003). The impact of customer trust and perception of security control on the acceptance of electronic commerce. *International Journal of Electronic Commerce, 7*(3), 135-162.

Sun Microsystems. (2001, May 22). Sun online privacy policy. Retrieved September 3, 2007, from http://www.sun.com/privacy/

Surry, D. W., & Gustafson, K. L. (1994). *The role of perceptions in the adoption of computer-based learning.* ERIC Clearinghouse on Information and Technology (ERIC Document Reproduction Service No. ED374788).

Sveiby, K.E. (1997). *The new organizational wealth: Managing & measuring knowledge-based assets.* San Francisco: Berrett-Koehler Publishers.

Swain, J.A., & Hellerstein, W. (2005). The political economy of the streamlined sales and use tax agreement. *National Tax Journal, 58*(3), 605-619.

Swaminathan, V., Lepkowska-White, E., & Rao, B. P. (1999). Browsers or buyers in cyberspace? An investigation of factors influencing electronic exchange. *Journal of Computer-Mediated Communication, 5*(2). Retrieved September 1, 2007, from http://jcmc.indiana.edu/

Swanson, E.B. (1994). Information systems innovation among organisations. *Management Science, 40*(9), 1069–1092.

Swatman, P. M. C., & Swatman, P. A. (1992). EDI system integration: A definition and literature survey. *The Information Society, 8*, 169-205.

Sweeney, T. (2000, November 13). Wireless LANs almost ready for widescale adoption. *Informationweek. com*, pp. 286-292.

Szymanski, D. M., & Hise, R. T. (2000). E-satisfaction: An initial examination. *Journal of Retailing, 76*(3), 309-322.

Tagliavini, M., Ravarini, A., Antonelli, A. (2001). An evaluation model for electronic commerce activities within SMEs. *Information Technology and Management, 2*, 211-230.

Tan, S. J. (1999). Strategies for reducing consumers' risk aversion in Internet shopping. *Journal of Consumer Marketing, 16*, 163-180.

Tan, Y., & Thoen, W. (2001). Toward a generic model of trust for electronic commerce. *International Journal of Electronic Commerce, 5*, 61-74.

Taylor, S., & Todd, P.A. (1995). Understanding information technology usage: A test of competing models. *Information Systems Research, 6*(2), 144-176.

Teltscher, S. (2002). *E-Commerce and Development Report 2002*. United Nations Conference on Trade and Development.

Teo, H. H., Wei, K. K., & Benbasat, I. (2003). Predicting intention to adopt interorganizational linkages: An institutional perspective. *MIS Quarterly, 27*, 19-49.

Teo, T., Tan, M., & Buk, W. (1998). A contingency model of Internet adoption in Singapore. *International Journal of Electronic Commerce, 2*(2), 95–118.

Tetteh, E., & Burn, J. (2001). Global strategies for SME-business: Applying the SMALL framework. *Logistics Information Management, 14*(1-2), 171-180.

The European Parliament and the Council of the European Union. (2000). Regulation (EC) No 45/2001 of the European Parliament and of the Council of 18 December 2000 on the protection of individuals with regard to the processing of personal data by the community institutions and bodies and on the free movement of such data. *Official Journal of the European Communities*. Retrieved September 2, 2007, from http://europa.eu.int/eur-lex/pri/en/oj/dat/2001/l_008/l_00820010112en00010022.pdf

Themistocleous, M., & Irani, Z. (2002). Towards a novel framework for the assessment of enterprise application integration packages. In *Proceedings of the 36th Hawaii International Conference on Systems Sciences*. Retrieved September 10, 2007, from http://www.computer.org/portal /site/ieeecs/

Thomas, W. I., & Znaniecki, F. (1927). *The Polish peasant in Europe and America*. New York: Knopf.

Thong, J. (1999). An integrated model of information systems adoption in small business. *Journal of Management Information Systems, 15*(4), 187–214.

Thong, J., & Yap, C. (1995). CEO characteristics, organisational, characteristics and information technology adoption in small business. *Omega, International Journal of Management Sciences, 23(*4), 429–442.

Thong, J., & Yap, C. (1996). Information technology adoption by small business: An empirical study. In K. Kautz, & J. Pries-Heje (Eds.), *Diffusion and adoption of information technology* (pp. 160–175). London: Chapman & Hall.

Thong, J., Yap, S., & Raman, K. (1994). Engagement of external expertise in information systems implementation. *Journal of Management Information Systems, 11*(2), 209.

Torkzadeh, G., & Dhillon, G. (2002). Measuring factors that influence the success of Internet commerce. *Information Systems Research, 13*(2), 187-204.

Tornatzky, L. G., & Fleischer, M. (1990). *The process of technological innovation*. Lexington, MA: Lexington Books.

Tornatzky, L. G., & Klein, K. J. (1982). Innovation characteristics and innovation adoption-implementation: A meta-analysis of findings. *IEEE Transactions on Engineering Management, 9*(1), 28-45.

Tribunalla, T. (2002, January). Twenty questions of e-commerce security. *The CPA Journal*, pp. 60-63.

TRUSTe. (2005). TRUSTe: Make privacy your choice. Retrieved September 5, 2007, from http://www.truste.org/businesses/Web_privacy_seal.php

Tung, L. L., & Rieck, O. (2005). Adoption of electronic government services among business organizations in Singapore. *The Journal of Strategic Information Systems, 14*(4), 417-440.

Tuunainen, V.K. (1998). Opportunities of effective integration of EDI for small businesses in the automotive industry. *Information & Management, 34*, 361-375.

Tuunainen, V.K. (1999). Opportunities of effective integration of EDI for small businesses in the automotive industry. *Information & Management, 36*(6), 361-375.

Tversky, A. (1995). Weighing risk and uncertainty. *Psychological Review, 102*(2), 269-283.

U.S. Census Bureau. (2004, February). *Retail e-commerce sales in second quarter 2004*. Retrieved September 7, 2007, from the Department of Commerce News, http://www.census.gov/mrts/www/ecom.pdf

U.S. SBA, Office of Advocacy. (2000). Small business expansions in electronic commerce. Retrieved September 1, 2007, from http://www.SBA.GOV/ADVO/STATS/

UMIST and the Office of the Information Commissioner. (2002). *Study of compliance with the Data Protection Act of 1998 by UK based Websites*. Retrieved September 2, 2007, from http://www.co.umist.ac.uk/research/tech_reports/trs_2002_008_lam.pdf

UNCTAD. (2001). *E-commerce and development report 2001*. Retrieved September 2, 2007, from http://r0.unctad.org/ecommerce/docs/edr01_en/edr01pt0_en.pdf

UNCTAD. (2002). *E-commerce and development report 2002*. Retrieved September 2, 2007, from http://r0.unctad.org/ecommerce/ecommerce_en/faq_en.htm

United Nations General Assembly. (1948). *Universal Declaration of Human Rights*. Retrieved September 2, 2007, from http://www.un.org/Overview/rights.html

UNSPSC. (2001). *Why coding and classifying products is critical to success in electronic commerce, using the UNSPSC* (White Paper). Granada Research

Use tech as a tool. (2002). *Men's Health*, p. 64.

Van Akkeren, J., & Cavaye, A.L.M. (1999, December 1-3). Factors affecting entry-level Internet technology adoption by small business in Australia: An empirical study. In *Proceedings of the 10th Australasian Conference on Information Systems*, Wellington, New Zealand.

Van Blokland, A. (2004). Killer apps from DoCoMo and KDDI. *J@pan Inc., 53*, 6

Van de Ven, A.H. (1976). On the nature, formation, and maintenance of relations among organizations. *The Academy of Management Review, 1*(4), 24-36.

Van Dyke, T. P., Midha, V., & Nemati, H. (2007). The effect of consumer privacy empowerment on trust and privacy concerns in e-commerce. *Electronic Markets, 17*(1), 68-81.

Vanhaverbeke, W., Duysters, G., & Noorderhaven, N. (2002). External technology sourcing through alliances or acquisitions: An analysis of the application-specific integrated circuits industry. *Organization Science, 13*(6), 714-733.

Varshney, U. (2001). Location management support for mobile commerce applications. *Proceedings of the 1st International Workshop on Mobile Commerce* (pp. 1-6).

Varshney, U., & Vetter, R. (2002). Mobile commerce: Framework, applications and networking support. *Mobile Networks and Applications, 7*(3), 185-198.

Veblen, T. (1899). *The theory of the leisure class*. New York: Macmillan.

Venkatesan, V.S., & Fink, D. (2002). Adoption of Internet technologies and e-commerce by small and medium enterprises (SMEs) in Western Australia. In *Proceedings of the Information Resource Management Association International Conference* (pp. 1136-1137).

Venkatesh, V., & Brown, S. A. (2001). A longitudinal investigation of personal computers in homes: Adoption determinants and emerging challenges. *MIS Quarterly, 25*(1), 71-102.

Venkatesh, V., Morris, M. G., Davis, G. B., & Davis, F. D. (2003). User acceptance of information technology: Toward a unified view. *MIS Quarterly, 27*(3), 425-478.

Venkatraman, N. (1989). The concept of fit in strategy research: Toward verbal and statistical correspondence. *Academy of Management Review, 14*(3), 423-444.

Venkatraman, N. (2000). Five steps to a dot-com strategy: How to find your footing on the Web. *Sloan Management Review, 41*, 15-28.

Verheul, I., Risseeuw, P., & Bartelse, G. (2002). Gender differences in strategy and human resource management. *International Small Business Journal, 20*(4), 443-476.

Verisign. (2002). Retrieved September 5, 2007, from http://www.verisign.com

Victor, C., & Jih, W-J. (2006). Fair or not? The taxation of e-commerce. *Information Systems Management, 23*(1), 68-72.

Vijayasarathy, L.R. (2002). Internet taxation, privacy and security: Opinions of the taxed and legislated. *Quarterly Journal of Electronic Commerce, 3*(1), 53-71.

Vlosky, R.P., Fontenot, R., & Blalock, L. (2000). Extranets: Impacts on business practices and relationships. *Journal of Business & Industrial Marketing, 15*(6), 438-457.

Walczuch, R., Braven, G., & Lundgren, H. (2000). Internet adoption: Barriers for small firms in the Netherlands. *European Management Journal, 18*(5), 561–572.

Walczuch, R., Van Braven, G., & Lundgren, H. (2000). Internet adoption barriers for small firms in The Netherlands. *European Management Journal, 18*(5), 561-572.

Walker, G., & Weber, D. (1987). Supplier competition, uncertainty, and make-or-buy decisions. *Academy of Journal Management, 30*(3), 589-596.

Wallace, D.W., Giese, J.L., & Johnson, J.L. (2004). Customer retailer loyalty in the context of multiple channel strategies. *Journal of Retailing, 80*(4), 249-263.

Wang, J.C., & Tsai, K.H. (2002). Factors in Taiwanese firms' decisions to adopt electronic commerce: An empirical study. *World Economy, 25*(8), 1145-1167.

Wang, R. Y., & Strong, D. M. (1996). Beyond accuracy: What data quality means to data consumers. *Journal of Management Information Systems, 12*(4), 5-34.

Wang, S., & Archer, N. (2004). Strategic choice of electronic marketplace functionalities: A buyer-supplier relationship perspective. *Journal of Computer Mediated Communication, 10*, 1-30. Retrieved September 1, 2007, from http://jcmc.indiana.edu/

Wang, W., Liew, S.C., & Li, V.O.K. (2005). Solutions to performance problems in VoIP over a 802.11 wireless LAN. *IEEE Transactions on Vehicular Technology, 54*(1), 366-384.

Ward, B.T., & Sipior, J.C. (2004). To tax or not to tax e-commerce: A United States perspective. *Journal of Electronic Commerce Research, 5*(3), 172-180.

Warren, S., & Brandeis, L. (1890). The right to privacy. Retrieved September 2, 2007, from http://www.louisville.edu/library/law/brandies/privacy.html (Originally published in *Harvard Law Review, 4*(5).

Welsh, J.A., & White, J.F. (1981, July-August). A small business is not a little big business. *Harvard Business Review*, 18-32.

Westbrook, R. A., et al. (1983). Value-percept disparity: An alternative to the disconfirmation of expectations theory of consumer satisfaction. *Advances in Consumer Research, 10*, 256-261.

Westhead, P., & Storey, D.J. (1996). Management training and small firm performance: Why is the link so weak? *International Small Business Journal, 14*(4), 13-24.

Westin, A. (1967). *Privacy and freedom.* New York: Antheneum.

Westin, A., & Maurici, D. (1998). E-commerce and privacy: What net users want. *PriceWaterhouseCoopers*, p. 15.

Whiting, R. (2003). A win-win combination? *Information Week*. Retrieved September 10, 2007, from http://www.informationweek.com.story/IWK20030314S0001

Wilkinson, I. (2001). A history of network and channels thinking in marketing in the 20th century. *Australasian Journal of Marketing, 9*(2), 23-53.

Williamson, O. (1979). Transaction cost economics: The governance of contractual relations. *Journal of Law and Economics, 22*(10), 233-261.

Williamson, O. (1981). The economics of organization: The transaction cost approach. *American Journal of Sociology, 87*(3), 549-577.

Williamson, O.E. (1991, June). Comparative economic organization: The analysis of "discrete structural alternatives." *Administrative Science Quarterly, 36*(2), 269-296.

Wilson, D.T., & Mummalaneni, V. (1986). Bonding and commitment in buyer-seller relationships: A preliminary conceptualisation. *Journal of Industrial Marketing & Purchasing, 1*(3), 44-58.

Wilson, H., Daniel, E., & McDonald, M (2002). Factors for success in customer relationship management (CRM) systems. *Journal of Marketing Management, 18*(1-2), 193-219.

Wolfingbarger, M., & Gilly, M. C. (2001). Shopping online for freedom, control, and fun. *California Management Review, 43*(2), 34-55.

Wolin, B. (2002). *Automatic classification in product catalogs.* ACM.

Wonglimpiyarat, J. (2002). *The business strategies in payment innovations.* Paper presented at the 1ˢᵗ National Conference on Electronic Business, Thailand.

Woodroof, J., & Burg, W. (2003). Satisfaction/dissatisfaction: Are users predisposed? *Information & Management, 40*(4), 317-324.

Woodside, A., & Wilson, E.J. (2003). Case study research methods for theory building. *Journal of Business & Industrial Marketing, 18*(6/7), 493-508.

Woudenberg, F. (1991). An evaluation of delphi. *Technological Forecasting and Social Change, 40*(2), 131-150.

Wright, M. (2005). WiMax wireless broadband. *EDN, 50*(7), 44-50.

Wuyts, S., & Geyskens, I. (2005). The formation of buyer-supplier relationships: Detailed contract drafting and close partner selection. *Journal of Marketing, 69,* 103-117.

Wynarczyk, P., Watson, R., Storey, D.J., Short, H., & Keasey, K. (1993). *The managerial labour market in small and medium sized enterprises.* London: Routledge.

Xing, Y., & Grant, D.B. (2006). Developing a framework for measuring physical distribution service quality of multi-channel and "Pure Player" Internet retailers. *International Journal of Retail & Distribution Management, 34*(4/5), 278-289.

Xu, B., & Walke, B. (2001). Design issues of self-organizing broadband wireless networks. *Computer Networks, 37*(1), 73-81.

Yang, B., & Lester, D. (2004). Attitudes toward buying online. *Cyber Psychology & Behavior, 7*(1), 85-91.

Yang, J., & Poon, W. (2001). Taxable base of Internet commerce. *Municipal Finance Journal, 22*(3), 70-80.

Yang, Z., & Fang, X. (2004). Online service quality dimensions and their relationships with satisfaction: A content analysis of customer reviews of securities brokerage services. *International Journal of Service Industry Management, 15*(3), 302-326.

Yellavalli, B., Holt, D., & Jandial, A. (2007). *Retail multi-channel integration. delivering a seamless customer experience* (Infosys White Paper). Retrieved September 7, 2007, from http://www.infosys.com/supplychain/InfosysMCIWhitePaperfinal.pdf

Yin, R. (1989). *Case study research.* Sage Publications.

Yin, R. (1994). *Case study research design and methods.* Thousand Oaks, CA: Sage Publications.

Young, D., & Benamati, J. (2000). Differences in public Web sites: The current state of large U.S. firms. *Journal of Electronic Commerce Research, 1*(3), 94-105.

Young, S. (2000, December 11). E-commerce (a special report): Buying in—In search of the killer app: As mobile commerce gets going, the question everybody wants to know is a simple one: What will get consumers to flock to it? *Wall Street Journal,* p. R.8.

Yousafzai, S.Y., Pallister, J.G., & Foxall, G.R. (2003). A proposed model of e-trust for electronic banking. *Technovation, 23*(11), 847-860.

Yuan, Y., & Zhang, J.J. (2003). Towards an appropriate business model for m-commerce. *International Journal of Mobile Communications, 1*(1/2), 35-56.

Zablah, A.R, Bellenger, D.N., & Johnston, W.J. (2004). An evaluation of divergent perspectives on customer relationship management: Towards a common understanding of an emerging phenomenon. *Industrial Marketing Management, 33*(6), 475-489.

Zahavi, A. (1975). Mate selection: A selection for a handicap. *Journal of Theoretical Biology, 53*(1), 205-214.

Zeithaml, V. A., & Bitner, M. J. (1997). *Services marketing* (p. 114). Singapore: McGraw-Hill.

Zhang, A. (2005). Transaction governance structure: Theories, empirical studies, and instruments. *International Journal of Commerce and Management, 16*(2), 59-85.

Zhang, A., Melcher, A., & Li, L. (2004). Mapping the relationships among product complexity, information technology, and transaction governance structure: A case study. *Journal of Management Systems, 16*(4), 41-54.

Zhang, X., Keeling, K. B., & Pavur, R. J. (2000). Information quality of commercial Web site home pages: An explorative analysis. In *Proceedings of the 21st International Conference on Information Systems*, Brisbane, Australia (pp. 164-175).

Zhu, K., Kraemer, K. L., Xu, S., & Derick, J. (2004). Information technology payoff in e-business environments: An international perspective on value creation of e-business in the financial services industry. *Journal of Management Information Systems, 21*(1), 17-54.

Zhu, K., Kraemer, K., & Xu, S. (2003). Electronic business adoption by European firms: A cross-country assessment of the facilitators and inhibitors. *European Journal of Information Systems, 12*(4), 251.

Zucker, L. (1986). Production of trust: Institutional sources of economic structure: 1840-1920. In B. Staw & L. Cummings (Eds.), *Research in organizational behavior* (pp. 53-111). Greenwich, CT: JAI Press.

About the Contributors

Sven Abels (sables@acm.org) started working as a freelancer about 12 years ago by founding his own software company Abelssoft. Within those activities, he conceptualized and implemented software products for end users and also offered IT consulting for small and midsized enterprises. Abels received a BSc, Dipl.-Inform, and a PhD from the University of Oldenburg (Germany). He organized several academic workshops and has over 40 publications in journals, proceedings, and books.

Lei-da Chen is associate professor of information systems and technology in the College of Business Administration of Creighton University. His research and consulting interests include electronic commerce, mobile e-commerce, Web-based systems development, data warehousing and mining, and diffusion of information technology in organizations. Dr. Chen is the author of a book, *Mobile Commerce Application Development*, and over 40 professional articles in refereed journals and national and international conference proceedings.

Jonathan Cowin is a business student of the College of Business Administration at Creighton University in Omaha, Nebraska, majoring in finance. Cowin was born and raised in Overland Park, Kansas, where he was the oldest of four children. Cowin plans to graduate from Creighton in May of 2009.

John R. Criswell II is a senior programmer with Shelter Insurance and adjunct faculty teaching computer information systems at Columbia College in Columbia, Missouri. He received a BS (computer information systems), MBA, and MS CIS from Missouri State University. His research has appeared in the *Journal of Electronic Commerce in Organizations* and *Journal of Business and Behavioral Sciences*. His current research interests include privacy policy statements, e-commerce, and ethics in information systems.

Martin D. "Marty" Crossland is the chairman of distance programs for the School of Business at Oral Roberts University. He earned a PhD in management information systems from Indiana University, an MBA from Oklahoma City University, and a BS in geology from Texas Tech University. His research interests include decision making effectiveness and human factors in decision support system usage, particularly with spatially reference information (geographic information systems), telecommunications and networking, and systems security. His research has been published in various journals, including *MIS Quarterly, Decision Support Systems, Journal of End User Computing,* and *Technology Studies.*

Yanqing Duan, PhD, is a reader in information systems at The University of Bedfordshire Business School. Her principal research interest is how the emerging information and communication technologies (ICT) can be effectively used in, and their impact on, supporting decision making, facilitating knowledge transfer, and improving skills development. This research focus is reflected in the context of ICT based knowledge management and transfer, use of intelligent systems in supporting organizational and individual decision making, small to medium enterprises (SMEs) adoption of e-commerce/e-business, and Web-based training systems for SMEs. She has coordinated many European Commission funded research projects and published about 90 papers in journals, books, and international conference proceedings.

Zetian Fu, PhD, is a professor and vice president of China Agriculture University, Beijing, China. He has a wide range of research interests, including agriculture systems engineering, agriculture information technologies, agriculture structure adjustment in China, agriculture policies and strategies, and so forth. He has received numerous research grants and supervised many doctoral students. He has over 100 publications in journals, books, and conference proceedings.

Axel Hahn (hahn@wi-ol.de) is head of the working group business information systems or the University of Oldenburg in northern Germany. He owns the professorship business informatics. His main research areas are interoperability in virtual organizations and information processing at the product development.

Qile He is a research associate at Middlesex University Business School, London. He received his first degree, a BA in economics, from the University of Colorado at Denver. Subsequently, he gained an MSc in financial decision management from the University of Luton and an MSc in research methods from Middlesex University. He is now pursuing his PhD at Middlesex University. His principal research interests include organizational learning, strategic partnership, and knowledge transfer processes and practices in the context of firms' supply chain management.

Luiz Antonio Joia is an associate professor and MBA head at the Brazilian School of Public and Business Administration, Getulio Vargas Foundation, and an adjunct professor at Rio de Janeiro State University, Brazil. He has published two books, several chapters, and more than 50 scientific papers in international journals and conferences. He holds a BSc in civil engineering from the Militar Institute of Engineering, Brazil, and an MSc in civil engineering and DSc in engineering management from the Federal University of Rio de Janeiro, Brazil. He also holds an MSc in management studies from Oxford University, UK.

Norbert Jurkiewicz is an undergraduate student in information sciences and technology at Penn State University and expects to graduate in May 2007. Currently he is an APL developer for The Carlisle Group, a Scranton, Pennsylvania-based software developer that provides solutions for the financial industry.

Young-Gul Kim is the director of the Knowledge Management Research Center at the Graduate School of Management of the Korea Advanced Institute of Science and Technology (KAIST). He has a BS and MS from Seoul National University and a PhD from University of Minnesota's Curtis L. Carlson School of Management. Before joining KAIST in 1993, Professor Kim taught at the Katz Graduate School of Business, University of Pittsburgh, USA as a faculty for three years. He has published in numerous academic journals such as *MIS Quarterly, Communications of the ACM, Journal of MIS, IEEE Transactions on Engineering Management, Business Process Management Journal, Journal of Strategic Information Systems*, and so on.

Kathryn M. Kimery is associate professor of information systems and chair of the Department of Finance, Information Systems, and Management Science at Saint Mary's University in Halifax, Nova Scotia. She earned her PhD from the Michael F. Price College of Business at the University of Oklahoma in 1998. Her research interests focus on electronic commerce, computer-assisted instruction in higher education, computing careers, and ethical issues in computing and business education. She has published articles in numerous journals, including the *Journal of Electronic Commerce in Organizations, Journal of Business Research, Journal of Information Technology Theory and Application, International Journal of Business and Economic Research*, and *Journal of Management Education.*

Assion Lawson-Body is an assistant professor at the University of North Dakota. He obtained his PhD and MBA in MIS from Laval **University, Quebec, Canada**. He also received a DESS-CTCI from IAE, University of Montpellier 2, France. His publications have appeared or will appear in the *Journal of Electronic Commerce in Organizations, Journal of Computer-Mediated Communication, Journal of E-Business, E-Business Review, Academy of Information and Management Science Journal, Encyclopedia of E-commerce, E-Government and M-commerce, Encyclopedia of Multimedia Technology and Networking, Journal of Comparative International Management, "Revue des Sciences de Gestion,"* and so forth. He has also published in several conference proceedings such as Association of Information Systems, IRMA, Association for Information and Management, Business, Economics and Management Disciplines, and so on. He has consulted for the Small Business Development Center (SBDC) and Government Rural Outreach Initiative (e-government) in North Dakota.

Daoliang Li, PhD, is a professor at the China Agricultural University. His principal research interest is the development and use of intelligent systems in environment and agriculture, especially for decision support systems, remote sensing, and GIS in revegetation/rehabilitation of abandoned lands. He is also interested in knowledge management and e-learning. He has published widely in international journals and books.

Robert MacGregor is an associate professor in the School of Information Technology and Computer Science at the University of Wollongong in Australia. He is also the former head of discipline in information systems. His research expertise lies in the areas of information technology (IT) and electronic commerce (e-commerce) in small to medium enterprises (SMEs). He has authored a number of journal and conference publications examining the use and adoption of IT in SMEs. MacGregor is also the founding editor of the *Australasian Journal of Information Systems* and was conference chair of the Australian Conference of Information Systems in 1992. In his spare time, Rob writes music. His most recent work is the symphony "Alba."

Maria Madlberger (maria.madlberger@wu-wien.ac.at) is an assistant professor at the Institute for Management Information Systems at the Vienna University of Economics and Business Administration.

She received her PhD in commerce from the Department of Retailing and Marketing at this university in 2002. Madlberger's research activities follow an interdisciplinary approach as she concentrates on the links between information systems and marketing, especially in the field of e-commerce. Her research interests are focused on the application of inter-organizational information systems and information sharing in supply chain management, strategic and operational benefits of electronic data interchange (EDI), multichannel retailing, distribution in B2C e-commerce, and Internet marketing. She has published her research results in journals and refereed conferences in the fields of e-commerce, marketing, and supply chain management. Her dissertation has been published as a book titled *Electronic Retailing*. Before Madlberger joined the institute, she gained practical experience as a specialized journalist at a trade journal for the grocery and FMCG sector. .

Mary McCord is associate professor of computer information systems at the University of Central Missouri. After an entrepreneurial career in oil and gas production, she received her PhD in business administration from the University of Oklahoma. Her research areas include e-commerce, service learning, and team-based learning. She is currently teaching management of information systems through the Integrative Business Experience program, which combines team-based learning methods with real world business endeavors. She has published articles in journals such as *Journal of Electronic Commerce in Organizations*, *Journal of Informatics Education Research*, *Journal of Information Technology Theory and Application*, *To Improve the Academy, MBAR Journal*, and *Handbook of Research on Electronic Surveys and Measurements*.

David B. Meinert is professor and director of the MS CIS Program at Missouri State University. Dr. Meinert received his doctorate in management information systems from the University of Mississippi in 1990. His professional background includes software development, systems integration, and project management. Dr. Meinert has published in a number of journals, including *Journal of Applied Business Research, Journal of Computer Information Systems, Information Strategy: The Executive's Journal, Information Resource Management Journal, End User Computing Management, Journal of Electronic Commerce in Organizations, Focus on Change Management, Journal of Marketing Management*, and *Journal of Marketing Theory and Practice*.

Ravi Nath is the associate dean for graduate programs and the holder of the Jack and Joan McGraw Endowed Chair of Information Technology Management in the College of Business Administration at Creighton University. He has published numerous research papers in the area of electronic commerce and information systems in various national and international publications. Dr. Nath teaches and conducts research in information systems, electronic commerce, and data mining. Also, Dr. Nath serves on the boards of several for-profit and nonprofit organizations. He holds a master's degree from Wichita State University and a PhD from Texas Tech University.

Timothy P. O'Keefe, PhD, is associate professor and chairman of the Department of Information Systems and Business Education at the University of North Dakota. He is an experienced IT consultant and cofounder of a successful Internet services company. His research interests include electronic business and commerce, database design and optimization benchmarking, Internet business efficacy and assessment, and the relationship between the information systems and records management functions in organizations, among others. He has published and presented at numerous national and international conferences as well as in journals ranging from *Communications of the ACM* to the *Journal of Forensic Accounting*. Recently, Dr. O'Keefe spent several months as a visiting professor at the University of Shanghai for Science and Technology teaching database design and management information systems. He has been actively involved in the Wuhan International Conference on E-Business and has been active in recruiting Chinese students to graduate programs in the United States.

Chung-Hoon Park is the senior consultant of the Office of Strategy Consulting at Samsung SDS. He has a BS, MS, and PhD from the Korea Advanced Institute of Science and Technology (KAIST). He has published in the *International Journal of Retailing and Distribution Management and Business Process Management Journal*. His interest is in customer relationship management, knowledge management, and electronic commerce. His paper on customer relationship management has received the best paper award from the *Business Process Management Journal* in 2004.

Alan R. Peslak is an assistant professor of information sciences and technology at Penn State University. He received his PhD in information systems from Nova Southeastern University, Fort Lauderdale, Florida. His research areas include information technology social, ethical, and economic issues as well as information technology pedagogy. Publications include the *Communications of the ACM, Information Resources Management Journal, Journal of Business Ethics, Journal of Computer Information Systems, Journal of Information Systems Education, Team Performance Management, Information Research,* and *First Monday.* He has over 25 years of diverse manufacturing and service industry experience. He is on the editorial boards of numerous journals.

Dane K. Peterson is a professor of quantitative business analysis at Missouri State University. He received his PhD in quantitative methods and applied psychology from Southern Illinois University. He has published in numerous journals such as *Journal of Applied Psychology, Organizational Behavior and Human Decision Processes, International Journal of Information Management, Business & Society, Journal of Electronic Commerce in Organizations, Information Resources Management Journal, Business & Psychology, Personnel Review,* and *Information Technology & People.*

Christopher G. Reddick is an assistant professor of public administration at the University of Texas at San Antonio. He was a recipient of the President's Distinguished Achievement Award for Research, UTSA 2005. He formerly taught at Murray State University in Kentucky where he was MPA director. Dr. Reddick's research interests are in e-government, public budgeting, and employee health benefits. Some of his publications can be found in the academic journals *Public Budgeting & Finance, Government Information Quarterly, Financial Accountability and Management, Social Science Computer Review, e-Service Journal, Journal of E-government, International Journal of Electronic Government Research, Municipal Finance Journal, and the Review of Public Personnel Administration.* Dr. Reddick holds a BA and MA in political science specializing in public administration, and a MBA in business studies at the University of Guelph in Canada. He has a PhD in political science from the University of Sheffield in the United Kingdom.

Han Reichgelt holds degrees in philosophy and psychology from the University of Nijmegen in The Netherlands, and a PhD in cognitive science from the University of Edinburgh in Scotland. Previously, he was a research fellow at the University of Edinburgh, lecturer in Psychology at the University of

Nottingham, and professor of computer science at the University of the West Indies, Mona, Jamaica. His current position is associate dean of the College of Information Technology at Georgia Southern University. Reichgelt is the (co-)author of over 70 journals and refereed conference papers, as well as of a textbook on knowledge representation in artificial intelligence. His research interests include IT and economic development, IT application delivery quality, and computing education. He currently chairs the ACM Special Interest Group on IT Education.

Jari Salo is currently an assistant professor of marketing at the University of Oulu. He received his DSc (econ. & bus. adm.) from the University of Oulu. Previously, he has published in *Business Process Management Journal, Journal of Business and Industrial Marketing, Journal of Euromarketing,* and other journals. Besides journal articles, Salo has also published several book chapters and has participated in leading conferences in the marketing and information technology area. He has served as a reviewer for many journals, conferences (AMA, HICSS, EMAC, ANZMAC, IRMA), and books. His present research interests include business relationship digitization, electronic commerce including mobile marketing, and new product development and innovation.

Paulo Sergio Sanz is a researcher at the Brazilian School of Public and Business Administration, Getulio Vargas Foundation, Brazil, and an IT consultant. He teaches executive education courses of the Getulio Vargas Foundation. He has published several papers in national and international journals and conferences. He holds a BSc in systems analysis and an MBA from the Brazilian School of Public and Business Administration of Getulio Vargas Foundation.

Lejla Vrazalic is an associate professor in information systems at the University of Wollongong in Dubai (UOWD). She is also the chair of the UOWD Research Committee and coordinator of the Program for the Enhancement of Learning and Teaching (PELT). Her research interests are in human computer interaction and e-commerce, and she was awarded the University Medal in 1999 for her research. Lejla received the Vice Chancellors Award for Outstanding Contribution to Teaching and Learning (OCTAL) in 2004 and a Carrick Citation for Outstanding Contributions to Student Learning in 2006. She is also the recipient of the 2004 Australian Prime Minister's Award for Excellence in Business Community Partnerships (NSW) for her work on community portals in Australia.

Aimao Zhang is a faculty member at Department of Information Technology, Georgia Southern University. She earned her Doctor of Philosophy from Southern Illinois University at Carbondale with a major in management information systems (2001) and a minor in production/operations management. She is specialized in teaching Web design, middle layer programming, and integrated Web applications. Her research covers e-commerce, industrial economics, banking and health care studies, and cross culture studies. Dr. Zhang's publications include book chapters, papers in refereed journals, national and international conferences.

Index